New Media: a critical introduction

New Media: A Critical Introduction is a comprehensive introduction to the culture, history, technologies and theories of new media. Written especially for students, the book considers the ways in which 'new media' really are new, assesses the claims that a media and technological revolution has taken place and formulates new ways for media studies to respond to new technologies.

The authors introduce a wide variety of topics including: how to define the characteristics of new media; social and political uses of new media and new communications; new media technologies, politics and globalisation; everyday life and new media; theories of interactivity; simulation; the new media economy; cybernetics and cyberculture; the history of automata and artificial life.

Substantially updated from the first edition to cover recent theoretical developments, approaches and significant technological developments, this is the best and by far the most comprehensive textbook available on this exciting and expanding subject.

Key features:

- fully immersive companion website **www.newmediaintro.com** including new international case studies, extra resources and multimedia features

- packed with pedagogical features to make the text more accessible and easier to use for students and simpler to teach from. These include: a user's guide – marginal notes – case studies – glossary of terms – an expanded and annotated bibliography to help with further study

New to this edition:

- a brand new preface and overview of the major approaches and arguments made in the book

- new case studies on videogames and television and technological change

- expanded conceptual discussions covering configuration, simulation, virtuality, mobile and networked media

- new chapters on: simulation – science and technology studies – the history of immersive media – music as new media – the economics of the 'Long Tail' – the viral – 'wikis' and Web 2.0 – technology, causality and culture

- a new user-friendly text design with even more illustrations

Martin Lister, **Jon Dovey**, **Seth Giddings** and **Kieran Kelly** are members of the Department of Culture, Media and Drama, in the Faculty of Creative Arts and **Iain Grant** is Head of Field in Philosophy, in the Faculty of Social Sciences and Humanities, all at the University of the West of England, Bristol.

New Media: a critical introduction

Second Edition

Martin Lister / Jon Dovey / Seth Giddings /
Iain Grant / Kieran Kelly

Routledge
Taylor & Francis Group

LONDON AND NEW YORK

First published 2003
This edition published 2009
by Routledge
2 Park Square, Milton Park, Abingdon, Oxon OX14 4RN

Simultaneously published in the USA and Canada
by Routledge
711 Third Ave, New York, NY 10017

Routledge is an imprint of the Taylor & Francis Group, an informa business

Typeset in Helvetica by
M Rules

British Library Cataloguing in Publication Data

A catalogue record for this book is available from the British Library

Library of Congress Cataloging-in-Publication Data

New media : a critical introduction / Martin Lister . . . [et al.]. – 2nd ed.
        p.   cm.
Includes bibliographical references and index.
1. Mass media—Technological innovations. I. Lister, Martin, 1947–

P96.T42N478 2008
302.23—dc22   2008026918

ISBN10: 0-415-43160-3 (hbk)
ISBN10: 0-415-43161-1 (pbk)
ISBN10: 0-203-88482-5 (ebk)

ISBN13: 978-0-415-43160-6 (hbk)
ISBN13: 978-0-415-43161-3 (pbk)
ISBN13: 978-0-203-88482-9 (ebk)

Contents

Illustrations

The following were reproduced with kind permission. While every effort has been made to trace copyright holders and obtain permission, this has not been possible in all cases. Any omissions brought to our attention will be remedied in future editions.

Case studies

Authors' biographies

Martin Lister, Jon Dovey, Seth Giddings and Kieran Kelly are members of the Department of Culture, Media and Drama, in the Faculty of Creative Arts. Iain Grant is Head of Field in Philosophy, in the Faculty of Social Sciences and Humanities. All at the University of the West of England, Bristol.

Martin Lister is Professor of Visual Culture in the Department of Culture, Media and Drama, at UWE, Bristol. He has written widely on photography, visual culture, and new media technologies and is a curator and media producer. He edited *The Photographic Image in Digital Culture* (Routledge, 1995) and produced the CD-ROM *From Silver to Silicon: A CD-ROM about photography, technology and culture*, London, ARTEC (both 1996). Recent publications include 'Photography in the Age of Electronic Imaging' *in Photography: A Critical Introduction* (Routledge 2003), and 'A Sack in the Sand: Photography and Information', *Convergence*, 13/3, Sage, 2007.

Jon Dovey is Professor of Screen Media in the Faculty of Creative Arts, UWE, Bristol. He is a writer, lecturer and producer. His research focus is on technology and cultural form; he edited *Fractal Dreams, New Media in Social Context*, one of the first UK academic books in the field in 1996. Subsequently he wrote *Freakshows – First Person Media and Factual TV* (2000) and co-authored *Game Cultures* (2006). His current work centres on Play, User Generated Content, and Pervasive Media through the Digital Cultures Research Centre which he leads at UWE.

Seth Giddings is Senior Lecturer in Digital Media and Critical Theory in the Department of Culture, Media and Drama at UWE, Bristol. He teaches critical media practice and new media studies, with a focus on popular new media and everyday life. His current research includes the production of ethnographies of play and technoculture, and is developed in both written and moving image form. His recent publications include: 'Dionysiac machines: videogames and the triumph of the simulacra', *Convergence*, 13(3), 2007; 'Playing with nonhumans: digital games as technocultural form', in Castells and Jenson (eds) *Worlds in Play: international perspectives on digital games research* (Peter Lang, 2007); 'Digital games as new media', in Rutter and Bryce (eds) *Understanding Digital Games* (Sage, 2006).

Iain Grant is Head of Field in Philosophy at UWE, where he specialises in Metaphysics, Contemporary French Philosophy, the Philosophy of Technology and the Philosophy of Nature. He has published widely on problems from post-Kantian European Philosophy and Science, and is the author of *On Grounds After Schelling* (forthcoming) and *Philosophies of Nature After Schelling* (Continuum, 2006), and co-author of *Idealism* (forthcoming, Acumen, 2009).

Kieran Kelly is a Senior Lecturer in Cultural Studies at UWE where he teaches media theory. He started working in public sector computing over 20 years ago. His academic background lies in economic history and the two are combined in his work on the political economy of new media.

Preface to the second edition

Preparing the second edition of this book has afforded the opportunity to consider several issues. These have been prompted, in equal part, by reviews of the book, debate about its perspectives, feedback from students, our own continuing collective and individual researches and, not least, by an ongoing history; a history that the first edition itself foregrounded and of which it has inevitably become a part. There have been changes in the field of new media and new media studies over the last decade. As we returned to our original project we were, in fact, testing the approach we adopted in the first edition, where we sifted out significant change, and ways of understanding that change, from the wider culture of continual upgrades, rapid obsolescence, marketing hype, shrill manifestos and disciplinary limits. We have been pleased to find that much of our thinking in the first edition still stands. Yet, this second edition contains many changes, some sections have been radically redrafted, others more subtly modified, and there are wholly new sections. But for good reasons, other parts of the book remain unchanged from the first edition.

The situation upon beginning the process of revisiting, revising and augmenting the first edition was daunting. Yet, as work progressed, the rudiments of an archaeology came into focus. We were able to perceive the overlay of 'new' technological artefacts and relations onto the schema that we constructed for the 2003 edition. As this became clear, the strong historical element of our project telescoped. The histories that figured in the first edition now became a part of longer histories by virtue of the subsequent accretion of time and change. In the period between the first and this edition, there has been argument and debate, competing viewpoints have emerged, new research has been undertaken, and theories have evolved. We, however, cannot emphasise enough the importance of the historical dimension of the study of technology (media or otherwise) in culture. Already reflectively addressed in the first edition, this has become even clearer now. Taking account of the historical dimension of technologies, and the cultures they inhabit and afford, avoids the pitfalls of identifying an essential change. Although much was made, around the turn of the present century, of the transformative potentials of technology, whether utopian or dystopian, when considered historically such moments can be seen to contribute to lines of development that have longer histories. Such moments of intense technological change add directions to these longer lineages, they prompt intentions, they select from the possibilities those lineages afford and the futures they shape.

Now that the first edition is itself a part of (new media) history, how has it fared? First, we have been gratified to learn that it has been widely read and adopted as core reading within university courses across three continents. This provides a welcome acknowledgement that the book's central aim of providing a survey of the most important problems raised by the issue of technology in culture have been essentially met. Second, it is used at different levels in university teaching, on both undergraduate and postgraduate degrees, indicating that the book's accounts, problematisations, and arguments have attained a balance of lucidity *and* generality to serve a variety of academic purposes. Third, unusually for a textbook, it has been critically reviewed and its arguments disputed and discussed in academic research literature (Kember 2005, Morley 2007). This tells us that our arguments hit home, that our characterisations of the core problems not only of New Media Studies, but more broadly, of technology and culture are, within always uncertain limits, accurate.

A certain anxiety inevitably arises in writing about a 'new' anything: by definition ephemeral, the new cannot remain new; we asked ourselves at the time of preparing the first edition how best to avoid this inevitable pitfall. We were, then, clear about the challenge a book on new media faced. We were also clear about the strategy that we would adopt. We decided it would be absurd to tie a discussion of 'new media' to those particular media which were new at the time of writing; our task was not to simply catalogue this and that new piece of kit and its uses but instead to concentrate on larger-scale historical trends and identify the core problems of technology and culture. What constitutes newness in media? Are there some key characteristics that allow us to distinguish the 'new' from the 'old'? What part does technological change play in that? What questions do new media pose to our available analytical frameworks? Which disciplines would help us?

In seeking to avoid producing a book that would be just an historical incident, the mere expression of a moment, we broadened our field of view to the history and philosophy of technology and culture as the informing context for our study of new media. In consequence, the continuing use, and the demand for a second edition, provide a testable record of the success of our aims for the first edition.

While working on this new edition we adopted a principle to guide us in deciding to include new material. It is this: the mere appearance of a new media device or newly named media practice would not in itself mean that we should devote a new section of the book to it. That way would lie the madness and kind of novelty-driven 'upgrade' scholarship which we wished to avoid in the first edition. This would have been to allow the tail to wag the dog. Instead we asked: does a new development require new conceptualisation? Which developments require new thinking because they present us with issues and questions which the first edition is not equipped to explain? Here, for instance, we decided that 'blogs' and 'blogging', a form and a practice that has developed exponentially since 2002, did not *substantially* require new thought and analysis beyond that we gave more generally to computer mediated communication, and specifically to the temporality and interactivity of email, in the first edition. On the other hand, the rapid growth of Social Network Sites since 2003 (Boyd 2007) or the significance of YouTube did present us with socio-technical practices which were not evident, or rather, were *not evolved*, in 2003. These would then require our attention. We have spoken already in this Preface about history, which formed one of the core lineaments of our considerations; the other consists of identifying the recurrent or perhaps transhistorical *problems* of techological cultures. While by no means an exhaustive or closed list, certain of these are worth drawing the reader's attention to. This is not simply because we think them interesting (although we certainly do); it is also because these provide the outlines of what we think *any and all* study of technology in culture *must* address.

At an early stage in the planning of the first edition, the project was criticised for paying excessive attention to a problem many academics and researchers considered over and done with or, maybe, simply a methodological diversion. This was a problem that we raised and characterised using the debates between Marshall McLuhan and Raymond Williams. Risking our colleagues' indifference, we insisted on the map these two scholars drew of the problem-field of technology and culture. While, as we point out below, it has been Williams's account that has held formative sway over the majority of the social, cultural and historical study of media, culture and technology, the problems to which this account provided its discipline-structuring conclusions remain live, indeed heightened, ones. Specifically, the debates focused on the role of *causes* in culture. While the by now traditional response to this issue is to deny that causes are active in, or pertinent to the study of, cultural phenomena, preferring instead to centre all upon human agency, more recent developments in a variety of fields of academic inquiry – we should mention in particular the considerable impact of Actor Network Theory in Science and Technology Studies – have in effect re-opened this debate by rethinking, indeed denying, a difference in kind between cultural and natural events. We address these points in what follows under the rubric of a *realism* in the study of technology in culture. We ask our readers, therefore, to be alert to the difference it would make to cultural studies in the broadest sense, if we no longer insist, as did Williams, on the essential separability of culture from nature. This is neither a dogmatic commandment, nor is the shape such studies of culture would assume determined in advance; rather, we maintain that this is a field open for contributions, and in which there are considerable opportunities for contributing to new accounts of cultural phenomena. Conceptual change, however, also involves change in our overall image of a culture and its elements. In the humanities and the social sciences in general, we are used to considering the concepts of 'subjects' and 'identities' as core in the study of culture; yet what *are* these, and how might they be altered, or even replaced, by drawing different maps of cultural entities?

A second important issue we are now in a position to consider, is that technology is not some occasional player in cultural events, but a permanent fixture. Without recording technologies of some kind (tablets, paper, wax, movable print, analogue and digital electronics and so forth), the cultures we all inhabit would not exist. Technology then is not peripheral to the concerns of analysts of culture, media and history, but an omnipresent element of them. In short, *all culture is technological*. While some may panic at this, fearing perhaps that cultural studies could be replaced by engineering diagrams, this reductive response is not the only one available. We should consider, however, in increasingly complex technological environments, entering into dialogue with all the players in our cultures' production – the sciences, the engineering, and the humanities and social sciences – and so should not reject engineering as culturally irrelevant simply out of fear and a desire for the comforts of our academic homes. As we note in what follows, for instance, the affects (the fear, rapture, or indifference) that accompany technology are themselves real elements in the cultures these technologies inhabit. One argument we offer that makes sense both of the engineering and the affect concerns the concept of *affordances*: technology is not all there is to culture, nor does it determine it in some predictable or absolute way; rather, technologies *afford* cultural possibilities, not all of which are exploited or actualised.

The first edition of this book was published in 2003, which means that it was researched and written in 2000–2002, and conceived even earlier. In that first edition, while recognising longer formative histories, we suggested that the mid-1980s were a useful marker for thinking about 'new media' (see p. 2 of Introduction). However, even then, some commentators found the term 'new media' a strange one to choose to refer to something that begun to be apparent in the 1980s. At the time, we recommended our choice of title by pointing out that it was a more serviceable term than the obvious alternatives: 'digital media', 'interactive media', or 'computer-mediated communication' etc. (see **1.1.4** for those reasons). To some, it will seem even stranger to retain the title for this second, 2008 edition. Now, a whole generation of readers, born in the 1980s, have come to maturity for whom so-called 'new media' were always a part of their world and the 'old' media to which they were originally compared now hardly exist in any distinct form untouched and transformed by the 'new'. This holds for the production of an ancient media form such as this book, and the way that it was written and produced, as much as to the existence of the persistent virtual world of Second Life. Of course, deliberately purist niches and minority cultures hold out against, or within, the ubiquitous restructurings of new media. Some people seek out Super 8 movie film, vinyl records, assiduously pursue chemical photography, write letters, paint pictures, play the acoustic guitar. Of course they do and specialist economies support them (ironically, often utilising the resources of the Internet). However, a generation exists, many of whom will be the readers of this book, who work, think, and play within a new media environment as naturally as fish swim in the sea. For them (for you), the epithet 'new' attached to their (your) media only makes sense with effort; with historical perspective. Critical enquiry into the formation and significance of the most naturalised and habituated phenomena benefit from a kind of distance or shock, from 'making strange'. It is remarkable, and a testament to the speed and depth of change, that we already need to achieve this 'making strange' in respect of 'new media' for, as McLuhan observed, 'One thing about which fish know exactly nothing is water, since they have no anti-environment which would enable them to perceive the element they live in' (McLuhan quoted in Federman 2003). With the greatest respect to fish, this book, in both its first and now its second edition strives to bring into view that which they are ignorant of.

'New media' is historical in an epochal as well as a biographical way. At the time of writing, a Google search for terms containing 'new media' yielded massive results: 'new media courses' found 49 million results, for 'new media jobs' 52 million results, for 'new media products' 51 million, and using Google Scholar, 'new media' as a topic of academic research offered over 31 million results. Rather like the 'new world' of the Americas 'discovered' by Europeans in the fourteenth century, the term has truly stuck. It is a historical marker. It locates a watershed.

In what follows, we propose and discuss certain types of history, some linear and 'teleological', or directed towards a particular outcome; some not linear in this sense, but involving twists and turns that only appear after they have done their work. We do not conclude by recommending a particular historical approach, but insist only that history is complex and convoluted. What appears simple and linear from a limited, present perspective, is always more complex. Technological history, in particular, is haunted by the 'corpses of dead machines', as Marx put it (see, for example, **2.1**). Part of addressing this history involves sorting through the immense present, and paying attention, therefore, to what is not immediately obvious, even though it stares us in the face. And in drawing up these histories, we are inevitably drawn into them. The inescapability of history is to be embraced, and our involvements in it examined. By engaging in this second edition, we have been afforded the opportunity to involve ourselves further in unpredictable developments; in messy forecasts and fuzzy understandings of the present. We do not escape this by mapping problems (there are always new problems to be identified), nor do we avoid it by grasping history whole, as it were, from outside (even were this possible, it would be history seen from outside at a certain point in history). But by attending to the history and problems of technology in culture, and by considering no issue settled in advance, we do make a serious attempt to understand our surroundings and how they have assumed the strange shapes they have. It is to this project that we would like to encourage contributions, and we offer this second edition, with its inevitable limits, in the hope that it may inspire you to do so.

Bibliography

Boyd, M. Danah 'Social Network Sites: Definition, History, and Scholarship', *Journal of Computer-Mediated Communication*, http://jcmc.indiana.edu/, 2007.

Federman, M. 'Enterprise Awareness: McLuhan Thinking', McLuhan Program in Culture and Technology, University of Toronto. http://www.utoronto.ca/mcluhan/EnterpriseAwarenessMcLuhanThinking.pdf, 2003.

Kember, S. 'Doing Technoscience as (New) Media' in J. Curran and D. Morley (eds) *Media and Cultural Theory*, Routledge, 2005.

Morley, D. *Media, Modernity and Technology: The Geography of the New*, Routledge, 2007.

Introduction

The book's purpose

The purpose of this book is to offer students conceptual frameworks for thinking through a range of key issues which have arisen over two decades of speculation on the cultural implications of new media. It is first and foremost a book about the questions, the ideas and debates – the critical issues – that the emergence of new media technologies has given rise to. In this, we hope that it is a genuine contribution to the study of the new media and technologies. There is no such thing, however, as a wholly impartial, objective work that sets about cataloguing the debates, one after the other, without arguing for one thing rather than another, or judging some aspects of the problems to be important, and others not. The reader should therefore note in advance that it is a necessary component of this book, as of any other, that its authors judge what is important and what is not, and that they argue for some theoretical positions, and against others. We do not aim to summarise blandly the state of the art in new media and **technology**, but to present for the reader some of the contested issues that are rife within this emerging field. You will find in the book arguments for different positions. Where this is so, we are overt about it, and we let you, the reader, know. Indeed, this is only to be expected, since the bodies of expertise this book uniquely brings to bear on its topic draw on our various disciplinary backgrounds in visual culture, media and cultural history, media theory, media production, philosophy and the history of the sciences, political economy and sociology. Finally, just as it is important to be aware of what differentiates the various arguments in this book, it is also crucial to note what all of our arguments share. This book's authors have in common a commitment to a synthetic approach to new media studies. We each individually hold that the field is so complex that it cannot be addressed other than by combining, or synthesising, knowledges. While this adds some complexity to the book as a whole, it all the more accurately embodies the contested field that is new media studies.

Our approach to the subject

Unlike some of the new media that we discuss in the following pages, this medium, the book, has clearly separated authors and readers. An author does not know her or his thousands of readers, yet an author must have some way of describing to themselves who they think their readers are likely to be. If they forget this then their publishers are likely to remind them, as they wish to sell the book; for them a successful identification of a body of readers is a market. In writing this book, how have we thought about our readership? We assume that the majority of our readers are students who have developed a special interest in the study of the new media forms that have appeared over the last fifteen years or so. We envisage them having some introductory knowledge of media studies or a related discipline.

Readers also want to know what to expect of their authors. This book has several, and we have something to say about this below. For the moment, however, we should recognise that the present occasion for a conjunction of authors and readers is the topic of this book: the new media. What, however, are they? We take them to be those methods and social practices of communication, representation, and expression that have developed using the digital, multimedia, **networked** computer and the ways that this machine is held to have transformed work in other media: from books to movies, from telephones to television. When did all this happen? What, in other words, is the period in which 'everything changed'? The process by which computerisation or 'digitisation' impacted upon the media of the twentieth century has moved on many fronts and at different speeds, so it is difficult to pinpoint a single date or decisive period for the emergence of new media. Even the key developments in computing, the core technology of this digitisation, which, over the long term, made this technically and conceptually possible, are many. We can get some idea of the period that mainly concerns us by considering the emergence of the personal computer. We can point to the mid-1980s as a watershed, when the **PC** began to be equipped with **interactive** graphic **interfaces**; to possess enough memory to run the early versions of image manipulation software; and when computer-mediated communications networks began to emerge. This was a moment when the ideas and concepts of earlier visionaries appeared to become real possibilities.

In turn, it is since that time, a period of less than thirty years, that speculation, prediction, theorisation and argument about the nature and potential of these new media began to proceed at a bewildering and breathless pace. A wide range of ideas, many of which challenged settled assumptions about media, culture and technology (and, indeed, nature) were generated and pulled along in the vortex of constant and rapid technological innovation. So too was a comparable quantity of 'hype' that accompanied the emergence of new media in the mid-1980s. This, of course, is still with us, but it has been met by some hard-headed reflection born of experience and enough time to recover some critical poise. New media have become a major focus of research and theory, an emerging field of media and cultural study which now possesses a complex body of thought and writing. Thinking about new media has become a critical and contested field of study.

Media studies, like any other field of study, thrives on problems. At the early stages in the study of any new phenomenon the very question of 'what the problems are' is part of the field of enquiry; the problems themselves are contested. What exactly is the problem? Which questions are worth bothering about? Which ideas are really significant? In this book, by bringing together a range of voices and disciplines, we have aimed to provide an initial map of the territory and its debates.

Such a project has its challenges. When we began to write this book we were conscious, above all, of the rapid pace of media-technological change that has characterised the end of the twentieth and the beginning of the twenty-first centuries. This became all the more apparent with the rise of what we might call 'upgrade culture': with the practice of upgrading, the computer itself becomes a technology in flux, rather than a finally achieved and stable piece of technology. Thus we were faced with the question of how to take a snapshot of a breaking wave. Constant technological and media change makes it absurd to tie a discussion of 'new media' to those particular media which are new at the time of writing. Rather, we set ourselves the task of investigating the more fundamental issues of what constitutes newness in media and what part technological change may play in that. Similarly, rather than taking notice only of those ideas that arise in the immediate context of discussions about '**cyber-culture**', we draw on a much wider range of historical and contemporary resources that offer to shed light on the present situation. So this book draws upon theories and frameworks – not only from media studies but also from art and cultural history, the study of popular culture, political economy, the sciences, and philosophy. It is our belief that this inclusiveness is the only way to begin to make sense of the cultural changes that new media are held to make. By taking this approach we try to get our heads above the tidal wave of media and techno-logical change, to survey what lies in the distance, and not simply to concentrate on the froth on the crest of the wave. Even surfers chart a wave's history, trying to catch it at the optimal moment of its emergence; only a stupid surfer would ignore it! This is not a book, then, that contents itself with clutching at the latest software upgrade, gizmo, avant-garde experiment, or marketing ploy. Rather, what we hope distinguishes this book is that it focuses not just on these disparate things but also on what forms of understanding are being brought to bear on them, and what meanings are being invested in them.

It is in this way that this book is a critical introduction to new media and technology. Being 'critical' does not mean adopting the view that 'there's nothing new under the sun'. The new-ness of new media is, in part, real, in that these media did not exist before now. But taking these changes into account does not mean abolishing all history because it (history) is full of similar moments of newness. By taking a critical and historical view of new media and tech-nology we hope this book will not forsake newness for history, nor history for newness. Rather, it begins with a history of newness itself.

To make this point clear, consider how some so-called critical approaches often effectively deny that there has been any substantial change at all, either in the media or in the cultures of which they form part. Such critical accounts of new media frequently stress the continuity in economic interests, political imperatives and cultural values that drive and shape the 'new' as much as the 'old' media. They seek to show that the dominant preoccupation with new media's difference, with the way that it outstrips and parts company with our old, passive, **analogue** media, is an ideological trick, a myth. They argue that new media can largely be revealed as the latest twist in capitalism's ruthless ingenuity for ripping us off with seductive **commodities** and the false promise of a better life. These are important voices, but com-puter and related digital technologies are at least candidates for inclusion in a list of cultural technologies (including the printing press and the book, photography, telephony, cinema and television) which, in complex and indirect ways, have played a major part in social and cul-tural change. While it is true that, because of some of their uses and contents, none of these media can be simply celebrated as great and benign human achievements, neither can they be reduced to evil capitalist scams!

On the other hand, consider those critics who insist uncritically that everything has changed. Or those who read digital technologies as already having brought about a **utopia**, the like of which has never previously existed. Or again, there are those who simply refuse all critical comment, and insist that the old theoretical tools are simply redundant in the face of the enormity of the technological sea-change taking place. While it is clear that some change has indeed occurred, if it were true that these changes are as fundamental as all that, then we would find it impossible to put into words what is happening!

Pursuing our earlier metaphor, we could say that the critical critics are so deep under-water that they don't see the wave. Meanwhile, the uncritical utopians are so focused on the crest of the wave itself that they cannot see the ocean of which it is part. Opposing these positions does not really represent a genuine dispute. It is not 'business as usual', but nor has all business collapsed. Rather, in this book, we both stand back from the hype and investigate the nature of change. There is, it seems to us, no real alternative. We draw our readers' attention to two other features of this book.

The book's historical dimension

It could seem that an introduction to thinking critically about new media, unlike one on, say, photography or film and cinema, would have little history to deal with. As we have already noted, we consider it a serious flaw not to engage with the histories of the technologies and media under discussion. New things do not have no history; rather, they make us search a little harder for their histories. Indeed, new things may bring out overlooked histories in order to answer the question of where they come from. Moreover, in the claims and ideas that currently surround new media, we can find many historical echoes. We need to consider that 'old' media technologies were themselves once new and held enormous significance for their contemporaries for that very reason. Attempts to come to terms with our own new machines and their products should prompt in us an awareness that we have been here before. Even printed books were once new. We can then ask, in what terms was this newness conceived, in what ways does it compare to our own, and what relation did it have to eventual outcomes? In responding to our contemporary 'new' we will learn something from other historical moments and times.

The book's emphasis on wider questions of culture and technology

In parts of the book we recognise how inextricable new media are from the technologies that have made them possible. This means that we needed to provide some bearings for thinking about the relationship of media and technology. This raises a larger topic and set of debates concerning the relationship between culture and technology; a matter that is precisely brought into focus in a term such as 'cyberculture'. It seems crucial that we have some ways of assessing the extent and intensity of the kind of changes that media technologies can bring about. If, as it seems, our contemporary culture is deeply immersed in changing technological forms, the important question is raised as to how far new media and communication technologies, indeed technologies in general, do actually determine the cultures that they exist within. Conversely we must also ask how cultural factors shape our use and experience of technological power. These are, as many commentators have noted recently and in the past, vexed and unsettled questions that new media put once again, firmly before us.

The book's organisation

Rather than dedicating each chapter to a discrete or separate new media form (for example a chapter on the **Internet** or another on computer games) the five major parts of the book are based upon different kinds of discussion and ways of thinking about new media. In this way, each part foregrounds a different set of critical issues and arguments, alongside more detailed discussion of particular media or technological forms, as the occasion demands. Each part of the book considers new media through the prism of different kinds of questions and theories. The reader will find that many forms of new media are discussed in a number of places in the book, quite possibly in several locations across the five parts. ('Virtual reality', for example, is briefly discussed in Part 1 as part of an analysis of the key or defining characteristics of new media, in Part 2 where changes in visual culture are explored, a history of immersive media is offered, and in Part 5 where philosophical arguments about the relationship of the 'virtual' to the 'real' are discussed.) To some extent, the different kinds of conceptual framework that are employed in each part of the book will reflect the kind of media studied. Part 3, for instance, presents studies of new media that use a political economy perspective and broadly sociological discussions of new media's role in the formation of **community** and identity. This part therefore has a good deal more to say about online media and communication networks, where these phenomena are thought to occur, than do other parts of the book.

How to use the book

As stated earlier, in considering our readership we have assumed a student reader who has some background in media studies or a related discipline and who now wishes to engage with the particular debates of new media studies. However, the very range of the issues which we introduce and consider in these pages means that much unfamiliar material will be met. To help the reader in this task we have adopted a number of strategies. We have tried to avoid the use of overly technical academic language wherever possible and we provide explanations of the concepts we use, both in the text as they arise or in the Glossary. At appropriate points, arguments are illustrated with case studies. Where a particularly difficult set of ideas is met we provide a short summary for the reader, sufficient for them to follow the discussion in hand, and point them to further reading where the ideas can be studied in more depth. Alongside the main text a running series of margin notes are provided. These serve two main functions. They add detail to the main argument without disrupting its flow, and they provide important bibliographical references related to the point being discussed. All references are listed in extensive bibliographies at the end of each chapter.

This is a large book that covers a great deal of ground. It is likely that most readers will consult one part or another at different times rather than read it in a linear fashion from cover to cover. Given this, we briefly restate some points in more than one place in the book in order that the reader can engage with their chosen section without having to chase supporting material that is elsewhere in the book. Also, throughout the book we provide cross references which are designed to alert the reader to where there is more material on the topic in hand or where they can find another viewpoint on it.

The book's parts

Part 1: New Media and New Technologies

In this part of the book some fundamental questions are asked about new media. Distinctions are made between the kinds of phenomena that are bundled up in the term 'new media' in order to make the field of study more manageable. Some key characteristics which have come to be seen as defining new media are mapped, discussed and exemplified and we ask how the 'newness' of new media is variously understood. In the latter sections, we discuss a number of ways in which new media have been given a history, and how, in that process, they are given significance. An important concept in the cultural study of media technology is introduced, 'the technological imaginary', and similarities between the ways that earlier twentieth-century 'new media' were received and current developments are discussed. Finally, in this part, we explore the roots of a contemporary debate about new media which centres upon the power of media to determine the nature of culture and society. We recognise the importance accorded to the work of Marshall McLuhan in much contemporary thinking about new media and revisit the terms in which Raymond Williams, and much academic media studies, contests this way of understanding new media. Contributions to understanding new media, from outside of traditional media studies are considered, especially from the perspective of science and technology studies.

Part 2: New Media and Visual Culture

In Part 2 we ask how new visual media and imaging technologies are bringing about contemporary changes in visual culture. Throughout the twentieth century, visual culture has been dominated by one technological medium after another: photography, narrative film and cinema, broadcast television and video. Each has been credited with leading us to see the world in different ways. More widely, the very nature of vision has come to be understood as historically variable. How are these processes extended into the age of new media? In order to explore this, we trace the history of virtual reality, immersive media, and digital cinema. As a part of the discussion of virtual reality the cultural implications of the historical intersection of simulation technologies, developed within computer science in the 1960s, and the deeply embedded traditions of Western visual representation are considered. The concepts of representation and simulation are discussed (as well as in **1.2.6**). Central issues for theories of photography, film and cinema have been their realism and the nature of visual representation. Following on from the argument that, in virtual reality, representation is displaced by another practice, simulation, these issues are considered in the context of computer-generated animation, special effects and digital cinema.

Part 3: Networks, Users and Economics

Part 3 deals with the networked forms of new media afforded by the Internet. It has a particular emphasis on the relationship between economics and the forms of media culture emerging through net based technologies. As such its aim is to demonstrate how we need to understand the relationships between human creativity, technological potential, and the possibilities offered by markets. The structure of the section itself is offered as a model for understanding these mutually determining relationships, moving between a generalised understanding of the macro-economic forces of globalisation and neo-liberalism to the specific instance of how this might affect the user of a social network site or the producer of online TV. The section looks at how the 'social shaping of technology' approach can be successfully applied to networked media through the traditional Media Studies tools of political economy. It critically analyses the identification between the internet and globalisation, emphasising the reality of a 'digital divide' as way of challenging the 'world wide' appellation of the WWW. More specifically it examines the way in which networked based businesses have been subject to the boom and bust cycle of the market as a way of understanding Web 2.0 developments as a direct response to the dot.com crash of 2000–2002. We include a new section on the way in which networked practices and technologies have affected the music industries which in many ways exemplifies the conflicts between users and owners of Intellectual Property which all media businesses have found so challenging in the early years of the new century. We argue that the economic theory of the 'Long Tail' has emerged as an important new model for understanding networked media, unlocking new possibilities for users and producers alike, leading to the new business practices of viral marketing, community management and web advertising. Interwoven with this background the reader will find a summary of the main traditions from the study of Computer Mediated Communication that offer paradigms for thinking about the kinds of personal investments afforded by the Internet; investments of time, passion and creativity that are also driving adaptations in media business practices. These investments are now often referred to as 'user-generated content' and this section looks at some of the forms which this explosion of media production takes, such as YouTube.

Part 4: New Media in Everyday Life

Claims for the revolutionary impact of new media technologies often assume profound trans-formations of everyday life, and the structures and relationships on which it is based: the sense of individual self or identity; consumption; the dynamics and politics of generation and gender in families and other households; connections between the global and the local. Part 4 is concerned with the study of popular new entertainment and communications media in everyday life. It looks at how the intersections of new media technologies and networks with the spaces and relationships of the home might be theorised. It explores how the 'newness' of new media might be understood as it meets the longer-established time and space of the family and the home. This part is particularly concerned with the description and theorisation of play as an under-researched cultural phenomenon that has, with new media such as videogames and mobile phones, shifted to the centre of everyday popular culture and lived experience for children and adults. We question some of the foundational theoretical positions that underpin studies of everyday media culture, particularly the culturalist assertion that everyday relationships and environments shape the nature and adoption of new media tech-nologies, but never vice versa. This section will synthesise and deploy some key alternative ways of thinking about everyday life, experience, play and bodies as profoundly technocul-tural, ways of thinking drawn from the emerging field of new media studies, including Science and Technology Studies, game studies and cybercultural studies.

Part 5: Cyberculture: Technology, Nature and Culture

Part 5 pursues problems posed elsewhere in the book and argues that the core dilemma facing any study of technology is how to understand the part played by a technology's sheer physical form in the shaping of history and culture, on the one hand, and – although this is principally addressed in Part 4 – how that culture is experienced. Here we consider argu-ments, some very old, that there is a tighter relationship between technology and culture than is often acknowledged. To demonstrate this, we consider three periods in the history of tech-nology, which can be named after their principal technologies: mechanical, steam, and cybernetic. We discuss the deep and structuring influence of each of these technologies on the cultures formed around them. The scientific, philosophical and historical contexts in which these technocultural relationships occur are also examined. Given the importance of intelli-gent agents in contemporary digital culture, particular attention will be paid to how the long history of efforts to understand and to build automata, or self-acting machines, exemplifies these relationships. Finally, drawing on materials and arguments presented throughout the book, Part 5 concludes with an argument for the kind of realism necessary to understand technology in culture, centring on the concept of causality.

1 New Media and New Technologies

1.1 New media: do we know what they are?

This book is a contribution to answering the question, 'What is new about "new media"?' It also offers ways of thinking about that question, ways of seeking answers. Here, at the outset, we ask two prior questions. First, 'What are media anyway?'. When you place the prefix 'new' in front of something it is a good idea to know what you are talking about and 'media' has long been a slippery term (we will also have a lot to say about that in various parts of the book). Second, what, at face value and before we even begin to interrogate them, do we include as 'new media'?

1.1.1 Media studies

For some sixty years the word 'media', the plural of 'medium', has been used as a singular collective term, as in 'the media' (Williams 1976: 169). When we have studied the media we usually, and fairly safely, have had in mind 'communication media' and the specialised and separate institutions and organisations in which people worked: print media and the press, photography, advertising, cinema, broadcasting (radio and television), publishing, and so on. The term also referred to the cultural and material products of those institutions (the distinct forms and **genres** of news, road movies, soap operas which took the material forms of newspapers, paperback books, films, tapes, discs: Thompson 1971: 23–24). When systematically studied (whether by the media institutions themselves as part of their market research or by media academics inquiring critically into their social and cultural significance) we paid attention to more than the point of media production which took place within these institutions. We also investigated the wider processes through which information and representations (the 'content') of 'the media' were distributed, received and consumed by audiences and were regulated and controlled by the state or the market.

We do, of course, still do this, just as some of us still watch 90-minute films, in the dark, at the cinema, or gather as families to watch in a fairly linear way an evening's scheduled 'broadcast' television. But many do not consume their 'media' in such ways. These are old habits or practices, residual options among many other newer ones. So, we may sometimes continue to think about media in the ways we described above, but we do so within a changing context which, at the very least, challenges some of the assumed categories that description includes.

For example, in an age of trans-mediality we now see the migration of content and intellectual property across media forms, forcing all media producers to be aware of and collaborate with others. We are seeing the fragmentation of television, the blurring of boundaries

For more on these particular developments see: **3.16**, **3.22**, **3.23**

(as in the rise of the 'citizen journalist'); we have seen a shift from 'audiences' to 'users', and from 'consumers' to 'producers'. The screens that we watch have become both tiny and mobile, and vast and immersive. It is argued that we now have a media economics where networks of many small, minority and niche markets replace the old 'mass audience' (see The Long Tail **3.13**). Does the term 'audience' mean the same as it did in the twentieth century? Are media genres and media production skills as distinct as they used to be? Is the 'point of production' as squarely based in formal media institutions (large specialist corporations) as it used to be? Is the state as able to control and regulate media output as it once was? Is the photographic (lens based) image any longer distinct from (or usefully contrasted to) digital and computer generated imagery?

However, we should note right now (because it will be a recurring theme in this book), that even this very brief indication of changes in the forms, production, distribution, and consumption of media is more complex than the implied division into the 'old' and 'new' suggest. This is because many of these very shifts also have their precedents, their history. There have long been minority audiences, media that escape easy regulation, hybrid genres and 'inter-texts' etc. In this way, we are already returned to the question 'What is "new" about "new media"?' What is continuity, what is radical change? What is truly new, what is only apparently so?

Despite the contemporary challenges to its assumptions, the importance of our brief description of 'media studies' above is that it understands media as fully social institutions which are not reducible to their technologies. We still cannot say that about 'new media', which, even after almost thirty years, continues to suggest something less settled and known. At the very least, we face, on the one hand, a rapid and ongoing set of technological experiments and entrepreneurial initiatives; on the other, a complex set of interactions between the new technological possibilities and established media forms. Despite this the singular term 'new media' is applied unproblematically. Why? Here we suggest three answers. First, new media are thought of as epochal; whether as cause or effect, they are part of larger, even global, historical change. Second, there is a powerful utopian and positive ideological charge to the concept 'new'. Third, it is a useful and inclusive 'portmanteau' term which avoids reducing 'new media' to technical or more specialist (and controversial) terms.

1.1.2 The intensity of change

The term 'new media' emerged to capture a sense that quite rapidly from the late 1980s on, the world of media and communications began to look quite different and this difference was not restricted to any one sector or element of that world, although the actual timing of change may have been different from medium to medium. This was the case from printing, photography, through television, to telecommunications. Of course, such media had continually been in a state of technological, institutional and cultural change or development; they never stood still. Yet, even within this state of constant flux, it seemed that the nature of change that was experienced warranted an absolute marking off from what went before. This experience of change was not, of course, confined only to the media in this period. Other, wider kinds of social and cultural change were being identified and described and had been, to varying degrees, from the 1960s onwards. The following are indicative of wider kinds of social, economic and cultural change with which new media are associated:

- *A shift from modernity to postmodernity*: a contested, but widely subscribed attempt to characterise deep and structural changes in societies and economies from the 1960s onwards, with correlative cultural changes. In terms of their aesthetics and economies new media are usually seen as a key marker of such change (see e.g. Harvey 1989).

- **Intensifying processes of globalisation**: a dissolving of national states and boundaries in terms of trade, corporate organisation, customs and cultures, identities and beliefs, in which new media have been seen as a contributory element (see e.g. Featherstone 1990).

- **A replacement, in the West, of an industrial age of manufacturing by a 'post-industrial' information age**: a shift in employment, skill, investment and profit, in the production of material goods to service and information 'industries' which many uses of new media are seen to epitomise (see e.g. Castells 2000).

- **A decentring of established and centralised geopolitical orders**: the weakening of mechanisms of power and control from Western colonial centres, facilitated by the dispersed, boundary-transgressing, networks of new communication media.

New media were caught up with and seen as part of these other kinds of change (as both cause and effect), and the sense of 'new times' and 'new eras' which followed in their wake. In this sense, the emergence of 'new media' as some kind of epoch-making phenomena, was, and still is, seen as part of a much larger landscape of social, technological and cultural change; in short, as part of a new **technoculture**.

1.1.3 The ideological connotations of the new

There is a strong sense in which the 'new' in new media carries the ideological force of 'new equals better' and it also carries with it a cluster of glamorous and exciting meanings. The 'new' is 'the cutting edge', the 'avant-garde', the place for forward-thinking people to be (whether they be producers, consumers, or, indeed, media academics). These connotations of 'the new' are derived from a modernist belief in social progress as delivered by technology. Such long-standing beliefs (they existed throughout the twentieth century and have roots in the nineteenth century and even earlier) are clearly reinscribed in new media as we invest in them. New media appear, as they have before, with claims and hopes attached; they will deliver increased productivity and educational opportunity (**4.3.2**) and open up new creative and communicative horizons (**1.3**, **1.5**). Calling a range of developments 'new', which may or may not be new or even similar, is part of a powerful ideological movement and a narrative about progress in Western societies (**1.5**).

4.3.2 Edutainment, edutainment, edutainment
1.3 Change and continuity
1.5 Who was dissatisfied with old media?

This narrative is subscribed to not only by the entrepreneurs, corporations who produce the media hardware and software in question, but also by whole sections of media commentators and journalists, artists, intellectuals, technologists and administrators, educationalists and cultural activists. This apparently innocent enthusiasm for the 'latest thing' is rarely if ever ideologically neutral. The celebration and incessant promotion of new media and **ICTs** in both state and corporate sectors cannot be dissociated from the globalising **neo-liberal** forms of production and distribution which have been characteristic of the past twenty years.

1.1.4 Non-technical and inclusive

'New media' has gained currency as a term because of its useful inclusiveness. It avoids, at the expense of its generality and its ideological overtones, the reductions of some of its

Case study 1.3 What is new about interactivity?

alternatives. It avoids the emphasis on purely technical and formal definition, as in '**digital**' or 'electronic' media; the stress on a single, ill-defined and contentious quality as in '**interactive** media', or the limitation to one set of machines and practices as in '**computer-mediated communication**' (CMC).

So, while a person using the term 'new media' may have one thing in mind (the Internet), others may mean something else (digital TV, new ways of imaging the body, a virtual environment, a computer game, or a blog). All use the same term to refer to a range of phenomena. In doing so they each claim the status of 'medium' for what they have in mind and they all borrow the glamorous connotations of 'newness'. It is a term with broad cultural resonance rather than a narrow technicist or specialist application.

There is, then, some kind of sense, as well as a powerful ideological charge, in the singular use of the term. It is a term that offers to recognise some big changes, technological, ideological and experiential, which actually underpin a range of different phenomena. It is, however, very general and abstract.

We might, at this point, ask whether we could readily identify some kind of fundamental change which underpins all new media – something more tangible or more scientific than the motives and contexts we have so far discussed. This is where the term 'digital media' is preferable for some, as it draws attention to a specific means (and its implications) of the registration, storage, and distribution of information in the form of digital binary code. However, even here, although digital media is accurate as a formal description, it presupposes an absolute break (between **analogue** and digital) where we will see that none in fact exists. Many digital new media are reworked and expanded versions of 'old' analogue media (**1.2.1**).

1.1.5 Distinguishing between kinds of new media

The reasons for the adoption of the abstraction 'new media' such as we have briefly discussed above are important. We will have cause to revisit them in other sections of this part of the book (**1.3**, **1.4**, **1.5**) as we think further about the historical and ideological dimensions of 'newness' and 'media'. It is also very important to move beyond the abstraction and generality of the term; there is a need to regain and use the term in its plural sense. We need to ask what the new media are *in their variety and plurality*. As we do this we can see that beneath the general sense of change we need to talk about a range of different kinds of change. We also need to see that the changes in question are ones in which the ratios between the old and the new vary (**1.3**).

Below, as an initial step in getting clearer about this, we provide a schema that breaks down the global term 'new media' into some more manageable constituent parts. Bearing in mind the question marks that we have already placed over the 'new', we take 'new media' to refer to the following:

- *New textual experiences*: new kinds of **genre** and **textual** form, entertainment, pleasure and patterns of media consumption (computer games, simulations, special effects cinema).

- *New ways of representing the world*: media which, in ways that are not always clearly defined, offer new representational possibilities and experiences (immersive virtual environments, screen-based interactive multimedia).

- *New relationships between subjects (users and consumers) and media technologies*: changes in the use and reception of image and communication media in everyday life and in the meanings that are invested in media technologies (**3.1–3.10** and **4.3**).

- **New experiences of the relationship between embodiment, identity and community**: shifts in the personal and social experience of time, space, and place (on both local and global scales) which have implications for the ways in which we experience ourselves and our place in the world.

- **New conceptions of the biological body's relationship to technological media**: challenges to received distinctions between the human and the artificial, nature and technology, body and (media as) technological prostheses, the real and the **virtual** (**5.1** and **5.4**).

- **New patterns of organisation and production**: wider realignments and integrations in media culture, industry, economy, access, ownership, control and regulation (**3.5–3.22**).

If we were to set out to investigate any one of the above, we would quickly find ourselves encountering a whole array of rapidly developing fields of technologically mediated production (user-generated content) and even a history of such as the site for our research. These would include:

- **Computer-mediated communications**: **email**, chat rooms, **avatar**-based communication forums, voice image transmissions, the World Wide Web, blogs etc., social networking sites, and mobile telephony.

- **New ways of distributing and consuming** media texts characterised by interactivity and hypertextual formats – the World Wide Web, CD, DVD, Podcasts and the various platforms for computer games.

- **Virtual 'realities'**: simulated environments and immersive representational spaces.

- **A whole range of transformations and dislocations of established media** (in, for example, photography, animation, television, journalism, film and cinema).

1.2 The characteristics of new media: some defining concepts

In **1.1** we noted that the unifying term 'new media' actually refers to a wide range of changes in media production, distribution and use. These are changes that are technological, textual, conventional and cultural. Bearing this in mind, we nevertheless recognise that since the mid-1980s at least (and with some changes over the period) a number of concepts have come to the fore which offer to define the key characteristics of the field of new media as a whole. We consider these here as some of the main terms in discourses about new media. These are: **digital**, **interactive**, **hypertexual**, **virtual**, **networked**, and **simulated**.

Before we proceed with this, we should note some important methodological points that arise when we define the characteristics of a medium or a media technology. What we are calling 'characteristics' here (digital, interactive, hypertexual etc.) can easily be taken to mean the 'essential qualities' of the medium or technology in question. When this happens being 'digital', for example, ceases to mean a source of possibilities, to be used, directed, and exploited. It becomes, instead, a totalising or overarching concept which wholly subsumes the medium in question. There is then a danger that we end up saying, 'Because a technology is like "this" (electronic, composed of circuits and pulses which transform colour, sound, mass or volume into binary digital code) it *necessarily* results in "that" (networked, fleeting and immaterial products)'. To make this move risks the accusation of 'essentialism' (an 'essentialist' being someone who argues that a thing is what it is because it possesses an unchanging and separable essence: see **5.4.6**).

(Bruno Latour,
'Alternative digitality'
at: http://www.bruno-
latour.fr/presse/presse_art
/GB-05%20DOMUS
%2005-04.html)

1.1 One of the complete human-headed lions from the entrance to the throneroom of Ashurnasirpal II now in the British Museum. The head of a corresponding sculpture can be seen in the foreground. These two figures were recorded using a NUB 3D Triple White light scanning system. They were recorded and milled at a resolution of 400 microns. Photograph by Factum Arte

With regard to 'digitality' an instructive example is offered by the work carried out by the artists and technicians of 'Factum–Arte', a group who use digital technology to reproduce ancient artefacts such as sculptures, monuments, bas-reliefs and paintings (http://www.factum-arte.com/eng/default.asp). These are not virtual, screen based replicas of the original works but material facsimiles ('stunning second originals') achieved by computers and digital technology driving and guiding powerful 3-D scanners, printers and drills. Here, the 'digital' produces hefty material objects rather than networked, fleeting and immaterial things (see **Figs 1.1** and **1.2**). This may be a rare case of digital technology being directly connected to the production of physically massive artefacts rather than flickering images on screens (the 'virtual') but it nevertheless warns against the kind of 'this therefore that' (digital) essentialism we warned of above.

On the other hand, while traditional media studies is wary of doing so (see **1.6–1.6.5**, **4.3.4**, and **5.1–5.1.10**), in **5.4.6** we also argue that it is very important to pay attention to the physical and material constitution of a technology (a digital media-technology no less than a heavy industrial manufacturing technology), not just its cultural meanings and social applications. This is because there is a real sense in which the physical nature and constitution of a technology encourages and constrains its uses and operation. To put this very basically, some technologies are tiny things, some are large and hefty. In terms of media technologies, compare an iPod to a 1980s 'ghetto-blaster' (**Fig 1.3**), or a 1940s 'radiogram' (**Fig 1.4**) and consider the influence that their sheer size has on how they are used, where and by whom, quite apart from matters such as the lifestyles and cultural meanings that may be attached to these objects.

Such physical properties of technologies are real. They change the environments and ecologies, natural and social, in which they exist. They seriously constrain the range of purposes to which they can be put and powerfully encourage others. Hence, recognising what a technology is – really and physically – is a crucial, if a partial and qualified aspect of a media technology's definition. This does not mean that we should reduce technology to its physical features because in doing that we would become essentialist about technological objects; we would arrive at a technological essentialism.

Let us take a final example from 'old' media: broadcast television (or radio). It is common

1.2 The feet of one of the human-headed lions from the entrance to the throneroom of Ashurnasirpal II now in the British Museum. The 3-dimensional data was recorded using a NUB 3D Triple White light scanning system and milled at a resolution of 400 microns. On the computer screen is an image of the scanned data which is directly compared to the facsimile to ensure accuracy. Photograph by Factum Arte

1.3 1980s ghetto-blaster. © Stone/Getty Images

1.4 1940s radiogram. England, 1940, WWII forces sweetheart, singer Vera Lynn places a record on her radiogram. Photo © Popperfoto/Getty Images

The question of determination (technological or other) is a more complex question, and is dealt with in **1.6.6** and **5.2**

(especially when contrasted to digital networked media) to think of television as a centralised medium – broadcasting out from a centre to a mass audience. This is not because the technology of television inevitably leads to centralisation (just as Factum-Arte's digitality doesn't inevitably lead to virtuality) but it does lend itself to such a use; it readily facilitates centralisation. Of course, alternative uses of broadcast media existed as in 'ham' and CB radio, in local television initiatives in many parts of the world, or even the use of the television receiver as a sculptural light-emitting object in the video installations of the artist Nam June Paik. Nevertheless television came to be developed and put to use dominantly in a centralising direction. That is, television came to be organised in this way within a social structure which needed to communicate from centres of power to the periphery (the viewer/listener). Recognising that a single media technology can be put to a multiplicity of uses, some becoming dominant and others marginal for reasons that can be cultural, social, economic or political as well as technological, is one important way of understanding what a medium is (**1.6**).

So, our approach here, in identifying new media's 'characteristics', is not meant to lead to or endorse essentialism but to take seriously the physical constitution and operation of technologies as well as the directions in which they have been developed. Being 'digital' is a real state and it has effects and potentialities. On the other hand, this does not mean that 'being digital' is a full description or wholly adequate concept of something. There is, then, a difference between assuming or asserting that we have detected the essence of something and recognising the opportunities or constraints that the nature of a media technology places before us. A useful term here, taken from design theory, is 'affordance' which refers to

> the perceived and actual properties of (a) thing, primarily those fundamental properties that determine just how the thing could possibly be used . . . A chair affords ('is for') support, and, therefore, affords sitting. A chair can also be carried. Glass is for seeing through, and for breaking.
>
> (Norman 2002: 9).

'Affordance' draws our attention to the actions that the nature of a thing 'invites' us to perform. It is in this spirit that we now discuss the defining characteristics of new media.

1.2.1 Digital

We need first of all to think about why new media are described as digital in the first place – what does 'digital' actually mean in this context? In addressing this question we will have cause to define digital media against a very long history of analogue media. This will bring us to a second question. What does the shift from analogue to digital signify for producers, audiences and theorists of new media?

In a digital media process all input data are converted into numbers. In terms of communication and representational media this 'data' usually takes the form of qualities such as light or sound or represented space which have already been coded into a 'cultural form' (actually 'analogues'), such as written text, graphs and diagrams, photographs, recorded moving images, etc. These are then processed and stored as numbers and can be output in that form from **online** sources, digital disks, or memory drives to be decoded and received as screen displays, dispatched again through telecommunications networks, or output as 'hard copy'. This is in marked contrast to analogue media where all input data is converted into another physical object. 'Analogue' refers to the way that the input data (reflected light from a textured surface, the live sound of someone singing, the inscribed marks of someone's handwriting) and the coded media product (the grooves on a vinyl disc or the distribution of magnetic particles on a tape) stand in an analogous relation to one another.

Analogues

'Analogue' refers to processes in which one set of physical properties can be stored in another 'analogous' physical form. The latter is then subjected to technological and cultural coding that allows the original properties to be, as it were, reconstituted for the audience. They use their skills at e.g. watching movies to 'see' the 'reality' through the analogies. *Analogos* was the Greek term which described an equality of ratio or proportion in mathematics, a transferable similarity that by linguistic extension comes to mean a comparable arrangement of parts, a similar ratio or pattern, available to a reader through a series of transcriptions. Each of these transcriptions involves the creation of a new object that is determined by the laws of physics and chemistry.

CASE STUDY 1.1: Analogue and digital type

Consider how this book would have been produced by the analogue print process which used discrete, movable pieces of metal type; *the way* of producing books in the 500 years between Gutenberg's mid fifteenth-century invention of the printing press and the effective introduction of digital printing methods in the 1980s. Handwritten or typed notes would have been transcribed by a typesetter who would have set the pages up using lead type to design the page. This type would then have been used with ink to make a physical imprint of the words onto a second artefact – the book proofs. After correction these would have been transcribed once more by the printer to make a second layout, which would again have been made into a photographic plate that the presses would have used to print the page. Between the notebook and the printed page there would have been several analogous stages before you could read the original notes. If, on the other hand, we write direct into word processing software every letter is immediately represented by a numerical value as an electronic response to touching a key on the keyboard rather than being a direct mechanical impression in paper caused by the weight and shape of a typewriter 'hammer' (see Hayles 1999: 26, 31). Layout, design and correction can all be carried out within a digital domain without recourse to the painstaking physical work of type manipulation.

Analogue media, mass production and broadcasting

The major media of the nineteenth and early twentieth centuries (prints, photographs, films and newspapers) were the products not only of analogue processes but also of technologies of mass production. For this reason, these traditional mass media took the form of industrially mass-produced physical artefacts which circulated the world as copies and commodities.

With the development of broadcast media, the distribution and circulation of such media as physical objects began to diminish. In broadcast media the physical analogue properties of image and sound media are converted into further analogues. These are wave forms of differing lengths and intensities which are encoded as the variable voltage of transmission signals. In live broadcast media such as pre-video television or radio there was a direct conversion of events and scenes into such electronic analogues.

This electronic conversion and transmission (broadcast) of media like film, which is a physical analogue, suggests that digital media technologies do not represent a complete break with traditional analogue media. Rather, they can be seen as a continuation and extension of a principle or technique that was already in place; that is to say, the principle of conversion from physical artefact to signal. However, the scale and nature of this extension are so significant that we might well experience it not as a continuation but as a complete break. We now look at why this is so.

For a detailed discussion of the differences between analogue and digital processes see T. Binkley, 'Reconfiguring culture' in P. Hayward and T. Wollen, *Future Visions: new technologies of the screen*, London: BFI (1993)

Digital media

In a digital media process the physical properties of the input data, light and sound waves, are not converted into another object but into numbers; that is, into abstract symbols rather than analogous objects and physical surfaces. Hence, media processes are brought into the symbolic realm of mathematics rather than physics or chemistry. Once coded numerically, the input data in a digital media production can immediately be subjected to the mathematical processes of addition, subtraction, multiplication and division through **algorithms** contained within software.

It is often mistakenly assumed that 'digital' means the conversion of physical data into binary information. In fact, digital merely signifies the assignation of numerical values to phenomena. The numerical values could be in the decimal (0–9) system; each component in the system would then have to recognise ten values or states (0–9). If, however, these numerical values are converted to binary numbers (0 and 1) then each component only has to recognise two states, on or off, current or no current, zero or one. Hence all input values are converted to binary numbers because it makes the design and use of the pulse recognition components that are the computer so much easier and cheaper.

This principle of converting all data into enormous strings of on/off pulses itself has a history. It is traced by some commentators from the late seventeenth-century philosopher Leibniz, through the nineteenth-century mathematician and inventor, Charles Babbage, to be formulated seminally by Alan Turing in the late 1930s (Mayer 1999: 4–21). The principle of binary digitality was long foreseen and sought out for a variety of different reasons. However, without the rapid developments in electronic engineering begun during the Second World War it would have remained a mathematical principle – an idea. Once the twin engineering goals of miniaturisation and data compression had combined with the principle of encoding data in a digital form massive amounts of data could be stored and manipulated.

In the last decades of the twentieth century the digital encoding of data moved out from the laboratories of scientific, military and corporate establishments (during the mainframe years) to be applied to communications and entertainment media. As specialist software, accessible machines and memory-intensive hardware became available, first text and then sound, graphics and images became encodable. The process swiftly spread throughout the analogue domain, allowing the conversion of analogue media texts to digital bit streams.

See W. J. Mitchell, *The Reconfigured Eye*, Cambridge, Mass.: MIT Press (1992), pp. 1–7, 18–19, and footnote on p. 231

The principle and practice of digitisation is important since it allows us to understand how the multiple operations involved in the production of media texts are released from existing only in the material realm of physics, chemistry and engineering and shift into a symbolic computational realm. The fundamental consequences of this shift are that:

- media texts are 'dematerialised' in the sense that they are separated from their physical form as photographic print, book, roll of film, etc. (However see the section 'Digital processes and the material world' for an account of why this does not mean that digital media are 'immaterial'.)

- data can be compressed into very small spaces;

- it can be accessed at very high speeds and in non-linear ways;

- it can be manipulated far more easily than analogue forms.

The scale of this quantitative shift in data storage, access and manipulation is such that it has been experienced as a qualitative change in the production, form, reception and use of media.

Fixity and flux

Analogue media tend towards being fixed, where digital media tend towards a permanent state of flux. Analogue media exist as fixed physical objects in the world, their production being dependent upon transcriptions from one physical state to another. Digital media may exist as analogue hard copy, but when the content of an image or text is in digital form it is available as a mutable string of binary numbers stored in a computer's memory.

The essential creative process of editing is primarily associated with film and video production, but in some form it is a part of most media processes. Photographers edit contact strips, music producers edit 'tapes'; and of course written texts of all kinds are edited. We can use the process of editing to think further about the implications of 'digitality' for media.

To change or edit a piece of analogue media involved having to deal with the entire physical object. For instance, imagine we wanted to change the levels of red on a piece of film as an analogue process. This would involve having to 'strike' new prints from the negative in which the chemical relationship between the film stock and the developing fluid was changed. This would entail remaking the entire print. If the original and inadequate print is stored digitally every pixel in every frame has its own data address. This enables us to isolate only the precise shots and even the parts of the frame that need to be changed, and issue instructions to these addresses to intensify or tone down the level of red. The film as a digital document exists near to a state of permanent flux until the final distribution print is struck and it returns to the analogue world of cinematic exhibition. (This too is changing as films get played out from servers rather than projectors in both on-demand digital TV and movie theatres.)

Any part of a text can be given its own data address that renders it susceptible to interactive input and change via software. This state of permanent flux is further maintained if the text in question never has to exist as hard copy, if it is located only in computer memories and accessible via the Internet or the web. Texts of this kind exist in a permanent state of flux in that, freed from authorial and physical limitation, any net user can interact with them, turning them into new texts, altering their circulation and distribution, editing them and sending them, and so on. This fundamental condition of digitality is well summarised by Pierre Lévy:

> The established differences between author and reader, performer and spectator, creator and interpreter become blurred and give way to a reading writing continuum that extends from the designers of the technology and networks to the final recipient, each one contributing to the activity of the other – the disappearance of the signature.
>
> (Lévy 1997: 366)

Digital processes and the material world

So digitisation creates the conditions for inputting very high quantities of data, very fast access to that data and very high rates of change of that data. However, we would not want to argue that this represents a complete transcendence of the physical world, as much digital rhetoric does. The limits of the physical sciences' ability to miniaturise the silicon chip may have already have been reached although current research on nano-circuits promises to reduce their current size by many times.

Although wireless connections between computers and servers and to networks are becoming increasingly common, many connections continue to rely upon cables and telephone lines, which have to be physically dug into the earth. On a more day-to-day level the constant negotiations that any computer-based media producer has to make between memory and compression are also testament to the continuing interface with the physical

For news on nano-chip developments see: http://www.science daily.com/releases/2006 /07/060708082927.htm

CASE STUDY 1.2: Email: the problem of the digital letter

One estimate suggests that there are now over 1.2 billion, and rising, email users in the world (see: http://www.radicati.com/). For those of us within that sixth of the world's population email is now an everyday medium; part of the everyday routines which have dropped below the level of conscious attention. Yet 'e-mail' (electronic mail) developed alongside or within the wider development of the Internet from its origins in more local networks such as ARPANET from the 1970s on. In this sense it was simply a way of writing terse notes or messages in much the same way as people wrote and sent notes or letters to one another with the advantage of much more rapid delivery. However, as the ownership of networked PCs grew, and email applications became widely available, commercially or as free downloads, the email came to replace the written letter for very large numbers of people. There is more to this than meets the eye (not least for the postal services that still exist worldwide) and it continues to be a useful case study in thinking about the significance of digitality.

The conventional letter had specific and valuable characteristics and an important history (and for some people, it still has. Indeed, some of the characterstics of email communication that we discuss below have led to a certain re-evaluation of the 'letter'). The letter requires physical production, it has to be written or typed, put into an envelope, licked, posted in a special box. It is then subject to the vast enterprise of the post office system in which each house is a physicalised data address.

In addition to these material properties the letter has an important history as a literary and cultural form. Until industrialisation interpersonal communication over distance by writing depended upon the physical transportation of the text by messenger, hand to hand. Public or private news took days or weeks to move from one part of a country, or empire, to another. This pace of transmission had an effect upon the status of the message: the arrival of a letter in pre-industrial society was an 'occasion', replete with significance.

The commercial and military imperatives of industrialisation and imperialism demanded greater speed and accuracy in person-to-person communications, leading to developments in telegraphy, telephony and the modern postal service. By contrast, we might characterise email in relation to the principles of digitality (i.e. speed, quantity and flexibility). The email process, though not instantaneous, is extremely fast compared to the physical transportation of a letter; so fast, in fact, that it might stand as one of the best examples of the kind of 'space–time compression' often referred to as typical of a **postmodern** communications environment. Distant locations are brought into the same communicative proximity as the office next door.

Additionally the email, because it exists only in digital not analogue form, is subject to multiple transformations and uses. Unlike the handwritten letter it can be multiply re-edited during composition, and the recipient can re-edit the original, interpolating comment and response. The email can be sent to individuals or groups, so the email might be written in any number of registers on a private–public scale. Writing an email to your co-workers will demand a different mode of address from writing an email to your extended friends and family network. A one-to-one email will have a different tone from a group email – in composing we are constantly negotiating different positions on a private–public scale.

This flexibility is enhanced by the possibility of making attachments to the email. These might be anything from another text document to photos, moving image files or music. More or less whatever can be digitised can be attached. Here we see email exemplifying **convergence** of previously discrete media forms.

These qualities have led to a massive increase in the quantity of communications information processed via the PC. There is a net increase in communicative actions, a perceived increase in productivity for organisations, and arguably an increase in social and familial communicative traffic (among what we have to remember is still a global minority with domestic online access). At the level of administration and management this use of email represents an intensification of the paper-based form of the memo. However, this increase in traffic creates new problems of data storage and management; the sheer volume of email received by organisational workers creates 'information overload'. 'No email days' have become a feature of corporate life as managers have come to understand that constant message checking is the enemy of concentration (see Wakefield 2007).

These changes have a number of qualitative implications. For instance, whereas the postal letter has evolved a whole series of formal codes and conventions in modes of address (inscribed as core topics within British schools' National Curriculum) the new forms of digital text communication have evolved a whole set of far less formal conventions:

Thoughts tend toward the experiential idea, the quip, the global perspective, the interdisciplinary thesis, the uninhibited, often emotional response. I Way [Internet] thought is modular, non-linear, malleable and co-operative. Many participants prefer internet writing to book writing as it is conversational, frank and communicative rather than precise and over written.

(Kevin Kelly, editor, *Wired* magazine in 'Guardian Online', 20 June 1994)

However, the responses prompted by the instantaneous availability of the reply button are not always so positive – hence the Internet-based practice of '**flaming**' – argumentative, hostile and insulting exchanges which can accelerate rapidly in a spiral of mutual recrimination. It is precisely the absence of the face-to-face exchange that leads to communication that can become dangerous. The carefully crafted diplomatically composed memo gives way to the collectively composed, often acrimonious, email debate.

With this kind of history in mind we can see how a consideration of even the banal case of email might give rise to a number of central critical questions:

1   Where does control over **authorship** lie when the email text can be multiply amended and forwarded?

2   What kind of authority should we accord the electronic letter? Why do we still insist on hard copy for contractual or legal purposes?

3   What are the possible consequences of an interpersonal communication system based increasingly not on face-to-face interaction but on anonymous, instant, interaction?

In attempting to answer such questions we might have recourse to different kinds of analytic contexts. First of all an understanding of the cultural history and form of the letter itself. Second, an understanding of the convergence of discrete media forms through the process of digitisation. Third, an attempt to assess those shifts through already existing analyses of culture – in this case theories of authorship and reading. Finally, the questions above would have to be answered with reference to the study of CMC (Computer Mediated Communications) in which the problem of the disappearance of face-to-face communication has been central.

world that has always been at the centre of media processing. For consumers worldwide, differences of wealth and poverty which underpin their highly differential access to other goods, services and technologies apply equally to digital media. The digital principle does not escape the demands of physics or the economic principles of scarcity.

> For a brief history of email see: http://www.livinginternet.com /e/ei.htm

1.2.2 Interactivity

Since the early 1990s, the term 'interactivity' has been much debated and has undergone frequent redefinition. Most commentators have agreed that it is a concept that requires further definition if it is to have any analytical purchase (see e.g. Downes and McMillan 2000; Jensen 1999; Schultz 2000; Huhtamo 2000; Aarseth 1997; Manovich 2001: 49–61). Subsequently there have been several main attempts to do so which we discuss below and in **Case Study 1.3**. The concept also carries a strong ideological charge: as Aarseth (1997: 48) observed, 'To declare a system interactive is to endorse it with a magic power.'

> Case study 1.3 What is new about interactivity?

At the ideological level, interactivity has been one of the key 'value added' characteristics of new media. Where 'old' media offered passive consumption new media offer interactivity. Generally, the term stands for a more powerful sense of user engagement with media texts, a more independent relation to sources of knowledge, individualised media use, and greater user choice. Such ideas about the value of 'interactivity' have clearly drawn upon the popular discourse of neo-liberalism (see **3.7**) which treats the user as, above all, a consumer. Neo-liberal societies aim to commodify all kinds of experience and offer more and more finely tuned degrees of choice to the consumer. People are seen as being able to make individualised lifestyle choices from a never-ending array of possibilities offered by the market. This

3.4 Political economy

For full discussions of the problems of defining interactivity see Jens F. Jensen's 'Interactivity – tracking a new concept in media and communication studies', in Paul Mayer (ed.) *Computer Media and Communication*, Oxford: Oxford University Press, (1999), which offers a comprehensive review of theoretical approaches, and E. Downes and S. McMillan, 'Defining Interactivity', *New Media and Society* 2.2 (2000): 157–179 for a qualitative ethnographic account of the difficulties of applying theoretical definitions in practice; and Lisbet Klastrup (2003) *Paradigms of interaction conceptions and misconceptions of the field today* (http://www.dichtung-digital.com/2003/issue/4/klastrup/) for a provocative study of the term's slipperiness

1.2.3 Hypertextual

1.2.5 Virtual
2.1–2.6 What happened to Virtual Reality; The virtual and visual culture; The digital virtual; Immersion: a history; Perspective, camera, software; Virtual images/Images of the virtual

ideological context then feeds into the way we think about the idea of interactivity in digital media. It is seen as a method for maximising consumer choice in relation to media texts.

However, in this section we are mainly concerned with the instrumental level of meanings carried by the term 'interactive'. In this context, being interactive signifies the users' (the individual members of the new media 'audience') ability to directly intervene in and change the images and texts that they access. So the audience for new media becomes a 'user' rather than the 'viewer' of visual culture, film and TV or a 'reader' of literature. In interactive multimedia texts there is a sense in which it is necessary for the user to actively intervene; to act as well as viewing or reading in order to produce meaning. This intervention actually subsumes other modes of engagement such as 'playing', 'experimenting', and 'exploring' under the idea of interaction. Hinting at the connection between instrumental definitions and ideological meanings, Rosanne Allucquere Stone suggests that the wide field of possibility suggested by the idea of interactivity has been 'electronically instantiated . . . in a form most suitable for commercial development – the user moves the cursor to the appropriate place and clicks the mouse, which causes something to happen' (Stone 1995: 8). We can break down this pragmatic account of interactivity further.

Hypertextual navigation

Here the user must use the computer apparatus and software to make reading choices in a database. (We are using the term 'database' in a general rather than specifically technical sense – a database is any collection of memory stored information, text, image, sound, etc.) In principle, this database could be anything from the entire World Wide Web to a particular learning package, an adventure game, or the hard drive on your own PC. The end results of such interactions will be that the user constructs for him or herself an individualised text made up from all the segments of text which they call up through their navigation process. The larger the database the greater the chance that each user will experience a unique text (**1.2.3**).

Immersive navigation

In the early 1990s Peter Lunenfeld (1993) usefully distinguished between two paradigms of interaction, which he called the 'extractive' and the 'immersive'. Hypertextual navigation (above) is 'extractive'. However, when we move from seeking to gain access to data and information to navigating representations of space or simulated 3D worlds we move into 'immersive' interaction. In some sense both kinds of interaction rely upon the same technological fact – the existence of a very large database which the user is called upon to experience. At one level, a more or less realistically rendered 3D space like the game world of 'Halo 3' or 'Grand Theft Auto IV' is just as much a big database as Microsoft's 'Encarta' encyclopaedia. We might say that the navigation of immersive media environments is similar to hypertextual navigation, but with additional qualities (**1.2.5, 2.1–2.6**).

When interacting in immersive environments the user's goals and the representational qualities of the media text are different. Immersive interaction occurs on a spectrum from 3D worlds represented on single screens through to the 3D spaces and simulations of virtual reality technologies. Although the point-and-click interactivity of hypertextual navigation may well be encountered in such texts, immersive interaction will also include the potential to explore and navigate in visually represented screen spaces. Here the purpose of interaction is likely to be different from the extractive paradigm. Instead of a text-based experience aimed at finding and connecting bits of information, the goals of the immersed user will include the visual and sensory pleasures of spatial exploration.

Registrational interactivity

Registrational interactivity refers to the opportunities that new media texts afford their users to 'write back into' the text; that is to say, to add to the text by registering their own messages. The base line of this kind of interactivity is the simple activity of registration (i.e. sending off details of contact information to a website, answering questions prompted in online transactions, or typing in a credit card number). However, it extends to any opportunity that the user has to input to a text. The original Internet bulletin boards and newsgroups were a good example – not interactive in the sense of face-to-face communication, yet clearly built up by successive inputs of users' comments. This 'input' or 'writing back' then becomes part of the text and may be made available to other users of the database.

Interactive communications

As we have seen in our case study of email (**Case study 1.2**), computer-mediated communications (CMC) have offered unprecedented opportunities for making connections between individuals, within organisations, and between individuals and organisations.

Much of this connectivity will be of the registrational interactivity mode (defined above) where individuals add to, change, or synthesise the texts received from others. However, when email and chat sites are considered from the point of view of human communication, ideas about the degree of reciprocity between participants in an exchange are brought into play. So, from a Communication Studies point of view, degrees of interactivity are further broken down on the basis of the kinds of communication that occur within CMC. Communicative behaviours are classified according to their similarity to, or difference from, face-to-face dialogue, which is frequently taken as the exemplary communicative situation which all forms of 'mediated' communication have to emulate. On this basis, the question and response pattern of a bulletin board or online forum, for instance, would be seen as less interactive than the free-flowing conversation of a chat site. This inflects the whole idea of interactivity by lending it a context of person-to-person connection.

Interactivity and problems of textual interpretation

Interactivity multiplies the traditional problems about how texts are interpreted by their readers. By the problem of interpretation we refer to the idea that the meaning of any given text is not securely encoded for all audiences to decode in the same way. This is based upon the recognition that the meanings of a text will vary according to the nature of its audiences and circumstances of reception. We all already have highly active interpretative relationships with the analogue (or linear) texts we encounter, such as books and movies. Under conditions of interactivity this problem does not disappear but is multiplied exponentially. This is because the producer of an interactive text or navigable database never knows for certain which of the many versions of the text their reader will encounter. For critics this has raised the essential question of how to evaluate or even conceptualise a 'text' that never reads the same way twice. For producers it raises essential problems of control and authorship. How do they make a text for a reader knowing that they have very many possible pathways through it?

What is the interactive text?

Established ways of thinking about how meaning is produced between readers and texts assumed a stability of the text but a fluidity of interpretation. Under conditions of interactivity this traditional stability of the text has also become fluid. Hence as critics we find ourselves having to reconceptualise the status of our own interpretations of the interactive text. From a theoretical point of view the traditional semiotic tools used for analysis of texts become

Case study 1.2 Email: the problem of the digital letter

See Lev Manovich 'What New Media is Not', *The Language of New Media*, Cambridge, Mass.: MIT Press (2001), pp. 49–61 and Espen Aarseth, 'We All Want to Change the World: the ideology of innovation in digital media', *Digital Media Revisited* (eds T. Rasmussen, G. Liestol and A. Morrison), Cambridge, Mass.: MIT Press (2002). Both authors argue that we have always had an 'interactive' relationship with texts of all kinds because of our individual interpretative relationships with them and that therefore 'interactivity' is a redundant term inadequate. Aarseth observed in his seminal study of the problem in *Cybertext*: '[t]he new [interactive digital media] consist of "interactive dynamic" elements, a fact that renders traditional semiotic models and terminology, which were developed for objects that are mostly static, useless in their present unmodified form' (Aarseth 1997: 26). Instead of the traditional text/user relations the many kinds of interactivity now available have suggested the need to think of the user as a component in cybernetic circuit of machine, text and body:

> Cybertext . . . is the wide range (or perspective) of possible textualities seen as a typology of machines, as various kinds of literary communication systems where the functional differences among the mechanical parts play a defining role in determining the aesthetic process . . . cybertext shifts the focus from the traditional threesome of author/sender, text/message, and reader/receiver to the cybernetic intercourse between the various part(icipant)s in the textual machine.
>
> (Aarseth 1997: 22)

Understandings of the role of the body in this circuit have become increasingly frequent following Marie-Laure Ryan's (2001) work calling for a phenomenology that analyses 'the sense of "presence" through which the user feels corporeally connected to the virtual world' (2001: 14). These approaches are particularly appropriate where the interactive pleasures on offer are primarily kinaesthetic rather than cognitive as in the case of the immersive interactions offered by computer games for example. As Dovey and Kennedy (2006: 106) argued, 'The idea of a disembodied spectator/viewer/reader is a fictional subject created by particular ways of conceptualising the relationship between "texts" and "readers". This fiction is founded on the Cartesian model of perception whereby consciousness is seen as separate to and distinct from embodiment.'

The cybernetic quality of interactions afforded by digital textualities has led some commentators (see Aarseth 2001, Eskelinen 2001 and Moulthrop 2004) to adopt the use of the term 'configuration' in preference to 'interaction'. This term carries the double force of its derivation from Actor Network Theory inflected study of technological design (Woolgar 1991) and its more colloquial meaning of the ways in which were all called upon to individually 'configure' or simply 'set up' our own technological environments. In his study of usability trials Woolgar defines configuration as designers' attempts to 'define, enable, and constrain' the user, through the design of an object which will 'define and delimit' the user's possible behaviours. In this sense technologies 'configure' us, affording particular kinds of behavioural patterns. So whereas the term 'interaction' implies a two-way communication, 'configuration' suggests a two-way, mutually constitutive process through which both user and software are dynamically engaged in refashioning one another in a feedback loop. Moulthrop argues that understanding computer gameplay helps to explain how we are all increasingly called upon to have configurative relationships with our media environments:

> Games – computer games in particular – appeal because they are configurative, offering the chance to manipulate complex systems within continuous loops of intervention, observation, and response. Interest in such activities grows as more people exchange email, surf the world wide web, post to newsgroups, build web logs, engage in chat and instant messaging, and trade media files through peer-to-peer networks. As in various sorts of gaming, these are all in some degree configurative practices, involving manipulation of dynamic systems that develop in unpredictable or emergent ways.
>
> (Moulthrop 2004: 64)

His argument makes a similar claim to the neo-Frankfurt School position on 'interaction' (see **Case study 1.3**) that 'configuration' is a necessarily active way for us to understand not just software systems but also political and cultural systems:

> If we conceive of configuration as a way of engaging not just immediate game elements, but also the game's social and material conditions – and by extension, the conditions of other rule-systems such as work and citizenship – then it may be very important to insist upon the difference between play and interpretation, the better to resist immersion.
>
> (2004: 66)

Problems for producers

If new media products pose new questions about textuality they also demand different relationships between producers and users. How do you design an interface that offers navigational choice but at the same time delivers a coherent experience? These problems will of course vary from one text to another. For instance, a website with many embedded links to other sites will offer users many opportunities to take different pathways. The reader/user is quite likely to click onto another site whilst only halfway through your own. On the other hand, within a downloaded interactive learning package, or one that runs off a discrete memory drive (i.e. CD-ROM/DVD) where there is a finite database, the user can be far more easily 'guided' in their navigation of pathways that the producers are able to pre-structure. This has meant that producers of interactive texts have gradually come to understand that they need to have collaborative and co-creative relationship with their audiences (see **3.22–3.23**). The digital media text (e.g. website, game, social network), is an *environment* supporting a range of user activities that emerge within the perimeters of the software. Producers therefore need, in Woolgar's terms, to 'configure' the user, to have some idea of the kinds of behaviours that they want their environment to afford, whilst simultaneously understanding that they can neither wholly predict nor control what users will do within it.

These rich forms of interaction therefore have a number of consequences for producers:

- they create the possibility for traditional media producers to collaborate with audiences by finding ways to incorporate 'user-generated content' in their corporate projects e.g. newspapers 'crowdsourcing' stories (see **3.21**)

- they also redefine the producer not as author but as 'experience designer'. Authors produced texts that readers interpreted. Interactive media designers are increasingly experience designers, creating open media spaces within which users find their own pathways (e.g. *The Sims* or *Second Life*)

- audiences' expectations of an interactive experience with a mediated world create the conditions for transmedial production in which for instance a TV programme can be repurposed across a range of platforms, a website with chat/forum capability, a box set DVD with additional material, a computer game etc.

1.2.3 Hypertextual

There are clear links between the navigational, explorative, and configurative aspects of interactivity and hypertextuality. Also, like interactivity, hypertextuality has ideological overtones and is another key term that has been used to mark off the novelty of new media from analogue media. Apart from its reference to non-sequential connections between all kinds of data facilitated by the computer, in the early 1990s the pursuit of literary hypertexts as novels and forms of non-linear fiction was much in evidence, becoming something of an artistic movement. Such literary hypertexts also attracted much attention from critics and theorists. This work now looks something like a transitional moment produced by the meeting between literary studies and new media potential. However, hypertext and hypertexuality remain an important part of the history of computing, particularly in the way they address ideas about the relationship of computer operating systems, software and databases, to the operation of the human mind, cognitive processes and learning.

Histories

The prefix 'hyper' is derived from the Greek 'above, beyond, or outside'. Hence, hypertext has come to describe a text which provides a network of links to other texts that are 'outside, above and beyond' itself. Hypertext, both as a practice and an object of study, has a dual history.

One history ties the term into academic literary and representational theory. Here there has long been an interest in the way any particular literary work (or image) draws upon or refers out to the content of others, the process referred to as intertextuality. This places any text as comprehensible only within a web of association that is at once 'above, beyond or outside' the text itself. At another level, the conventional means of footnoting, indexing, and providing glossaries and bibliographies – in other words the navigational apparatus of the book – can be seen as antecedents of hypertexts, again guiding the reader beyond the immediate text to necessary contextualising information.

The other history is derived from the language of the computer development industry. Here, any verbal, visual or audio data that has, within itself, links to other data might be referred to as a hypertext. In this sense the strict term 'hypertext' frequently becomes confused with the idea and rhetoric of hypermedia (with its connotations of a kind of super medium which is 'above, beyond, or outside' all other media connecting them all together in a web of convergence).

Defining hypertexts

We may define a hypertext as a work which is made up from discrete units of material, each of which carries a number of pathways to other units. The work is a web of connection which the user explores using the navigational aids of the interface design. Each discrete 'node' in the web has a number of entrances and exits or links.

1.2.1 Digital

As we have seen (**1.2.1**), in a digitally encoded text any part can be accessed as easily as any other so that we can say that every part of the text can be equidistant from the reader. In an analogue system like traditional video, arriving at a particular frame ten minutes into a tape involved having to spool past every intervening frame. When this information came to be stored digitally this access became more or less instantaneous. Such technology offers the idea that any data location might have a number of instantly accessible links to other locations built into it. Equally the many interventions and manipulations enabled by this facility create the qualities of interactivity (**1.2.2**).

Hypertext and a model of the mind

Vannevar Bush's 1945 essay 'As We May Think' is often seen as a seminal contribution to the idea of hypertext. Bush was motivated by the problem of information overload; the problem of the sheer volume of knowledge that specialists, even in the late 1940s, had to access and manipulate. Bush proposed that science and technology might be applied to the

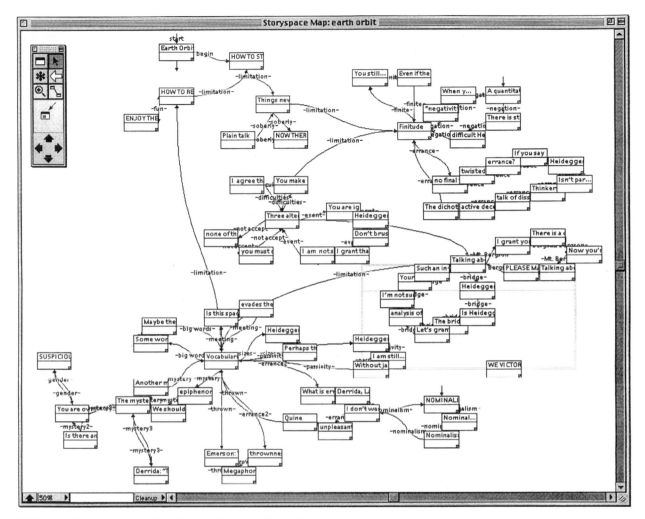

1.5 Diagram of an early hypertextual architecture – Storyspace Map: earth orbit, www.eastgate.com

management of knowledge in such a way as to produce novel methods for its storage and retrieval. He conceptualised a machine, the 'Memex', in which data could be stored and retrieved by association rather than by the alphabetical and numerical systems of library indices. Bush argued that,

> The human mind operates by association. With one item in its grasp, it snaps instantly to the next that is suggested by the association of thoughts, in association with some intricate web of trails carried by the cells of the brain.
>
> (Bush in Mayer 1999: 33)

The data in the Memex would be individually coded according to the associative links that a user found meaningful to his or her own work,

> It [the Memex] affords an immediate step . . . to associative indexing, the basic idea of which is a provision whereby any item may be caused at will to select immediately and automatically another . . . The process of tying two items together is the important thing.
>
> (Bush in Mayer 1999: 34)

See Pierre Lévy, *Collective Intelligence: Mankind's Emerging World in Cyberspace*, Cambridge: Perseus (1997) and D. Tapscott and A. Williams, *Wikinomics: How Mass Collaboration Changes Everything*, London: Penguin Books (2006) for the ways in which these utopian aspirations have been absorbed into business practice

Bush's argument from 1945 carries within it many of the important ideas that have subsequently informed the technology and practice of hypertext. In particular his position rests upon the assertion that associative linkage of data is a more 'natural' model of information management than the conventional linear alphabetical methods of bibliography such as the Dewey library system. Associative linkage, argues Bush, replicates more accurately the way the mind works. The continuing appeal of hypertext as both information storage and creative methodology has been that it appears to offer a better model of consciousness than linear storage systems. We can observe this appeal continuing in speculation about the development of a global 'neural net' that follows on from Nelson's arguments below. These ideas also resurface in a different form in the arguments of Pierre Lévy calling for a global 'collective intelligence' and in the daily practice of using a site like Wikipedia. Such an enterprise appears in many ways to conform to the idea that knowledge can be produced through associative rather than linear linkage and that, moreover, this knowledge can be collectively authored.

Hypertext as non-sequential writing

The microfiche technologies of the postwar period were unable to create Bush's vision. However, twenty years later, as digital computing began to be more widespread, his ideas were revived, most notably by Ted Nelson. His 1982 paper 'A New Home for the Mind' argues for the wholesale reorganisation of knowledge along hypertextual lines:

> This simple facility – call it the jump-link capability – leads immediately to all sorts of new text forms: for scholarship, for teaching, for fiction, for poetry . . . The link facility gives us much more than the attachment of mere odds and ends. It permits fully non sequential writing. Writings have been sequential because pages have been sequential. What is the alternative? Why hypertext – non sequential writing.
>
> (Nelson 1982, in Mayer 1999: 121)

However, Nelson does not stop at the idea of non-sequential writing, he also foresees, ten years before browser software made Internet navigation a non-specialist activity, a medium very close to contemporary website forms of the Internet. In this medium 'documents window and link freely to one another', 'every quotation may be traced instantly', and 'minority interpretations and commentary may be found everywhere'. He envisages

> a hyperworld – a new realm of published text and graphics, all available instantly; a grand library that anybody can store anything in – and get a royalty for – with links, alternate visions, and backtrack available as options to anyone who wishes to publish them.
>
> (Nelson 1982, in Mayer 1999: 124)

So, the postwar challenge of managing information overload, a model of the mind as a web of trails and associations, and a concept of non-linear writing then extended to a freely accessible 'grand library' of all kinds of media, finally lead us to the concept of hypermedia. Nelson's vision of the potential of hypertext opens out to encompass an emancipatory configuration of human knowledge based in accessibility and manipulation through associative links.

Hypermediacy

More recently the very specific application of hypertext as an information management principle expanded to suggest all kinds of non-linear, networked paradigms. Here the term began
to overlap with the idea of hypermediacy. The ideological investment in the idea of hypertext
spills over into use of the term 'hypermedia' to describe the effects of hypertextual methods
of organisation on all mediated forms. By the end of the 1990s, hypermediacy emerged as
an important term in a theory of new media:

> the logic of hypermediacy acknowledges multiple acts of representation and makes them
> visible. Where immediacy suggests a unified visual space, contemporary hypermediacy
> offers a heterogeneous space, in which representation is conceived of not as a window on
> the world, but rather as 'windowed' itself – with windows that open on to other repre-
> sentations or other media. The logic of hypermediacy multiplies the signs of mediation and
> in this way tries to reproduce the rich sensorium of human experience.
>
> (Bolter and Grusin 1999: 33–34)

Reproducing the 'rich sensorium of human experience' is the kind of claim that recalls
Marshall McLuhan's view that media should be understood as extensions of the human body
(**1.6.2**). As we have seen, it is a claim that that was present in the original formulations of ideas
of hypertextuality – the assumptions about cognition in Vannevar Bush and Ted Nelson here
become a principle in which hypermedia are valorised as somehow representing the ultimate
augmentation of human consciousness.

1.6.2 Mapping Marshall
McLuhan

From the library to Google – critical questions in hypertext

Much of the debate arising from the application of hypertext overlapped with discussions
about the consequences of interactivity. However, debates about the issues and questions
arising from hypertext practices have been conducted with reference to literary theory while
questions of interactivity tended to reference human computer interface studies and communication studies.

Clearly, considerations of interactivity and hypertext share a concern with the status and
nature of the text itself. What happens when conventional ways of thinking about the text
derived from literature or media studies are applied to texts that, allegedly, work in entirely
new ways? If the existing structures of knowledge are built upon the book, what happens
when the book is replaced by the computer memory and hypertextual linking?

Since the Middle Ages human knowledge and culture has been written, recorded and in
some sense produced by the form of the book (see, for example, Ong 2002; Chartier 1994). The
printed word has established an entire taxonomy and classification system for the management
and production of knowledge (e.g. contents, indices, reference systems, library systems, cita-
tion methods, etc.). It is argued that this literary apparatus of knowledge is defined around
sequential reading and writing. When we write, we order our material into a linear sequence in
which one item leads into another within recognised rhetorical terms of, for example, argument,
narrative or observation. Similarly the reader follows, by and large, the sequencing established
by the author. Now, it was argued, hypertext offered the possibility of non-sequential reading and
writing. There is no single order in which a text must be encountered.

Each 'node' of text carries within it variable numbers of links that take the reader to different successive nodes, and so on. Thus the reader is offered a 'non-linear' or, perhaps more
accurately, a 'multilinear' experience. (Following a link is a linear process; however the variable number of links on offer in any given text produce high numbers of possible pathways.)

Knowledge constructed as multilinear rather than monolinear, it is argued, threatens to overturn the organisation and management of knowledge as we have known it to date, since all existing knowledge systems are founded upon the principle of monolinearity.

Thus the very status of the text itself is challenged. The book which you hold in your hand is dissolved into a network of association – within the book itself numerous crosslinkages are made available which facilitate many different reading pathways; and the book itself becomes permeable to other texts. Its references and citations can be made instantly available, and other related arguments or converse viewpoints made available for immediate comparison. In short, the integrity of the book and of book-based knowledge systems is superseded by network knowledge systems. The superstructure of knowledge storage that formed library systems (Dewey classification, indices, paper based catalogues) is replaced by the design of the search engine with its associated systems of metadata, tagging and user-generated taxonomies of knowledge.

Hypertext scholarship

We can identify two trajectories in the first wave of hypertext scholarship that began to try and understand the significance of these developments.

The first was the return to previously marginal works in the history of literature which had themselves sought to challenge the linearity of text – these often experimental works are then constructed as 'proto-hypertexts'. So, for instance, works as diverse as the I Ching, Sterne's *Tristram Shandy*, Joyce's *Ulysses*, stories by Borges, Calvino, and Robert Coover and literary experiments with the material form of the book by Raymond Queneau and Marc Saporta are all cited as evidence that hypertextual modes of apprehension and composition have always existed as a limit point and challenge to 'conventional' literature. For students of other media we might begin to add the montage cinema of Vertov and Eisenstein, experiments with point of view in films like Kurosawa's *Rashomon* and time in a film like *Groundhog Day* (see, for example, Aarseth 1997: 41–54 and Murray 1997: 27–64). Equally, the montage of Dada, Surrealism and their echoes in the contemporary collage of screen-based visual culture might also be seen as 'hypermediated' in Bolter and Grusin's sense. Here then is another important point at which the history of culture is reformulated by the development of new media forms (**1.4**).

1.2.4 Networked

During the late 1970s and throughout the 1980s, capitalist economies experienced recurring crises, caused by the rigidity of their centralised production systems. These were crises in the profitability of the mass production of homogeneous commodities for mass consumer markets. In his detailed analysis of a shift from the 'modern' to the 'postmodern' mode of production, the Marxist cultural geographer David Harvey traced the manner in which these rigidities of centralised 'fordist' economies were addressed. Writing in 1989, he noted,

> what is most interesting about about the current situation is the way that capitalism is becoming ever more tightly organized *through dispersal*, geographical mobility, and flexible responses in labour markets, labour processes and consumer markets, all accompanied by hefty doses of institutional, product, *and technological innovation* [our emphases]

> (Harvey 1989: 159)

The primary literature and debates arising are by now extensive, and have become one of the most important points of contact between European critical theory and American **cyberculture** studies. This section offers a brief introductory overview of the key questions. For further study see, for example, Jay David Bolter, *Writing Space: The Computer, Hypertext and the History of Writing*, New York: Erlbaum (1991); George Landow and Paul Delaney (eds), *Hypermedia and Literary Studies*, Cambridge, Mass.: MIT Press (1991); George Landow, *Hypertext: The Convergence of Contemporary Literary Theory and Technology*, Baltimore and London: Johns Hopkins University Press (1992) (especially pp. 1–34); George Landow (ed.) *Hyper/Text/Theory*, Baltimore and London: Johns Hopkins University Press (1994); Mark Poster, *The Mode of Information*, Cambridge: Polity Press (1990), pp. 99–128

These changes were felt in the organisation of media production. In 1985, Françoise Sabbah observed the tendency of the then emerging 'new media' toward decentralisation of production, differentiation of products, and segmentation of consumption or reception:

> the new media determine a segmented, differentiated audience that, although massive in terms of numbers, is no longer a mass audience in terms of simultaneity and uniformity of the message it receives. The new media are no longer mass media . . . sending a limited number of messages to a homogeneous mass audience. Because of the multiplicity of messages and sources, the audience itself becomes more selective. The targeted audience tends to choose its messages, so deepening its segmentation . . .
>
> (Sabbah 1985: 219; quoted in Castells 1996: 339)

Now, in the first decade of the twenty-first century, these have become key aspects of our networked and dispersed mediasphere. Over the last twenty-five years or so, the development of decentralised networks has transformed media and communication processes. Indeed, some commentators now argue, we have recently entered a new phase in which these characteristics become even more pronounced. Here, not only are the markets and audiences for media of all kinds de-massified, increasingly specialist and segmented, and involving a blurring of producer and consumer, but whole sectors of the new media industries are learning to see their role as providing the means and opportunities for 'users' to generate their own content. Simultaneously, a new media economics is being recognised, one that does not aim to address large single audiences but instead seeks out the myriad of minority interests and niche markets that the net is able to support (see **3 .13**, The Long Tail).

The World Wide Web, corporate intranets, Virtual Learning Environments, MPORPGs, 'persistent worlds', Social Network Sites, blog networks, online forums of all kinds, and humble email distribution lists, are all networks of various scales and complexities that nestle within or weave their way selectively through others. All are ultimately connected in a vast, dense and (almost) global network (the Internet itself) within which an individual may roam, if policed and limited by firewalls, passwords, access rights, available bandwidths and the efficiency of their equipment. This is a network that is no longer necessarily accessed at fixed desktop workstations plugged into terrestrial phone lines or cables, but also wirelessly and on the move, via laptops, PDAs, GPS devices, and mobile phones.

There are intricacies, unforeseen contradictions and social, political, economic and cultural questions that arise with these developments. These issues are more fully discussed in Part 3 of this book. For the moment our task is to see how, in recent history, there has been a shift from media centralisation to dispersal and networking.

Consumption

From our present position we can see that from the 1980s on, our consumption of media texts has been marked by a shift from a limited number of standardised texts, accessed from a few dedicated and fixed positions, to a very large number of highly differentiated texts accessed in multifarious ways. The media audience has fragmented and differentiated as the number of media texts available to us has proliferated. For instance, from an era with a limited number of broadcast TV stations, containing no time-shifting VCRs or DVD players, with very limited use of computers as communication devices and no mobile media at all, we now find ourselves confronted by an unprecedented penetration of media texts into everyday life. 'National' newspapers are produced as geographically specific editions; they can be

For further accounts of the development of an approach to hypertext that goes beyond the post-structuralist paradigm, see especially Aarseth (1997), but also Michael Joyce, *Of Two Minds: hypertext pedagogy and poetics*, Ann Arbor: University of Michigan Press (1995); Stuart Moulthrop, 'Toward a rhetoric of informating texts in hypertext', *Proceedings of the Association for Computing Machinery*, New York (1992), 171–179; M. Rieser and A. Zapp (eds) *New Screen Media: cinema/art/narrative*, London: British Film Institute, 2002; M.-L. Ryan, *Possible Worlds, Artificial Intelligence, and Narrative Theory*, Bloomington and Indianapolis: Indiana University Press, (1991); P. Harrigan and N. Wardrip-Fruin (eds) *First Person, New Media as Story, Performance and Game*, Cambridge, Mass.: MIT Press, (2003.)

interactively accessed, archived online, we can receive 'alerts' to specific contents. Network and terrestrial TV stations are now joined by independent satellite and cable channels. Alongside real-time broadcasts we have TV 'on demand', time shifted, downloaded and interactive. The networked PC in the home offers a vast array of communication and media consumption opportunities; mobile telephony and mobile computing have begun to offer a future in which there are no media free zones, at least in the lives of the populations of the 'developed' world. Technologists are currently conceptualising what a 'pervasive' media environment will be, when all media is available on a variety of wireless platforms and devices.

See e.g.
http://interactive.usc.
edu/research/mobile/

The 'mass media', which were transformed in this way, were the products of the communication needs of the first half of the twentieth century in the industrialised world and as such they had certain characteristics. They were centralised, content was produced in highly capitalised industrial locations such as newspaper printworks or Hollywood film studios. In broadcast media, press and cinema, distribution was tied to production, film studios owned cinema chains, newspapers owned fleets of distribution vans, the BBC and other national 'broadcasters' owned their own transmission stations and masts. Consumption was characterised by uniformity: cinema audiences all over the world saw the same movie, all readers read the same text in a national newspaper, we all heard the same radio programme. And we did these things at the same scheduled times. Twentieth-century mass media were characterised by standardisation of content, distribution and production process. These tendencies toward centralisation and standardisation in turn reflected and created the possibility for control and regulation of media systems, for professionalisation of communicative and creative processes, for very clear distinctions between consumers and producers, and relatively easy protection of intellectual property.

See Brian Winston,
*Media, Technology and
Society: a History: from
the Telegraph to the
Internet*, London and
New York: Routledge
(1998), pp. 243–275, for
a history of broadcast
networks.

The centre of a circle

A useful way to conceptualise the difference between centralised and dispersed media distribution systems is to think about the differences between radio and television broadcast *transmissions* and computer media *networks*. The technology at the heart of the original radio and TV broadcast systems is radio wave transmission; here transmission suites required high investment in capital, plant, buildings, masts, etc. Airwave transmission was supplemented by systems of coaxial cable transmission, where massive investments throughout the twentieth century led to the establishment of a global network of cable systems crossing whole continents and oceans. At the core of this technology of transmission there was a central idea, that of transmission from 'one to many': one input signal was relayed to many points of consumption. The radio transmitter, then, works (for social and technological reasons) on a centralised model.

Nodes in a web

In contrast, the computer **server** is the technology at the heart of the dispersed systems of new media. A server, by contrast to a transmission mast, is a multiple input/output device, capable of receiving large amounts of data as input as well as making equally large quantities available for downloading to a PC. The server is a networked device. It has many input connections and many output connections, and exists as a node in a web rather than as the centre of a circle.

A radio transmitter capable of handling broadcast radio and TV signals is an expensive capital investment way beyond the reach of most enterprises or individuals. The server, on the other hand, is relatively cheap, being commonplace in medium or large enterprises of all kinds. Access to server space is commonly domestically available as part of online sub-scription packages.

However, this simple opposition between the centralised and the networked prompts questions. Most interestingly, it points up how there is no radical and complete break between 'old' and 'new' media. This is because networked media distribution could not exist without the technological spine provided by existing media routes of transmission, from tele-phone networks to radio transmission and satellite communications. 'Old' media systems of distribution are not about to disappear, although they become less visible, because they are the essential archaeological infrastructure of new media.

New media networks have been able to reconfigure themselves around this 'old' core to facilitate new kinds of distribution that are not necessarily centrally controlled and directed but are subject to a radically higher degree of audience differentiation and discrimination. Many different users can access many different kinds of media at many different times around the globe using network-based distribution. Consumers and users are increasingly able to cus-tomise their own media use to design individualised menus that serve their particular and specific needs.

This market segmentation and fragmentation should not be confused with a general democratisation of the media. As Steemers, Robins and Castells have argued, the multipli-cation of possible media choices has been accompanied by an intensification of merger activities among media corporations: 'we are not living in a global village, but in customised cottages globally produced and locally distributed' (Castells 1996: 341); (see **3.4–3.10**).

Production

This increased flexibility and informality of our interaction with media texts of all kinds is equally present in the field of media production. Here, too, we have seen the development of pro-duction technologies and processes that have challenged the older centralised methods of industrial organisation and mass media production sectors. These changes can be perceived within the professional audiovisual industries as well as within our everyday domestic spheres.

Today, media industries are facing the fact that the conjunction of computer-based com-munications and existing broadcast technologies has created a wholly new and fluid area of media production. The traditional boundaries and definitions between different media processes are broken down and reconfigured. The specialist craft skills of twentieth-century media production have become more generally dispersed throughout the population as a whole, in the form of a widening baseline of 'computer literacy', information technology skills, and especially the availability of software that increasingly affords the production of 'user-generated content' (see **3.21**) .

Across the period, the range of sites for the production of media content has expanded – production has been dispersing itself more thoroughly into the general economy, now fre-quently dubbed 'the knowledge economy' or the 'information society'. This dispersal of production can also be observed from the perspective of the everyday worlds of work and domesticity. Consider the proximity of media production processes to a twentieth-century cit-izen. In the UK during the 1970s, for instance, the nineteenth-century media processes of print and photography would probably have been the only kind of media production processes that might be used or discussed in everyday life as part of civic, commercial, cul-tural or political activity. Broadcasting and publishing systems (the 'press') were mostly very distant from the lives of ordinary people. However, by the end of the century, print production was easier than ever through digitised desktop publishing, and editorial and design tech-nologies were all available in domestic software packages. Photographic production through

An extraordinary but little noticed and eccentric example of this is the use of a subterranean system of conduits designed to provide hydraulically (waterpowered) generated electricity to London households in the 1890s. The conduits were designed to hold water under pressure which powered generators placed at the threshold of each subscribing home. This system, owned until the 1970s by the long defunct 'London Hydraulic Power Company', was purchased by Mercury Telecommunications in 1992. Under Mercury's ownership these conduits originally designed to carry water were used as a means to deliver Internet cable services to those same homes (Gershuny 1992)

See also Jeanette Steemers, 'Broadcasting is dead, long live digital choice', *Convergence* 3.1 (1997) and J. Cornford and K. Robins, 'New media', in J. Stokes and A. Reading (eds) *The Media in Britain*, London: Macmillan (1999)

digital cameras, post-production processes, and distribution through file compression and networks, have transformed domestic photography (see Rubinstein and Sluis 2008). Television production has moved much closer to the viewer in the sense that very many of us 'shoot' digital video which can now be distributed online by, for example, YouTube (see **3.23**). There may be limitations to this self production of media images, although new conventions and forms are also emerging to which the once mainstream media respond reflexively, but, as Castells recognised, it has also modified the older 'one way flow' of images and has 'reintegrated life experience and the screen' (1996: 338).

The integration of media process into everyday life is not confined to the domestic sphere. As work has increasingly moved towards service rather than production economies all kinds of non-media workers find themselves called upon to be familiar with various kinds of media production processes from web design to Powerpoint presentation and computer-mediated communication software. Both at home and at work media production processes are far closer to the rhythms of everyday life. While we certainly would not wish to over-emphasise the degree of this proximity by echoing claims of cyber pioneers for the total collapse of the distinction between consumption and production, it is certainly the case that the distance between the elite process of media production and everyday life is smaller now than at any time in the age of mass media.

Consumption meets production

Across a range of media we have seen the development of a market for 'prosumer' technologies; that is, technologies that are aimed at neither the professional nor the (amateur) consumer market but both – technologies that enable the user to be both consumer and producer. This is true in two senses; the purchaser of a £2,000 digital video camera is clearly a consumer (of the camera), and may use it to record home movies, the traditional domain of the hobbyist consumer. However, they may equally use it to record material of a broadcast quality for a Reality TV show, or to produce an activist anti-capitalist video that could have global distribution or pornographic material that could equally go into its own circuit of distribution. Until the 1990s the technological separation between what was acceptable for public distribution and what was 'only' suitable for domestic exhibition was rigid. The breakdown of the professional/amateur category is a matter ultimately of cost. The rigid distinction between professional and amateur technologies defined by engineering quality and cost has now broken down into an almost infinite continuum from the video captured on a mobile phone to the high-definition camera commanding six-figure prices.

The impact of these developments has been most clearly seen in the music industry. Digital technologies have made possible a dispersal and diffusion of music production that has fundamentally changed the nature of the popular music market. The apparatus of analogue music production, orchestral studios, 20-foot sound desks and 2-inch rolls of tape can all now be collapsed into a sampling keyboard, a couple of effects units, and a computer. The bedroom studio was clearly one of the myths of 'making it' in the 1990s; however, it is not without material foundation. The popular success of dance music in all its myriad global forms is in part the consequence of digital technologies making music production more accessible to a wider range of producers than at any time previously.

The PC itself is in many ways the ultimate figure of media 'prosumer' technology. It is a technology of distribution, of consumption, as well as a technology of production. We use it to look at and listen to other people's media products, as well as to produce our own, from ripping CD compilations to editing videotape, mixing music or publishing websites. This overlap between consumption and production is producing a new networked zone of media exhibition that is neither 'professionalised' mainstream nor amateur hobbyist. Jenkins argues that

> it is clear that new media technologies have profoundly altered the relations between media producers and consumers. Both culture jammers and fans have gained greater visibility as they have deployed the web for community building, intellectual exchange, cultural distribution, and media activism. Some sectors of the media industries have embraced active audiences as an extension of their marketing power, have sought greater feedback from their fans, and have incorporated viewer generated content into their design processes. Other sectors have sought to contain or silence the emerging knowledge culture. The new technologies broke down old barriers between media consumption and media production. The old rhetoric of opposition and cooptation assumed a world where consumers had little direct power to shape media content and where there were enormous barriers to entry into the marketplace, whereas the new digital environment expands their power to archive, annotate, appropriate, and recirculate media products.
>
> (Jenkins 2002: see **3.21**)

In the media industries the craft bases and apprenticeship systems that maintained quality and protected jobs have broken down more or less completely, so that the question of how anyone becomes 'qualified' to be a media producer is more a matter of creating a track record and portfolio for yourself than following any pre-established routes. This crisis is also reflected in media education. Here, some argue for a pressing need for a new vocationalism aimed at producing graduates skilled in networking and the production of intellectual and creative properties. Others argue that, in the light of the new developments outlined above, media studies should be seen as a central component of a new humanities, in which media interpretation and production are a core skillset for all kinds of professional employment. Yet others argue for a 'Media Studies 2.0' which would break with the traditional media studies emphasis on 'old' broadcasting models and would embrace the new skills and creativity of a 'YouTube' generation (see Gauntlett 2007, Merrin 2008).

In summary, new media are networked in comparison to mass media – networked at the level of consumption where we have seen a multiplication, segmentation and resultant individuation of media use; dispersed at the level of production where we have witnessed the multiplication of the sites for production of media texts and a greater diffusion within the economy as a whole than was previously the case. Finally, new media can be seen as networked rather than mass for the way in which consumers can now more easily extend their participation in media from active interpretation to actual production.

1.2.5 Virtual

Virtual worlds, spaces, objects, environments, realities, selves and identities, abound in discourses about new media. Indeed, in many of their applications, new media technologies produce virtualities. While the term 'virtual' (especially 'virtual reality') is readily and frequently used with respect to our experience of new digital media it is a difficult and complex term. In this section we make some initial sense of the term as a characteristic feature of new media. A fuller discussion and history will be found in Part 2 (**2.1–2.6**). In terms of new digital media we can identify a number of ways in which the virtual is used.

First, throughout the 1990s, the popular icon of 'virtual reality' was not an image of such a reality itself but of a person experiencing it and the apparatus that produced it. This is the image of a head-set wearing, crouching and contorted figure perceiving a computer-generated 'world' while their body, augmented by helmets carrying stereoscopic LCD screens, a device that monitors the direction of their gaze, and wired gloves or body suits providing tactile and positioning feedback, moves in physical space.

Equally powerful have been a series of movies, cinematic representations of virtual reality, from the early 1980s onwards, in which the action and narrative takes place in a simulated, computer generated world (*Tron*: 1982, *Videodrame*: 1983, *Lawnmower Man*: 1992, *The Matrix*: 1999, *eXistenZ*: 1999).

The 'virtual reality' experienced by the wearer of the apparatus is produced by **immersion** in an environment constructed with computer graphics and digital video with which the 'user' has some degree of interaction. The movies imagine a condition where human subjects inhabit a virtual world which is mistaken for, or has replaced, a 'real' and physical one.

Second, alongside these immersive and spectacular forms of virtual reality, another influential use of the term refers to the space where participants in forms of online communication feel themselves to be. This is a space famously described as 'where you are when you're talking on the telephone' (Rucker *et al.* 1993: 78). Or, more carefully, as a space which 'comes into being when you are on the phone: not exactly where you happen to be sitting, nor where the other person is, but somewhere in between' (Mirzoeff 1999: 91).

As well as these uses, the 'virtual' is frequently cited as a feature of postmodern cultures and technologically advanced societies in which so many aspects of everyday experience are technologically simulated. This is an argument about the state of media culture, postmodern identity, art, entertainment, consumer and visual culture; a world in which we visit virtual shops and banks, hold virtual meetings, have virtual sex, and where screen-based 3D worlds are explored or navigated by videogame players, technicians, pilots, surgeons etc.

Increasingly we also find the term being used retrospectively. We have already noted the case of the telephone, but also the experience of watching film and television, reading books and texts, or contemplating photographs and paintings are being retrospectively described as virtual realities (see Morse 1998; Heim 1993: 110; Laurel in Coyle 1993: 150; Mirzoeff 1999: 92–99). These retrospective uses of the term can be understood in two ways: either as a case of the emergence of new phenomena casting older ones in a new light (Chesher 1997: 91) or that, once it is looked for, experience of the 'virtual' is found to have a long history (Mirzoeff 1999: 91 and Shields 2003).

As Shields has pointed out (2003: 46) in the digital era the meaning of 'virtual' has changed. Where, in everyday usage, it once meant a state that was 'almost' or 'as good as' reality, it has now come to mean or be synonymous with 'simulated' (see **1.2.6**). In this sense, rather than meaning an 'incomplete form of reality' it now suggests an alternative to the real and, maybe, 'better than the real' (46). However, some older meanings of 'virtual' still find echoes in modern usage. One of these is the connection between the virtual and the 'liminal' in an anthropological sense, where the liminal is a borderline or threshold between different states such as the carnivals or coming of age rituals held in traditional societies. Such rituals are usually marked by a period in which the normal social order is suspended for the subject who is passing from one status or position to another. The more recent interest in virtual spaces as spaces of identity performance or places where different roles can be played out appears continuous with older liminal zones (Shields 2003: 12).

The rise of the digital virtual (the virtual as simulation and as an alternative reality) has also

See http://www.cyberpunk review.com/virtual-reality-movies/ for a full list of movies about VR

3.17–3.20
5.4 Theories of cyberculture

For a view which challenges the idea that the Internet is a space, or should be thought of as a space at all, see Chesher (1997): 91

The experience of acting remotely via robotics on a simulation can more accurately be described as telepresence. While telepresence is often subsumed as a kind of VR, see Ken Goldberg, 'Virtual reality in the age of telepresence', *Convergence* 4.1 (1998) for a fuller discussion of the difference led to interest in philosophical accounts of the virtual. Here, particularly in the thought of the philosopher Gilles Deleuze, we are urged to see that the virtual is not the opposite of the real but is itself a kind of reality and is properly opposed to what is 'actually' real. This is an important argument as, in a world in which so much is virtual, we are saved from concluding that this is tantamount to living in some kind of un-real and immaterial fantasy world. In networked, technologically intensive societies we increasingly pass between actual and virtual realities; in such societies we deal seamlessly with these differing modes of reality (see **3.20**).

There is a common quality to the two kinds of virtual reality with which we started above (that produced by technological immersion and computer generated imagery and that imagined space generated by online communications). This is the way that they give rise to puzzling relationships between new media technologies and our experiences and conceptions of space, of **embodiment** (literally: of having and being conscious of having bodies) and identity (see **4.4**). The generic concept which has subsumed both kinds of virtual reality has been 'cyberspace'. It is now arguable that the widespread and deep integration of new technologies into everyday life and work means that the concept of 'cyberspace' (as an other space to 'real' physical space) is losing its force and usefulness. Nevertheless, the promise of a fusion of these two kinds of virtual reality – the sensory plenitude of immersive VR and the connectivity of online communication – has been an important theme in the new media imaginary (see **1.5.2**) because, in such a scenario, full sensory immersion would be combined with extreme bodily remoteness.

The middle term, the ground for anticipating such a fusion of the two VRs, is the digital simulation of 'high resolution images of the human body in cyberspace' (see Stone 1994: 85). The empirical grounds for venturing such a claim are seen in the form of virtual actors or synthespians (computer simulations of actors) that appear in cinema, TV, and videogames. However, the computing power and the telecommunications bandwidth necessary to produce, transmit and refresh simulations of human beings and their environments, let alone the programming that would enable them to interact with one another in real time, remains a technological challenge. Instead we find the body digitally represented in a host of different ways. In popular culture for instance we see increasing hybridisation of the human body in performance as real actors create the data for a performance which is finally realised in CGI form through various techniques of motion capture. In the realm of MMORPGs we see the body of the user represented through avatars that are the subject of intense and intricate work by their users.

If we were to understand these digitisations of the body as partial realisations of the fully immersive 3-D Avatar, interesting questions arise. Where does the desire for such developments lie? And, what goals or purposes might attract the financial investment necessary for such technological developments? In thinking about these developments, their desirability and purpose, we have to take into account the **technological imaginary** (**1.5.2**) which so powerfully shapes thinking about new media of all kinds. We are also reminded of the part played by science fiction in providing us with ideas and images with which to think about cyberspace and the virtual. Writing in the mid-1990s, Stone (1994: 84), suggested that when the first 'virtual reality' environments came online they would be realisations of William Gibson's famous definition of cyberspace, in his novel *Neuromancer*, as a 'consensual hallucination'. The current examples of persistent online worlds such as '*Second Life*' or games like *World of Warcraft* mark the current stage of this vision and project.

> The way in which media history is more generally recast in the light of present preoccupations is discussed in 1.4, What kind of history?

> Related to this interest in virtual reality, a more general quality or mode of existence, 'the virtual', has seen revived interest. The concept has a long history in philosophy and theology (see Pierre Lévy, *Becoming Virtual: Reality in the Digital Age*, New York: Perseus, 1998). See also R. Shields, *The Virtual*, London and New York: Routledge (2003), and **5.4.2**

1.5.2 The technological imaginary

> See also: **2.1** What happened to Virtual Reality?

William Gibson, in *Neuromancer* (1986: 52), describes cyberspace as 'a consensual hallucination experienced daily by billions of legitimate operators in every nation . . . a graphic representation of data abstracted from the banks of every computer in every human system. Unthinkable complexity. Lines of light ranged in the nonspace of the mind, clusters and constellations of data. Like city lights receding.' This has become the standard science fictional basis for imagining cyberspace as an architectural (Cartesian) space, in which 'a man may be seen, and perhaps touched as a woman and vice versa – or as anything else. There is talk of renting pre-packaged body forms complete with voice and touch . . . multiple personality as commodity fetish!' (Stone 1994: 85)

This is very clear as regards the functional character of VR, which we discuss in **2.1–2.6** below

1.2.6 Simulated

We saw in the previous section that uses of the concept 'virtual' have, in a digital culture, close relationships with 'simulation'. Simulation is a widely and loosely used concept in the new media literature, but is seldom defined. It often simply takes the place of more established concepts such as 'imitation' or 'representation'. However where the concept is paid more attention, it has a dramatic effect on how we theorise cultural technologies such as VR (**2.1–2.6**) and cinema (**2.7**). For the moment, it is important to set out how the term has been used in order to make the concept of simulation, and how we will subsequently use it, clear.

Looser current uses of the term are immediately evident, even in new media studies, where it tends to carry more general connotations of the illusory, the false, the artificial, so that a simulation is cast as an insubstantial or hollow copy of something original or authentic. It is important to invert these assumptions. A simulation is certainly artificial, synthetic and fabricated, but it is not 'false' or 'illusory'. Processes of fabrication, synthesis and artifice are real and all produce new real objects. A videogame world does not necessarily imitate an original space or existing creatures, but it exists. Since not all simulations are imitations, it becomes much easier to see simulations as things, rather than as representations of things. The *content* of simulations may of course (and frequently does) derive from 'representations'. This is what lies at the core of Umberto Eco's analysis of Disneyland for instance: the houses in Disneyland's version of an ideal American Main Street are fakes, deceits, they look something like real houses yet are something quite different (in this case supermarkets or gift shops) (Eco 1986: 43). But noticing a gap between the representational content of a simulation (shops, space invaders) and its architectural or mechanical workings should not lead us to discount and ignore the latter. The simulation exists regardless of whether we are fooled by its content or not. Thus the problem to which simulation draws our attention is not that of the difference between 'simulated' and 'real' content, but rather that of the material and real existence of simulations as part of the furniture of the same real world that has been so thoroughly 'represented' throughout the history of the arts and media. In other words a simulation is real *before* it imitates or represents anything.

For the present, however, as things stand in new media studies, not only is there no agreement that simulation does in fact differ from representation or imitation, but the simple profusion of answers to the question of what simulation really is and how, or if it differs at all from representation or imitation, has led many commentators to give up seeking any specificity to the concept and to concede that

> [t]he distinction between simulation and imitation is a difficult and not altogether clear one. Nevertheless, it is vitally important. It lies at the heart of virtual reality.
>
> (Woolley 1992: 44)

Yet if the concept is, as Woolley here notes, 'vitally important', it surely becomes all the more important to seek some clarity. We should then examine the ways in which the term is in use with regard to the analysis of new media. There are three very broad such ways, which we will call Postmodernist, Computer, and Game simulation.

Postmodernist simulation
Here the term is drawn principally from Jean Baudrillard's identification of simulation with hyperreality (Baudrillard 1997). According to Baudrillard, simulacra are signs that cannot be exchanged with 'real' elements outside a given system of other signs, but only with other

signs within it. Crucially, these sign-for-sign exchanges assume the functionality and effectiveness of 'real' objects, which is why Baudrillard calls this regime of signs hyperreal. When, under these conditions, reality is supplanted by hyperreality, any reality innocent of signs disappears into a network of simulation.

In postmodernist debates over the past few decades claims that simulation is superseding representation have raised fundamental questions of the future of human political and cultural agency. Baudrillard himself, however, is no fan of postmodernist theory: 'The postmodern is the first truly universal conceptual conduit, like jeans or coca-cola . . . It is a world-wide verbal fornication' (Baudrillard 1996a: 70). This is in stark contrast to those who use Baudrillard's theorising as the exemplification of postmodern thought. Douglas Kellner, for instance, considers Baudrillard as resignedly telling the story of the death of the real without taking political responsibility for this story. Others consider him the media pessimist *par excellence*, who argues that the total coverage of the real with signs is equivalent to its absolute disappearance. Still others celebrate Baudrillard as an elegant 'so what?' in the face of the collapse of all values. All, however, omit the central point regarding his theory of simulation: that it functions and has effects – it is operational – and is therefore hyper-*real* rather than hyper-*fictional*. The grounds of this operativity are always, for Baudrillard, technological: 'Only technology perhaps gathers together the scattered fragments of the real' (Baudrillard 1996b: 4). 'Perhaps', he adds, 'through technology, the world is toying with us, the object is seducing us by giving us the illusion of power over it' (1996b: 5).

Baudrillard, who published an early (1967) and positive review of McLuhan's *Understanding Media*, makes it clear that the ground of hyperrealism is technology as a complex social actor over which we maintain an illusion of control. To cite a typically contentious Baudrillardian example, electoral systems in developed democratic states do not empower an electorate, but rather determine the exercise of democracy in cybernetic terms: voting for party X rather than party Y consolidates the governance of binary coding over political systems. This constitutes a 'simulation' of democracy not in the sense that there are really and in fact more complex political issues underlying this sham democracy; but rather in the sense that real and effective politics is now conducted in precisely this new scenario. Choice has become the only reality that matters, and it is precisely quantifiable. Thus the simulation, or transposition of democracy onto another scene, concerned exclusively with a hypertrophied 'choice', is the only political reality there is. It is for this reason that simulations constitute, for Baudrillard, the hyperreality of cybernetic governance. The 'perfect crime' to which the title of one of Baudrillard's works alludes is not the destruction of reality itself, but the destruction of an illusory reality beyond the technologies that make it work (Baudrillard 1996b). The effect is not a loss of reality, but the consolidation of a reality without an alternative.

Where commentators on contemporary cultural change have seized upon the concept of simulation is in noting a shift from 'representation' to simulation as dominant modes of the organisation of cultural objects and their signifying relationships to the world. According to such scholars 'representation' was conceived to be a cultural act, an artefact of negotiated meanings, pointing, however unsuccessfully or incompletely, to a real world beyond it. 'Simulation', they assert, supplants these negotiated relationships between social and cultural agents *and reality*, replacing them with relationships that operate *only within culture* and its mediations:

> The theory of simulation is a theory of how our images, our communications and our media have usurped the role of reality, and a history of how reality fades.
>
> (Cubitt 2001: 1)

Such critical approaches draw on theories that identify profound cultural, economic and polit-ical shifts taking place in the developed world in recent decades. A defining moment in the development of this approach is Guy Debord's *Society of the Spectacle* (1967), which argues that the saturation of social space with mass media has generated a society defined by spec-tacular rather than real relations. Although there are various approaches and positions within this broad trend, they generally share the assumption that the emergence in the postwar period of a consumption-led economy has driven a culture which is dominated and colonised by the mass media and commodification. The rise of this commercialised, mediated culture brings with it profound anxieties about how people might know, and act in, the world. The sheer proliferation of television screens, computer networks, theme parks and shopping cen-tres, and the saturation of everyday life by spectacular images so thoroughly mediated and processed that any connection with a 'real world' seems lost, adds up to a simulated world: a hyperreality where the artificial is experienced as real. Representation, the relationship (how-ever mediated) between the real world and its referents in the images and narratives of popular media and art, withers away. The simulations that take its place also replace reality with spectacular fictions whose lures we must resist. In broad outlines, this remains the stan-dard view of Baudrillard's theses.

Accordingly, Baudrillard's controversial and often poorly-understood versions of simula-tion and simulacra have proved very influential on theories and analysis of postwar popular and visual culture. The nature of the ascendency of this order of simulation over that of rep-resentation has been posited as being of fundamental importance to questions of the future of human political and cultural agency. Cultural and critical theory, when faced with the man-ufactured, the commodified and the artificial in modern culture, has identified the simulational and simulacral character of postwar culture in the developed world – a culture, it is claimed, that is increasingly derealised by the screens of the mass media, the seductions and veilings of commodification, and (more recently) the virtualisations of digital culture. For instance, Fredric Jameson describes the contemporary world as one in which all zones of culture and everyday life are subsumed by the commodifying reach of consumer capitalism and its spec-tacular media:

> a whole historically original consumers' appetite for a world transformed into sheer images of itself and for pseudo-events and 'spectacles' . . . It is for such objects that we reserve Plato's concept of the 'simulacrum', the identical copy for which no original has ever existed. Appropriately enough, the culture of the simulacrum comes to life in a society where exchange value has been generalized to the point at which the very memory of use value is effaced, a society of which Guy Debord has observed, in an extraordinary phrase, that in it 'the image has become the final form of commodity reification . . .'.
>
> (Jameson 1991: 18)

Similarly, for Cubitt, as reality fades, the materiality of the world around us becomes unsteady, 'the objects of consumption are unreal: they are meanings and appearances, style and fash-ion, the unnecessary and the highly processed' (Cubitt 2001: 5).

What is at stake for these theorists is that any sense of political agency or progressive knowledge is lost in this seductive, consumerist apocalypse. The relationship between the real and the mediated, the artificial and the natural, implodes. It is also clear how the tech-nological sophistication, seductive/immersive and commercial nature of videogames might be seen as a particularly vivid symptom of this postmodernist condition (Darley 2000). It is equally clear, however, that these critics' conceptions of Baudrillard in general and simulation in particular are at best partial, and at worst wholly misleading. For these reasons, it is wholly appropriate to refer to such a constellation of theories as 'postmodernist', as it is to argue that Baudrillard's simulation is not postmodernist. Far from providing any specificity to the concept of simulation, the postmodernist approach generalises it to the point where it becomes an entire theory of culture (the pervasiveness of technological visual culture is further discussed in **1.5.3**, and with specific regard to the theory of the 'virtual' in **2.1–2.6**).

Computer simulation

The second use of the concept reflects a more specific concern with simulation as a particular form of computer media (Woolley 1992, Lister *et al.* 2003, Frasca 2003, Prensky 2001). Just as a confusion of imitation, representation or mimesis with simulation arises in postmodernist uses, critical approaches to computer simulation tend to take a more nuanced attitude to the mimetic elements sometimes (but not always) present in simulation. The principal difference is, in this case, that simulation is not a dissembling, illusory distraction from the real world (like Eco's Disneyland) but rather a model of the world (or of some aspect of it). This context presents a more specific and differentiated use of simulation than that of the postmodernists. For some (writers, engineers, social scientists, military planners, etc.) the computer simulation models complex and dynamic systems over time in ways impossible in other media.

Marc Prensky, in a book that espouses the use of computer games in education and training, offers three definitions of simulation:

- any synthetic or counterfeit creation

- creation of an artificial world that approximates the real one

- a mathematical or algorithmic model, combined with a set of initial conditions, that allows prediction and visualisation as time unfolds (Prensky 2001: 211)

The first and second of these definitions recall the confusion of some aspects of simulation with imitation. That a simulation is a 'counterfeit' (definition 1) suggests it may be smuggled in, unnoticed, to stand in for 'the real thing'. That it is 'synthetic', by contrast, suggests only that it has been manufactured. Just as it would be false to say that any manufactured product, by virtue of being manufactured, counterfeits a reality on which it is based (what does a car counterfeit?), so it would be equally false to argue that all simulations 'counterfeit' a reality. In short, if manufacturing goods adds additional elements to reality, so too, surely, should manufacturing simulations.

Definition 2 repeats this error: an artificial world does not necessarily approximate the real one. Consider, for example, the work of exobiologists – biologists who research the possible forms life on other worlds might take. An exobiologist, for instance, might simulate a world with denser gravity than ours; this would entail that, if life evolved on such a world, it would take a different form, with creatures perhaps more horizontally than vertically based, replacing legs with other means of locomotion, and so forth. Undoubtedly such a world is simulated, but it precisely does not approximate ours. In a more familiar sense, this is what we encounter in videogame-worlds, and the rules governing the motion of characters, the impact and consequence of collisions, and so on. In particular, the issue of 'virtual gravity' (generally weaker than the terrestrial variety with which we are familiar) demonstrates the extent to which such simulations owe their contribution to reality to their differences from, rather than approximations of, our own. We will see in section **5.3** that historians and theorists of automata quite specifically differentiate between automata proper and simulacra – in brief, not all automata are simulacra, insofar as they do not necessarily approximate the human form. These examples alone ought to make us wary of suggesting any equivalence between imitation and simulation.

For the task in hand – the identification of analytical concepts and approaches in the study of computer simulation in the context of a general account of new media studies – Prensky's third definition of simulations as material (and mathematical) technologies and media is very useful. It recalls, for instance, both the temporal aspects of simulation (see below) and the Baudrillardian sense, reflecting on the notion of simulation as productive of reality, neither a 'counterfeit' nor necessarily an approximation of a real world beyond them. This is helpful in that such an account makes more obvious sense of those simulations used in many different contexts, for example by economists to predict market fluctuations, and by geographers to analyse demographic change. Unlike the postmodernist use of the term, this gain in applicability does not cost a loss of specificity. The processes of simulation are also foregrounded in gaming, since all digital games are simulations to some extent. Prensky cites Will Wright (the creator of *SimCity*, *The Sims*, and numerous other simulation games) discussing simulations as models quite different from, for example, balsa wood models. The simulation is temporal, modelling processes such as decay, growth, population shifts, not physical structures. The model, we might say in more familiar terms, really does precede the reality it produces (see again section **2.6** below).

Simulation games

In recent years, game studies has adopted analytical, formal and descriptive approaches to the specificity of computer simulation software. 'Simulation' here refers to the particular character and operations of games, particularly computer and videogames, as processual, algorithmic media. Distinctions are made between simulation as a media form that models dynamic, spatio-temporal and complex relationships and systems (for example, of urban development and economics in SimCity) and the narrative or representational basis of other, longer-established, media (literature, film, television, etc.).

> unlike traditional media, video games are not just based on representation but on an alternative semiotical structure known as simulation. Even if simulations and narrative do share some common elements – character, settings, events – their mechanics are essentially different. More importantly, they also offer distinct rhetorical possibilities.
>
> (Frasca 2003: 222)

Gonzalo Frasca's simulations are media objects that model complex systems. They are not limited to computer media (pre-digital machines and toys can simulate) but come into their own with the processing affordances of computing. This emphasis on the simulational character of computer and videogames has proven to be productive in the task of establishing the distinctiveness of the videogame as a hybrid cultural form, emphasising features, structures and operations inherited from both its computer science and board game forebears over other sides of its family – notably its media ancestors (literature, cinema, television).

What distinguishes the computer simulation is precisely what video games remind us of: it is a dynamic real-time experience of intervening with sets of algorithms that model any environment or process (not just imitating existing ones) – playing with parameters and variables.

So simulation in a videogame could be analysed thus:

In computer game culture the term 'simulation games' refers to a specific genre in which the modelling of a dynamic system (such as a city in *SimCity* or a household in *The Sims*) provides the main motive of the game as structure and gameplay experience

1   productive of reality – so in *Doom*, *Tomb Raider*, or *Grand Theft Auto* the game is representational on one level – tunnels, city streets, human figures, monsters and vehicles – part of the universe of popular media culture, but the experience of playing the game is one of interacting with a profoundly different kind of environment. These maps are not maps of any territory, but interfaces to a database and the algorithms of the computer simulation;

2   this 'reality' then is mathematically structured and determined. As Prensky points out, *The Sims* adds a fun interface to a cultural form rooted in science and the mathematical and traditionally presented only as numbers on the screen. Games such as SimCity incorporated

> a variety of ways of modelling dynamic systems – including linear equations (like a spreadsheet), differential equations (dynamic system-based simulations like Stella) and cellular automata – where the behaviors of certain objects come from their own properties and rules for how those properties interacted with neighbors rather than from overall controlling equations.
>
> (Prensky 2001: 210–211).

Note: Prensky makes a clear connection here between the playful simulation of popular videogames and the computer science of Artificial Life. For more on ALife and cellular automata see **5.3.5**.

3   as we have seen, exobiology and some videogames clearly indicate that simulations can function without simulating or representing already existing phenomena and systems. The mimetic elements of *Tetris*, *Minesweeper* and *Donkey Kong* are residual at best, yet each of these games is a dynamic simulated world with its own spatial and temporal dimensions and dynamic relationships of virtual forces and effects. They simulate only themselves.

4   thinking of videogames as simulations also returns us to the assertion that the player's experience of cyberspace is one not only of exploration but of realising or bringing the gameworld into being in a semiotic and cybernetic circuit:

> The distinguishing quality of the virtual world is that the system lets the participant observer play an active role, where he or she can test the system and discover the rules and structural qualities in the process.
>
> (Espen Aarseth 2001: 229)

> For the cybernetic nature of videogame play see **4.5.6** and **5.4.4**

Summary

Ostensibly, these three positions have quite different objects of concern: the computer simulation of interest to game studies is not postmodernist simulation. Game studies is more modest – keen to establish the difference of games and simulations from narrative or representational media forms, rather than claiming simulation as an overarching model of contemporary culture. To analyse a videogame as a computer simulation is to understand it as an instance in everyday life, rather than as an all-encompassing hyperreality. Moreover, the screen metaphors of the postmodernist simulation carry little sense of the dynamic and procedural characteristics of computer simulation. Studied as such, computer simulations can be seen not only as the visual presentation of artificial realities (as, again, the screens of hyperreality suggest) but as the generation of dynamic systems and economies, often with (and always in videogames) an assumption of interactive engagement written into the models and processes.

The three broad concepts of simulation outlined above overlap however. Postmodernist simulation, though formulated before the rise of computer media to their current predominance and predicated on – crudely speaking – the electronic media and consumer culture, is now widely applied to the Internet, Virtual Reality and other new media forms. Discussions of the nature of computer simulations often also entail a consideration of the relationships (or lack of) between the computer simulation and the real world. Both make a distinction between 'simulation' (where a 'reality' is experienced that does not correspond to any actually existing thing), and 'representation' (or 'mimesis', the attempt at an accurate imitation or representation of some real thing that lies outside of the image or picture) – though often with very different implications and intentions.

To sum up: within all of these approaches to simulation there is a tendency to miss a key point: simulations are real, they exist, and are experienced within the real world which they augment. Since, as *Donkey Kong* and the alien creatures of exobiology teach us, not all simulations are imitations, it becomes much easier to see simulations as things in their own right, rather than as mere representations of other ('realer') things.

1.2.7 Conclusion

The characteristics which we have discussed above should be seen as part of a matrix of qualities that we argue is what makes new media different. Not all of these qualities will be present in all examples of new media – they will be present in differing degrees and in different mixes. These qualities are not wholly functions of technology – they are all imbricated into the organisation of culture, work and leisure with all the economic and social determinations that involves. To speak of new media as networked, for instance, is not just to speak of the difference between server technology and broadcast transmitters but also to talk about the deregulation of media markets. To talk about the concept of the virtual is not just to speak of head-mounted display systems but also to have to take into account the ways in which experiences of self and of identity are mediated in a 'virtual' space. Digitality, Interactivity, Hypertextuality, Virtuality, Networked Media and Simulation are offered as the beginnings of a critical map. This discussion of the 'characteristics' of new media has merely established the grounds upon which we might now begin substantially to address the questions that they raise.

1.3 Change and continuity

From this section to the end of Part 1 (**1.3–1.6.6**) we now change our tack. So far we have considered, as promised at the outset, what it is that we take to be 'new media' and we have gone as far as to suggest some defining characteristics. We now take up the question of what is involved in considering their 'newness'. Enthusiastic students of media technologies might wonder why this is a necessary question. Why do we not simply attempt to describe and analyse the exciting world of media innovation that surrounds us? Writing in this manner would be at the mercy of what we referred to in the introduction as permanent 'upgrade culture' – no sooner published than out of date because it failed to offer any critical purchase on the field. There are plenty of existing sites for readers to catch up on latest developments most of which are designed to facilitate the reader's consumption. Our purpose is to facilitate critical thinking. In order to do that we need to get beyond the banal pleasures of novelty to reveal how the 'new' is constructed. Our aim here is to enable a clarity of thought often *disabled* by the shiny dazzle of novelty. We hope to show that this centrally involves knowing something about the history of media, the history of newness, and the history of our responses to media and technological change. But there is more to it than that. Here is a checklist and overview of what is to come, and why, in these last sections of Part 1.

- 'Newness' or what it is 'to be new' is not the simple quality we may take it to be and can be conceived of in several ways. This is discussed in **1.3–1.3.2**.

- New media 'arrives', has already been provided with, a history, or histories and these often seek to explain new media's 'newness'. Some of these histories are what are known as 'teleological' while others argue that a better approach is 'genealogical'. Essentially, to consider the nature of the 'new' we have to become involved in theories 'of' history (or historiography). This is explained, with examples in **1.4** and **1.4.1**.

- Frequently, 'new media' (or indeed any media, 'film' for example) are thought, by some, to each have a defining essence. It is then argued that to realise this essence, to bring it into its own, requires a break with the past and old habits and ways of thinking. This too, is often associated with a sense of 'progress'. Each medium is better (affording greater realism, greater imaginative scope, more efficient communication etc.) than those that proceed it. We examine these ideas as a 'modernist concept of progress' in **1.4.2**.

- Far from being the latest stage in a linear progression, much about new media recalls some much older, even ancient practices and situations. They appear to repeat or revive historical practices that had been forgotten or become residual. There is something like an 'archaeology' of new media. This is dealt with in **1.4.3–1.4.4**.

- New media are frequently contrasted (usually favourably) with 'old media'. It is as if there is an implied critique of old media in new media. Old media are suddenly thrown into a bad light. This issue is raised in **1.5–1.5.1**, and leads us to:

- The discursive construction of media and The Technological Imaginary. Here we explore, through a number of case studies, the various ways in which media technologies are invested with significance as they are expected to realise hopes, satisfy desires, resolve social problems etc.; **1.5.2**, **1.5.3**, **1.5.4**, **1.5.5** and **Case studies 1.4–1.7**.

- In this way we are brought to face a key question and a debate which typically becomes urgent as new media and new technologies emerge: do media technologies have the power to transform cultures? Or, are they just dumb tools, pieces of kit which reflect a society's or a culture's values and needs. In short, are 'media' determined or determining? As our media and communication technologies become more complex, powerful and pervasive, even (if contentiously) intelligent and self organising, this is an ever more important question and debate. Through a discussion of an earlier and informative debate between two major theorists of media (Raymond Williams and Marshall McLuhan) we open up this issue in some detail in **1.6–1.6.6**. This will prepare us to consider theories about culture, technology and nature (particularly those coming from Science and Technology Studies) which offer to avoid this vexed dichotomy.

1.3.1 Introduction

Media theorists, and other commentators, tend to be polarised over the degree of new media's newness. While the various camps seldom engage in debate with each other, the argument is between those who see a media revolution and those who claim that, on the contrary, behind the hype we largely have 'business as usual'. To some extent this argument hinges upon the disciplinary frameworks and **discourses (1.5.3)** within which proponents of either side of the argument work. What premises do they proceed from? What questions do they ask? What methods do they apply? What ideas do they bring to their investigations and thinking?

In this section we simply recognise that while the view is widely held that new media are 'revolutionary' – that they are profoundly or radically new in kind – throughout the now extensive literature on new media there are also frequent recognitions that any attempt to understand new media requires a historical perspective. Many reasons for taking this view will be met throughout the book as part of its detailed case studies and arguments. In this section we look at the general case for the importance of history in the study of new media.

1.3.2 Measuring 'newness'

The most obvious question that needs to be asked is: 'How do we know that something is new or in what way it is new if we have not carefully compared it with what already exists or has gone before?' We cannot know with any certainty and detail how new or how large changes are without giving our thinking a historical dimension. We need to establish from what previous states things have changed. Even if, as Brian Winston observes, the concept of a 'revolution' is implicitly historical, how can one know 'that a situation has changed – has revolved – without knowing its previous state or position?' (Winston 1998: 2). In another context, Kevin Robins (1996: 152) remarks that, 'Whatever might be "new" about digital technologies, there is something old in the imaginary signification of "image revolution".' Revolutions then, when they take place, are historically relative and the idea itself has a history. It is quite possible to take the view that these questions are superfluous and only divert us from the main business. This certainly seems to be the case for many new media enthusiasts who are (somewhat arrogantly, we may suggest) secure in their conviction that the new is new and how it got to be that way will be of a lot less interest than what comes next!

However, if asked, this basic question can help us guard against missing at least three possibilities:

1   Something may appear to be new, in the sense that it looks or feels unfamiliar or because it is aggressively presented as new, but on closer inspection such newness may be revealed as only superficial. It may be that something is new only in the sense that it turns out to be a new version or configuration of something that, substantially, already exists, rather than being a completely new category or kind of thing. Alternatively, how can we know that a medium is new, rather than a hybrid of two or more older media or an old one in a new context which in some ways transforms it?

2   Conversely, as the newness of new media becomes familiar in everyday use or consumption (see **4.2** and **4.3**) we may lose our curiosity and vigilance, ceasing to ask questions about exactly what they do and how they are being used to change our worlds in subtle as well as dramatic ways.

3   A final possibility that this simple question can uncover is that on close inspection and reflection, initial estimates of novelty can turn out not to be as they seem. We find that some kinds and degrees of novelty exist but not in the ways that they were initially thought to. The history of what is meant by the new media buzzword 'interactivity' is a prime

example of the way a much-lauded quality of new media has been repeatedly qualified and revised through critical examination.

Case study 1.3: What is new about interactivity?

The overall point is that the 'critical' in the critical study of new media means not taking things for granted. Little is assumed about the object of study that is then illuminated by asking and attempting to answer questions about it. An important way of doing this – of approaching something critically – is to ask what its history is or, in other words, how it came to be as it is.

Lastly, in this review of reasons to be historical in our approach to new media, we need to recall how extensive and heterogeneous are the range of changes, developments, and innovations that get subsumed under the term 'new media'. This is so much the case that without some attempt to break the term or category down into more manageable parts we risk such a level of abstraction and generalisation in our discussions that they will never take us very far in the effort to understand one or another of these changes (see **1.1**). A better approach is to look for the different ratios of the old and the new across the field of new media. One way of doing this is, precisely, historical. It is to survey the field of new media in terms of the degree to which any particular development is genuinely and radically new or is better understood as simply an element of change in the nature of an already established medium.

Old media in new times?
For instance, it can be argued that 'digital television' is not a new medium but is best understood as a change in the form of delivering the contents of the TV medium, which has a history of some fifty years or more. This would be a case of what Mackay and O'Sullivan describe as an 'old' medium 'in new times' as distinct from a 'new medium' (1999: 4–5). On the other hand, immersive virtual reality or massively multi-player online gaming look to be, at least at first sight, mediums of a radically and profoundly new kind. This, however, still leaves us with the problem of defining what is truly new about them.

Before we accept this 'new/old' axis as a principle for distinguishing between kinds of new media, we have to recognise immediately that the terms can, to some extent, be reversed. For instance, it can be argued that some of the outcomes of producing and transmitting TV digitally have had quite profound effects upon its programming and modes of use and consumption such that the medium of TV has significantly changed (**Case study 1.7**). It could also be claimed that the increased image size, high definition, programmes on demand, interactive choice etc., of contemporary television effectively transforms the medium. Whether we would want to go as far as saying that it will be an entirely new medium still seems unlikely, if not impossible. On the other hand, the apparently unprecedented experiences offered by the technologies of immersive VR or online, interactive, multimedia can be shown to have histories and antecedents, both of a technological and a cultural kind, upon which they draw and depend (**1.2**, **1.3**). Whether, in these cases, however, we would want to go as far as saying that therefore VR is adequately defined by tracing and describing its many practical and ideological antecedents is another matter.

The idea of 'remediation'
A third possibility is that put forward by Jay Bolter and Richard Grusin (1999) who, following an insight of Marshall McLuhan, effectively tie new media to old media as a structural condition of all media. They propose and argue at some length that the 'new', in turn, in new media is the manner in which the digital technologies that they employ 'refashion older media', and then these older media 'refashion themselves to answer to the challenges of new media'

(p. 15). It seems to us that there is an unassailable truth in this formulation. This is that new media are not born in a vacuum and, as media, would have no resources to draw upon if they were not in touch and negotiating with the long traditions of process, purpose, and signification that older media possess. Yet, having said this, many questions about the nature and extent of the transformations taking place remain.

CASE STUDY 1.3: What is new about interactivity?

From the 1990s onward, 'interactivity' became a key buzzword in the world of new media. The promise and quality of interactivity has been conceived in a number of ways.

The creative management of information

This concept of interactivity has roots in the ideas of early computer visionaries dating back as far as the 1940s, such as Vannevar Bush (1945) and Alan Kay and Adele Goldberg (1977) (both in Mayer 1999). These are visions of interactive computer databases liberating and extending our intellects. Such concepts, conceived in the years after the Second World War, were in part responses to the perceived threat of information overload in the modern world. Searchable databases that facilitated a convergence of existing print and visual media and the information they contained were seen as a new way for the individual to access, organise, and think with information.

Interactivity as consumer choice technologically embodied

We saw in our discussion of the concept in **1.2** how it has been central to the marketing of personal computers by linking it to contemporary ideas about consumer choice. On this view, being interactive means that we are no longer the passive consumers of identical ranges of mass-produced goods, whether intellectual or material. Interactivity is promoted as a quality of computers that offers us active choices and personalised commodities, whether of knowledge, news, entertainment, banking, shopping and other services.

The death of the author

During the 1990s, cybertheorists were keen to understand interactivity as a means of placing traditional authorship in the hands of the 'reader' or consumer (Landow 1992). Here, the idea is that interactive media are a technological realisation of a theory, first worked out mainly in relation to literature, known as 'post-structuralism'. We had, it was suggested, witnessed the 'death of the author', the central, fixed and god-like voice of the author behind the text (see, for example, Landow 1992). Interactivity meant that users of new media would be able to navigate their way across uncharted seas of potential knowledge, making their own sense of a body of material, each user following new pathways through the matrix of data each time they set out on their journeys of discovery.

A related idea is that the key property of interactivity is a major shift in the traditional relationship between the production and reception of media. This resides in the power that computers give the reader/user to 'write back' into a text. Information, whether in the form of text, image, or sound, is received within software applications that allow the receiver to change – delete, add, reconfigure – what they receive. It has not been lost on many thinkers that this practice, while enabled by electronic digital technology, resembles the medieval practice of annotating and adding extensive marginalia to manuscripts and books so that they became palimpsests. These are surfaces upon which generations of additions and commentaries are overwritten on texts, one on the other. While this is true it has only a limited sense. There is after all a tremendous difference between the operation of the Internet and the highly selective access of the privileged class of medieval monks to sacred texts.

More recently, in the face of exaggerated claims for the almost magical powers of interactivity and on the basis of practice-based critical reflection, more critical estimations have been made. As the artist Sarah Roberts has put it:

the illusion that goes along with [interactivity] is of a kind of democracy . . . that the artist is sharing the power of choice with the viewer, when actually the artist has planned every option that can happen . . . it's a great deal more complex than if you [the user] hadn't had a sort of choice, but it's all planned.

(Penny 1995: 64)

These concepts of interactivity are less descriptions of particular technical, textual, or experiential properties and more claims or propositions rooted in the inspired founding visions, imaginative marketing strategies, and the sophisticated analogies of academic theorists about new, real or imagined, possibilities of human empowerment. However, whatever merits these ideas have, whether visionary or opportunistic, they have been subjected to methodical enquiry from within a number of disciplines which we need to attend to if we are to get beyond these broad characterisations of interactivity.

Human–computer interaction: intervention and control

A technical idea of interactivity has taken shape most strongly within the discipline of human–computer interaction (HCI). This is a scientific and industrial field which studies and attempts to improve the interface between computers and users.

An 'interactive mode' of computer use was first posited during the years of mainframe computers when large amounts of data were fed into the machine to be processed. At first, once the data was entered, the machine was left to get on with the processing (batch processing). Gradually however, as the machines became more sophisticated, it became possible to intervene into the process whilst it was still running through the use of dialogue boxes or menus. This was known as operating the computer in an 'interactive' mode (Jensen 1999: 168). This ability to intervene in the computing process and see the results of your intervention in real time was essentially a *control* function. It was a one-way command communication from the operator to the machine. This is a very different idea of interaction from the popularised senses of hypertextual freedom described above (Huhtamo 2000).

This idea of *interaction as control* continued to develop through the discipline of HCI and was led by the ideas of technologists like Licklider and Engelbart (Licklider and Taylor 1999 [orig: 1968]; Engelbart 1999 [orig: 1963]). If the kind of symbiosis between operator and machine that they envisaged was to take place then this interactive mode had to be extended and made available outside of the small groups who understood the specialised programming languages. To this end, during the early 1970s, researchers at the Xerox Palo Alto Research Center developed the GUI, the graphical user interface, which would work within the simultaneously developed standard format for the PC: keyboard, processor, screen and mouse. In what has become one of the famous moments in the history of Xerox, they failed to exploit their remarkable breakthroughs. Later, Apple were able to use the GUI to launch their range of PCs in the early 1980s: first the Apple Lisa, then in 1984 the celebrated Apple Mac. These GUI systems were then widely imitated by Microsoft.

Communication studies and the 'face-to-face' paradigm

However, this idea of *interaction as control*, as interface manipulation, is somewhat at odds with the idea of interactivity as a mutually reciprocal communication process, whether between user and machine/database or between user and user. Here we encounter an understanding of the term derived from sociology and communications studies. This tradition has attempted to describe and analyse interactivity and computers in relation to interactivity in face-to-face human communication. In this research interaction is identified as a core human behaviour, the foundation of culture and community. For communications theorists interaction is a quality present in varying degrees as a quality of communication. So a question and answer pattern of communication is somewhat 'less' interactive than an open-ended dialogue (see, for example, Shutz 2000; Jensen 1999). Similarly the modes of interactivity described in **1.2** would here be classified on a scale of least to most interactive, with the various kinds of CMC 'most' interactive and the navigational choices 'least' interactive.

Various commentators (for example, Stone 1995: 10; Aarseth 1997: 49) quote Andy Lippman's definition of interactivity generated at MIT in the 1980s as an 'ideal'. For Lippman interactivity was 'mutual and simultaneous activity on the part of both participants, usually working toward some goal, but not necessarily'. This state needed to be achieved through a number of conditions:

Mutual interruptibility
limited look ahead (so that none of the partners in the interaction can foresee the future shape of the interaction)
no default (there is no pre-programmed route to follow)
the impression of an infinite database (from the participants' point of view).

(Stone 1995: 10–11)

This sounds like a pretty good description of conversation, but a very poor description of using a point-and-click interface to 'interact' with a computer.

The study of artifical intelligence

There seem to us to be some real problems with the application of communications theories based in speech to technologically medi-ated communications. Unresolved, these problems lead to impossible expectations of computers, expectations that open up a gap between what we experience in computer-based interaction and what we might desire. Often this gap gets filled by predictions drawn from yet another methodological field – that of artificial intelligence (AI). The argument usually goes something like this. Ideal human–computer interaction would approach as close as possible to face-to-face communication; however, computers obviously can't do that yet since they are (still) unable to pass as human for any length of time. Futuristic scenarios (scientific and science fictional) pro-pose that this difficulty will be resolved as chips get cheaper and computing enters into its ubiquitous phase (see **ubiquitous computing** and pervasive media). In the meantime we have to make do with various degrees along the way to 'true' (i.e. conversa-tional) interaction. In this construction interactivity is always a failure awaiting rescue by the next development on an evershifting technological event horizon.

Media studies

Understandings of interactivity not only draw on HCI, communications studies, and AI research but often call up debates around the nature of media audiences and their interpretations of meanings that have been generated within media studies. Influential strands within media studies teach that audiences are 'active' and make multiple and variable interpretative acts in response to media texts:

> the meaning of the text must be thought of in terms of which set of discourses it encounters in any particular set of circumstances, and how this encounter may restructure both the meaning of the text and the discourses which it meets.
>
> (Morley 1980: 18)

This reading of audience behaviour is sometimes referred to as an 'interactive' activity. Prior to the emergence of computer media, it is argued that as readers we already had 'interactive' relationships with (traditional analogue) texts. This position is then extended to argue that not only do we have complex interpretative relationships with texts but active material relationships with texts; we have long written marginalia, stopped and rewound the videotape, dubbed music from CD to tape, physically cut and pasted images and text from print media into new arrangements and juxtapositions. In this reading, interactivity comes to be understood as, again, a kind of technological correlative for theories of textuality already established and an extension of material practices that we already have. So, for instance, even though we might not all share the same experience of a website we may construct a version of 'the text' through our talk and discussion about the site; similarly it is argued we will not all share the same experience of watching a soap opera. Indeed, over a period of weeks we will almost certainly not see the same 'text' as other family members or friends, but we can construct a common 'text' through our responses and talk about the programme. The text and the meanings which it produces already only exist in the spaces of our varied interpretations and responses.

In other words there is a perspective on interactivity, based in literary studies and media studies, that argues that nothing much has changed in principle. We are just offered more opportunities for more complex relationships with texts but these relationships are essentially the same (Aarseth 1997: 2). However, we would argue that the distinction between interaction and interpretation is even more important now than previously. This is because the problems which face us in understanding the processes of mediation are mul-tiplied by new media: the acts of multiple interpretation of traditional media are not made irrelevant by digital and technological forms of interactivity but are actually made more numerous and complex by them. The more text choices available to the reader the greater the possible interpretative responses. The very necessity of intervention in the text, of manipulation of the text's forms of interaction, requires a more acute understanding of the act of interpretation.

Grassroots democratic exchange

Beyond the particular ways of understanding interactivity that flow from the four methodologies we have discussed, there lies another, more diffuse yet extremely powerful, discourse about interactivity that is so pervasive as to have become taken for granted. Within this usage 'interactive' equals automatically better – better than passive, and better than just 'active' by virtue of some implied reciprocity. This diffuse sense of the virtue of interactivity also has a social and cultural history, dating from the late 1960s and early 1970s. In this history, democratising challenges to established power systems were led by constant calls for dialogue and increased lateral, rather than vertical and hierarchical, communications as a way of supporting social progress. This ideological attack on one-way information flows in favour of lateral or interactive social communications lay behind much of the radical alternative rhetorics of the period. A community arts and media group active in London through the 1970s and 1980s, under the name of 'Interaction', is characteristic of the period in its analysis:

> The problems of a pluralist urban society (and an over populated one dependent on machines as well) are very complex. Answers, if there are any, lie in the ability to relate, to inform, to listen – in short the abilities of creative people.
>
> (Berman 1973: 17)

The abilities to 'relate' and to 'listen' are the skills of face-to-face dialogue and social interaction recast as a progressive force. This valorisation of social dialogue was 'in the air' in the early 1970s. It informed a radical critique of mainstream media which took root not only in the burgeoning of alternative and community media practices of the period but also in early ideas about computer networking. As was pointed out by Resource One, a community computing facility based in the Bay area of San Francisco:

> Both the quantity and content of available information is set by centralised institutions – the press, TV, radio, news services, think tanks, government agencies, schools and universities – which are controlled by the same interests which control the rest of the economy. By keeping information flowing from the top down, they keep us isolated from each other. Computer technology has thus far been used . . . mainly by the government and those it represents to store and quickly retrieve vast amounts of information about huge numbers of people. . . . It is this pattern that convinces us that control over the flow of information is so crucial.
>
> (*Resource One Newsletter*, 2 April 1974, p. 8)

This support for 'democratic media' is a kind of popular and latter-day mobilisation of ideas derived from the **Frankfurt School**, with its criticisms of the role of mass media in the production of a docile population seduced by the pleasures of consumption and celebrity (**1.5.4**). In this reading 'interactive' media are constructed as a potential improvement on passive media in that they appear to hold out the opportunity for social and political communications to function in a more open and democratic fashion which more closely approaches the ideal conditions of the public sphere.

We are now in a position to see that the idea of interactivity, as one of the primary 'new' qualities of new media, comes to us as an automatic asset with a rich history. Yet, as we have also seen, it is a term that carries the weight of a number of different, and contradictory, histories. It may be possible to argue that it is precisely this lack of definition which makes it such a suitable site for our investment in the idea of 'the new'.

1.5.4 The return of the Frankfurt School critique in the popularisation of new media

1.4 What kind of history?

'"I Love Lucy" and "Dallas", FORTRAN and fax, computer networks, comsats, and mobile telephones. The transformations in our psyches triggered by the electronic media thus far may have been preparation for bigger things to come' (Rheingold 1991: 387).

In **1.3** we posed a number of basic questions that need to be asked if critical studies of new media are to proceed without being based upon too many assumptions about what we are dealing with. We strongly suggested that asking these questions requires us to take an interest in the available histories of older media. There is, however, another important reason why the student of new media may need to pay attention to history. This is because, from their very inception, new media have been provided with histories, some of which can be misleading.

From the outset, the importance of new media, and the kind of futures they would deliver, has frequently been conceived as part of a historical unfolding of long-glimpsed possibilities. As the quote above suggests, such accounts imply that history may only have been a preparation for the media technologies and products of our time. In other words, a historical imagination came into play at the moment we began to strive to get the measure of new media technologies. These historical perspectives are often strongly marked by paradoxically old-fashioned ideas about history as a progressive process. Such ideas rapidly became popular and influential. There is little exaggeration in saying that, subsequently, a good deal of research and argument in the early years of 'new media studies' has been concerned with criticising these 'histories' and outlining alternative ways of understanding media change.

This section

While this book is not the place to study theories of history in any depth, a body of historical issues now attaches itself to the study of new media. Some examples, and an idea of the critical issues they raise, are therefore necessary. In this section we first consider what are known as **teleological** accounts of new media (**1.4.1**). The meaning of this term will become clearer through the following discussion of some examples but, broadly, it refers to the idea that new media are a direct culmination of historical processes. In this section, by taking an example of work on the history of new media we seek to show that there can be no single, linear historical narrative that would add to our understanding of all that 'new media' embraces. Instead, we are clearly faced with a large number of intersecting histories. These are unlikely to fall into a pattern of tributaries all feeding regularly and incrementally into a main stream. We would be hard put to think, let alone prove, that all of the developments, contexts, agents and forces that are involved in these histories had anything like a shared goal or purpose. We then outline the approaches of some theorists of new media who, rejecting the idea that new media can simply be understood as the utopian end point of progressive historical development, seek alternative ways of thinking about the differences and the complex connections between old and new media. In doing this we will consider how Michel Foucault's influential 'genealogical' theory of history has found a place in studies of new media (**1.4.1**).

Lastly, we consider a view derived from modernist aesthetics, which argues that for a medium to be genuinely new its unique essence has to be discovered in order for it to break itself free from the past and older media (**1.4.2**). In questioning this idea we introduce a number of examples in which new media are seen to recall the past, rather than break with it (**1.4.3**).

1.4.1 Teleological accounts of new media

From cave paintings to mobile phones

In a once popular and influential history of 'virtual reality', Howard Rheingold takes us to the Upper Palaeolithic cave paintings of Lascaux, where 30,000 years ago, 'primitive but effective cyberspaces may have been instrumental in setting us on the road to computerized world building in the first place' (Rheingold 1991: 379). He breathlessly takes his reader on a journey which has its destination in immersive virtual environments. En route we visit the origins of Dionysian drama in ancient Greece, the initiation rites of the Hopi, Navajo, and Pueblo tribes 'in the oldest continuously inhabited human settlements in North America', the virtual worlds of TV soap operas like *I Love Lucy* and *Dallas*, arriving at last to meet the interactive computing pioneers of Silicon Valley, major US universities and Japanese corporations. In Rheingold's sweeping historical scheme, the cave painting appears to hold the seeds of the fax machine, the computer network, the communications satellite and the mobile phone (Rheingold 1991: 387)!

Few examples of this way of understanding how we came to have a new medium are as mind-boggling in their Olympian sweep as Rheingold's. But, as we shall see, other theorists and commentators, often with more limited ambitions, share with him the project to understand new media as the culmination or present stage of development of all human media over time. When this is done, new media are placed at the end of a chronological list that begins with oral communication, writing, printing, drawing and painting, and then stretches and weaves its way through the image and communication media of the nineteenth and twentieth centuries, photography, film, TV, video and semaphore, telegraphy, telephony and radio. In such historical schemas there is often an underlying assumption or implication – which may or may not be openly stated – that new media represent a stage of development that was already present as a potential in other, earlier, media forms. A further example will help us see how such views are constructed and the problems associated with them.

From photography to telematics: extracting some sense from teleologies
Peter Weibel, a theorist of art and technology, former director of Ars Electronica and now director of a leading centre for new media art (ZKM, the Zentrum für Kunst und Medientechnologie, in Karlsruhe, Germany), offers an 8-stage historical model of the progressive development of technologies of image production and transmission which, having photography as its first stage, spans 160 years (1996: 338–339).

Weibel notes that in 1839 the invention of photography meant that image making was freed for the first time from a dependence upon the hand (this is Stage 1). Images were then further unfixed from their locations in space by electronic scanning and telegraphy (Stage 2). In these developments Weibel sees 'the birth of new visual worlds and telematic culture' (1996: 338).

Then, in Stages 3–5, these developments were 'followed by' film which further transformed the image from something that occupied space to one that existed in time. Next, the discovery of the electron, the invention of the cathode ray tube, and magnetic recording brought about the possibility of a combination of film, radio, and television – and video was born. At this stage, Weibel observes, 'the basic conditions for electronic image production and transfer were established' (1996: 338).

In Stage 6, transistors, integrated circuits and silicon chips enter the scene. All previous developments are now revolutionised as the sum of the historical possibilities of machine-aided image generation are at last united in the multimedia, interactive computer. This newly interactive machine, and the convergence of all other technological media within it, then join with telecommunications networks and there is a further liberation as 'matterless signs' spread like waves in global space (Stage 7). A new era (first glimpsed at Stage 2) now dawns: that of post-industrial, telematic civilisation.

So, Stage 7, Weibel's penultimate stage, is that of interactive telematic culture, more or less where we may be now at the end of the first decade of the twenty-first century. His final Stage 8 tips us into the future, a stage 'until now banished to the domain of science fiction' but 'already beginning to become a reality' (1996: 339). This is the sphere of advanced sensory technologies in which he sees the brain as directly linked to 'the digital realm' (ibid.).

Weibel clearly sees this history as progressive, one in which 'Over the last 150 years the mediatisation and mechanisation of the image, from the camera to the computer have advanced greatly' (1996: 338). There is a direction, then, advancing toward the present and continuing into the future, which is revealed by the changing character of our media over time.

As we look back over Wiebel's eight stages we see that the 'advances' all concern the increasing dematerialisation of images and visual signs, their separation from the material vehicle which carries them. The final, culminating stage in this dynamic is then glimpsed: neurological engineering which is about to usher in a direct interfacing of the brain with the world – a world where no media, material or immaterial, exist. We have the end of media or, as his title states, The World as Interface.

What kind of history is being told here?

- Each of Weibel's stages points to real technological developments in image media production and transmission. These technologies and inventions did happen, did and do exist.

- Moving out from the facts, he then offers brief assessments of what these developments have meant for human communication and visual culture. In these assessments, the insights of other media theorists show through.

- Overall, Weibel organises his observations chronologically; the stages follow each other in time, each one appearing to be born out of the previous one.

- There is an ultimate point of origin – photography. The birth of this image technology is placed as a founding moment out of which the whole process unfolds.

- He finds a logic or a plot for his unfolding story – his sequential narrative of progress. This is the story of the increasing automation of production and increasing separation of signs (and images) from any physical vehicle that carries them.

This story is not without sense. But it is important to see that it is, in actuality, an argument. It is an organisation and integration of facts and ways of thinking about those facts. Facts? Photography and then telecommunications were invented. Hard to contest. Ways of thinking about the significance of those facts? Photography and telecommunications converged to mean that reality (real, material, physically tangible space) disappeared. A dramatic pronouncement that, at the very least, we may want to debate.

By selectively giving each fact a particular kind of significance (there are many others that he could have found), Weibel is making a case. Although it is more focused than the example we took from Rheingold's 'history' of VR, it is basically similar in that an argument is made in the form of a historical narrative. Within Weibel's 'history' he foregrounds and makes us think about some very important factors. Good, perceptive and well-researched stories have always done this.

However, at the same time, there are some big problems with Weibel's account if we take it as a credible historical account without asking further questions about its implications. This is because he does not tell us why and how the apparent unfolding of events takes place. What drives this march of media from machine-aided production of material images (photography) to the simulation of 'artificial and natural worlds', and even the coming simulation of the 'brain itself'? What, in this pattern of seamless evolution, has he detected? How was the bloom of interactive 'telematic civilisation' always contained in the seed of photography?

Historical narratives of the kind that Rheingold and Weibel tell are forms of teleological argument. These are arguments in which the nature of the past is explained as a preparation for the present. The present is understood as being prefigured in the past and is the culmination of it. Such arguments seek to explain how things are in terms of their 'ends' (their outcomes or the purposes, aims and intentions that we feel they embody) rather than in prior causes. There have been many versions of such teleological historical explanation, beginning with those that saw the world as the outcome of God's design, through various kinds of secular versions of grand design, of cosmic forces, the unfolding of a world soul, through to dialectical explanation in which the present state of things is traceable to a long historical interplay of opposites and contradictions which inevitably move on toward a resolution. Related, if slightly less deterministically teleological, versions of historical explanation think in terms of history as a process of problem solving. Often a kind of relay race of great geniuses, in which each one takes up the questions left by their predecessors and, in each case, it is implied that the project is somehow communicated across and carried on over centuries of time as the final answer is sought.

Such attempts to find a (teleo)logic in history were strong in the nineteenth century, particularly in Western Europe and North America. Here, a dominant sense of optimism and faith in the progress of industry and science encouraged the view that history (as the growth, evolution and maturing of human societies) was drawing to a close.

Operating over very different timescales, both Rheingold and Weibel continue to tell stories about the rise of new media by adopting a kind of historical perspective which is as old as the hills. There is something of a paradox in the way in which new media have rapidly been provided with histories of a rather naive and uncritical (we are tempted to say old-fashioned) kind.

While we have stressed the importance of historical knowledge and research to understanding the contemporary field of new media, it does not, in our view, readily include these kinds of **teleology** which can be highly misleading in their grand sweep and the way in which they place new media, far too simply, as the end point of a long process of historical development.

Seeing the limits of new media teleologies

We now look at a third and recent contribution to the history of new media. This is a historical overview, in which Paul Mayer identifies the 'seminal ideas and technical developments' that lead to the development of computer media and communication. He traces the key concepts which lead from an abstract system of logic, through the development of calculating machines, to the computer as a 'medium' which can 'extend new possibilities for expressions, communication, and interaction in everyday life' (Mayer 1999: 321).

The important point for our present discussion is that as Mayer's thorough historical outline of 'pivotal conceptual insights' proceeds, we can also see how other histories that are quite distinct from that of the conceptual and technical development of computing itself are entwined with the one he traces. At various points in his history, doors are opened through which we glimpse other factors. These factors do not contribute directly to the development of computer media, but they indicate how quite other spheres of activity, taking place for other reasons, have played an essential but contingent part in the history of new media. We will take two examples.

In the first section of his history Mayer traces the conceptual and practical leaps which led to the building of the first mainframe computers in the 1940s. He begins his history with the project of the late-seventeenth-century philosopher, Leibniz, to formulate a way of reasoning logically by matching concepts with numbers, and his efforts to devise a 'universal logic machine' (Mayer 1999: 4). He then points to a whole range of other philosophical, mathematical, mechanical, and electronic achievements occurring in the 300-year period between the 1660s and the 1940s. The history leads us to the ideas and practical experiments in hypermedia carried out by Vannevar Bush and Ted Nelson (**1.2.3**) in the mid-twentieth century. It is a history which focuses on that part of technological development that involves envisioning: the capacity to think and imagine possibilities from given resources.

Clearly, many of these achievements, especially the earlier ones, were not directed at developing the computer as a medium as we would understand it. Such a use of the computer was not part of the eighteenth- and nineteenth-century frame of reference: it was not a conceivable or imaginable project. As Mayer points out, Leibniz had the intellectual and philosophical ambitions of his period (the late seventeenth and early eighteenth centuries) as one of the 'thinkers who advanced comprehensive philosophical systems during the Age of Reason' with its interest in devising logical scientific systems of thought which had universal validity (Mayer 1999: 4). Neither were our modern ideas about the interpersonal communications and visual-representational possibilities of the computer in view during the nineteenth-century phase of the Industrial Revolution. At this time the interest in computing was rooted in the need for calculation, 'in navigation, engineering, astronomy, physics' as the demands of these activities threatened to overwhelm the human capacity to calculate. (This last factor is an interesting reversal of the need that Vannevar Bush saw some 100 years later, in the 1950s, for a machine and a system that would augment the human capacity to cope with an overload of data and information [**1.2.3**].)

Hence, as we follow Mayer's historical account of key figures and ideas in the history of computing, we also see how the conceptual development of the modern computer as medium took place for quite other reasons. At the very least these include the projects of eighteenth-century philosophers, nineteenth-century industrialisation, trade and colonisation, and an early twentieth-century need to manage statistics for the governance and control of complex societies. As Mayer identifies, it is only in the 1930s when, alongside Turing's concept of 'the universal machine' which would automatically process any kind of symbol and not just numbers, the moment arrives in which, 'the right combination of concepts, technology and political will colluded to launch the construction of machines recognisable today as computers in the modern sense' (1999: 9). In short, while Mayer traces a set of chronological connections between 'pivotal concepts' in the history of computing, we are also led to see:

1   That the preconditions were being established for something that was not yet conceived or foreseen: the computer as a medium.

2   That even the conceptual history of computing, formally presented as a sequence of ideas and experiments, implies that other histories impact upon that development.

To sum up, we are led to see that a major factor in the development of computer media is the eventual impact of one set of technologies and practices – those of computing numbers – on other sets: these being social and personal practices of communication and aural, textual and visual forms of representation. In short, a set of technological and conceptual developments which were undertaken for one set of reasons (and even these, as we have seen, were not stable and sustained, as the philosophical gave way to the industrial and the commercial, and then the informational) have eventually come to transform a range of image and communication media. It is also apparent that this happened in ways that were completely unlooked for. New image and communications media were not anticipated by the thinkers, researchers, technologists and the wider societies to which they belonged, during the period between the eighteenth and the mid-twentieth century in which digital computing develops (Mayer 1999).

If this first example begins to show how teleological accounts obscure and distort the real historical contingency of computer media, our second example returns us to the greater historical complexity of what are now called new media. Mayer's focus is on the computer as a medium itself: the symbol-manipulating, networked machine through which we communicate with others, play games, explore databases and produce texts. Returning to our initial breakdown of the range of phenomena that new media refers to (**1.1**), we must remind ourselves that this is not all that new media has come to stand for. Computer-mediated communication, Mayer's specific interest, is only one key element within a broader media landscape that includes convergences, hybridisations, transformations, and displacements within and between all forms of older media. These media, such as print, telecommunications, photography, film, television and radio, have, of course, their own, and in some cases long, histories. In the last decades of the twentieth century these histories of older media become precisely the kinds of factors that began to play a crucial role in the development of computer media, just as the demands of navigators or astronomers for more efficient means of calculating did in the nineteenth.

This is a vital point as Mayer's historical sketch of the conceptual development of the computer ends, with Alan Kay and Adele Goldberg's 1977 prototype for an early personal computer named the 'Dynabook'. He observes that the 'Dynabook' was conceived by its designers as 'a metamedium, or a technology with the broadest capabilities to simulate and expand the functionality and power of other forms of mediated expression' (Mayer 1999: 20). Kay and Goldberg themselves make the point somewhat more directly when they write that 'the computer, viewed as a medium itself, can be all other media'. In the late 1970s, Kay and Goldberg's vision of the media that the Dynabook would 'metamediate' was restricted to text, painting and drawing, animation and music. (Subsequently, of course, with increased memory capacity and software developments, the 'other media' forms which the computer 'can be' would include photography, film, video and TV.)

On the face of it, this seems simple enough. What Kay and Goldberg are saying is that the computer as a 'medium' is able to simulate other media. However, both they and Mayer, in his history, seem to assume that this is unproblematic. As Mayer puts it, one of the great things about the Dynabook as a prototype computer medium, is that it is an 'inspiring realisation of Leibniz's generality of symbolic representation' (1999: 21) due to its ability to reduce all signs and languages – textual, visual, aural – to a binary code (**1.2.1**). It does a great deal more besides, of course: it 'expand[s] upon the functionality and power of other forms of mediated expression' (1999: 20). However, this convergence and interaction of many previously separate media actually makes the picture far more complicated. We have to remind ourselves that this range of 'old' media, that the computer carries and simulates, have in turn their own histories. Ones which parallel, and in some cases are far older than that of the computer.

The media which the computer 'simulates and expands' are also the result of conceptual and technical, as well as cultural and economic, histories which have shaped them in certain ways. In an expanded version of Mayer's history, space would need to be made for the ways in which these traditional media forms contributed to thinking about the Dynabook concept itself. For, if we are to understand the complex forms of new media it is not enough to think only in terms of what the computer might have offered to do for 'other forms of mediated expression' but also to ask how these other media forms shaped the kind of 'metamediating' that Goldberg and Kay envisaged. The universal symbol-manipulating capacity of the computer could not, by itself, determine the forms and aesthetics of the computer medium. This is because the very media that the computer (as medium) incorporates (or metamediates) are not neutral elements: they are social and signifying practices. We would want to know, for instance, what the outcomes of other histories – the conventions of drawing, the genres of animation, the trust in photographic realism, the narrative forms of text and video, and the languages of typography and graphic design, etc. – brought to this new metamedium. These are, in fact, the very issues which have come to exercise practitioners and theorists of new media, and which the various parts of this book discuss.

Foucault and genealogies of new media

A widely read theorist of new media, Mark Poster, has suggested:

> The question of the new requires a historical problematic, a temporal and spatial framework in which there are risks of setting up the new as a culmination, telos or fulfillment of the old, as the onset of utopia or **dystopia**. The conceptual problem is to enable a historical differentiation of old and new without initialising a totalising narrative. Foucault's proposal of a genealogy, taken over from Nietzsche, offers the most satisfactory resolution.
>
> (Poster 1999: 12)

In this way, Poster sums up the problems we have been discussing. How do we envisage the relationship of new and old media over time, sequentially, and in space (what kind of co-existence or relationship with each other and where?) without assuming that new media bring old media to some kind of concluding state for good or bad? How do we differentiate between them without such sweeping, universalising schemas as we met above? Foucault's concept of genealogy is his answer.

   Jay Bolter and Richard Grusin introduce their book on new media, entitled *Remediation*, with an explicit acknowledgement of their debt to Foucault's method:

> The two logics of remediation have a long history, for their interplay defines a genealogy that dates back at least to the Renaissance and the invention of linear perspective. Note 1: Our notion of genealogy is indebted to Foucault's, for we too are looking for historical affiliations or resonances, and not of origins. Foucault . . . characterised genealogy as 'an examination of descent', which 'permits the discovery, under the unique aspect of a trait or a concept of the myriad events through which – thanks to which, against which – they were formed'.
>
> (Bolter and Grusin 1999: 21)

How does an idea or a practice, which for Bolter and Grusin is the concept and practice of remediation (the way that one medium absorbs and transforms another), reach us (descend)? What multiple factors have played a part in shaping that process?

   We should note that Poster is particularly keen to avoid thinking of history as a process with a 'culmination' and end point. Bolter and Grusin, like Foucault, are not interested in the origins of things. They are not interesting in where things began or where they finished. They are interested in 'affiliations' (the attachments and connections between things) and 'resonances' (the sympathetic vibrations between things). They want to know about the 'through' and 'against' of things. Instead of images of linear sequences and chains of events we need to think in terms of webs, clusters, boundaries, territories, and overlapping spheres as our images of historical process.

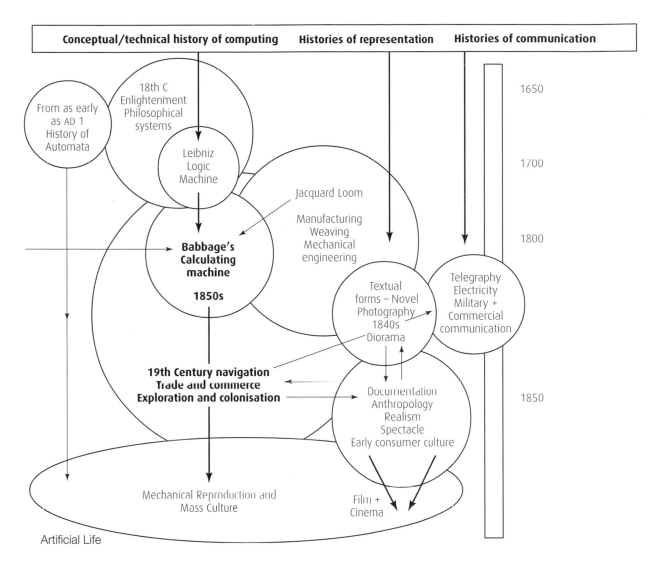

Conceptual/technical history of computing	Histories of representation	Histories of communication

1650

18th C Enlightenment Philosophical systems

From as early as AD 1 History of Automata

Leibniz Logic Machine

1700

Jacquard Loom

Manufacturing Weaving Mechanical engineering

1800

Babbage's Calculating machine

1850s

Textual forms – Novel Photography 1840s Diorama

Telegraphy Electricity Military + Commercial communication

19th Century navigation Trade and commerce Exploration and colonisation

Documentation Anthropology Realism Spectacle Early consumer culture

1850

Mechanical Reproduction and Mass Culture

Film + Cinema

Artificial Life

1.6 A simple model of the complex of histories 'through' and 'against' which new media emerge.

Theorists of new media seeking alternative ways of thinking about the differences and the complex connections between old and new media have drawn upon the influential 'genealogical' theory of history, as argued and put into practice in a number of major works of cultural history by the philosopher-historian Michel Foucault. It is a historical method which offers the possibility of thinking through new media's relationship to the past while avoiding some of the problems we have met above. In doing this, theorists of new media are following in the footsteps of other historians of photography, film, cinema and visual culture such as John Tagg (1998), Jonathan Crary (1993) and Geoffrey Batchen (1997) who have used what has become known as a 'Foucauldian' perspective.

1.4.2 New media and the modernist concept of progress

the full aesthetic potential of this medium will be realised only when computer artists come to the instrument from art rather than computer science . . . Today the kind of simulation envisioned . . . requires a $10 million Cray-1 supercomputer, the most powerful computer in the world . . . [T]he manufacturers of the Cray-1 believe that by the early 1990s computers with three-fourths of its power will sell for approximately $20,000 less than the cost of a portapak and editing system today . . . [F]inally accessible to autonomous individuals, the full aesthetic potential of computer simulation will be revealed, and the future of cinematic languages . . . will be rescued from the tyranny of perceptual imperialists and placed in the hands of artists and amateurs.

(Youngblood 1999: 48)

In the name of 'progress' our official culture is striving to force the new media to do the work of the old.

(McLuhan and Fiore 1967a: 81)

In order to conceive a properly genealogical account of new media histories we need not only to take account of the particular teleologies of technohistory above but also the deeply embedded experience of **modernism** within aesthetics.

Commentators on new media, like Gene Youngblood, frequently refer to a future point in time when their promise will be realised. Thought about new media is replete with a sense of a deferred future. We are repeatedly encouraged to await the further development of the technologies which they utilise. At times this takes the simple form of the 'when we have the computing power' type of argument. Here, the present state of technological (under)development is said to constrain what is possible and explains the gap between the potential and actual performance (see for example, our discussion of virtual reality, **2.1**) .

Related to views of this kind, there are some which embody a particular kind of theory about historical change. It is not technological underdevelopment *per se* that is blamed for the failure of a new medium to deliver its promise; rather, the culprit is seen to be ingrained cultural resistance. Here, the proposal is that in their early phases new media are bound to be used and understood according to older, existing practices and ideas, and that it is largely such ideological and cultural factors that limit the potential of new media. (See also **1.6**.) The central premiss here is that each medium has its own kind of essence; that is, some unique and defining characteristic or characteristics which will, given time and exploration, be clearly revealed. As they are revealed the medium comes into its own. This kind of argument adds ideas about the nature of media and culture to the simpler argument about technological underdevelopment.

Such a view has quite a long history itself, as will be seen in the example from the pioneering writer on 'expanded' cinema, Gene Youngblood, quoted at the beginning of this section. Writing in 1984, in an essay on the then emerging possibilities of digital video and cinema (in Druckery 1999), he looks forward to the 1990s when he foresees affordable computers coming to possess the kind of power that, at his time of writing, was only to be found in the $10 million Cray-1 mainframe supercomputer. Then, in a clear example of the modernist argument that we have outlined, he adds that we must also look forward to the time when the 'full aesthetic potential of the computer simulation will be revealed', as it is rescued from 'the tyranny of perceptual imperialists' (in Druckery 1999: 48). Such imperialists being, we can assume, those scientists, artists and producers who impose their old habits of vision and perception upon the new media (see **2.3**).

In a more recent example, Steve Holzmann (1997: 15) also takes the view that most existing uses of new media fail to 'exploit those special qualities that are unique to digital worlds'. Again, this is because he sees them as having as yet failed to break free of the limits of 'existing paradigms' or historical forms and habits. He, too, looks forward to a time when new media transcend the stage when they are used to fulfil old purposes and when digital media's 'unique qualities' come to 'define entirely new languages of expression'.

As Bolter and Grusin have argued (1999: 49–50), Holzmann (and Youngblood before him in our other example) represent the modernist viewpoint. They believe that for a medium to be significantly new it has to make a radical break with the past.

A major source of such ideas is to be found in one of the seminal texts of artistic modernism: the 1961 essay 'Modernist Painting' by art critic and theorist Clement Greenberg. Although the new, digital media are commonly understood as belonging to a postmodern period, in which the cultural projects of modernism are thought to have been superseded, Greenbergian ideas have continued to have a considerable pull on thinking about new media. Clearly, the point of connection is between the sense that new media are at the cutting edge of culture, that there is an opening up of new horizons and a need for experimentation, and the ideology of the earlier twentieth-century artistic avant-garde movements in painting, photography, sculpture, film and video.

We meet these modernist ideas whenever we hear talk of the need for new media to break clear of old habits and attitudes, the gravity field of history and its old thought patterns and practices. It is also present when we hear talk about the essential characteristics of new media; when the talk is of the distinctive essence of 'digitality' as against the 'photographic', the 'filmic' or the 'televisual' (**1.2**).

Greenberg himself did not think that modern art media should or could break with the past in any simple sense. But he did think they should engage in a process of clarifying and refining their nature by not attempting to do what was not proper to them. This process of refinement included ditching old historical functions that a medium might have served in the past. Painting was the medium that interested him in particular, and his efforts were part of his search to identify the importance of the painting in an age of mechanical reproduction – the age of the then relatively 'new' media of photography and film. He argued that painting should rid itself of its old illustrative or narrative functions to concentrate on its formal patterning of colour and surface. Photography was better suited to illustrative work and showed how it was not, after all, appropriate to painting. Painting could now realise its true nature.

Greenberg also made his arguments in the mid-twentieth-century context of a critique of the alienating effects of capitalism on cultural experience. He shared with other critics the view that the heightened experiences that art had traditionally provided were being eroded and displaced by a levelling down to mere 'entertainment' and popular kitsch. He argued that the arts could save their higher purpose from this fate 'by demonstrating that the kind of experience they provided was valuable in its own right and not obtained from any other kind of activity' (Greenberg 1961, in Harrison and Wood 1992: 755). He urged that this could be done by each art determining, 'through the operations peculiar to itself, the effects peculiar and exclusive to itself' (ibid.). By these means each art would exhibit and make explicit 'that which was unique and irreducible' to it (ibid.). The task of artists, then, was to search for the fundamental essence of their medium, stripping away all extraneous factors and borrowings from other media. It is often thought that this task now falls to new media artists and forward-looking experimental producers.

However, the manner in which a new medium necessarily adopts, in its early years, the conventions and 'languages' of established media is well known. There is the case of the early photographers known as the Pictorialists, who strove to emulate the aesthetic qualities of painting, seeing these as the standards against which photography as a medium had to be judged. In Youngblood's terms they would be examples of 'perceptual imperialists' who acted as a brake on the exploration of the radical representational possibilities afforded by photography as a new medium. Similarly, it is well known that early cinema adopted the conventions of the theatre and vaudeville, and that television looked for its forms to theatre, vaudeville, the format of the newspaper, and cinema itself.

As we have seen, Bolter and Grusin's theory of 'remediation' (1999) deploys a Foucauldian historical perspective to argue against the 'comfortable modernist rhetoric' of authentic media 'essences' and 'breaks with the past' that we have discussed here. They follow McLuhan's insight that 'the content of a medium is always another medium' (1999: 45). They propose that the history of media is a complex process in which all media, including new media, depend upon older media and are in a constant dialectic with them (1999: 50). Digital media are in the process of representing older media in a whole range of ways, some more direct and 'transparent' than others. At the same time, older media are refashioning themselves by absorbing, repurposing, and incorporating digital technologies. Such a process is also implied in the view held by Raymond Williams, whose theory of media change we discuss fully later (**1.6.3**). Williams argues that there is nothing inherent in the nature of a media technology that is responsible for the way a society uses it. It does not, and cannot, have an 'essence' that would inevitably create 'effects peculiar and exclusive to itself'. In a closely argued theory of the manner in which television developed, he observes that some 20 years passed before, 'new kinds of programme were being made for television and there were important advances in the productive use of the medium, including . . . some kinds of original work' (Williams 1974: 30). Productive uses of a new medium and original work in them are not precluded, therefore, by recognising their long-term interplay with older media.

We need, then, to ask a number of questions of the modernist and avant-garde calls for new media to define itself as radically novel. Do media proceed by a process of ruptures or decisive breaks with the past? Can a medium transcend its historical contexts to deliver an 'entirely new language'? Do, indeed, media have irreducible and unique essences (which is not quite the same as having distinguishing characteristics which encourage or constrain the kind of thing we do with them)? These seem to be especially important questions to ask of new digital media which, in large part, rely upon hybrids, convergences and transformations of older media.

> The term 'affordance', taken from design theory may be relevant here. For example, '. . . the term affordance refers to the perceived and actual properties of the thing, primarily those fundamental properties that determine just how the thing could possibly be used . . . A chair affords ("is for") support, and, therefore, affords sitting. A chair can also be carried. Glass is for seeing through, and for breaking' (Norman 2002: 9)

1.4.3 The return of the Middle Ages and other media archaeologies

This section looks at yet another historicising approach to new media studies; here, however, insights from our encounters with new media are drawn upon to rethink existing media histories. Such revisions imply a view of history that is far from teleological, or a basis in the belief in inevitable 'progress'. Unlike the previous examples we turn here to a kind of historical thinking that neither looks at new media as the fulfilment of the recent past nor does it assume a future time in which new media will inevitably transcend the old. Rather, it is suggested that certain uses and aesthetic forms of new media significantly recall residual or suppressed intellectual and representational practices of relatively, and in some cases extremely, remote historical periods. In the context of his own argument against 'sequential narratives' of change in image culture, Kevin Robins observes that:

It is notable that much of the most interesting discussion of images now concerns not digital futures but, actually, what seemed until recently to be antique and forgotten media (the panorama, the camera obscura, the stereoscope): from our postphotographic vantage point these have suddenly acquired new meanings, and their reevaluation now seems crucial to understanding the significance of digital culture.

(Robins 1996: 165)

The ludic: cinema and games

A major example of this renewed interest in 'antique' media is in the early cinema of circa 1900–1920 and its prehistory in mechanical **spectacles** such as the panorama. Its source is in the way the structures, aesthetics and pleasures of computer games are being seen to represent a revival of qualities found in that earlier medium. It is argued that this 'cinema of attractions' was overtaken and suppressed by what became the dominant form of narrative cinema, exemplified by classical Hollywood in the 1930s–1950s. Now, at the beginning of the twenty-first century, changes in media production and in the pleasures sought in media consumption, exemplified in the form of the computer game and its crossovers with special effects 'blockbuster' cinema, indicate a return of the possibilities present in early cinema. These ideas and the research that supports them are discussed in more detail later (see **2.7**). What is significant in the context of this section is the way that noticing things about new media has led some of its theorists to find remarkable historical parallels which cannot be contained within a methodology of technological progress, but rather of loss, suppression or marginalisation, and then return.

Rhetoric and spatialised memory

Benjamin Woolley, writing about Nicholas Negroponte's concept of 'spatial data management', exemplified in computer media's metaphorical desktops, and simulated 3D working environments, draws a parallel with the memorising strategies of ancient preliterate, oral cultures. He sees the icons and spaces of the computer screen recalling the 'mnemonic' traditions of classical and medieval Europe. Mnemonics is the art of using imaginary spaces or 'memory palaces' (spatial arrangements, buildings, objects, or painted representations of them) as aids to remembering long stories and complex arguments (Woolley 1992: 138–149). Similarly, with a focus on computer games, Nickianne Moody (1995) traces a related set of connections between the forms and aesthetics of role play games, interactive computer games and the allegorical narratives of the Middle Ages.

Edutainment and the eighteenth-century Enlightenment

Barbara Maria Stafford observes that with the increasingly widespread use of interactive computer graphics and educational software packages we are returning to a kind of 'oral-visual culture' which was at the centre of European education and scientific experiment in the early eighteenth century (1994: xxv). Stafford argues that during the later eighteenth century, and across the nineteenth, written texts and mass literacy came to be the only respectable and trustworthy media of knowledge and education. Practical and the visual modes of enquiry, experiment, demonstration and learning fell into disrepute as seductive and unreliable. Now, with computer animation and modelling, virtual reality, and even email (as a form of discussion), Stafford sees the emergence of a 'new vision and visionary art-science', a form of visual education similar to that which arose in the early eighteenth century, 'on the boundaries between art and technology, game and experiment, image and speech' (ibid.). However, she argues, in order for our culture to guide itself through this 'electronic upheaval' (ibid.) we will need 'to go backward in order to go forward', in order to 'unearth a past material world that had once occupied the centre of a communications network but was then steadily pushed to the periphery' (ibid.: 3).

Stafford's case is more than a formal comparison between two periods when the oral, visual and practical dominate over the literary and textual. She also argues that the use of images and practical experiments, objects and apparatuses, that characterised early **Enlightenment** education coincided with the birth of middle-class leisure and early forms of consumer culture (1994: xxi). Stafford also suggests that our late twentieth- and early twenty-first-century anxieties about 'dumbing down' and 'edutainment' are echoed in eighteenth-century concerns to distinguish authentic forms of learning and scientific demonstration from quackery and charlatanism. Her argument, overall, is that the graphic materials of eighteenth-century education and scientific experiment were the 'ancestors of today's home- and place-based software and interactive technology' (ibid.: xxiii).

In each of these cases, history is not seen simply as a matter of linear chronology or uni-linear progress in which the present is understood mainly as the superior development of the immediate past; rather, short-circuits and loops in historical time are conceived. Indeed, it chimes with the postmodern view that history (certainly social and cultural history) as a continuous process of progressive development has ceased. Instead, the past has become a vast reservoir of styles and possibilities that are permanently available for reconstruction and revival. The most cursory glance at contemporary architecture, interior design and fashion will show this process of retroactive culture recycling in action.

We can also make sense of this relation between chronologically remote times and the present through the idea that a culture contains dominant, residual, and emergent elements (Williams 1977: 121–127). Using these concepts, Williams argues that elements in a culture that were once dominant may become residual but do not necessarily disappear. They become unimportant and peripheral to a culture's major concerns but are still available as resources which can be used to challenge and resist dominant cultural practices and values at another time. We might note, in this connection, how cyber-fiction and fantasy repeatedly dresses up its visions of the future in medieval imagery. The future is imagined in terms of the past. As Moody puts it:

> Much fantasy fiction shares a clearly defined quasi-medieval diegesis. One that fits snugly into Umberto Eco's categorisation of the 'new middle ages' . . . For Eco it would be entirely logical that the 'high tech' personal computer is used to play dark and labyrinthine games with a medieval diegesis.
>
> (Moody 1995: 61)

For Robins, the significance of these renewed interests in the past, driven by current reflections on new media, is that they allow us to think in non-teleological ways about the past and to recognise what 'modern culture has repressed and disavowed' (1996: 161) in its over-riding and often exclusive or blind concern for technological rationalism. The discovery of the kind of historical precedents for new media which our examples stand for, may, in his terms, be opportunities for grasping that new media are not best thought of as the narrow pinnacle of technological progress. Rather, they are evidence of a more complex and richer co-existence of cultural practices that the diverse possibilities of new media throw into fresh relief.

1.4.4 A sense of déjà vu

The **utopian**, as well as **dystopian**, terms in which new media have been received have caused several media historians to record a sense of déjà vu, the feeling that we have been here before. In particular, the quite remarkable utopian claims made for earlier new media technologies such as photography and cinema have been used to contextualise the widespread technophilia of the last fifteen or so years (e.g. Dovey 1995: 111). So, the history in question this time is not that of the material forerunners of new image and communication media themselves but of the terms in which societies responded to and discussed earlier 'media revolutions'. This is discussed more fully later (**1.5**).

Two kinds of historical enquiry are relevant here. The first is to be found in the existing body of media history, such as: literacy (Ong 2002), the printing press (Eisenstein 1979), the book (Chartier 1994), photography (Tagg 1998), film and television (Williams 1974). These long-standing topics of historical research provide us with detailed empirical knowledge of what we broadly refer to as earlier 'media revolutions'. They also represent sustained efforts to grasp the various patterns of determination, and the surprising outcomes of the introductions, over the long term, of new media into particular societies, cultures and economies. While it is not possible to transfer our understanding of the 'coming of the book' or of 'the birth of photography' directly and wholesale to a study of the cultural impact of the computer, because the wider social context in which each occurs is different (**1.5**), such studies provide us with indispensable methods and frameworks to guide us in working out how new technologies become media, and with what outcomes.

Second, a more recent development has been historical and ethnographic research into our imaginative investment in new technologies, the manner in which we respond to their appearance in our lives, and the ways in which the members of a culture repurpose and subvert media in everyday use (regardless of the purposes which their inventors and developers saw for them). This is also discussed more fully in (**1.5**), where we deal with the concept of the 'technological imaginary'(**1.5.2**).

1.4.5 Conclusion

Paradoxically, then, it is precisely our sense of the 'new' in new media which makes history so important – in the way that something so current, rapidly changing and running toward the future also calls us back to the past. This analytic position somewhat challenges the idea that new media are 'postmodern' media; that is, media that arise from, and then contribute to, a set of socio-cultural developments which are thought to mark a significant break with history, with the 'modern' industrial period and its forerunner in the eighteenth-century age of Enlightenment. We have seen that thinking in terms of a simple separation of the present and the recent past (the postmodern) from the 'modern' period may obscure as much as it reveals about new media. We have argued instead for a history that allows for the continuation of certain media traditions through 'remediation', as well as the revisiting and revival of suppressed or disregarded historical moments in order to understand contemporary developments. Our review of (new) media histories is based in the need to distinguish between what may be new about our contemporary media and what they share with other media, and between what they can do and what is ideological in our reception of new media. In order to be able to disregard what Langdon Winner (1989) has called 'mythinformation' we have argued that history has never been so important for the student of media.

1.5 Who was dissatisfied with old media?

We live in this very weird time in history where we're passive recipients of a very immature, noninteractive broadcast medium. Mission number one is to kill TV.

(Jaron Lanier, quoted in Boddy 1994: 116)

Photographers will be freed from our perpetual restraint, that of having . . . to record the reality of things . . . freed at last from being the mere recorders of reality, our creativity will be given free rein.

(Laye, quoted in Robins 1991: 56)

1.5.1 The question

The question that forms the title of this section is asked in order to raise a critical issue – what were the problems to which new communications media are the solutions? We might, of course, say that there were none. 'New' media were simply that – 'new' – in themselves and have no relation to any limits, shortcomings, or problems that might have been associated with 'old' media. But, the two quotes above, one referring to television and the other to photography, can stand for many other views and comments that strongly suggest that they do.

In thinking about such a question we will find ourselves considering the discursive frameworks that establish the conditions of possibility for new media. This in turn will allow us to look at some of the ways in which previously 'new' media have been considered in order to understand the discursive formations present in our contemporary moment of novelty.

In the rumours and early literature about the coming of multimedia and virtual reality, and as soon as new media forms themselves began to appear, they were celebrated as overcoming, or at least as having the promise to overcome, the negative limits and even the oppressive features of established and culturally dominant analogue media. As the above statements about television and photography imply, in the reception of new media there was, and still is, an implication that we needed them in order to overcome the limits of the old.

On this basis it could seem reasonable to ask whether media were in such bad odour in pre-digital days, that a mass of criticism and dissatisfaction formed a body of pressure such that something better was sought. Or, alternatively, we might ask whether ideas about the superiority of new media are merely retrospective projections or post-hoc rationalisations of change; simply a case of wanting to believe that what we have is better than what went before.

However, these questions are too reductive to arrive at an understanding of how our perceptions and experiences of new media are framed. In order to arrive at a better explanation, this section considers how the development and reception of new media have been shaped by two sets of ideas. First, the socio-psychological workings of the 'technological imaginary'; second, earlier twentieth-century traditions of media critique aimed at the 'mass' broadcast media and their perceived social effects. We will be interested in these traditions to the extent that they are picked up and used in the evaluation of new media.

1.5.2 The technological imaginary

The phrase the 'technological imaginary', as it is used in critical thought about cinema in the first place (De Lauretis *et al.* 1980) and now new media technologies, has roots in psychoanalytic theory. It has migrated from that location to be more generally used in the study of culture and technology. In some versions it has been recast in more sociological language and is met as a 'popular' or 'collective' imagination about technologies (Flichy 1999). Here, tendencies that may have been originally posited (in psychoanalytical theory) as belonging to individuals are also observed to be present at the level of social groups and collectivities. However, some of the specific charge that the word has in psychoanalytic theory needs to be retained to see its usefulness. The French adjective *imaginaire* became a noun, a name for a substantive order of experience, the *imaginaire*, alongside two others – the 'real' and the 'symbolic' – in the psychoanalytic theories of Jacques Lacan. After Lacan, *imaginaire* or the English 'imaginary' does not refer, as it does in everyday use, to a kind of poetic mental faculty or the activity of fantasising (Ragland-Sullivan 1992: 173–176). Rather, in psychoanalytic theory, it refers to a realm of images, representations, ideas and intuitions of fulfilment, of wholeness and completeness that human beings, in their fragmented and incomplete selves, desire to become. These are images of an 'other' – an other self, another race, gender, or significant other person, another state of being. Technologies are then cast in the role of such an 'other'. When applied to technology, or media technologies in particular, the concept of a technological imaginary draws attention to the way that (frequently gendered) dissatisfactions with social reality and desires for a better society are projected onto technologies as capable of delivering a potential realm of completeness.

This can seem a very abstract notion. The Case studies in this section show how, in different ways, new media are catalysts or vehicles for the expression of ideas about human existence and social life. We can begin to do this by reminding ourselves of some typical responses to the advent of new media and by considering the recurring sense of optimism and anxiety that each wave of new media calls up.

As a new medium becomes socially available it is necessarily placed in relation to a culture's older media forms and the way that these are already valued and understood. This is seen in expressions of a sense of anxiety at the loss of the forms that are displaced. Well-known examples of this include the purist fears about the impact of photography on painting in the 1840s, and of television and then video on cinema in the 1970s. More recently, regret has been expressed about the impact of digital imaging on photography (Ritchen 1990) and graphics software on drawing and design as they moved from the traditional craft spaces of the darkroom and the drawing board to the computer screen. In terms of communication media this sense of loss is usually expressed in social, rather than aesthetic or craft terms. For instance, during the last quarter of the nineteenth century it was feared that the telephone would invade the domestic privacy of the family or that it would break through important settled social hierarchies, allowing the lower classes to speak (inappropriately) to their 'betters' in ways that were not permitted in traditional face-to-face encounters (Marvin 1988). (See **Case study 1.5**.) Since the early 1990s, we have seen a more recent example in the widespread shift that has taken place between terrestrial mail and email. Here anxieties are expressed, by some, about the way that email has eradicated the time for reflection that was involved in traditional letter writing and sending leading to notorious email 'flaming' and intemperate exchanges (see also **Case study 1.2**).

Conversely, during the period in which the cultural reception of a new medium is being worked out, it is also favourably positioned in relation to existing media. The euphoric celebration of a new medium and the often feverish speculation about its potential is achieved, at least in part, by its favourable contrast with older forms. In their attempts to persuade us to invest in the technology advertisers often use older media as an 'other' against which the 'new' is given an identity as good, as socially and aesthetically progressive. This kind of comparison draws upon more than the hopes that a culture has for its new media, it also involves its existing feelings about the old (Robins 1996).

Traditional chemical photography has played such a role in recent celebrations of digital imaging (see Lister 1995; Robins 1995), as has television in the talking-up of interactive media. Before the emergence and application of digital technologies, TV, for instance, was widely perceived as a 'bad object' and this ascription has been important as a foil to celebrations of interactive media's superiority over broadcast television (Boddy 1994; see also **Case study 1.5**). Television is associated with passivity, encapsulated in the image of the TV viewer as an inert 'couch potato' subject to its 'effects', while the interactive media 'user' (already a name which connotes a more active relation to media than does 'viewer') conjures up an image of someone occupying an ergonomically designed, hi-tech swivel chair, alert and skilled as they 'navigate' and make active choices via their screen-based interface. Artists, novelists, and technologists entice us with the prospect of creating and living in virtual worlds of our own making rather than being anonymous and passive members of the 'mass' audience of popular television. As a broadcast medium, TV is seen as an agent for the transmission of centralised (read authoritarian or incontestable) messages to mass audiences. This is then readily compared to the new possibilities of the one-to-one, two-way, decentralised transmissions of the Internet or the new possibilities for narrowcasting and interactive TV. Similar kinds of contrast have been made between non-linear, hot-linked, hypertext and the traditional form of the book which, in this new comparison, becomes 'the big book' (like this one), a fixed, dogmatic text which is the prescriptive voice of authority.

So, a part of understanding the conditions in which new media are received and evaluated involves (1) seeing what values a culture has already invested in old media, and this may involve considering whose values these were, and (2) understanding how the concrete objects (books, TV sets, computers) and the products (novels, soap operas, games) of particular media come to have good or bad cultural connotations in the first place (see **Case studies 1.5**, **1.6**). In order to do this we first consider how apparent the technological imaginary is in the ways we talk and write about media.

Case study 1.5 New media as arenas for discussing old problems

1.5.3 The discursive construction of new media

It is essential to realise that a theory does not find its object sitting waiting for it in the world: theories constitute their own objects in the process of their evolution. 'Water' is not the same theoretical object in chemistry as it is in hydraulics – an observation which in no way denies that chemists and engineers alike drink, and shower in, the same substance.

(Burgin 1982: 9)

Victor Burgin offers this example of the way that the nature of a common object of concern – water – will be differently understood according to the specific set of concepts which are used to study it. A key argument of post-structuralist theory is that language does not merely describe a pre-given reality (words are matched to things) but that reality is only known through language (the words or concepts we possess lead us to perceive and conceive the world in their terms). Language, in this sense, can be thought of as operating as microscopes, telescopes and cameras do – they produce certain kinds of images of the world; they construct ways of seeing and understanding. Elaborated systems of language (conversations, theories, arguments, descriptions) which are built up or evolved as part of particular social projects (expressing emotion, writing legal contracts, analysing social behaviour, etc.) are called discourses. Discourses, like the words and concepts they employ, can then be said to construct their objects. It is in this sense that we now turn to the discursive construction of new media as it feeds (frames, provides the resources for) the technological imagination.

In sections **1.3** and **1.4** we considered some ways in which histories of media form part of our contemporary responses to new media. On meeting the many claims and predictions made for new media, media historians have expressed a sense of déjà vu – of having 'seen this' or 'been here' before (Gunning 1991). This is more than a matter of history repeating itself. This would amount to saying that the emergence and development of each new medium occurs and proceeds technologically and socio-economically in the same way, and that the same patterns of response are evident in the members of the culture who receive, use and consume it. There are, indeed, some marked similarities of this kind, but it would be too simple to leave the matter there. To do this would simply hasten us to the 'business as usual' conclusion which we have rejected as conservative and inadequate (**1.1** and **1.3**). More importantly, it would be wrong. For, even if there are patterns that recur in the technological emergence and development of new media technologies, we have to recognise that they occur in widely different historical and social contexts. Furthermore, the technologies in question have different capacities and characteristics.

For example, similarities are frequently pointed out between the emergence of film technology and the search for cinematic form at the end of the nineteenth century and that of multimedia and VR at the end of the twentieth century. However, film and cinema entered a world of handmade images and early kinds of still photographic image (at that time, a difficult craft), of venue-based, mechanically produced theatrical spectacles in which the 'movement' and special effects on offer were experienced as absolutely novel and would seem primitive by today's standards. There was no broadcasting, and even the telephone was a novel apparatus. And, of course, much wider factors could be pointed to: the state of development of mass industrial production and consumer culture, of general education, etc. The world into which our new media have emerged is very different; it has seen a hundred years of increasingly pervasive and sophisticated technological visual culture (Darley 1991).

It is a world in which images, still and moving, in print and on screens, are layered so thick, are so intertextual, that a sense of what is real has become problematic, buried under the thick sediment of its visual representations. New media technologies which emerge into this context enter an enormously complex moving image culture of developed genres, signifying conventions, audiences with highly developed and 'knowing' pleasures and ways of 'reading' images, and a major industry and entertainment economy which is very different from, even if it has antecedents in, that of the late nineteenth century.

What then gives rise to the sense of déjà vu mentioned above? It is likely that it does not concern the actual historical repetition of technologies or mediums themselves – rather, it is a matter of the repetition of deeply ingrained ways in which we think, talk, and write about new image and communication technologies. In short, their discursive construction. Whatever the actual and detailed paths taken by a new media technology in its particular historical context of complex determinations (the telephone, the radio, TV, etc.) it is a striking matter of record that the responses of contemporaries (professionals in their journals, journalists, academic and other commentators) are cast in uncannily similar terms (Marvin 1988; Spiegel 1992; Boddy 1994).

In noticing these things, the experience of loss with the displacement of the old, the simultaneous judgement of the old as limited, and a sense of repetition in how media and technological change is talked and written about, we are ready to consider some more detailed examples of the 'technological imaginary' at work.

CASE STUDY 1.4: The technological imaginary and the 'new media order'

Key text: Kevin Robins, 'A touch of the unknown', in K. Robins (1996) *Into the Image*, Routledge, London and New York.

> Entering cyberspace is the closest we can come to returning to the Wild West . . . the wilderness never lasts long – you had better enjoy it before it disappears.
>
> (Taylor and Saarinen 1994: 10)

As we have seen, a broad definition of the 'technological imaginary' refers us to the way that new technologies are taken up within a culture and are hooked into, or have projected onto them, its wider social and psychological desires and fears. Kevin Robins has applied the ideas of the psychoanalyst Wilfred Bion and other philosophers and political theorists to argue this case. He has returned to this theme in a number of essays dealing with new media and cyberculture, especially VR and new image and vision technologies (Robins 1996). In these essays he seeks to show how the dominant way in which we are asked to understand new media is exclusively driven by utopian, rationalist and transcendental impulses to escape the difficulties of social reality, and that these have deep roots in Western capitalist societies:

> The new image and information culture is now associated with a renewed confidence in technological solutions to the problems of human culture and existence. The new technologies have revitalised the utopian aspirations in the modern techno-rationalist project. The progressivist and utopian spirit is articulated through ordinary, spontaneous and commonsensical accounts of what is happening: through the culture, there is a sense of almost limitless possibilities inherent in the 'cyber-revolution'. *Indeed, such is the dominant technological imaginary, that it is almost impossible to discuss the new techno-culture in any other way.*
>
> (Robins 1996: 13; emphasis added)

He argues that behind the transcendental rhetorics of late twentieth- and early twenty-first-century techno-culture is an old human project to contain and master the ever present threat of **chaos** and disorder.

> What is psychically compelling about the technologies I am considering here . . . is their capacity to provide a certain security and protection against the frightful world and against the fear that inhabits our bodies. They provide the means to distance and detach ourselves from what is fear provoking in the world and in ourselves.
>
> (Robins 1996: 12)

For Robins, the technological imaginary of the 'new media order' is but the latest instance of a long history of similar 'psychic investments we make in technological forms'. He sees the modern (nineteenth- and early twentieth-century) 'social imaginary' as having always been expansionist and utopian, leading us to seek out new frontiers, the other side of which lie better worlds. As real places and frontiers become exhausted, the cyberspaces and places of virtual life promised by new media become the new utopias which we reach for across a new technological frontier (1996: 16). Now, assessments of the value of computer-mediated communication, online communities, and the new virtual selves that await us in cyberspace can be understood as elements of a 'distinctive social vision' born of the contemporary technological imaginary (1996: 24).

Robins argues that this desire for better, less problematic (cyber) spaces is driven by a deep fear of disorder, of the unknown and meaninglessness. In a manner that is reminiscent of McLuhan, Robins sees the modern world 'surveyed by absolute vision', as a world which could be ordered, controlled, surveilled and manipulated from an omnipotent distance. This has been, and continues to be, 'massively facilitated by the development of a succession of new technological means' (1996: 20). Co-existing with this desire for technologically empowered control, the technological imagination leads us to dream of the pleasure of shifting our existence to 'an alternative environment, one that has been cleansed of the real world's undesirable qualities' by entering 'into the image'. This is now achieved through the IMAX screen and lies behind our fascination with the prospect of immersive VR; formerly it was sought in the form of Hayles tours, panoramas, and early cinema (1996: 22). (See **2.7**.)

2.7 Digital cinema

CASE STUDY 1.5: New media as arenas for discussing old problems

Key text: Carolyn Marvin (1988) *When Old Technologies Were New: Thinking About Electric Communication in the Nineteenth Century*, Oxford University Press, New York and Oxford.

> Discussions of electrical and other forms of communication in the late nineteenth century begin from specific cultural and class assumptions about what communication ought to be like among particular groups of people. These assumptions informed the beliefs of nineteenth-century observers about what these new media were supposed to do . . .
>
> (Marvin 1988: 6)

If Robins's understanding of the contemporary technological imaginary of the 'new media order' stresses its utopian character, Carolyn Marvin, in her research into the early history of electric communications technologies, sees them as 'arenas for negotiating issues crucial to the conduct of social life'. She argues that beneath their more obvious functional meanings (the ways in which new media offer greater speed, capacity, and better performance) a whole range of 'social meanings can elaborate themselves' (Marvin 1988: 4). She describes the varied, surprising and furious experiments that were undertaken to see how the new technologies might extend existing social and cultural practices. In its early years, the telephone was used to relay orchestral concerts to the homes of the wealthy and privileged, it was informally co-opted by groups of lonely musicians in order to 'jam' together over the telephone lines, and telephone operators used their vantage point to gossip and spread private information within small communities. As such things happened, questions were raised about who, in society, has the power to define the use of technologies, who should use them and to what ends, what their implications are for settled patterns of social life, what needs to be defended, and whose interests should be furthered.

For Carolyn Marvin, 'the introduction of new media is a special historical occasion when patterns anchored in older media that have provided the stable currency of social exchange are re-examined, challenged, and defended' (Marvin 1988: 4). While an orthodox way of studying new communication technologies, like the telephone, involves examining how the new machine or instrument may introduce new practices and contribute to the building of new social relationships, Marvin sees new media as 'providing new platforms on which old groups confront one other'. The appearance of a new medium becomes a kind of occasion for a 'drama', whereby the existing groups and hierarchies within a society attempt to assimilate the new technology into their familiar worlds, rituals and habits. On the one hand, a society works to use the new technology to fulfil old and existing social functions, while at the same time it projects onto the technology its fears about its own stability and already existing social tensions.

Marvin shows how a technological imaginary is at work long before a new communications technology settles into a stable form. The new groups of 'experts' and professionals who formed around new media technologies, with their particular visions and imaginaries (such as Negroponte or the French HDTV researchers discussed in **Case study 1.7**), are only one group in a wider society that seeks to experiment with and imagine the possibilities of the new medium in order to 'reduce and simplify a world of expanding cultural variety to something more familiar and less threatening' (1988: 5).

CASE STUDY 1.6: The technological imaginary and the cultural reception of new media

Television and the gendering of a 'bad' object

Key text: William Boddy (1994) 'Archaeologies of electronic vision and the gendered spectator', *Screen* 35.2 (Summer): 105–122.

> the . . . exploration of the history of technology is more than technical . . . technology can reveal the dream world of society as much as its pragmatic realisation.
>
> (Gunning, quoted in Boddy 1994: 105)

William Boddy has adopted Marvin's approach to examine how, earlier in the twentieth century, a technological imaginary shaped our perceptions of radio and television in ways which now inform our ideas about the value of new digital media.

Radio and, later, television were media technologies that had to be 'filled' with content after they were designed (Williams 1974: 25). With its beginnings in the transmission of 'one-to-one' secret messages for military and trading purposes, radio started its civil life in the 'attic' as a hobby or an enthusiast's activity. In the 1920s radio receivers of various kinds of complexity were self-assembled by men and boys from parts and kits. Isolated from the rest of the family by their headphones, these male enthusiasts 'fished' the airwaves. 'The radio enthusiasts . . . envisioned radio as an active sport . . . in which the participant gained a sense of mastery – increased masculinity – by adjusting the dials and "reeling" in the distant signals' (Spiegel 1992: 27). This was a gendered activity, being almost exclusively pursued by men. During this period radio was also hailed for its potential social good. A medium to weld a nation together in solidarity, and to build community where none existed or where it was threatened by racist tensions (the parallels with the Internet are strong).

From the mid-1920s, in the US and Europe, sound broadcasting was transformed by investment in the production of 'user friendly' domestic receivers in order to open up the growing markets for consumer durables in the family home – the box camera, washing machine, the gas range, and the vacuum cleaner. There was a determined attempt on the part of broadcasters and hardware manufacturers to shift the popular perception of the radio away from an untidy mass of wires, valves and acid-filled batteries used in intense isolation by men in their attics. Instead it was marketed as a piece of furniture suitable for siting in the living room and audible through camouflaged speakers. Radio came to be perceived as background atmosphere, a cosmetic domestic addition to furniture and wallpaper, for the distracted housewife (Boddy 1994: 114). As a 1923 trade journal advised the retailers who were to sell the new sets, 'don't talk circuits. Don't talk in electrical terms . . . You must convince everyone . . . that radio will fit into the well appointed home' (Boddy 1994: 112).

The reaction of the male radio enthusiast was predictable (and foreshadows that of the hackerish Internet users' response to the mid-1990s emergence of the commercialised, animated banner-ad commodification of the 'information wants to be free' Internet). Radio amateurs bemoaned the loss of an engrossing hobby and the thrilling business of 'conquering time and space', while wrestling ingeniously with the technology (Boddy 1994: 113).

Instead, with the 'distracted housewife' as the ideal audience, radio came to be seen as 'passive listening', a matter of 'mere' enjoyment. A commercialised, trivial regime of 'programmes' aimed at an 'average woman listener [who] is neither cosmopolitan nor sophisticated. Nor does she have much imagination' (Boddy 1994: 114). Fears grew that radio would isolate and lead to the stagnation of family life. After its heroic 'attic days' radio was judged to have become a pacifying, emasculating and feminising activity.

1.2 The characteristics of
new media: some defining
concepts

CASE STUDY 1.7: The technological imaginary and the shaping of new media

Key text: Patrice Flichy (1999) 'The construction of new digital media', *New Media and Society* 1.1: 33–39.

> communication technologies, in particular, like network technologies, are often the source of an abundant production by the collective imagination . . . in which innovations are celebrated by the media even before being launched.
>
> (Flichy 1999: 33)

Patrice Flichy proposes that the technological imaginary plays a role in the very creation of a new medium. It is a factor that interplays with actual technological developments, planning, and the lifestyles and modes of work into which the technology is designed to fit. It is an element which owes more to certain ideologies and desires that circulate within a culture than to hard-headed calculations and credible expectations of how a medium is likely to be used (Flichy 1999: 34). Flichy uses recent debates over the future of digital television as one of his examples (see also Winston 1996). In the 1990s three views on how digitisation should be applied to the medium of television competed with each other. These were:

- HDTV (high-definition digital television)

- personalised, interactive television (push media)

- multi-channel cable and satellite television

HDTV involved the use of digitisation to give television a high-resolution image. This was, initially, a primarily European concept and Flichy traces it to a French habit of thinking of television 'cinematographically'; that is, rather than thinking of television in terms of its flow of images, to be preoccupied instead with the quality of the framed image 'on the screen'.

The second conception, that championed by Nicolas Negroponte, the 'digital guru' from MIT, envisions the future of TV as a 'gigantic virtual video library' delivering personalised contents to its interacting users. This concept of TV as breaking free of linear, centralised programming and scheduling, and emphasising 'user choice', is related to a sort of interactive 'essence' of digital technology (**1.2**).

The third option, to use increased digital bandwidth to multiply the number of TV channels, is technologically and economically driven in the sense that it builds upon previous corporate investments in cable and satellite transmission. This option, which in many ways is to 'provide more of the same', now appears to be the direction actually being taken by the early operators of digital television.

The degree to which each of these visions of what television 'could be' has been subsequently realised is not at issue. The point is that such visions are driven by cultural values upon which a technological imaginary is based and not on technological necessities; it is possible that the technology could deliver any or all of the options.

The debate and practical competition over how to employ digital technology in relation to the existing medium of television was based upon three kinds of technological imaginary: the desire to elevate television to the status of cinema by providing it with the detail and beauty of the film image; a conviction that television should be radically transformed in line with the new principles of digital culture; and, finally, the profit-driven ambition to use technology to provide more of the same while creating more television 'niche' markets.

The examples above argue that the processes that determine the kind of media we actually get are neither solely economic nor solely technological, but that all orders of decision in the development process occur within a discursive framework powerfully shaped by the technological imaginary. The evidence for the existence of such a framework can be tracked back through the introduction of numerous technologies and goods throughout the modern period.

1.5.4 The return of the Frankfurt School critique in the popularisation of new media

We now return to a broader consideration of the points raised in **Case study 1.3** concerning the allegedly 'democratic' potential of interactivity. Here, however, we point out how a tradition of criticism of mass media finds itself reappropriated as another discursive framework that shapes our ideas about what new media are or could be.

This tradition of media critique expressed profound dissatisfaction with the uses and the cultural and political implications of broadcast media throughout the early and mid-twentieth century. Such critics of the effects of twentieth-century mass media did not normally think that there was a technological solution to the problems they identified. They did not suggest that new and different media technologies would overcome the social and cultural problems they associated with the media they were familiar with. To the extent that they could conceive of change in their situation they saw hope lying in social action, whether through political revolution or a conservative defence of threatened values. In another tradition it was more imaginative and democratic uses of existing media that were seen as the answer. Nevertheless, the critique of mass media has become, in the hands of new media enthusiasts, a set of terms against which new media are celebrated. The positions and theories represented by these media critics have been frequently rehearsed and continue to be influential in some areas of media studies and theory. Because of this they need not be dealt with at great length here as many accessible and adequate accounts already exist (Strinati 1995; Stevenson 1995; Lury 1992).

The 'culture industry', the end of democratic participation and critical distance

From the 1920s until the present day the mass media (especially the popular press and the broadcast media of radio and television) have been the object of sustained criticism from intellectuals, artists, educationalists, feminists and left-wing activists. It is a (contentious) aspect of this critique, which sees mass culture as disempowering, homogenising, and impositional in nature, that is of relevance in this context. Strinati sums up such a view:

> [there] is a specific conception of the audience of mass culture, the mass or the public which consumes mass produced cultural products. The audience is conceived of as a mass of passive consumers . . . supine before the false pleasures of mass consumption . . . The picture is of a mass which almost without thinking, without reflecting, abandoning all critical hope, buys into mass culture and mass consumption. Due to the emergence of mass society and mass culture it lacks the intellectual and moral resources to do otherwise. It cannot think of, or in terms of, alternatives.
>
> (Strinati 1995: 12)

Such a conception and evaluation of the 'mass' and its culture was argued by intellectuals who were steeped in the values of a literary culture. Alan Meek has described well a dominant kind of relationship which such intellectuals and artists had to the mass media in the early and mid-twentieth century:

> The modern Western intellectual appeared as a figure within the public sphere whose technological media was print and whose institutions were defined by the nation state. The ideals of democratic participation and critical literacy which the intellectual espoused

have often been seen to be undermined by the emerging apparatus of electronic media, 'mass culture', or the entertainment industry.

(Meek 2000: 88)

Mass society critics feared four things:

- the debasement and displacement of an authentic organic folk culture;

- the erosion of high cultural traditions, those of art and literature;

- loss of the ability of these cultural traditions (as the classical 'public sphere') to comment critically on society's values;

- the indoctrination and manipulation of the 'masses' by either totalitarian politics or market forces.

The context within which these fears were articulated was the rise of mass, urban society. Nineteenth- and early twentieth-century industrialisation and urbanisation in Western Europe and America had weakened or destroyed organic, closely knit, agrarian communities. The sense of identity, community membership and oral, face-to-face communication fostered and mediated by institutions like the extended family, the village, and the Church were seen to be replaced by a collection of atomised individuals in the new industrial cities and workplaces. At the same time the production of culture itself became subject to the processes of industrialisation and the marketplace. The evolving Hollywood mode of film production, popular 'pulp' fiction, and popular music were particular objects of criticism. Seen as generic and formulaic, catering to the lowest common denominators of taste, they were assembly line models of cultural production. Radio, and later television, were viewed as centralised impositions from above. Either as a means of trivialising the content of communication, or as a means of political indoctrination, they were seen as threats to democracy and the informed critical participation of the masses in cultural and social life. How, feared the intellectuals, given the burgeoning of mass electronic media, could people take a part in a democratic system of government in which all citizens are active, through their elected representatives, in the decisions a society makes?

With the erosion of folk wisdom and morality, and the trivialisation, commercialisation and centralisation of culture and communications, how could citizens be informed about issues and able, through their educated ability, to think independently and form views on social and political issues? Critical participation demanded an ability and energy to take issue with how things are, to ask questions about the nature or order of things, and a capacity to envision and conceive of better states as a guide to action. In the eyes of theorists such as those of the Frankfurt School, such ideals were terminally threatened by the mass media and mass culture.

Further, such developments took place in the context of twin evils. First, the twin realities of Fascism and Stalinism which demonstrated the power of mass media harnessed to totalitarianism. Second, the tyranny of market forces to generate false needs and desires within the populations of capitalist societies where active citizens were being transformed into 'mere' consumers.

This 'mass society theory', and its related critiques of the mass media, has been much debated, challenged and qualified within media sociology, **ethnography**, and in the light of postmodern media theory in recent years (see, for example, our discussion of audience interaction with mass media texts in **Case study 1.3**). Despite the existence of more nuanced accounts of the mass media which offer a more complex view of their social significance, it has now become clear that some of the main proponents of the twenty-first century's new communications media are actually celebrating their potential to restore society to a state where the damage perceived to be wrought by mass media will be undone. In some versions there is an active looking back to a pre-mass culture golden age of authentic exchange and community. We can especially note the following:

- The recovery of community and a sphere of public debate. In this formulation the Internet is seen as providing a vibrant counter public sphere. In addition, shared online spaces allegedly provide a sense of 'cyber community' against the alienations of contemporary life.

- The removal of information and communication from central authority, control and censorship.

- The 'fourth estate' function of mass media, seen here to be revived with the rise of the 'citizen journalist' as alternative sources of news and information circulate freely through 'blogs', online publishing, camera-phone photography etc.

- The creative exploration of new forms of identity and relationship within virtual communities and social networking sites.

Online communication is here seen as productive not of 'passive' supine subjects but of an active process of identity construction and exchange. These arguments all in some way echo and answer ways in which conventional mass media have been problematised by intellectuals and critics.

The Brechtian avant-garde and lost opportunities

These 'answers' to a widespread pessimism about mass media can be seen in the light of another tradition in which the emancipatory power of radio, cinema, and television (also the mass press) lay in the way that they promised to involve the workers of industrial society in creative production, self-education and political expression. A major representative of this view is the socialist playwright Bertolt Brecht. Brecht castigated the form that radio was taking in the 1930s as he saw its potentials being limited to 'prettifying public life' and to 'bringing back cosiness to the home and making family life bearable'. His alternative, however, was not the male hobby, as described by Boddy above (**Case study 1.6**), but a radical practice of exchange and networking. It is interesting to listen to his vision of radio conceived as a 'vast network' in 1932:

> radio is one-sided when it should be two. It is purely an apparatus for distribution, for mere sharing out. So here is a positive suggestion: change this apparatus over from distribution to communication. The radio would be the finest possible communication apparatus in public life, a vast network of pipes. That is to say, it would be if it knew how to receive as well as submit, how to let the listener speak as well as hear, how to bring him into a relationship instead of isolating him.
>
> (Brecht 1936, in Hanhardt 1986: 53)

Brecht's cultural politics have lain behind radical movements in theatre, photography, television and video production from the 1930s to the 1980s. In a final or latest resurgence they now inform politicised ideas about the uses of new media. Here it is argued that new media can be used as essentially two-way channels of communication that lie outside of official control. Combined with mobile telephony and digital video anti-capitalist demonstrators are now able to webcast near live information from their actions, beating news crews to the action and the transmission.

Finally, it is necessary to mention the influential ideas of a peripheral member of the Frankfurt School, Walter Benjamin. He took issue, in some of his writing, with the cultural pessimism of his colleagues. In 'The Work of Art in the Age of Mechanical Reproduction', and 'The Author As Producer', he argues that photography, film, and the modern newspaper, as media of mass reproduction, have revolutionary potential. Benjamin roots his argument in noticing some of the distinctive characteristics of these media, and the implications that he draws from them can be heard to echo today in the more sanguine estimations of the potential of new (digital) media. However, Benjamin sees that whether or not this potential will be realised is finally a matter of politics and not technology.

1.5.5 Conclusion

Section 5 has served to illustrate how the debates about new media, what it is, what it might be, what we would like it to be, rehearse many positions that have already been established within media studies and critical theory. Though the debates above are largely framed in terms of the amazing novelty of the possibilities that are opening up, they in fact revisit ground already well trodden. The disavowal of the history of new media thus appears as an ideological sleight of hand that recruits us to their essential value but fails to help us understand what is happening around us.

1.6 New media: determining or determined?

In previous sections of Part 1 of this book we have been looking at what kinds of histories, definitions and discourses shape the way we think about new media. We begin this final section by turning to examine two apparently competing paradigms, or two distinct approaches to the study of media, both of which underlie different parts of what will follow in this volume.

At the centre of each of these paradigms is a very different understanding of the power media and technology have to determine culture and society. The long-standing question of whether or not a media technology has the power to transform a culture has been given a very high profile with the development of new media. It will repay the good deal of attention that we give it here and in Part 5. In this section we will investigate this issue and the debates that surround it by turning back to the writings of two key but very different theorists of media: Marshall McLuhan and Raymond Williams. It is their views and arguments about the issue, filtered through very different routes, that now echo in the debate between those who see new media as revolutionary or as 'business as usual' that we pointed to in (**1.1**).

Although both authors more or less ceased writing at the point where the PC was about to 'take off' their analysis of the relationships between technology, culture and media continues to resonate in contemporary thought. As media theorists, both were interested in new media. It is precisely McLuhan's interest to identify and 'probe' what he saw as big cultural shifts brought about by change in media technologies. Williams, too, speaks of 'new media' and is interested in the conditions of their emergence and their subsequent use and control. While McLuhan was wholly concerned with identifying the major cultural effects that he saw new technological forms (in history and in his present) bringing about, Williams sought to show that there is nothing in a particular technology which guarantees the cultural or social outcomes it will have (Williams 1983: 130). McLuhan's arguments are at the core of claims that 'new media change everything'. If, as McLuhan argued, media determine consciousness then clearly we are living through times of profound change. On the other hand, albeit in a somewhat reduced way, the 'business as usual' camp is deeply indebted to Williams for the way in which they argue that media can only take effect through already present social processes and structures and will therefore reproduce existing patterns of use and basically sustain existing power relations.

1.6.1 The status of McLuhan and Williams

In the mainstream of media studies and much cultural studies the part played by the technological element that any medium has is always strongly qualified. Any idea that a medium can be reduced to a technology, or that the technological element which is admitted to be a part of any media process should be central to its study, is strongly resisted. The grounds for this view are to be found in a number of seminal essays by Raymond Williams (1974: 9–31; 1977: 158–164; 1983: 128–153), which, at least in part, responded critically to the 'potent observations' (Hall 1975: 81) of the Canadian literary and media theorist Marshall McLuhan. Williams's arguments against McLuhan subsequently became touchstones for media studies' rejection of any kind of **technological determinism**.

Yet, and here we meet one of the main sources of the present clash of discourses around the significance of new media, McLuhan's ideas have undergone a renaissance – literally a rebirth or rediscovery – in the hands of contemporary commentators, both popular and academic, on new media. The **McLuhanite** insistence on the need for new non-linear ('mosaic' is his term) ways of thinking about new media, which escape the intellectual protocols, procedures and habits of a linear print culture, has been taken up as something of a war cry against the academic media analyst. The charge that the neo-McLuhan cybertheorists make about media studies is made at this fundamental, epistemological level; that they simply fail to realise that its viewpoints (something, in fact, that McLuhan would claim we can no longer have) and methodologies have been hopelessly outstripped by events. As an early critic of McLuhan realised, to disagree with McLuhanite thinking is likely to be seen as the product of 'an outmoded insistence on the logical, ABCD minded, causality mad, one-thing-at-a-time method that the electronic age and its prophet have rendered obsolete' (Duffy 1969: 31).

Both Williams and McLuhan carried out their influential work in the 1960s and 1970s. Williams was one of the founding figures of British media and cultural studies. His rich, if at times abstract, historical and sociological formulations about cultural production and society provided some of the master templates for what has become mainstream media studies. Countless detailed studies of all kinds of media are guided and informed by his careful and penetrating outlines for a theory of media as a form of cultural production. His work is so deeply assimilated within the media studies discipline that he is seldom explicitly cited; he has become an invisible presence. Wherever we consider, in this book, new media as subject to control and direction by human institutions, skill, creativity and intention, we are building upon such a Williamsite emphasis.

On the other hand, McLuhan, the provoking, contentious figure who gained almost pop status in the 1960s, was discredited for his untenable pronouncements and was swatted away like an irritating fly by the critiques of Williams and others (see Miller 1971). However, as Williams foresaw (1974: 128), McLuhan has found highly influential followers. Many of his ideas have been taken up and developed by a whole range of theorists with an interest in new media: Baudrillard, Virilio, Poster, Kroker, De Kerckhove. The work of McLuhan and his followers has great appeal for those who see new media as bringing about radical cultural change or have some special interest in celebrating its potential. For the electronic counter-culture he is an oppositional figure and for corporate business a source of propaganda – his aphorisms, 'the global village' and 'the medium is the message', 'function as globally recog-nised jingles' for multinational trade in digital commodities (Genosko 1998). The magazine *Wired* has adopted him as its 'patron saint' (*Wired*, January 1996).

Williams's insights, embedded in a grounded and systematic theory, have been a major, shaping contribution to the constitution of an academic discipline. McLuhan's elliptical, unsys-tematic, contradictory and playful insights have fired the thought, the distinctive stance, and the methodological strategies of diverse but influential theorists of new media. We might say that Williams's thought is structured into media studies while, with respect to this discipline, McLuhan and those who have developed his ideas stalk its margins, sniping and provoking in ways that ensure they are frequently, if sometimes begrudgingly, referenced. Even cautious media academics allow McLuhan a little nowadays. He is seen as a theoretically unsubtle and inconsistent thinker who provokes others to think (Silverstone 1999: 21). It matters if he is wrong. One or another of his insights is often the jumping-off point for a contemporary study.

McLuhan's major publications appeared in the 1960s, some two decades before the effective emergence of the PC as a technology for communications and media production. It is a shift from a 500-year-old print culture to one of 'electric' media, by which he mainly means radio and television, that McLuhan considers. He only knew computers in the form of the mainframe computers of his day, yet they formed part of his bigger concept of the 'elec-tric environment', and he was sharp enough to see the practice of timesharing on these machines as the early signs of their social availability. By the 1990s, for some, McLuhan's ideas, when applied to developments in new media, had come to seem not only potent but extraordinarily prescient as well. It is quite easy to imagine a student at work in some future time, who, failing to take note of McLuhan's dates, is convinced that he is a 1990s writer on cyberculture, a contemporary of Jean Baudrillard or William Gibson. While this may owe something to the way that his ideas have been taken up in the postmodern context of the last two decades of the twentieth century by writers such as Baudrillard, Virilio, De Kerckhove, Kroker, Kelly, and Toffler, this hardly undermines the challenging and deliberately perverse originality of his thought.

The debate between the Williams and McLuhan positions, and Williams's apparent victory in this debate, left media studies with a legacy. It has had the effect of putting paid to any 'good-sense' cultural or media theorist raising the spectre of the technological determinism associated with the thought of McLuhan. It has also had the effect of foreclosing aspects of the way in which cultural and media studies deals with technology by implicitly arguing that technology on its own is incapable of producing change, the view being that whatever is going on around us in terms of rapid technological change there are rational and manipula-tive interests at work driving the technology in particular directions and it is to these that we should primarily direct our attention. Such is the dismissal of the role of technology in cultural change that, should we wish to confront this situation, we are inevitably faced with our views being reduced to apparent absurdity: 'What!? Are you suggesting that machines can and do act, cause things to happen on their own? – that a machine caused space flight, rather than the superpowers' ideological struggle for achievement?'

However, there are good reasons to believe that technology cannot be adequately analysed only within the **humanist** frame Williams bequeathed cultural and media theorists. Arguments about what causes technological change may not be so straightforward as cul-turalist accusations of political or theoretical naivety seem to suggest. In this section, therefore, we review Williams's and McLuhan's arguments about media and technology. We

Eventually the intellectual distance between Williams and McLuhan was great, but this was not always so. In a review of McLuhan's *Gutenberg Galaxy*, published in 1962, Williams writes of his preoccupation with the book (Stearn 1968: 188). He considers it to be 'a wholly indispensable work'. It was a work that stayed in his mind for months after he first read it and to which he returned frequently; but he was already uneasy about McLuhan's singling out of the medium of print as the single causal factor in social change (Stearn 1968: 190). However, by 1974 his estimation of McLuhan's importance had deteriorated markedly. He saw McLuhan's projection of totalising images of society – its 'retribalisation', the electronic age, 'the global village' – projected from his 'unhistorical and asocial' study of media as 'ludicrous' (Stearn 1968: 128) then examine the limits of the humanist account of technology that Williams so influentially offered and ask whether he was correct in his dismissal of McLuhan as a crude technological determinist. Finally, we explore other important nonhumanist accounts of technology that are frequently excluded from the contemporary study of media technologies. The latter are then more fully elaborated in Part 5.

Humanism

'**Humanism**' is a term applied to a long and recurring tendency in Western thought. It appears to have its origins in the fifteenth- and sixteenth-century Italian Renaissance where a number of scholars (Bruno, Erasmus, Valla, and Pico della Mirandola) worked to recover elements of classical learning and natural science lost in the 'dark ages' of the medieval Christian world. Their emphasis on explaining the world through the human capacity for rational thought rather than a reliance on Christian theology fostered the '[b]elief that individual human beings are the fundamental source of all value and have the ability to understand – and perhaps even to control – the natural world by careful application of their own rational faculties' (*Oxford Companion to Philosophy*). This impetus was added to and modified many times in following centuries. Of note is the seventeenth-century Cartesian idea of the human subject, 'I think, therefore I am. I have intentions, purposes, goals, therefore I am the sole source and free agent of my actions' (Sarup 1988: 84). There is a specifically 'Marxist humanism' in the sense that it is believed that self-aware, thinking and acting individuals will build a rational socialist society. For our purposes here it is important to stress that a humanist theory tends only to recognise human individuals as having agency (and power and responsibility) over the social forms and the technologies they create and, even, through rational science, the power to control and shape nature.

1.6.2 Mapping Marshall McLuhan

Many of McLuhan's more important ideas arise within a kind of narrative of redemption. There is little doubt that much of McLuhan's appeal to new media and cyber enthusiasts lies in the way that he sees the arrival of an 'electronic culture' as a rescue or recovery from the fragmenting effects of 400 years of print culture. McLuhan has, indeed, provided a range of ideological resources for the technological imaginary of the new millennium.

Here, we outline McLuhan's grand schema of four cultures, determined by their media forms, as it is the context in which some important ideas arise; ideas which are, arguably, far more important and useful than his quasi-historical and extremely sweeping narrative. We then concentrate on three key ideas. First, 'remediation', a concept that is currently much in vogue and finds its roots in McLuhan's view that 'the content of any medium is always another medium' (1968: 15–16). Second, his idea that media and technologies are extensions of the human body and its senses. Third, his famous (or notorious) view that 'the medium is the message'. This section is the basis for a further discussion, in **1.6.4**, of three 'theses' to be found in McLuhan's work: his extension thesis, his environmental thesis, and his anti-content thesis.

A narrative of redemption

McLuhan's view of media as technological extensions of the body is his basis for conceiving of four media cultures which are brought about by shifts from oral to written communication, from script to print, and from print to electronic media. These four cultures are: (1) a primitive culture of oral communication, (2) a literate culture using the phonetic alphabet and hand-written script which co-existed with the oral, (3) the age of mass-produced, mechanical printing (*The Gutenberg Galaxy*), and (4) the culture of 'electric media': radio, television, and computers.

'PRIMITIVE' ORAL/AURAL CULTURE

In pre-literate 'primitive' cultures there was a greater dominance of the sense of hearing than in literate cultures when, following the invention of the phonetic alphabet (a visual encoding of speech), the ratio of the eye and the ear was in a better state of equilibrium. Pre-literate people lived in an environment totally dominated by the sense of hearing. Oral and aural communication were central. Speaking and hearing speech was the 'ear-man's' main form of communication (while also, no doubt, staying alert to the sound of a breaking twig!). McLuhan is not enthusiastic about this kind of culture. For him it was not a state of 'noble savagery' (Duffy 1969: 26).

> Primitive man lived in a much more tyrannical cosmic machine than Western literate man has ever invented. The world of the ear is more embracing and inclusive than that of the eye can ever be. The ear is hypersensitive. The eye is cool and detached. The ear turns man over to universal panic while the eye, extended by literacy and mechanical time, leaves some gaps and some islands free from the unremitting acoustic pressure and reverberation.
>
> (McLuhan 1968: 168)

THE CULTURE OF LITERACY

McLuhan says that he is not interested in making judgements but only in identifying the con-figurations of different societies (1968: 94). However, as is implied in the above passage, for McLuhan the second culture, the culture of literacy, was an improvement on pre-literate, oral culture. For here, via the alphabet and writing, as extensions of the eye, and, in its later stages, the clock, 'the visual and uniform fragmentation of time became possible' (1968: 159). This released 'man' from the panic of 'primitive' conditions while maintaining a balance between the aural and the visual. In the literate, scribal culture of the Middle Ages McLuhan sees a situation where oral traditions coexisted alongside writing: manuscripts were individ-ually produced and annotated by hand as if in a continual dialogue, writers and readers were hardly separable, words were read aloud to 'audiences', and the mass reproduction of uni-form texts by printing presses had not led to a narrowing dominance and authority of sight over hearing and speaking. Writing augmented this culture in specialised ways without wholly alienating its members from humankind's original, participatory, audio-tactile universe (Theal 1995: 81).

PRINT CULTURE

For McLuhan, the real villain of the piece is print culture – the Gutenberg Galaxy with its 'typo-graphic man', where the sensory alienation which was avoided in literate culture occurs. Here we meet the now familiar story of how the mass reproduction of writing by the printing press, the development of perspectival images, the emerging scientific methods of observation and measurement, and the seeking of linear chains of cause and effect came to dominate modern, rationalist print culture. In this process its members lost their tactile and auditory rela-tion with the world, their rich sensory lives were fragmented and impoverished as the visual sense dominated. In McLuhan's terms this is a culture in which the 'stepping up of the visual component in experience . . . filled the field of attention' (1962: 17). The culture was hypno- tised by vision (mainly through its extensions as typography and print) and the 'interplay of all the senses in haptic harmony' dies. Fixed points of view and measured, separating distances come to structure the human subject's relation to the world. With this 'instressed concern with one sense only, the mechanical principle of abstraction and repetition emerges', which means 'the spelling out of one thing at a time, one sense at a time, one mental or physical operation at a time' (1962: 18). If the primitive pre-literate culture was tyrannised by the ear, Gutenberg culture is hypnotised by its eye.

ELECTRONIC CULTURE

The fourth culture, electronic culture, is 'paradise regained' (Duffy 1969). Developing from the invention of telegraphy to television and the computer, this culture promises to short-circuit that of mechanical print and we regain the conditions of an oral culture in acoustic space. We return to a state of sensory grace; to a culture marked by qualities of simultaneity, indivisibil- ity and sensory plenitude. The haptic or tactile senses again come into play, and McLuhan strives hard to show how television is a tactile medium.

> McLuhan's ideas about television received very short shrift from British cultural and media studies, even in its formative period (see Hall 1975)

The terms in which McLuhan described this electric age as a new kind of primitivism, with tribal-like participation in the 'global village', resonates with certain strands of New Age media culture. McLuhan's all-at-onceness or simultaneity, the involvement of everyone with every- one, electronic media's supposedly connecting and unifying characteristics, are easy to recognise in (indeed, in some cases have led to) many of the terms now used to characterise new media – connectivity, convergence, the network society, wired culture, and interaction.

> 1.1.4 Non-technical and inclusive
> 1.3 Change and continuity

Remediation (see also 1.1.4 and 1.3)

First, and most uncontentiously because it was an idea that McLuhan and Williams shared, is the idea that all new media 'remediate' the content of previous media. This notion, as developed by McLuhan in the 1960s, has become a key idea, extensively worked out in a recent book on new media. In *Remediation: Understanding New Media* (1999), Jay David Bolter and Richard Grusin briefly revisit the clash between Williams and McLuhan as they set out their own approach to the study of new media. They define a medium as 'that which remediates'. That is, a new medium 'appropriates the techniques, forms, and social signif- icance of other media and attempts to rival or refashion them in the name of the real' (ibid.: 65). The inventors, users, and economic backers of a new medium present it as able to rep- resent the world in more realistic and authentic ways than previous media forms, and in the process what is real and authentic is redefined (ibid.). This idea owes something to McLuhan, for whom 'the "content" of any medium is always another medium' (1968: 15–16).

> See Williams (1974) on music hall and parlour games in broadcasting

Bolter and Grusin have something interesting to say about Williams and McLuhan which bears directly upon our attempt to get beyond the polarised debates about new media. They agree with Williams's criticism that McLuhan is a technological determinist who single- mindedly took the view that media technologies act directly to change a society and a culture, but they argue that it is possible to put McLuhan's 'determinism' aside in order to appreciate 'his analysis of the remediating power of various media'. Bolter and Grusin encourage us to see value in the way that McLuhan 'notices intricate correspondences involving media and cultural artefacts' (1999: 76), and they urge us to recognise that his view of media as 'exten- sions of the human sensorium' has been highly influential, prefiguring the concept of the **cyborg** in late twentieth-century thought on media and cyberculture or technoculture. It is precisely this ground, and the question of the relationship between human agency and technology in the age of cybernetic culture, which the neo-McLuhanites attempt to map.

Extending the sensorium

McLuhan reminds us of the technological dimension of media. He does so by refusing any distinction between a medium and a technology. For him, there is no issue. It is not accidental that he makes his basic case for a medium being 'any extension of ourselves' (1968: 15) by using as key examples the electric light (ibid.) and the wheel (ibid.: 52) – respectively a system and an artefact which we would ordinarily think of as technologies rather than media. Basically, this is no more than the commonplace idea that a 'tool' (a name for a simple technology) is a bodily extension: a hammer is an extension of the arm or a screwdriver is an extension of the hand and wrist.

In *The Medium is the Massage* (McLuhan and Fiore 1967a) McLuhan drives this point home. We again meet the wheel as 'an extension of the foot', while the book is 'an extension of the eye', clothing is an extension of the skin, and electric circuitry is an 'extension of the central nervous system'. In other places he speaks of money (1968: 142) or gunpowder (ibid.: 21) as a medium. In each case, then, an artefact is seen as extending a part of the body, a limb or the nervous system. And, as far as McLuhan is concerned, these are 'media'.

McLuhan conflates technologies and mediums in this way because he views both as part of a larger class of things; as extensions of the human senses: sight, hearing, touch, and smell. Wheels for instance, especially when driven by automotive power, radically changed the experience of travel and speed, the body's relationship to its physical environment, and to time and space. The difference between the view we have of the world when slowly walking, open on all sides to a multisensory environment, or when glimpsed as rapid and continuous change through the hermetically sealed and framing window of a high-speed train, is a change in sensory experience which did and continues to have cultural significance. (See, for instance, Schivelbusch 1977.) It is this broadening of the concept of a medium to all kinds of technologies that enabled McLuhan to make one of his central claims: that the 'medium is the message'. In understanding media, it matters not, he would claim, why we are taking a train journey, or where we are going on the train. These are irrelevant side issues which only divert us from noticing the train's real cultural significance. Its real significance (the message of the medium itself) is the way it changes our perception of the world.

McLuhan also asserts (he doesn't 'argue') that such extensions of our bodies, placed in the context of the body's whole range of senses (the sensorium), change the 'natural' relationships between the sensing parts of the body, and affect 'the whole psychic and social complex' (1968: 11). In short, he is claiming that such technological extensions of our bodies affect both our minds and our societies. In *The Gutenberg Galaxy* (1962: 24) he expresses the idea of technological extension more carefully when he says, 'Sense ratios change when any one sense or bodily or mental function is externalised in technological form.' So, for McLuhan, the importance of a medium (seen as a bodily extension) is not just a matter of a limb or anatomical system being physically extended (as in the hammer as 'tool' sense). It is also a matter of altering the 'ratio' between the range of human senses (sight, hearing, touch, smell) and this has implications for our 'mental functions' (having ideas, perceptions, emotions, experiences, etc.).

Media, then, change the relationship of the human body and its sensorium to its environment. Media generally alter the human being's sensory relationship to the world, and the specific characteristics of any one medium change that relationship in different ways. This is McLuhan's broad and uncontestable premise upon which he spins all manner of theses –

There is also an important reversal of this idea as with industrial mechanisation we come to think of the human body as a mere extension of the machine. An idea powerfully represented by Charlie Chaplin in *Modern Times* and theorised by Marx and Benjamin amongst others (see also **1.6.4**) some far more acceptable than others. It is not hard to see how such a premiss or idea has become important at a time of new media technologies and emergent new media forms.

The medium is the message

As we saw above, in what has been widely condemned as an insupportable overstatement, McLuhan concludes from his idea of media as extensions of man that 'understanding media' has nothing to do with attending to their content. In fact he maintains that understanding is blocked by any preoccupation with media content and the specific intentions of media producers. He views the 'conventional response to all media, namely that it is how they are used that counts', as 'the numb stance of the technological idiot. For the "content" of a medium is like the juicy piece of meat carried by the burglar to distract the watchdog of the mind' (1968: 26).

McLuhan will have no truck with questions of intention whether on the part of producers or consumers of media. In a seldom referred to but telling passage in *Understanding Media* (1968: 62) he makes it clear that 'It is the peculiar bias of those who operate the media for the owners that they be concerned about program content.' The owners themselves 'are more concerned about the media as such'. They know that the power of media 'has little to do with "content"'. He implies that the owner's preoccupation with the formula 'what the public wants' is a thin disguise for their knowing lack of interest in specific contents and their strong sense of where the media's power lies.

Hence his deliberately provocative slogan 'The medium is the message'. This is where his use of the electric light as a 'medium' pays off. It becomes the exemplary case of a 'medium without a message' (1968: 15). McLuhan asserts that neither the (apparent and irrelevant) messages that it carries (the words and meanings of an illuminated sign) nor its uses (illuminating baseball matches or operating theatres) are what is important about electric light as a medium. Rather, like electricity itself, its real message is the way that it extends and speeds up forms of 'human association and action', whatever they are (1968: 16). What is important about electric light for McLuhan is the way that it ended any strict distinction between night and day, indoors and outdoors and how it then changed the meanings (remediated) of already existing technologies and the kinds of human organisation built around them: cars can travel and sports events can take place at night, factories can operate efficiently around the clock, and buildings no longer require windows (1968: 62). For McLuhan, the real '"message" of any medium or technology is the change of scale or pace or pattern that it introduces into human affairs' (1968: 16). Driving his point home, and again moving from technology to communication media, he writes:

> The message of the electric light is like the message of electric power in industry. Totally radical, pervasive, and decentralised. For the electric light and power are separate from their uses, yet they eliminate time and space factors in human association exactly as do radio, telegraph, telephone and TV, creating involvement in depth.
>
> (McLuhan 1968: 17)

Also, like the effects of the electric light on the automobile, McLuhan claims that the content of any medium is another medium which it picks up and works over (the medium is the message).

McLuhan's absolute insistence on the irrelevance of content to understanding media needs to be seen as a strategy. He adopts it in order to focus his readers upon:

1　the power of media technologies to structure social arrangements and relationships, and

2　the mediating aesthetic properties of a media technology. They mediate our relations to one another and to the world (electronic broadcasting as against one-to-one oral communication or point-to-point telegraphic communication for instance). Aesthetically, because they claim our senses in different ways, the multidirectional simultaneity of sound as against the exclusively focused attention of a 'line' of sight, the fixed, segmenting linearity of printed language, the high resolution of film or the low resolution of TV, etc.

> It is McLuhan's view that these mediating factors are qualities of the media technologies themselves, rather than outcomes of the way they are used, which is criticised by Williams and many in media studies

We should now be in a better position to see what McLuhan offers us in our efforts to 'understand new media', and why his work has been seen to be newly important in the context of new media technologies:

- McLuhan stresses the physicality of technology, its power to structure or restructure how human beings pursue their activities, and the manner in which extensive technological systems form an environment in which human beings live and act. Conventional wisdom says that technology is nothing until it is given cultural meaning, and that it is what we do with technologies rather than what they do to us that is important and has a bearing on social and cultural change. However, McLuhan's project is to force us to reconsider this conventional wisdom by recognising that technology also has an agency and effects that cannot be reduced to its social uses.

- In his conception of media as technological extensions of the body and its senses, as 'outerings' of what the body itself once enclosed, he anticipates the networked, converging, cybernetic media technologies of the late twentieth/early twenty-first centuries. He also distinguishes them from earlier technologies as being more environmental. In his words, 'With the arrival of electric technology, man extended, or set outside himself, a live model of the central nervous system itself' (1968: 53). This is qualitatively different from previous kinds of sensory extension where 'our extended senses, tools, and technologies' had been 'closed systems incapable of interplay or collective awareness'. However, 'Now, in the electric age, the very instantaneous nature of co-existence among our technological instruments has created a crisis quite new in human history' (1962: 5). McLuhan's sweeping hyperbolic style is much in evidence in that last statement. However, the evolution of networked communication systems and present anticipations of a fully functioning, global neural net is here prefigured in McLuhan's observations of broadcast culture in the 1960s.

- McLuhan's ideas have been seen as the starting point for explanation and understanding of the widely predicted conditions in which cybernetic systems have increasingly determining effects upon our lives. At a point in human history where for significant numbers of people 'couplings' with machines are increasingly frequent and intimate, where our subjectivity is challenged by this new interweaving of technology into our everyday lives, he forces us to reconsider the centrality of human agency in our dealings with machines and to entertain a less one-sided view.

1.6.3 Williams and the social shaping of technology

We noted at the outset of this section that media studies has by and large come to ignore or reject the views of Marshall McLuhan in favour of Raymond Williams's analysis of similar terrain. In this section we draw out the major differences in their approaches to the question of technology's relation to culture and society.

Human agency versus technological determination

Williams clearly has McLuhan's concept of the 'extensions of man' in mind when he writes that 'A technology, when it has been achieved, can be seen as a general human property, an extension of a general human capacity' (1974: 129; our italics). McLuhan is seldom interested in why a technology is 'achieved', but this is a question that is important for Williams. For him 'all technologies have been developed and improved to help with known human practices or with foreseen and desired practices' (ibid.). So, for Williams, technologies involve precisely what McLuhan dismisses. First, they cannot be separated from questions of 'practice' (which are questions about how they are used and about their content). Second, they arise from human intention and agency. Such intentions arise within social groups to meet some desire or interest that they have, and these interests are historically and culturally specific.

McLuhan holds that new technologies radically change the physical and mental functions of a generalised 'mankind'. Williams argues that new technologies take forward existing practices that particular social groups already see as important or necessary. McLuhan's ideas about why new technologies emerge are psychological and biological. Humans react to stress in their environment by 'numbing' the part of the body under stress. They then produce a medium or a technology (what is now frequently called a prosthesis) which extends and externalises the 'stressed out' sense or bodily function. Williams's argument for the development of new technologies is sociological. It arises from the development and reconfiguration of a culture's existing technological resources in order to pursue socially conceived ends.

McLuhan insists that the importance of a medium is not a particular use but the structural way that it changes the 'pace and scale' of human affairs. For Williams, it is the power that specific social groups have that is important in determining the 'pace and scale' of the intended technological development – indeed, whether or not any particular technology is developed (see Winston 1998). Williams's emphasis called for an examination of (1) the reasons for which technologies are developed, (2) the complex of social, cultural, and economic factors which shape them, and (3) the ways that technologies are mobilised for certain ends (rather than the properties of the achieved technologies themselves). This is the direction which the mainstream of media studies came to take.

The plural possibilities and uses of a technology

Where, for the most part, McLuhan sees only one broad and structuring set of effects as flowing from a technology, Williams recognises plural outcomes or possibilities. Because he focuses on the issue of intention, he recognises that whatever the original intention to develop a technology might be, subsequently other social groups, with different interests or needs, adapt, modify or subvert the uses to which any particular technology is put. Where, for McLuhan, the social adoption of a media technology has determinate outcomes, for Williams this is not guaranteed. It is a matter of competition and struggle between social groups. For Williams, the route between need, invention, development, and final use or 'effect' is not straightforward. He also points out that technologies have uses and effects which were unforeseen by their conceivers and developers. (A point with which McLuhan would agree.) Overall, Williams's critique of McLuhan adds up to the premise that there is nothing in a particular technology which guarantees or causes its mode of use, and hence its social effects. By viewing media the way he does, he arrives at the opposite conclusion to McLuhan: what a culture is like does not directly follow from the nature of its media.

Concepts of technology

We have noted how broadly, following a basic (nineteenth-century) anthropological concept of 'man' as a tool user, McLuhan defines a technology and how he subsumes media within this definition without further discussion. Williams does not. First, he distinguishes between various stages or elements in a fully achieved technology. The outcome of this process is subject to already existing social forces, needs and power relations.

In line with the 'social shaping of technology' school of thought (Mackenzie and Wajcman 1999), Williams is not content to understand technologies only as artefacts. In fact the term 'technology' makes no reference to artefacts at all, being a compound of the two Greek roots *techne*, meaning art, craft or skill, and *logos*, meaning word or knowledge (Mackenzie and Wajcman 1999: 26). In short, technology in its original form means something like 'knowledge about skilful practices' and makes no reference at all to the products of such knowledge as tools and machines. So, for Williams, the knowledges and acquired skills necessary to use a tool or machine are an integral part of any full concept of what a technology is. McLuhan is largely silent on this, his attention being fully centred upon the ways in which technologies 'cause' different kinds of sensory experience and knowledge ordering procedures.

CASE STUDY 1.8: The social nature of a media technology

Williams takes the technology of writing, which was so important in McLuhan's scheme of things, as an example (Williams 1981: 108). He differentiates between:

- **Technical inventions and techniques** upon which a technology depends, the alphabet, appropriate tools or machines for making marks, and suitable surfaces for accurately retaining marks;

- **The substantive technology** which, in terms of writing, is a distribution technology (it distributes language) and this requires a means or form – scrolls of papyrus, portable manuscripts, mass-produced printed books, letters, or emails and other kinds of electronic text;

- **The technology in social use**. This includes (a) the specialised practice of writing which was initially restricted to 'official' minorities and then opened up, through education, to larger sections of society. But always, each time this happened, it was on the basis of some kind of argued need (the needs of merchants, of industrial workers, etc.), and (b) the social part of the distribution of the technologically reproduced language (reading) which again was only extended in response to perceived social needs (efficient distribution of information, participation in democratic processes, constituting a market of individuals with the ability to consume 'literature', etc.).

As Williams points out, at the time of his writing in 1981, after some thousands of years of writing and 500 years of mass reproduction in print, only 40 per cent of the world's population were able to read and hence had access to written texts. In this way, Williams argues that having noted the strictly technical and formal aspects of a technology we are still crucially short of a full grasp of what is involved. For these basic techniques and forms to be effective as a technology within a society, we also have to add the ability to read and to be constituted as part of a readership or market by publishers. Simply put, writing cannot be understood as a communications technology unless there are readers. The ability to read, and the control of, access to, and arrangements for learning to read, are part of the distributive function of the technology of writing. In this sense, Williams argues, a full description of a technology, both its development and its uses, is always social as well as technical and it is not simply a matter of the 'social' following the technological as a matter of 'effects'. Clearly this is an argument that can be extended to new media as policy debates about the growing existence of a 'digital divide' illustrate. The extent to which the technology can have transformative 'effects' is more or less in relation to other pre-existing patterns of wealth and power.

The concept of a medium

While McLuhan uses the term 'medium' unproblematically and is quite happy to see it as a kind of technology, Williams finds the term problematic and he shares with some other theorists (Maynard 1997) an uneasiness about conflating 'media' and 'technology'. It is often implicit for Williams that a medium is a particular use of a technology; a harnessing of a technology to an intention or purpose to communicate or express.

CASE STUDY 1.9: When is a technology a medium?

Here we might take the much-considered case of photography. Clearly there is a photographic technology; one in which optical and mechanical systems direct light onto chemically treated surfaces which then become marked in relation to the way that configurations of light fall on that surface. This, however, is not a medium. The manufacture of silicon chips, a technical process upon which the manufacture of computers now depends, uses this photographic technology. It is used to etch the circuits on the microscopic chips. This is a technological process – a technology at work. However, another use of the photographic technology is to make pictures – to depict persons or events in the world. This may also be a technology at work. However, when it is said that these pictures or images provide us with information, represent an idea, express a view, or in some way invite us to exercise our imaginations in respect to the contents and forms of the image, then we may say that photography is being used as a medium. Or, more accurately, the technology of photography is being used as a medium of communication, expression, representation or imaginative projection. On this line of argument, a medium is something that we do with a technology. Clearly, what we do needs to be of an order that the technology can facilitate or support but it does not necessarily arise from the technology itself. Having an intention for a technology is not synonymous with the technology per se. A technology becomes a medium through many complex social transformations and transitions; it is, in Williams's reading, profoundly the product of culture and not a given consequence of technology.

5.1.8 A problem with binary definitions
1.6.2 Mapping Marshall McLuhan

Williams is also wary about the theoretical implications that the term 'medium' has come to carry. First, he criticises and virtually dismisses it as always being a misleading reification of a social process. Second, he sees that it is also a term that is used to recognise the part that materials play in a practice or process of production, as in artistic processes where the very nature of paint, ink, or a certain kind of camera will play a part in shaping the nature of an artistic product (1977: 159).

Medium as a reification of a social process

When he thinks about the sense in which a medium is a reification, McLuhan can be seen as very much in the centre of Williams's line of fire. Williams uses the following seventeenth-century statement about the nature of vision to demonstrate what he sees to be the major difficulty, still present in contemporary thought, with the concept of a 'medium': 'to the sight three things are required, the Object, the Organ and the Medium' (1977: 158).

The problem, he argues, is that such a formulation contains an inherent duality. A 'medium' is given the status of an autonomous object (or the process of mediation is given the status of a process that is separate from what it deals with) which stands between and connects two other separate entities: that which is mediated (an object) and that which receives the results of the mediating process (the eye). With language as his example, Williams points out that when this concept of a medium is being used, 'Words are seen as objects, things, which men [sic] take up and arrange into particular forms to express or communicate information which, before this work in the "medium" they already possess' (1977: 159).

Williams argued against this position – for him the process of mediation is itself constitutive of reality; it contributes to the making of our realities. Communication and interaction are what we do as a species. The 'medium' is not a pre-given set of formal characteristics whose effects can be read off – it is a process that itself constitutes that experience or that reality. So for Williams to argue that 'the medium is the message' is to mistake and to reify an essentially social process taking place between human agents and their interests as if it were a technological object outside of human agency. As a theoretical conception which structures thought it necessarily leaves us with sets of binary terms: the self and the world, subject and object, language and reality, ideology and truth, the conscious and unconscious, the economic base and the cultural superstructure, etc. (see **5.1.8** for some problems with binary terms).

Medium as material

One way of avoiding this problem is to narrow the definition of a medium. This is the other direction which Williams's thought on the subject takes. He recognises that a 'medium' can also be understood as 'the specific material with which a particular kind of artist worked', and 'to understand this "medium" was obviously a condition of professional skill and practice' (Williams 1977: 159). The problem here, writes Williams, is that even this down to earth sense of a medium is often extended until it stands in for the whole of a practice, which he famously defines as 'work on a material for a specific purpose within certain necessary social conditions' (1977: 160). Once again we see that Williams wants to stress that a medium is only part of a wider practice, a material that is worked upon to achieve human purposes pursued in determining social contexts; a means to an end.

1.6.4 The many virtues of Saint McLuhan

Introduction

Following our 'mapping' of McLuhan's ideas in **1.6.2**, we will now move on to a discussion of three core theses that emerge from those ideas. These are:

1   the extension thesis: technology is an 'extension of man' (1964);

2   the environmental thesis: 'the new media are not bridges between man and nature: they are nature' (1969: 14);

3   the anti-content thesis: 'Societies have always been shaped more by the nature of the media by which men communicate than by the content of the communication' (1964: 1).

If Williams, as we noted in **1.6.1**, has become, as it were, the 'deep structure' of cultural and media studies' address to technology, McLuhan's theses spring up, barely disguised, whenever a new medium arises and draws attention to the question of technology. It is important to note, then, that while the debate between Williams and McLuhan centres around the 'old medium' of TV, that debate continues to frame contemporary cultural discussions of technology in general, and of cyberculture in particular.

Since his 1967 review of *Understanding Media*, for instance, McLuhan has been one of the constant references in the work of Jean Baudrillard. One of Baudrillard's most famous theses, concerning 'The Implosion of Meaning in the Media' (in Baudrillard 1997), is precisely concerned to analyse further McLuhan's anti-content thesis. Similarly, Baudrillard's critics (see, for example, Kellner 1989; Gane 1991; Genosko 1998) have consistently drawn attention to his debt to, and criticisms of, McLuhan: if he rejects McLuhan's optimistic neo-tribal future, Baudrillard extends the idea that 'the medium is the message' further than McLuhan ever did. Moreover, as Istvan Csisery-Ronay (in McCaffery 1992: 162) has noted, it is precisely his concern with systems over meaning in his analyses of media that makes him a 'philosopher of **cyberpunk** and a practitioner of cybercriticism'.

Again, Arthur Kroker's analysis of technology and postmodernity places McLuhan's extension thesis at the centre of that discussion, quoting from *Counterblast* (1969: 42) McLuhan's assertion that the rise of electronic technologies makes the technological environment one composed from 'the externalisation of the human nervous system' (Kroker 1992: 64). Finally, the extension thesis recurs wherever cyborgs, 'couplings of organisms and machines' (Haraway 1991: 150), are concerned (and, as we shall see below, the longest-lived theory of technology in general is precisely the extension thesis). These examples are far from exhaustive. Indeed, while some theorists make partial use of McLuhan's work, others (De Kerckhove 1997; Genosko 1998; Levinson 1999) maintain simply that McLuhan is the theorist of cyberculture. We are not asking, however, whether Williams or McLuhan provides the more accurate or 'correct' theory. Rather, what we want to show is that this 'old media' debate continues to provide essential co-ordinates on the map of new media and cybercultural studies. As we show in **1.1**, we have been here before: debates about 'new media' have been around for a long time!

We shall examine each of McLuhan's three theses in turn.

The extension thesis

1.6.1 The status of McLuhan and Williams

The 'extensions of man', although widely recognised as McLuhan's coinage, expresses the functional differences in human capabilities introduced by the (then) new media. It was not, however, a new idea. In fact, it stretches back to Aristotle in the fifth century BC. By tracing the long history of this thesis, however, we will see that it is clearly based in the nature of the human body. We will look at four versions of this thesis: Aristotle, Marx, Ernst Kapp, and Henri Bergson.

Donald MacKenzie and Judy Wajcman's influential collection, *The Social Shaping of Technology* ([1985] 1999), for example, while it does not use Williams overtly, mounts a clearly Williamsite challenge to the question of technological determinism

ARISTOTLE

In two works on practical philosophy – the *Eudemian Ethics* and the *Politics* – Aristotle discusses the idea that tools are extensions of soul and body. Thus, in the former work he writes:

> For the body is the soul's natural tool, while the slave is as it were a part and detachable tool of the master, the tool being a sort of inanimate slave.
>
> (*Eudemian Ethics*, book VII, 1241b; in Barnes 1994: 1968)

1.1 New media: do we know what they are?
5.3 Biological technologies: the history of automata

And he repeats the point in the *Politics*:

> Now instruments are of various sorts; some are living, others lifeless; in the rudder, the pilot of the ship [the *kybernetes*] has a lifeless, in the look-out man, a living instrument; for in arts [*techne*], the servant is a kind of instrument.
>
> (*Politics* book I, 1253b; in Everson 1996: 15)

We can see a certain prefiguration of cybernetics in these passages (see **5.3**), if not of cyborgs: detachable tools, inanimate slaves, living and lifeless instruments. The core of the idea is, however, that instruments extend the functions of the labouring body.

MARX

This idea receives a further twist in Marx, where he proposes that technology is a human means of self-extension. Where Aristotle sees instruments as lifeless servants, and servants as living instruments, Marx, in *Grundrisse*, although continuing to root the thesis in the human body, is simultaneously concerned to distance the technological world from the natural realm:

> Nature builds no machines, no locomotives, railways, electric telegraphs, self-acting mules, etc. These are the products of human industry; natural material transformed into organs of the human will over nature . . . They are organs of the human brain, created by the human hand.
>
> (Marx [1857] 1993: 706)

While part of nature, the technological extension of human industry creates non-natural organs that in turn extend the human brain's dominion over nature. Political economist that he was, however, Marx would also note the cost of these benefits, insofar as they also transform the relation between the labouring individual and the method of working. When using hand tools, Marx writes, the labouring individual retains an independent capacity to labour; on the other hand, when it is a question of larger machines and systems of machinery (such as are found in factories; ibid.: 702), then

> The worker's activity . . . is determined and regulated on all sides by the movement of machinery, and not the opposite . . . The science which compels the inanimate limbs of the machinery, by their construction, to act purposively, as an automaton . . . acts upon [the worker] through the machine as an alien power, as the power of the machine itself.
>
> (ibid.: 693)

By extending the natural body, then, that body becomes transformed by its own extensions. If the question of who is in control of the machine is unambiguous in Aristotle, it becomes highly complex in Marx, and the socially structuring force forming the labouring body in industrial capitalism.

KAPP

A mere twenty years after Marx's *Grundrisse*, Ernst Kapp wrote *Outlines of a Philosophy of Technology* (1877), in which the phrase 'philosophy of technology' was coined for the first time. In it Kapp wrote, apparently presciently, of a 'universal telegraphics' that would transform (i.e., shrink) time and (manipulate) space. Kapp argues that telegraphics is an extension of the nervous system, just as railways extend the circulatory system. So, like Aristotle and Marx, he viewed technology as a form of 'organ projection'. Thus:

> [s]ince the organ whose utility and power is to be increased is the controlling factor, the appropriate form of a tool can be derived only from that organ. A wealth of intellectual creations thus springs from hand, arm and teeth. The bent finger becomes a hook, the hollow of the hand a bowl; in the sword, spear, oar, shovel, rake, plough and spade, one observes the sundry positions of arm, hand, and fingers.
>
> (Kapp 1877: 44–45; cited in Mitcham 1994: 23–24)

As can be seen from this passage, Kapp is more concerned to demonstrate that the forms of tools recapitulate those of human organs. He thus echoes a well-known principle of nineteenth-century biology, but draws no more lessons from this other than to 'naturalise' the production of technological artefacts.

BERGSON

At the turn of the twentieth century we find the same idea in Henri Bergson's *Creative Evolution* ([1911]1920), where the philosopher notes that technology 'reacts on the nature of the being that constructs it', much as Marx indicates, insofar as it 'confers on him . . . a richer organisation, being an artificial organ by which the natural organism is extended' ([1911] 1920: 148). In Bergson ([1911] 1920: 148) as in Marx, the extension is thus extended itself, as this later passage makes clear:

> If our organs are natural instruments, our instruments must then be artificial organs. The workman's tool is the continuation of his arm, the tool-equipment of humanity is therefore a continuation of its body. Nature, in endowing each of us with an essentially tool-making intelligence, prepared for us in this way a certain expansion. But machines which run on oil or coal . . . have actually imparted to our organism an extension so vast, have endowed it with a power so mighty, so out of proportion with the size and strength of that organism, that surely none of all this was foreseen in the structural plan of our species.
>
> ([1932] 1935: 267–268)

Here extension has run full circle: the extensions, although grounded in the human body, extend themselves in such a way as to alter that body. While nature endowed that body, say Marx and Bergson, with a tool-making capacity with which to extend itself, that capacity has grown in scale so much that it must act on its own plans, having outstripped nature.

The basis of the extension thesis becomes clear: it is rooted in the nature of the human body. In all the accounts of this thesis we have examined, technology is rooted in the natural capacities or forms of that body. In some, particularly Marx and Bergson, it feeds back on that body and alters it, and thereby alters its environment. Thus we arrive at the second of McLuhan's theses: the environmental thesis.

The environmental thesis

> [T]he new media are not bridges between man and nature: they are nature.
>
> (McLuhan 1969: 14)

Whereas Marx and Bergson make explicit their claims concerning the difference between hand-tools and large-scale machines or systems of machinery, Aristotle and Kapp do not: all technology simply extends the body. However, the key question that Marx and Bergson pose concerns the scale of technological extension, or what sociologist Jacques Ellul called 'the selfaugmentation of technology' ([1954] 1964: 85ff.). This thesis entails two main things:

- first, that above a certain threshold of quantitative change (the number of technologies a society uses) there arises a qualitative change in the structure and functioning of that society;

- second, that technology, at that point, becomes autonomous, determining its own future and that of the society it shapes.

We can see a very different account of technological determinism arising here than that Williams ascribed to McLuhan. We shall return to this account when we revisit the issue of

---

Marginal notes:

Bergson was no techno-enthusiast on the contrary, he astutely criticised a technologically dominated way of thinking as mere 'cinematographic thought' ([1911)] 1920: 287ff.), and delivered thereby one of the first critical analyses of the technology and effects of cinema

5.2.4 Determinisms

determinism in **5.2.4**. We can immediately note, however, that the qualitative change Ellul describes evokes a relationship between what Bergson describes as the scale of a given technology once it has left the category of the hand-tool, and that of technology's environmental impact: we hold a hammer, but we work in a printing press. In this sense alone, technology clearly changes society, not only in the environmental scale of its impact but in the changes to the working relationships between human and machine this entails.

When McLuhan considers the technological environment, however, he means something quite different from the obvious, physical bulk of a factory. This means, in turn, that McLuhan does not make any qualitative distinction between tools and systems of machinery. His sense of the technological environment remains physical, but in a far more subliminal, hard-to-perceive way. When writing about the electronic media, McLuhan coins the phrase 'the hidden environment' (1969: 20–21) to describe the effects of their presence:

> Media of all kinds exert no effect on ordinary perception. They merely serve human ends (like chairs!) . . . Media effects are new environments as imperceptible as water to a fish, subliminal for the most part.

> (McLuhan 1969: 22)

In other words, McLuhan's idea of media effects is not of the tabloid type: Rambo machine-guns a Vietcong village, therefore an impressionable but disaffected teenager runs amok in suburbia. Rather, they subtly alter everything, so that now all human actions take place in a technologically saturated environment that has become the natural world, never rising above the threshold of perception.

An excellent illustration of what McLuhan is getting at here can be found in Paul Verhoeven's *Robocop* (1984). After Murphy (Peter Weller), a cop in soon-to-be New Detroit, is gunned down, his dying body is taken to hospital where he is 'prepped' for various cybernetic implants: titanium-cased arms and legs, capable of exerting enormous pressures, their muscular power amplified by servo-motors; a microchip memory, and so on. The last implant we witness being fitted is his visual grid, which the viewer sees being bolted down over his face plate. The grid itself becomes increasingly visible as it is screwed into place, but disappears again once fully fitted. Robocop has utterly absorbed this visual filter, no longer seeing it, but actually seeing through it.

Just as Kapp sought to naturalise the forms of tools and technologies, so McLuhan points to the naturalisation of effects: if we want to understand the scale of the impact of technological change on culture, we must dig deeper than the content of the media and look at the technological effects of the media themselves. This, then, brings us to the third of Saint McLuhan's many virtues: the elevation of the media above the message. Before we move on, however, note the difference between the technological environments Marx, Bergson and Ellul describe, and that which McLuhan describes: the first is a process that necessarily gets out of hand, spiralling beyond human control; the second is like the screen fitted to Robocop's ocular implants – you notice it on its way in, but not once it becomes the preconscious experiential filter.

THE ANTI-CONTENT THESIS: 'THE MEDIUM IS THE MASSAGE'

The above phrase is the real title of McLuhan's often misquoted but most famous work (1967). The 'massage' brings out the tactile, sensory effects of the media, as discussed above. At the beginning of that book, a very hypertextual collage of image and text, he writes,

Societies have always been shaped more by the nature of the media by which men communicate than by the content of the communication.

(McLuhan and Fiore 1967a: 1)

In other words, McLuhan is arguing that it is not the content of the media that matters at all: whatever the narrative, representational strategy or the ideological mystifications taking place in media narratives, they are decidedly unimportant next to the constant sensory assault stemming from radio and television. As he puts it in an interview, the 'massage' of his 1964 work is created by

> the shaping, the twisting, the bending of the whole human environment by technology . . . a violent process, like all new technologies, often revolting, as well as revolutionary.

(McLuhan, in Stearn 1968: 331)

In contrast to this 'violent massage', to pay attention to the content of a medium or a text deludes the viewer, reader or listener into a sense of mastery over these machines. McLuhan delivers his scornful verdict on those (academics) who practise this: 'Content analysis divorces them from reality' (in Stearn 1968: 329). In this view, media effects do not so much provoke violence in viewers as exert violence on them. The human sensorium is under assault from the very media into which it extended itself.

> McLuhan's critical element is often left out. He is not arguing, as do Adorno and Horkheimer (1996), for example, that popular media are formally repetitive and therefore a cultural evil, but that, materially, their effects constitute a violent alteration of the sensory environment humans inhabit

If we take all three theses together, the same set of concerns emerges: the body is physically extended by the media; the senses and the environment they sense undergo a 'revolution' (Stearn 1968: 331) with every new piece of media technology. McLuhan's analyses are based on the body, the senses, and the technological environment. What unites all three is what we might call their physicalist emphasis – precisely what humanism in cultural and media studies has been unable to address! We will continue our discussion of the **physicalism** of new media and cybercultural studies in Part 5.

5.2.2 Causalities

In **5.2.2** we will have one further occasion to return to the McLuhan–Williams problematic, in the context of a thorough examination of what is entailed by the idea of technological determinism. Since any determinism relies on a conception of causality (to say 'X is determined by Y', is to argue that X causes Y), and since there are many accounts of causality, we have yet to establish what notion of causality Williams ascribes to McLuhan and what notion of causality McLuhan is working with.

1.6.5 The extent of the 'extensions of man'

At the root of the McLuhan/Williams debate lies the question of whether it is a machine's users that are in control of what they are using, or whether the machine in some sense determines its uses. In the first case, a more or less free human agency governs all historical processes, so that any event that takes place can be traced back to the actions of groups and individuals holding a certain view of things. Thus how we use technology is the only question we need ask of it, creating a gulf between the technology itself and its uses: it is as if technology simply does not exist until it is used. We tend, therefore, not to ask what a technology is, but what purposes it serves. That a technology is used in a particular way (the bomb to kill, television to reproduce the ideological status quo) is an accident of the views held by the controlling group. Therefore the point of studying the uses of a technology is not to study the technology but to analyse and contest the governing ideology that determines its uses. On this view, every technology is a tool.

While such a view works well for individual technologies (especially for isolated communications technologies – consider the displacement of the military ARPANET system into the Internet), it works less well if we consider the extent to which technology becomes environmental. In other words, there are quantitative changes in the scale of the work that can be accomplished in the shift from the tool to the machine, but as a consequence there are also fundamental qualitative shifts that alter the relation of human and machine. Rather than being reducible to tools for human purposes, when technology becomes environmental it can no longer be localised, isolated from the networks it forms the material basis of. This is the point from which McLuhan begins. Moreover, 'the medium is the massage' indicates the physical basis of the effects of technology: it is less concerned with a specific or isolated medium in the classical media studies sense (television, radio, film, etc.) than with the sense in which technology becomes the medium we inhabit. Thus, 'the new media are not bridges between man and nature: they are nature' (McLuhan 1969: 14). Accordingly, we need pay less attention to the content of a medium than its physical effects (hence 'massage' rather than message). These are effects principally on the body, since, beginning from the same tool-based conception of technology as does Williams, McLuhan famously views technology as 'extensions' of human capacities and senses. Technology therefore becomes a physical medium that alters the physical capacities of the human body. What therefore has traditionally within media studies been disparaged as technological determinism turns out merely to be taking the physical constitution and effects of a technologically saturated civilisation or culture seriously.

We have thus returned to the point from which section **1.6.4** began: the view that technology is an 'extension' of human capacities, senses, labour, and so on, a view that has such a long history in how human cultures have conceived their technologies. If, however, we seem merely to have come full circle, we need to re-examine what we have found out along the way. Thus we see that this definition of technology poses increasingly complex questions as technology itself becomes more complex. It is worth reiterating the points at which technology has become more complex:

1   Materially: the relation between biological and technological things (between humans and machines) gives rise to several questions. Have our interactions with technology become so all-pervasive as to produce hybrids of biological and technological components, thus unsettling the distinction between the natural and the artificial, or do they result in large-scale actor-networks that resist reduction either to biological or technological bases?

2   Causally: if biology is becoming increasingly inseparable from technology (as for example in the case of the Human Genome Project), what sort of causality is involved in technology producing effects? If in a determinist sense, then how? Does technology now, or will it, possess or acquire agency? If so, of what kind?

3   We have seen that conceiving of technology in this way constitutes a critique of humanism, which imagines the agent as separable, isolable from his/her/its physical, causal environment. If we do not thus imagine the agent, then in what sense is technology reducible to an 'extension of man', and at what point does it begin to become 'self-extending'?

4   We therefore see that studying the question of technology in culture entails opening questions regarding what culture is, and whether it is isolable from its physical environment and the forces therein, as Williams insists it is.

1.6.4 The many virtues of Saint McLuhan

For example, cloning, xenotransplantation, increasingly technological reproductive therapies, genetic engineering, artificial organs, genomics in general and the human genome in particular: the biosciences or biotechnologies seem to produce precisely such hybrids, but the possibilities go further. Cyberneticist Kevin Warwick, for example, recently conducted a year-long experiment using subcutaneously implanted microchips in his own body. Do such technologies extend or alter biological bodies?

1.4 What kind of history?
1.5 Who was dissatisfied with old media?

5.2.4 Determinisms

5 Cyberculture: technology, nature and culture

If we answer (4) in the negative, then we see how the question of technology opens onto the question of the physical basis of culture. It also therefore opens onto scientific and, in the strictest sense, metaphysical issues. One such metaphysical issue, which has enormous consequences in the sciences, is causality. We have seen that some forms of determinism (of the sort that Williams accused McLuhan of holding) presuppose a linear causality (of the sort that McLuhan argues so strenuously against). For Williams, it is essential to pose the problem of technological effects on culture in this manner if what he called 'cultural science' is to be separable from physical science. A second such problem concerns realism and **nominalism**. Generally speaking, nominalists argue that general terms such as 'technology' constitute nothing more than collective names to designate the totality of actually existing technological artefacts. This view is called nominalism because it believes that general terms such as 'technology' are nothing but names for collections of specific individuals. When nominalists talk about technology itself (or when they spot others talking in this way), then they say this amounts to nothing other than talk about empty names. Some nominalists suggest that such terms therefore be eradicated, voided of all but numerical or grammatical sense; others accept this lack of reference to the real world as an inescapable condition of human knowledge, since it is linguistically mediated, and the reference of a term is merely a structural artefact. Realists, by contrast, argue that 'technology' as such has characteristics not necessarily instantiated in all or even in some individual and actual artefacts. Many things are technological: not only mechanical, steam, electrical or digital machines, but also social structures or 'soft technologies' as Jacques Ellul calls them (Ellul [1954] 1964). Moreover, the realist may include in the concept of technology things that do not have any actual instantiation, but that remain real in some other form or function (a good example here is Babbage's Difference Engine, which was not fully constructed until 1991: prior to that date, did such technology really exist?). The crucial difference, however, is that realists need not view language either as simply naming things, or as a screen that either frames or obscures the stuff and matter of things and forces: physics.

Both these issues come clearly into focus when we consider history in general, and the history of technology in particular. Before moving on to a discussion of these topics, which pick up from sections **1.4** and **1.5**, we must also note the consequences of another aspect of the extension thesis as regards technology: that is, that as technology becomes simultaneously less massive and more environmental, deterministic consequences become correspondingly more likely. This is something McLuhan missed, but that Lyotard picks clearly up on. This position, known as 'soft determinism' (determinist consequences resulting from indeterminate causes; see **5.2.4**), recognises the difference in outcome of introducing a new tool into an agrarian culture, a new power source into an industrial culture, or a new programme into a digital culture. Such considerations give rise to the view that technological determinism is not a historical constant (as hard determinists, if they exist anywhere, would argue), but is historically specific to a degree of technological complexity in a given cultural frame. Moreover, it poses the question of what it is that is thus extended: is it the human sensorium, will, muscles, or bodies, as Aristotle, McLuhan and Marx say, or is it technology itself, as Ellul and Lyotard argue? If the latter, is there any such place as 'nature' or 'culture' that remains exempt from the actions of technology, or do we require, as Latour demands, a new constitution for the actor-networks, neither reducibly human nor machinic, but instead, bio-socio-technical?

What then are the consequences of taking the physical effects of technology seriously? First, as we shall see in Part 5, it entails that we can no longer separate physical from cultural processes, or matter from meaning. We can thus see how in attempting to answer the question 'what is technological determinism?' we are led to pose questions that carry us nec-essarily from the sphere of culture to those of technology and, finally, nature.

1.6.6. A new focus for old debates: Science and Technology Studies

> [S]cientists shout at sociologists, who shout back. You almost forget that there are issues to discuss.
>
> (Hacking 1999: vii)

One of the crucial issues to arise from the problems discussed in **1.6** concerns the relation between the natural and the human sciences. Broadly speaking, we may characterise the issue thus: if Williams's account is correct, then the cultural sciences focus on different enti-ties altogether than the natural sciences; if, conversely, McLuhan's concerns become the model of the cultural analysis of technological entities, then no such division of the 'natural' and 'cultural' sciences is viable. Since the 1980s, the character of this division of scientific labour has received renewed focus through the field known as Science and Technology Studies (STS). This simple fact attests to the crucial relevance of the McLuhan–Williams debates, which continue, as we shall see, to map the available positions in this newer field.

The problem with a media studies that follows Williams's model of 'cultural science' is that it eliminates any relationship at all between cultural and natural phenomena. Because STS has drawn renewed attention to this problem, it is a corrective to any presumed insulation of cultural from natural phenomena.

This is not to argue, however, that all practitioners of STS occupy the McLuhanite posi-tion; quite the contrary. The historian Steven Shapin, for instance, a notable participant in the STS debates, announces 'I take it for granted that science is a historically situated and social activity' (Shapin 1996: 7). Although he may take this for granted, Shapin nevertheless deemed a statement of this fact to be necessary. It is *the fact of the statement* that is impor-tant to the constitution of STS. Accordingly, it will be helpful to characterise STS as that field for which the relation of the natural and cultural sciences remains a *problem*, and STS itself therefore as a *problem field*. A brief examination of *how* these problems have been discussed will therefore provide a useful outline of STS from its inception to its more recent forms.

STS is generally held to have begun with the journal *Radical Science* (cf. Haraway 1989: 7) and the work of the 'Edinburgh School' (see Barnes, Bloor and Henry 1996) in the 1970s, followed by the 'Bath School' of what was called the 'sociology of scientific knowledge' in the 1980s (see Collins and Pinch 1993).

Although both schools might be broadly characterised as favouring the orientation Williams offers towards a specifically cultural science, arguing (again, generally speaking) for a species of social constructivism (**5.1.9–5.1.10**), the two founding schools of STS dispute the isolation of cultural from natural science, at least by submitting the latter to cultural analy-sis. Importantly, while thereby relativising the practice of science to historical and social locations, neither school advocates the extension of such a constructivism to the conclusions reached by those sciences. Rather, they seek to demonstrate that while the social domain importantly *includes* the address to physical nature, and while this fact entails the applicabil-ity of sociological modes of analysis to scientific practices and institutions, it does *not* entail that natural phenomena are therefore *nothing more than* cultural products.

An instructive example of the approach of these schools is provided by Barnes' *Interests and the Growth of Knowledge* (1977) and Collins and Pinch's *Frames of Meaning: the Social Construction of Extraordinary Science* (1982). These works follow the philosopher of science

Imre Lakatos (1970) in proposing that sociological constraints (teaching and research institutions, politics, funding, and so forth) play a decisive role in establishing scientific research programmes. This means that there is no such thing as pure research into nature, since such research is always conducted under the auspices of social pressures. Facing this problem, however, scientists differentiate between what is internal and what external to scientific practice and research, insulating a scientific 'core' from a social 'periphery'. What became known, following David Bloor (1991: 3–23) as the 'Strong Programme in the Sociology of Knowledge' therefore seeks to demonstrate the socially and scientifically complex 'framing' of scientific cores, and to draw out what this means for the constitution of scientific knowledge. However, acknowledging this social dimension to the construction of scientific research programmes is entirely different, as Hacking (1999: 68) notes, to 'doubting the truth . . . of propositions widely received in the natural sciences'. Science studies actual nature, albeit in an irreducibly social context.

Its influence on Cultural Studies in North America is marked (often through the work of Donna Haraway), though its emphasis on the operations and agency of technology and other material phenomena marks its difference from the articulations of technology and the human usually offered by the (social constructionist – see below) humanities and social sciences. Anne Balsamo (1998) and Jennifer Slack and J. Macgregor Wise (2002) offer accounts of the influence of STS on North American Cultural Studies. It has yet to register significantly in British Cultural Studies and has – as yet – had little to say on computers, and next to nothing on popular media or media technologies. It does though offer rich theoretical resources for theorising relationships and agency in popular new media and technoculture.

The approach pioneered by these sociologists of scientific knowledge remains very much alive, as illustrated by the opening of archaeologist and STS contributor Marcia-Anne Dobres' *Technology and Social Agency*: 'This is a book about technology. It is therefore, first and foremost a book about people' (Dobres 2000: 1). Just as Dobres' forerunners did not extend the social construction of scientific research programmes to a socially constructed natural world, Dobres does not think that the priority she considers must be accorded human actions and intentions in the analysis of a technology-rich environment entails that all agents are necessarily human. In 'making and remaking of the material world' is included the manufacture of *agents* (2000: 3). Similarly, although Dobres is clear that her book is primarily concerned with people and their interaction – with, that is, the cultural dimension – this culturalist perspective must be augmented, 'as all archaeologists know', by the *material* dimensions of culture. In consequence, Dobres' book 'places special emphasis on the intertwined sociality *and* materiality of technology' (2000: 7; emphasis added); she proposes, that is, that culture is necessarily informed by its physical (natural and technological) context. Clearly, it is the combination of attention to physical and social reality that distinguishes these approaches.

Many notable recent contributions to STS have followed Bruno Latour (1993) in taking as their focus the problem of how exactly this combination occurs. Although Latour began his contributions to STS with a constructionist focus on the function of inscription in science (cf. Latour and Woolgar 1979), in subsequent work he has pursued what he calls 'a more realistic realism' (1999: 15), developing what has become known as Actor-Network Theory (ANT). ANT is premised on two main points: that social actors are not exclusively human; and that it is not things but *networks* that constitute actors, human and non-human. It is precisely because the human and social sciences take it for granted that social agency is exclusively human that Latour's first thesis strikes many in those fields as 'treacherous', as he puts it (1999: 18). To be a social actor is, for such sciences, to be capable of reason, and therefore of choice. At root, agency rests on a notion of free will, that is, of a will uncon-strained by physical causes external to it. Since technological artefacts are incapable of such a will, they cannot be social agents. Latour's counter to this is that social networks, the envi-ronments in which humans act, are already technological, physical, *and* cultural, opening *We Have Never Been Modern* with a list of the items singled out for attention in an edition of a daily newspaper: strikes, the threats of war and famine, transportation systems, the HIV virus, photographs taken from the Hubble Space Telescope, political speeches, sports, arts, and so on. Realistically, reality is made up of *networks* of human and non-human things, rather than being divided into entities that are or are not agents regardless of their contexts. Latour's work therefore moves from the constructionist focus of Williams's cultural science to the socially determining pole occupied by McLuhan.

While ANT proposes that reality is made up of nature and culture, rather than one or the other, it arguably does not answer, as Sardar (2000: 41) has noted, the question of 'the degree to which . . . construction' is constrained by some objective reality 'out there'. In con-sequence, 'science wars' still rage, polarising the sciences and the humanities so that, as Hacking (1999: vii) sadly notes, 'you almost forget that there are issues to discuss' – almost, but not quite. STS has become a vibrant critical forum for the important exchanges between the natural and the human and social sciences, capable of combining with important phe-nomena such as stem-cell research or the 'visible human project' (Biagioli 1999 is a superb anthology showing the diversity and energy of contemporary Science Studies) from scientific, historical and cultural perspectives

It is precisely because STS reorients cultural attention towards its forgotten physical dimension that it reveals the contemporary importance of the debate between McLuhan and Williams. Rather, therefore, than amounting merely to an interesting historical curiosity, these debates are core to the future of cultural and media studies. It is precisely because Williams's account of cultural science crucially informs the settled form of cultural and media studies, that STS highlights the 'blind spots' (**5.1.1**) and assumptions inherent in such approaches to technology. STS not only provides an important corrective to such approaches, but becomes a vital contributor to the cultural study of physical and technological phenomena.

Among the issues that remain in the light of this brief history of STS, the problem of the precise relation between nature and culture remains to be interrogated. If, according to ANT, social networks are assembled from technological, physical, political, intentional and discur-sive elements, do these networks themselves owe their existence to nature or to culture? Are some elements more essential than others? Even if we assume that networks have priority over elements (that is, that elements do not exist without the networks that make them), we still do not know whether these networks can be said to exist without culture. Although there-fore ANT provides what many agree is a 'realistic' and thought-provoking *description* of reality, the question Latour's 'more realistic realism' has yet satisfactorily to answer, concerns reality itself.

Bibliography

Aarseth, Espen *Cybertext – Experiments in Ergodic Literature*, Baltimore, Md.: Johns Hopkins University Press, 1997.

Aarseth, Espen 'Computer Game Studies Year One', in *Game Studies: The International Journal of Computer Game Research*, vol. 1, no.1 (2001). Available online at http://gamestudies.org/0101/editorial.html

Aarseth, Espen 'We All Want to Change the World: the ideology of innovation in digital media', in *Digital Media Revisited*, (eds) T. Rasmussen, G. Liestol and A. Morrison, Cambridge, Mass.: MIT Press, 2002.

Adorno, Theodor and Horkheimer, Max *Dialectic of Enlightenment*, trans. John Cumming, London: Verso, 1996.

Balsamo, Anne 'Introduction', *Cultural Studies* 12, London: Routledge, 1998.

Barnes, Barry *Interests and the Growth of Knowledge*, London: Routledge, 1977.

Barnes, Barry, David Bloor and John Henry *Scientific Knowledge: A Sociological Analysis*, Chicago: University of Chicago Press, 1996.

Barnes, Jonathan *The Complete Works of Aristotle*, vol 2, Princeton, NJ: Princeton University Press, 1994.

Batchen, G. *Burning with Desire: The Conception of Photography*, Cambridge, Mass. and London: MIT Press, 1997.

Baudrillard, Jean *Cool Memories II*, trans. Chris Turner, Cambridge: Polity, 1996a.

Baudrillard, Jean *The Perfect Crime*, trans. Chris Turner, London: Verso, 1996b.

Baudrillard, Jean *Simulacra and Simulations*, trans. Sheila Faria Glaser, Ann Arbor: University of Michigan Press, 1997.

Benjamin, Walter 'The work of art in the age of mechanical reproduction', in *Illuminations*, ed. H. Arendt, Glasgow: Fontana, 1977.

Benjamin, Walter 'The Author as Producer', in *Thinking Photography*, ed. V. Burgin, London and Basingstoke: Macmillan, 1983.

Bergson, Henri *Creative Evolution*, trans. Arthur Mitchell, London: Macmillan, [1911] 1920.

Bergson, Henri *The Two Sources of Morality and Religion*, trans. R. Ashley Andra and Cloudesley Brereton, London: Macmillan, [1932] 1935.

Berman, Ed *The Fun Art Bus – An InterAction Project*, London: Methuen, 1973.

Biagioli, Mario *The Science Studies Reader*, New York: Routledge, 1999.

Binkley, T. 'Reconfiguring culture' in P. Hayward and T. Wollen, *Future Visions: new technologies of the screen*, London: BFI, 1993.

Bloor, David *Knowledge and Social Imagery*, Chicago: University of Chicago Press, 1991.

Boddy, William 'Archaeologies of electronic vision and the gendered spectator', *Screen* 35.2 (1994): 105–122.

Bolter, Jay David *Writing Space: the computer, hypertext and the history of writing*, New York: Lawrence Erlbaum Associates, 1991.

Bolter, J. and Grusin, R. *Remediation: understanding new media*, Cambridge, Mass. and London: MIT Press, 1999.

Brecht, Bertolt 'The radio as an apparatus of communication', in *Video Culture*, ed. J. Hanhardt, New York: Visual Studies Workshop, 1986.

Burgin, Victor *Thinking Photography*, London: Macmillan Press, 1982.

Bush, Vannevar 'As we may think' [*Atlantic Monthly*, 1945], in P. Mayer, *Computer Media and Communication: a reader*, Oxford: Oxford University Press, 1999.

Castells, M. *The Rise of the Network Society*, Oxford: Blackwell, [1996] 2000.

Chartier, R. *The Order of Books*, Cambridge: Polity Press, 1994.

Chesher, C. 'The ontology of digital domains', in D. Holmes (ed.) *Virtual Politics*, London, Thousand Oaks (Calif.), New Delhi: Sage, 1997.

Collins, Harry M. and Pinch, Trevor J. *Frames of Meaning: the Social Construction of Extraordinary Science*, London: Routledge, 1982.

Collins, Harry and Pinch, Trevor J. *The Golem: What Everyone Should Really Know about Science*, Cambridge: Cambridge University Press, 1993.

Cornford, J. and Robins, K. 'New media', in *The Media in Britain*, eds J. Stokes and A. Reading, London: Macmillan, 1999.

Coyle, Rebecca 'The genesis of virtual reality', in *Future Visions: new technologies of the screen*, eds Philip Hayward and Tana Woollen, London: BFI, 1993.

Crary, Jonathan *Techniques of the Observer: on vision and modernity in the nineteenth century*, Cambridge, Mass. and London: MIT Press, 1993.

Cubitt, Sean *Simulation and Social Theory*, London: Sage, 2001.

Darley, A. 'Big screen, little screen: the archeology of technology', *Digital Dialogues. Ten* 8 2.2 (1991): 78–87.

Darley, Andrew *Visual Digital Culture: surface play and spectacle in new media genres*, London and New York: Routledge, 2000.

Debord, Guy *The Society of the Spectacle*, Detroit: Red and Black, 1967.

De Kerckhove, Derrick *The Skin of Culture*, Toronto: Somerville House, 1997.

De Lauretis, T., Woodward, K. and Huyssen, A. *The Technological Imagination: theories and fictions*, Madison, Wis.: Coda Press, 1980.

Dobres, Marcia-Anne *Technology and Social Agency*, Oxford: Blackwell, 2000.

Dovey, J. ed. *Fractal Dreams*, London: Lawrence and Wishart, 1995.

Dovey, J. and Kennedy, H. W. *Game Cultures*, Maidenhead: McGraw-Hill, 2006.

Downes, E. J. and McMillan, S. J. 'Defining Interactivity: A Qualitative Identification of Key Dimensions', *New Media and Society* 2.2 (2000): 157–179.

Druckrey, T. ed. *Ars Electronica Facing the Future*, Cambridge, Mass. and London: MIT Press, 1999.

Duffy, Dennis *Marshall McLuhan*, Toronto: McClelland and Stuart Ltd, 1969.

Eastgate Systems. http://www.eastgate.com Hypertext Fiction.

Eco, Umberto *Travels in Hyperreality*, London: Pan, 1986.

Eisenstein, E. *The Printing Press as an Agent of Change*, Cambridge: Cambridge University Press, 1979.

Ellul, Jacques *The Technological Society*, New York: Vintage, [1954] 1964.

Engelbart, Douglas 'A conceptual framework for the augmentation of man's intellect', in *Computer Media and Communication*, ed. Paul Mayer, Oxford: Oxford University Press, 1999.

Enzenberger, Hans Magnus 'Constituents of a theory of mass media', in *Dreamers of the Absolute*, London: Radius, 1988.

Eskelinen, M. *The Gaming Situation* in *Game Studies: The International Journal of Computer Game Research*, vol. 1, no.1, (2001). Available online at http://gamestudies.org/0101/eskelinen/

Everson, Stephen ed. *Aristotle, The Politics and The Constitution of Athens*, Cambridge: Cambridge University Press, 1996.

Featherstone, M. ed. *Global Culture*, London, Thousand Oaks, New Delhi: Sage, 1990.

Featherstone, M. and Burrows, R. *Cyberspace, Cyberbodies, Cyberpunk: Cultures of Technological Embodiment*, London, Thousand Oaks, New Delhi: Sage, 1995.

Flichy, P. 'The construction of new digital media', *New Media and Society* 1.1 (1999): 33–38.

Foucault, Michel *The Archaeology of Knowledge*, London: Tavistock, 1972.

Frasca, Gonzalo 'Simulation Versus Narrative: An Introduction to Ludology', in *The Video Game Theory Reader*, eds Mark J. P. Wolf and Bernard Perron, London: Routledge, 2003, pp. 221–235.

Gane, Mike *Baudrillard: critical and fatal theory*, London: Routledge, 1991.

Gauntlett, David *Media Studies 2.0* (2007) http://www.theory.org.uk/mediastudies2-print.htm

Genosko, Gary *McLuhan and Baudrillard: the masters of implosion*, London: Routledge, 1998.

Gershuny, J. 'Postscript: Revolutionary technologies and technological revolutions', in *Consuming Technologies: Media and Information in Domestic Spaces*, eds R. Silverstone and E. Hirsch, London and New York: Routledge, 1992.

Gibson, W. *Neuromancer*, London: Grafton, 1986.

Giddings, Seth 'Dionysiac machines: videogames and the triumph of the simulacra', *Convergence*, 12(4) (2007): 419–443

Goldberg, K. 'Virtual reality in the age of telepresence', *Convergence* 4.1 (1998): 33–37.

Greenberg, Clement 'Modernist painting' in *Modern Art and Modernism: a critical anthology*, eds Francis Frascina and Charles Harrisson, London: Harper & Row, [1961] 1982.

Gunning, Tom 'Heard over the phone: the lonely villa and the De Lorde tradition of the terrors of technology', *Screen* 32.2 (1991): 184–196.

Hacking, Ian *The Social Construction of What?* Cambridge, Mass: Harvard University Press, 1999.

Hall, S. 'Television as a Medium and its Relation to Culture', Occasional Paper No. 34, Birmingham: The Centre for Contemporary Cultural Studies, 1975.

Hanhardt, J. G. *Video Culture*, Rochester, N.Y.: Visual Studies Workshop Press, 1986.

Haraway, Donna J. *Primate Visions. Gender, Race and Nature in the World of Modern Science*, London: Verso, 1989.

Haraway, Donna *Simians, Cyborgs and Women: the reinvention of nature*, London: Free Association, 1991.

Harrigan, P. and Wardrip-Fruin, N. eds *First Person, New Media as Story, Performance and Game*, Cambridge, Mass.: MIT Press, 2003.

Harrison, C. and Wood, P. *Art in Theory: 1900–1990*, Oxford and Cambridge, Mass.: Blackwell, 1992.

Harvey, D. *The Condition of Postmodernity*, Oxford: Blackwell, 1989.

Hayles, N. Katherine 'Virtual bodies and flickering signifiers', in *How We Became Post-Human*, ed. N. Katherine Hayles, Chicago and London: University of Chicago Press, 1999.

Heim, Michael 'The erotic ontology of cyberspace', in *Cyberspace: the first steps*, ed. Michael Benedikt, Cambridge, Mass.: MIT Press, 1991.

Heim, Michael *The Metaphysics of Virtual Reality*, New York and Oxford: Oxford University Press, 1993.

Holzmann, Steve *Digital Mosaics: the aesthetics of cyberspace*, New York: Simon and Schuster, 1997.

Huhtamo, Erkki 'From cybernation to interaction: a contribution to an archeology of interactivity', in *The Digital Dialectic*, ed. P. Lunenfeld, Cambridge, Mass.: MIT Press, 2000.

Jameson, Fredric *Postmodernism, or the cultural logic of late capitalism*, London: Verso, 1991.

Jenkins, H. *Interactive Audiences? The 'Collective Intelligence' Of Media Fans* (2002) http://web.mit.edu/cms/People/henry3/collective%20intelligence.html

Jensen, Jens F. 'Interactivity – tracking a new concept in media and communication studies', in *Computer Media and Communication*, ed. Paul Mayer, Oxford: Oxford University Press, 1999.

Joyce, Michael *Of Two Minds: hypertext pedagogy and poetics*, Ann Arbor: University of Michigan, 1995.

Kapp, Ernst *Grundlinien einer Philosophie des Technik. Zur Entstehungsgeschichte der Kultur ans neuen Gesichtspunkten* [Outlines of a Philosophy of Technology: new perspectives on the evolution of culture], Braunschweig: Westermann, 1877.

Kay, Alan and Goldberg, Adele 'Personal dynamic media', *Computer*, 10 March 1977.

Kay, Alan and Goldberg, Adele 'A new home for the mind', in *Computer Media and Communication*, ed. P. Mayer, Oxford: Oxford University Press, 1999.

Kellner, Douglas *Jean Baudrillard: from Marxism to postmodernism and beyond*, Cambridge: Polity Press, 1989.

Klastrup Lisbet *Paradigms of interaction conceptions and misconceptions of the field today* (2003) (http://www.dich-tung-digital.com/2003/issue/4/klastrup/)

Kroker, Arthur *The Possessed Individual*, New York: Macmillan, 1992.

Lakatos, Imre *Criticism and the Growth of Knowledge*, Cambridge: Cambridge University Press, 1970.

Landow, George *Hypertext: the convergence of contemporary literary theory and technology*, Baltimore, Md.: John Hopkins University Press, 1992.

Landow, George ed. *Hyper/Text/Theory*, Baltimore, Md.: Johns Hopkins University Press, 1994.

Landow, George and Delaney, Paul eds *Hypermedia and Literary Studies*, Cambridge, Mass.: MIT Press, 1991.

Latour, Bruno *We Have Never Been Modern*, trans. Catherine Porter, Hemel Hempstead: Harvester Wheatsheaf, 1993.

Latour, Bruno *Pandora's Hope: Essays on the Reality of Science Studies*, Cambridge, Mass.: Harvard University Press, 1999.

Latour, Bruno and Woolgar, Steven *Laboratory Life. The Social Construction of Scientific Facts*, London: Sage, 1979.

Latour, B. 'Alternative digitality' at: http://www.bruno-latour.fr/presse/presse_art/GB-05%20DOMUS%2005-04.html

Levinson, Paul, *Digital McLuhan*, London: Routledge, 1999.

Lévy, Pierre 'The aesthetics of cyberspace', in *Electronic Culture*, ed. T. Druckrey, New York: Aperture, 1997.

Lévy, Pierre *Collective Intelligence: Mankind's Emerging World in Cyberspace*, Cambridge: Perseus, 1997.

Lévy, Pierre *Becoming Virtual: Reality in the Digital Age*, New York: Perseus, 1998.

Licklider, J. C. R. 'Man computer symbiosis' in *Computer Media and Communication*, ed. Paul Mayer, Oxford: Oxford University Press, 1999.

Licklider, J. C. R. and Taylor, R. W. 'The computer as communication device', in *Computer Media and Communication*, ed. Paul Mayer, Oxford: Oxford University Press, 1999.

Lister, M. 'Introductory essay', in *The Photographic Image in Digital Culture*, London and New York: Routledge, 1995.

Lister, M., Dovey, J., Giddings, S., Grant, I. and Kelly, K. *New Media: A Critical Introduction*, (1st edn), London and New York: Routledge, 2003.

Lunenfeld, Peter 'Digital dialectics: a hybrid theory of computer media', *Afterimage* 21.4 (1993).

Lury, Celia 'Popular culture and the mass media', in *Social and Cultural Forms of Modernity*, eds Bocock and Thompson, Cambridge: Polity Press and the Open University, 1992.

Mackay, H. and O'Sullivan, T. eds *The Media Reader: continuity and transformation*, London, Thousand Oaks (Calif.), New Delhi: Sage, 1999.

MacKenzie, Donald and Wajcman, Judy *The Social Shaping of Technology*, Buckingham and Philadelphia: Open University Press, 1999.

Manovich, Lev *The Language of New Media*, Cambridge, Mass.: MIT Press, 2001.

Marvin, C. *When Old Technologies Were New*, New York and Oxford: Oxford University Press, 1988.

Marx, Karl *Grundrisse*, trans. Martin Nicolaus, Harmondsworth: Penguin, [1857] 1993.

Mayer, Paul *Computer Media and Communication: a reader*, Oxford: Oxford University Press, 1999.

Maynard, Patrick *The Engine of Visualisation*, Ithaca, N.Y.: Cornell University Press, 1997.

McCaffrey, Larry ed. *Storming the Reality Studio: a casebook of cyberpunk and postmodernism*, Durham, N.C.: Duke University Press, 1992.

McLuhan, Marshall *The Gutenberg Galaxy: the making of typographic man*, Toronto: University of Toronto Press, 1962.

McLuhan, Marshall *Understanding Media: the extensions of man*, Toronto: McGraw Hill, 1964.

McLuhan, Marshall *Understanding Media*, London: Sphere, 1968.

McLuhan, Marshall *Counterblast*, London: Rapp and Whiting, 1969.

McLuhan, M. and Carpenter, E. 'Acoustic space', in *Explorations in Communications*, eds M. McLuhan and E. Carpenter, Boston: Beacon Press, 1965.

McLuhan, Marshall and Fiore, Quentin *The Medium is the Massage: an inventory of effects*, New York, London, Toronto: Bantam Books, 1967a.

McLuhan, Marshall and Fiore, Quentin *War and Peace in the Global Village*, New York, London, Toronto: Bantam Books, 1967b.

Meek, Allen 'Exile and the electronic frontier', *New Media and Society* 2.1 (2000): 85–104.

Merrin, W. *Media Studies 2.0 My Thoughts* (2008) http://mediastudies2point0.blogspot.com/

Miller, J. *McLuhan*, London: Fontana, 1971.

Mitcham, Carl *Thinking Through Technology*, Chicago: University of Chicago Press, 1994.

Mitchell, W. J. *The Reconfigured Eye*, Cambridge, Mass.: MIT Press, 1992.

Mirzoeff, N. *An Introduction to Visual Culture*, London and New York: Routledge, 1999.

Moody, Nickianne 'Interacting with the divine comedy', in *Fractal Dreams: new media in social context*, ed. Jon Dovey, London: Lawrence and Wishart, 1995.

Morley, David *The Nationwide Audience*, London: British Film Institute, 1980.

Morse, Margaret *Virtualities: television, media art, and cyberculture*, Bloomington: Indiana University Press, 1998.

Moulthrop, Stuart 'Toward a rhetoric of informating texts in hypertext', *Proceedings of the Association for Computing Machinery*, New York, 1992.

Moulthrop, Stuart 'From Work to Play: Molecular Culture in the Time of Deadly Games', in *First Person: New Media as Story, Performance and Game*, eds P. Harrigan and N. Wardrip-Fruin, Cambridge, Mass. and London: MIT Press, 2004.

Murray, Janet *Hamlet on the Holodeck – The Future of Narrative in Cyberspace*, Cambridge, Mass. and London: MIT Press, 1997.

Nelson, Ted 'A new home for the mind' [1982], in *Computer Mediated Communications*, ed. P. Mayer, Oxford: Oxford University Press, 1999.

Norman, Donald A. *The Design of Everyday Things*, New York: Basic Books, 2002.

Ong, W. *Orality and Literacy*, London and New York: Routledge, 2002.

Penny, Simon 'The Darwin machine: artifical life and interactive art', *New Formations*, TechnoScience 29.64 (1966): 59–68.

Penny, Simon *Critical Issues in Electronic Media*, New York: SUNY Press, 1995.

Poster, Mark *The Mode of Information*, Cambridge: Polity Press, 1990.

Poster, Mark 'Underdetermination', *New Media and Society* 1.1 (1999): 12–17.

Prensky, Marc *Digital Games Based Learning*, New York: McGraw-Hill, 2001.

Ragland-Sullivan, Ellie 'The imaginary', in *Feminism and Psychoanalysis: a critical dictionary*, ed. E. Wright, Oxford: Basil Blackwell, 1992.

Rheingold, Howard *Virtual Worlds*, London: Secker and Warburg, 1991.

Rieser, M. and Zapp, A. eds *Interactivity and Narrative*, London: British Film Institute, 2001.

Rieser, M. and Zapp, A. eds *New Screen Media: Cinema/Art/Narrative*, London: British Film Institute, 2002.

Ritchen, Fred *In Our Own Image: the coming revolution in photography*, New York: Aperture, 1990.

Robins, K. 'Into the image', in *PhotoVideo: photography in the age of the computer*, ed. P. Wombell, London: River Orams Press, 1991.

Robins, K. 'Will images move us still?', in *The Photographic Image in Digital Culture*, ed. M. Lister, London and New York: Routledge, 1995.

Robins, Kevin *Into the Image: Culture and Politics in the Field Of Vision*, London and New York: Routledge, 1996.

Rubinstein, D. and Sluis, K. 'A Life More Photographic', in *Photographies*, Vol. 1, Issue 1, March 2008, pp. 9–28.

Rucker, R., Sirius, R. V. and Queen, M. eds *Mondo 2000: A User's Guide to the New Edge*, London: Thames and Hudson, 1993.

Ryan, M.-L. *Possible Worlds, Artificial Intelligence, and Narrative Theory,* Bloomington and Indianapolis: Indiana University Press, 1991.

Ryan, M.-L. *Narrative as Virtual Reality: Immersion and Interactivity in Literature and Electronic Media*, Baltimore, Md.: Johns Hopkins University Press, 2001.

Sabbah, Françoise 'The new media', in *High Technology Space and Society*, ed. Manuel Castells, Beverly Hills, Calif.: Sage, 1985.

Sardar, Ziauddinn *Thomas Kuhn and the Science Wars*, London: Icon, 2000.

Sarup, M. *Post-structuralism and Postmodernism*, Hemel Hempstead: Harvester Wheatsheaf, 1988.

Schivelbusch, Wolfgang *The Railway Journey: the industrialisation of time and space in the 19th century*, Berkeley and Los Angeles: University of California Press, 1977.

Schultz, Tanjev 'Mass media and the concept of interactivity: an exploratory study of online forums and reader email', *Media, Culture and Society* 22.2 (2000): 205–221.

Shapin, S. *The Scientific Revolution*, Chicago: University of Chicago Press, 1996.

Shields, R. *The Virtual*, London and New York: Routledge, 2003

Silverstone, Roger *Why Study the Media*, London, Thousand Oaks (Calif.) and New Delhi: Sage, 1999.

Slack, Jennifer Daryl and Wise, J. Macgregor 'Cultural studies and technology', in *The Handbook of New Media*, eds Leah Lievrouw and Sonia Livingstone, London: Sage, 2002, pp. 485–501.

Spiegel, Lynn *Make Room for TV: television and the family ideal in postwar America*, Chicago: University of Chicago Press, 1992.

Stafford, Barbara Maria *Artful Science: enlightenment entertainment and the eclipse of visual education*, Cambridge, Mass. and London: MIT Press, 1994.

Stearn, G. E. *McLuhan: hot and cool*, Toronto: Signet Books, 1968.

Steemers J, 'Broadcasting is dead, long live digital choice', *Convergence* 3.1 (1997).

Stevenson, Nick *Understanding Media Cultures: social theory and mass communication*, London: Sage, 1995.

Stone, Roseanne Allucquere 'Will the real body please stand up', in *Cyberspace: First steps*, ed. Michael Benedikt, Cambridge, Mass. and London: MIT Press, 1994.

Stone, Rosanne Allucquere *The War of Desire and Technology at the Close of the Mechanical Age*, Cambridge, Mass.: MIT Press, 1995.

Strinati, Dominic 'Mass culture and popular culture and The Frankfurt School and the culture industry', in *An Introduction to Theories of Popular Culture*, London and New York: Routledge, 1995.

Tagg, J. *The Burden of Representation*, London: Macmillan, 1998.

Taylor, M. C. and Saarinen, E. *Imagologies: media philosophy*, London and New York: Routledge, 1994.

Theal, Donald *The Medium is the RearView Mirror*, Montreal and London: McGill-Queens University Press, 1995.

Thompson, J. B. *The Media and Modernity: a social theory of the media*, Cambridge: Polity Press, 1971.

Wakefield, J. *Turn off e-mail and do some work* (2007) http://news.bbc.co.uk/1/hi/technology/7049275.stm

Weibel, Peter 'The world as interface', in *Electronic Culture*, ed. Timothy Druckrey, New York: Aperture, 1996.

Williams, Raymond *The Long Revolution*, London: Penguin, 1961.

Williams, R. *Television, Technology and Cultural Form*, London: Fontana, 1974.

Williams, R. *Keywords: a vocabulary of culture and society*, Glasgow: Fontana, 1976.

Williams, R. *Marxism and Literature*, Oxford: Oxford University Press, 1977.

Williams, R. *Culture*, London: HarperCollins, 1981.

Williams, R. *Towards 2000*, Harmondsworth: Penguin, 1983.

Williams, R. 'Means of production', in *Culture*, London: Fontana, 1986.

Winner, Langdon *Computers in the human context: information technology, productivity, and people*, Cambridge Mass.: MIT Press, 1989.

Winston, Brian 'The case of HDTV: light, camera, action: Hollywood and Technology', in *Technologies of Seeing: photography, cinematography and television*, London: BFI, 1996.

Winston, B. *Media, Technology and Society: a history from the telegraph to the internet*, London and New York: Routledge, 1998.

Woolley, B. *Virtual Worlds: A Journey in Hype and Hyperreality*, Oxford and Cambridge, Mass.: Blackwell, 1992.

Woolgar, S. 'Configuring the User: The Case of Usability Trials' in *A Sociology of Monsters. Essays on Power, Technology and Domination*, ed. J. Law, London: Routledge, 1991.

Youngblood, Gene 'A medium matures: video and the cinematic enterprise' in *Ars Electronica Facing the Future*, ed. T. Druckrey, Cambridge, Mass. and London: MIT Press, 1999.

2 New Media and Visual Culture

2.1 What happened to Virtual Reality (VR)?

2.1 The *Daily Telegraph* front page: 'Dawn of another World'.

2.2 Nintendo Wii. Courtesy of AFP/Getty Images

In hls 1984 novel, *Neuromancer,* William Gibson coined the term 'cyberspace' and offered his seminal vision of an immersive virtual world. Some twenty-three years later, in his latest novel (*Spook Country*, 2007) Hollis, his heroine (an ex-member of an avant-garde rock band turned techno-art journalist) interviews an artist who works with GPS and computer simulations, in Los Angeles:

> 'What's here, Alberto? What are we here to see?' Hollis demanded, as they reached the corner. He knelt and opened the case. The interior was padded with blocks of foam. He extracted something that she at first mistook for a welder's protective mask. 'Put this on.' He handed it to her. A padded headband, with a sort of visor. 'Virtual Reality?' She hadn't heard that term spoken aloud in years, she thought, as she pronounced it. 'The software lags behind,' he said. 'At least the kind I can afford.'
>
> (Gibson 2007: 7)

In Gibson's latest novel, 'VR' has become a memory. Its once futuristic apparatus is mistaken for a clumsy welder's mask and for those who still bother, like the artist Alberto, the software is still defective.

In a 2007 entry in his blog '10zenmonkies', R. U. Sirius, one-time editor of the leading cyberculture magazine *Mondo 2000*, recalls the interest and excitement that was once aroused by Virtual Reality or 'VR'. With a hint of disbelief he recalls how, in the emerging digital culture of the early 1990s, the promise of interacting with other people in shared 3-D worlds was as much a talking point as was the novelty of the Internet. He writes:

> 3-D worlds would be accessed through head-mounted displays. The idea was to put the user literally *inside* computer-created worlds, where she could move around and see and hear the goings on in a fully dimensional alternative reality and have the sensation of being in another world. The eyes were the primary organs of entrance into these other worlds, although touch, motion and sound were all also involved.

He then observes that the popular virtual world of 'Second Life' is a 'timid' example of what was then envisioned (http://www.10zenmonkeys.com/2007/03/09/whatever-happened-to-virtual-reality/).

In the first edition of this book, written in 2001–2002 when interest in VR was still relatively strong, we outlined its history and discussed the debate that surrounded it (Lister *et al*. 2003: 107–124). At that time we were able to raise the question of the future viability and status of VR as a 'medium', pointing to a number of factors which gave pause for thought. We argued that some careful analysis was needed to grasp what was actually happening in the development of VR technology and the social conditions for its use (see Box, 'Is VR a new medium?').

In virtual reality we have an example of a 'new medium' (or at least a candidate for one) which was once as absorbing and hyped as the Internet but which, unlike the Internet and WWW, seems not to have delivered (however disappointed some have been in what they have delivered). Nevertheless, throughout the 1990s, little can have exercised the minds and imaginations of technologists, journalists, artists, film directors, or academics as much as 'VR'. How are we to account for this waning of interest; this 'rise and fall' of Virtual Reality within the short history of new media?

From our present standpoint, we can now revisit the analysis that we undertook in 2001–2002. The populist hype, widespread experiment, the frequent conferences and artists' projects that explored VR with such excitement through the 1980s and 1990s has waned. Apart from the reasons we gave in our original analysis ('Is VR a new medium?') it is also now clear that the enthusiasm for VR was part of the euphoric techno-utopian expectations of the period, and the heady mix of the computer counter-culture and neo-liberal Silicon Valley entrepreneurship – a period that was brought to a fairly abrupt end by the dotcom bust of 2000 (see **3.10**).

In this context, VR has returned to whence it came – the laboratories of the military–industrial complex, where research and development steadily continues. It is taking place, for instance, in the Advanced Displays and Spatial Perception Laboratory at NASA's Ames Research Centre, where the lead researcher, Stephen Ellis, explains '(t)he technology of the 1980s was not mature enough'. His message is that the earlier period of intense activity was premature because vision ran ahead of the available hardware and software and too little was understood about how the human sensorium responded to the degree of bodily immersion that was attempted. Now, as computers have become many times faster, peripherals more lightweight, and further research into the biology and psychology of perception can be drawn upon, renewed and serious interest is being shown again (http://science.nasa.gov/headlines/y2004/21jun_vr.htm).

Research continues not only at NASA, but in ARPA's (Advanced Research Projects Agency) National Research Agenda for Virtual Reality, the US Airforce Office for Scientific Research and other military/industrial research centres (Grau 2003: 22).

Is VR a new medium?

While 'immersive VR' has been thought of as a 'medium' we should be cautious in doing so. It may be more accurate to see VR as a prime example of a technology (or collection of technologies) which is a stage where development and investment are taking place for a variety of speculative reasons.

However, whether the technology merits the status of a visual 'medium', in the widely accepted social sense, is open to question. An important way to understand a medium is as a set of social, institutional and aesthetic (as well as technological) arrangements for carrying and distributing information, ideas, texts, and images. Immersive VR has no firmly settled institutional pattern of distribution, exhibition or use and for this reason it is difficult to describe as a medium in a fully social sense. A medium is more than the technology it depends upon; it is also a practice. It is a kind of skilled work on raw materials (whether they be words, photographic materials or digitised analogue media) which uses conventions, structures and sign systems to make sense, to convey ideas and construct experiences. The jury must still be out on whether or not VR will ever achieve the status of a medium in this sense. Whether, in other words, it will become a form of social communication and representation in the manner of radio, cinema or television. We have already briefly discussed Stone's conviction that immersive or simulational VR will fuse with online forms at a future time to become a medium of a new and dramatic kind (**1.2.2**). The important point here is that neither visionary speculation nor sheer technological potential is itself a sufficient guarantee that a medium will actually be the outcome of a technology.

The social development of technologies as media
This takes us directly onto the terrain researched in considerable historical detail (with a primary interest in communications media) by Brian Winston in *Media, Technology and Society: A History: From the Telegraph to the Internet* (1999). On the basis of his research, Winston formulates and tests a number of stages through which potential communications technologies or 'media' will pass. In a simplified form they are these:

1   There must be a basis in a society's general scientific competence so that a certain kind of technology is feasible. This is the ground for a technology's possibility.

2   Next, there is the stage of 'ideation' when an idea or concept of how that available scientific competence may be given a technological application is envisaged – typically not by one inspired individual but by several in their supporting contexts and in a number of locations. This may lead to the building of prototypes, but these, as merely modelled potentialities, are not yet widely recognised or confirmed as useful social technologies by the social groups with the will to invest in them or the power to realise them.

3   Then there is the stage of a technology's 'invention'. Invention, on this view, is clearly not an original idea, an unprecedented inspiration, or an occasion for shouting 'Eureka!'. This is when a technology can be said to exist properly as it moves beyond an idea, and the prototype stage, as a clear necessity or use is seen and it finds social acceptance.

Even VR's status as a single technology is suspect. As Hillis (1996: 70) asks, does anything set VR apart from 'TV and telephony from which [it] is partly cobbled, imagined and extended?'

This, however, is not to imply that a medium, so defined, is neutral. Whether or not we want to go so far as Marshall McLuhan in proclaiming that the 'medium is the message', a medium is never separable from the information or content it carries; it contributes to, shapes, allows or disallows meaning

There is no smooth passage between these stages. Winston's research demonstrates that there is no guarantee that a technology will successfully pass through each of these stages to full social realisation and use. Prototypes do not proceed to be inventions unless a social purpose or need is evident. Further, even those which do can then be 'suppressed'. History is replete with technologies that could have been, for which prototypes existed but social need or commercial interest did not. There are also cases of technologies being invented twice, the telegraph being a case in point. The 'invention' a second time around succeeded because it was received into a social moment where there was a perceived need for it. The earlier invention was possible but redundant – to coin a phrase, 'ahead of its time' (Winston 1999: 5).

1.3. Change and continuity

The development of VR has a complex and contingent genealogy of the kind that we outline in **1.3**. From the 1950s onwards, several spheres of 'blue-sky' research in universities linked to programmes of military–industrial research into flight simulators and trainers, and related economic and cultural activity overlap one another. It is only latterly, in the late 1980s, that VR begins to constitute something like a media industry as well as an intense focus of cultural interest. With regard to the virtual space of the Internet we have to remember that it was 'Designed by a confluence of communities which appear to have little in common – such as Cold War defence departments, the counter-cultural computer programming engineer community, and university research throughout the world – the Internet's infrastructure was designed to withstand nuclear attack' (Hulsbus 1997). Immersive VR's history dates from circa 1989 (the SIGGRAPH conference of that year), with foundational experiments being traced to Ivan Sutherland's experiments in the 1960s (see Coyle 1993: 152; Woolley 1992: 41).

The social availability of VR
Using Winston's terms, we might say that, currently, the hybrid technologies of immersive VR appear to be teetering between repeatedly reinvented prototype and invention. VR occasionally flickers into life (often for no more than an hour or two) at prestigious art or media festivals and trade shows. Each such event or 'exhibition' is unique and of short duration. The construction of 'state of the art' virtual spaces and environments is intensive in its use of technology and hence, outside of the military–industrial sphere, such realisations are restricted to a few fleeting occasions, usually requiring expensive travel and maintenance in real time and space for those who wish to participate. Ironically, the viewer or user has to be in a precise (and expensive) institution or place in the real world if they wish to be in 'virtual' reality.

CASE STUDY 2.1 VR, art and technology

Douglas MacLeod, director of 'The Art and Virtual Environments Project' held in 1994 at the Banff Centre for Arts, Canada, explains that it took two years of intensive and groundbreaking work for artists and technologists to bring a range of VR projects to completion. Reflecting on the practical dimensions of the project, MacLeod writes, 'It was like staging nine different operas in two years while at the same time trying to invent the idea of opera.' Judging that this huge effort had only provided 'a suggestion of what this medium could be', he then worries that the works will never be shown again; 'Some are simply too complex to remount. In other cases, the team of artists and programmers that produced the piece has dispersed, taking with them the detailed knowledge of the assembly and installation of a particular work' (Moser and MacLeod 1996: xii; also see Morse 1998: 200).

In terms of spatial or geographical distribution, it is very likely that VR is rarer than hand-made pictures were in the era before photography and mass reproduction. A popular work on VR (Rheingold 1991) reads like a personal world tour of university research departments and the R&D divisions of major multinational entertainment and communications corporations: the University of North Carolina; Kansai Science City, Kyoto; NASA, Massachusetts; MIT; Tsukuba Japan; the US Marine Corps research facility in Honolulu; an inventor's house in Santa Monica; companies in California's Silicon Valley; a computer science laboratory in Grenoble, France (Rheingold 1991: 18–19). Such places arc hardly public or even semi-public venues for the consumption of a new medium.

Few can travel to expensive installations and exclusive institutions; so how is VR experienced as a medium in the social sense? The most ubiquitous form of VR is the stripped-down version seen in 'shoot-em-up' arcades. While this genre of VR may be of social and cultural significance it barely matches the promise of VR's advocates, whom we shall meet shortly. Outside of commercial arcades and theme parks, university or corporate research departments, immersive VR is hardly accessible to most of us.

We can contrast this situation with the ubiquity of the personal computer. It is possible to say that the PC is used for 'entertainment, interpersonal communication, self-expression, and access to information of many kinds', and therefore 'Computers are being used as media' (Mayer 1999: xiii). It is also clear that such uses have developed distinct genres, institutional frameworks (service providers, user groups, training in software use) and patterns of consumption (browsing, surfing, gaming, participation in online communities, networks, newsgroups). It is difficult to say the same for immersive VR. The importance of VR as a prototechnology must lie elsewhere. This, we will argue, is an implied challenge to settled historical practices of image making and receiving, and to the technological conditions which augment our visual and related aural and tactile experiences. However, for the same reasons that immersive VR is not a generally available experience, the basis or evidence for such claims needs careful inspection.

2.2 The virtual and visual culture

Cumbersome 'head sets' may have receded but Nintendo's new Wii computer game (**Fig 2.2**) finds its players whirling and lunging athletically in their domestic spaces with immediate and co-ordinated effects taking place on a simulated tennis court or baseball field. All these examples may be weaker ('timid' in R.U. Sirius's terms) than the immersions and simulations promised by the 'head mounted displays' or CAVE environments of Virtual Reality.

They nevertheless present us with visual (and sometimes haptic) experiences that attract the description of 'virtual'. Over the last twenty years or so, there have been some dramatic changes in the way that images are produced, in the ways we meet and access them, and in the kind of relationship we have to them. The fact that we are not immersed in virtual worlds while wearing old style head-sets and retro data-gloves does not mean that the virtual (as a quality or mode of experience) has not become an important characteristic of visual culture.

This retreat of 'VR' notwithstanding, it remains important because the virtual (as in virtual 'worlds', 'spaces', 'environments') abounds in contemporary media and visual culture. We need only think of the immersive quality of videogames that have a mobile first-person point

See Heim (1994: 65–77), who discusses the 'profound' difference between 'HMD' (headmounted display) VR and 'CAVE' VR in which the body is unencumbered by a headset and can move in a 'surround screen' projection

2.3 Sony Playstation 3: 'Virtual Tennis' video game (computer generated image, with 'photographic' backlighting and depth of field)

of view or use an avatar, both of which allow us to project into and move 'within' the game world; IMAX cinema that fills our field of vision; the vortex of special effects and simulated news studios of contemporary television with their deep space and lustrous surfaces (inhabited by real newscasters) (**Figs 2.4** and **2.5**); the programmed video displays, signs, and images of a shopping mall or metropolitan city centre which all but hide or dissolve (and are intended to dissolve) the physical architecture which supports them (**Fig 2.6**), the networks of webcams monitoring public spaces, online image-banks and virtual galleries etc.

VR as an object to think with

Full blown VR remains then, a paradigm for these more socially distributed virtual forms; it is an example of a discursive object – an object to think with (Crary 1993: 25–66). It is an apparatus which produces a kind of experience that raises questions about the nature of reality,

2.4 ITV virtual news studio, 2006

2.5 ITV Virtual set for election coverage, 2005

2.6 Chris Kitze, New York City, from
'The Electric Image' 2008. powerHouse Cultural
Entertainment, Inc.

perception, embodiment, representation and simulation. In the eighteenth century the
'camera obscura' was such an object, just as the cinematic projector was in the mid twentieth century (Metz 1975).

Today, we mainly think of the camera obscura as an instrumental technology, and a forerunner to the photographic camera, a kind of camera without film, which was used by
painters and draughtsmen as an aid to constructing images in perspective. However, as
Crary has argued, we think of the camera obscura predominantly in these terms because it
has mainly been art historians who have paid attention to it. He argues that throughout the
eighteenth century the main use of the camera obscura was not instrumental, it was not for
making images. More frequently, it was an object which was possessed by people (particularly philosophers and natural scientists) in order to stimulate philosophical reflection and
speculation on the nature of visual perception and knowledge. It provided a model for, and
raised questions about, the relationships of the external world, the eye and the brain (Crary
1993: 29). It was a practical model and a point of conversation and discourse, used in the
effort to understand the processes of perception and our experience of the visual world more
generally. It looks as if both apparatuses serve similar functions, some two and a half centuries apart, in the way that they promote intense speculation about vision, embodiment and
the nature of experience. This discursive status of VR is also fuelled by its representation in
other media: cinema, TV, novels, and comics, in what we might call 'the Matrix factor' rather
than frequent first-hand experience and use (Hayward 1993; Holmes 1997).

The 'virtual' is now a major trope or theme in media culture. The concept has close relationships with others, particularly **simulation** and **immersion**. And, at the same time, other
and older concepts associated with the study of images, including representation, illusion,
mimesis, even picture, copy, and fiction are drawn into the sphere of the virtual. In the

process, the relatively settled definitions of these older concepts become unstable. We can particularly note a lack of clarity now, in the relationship or difference between representation and reality, between representation and **simulation**, and between 'looking' or gazing and **immersion**.

2.3 The digital virtual

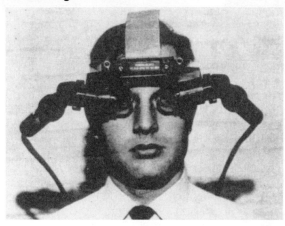

2.7 Sutherland's Head Mounted Display

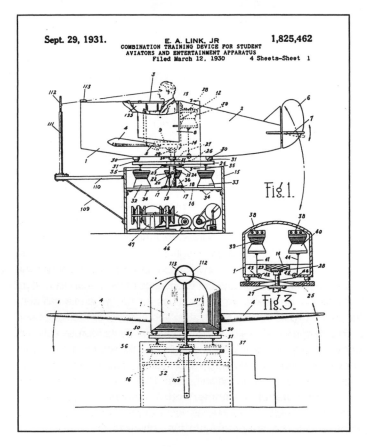

2.8 A Link Jnr Combination Training device

Effectively the digital 'virtual' enters into visual culture with early experimentation in human–computer interface design; the means by which a human interacts with the machine. Early forms of 'VR' offered to provide an interface that removes all signs of a mediating apparatus between the user and computer generated or stored image, information or content.

It was seen as promising to dispense with the residual forms of the computer screen, keyboard, and mouse (hang-overs from television, typewriters and mechanical controls). As the 1960s pioneer of graphic and immersive computer interfaces Ivan Sutherland put it, we should 'break the glass and go inside the machine' (quoted in Hillis 1996), or, in the words of the more recent developer of VR systems, Jaron Lanier: in VR 'the technology goes away' because 'we are inside it' (quoted in Penny 1995: 237).

Ivan Sutherland was a key figure in the operational and conceptual history of VR, and a pioneer of computer graphics and simulation technologies, who worked within militarily funded research programmes. In this context, Sutherland tackled the question of what symbolic form a computer's output might take or, as we would now put it, what would be the form of the human–computer interface? Given that a computer's internal activity is a vast and continuous stream of electrical impulses, Sutherland asked how the results of this invisible activity might be 'output' or externalised. What form – language or sign system – should be used to display the results of computation? Sutherland demonstrated that these impulses could be translated into an electron beam that was visible on a visual display unit – a screen. The origin of contemporary computer graphic interfaces, such as those used by the Apple operating systems or Microsoft Windows, is first seen in his now famous prototype 'Sketchpad'.

Sutherland also envisaged the possibility of going beyond graphic display to make the results of computation tangible. He conceived that if a computer reduced and processed any kind of information as a series of impulses, given the appropriate algorithms and programming, the physical movement of the human body – and even material resistance to that movement – could also be encoded as information which the computer could process.

From imitation to simulation

Sutherland's inspiration was the joystick of a Link Flight Trainer in which 'the feel' of a mocked-up aircraft's parts, moving as if against wind and air pressure, was mechanically fed back to the trainee pilot. In working upon the development of flight simulators, Sutherland drew upon several breakthroughs in technology and mathematics (see Woolley 1992: 42–48). Sutherland's work showed how human actions could become computable information that was then passed back to the human subject, via servo mechanisms and sensors, to then inform or control their further actions. This took a graphic and tactile form in a cybernetic 'feedback loop' between computer and human being (see **5.1**).

Where Sutherland's inspiration makes empirical references to a real aeroplane by a functionally quite unnecessary copying of its wings and tailplane, after Sutherland the flight simulator eventually becomes an enclosed environment, a 'black box', with no external, morphological reference to aeroplanes at all. Yet once such a 'black box' is entered the sensory conditions experienced in real flight can be more fully generated to include, for instance, the programmed vicissitudes of the weather, or engine failure, acting upon the virtual aircraft. Such simulators, without any external mimetic reference to real planes, can then simulate planes that have not yet been built or flights that have not yet been taken. Let alone there being no imitation of wings or tailfins as in the Link Trainer, there are no particular planes to imitate. Here we meet the distinction between imitation and simulation: the notion that in simulation (as against imitation or mimesis) the model now, in some senses, precedes the

See Bolter and Grusin (1999: 161–167) for a brief discussion of VR in these terms or as 'the end of mediation'

From the end of the Second World War, the US government began serious funding of research aimed at improving flight simulation and the computation of ballistic tables, the calculation of the trajectory of shells and missiles necessary to accurate targeting. The great cost of modern military aircraft, and the enormous demand for ballistic calculation, fuelled the development of electronic/digital computation. This was not the first time that the demand for calculation threatened to outstrip the human capacity to produce tabulated data fast enough and then drove the development of computers. See Mayer (1999: 506) on Babbage's Difference Engine (a version of which was completed in 1854), a mechanical computer which was partly a response to the demands for maritime navigation in the nineteenth century. Woolley (1992: 49) reports that in the 1940s the 60-second trajectory of a single missile would take twenty hours to work out by hand. One of the first electronic mainframe computers, the ENIAC (1944) took 30 seconds. For more on the military origins of cybernetics, and therefore contemporary computing, see Part 5 reality – a reversal of the expectation that 'models' are built (imitate) pre-existing realities. (See Woolley 1992: 42–44 for a more detailed discussion.)

This is a distinction that can be hard to grasp. For present purposes we will be content with the following recognition: what distinguishes simulation from imitation is that an artefact that is a simulation (rather than a copy) can be experienced as if it were real, even when no corresponding thing exists outside of the simulation itself. We are, after all, now familiar with such simulated reality effects from watching the seamless insertion of computer animations and special effects in contemporary blockbuster movies and television adverts. (For more on 'simulation', see **1.2.6**, and later in this section.)

'A head-mounted three dimensional display'

In a 1968 scientific paper of this name, Sutherland reported on an apparatus that would, in effect, generalise the flight simulator. Here, Sutherland made a conceptual move similar to that made by Alan Turing when he conceived of the computer as a 'universal' machine. Sutherland built an apparatus that included a rudimentary head-mounted display. The HMD's basic purpose was to 'present the user with a perspective image which changes as he moves' (Sutherland 1968: 757). The space that the wearer of the helmet 'saw', and which shifted as they moved their head, was generated mathematically. It was structured by a three-dimensional **Cartesian grid** with its three spatial co-ordinates imaged stereoscopically on the binocular TV screens held close before their eyes.

For Sutherland, this apparatus had no specific purpose such as flight simulation. It was a visual and tactile interface with a computer, an alternative to the early punch cards, or to a keyboard, light pen and screen. Instead of human–computer interfaces being holes punched in paper tape or two-dimensional manipulable graphics displayed on a VDU, this interface was, however rudimentary, spatial, visual, tactile and kinaesthetic. An important element in the history of Western visual culture makes an appearance in our brief account of Sutherland's work; a conception of space which is historically and culturally specific to Western art and science – in the form of a Cartesian grid which appeared to the wearer of Sutherland's head-mounted display.

2.4 Immersion: a history

As the inventor of the earliest HMD, Ivan Sutherland saw its purpose as continuous with a long tradition of pictorial representation. He intended his system to compute and present its user with 'a perspective image which changes as he moves' (Sutherland 1968: 757). The space that the wearer of his helmet 'saw', and which shifted as they moved their head, was the traditional three-dimensional Cartesian grid which perspective presupposes. However, in the 1990s, as the experience provided by developments in VR became more widely known to scholars of visual culture, the novelty and difference of the experience, rather than Sutherland's sense of continuity, was stressed. Again and again it is an experience of immersion, of being 'in' rather then before an image that is expressed. '(I)n virtual reality, the television swallows the viewer headfirst' (Dery 1993), or as Margaret Morse put it, 'VR is like passing through the movie screen to enter the fictional world of the "film"', and entering a virtual environment is like 'being able to walk through one's TV or computer, through the vanishing point or vortex and into a three-dimensional field of symbols' (1998: 181). In fact, concludes Morse, VR may herald the end, not the continuation of traditional forms as it 'may even be considered the last gasp of Renaissance space'. The VR user is a spectator whose 'station point is inside the projection of an image, transformed from a

The 'universal machine' is Turing's term for what we now call a 'computer': a machine with no dedicated purpose. Turing saw that a computer could be more than a numerical calculator; potentially it could be a machine open to a whole range of tasks – a machine that could become any other machine

For a discussion of the scopic regime of Cartesian perspectivalism in Western representation see Jay (1988)

monocular and stationary point of view into mobile agency in three-dimensional space' (1998: 182).

Jonathan Crary also sees a historical break occurring with VR, as a 'vast array of computer graphics techniques' brought about an 'implantation of fabricated visual "spaces"'. These produce images in a different way to film, photography, and television (they do not copy a reality before their lenses) and he sees them as bringing about a transformation in visual culture that is 'probably more profound than the break that separates medieval imagery from Renaissance perspective'. This break with tradition was 'relocating vision to a plane severed from a human observer' and supplanting 'most of the historically important functions of the human eye' (1993: 1–2). Yet another commentator, a scientist and literary scholar, considers that in VR we were witnessing a 'quantum leap into the technological construction of vision' (Hayles 1999: 38). And in the view of a sociologist,

> (o)f the myriad technological and cultural transformations taking place today, one has emerged to provide perhaps the most tangible opportunity for understanding the political and ethical dilemma of contemporary society. The arrival of virtual reality and virtual communities, both as metaphors for broader cultural processes and as the material contexts which are beginning to enframe the human body and human communication.
>
> (Holmes 1997: 1)

What underpins all these evaluations of VR's significance is a stress on the immersive experience that it provides and (in some) a shift of vision from its dependence upon the spatially positioned human eye to its production by machines and technologies.

Common to these attempts to describe the immersive experience of VR lies the key idea of passing through the surface of an image or picture to enter the very space that is depicted on the surface. Frequently, this is expressed as 'stepping through Alberti's window'. Leon Battista Alberti was an early fifteenth-century art theorist who is widely credited with formulating an influential method of constructing images using perspective. At the risk of considerable oversimplification, we may say that Alberti's method established the ground for a whole tradition of pictorial representation, the subsequent history of Western art, which eventually leads to the photographic camera. We can immediately glimpse here, why comparisons are drawn between the scale of change (in the nature of images) that took place in the Renaissance and at the end of the twentieth century.

2.4.1 Alberti's window

As Shields notes, 'the decoupling of space from place accomplished through the use of the telephone implies that "virtual life" has been coming for a long time', and, he continues, for longer than we thought because 'perspective', as used in images since the Renaissance, is a technology for producing the virtual (Shields 2003: 42). In *The Psychology of Perspective and Renaissance Art*, the experimental psychologist, Michael Kubovy examines the perspectival design of a fifteenth-century fresco painting and he describes the space created within the picture as 'virtual space' (Kubovy 1986: 140, fig 8.8).

He explains the manner in which the artist (Mantegna) contrived to make a viewer of his picture feel as if they were positioned beneath a stage on which the scene they are viewing (the picture itself) takes place (**Fig 2.9**). The view we are given is much like that we would have of a theatre stage from a position in the orchestra pit (see **Fig 2.10** and imagine being placed, virtually, in the orchestra pit, looking up at the stage). The result is that the feet of figures

Such references can be found in Morse (1998), Mirzoeff (1998), Heim (1993), Bolter and Grusin (1999), Marchessault (1996), Nunes (1997), Hillis (1996)

Della Pittura, first published 1435–6: a key, founding text on pictorial perspective. See Alberti (1966)

depicted as further away from the viewer are cut off from view. Only the feet of the figure standing right at the front edge of the stage are visible. To emphasise the point, Mantegna paints this foot as if it protrudes slightly over the edge of the stage. The intricate details of how this was achieved need not concern us here but they depend upon managing the relationship between the viewer's position in the physical space and the position of the depicted figures in a kind of virtual space.

2.10 An orchestra pit. To see what Mantegna has achieved in Fig 9, imagine the view of the stage available to a viewer in the orchestra pit. Image © Owen Franken/Corbis

2.9 St James the Great on his Way to Execution (fresco) (b/w photo) (detail), Mantegna, Andrea (1431–1506). Courtesy of Ovetari Chapel, Eremitani Church, Padua, Italy, Alinari/The Bridgeman Art Library

> This formulation of perspective in the fifteenth century was partly a recovery and systematisation of a less systematic and consistent form of pictorial perspective evident in the 'classical world' some 1,500 years before

At this time in the fifteenth century such relationships – such positions from which to view depicted 'worlds' – were being achieved by avant-garde artists who used one version or another of Alberti's method. As the diagram (**Fig 2.11**) shows, Alberti thought of a picture as a vertical plane (AB–CD) that was inserted at a certain point within a cone of vision centred on the spectator's eye. It is this plane that is referred to as 'Alberti's window'. The part of the cone between the spectator's given position and the picture plane or 'window' represents the physical distance between the viewer and the painting. It also gives the spectator a fixed viewpoint and an eye-level. The part of the cone extending between the picture plane and the figure (S) represents the space that will be depicted in the image – the space 'seen' through the window. Traditionally this is referred to as 'pictorial space'. It is this space that Kubovy describes as 'virtual'.

This is sensible, as Alberti's schema seeks to connect two kinds of space: that from which the image is viewed and that which is viewed within the image. The former is the actual space which the viewer physically inhabits while the latter seeks to be 'as good as' and continuous with that space. Artists of the time seemed to be acutely aware of this distinction between the actual and virtual spaces with which they worked. This is precisely what Mantegna is hinting at in making that foot protrude as if crossing from one space to another and, elsewhere, in

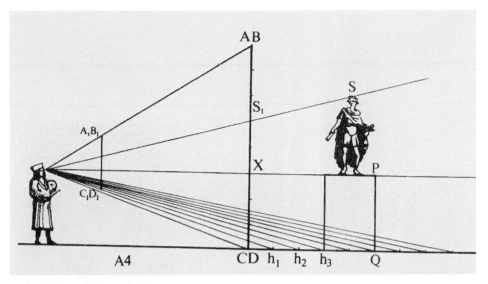

2.11 Diagram of Alberti's system. Beineke Library

depicting a head and an elbow protruding through a window as if bridging the physical and the virtual (**Fig 2.12**). From the early fifteenth century onwards, using versions of Alberti's method artists working in the developing Western pictorial tradition, articulated physical space and such 'virtual' space in all kinds of ways. In an early but effective example, in the Brancacci Chapel, the artist Masaccio connects the virtual spaces of his frescoes to the physical space of the chapel itself. He makes the image-space appear as an extension of the 'bricks and mortar' chapel (**Figs 2.15** and **2.16**).

2.12 Mantegna's 'window': detail from Andrea Mantegna, 'St Christopher's Body Being Dragged Away after His Beheading' (1451–5), Ovetari Chapel, Eremitani Church, Padua.

There have been a number of moments in the history of Western art when perspectival space and representation have been challenged or subverted. Clear examples are (1) the Baroque in the seventeenth century, where images are expressively distorted and the space of a picture is shot through with inconsistencies, (2) the exploration of multiple perspectives, and a deliberate play between surface and illusion, the visual and the tactile, in Cubism during the first two decades of the twentieth century, and (3) the rigorous denial of any illusion of three-dimensional depth in favour of the material, painted surface (an exploration of the 'plane' rather than the 'window') in much mid and late twentieth-century 'abstract' art. However, these styles and experiments are exceptions which prove the rule in that they self-consciously attempt to depart from the dominant perspectival tradition. See Jay (1988) for a discussion of this tradition

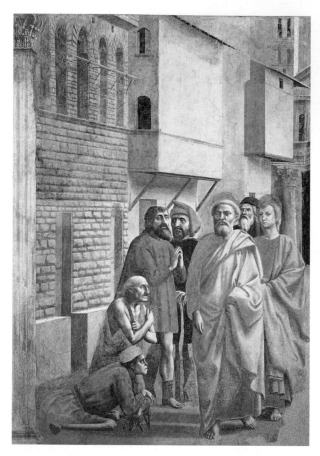

2.13 Fresco section: 'St Peter raises the cripples with his own shadow'.
Courtesy of Scala/Brancacci Chapel

2.14 Fresco section: 'The Baptism of the Neophytes'. Courtesy of
Scala/Brancacci Chapel

> We might even think of
> perspective as a kind of
> 'software'. The
> knowledge and
> technique once held in
> the painter's 'head' is
> now not only replicated
> in the optical lenses of
> mechanical cameras, it is
> replicated in the form of
> the algorithms and
> programming which
> guide digital virtual
> cameras in 3-D software
> applications

We are now in a position to think of pictorial perspective (Alberti's system) as a technology for constructing the space within an image and for managing the relationship of a viewer in physical space to the virtual space of the image.

2.4.2 Perspective as symbolic form

In the images by Masaccio and the accompanying diagrams we see that more than the extension of physical or actual space into virtual space is achieved. Masaccio's ability to do this also enables him to extend the representational possibilities of painting. By implying some degree of continuity or passage between the actual and the virtual he is able to build a temporal dimension into his static images.

He uses the depth axis of perspective to solve a narrative problem: how to depict the unfolding of an act over time, in a single, static scene which depicts space as a unified continuum. In 'The Baptism of the Neophytes' (**Fig 2.14**) we see one neophyte in the process of undressing, another waits, naked and shivering, and a third receives baptism. These three images can also be read as three moments in a continuous process. We can read this as an image of three men doing different things or as stages of one man's actions. Elsewhere in the 1420s such narrative conventions take place 'simultaneously' on the picture plane but in

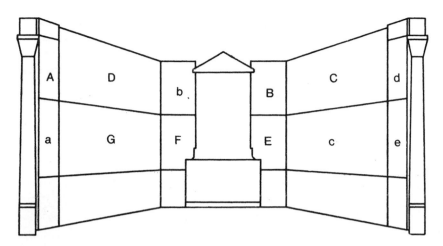

2.15 Diagram of fresco sections. Fig 2.13 above occupies position 'F' in diagram. Fig 2.14 occupies position 'E'.

See Erwin Panofsky, *Perspective as Symbolic Form*, New York: Zone Books (1997)(Published in English in 1991)

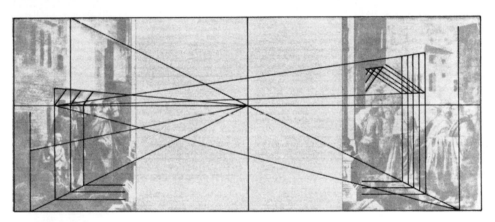

2.16 Diagram of perspective construction of Brancacci Chapel frescoes – vanishing points.

different spaces. Telling stories by painting a sequence of separate moments, rather like a series of frames in an animation or the panels in a comic book, was a common practice in the fifteenth century. Normally, however, each moment would be separately framed or placed on a separate part of the picture plane. In Masaccio's work, they become embodied and embedded in virtual space, and a sense of anticipation as well as physical experience is expressed.

In the first picture, 'St Peter raises the Cripples with his Own Shadow' (**Fig 2.13**) the perspective which integrates pictorial and architectural space also enables Masaccio to represent St Peter as walking past three beggars, and as he does the cripples are cured and rise up. They appear to be cured in the time that he passes by: the cripple furthest back in space, whom Peter has passed, now stands upright while the man he is about to draw level with is still unable to stand but will (so the narrative promises) imminently be cured. More than this, Peter looks ahead, out of the picture space and above the head of the spectator, whose viewpoint (also constructed by the image as we have seen) is beneath the saint. He appears to walk, curing the sick as he passes, and with a powerful implication that he is about to enter into (our) real space. Are we, it is therefore suggested, next in line?

We have seen how the pictorial or virtual space that perspective constructs is used to extend material, architectural space. We have seen how it can also be used to give expressive force and add meaning to what is represented. It also reaches out, as it were, to position the embodied viewer in real space, in relation to what is depicted or represented. In one case, that of 'St Peter raising the Cripples', the pictorial space effectively 'envelops' (if it does not yet 'immerse') the spectator as it is implied, visually, that the saint's progress through space (and time) continues toward the spectator.

Sixteenth-century architectural space and image space

2.17 The 'Sala delle Prospettive' (Hall of Perspective) designed by Baldassarre Peruzzi (1481–1536) c.1510 (photo)/Villa Farnesina, Rome, Italy/The Bridgeman Art Library

By the early sixteenth century we find a number of concentrated attempts to seamlessly fuse architecture and interior design with images as in the frescoes of the Sala delle Prospettive of 1516. Here, part of the architecture of the grand room is physical and part is painted illusion. An inhabitant of the room is afforded a (painted) view of the Roman landscape below them, glimpsed through massive painted pillars which appear to hold up the room's actual ceiling. As Grau (2003) observes, 'three dimensional architectural features with a real function combine with purely pictorial elements in a total effect where nothing interferes with the illusion or interrupts the effect' (p. 39).

Baroque

Later in the sixteenth century, fuelled by the zeal of the Counter-Reformation, the ideological fight-back of the Catholic Church against the Protestant reformation, the perspectival and illusionist skills of painters were harnessed in the heady, vertiginous style known as the Baroque. In this context we find ceiling paintings like Andrea Pozzo's in which the roof of the church of St Ignazio in Rome has been effectively dissolved as the viewer looks up to an image of heaven with bodies ascending in perspective. In each of these examples and the wider traditions and bodies of work to which they belong, 'Alberti's window' and its frame have begun to disappear. The frame which had been the very condition of constructing a perspectival image now ceases to mark the extent of an image 'arbitrarily' and instead, coincides with an aperture or opening in architectural space.

These Baroque paintings invite the spectator to enter a virtual space; they draw the viewer into a space that changes with their movements. They are 'navigable . . . "spaces of persuasion"' (Maravall, 1986: 74–75, quoted in Shields 2003).

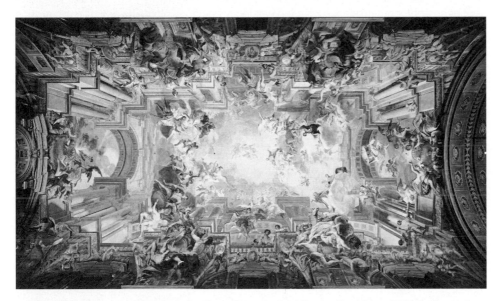

2.18 Fresco in a Baroque cathedral: Fra Andrea Pozzo, St Ignatius Being Received into Heaven (1691–4). Church of Sant Ignazio, Rome. Courtesy of Scala.

The Panorama

Using a method, developed at the end of the eighteenth century, for constructing accurate perspectives on curved surfaces, the nineteenth century saw the installation of 360-degree images in purpose built sites known as 'Panoramas'. Static and mobile touring Panoramas proliferated across Europe and North America as a form of spectacular entertainment. The painted illusions and virtual spaces of the fifteenth and sixteenth centuries now left the palaces and private villas of aristocrats and entered the public sphere as an early kind of mass entertainment. The building, marketing and operating of Panoramas became a lucrative industry. The spectator was positioned in the centre of the Panorama, surrounded completely by a seamless, illusionistic painting of a landscape, an historical event, or battle. There is a clear relationship between the subjects chosen for Panoramas and an age of 'empire', a taste for the exotic, the 'other', and the picturesque and the sublime.

2.19 Jeff Wall 'Restoration', 1993. (Showing the restoration of the 'Bourbaki' Panorama of 1881, painted in Lucerne by Edouard Castres). Courtesy of Kunst Museum, Lucerne

Either free to move and turn themselves or moved by a rotating mechanical floor, the spectator's gaze was mobile. Their central viewing position in a gallery ensured that they were kept at an appropriate distance from the painted scene (to reinforce its optical realism). This gallery also ensured that the upper and lower limits of the circular image could not be seen, as if hidden from view by the floor and ceiling of the 'room' from which they looked (an effect anticipated in Mantegna's fresco above, **Fig 2.9**). The image was luminous being lit by an invisible source from above. As they developed throughout the nineteenth century the visual illusion was enhanced as appropriate with sound and lighting effects, artificial wind, and smoke or 'mist'. In entering the Panorama, the paying spectator entered an artificial world, where all distracting or disruptive 'real world' cues were removed, to take up a viewing position in the dark and gaze at a luminous, moving and enveloping scene. 'The panorama installs the observer *in* the picture' (Grau 2003: 57). The Panorama was an industrial, entertainment apparatus that immersed the viewer within the image.

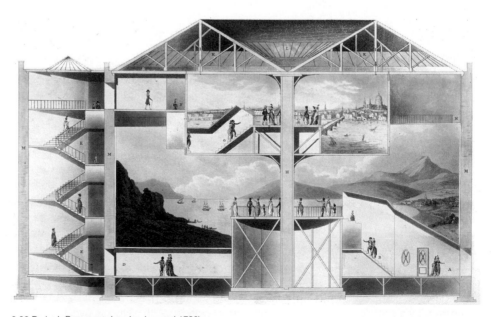

2.20 Barker's Panorama, London (opened 1793).

The 'peep show', the stereoscope, and the head mounted display

The utilisation of perspective in fresco cycles, in illusionistic interior design, vast Baroque ceiling paintings, and the design of the fully developed Panorama indicate that the immersive virtual realities of the late twentieth and early twenty-first centuries are part of a continuum of technological development, rather than an absolute and revolutionary break with earlier image forms.

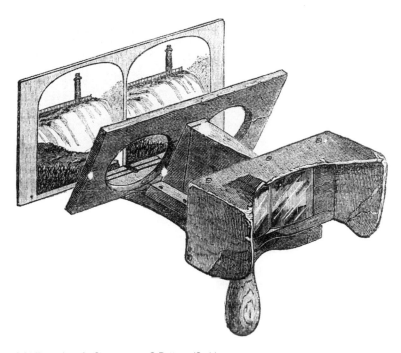

2.21 Illustration of a Stereoscope. © Bettman/Corbis

If the Panorama is a forerunner of immersive image environments we should also note a parallel history of devices; the peep show and the stereoscope. The peep show, small boxes held to the eyes which contained perspectival images lit from above (see Grau 2003: 51–52) pre-dates the Panorama. Others, contemporary with the large-scale Panorama, contrived to have a moving image scroll past the viewer's eyes. In the early nineteenth century one of the most popular ways of viewing the new 'photographs' was the stereoscope, 'an early nineteenth-century technology of seeing that would appear to parallel closely the VR experience' (Batchen 1998: 276). Contemporary responses to the stereoscope's image testify to the sense of disembodiment that it created: '[I] leave my outward frame in the arm-chair at my table, while in spirit I am looking down upon Jerusalem from the Mount of Olives' (Holmes 1859, quoted in Batchen 1998: 275–276). The three-dimensionalisation of photography which the stereoscope achieved is only one way in which, at the beginning of the nineteenth century, a number of boundaries between what was real and what was represented began to blur: 'the very dissolution which some want to claim is peculiar to a newly emergent and postmodern VR' (p. 276).

Importantly, these small devices did not enclose the body and hide the limits of the surrounding images by architectural design but by placing binocular images very close to the viewer's eyes. This is the arrangement that will be utilised, in the mid-twentieth century, in the Sutherland's 'head-mounted display' (**Fig 2.7**).

2.5 Perspective, camera, software

The age of the Panorama came to an end in the early twentieth century, principally because it was unable to compete with the spectacle of the new cinema. It was of course one among several antecedents for the cinema and has recently seen a revival in the immersive cinematic form of the IMAX (**Fig 2.26**) and techniques such as spherical projection where projected images fill or exceed the field of human vision. The Panorama's demise was possibly hastened by a challenge to another of its functions: the new popular magazines of the time, illustrated with photographs which served more rapidly than the Panorama to satisfy the appetite of a 'tourist gaze' for images of the exotic and of empire.

Between these handcrafted and mechanical immersive spaces and those of digital virtual reality and 'cyberspace', set apart as they are by centuries, lie the media of photography and film, about which we should say a little. The photographic camera was heir to Renaissance perspectival space and, via the establishment of 'photo-realism', it is the vehicle through which perspective and Cartesian space become encoded into computer software and the computer's 'virtual camera'.

The camera obscura, a filmless camera or room ('camera' means room in Italian), was, amongst other things, the photographic camera's forerunner and 'the very instrument for the mechanical production of monocular perspective' (Neale 1985: 20). Eventually, photography itself became the 'means by which it [a perspectival image] could be mechanically and chemically fixed, printed, marked and inscribed' (ibid.). Camera lenses are designed and engineered to produce perspectival vision, and were intended to do so from the very invention of photography. One of photography's pioneers, Nicephore Niepce, explicitly stated his aim as being to discover an 'agent' that would durably imprint the images of perspectival representation. This would no longer be a system of drawing and painting (à la Alberti), but a machine – the photographic camera.

With the rapid spread of photography in the first decades after its invention it was possible to conclude, as 'Strong as the mathematical convention of perspective had become in picture making before the pervasion of photography, that event definitely clamped it on our vision and our beliefs' (Ivins 1964: 108, cited in Neale 1985). In short, after several hundreds of years of perspective as a pictorial technology, the photographic camera industrialised perspective.

2.6 Virtual images/Images of the virtual

2.6.1 The virtual and the real

The virtual as a philosophical concept is discussed in **5.4.2**, where it is argued that it is not the opposite of the real but a kind of reality itself. We should not oppose the virtual – thinking of it as some kind of illusory world – to reality. Indeed, if we think about what we mean by the virtual when we use the term in everyday language this is clear. For instance, in response to the question 'Have you finished your essay' you might reply, 'Yes, virtually' meaning that for all intents and purposes you have finished, you are 'as good as' finished. Maybe you still have to check the spelling, add a short introduction and bibliography, and print it out. Otherwise the essay exists. It 'virtually' exists, the substantial work is done, and when you have completed these final tasks and it has become a sheaf of papers bearing printed words which successfully communicate your research and thought, it will 'actually' exist. You will hand it to your tutor.

The virtual has a long history too. In the fifteenth century a debate arose between Catholics and Protestants about what happened when people took Holy Communion in the Christian church. In partaking of bread and wine, did they actually consume Christ's flesh and blood or do so 'virtually' or symbolically and by way of their belief? This was an argument over which people literally lost their heads (Shields 2003: 5–6).

We learn something about the virtual from these, among many other examples. We learn that the 'virtual' isn't the same as an 'illusion'. The not quite finished essay wasn't an illusion, it wasn't unreal – it was just not complete, in the sense that it was not yet in its finished material form. Neither was the virtual 'taking of Christ's body' meant to signify an 'illusion'. Those who dissented from the belief that they were actually taking Christ's body by mouth, and that to think otherwise was unnecessary, did not intend, on the other hand, to suggest that it was a mere trick or sleight of hand. Rather, they wanted to recognise that they did not think that they were actually eating Christ's body but, in good faith, they were virtually and symbolically doing so and their action was 'real' in that sense.

Looking back on these examples, we can notice that not only is the 'virtual' not being taken as an 'illusion', neither is it being directly opposed to the 'real'. Rather, what is suggested by these examples is that the 'virtual' is different from the 'actual' but both are real in different ways.

It seems also to be the case, maybe increasingly, that the virtually real and the actually real are not completely distinct or separate worlds; they overlap or coexist and in technologically developed societies we move between them. Indeed, one theorist of virtual reality, N. Katherine Hayles, defines 'virtuality' as it exists pervasively in digital culture, as the 'perception that material objects are interpenetrated by information patterns' (1999: 13). As we move around our physical (literally our 'concrete' environments) we encounter and engage with the products of computed information at every turn. We can take the example of the ATM (Automatic Telling Machine), otherwise referred to in English as a 'cash dispenser' or in slang as a 'hole in the wall' (but a hole leading where we might ask?). This is a useful example because while there is a physical and actual reality to the ATM, through it we also enter the world of virtual banking and it is clear that we cannot easily call one real and the other illusory. At the ATM we simultaneously inhabit the actually real and the virtually real. The ATM's keyboard and screen, housed in stainless steel and mortared into the brick wall of a bank or supermarket, together with the pavement we stand on as we press the keys, are all actually and materially real. The access these technologies give us to computer servers and workstations in remote buildings, and the cable, wireless, and satellites that we connect to, are also real but the networks they comprise give rise to an experience of the virtual. The world of online banking and our 'virtual' cash which we access are also quite real. If we find that the online (virtual) banking system tells us that our account is empty then we are really without money. Maybe we cannot pay the rent or buy food. In this sense, being virtual is not 'being unreal', it is a state produced by actual and material technologies; it can engage our physical senses as they do, and it can have real world consequences that are definitely not illusory, such as being homeless or hungry.

But, the virtual reality or world which the ATM connects us to (which we may feel we 'enter') is a different reality from that of the actual ATM itself. It is not concretely present, we cannot grasp it physically. It is where our real (but virtual) money is (or just as importantly, isn't). We are at the ATM because we want to actualise that money, we want to exchange it for printed pieces of paper with authentic legitimating watermarks; for euros, pound notes or dollar bills. Until we do this the 'virtual reality' which our money has (it is not false or illusory, we know that we banked it!) has a kind of existence which, as Rob Shields has put it, is not typical of the 'phenomenologically present-at hand' but more like 'the non existent and non-present' (Shields: http://virtualsociety.sbs.ox.ac.uk/text/events/pvshields.htm undated). It is a latent world that can be called up with the 'speed of electrons' (2003: 22) and shut down again with the flick of a switch, just as online conversations, meetings, tours, walkthroughs, persistent worlds or the websites we browse can be.

In this sense, before they are actualised by printing, projection, or emission, digitally produced and stored images are themselves virtual. This is because they do not have, in their latent state, the obvious physical and material reality of analogue images. An analogue image is a transcription of one set of physical qualities (belonging to the object represented) into another set, those of the image or artifact (see **1.2.1**). A digital image resides in a computer file, it is a code or a set of information, a kind of latent image awaiting visibility and material form when it is loaded into appropriate software and projected or printed. We should be careful about this distinction as digital images are, of course, the products of hardware and must gain a material form of some kind (even if only light emitted from a screen) to become visible. In this contrast between the analogue and the digital we may be noting no more than a recent stage in the historical abstraction and relative dematerialisation of the substance on which an image is registered: a process that spans from the obdurate materiality of signs and images inscribed on stone tablets, animal skin, canvas or wood, paper, celluloid, or electro magnetic tape. There are some important implications here that concern the stability, longevity, and the ability to archive and then access, images. (See, for example, Besser, Feb 2001, 'Longevity of Electronic Art', http://www.gseis.ucla./~howard/Papers/elect-art-longevity.html.)

However, as we have seen, and this is what will mainly concern us here, images have long been involved in producing virtual spaces and environments. These have been understood as particular kinds of visual *representations*, a fact that immediately returns us to the discussion of *simulation* (in **1.2.6**) to which representations are contrasted. We have seen that pictorial perspective with its 500-year history is itself a technology of the virtual. It has been the dominant 'scopic regime' (Jay 1988) of visual representation in the Western tradition. We have also seen that within that tradition there have been a series of genres in which the aim has been to immerse the spectator 'as if' they were within the space of the image. This has taken two major forms. One is what we might call environmental and seen in the ambitious architectural schemes exemplified by Baroque ceiling paintings and the Panorama. The other is the history of devices from the peep show to the stereoscope which place images (in the latter case in a binocular manner) close to the human eye. Both histories feed into the image technologies of our digital visual culture.

2.6.2 Virtual, simulation, representation

In our 'new media' or digital culture, the virtual has come to equal the 'simulated' (Shields 2003: 46). The terms have become (virtually) synonymous. Virtual realities and virtual environments are produced by simulation technologies, principally: computer graphics software and telecommunications networks. Shared spaces are simulated in which we can interact with simulated 3-D objects and our view of such spaces and places changes in response to our simulated (but not physically actual) viewpoint. We are all now more or less familiar, through report or first-hand experience, with the following:

- computer-aided design and the simulation of objects and events that do not actually exist;

- software techniques such as 'ray tracing' and 'texture mapping' which digitally generate the visual forms and surfaces of invented objects 'as if' they conformed to the physical laws of optics;

- the production, animation and seamless fusion of still and moving photo-realistic images;

- the equipping of robot machines with the ability to see;

- the hybrid collection of technologies that produce the illusion of inhabiting and moving within virtual places;

- the technologies of telepresence that allow the body to act, through vision and touch, on remote objects;

- new forms of medical and scientific imaging (such as magnetic resonance imaging) that allow the interior spaces of the human body to be non-invasively seen and imaged;

- synoptic images of the Earth and space in which a range of data gathered by satellites is translated into photographic form.

In **1.2.6**, we introduced 'simulation' as one of the key characteristics of new media and sought a definition of the term. A number of points were made which rescued 'simulation' and 'simulacra' from the assumption that they are 'illusions' or 'false images' (much as we did above for the 'virtual'). We called attention to the fact that a simulation is itself an existing and material thing, a kind of object in the world (the 'virtual reality' apparatuses that we discussed above are a prime example). In short, whatever is simulated, the simulations are real things in themselves. Second, we pointed out that simulations do not necessarily imitate things, a simulation may model a process or a system (the stock market or climate change) rather than represent them with any kind of optical realism. In the special case of computer games (or our 'flight trainer' example, see **2.3**) what is simulated may not correspond to any actually existing thing beyond the simulation itself. We concluded, 'simulations are things rather then representations of things' and they can add new things to the world, as any process of production does, rather than represent (however mediated) existing things. In short, one of the ways of defining 'simulation' was to contrast it with 'representation'.

2.6.3 Representation, media studies, visual culture

Now, 'representation' is a key idea in traditional media studies where it points to the role of ideology, belief, and selective perception in the act of communicating ideas about and experiences of the 'real' world (in photography, television, film and cinema, advertisements etc.). It also draws our attention to the role of language, and in the realm of visual representation, the signs and codes that we necessarily employ in making images. In using the concept 'representation' we stress the way that the words or visual signs we use (the signifying processes) necessarily mediate or change the objects in the world that we communicate about. In its strongest form we go so far as to argue that the world only has meaning for us because of the concepts that we employ to make it meaningful. Changes in ways of visually representing the world, and the relationship of the resulting images to historically changing 'ways of seeing' are also central to the study of visual culture. Images both lead us to 'see' the world in certain ways and are themselves shaped by our ideas and a culture's priorities and interests. The technologies available to a culture also play a role in these processes. Further, the nature of an image or a visual representation can be said to constitute a viewer or spectator, largely by the way they give us a position and an identity from which to view the world (although, of course, we may reject the identities that a particular kind of image encourages us to adopt). In these and other ways, 'representation' has long been a very important concept in the study of art and media.

In **1.2.6**, we identified three broad ways in which simulation is used in the analysis of new media. In the version which we call 'Postmodernist' (see pages 38–41) we noted that many commentators on contemporary cultural change tend to agree that during the last decades of the twentieth century there has been a shift, in visual culture, from 'representation' to 'simulation'. Given the centrality, that we just noted, of the concept of 'representation' in the study of art and media this should be a change of some moment. Yet, surprisingly, there is simultaneously 'no agreement that simulation does in fact differ from representation or imitation'. By narrowing our definition of simulation, particularly by using the meaning it has in the study of computer simulations and computer games studies (definitions 2 and 3, pages 41–43) , some clarity was introduced into this otherwise confusing situation. In the study of computer simulations, a simulation is taken to be a 'modelling of a dynamic system'. This model is a structured environment, a universe with its own rules and properties with which the user or player interacts. It is not confined to imitating existing worlds or processes, although it may also do that in part. Here then, we have a kind of simulation (temporal, algorithmic, not necessarily mimetic, and interactive) that is clearly different from any visual representation that we can think of.

However, outside of these important cases, the distinction between simulation and representation remains unclear. Once we return to the kinds of virtuality and simulation that digital and networked image technologies produce, to the wider changes in visual culture which our 'postmodern' theorists celebrate or regret, confusion again reigns. If we think about our wider 'digital' visual culture the distinctions between representation and simulation that make sense in the study of computer games do not really hold for the following reasons.

Not only simulations are real

We saw above that it is important to see that simulations are not adequately thought of as 'illusions' both because they have their own reality (as hardware, as machines) and because they may model real processes. But while images that 'represent' in a traditional sense may not offer us an interactive engagement with virtual worlds in this way, they too are real things. They are also artefacts and are composed of material stuff (just as the things they represent usually are) – paint (coloured mud), ink (ground up shells), silver salts (mined) and spread on celluloid strips in factories, electro-magnetic particles, electronic pulses in hardwired circuits etc. However 'realistically' such images may represent or depict things they also have their own physical reality. In this sense, while it may be very important to insist on the materiality of simulations this is not an adequate basis to distinguish them from representations. We cannot simply say that a simulation is the product of a simulating machine while a representation is only a mental process or the product of ideas. It simply is not true. Both involve work on materials and utilise tools and technologies, and both are artefacts.

Mimesis

Further, defining simulation by contrasting it to representation depends upon associating representation with imitation. This involves resurrecting one particular, if persistent, theory of representation – that of 'mimesis'. In this ancient theory of representation, meaning is thought to lie in real things themselves and hence the work of representation is to faithfully copy the appearance of that thing. In this theory (and practice) of representation, the aim is to convey meaning rather in the way that a mirror reflects reality. It was a founding move of media studies to subject this ancient (and in many ways 'commonsense') 'reflective' approach to representation to a thorough going critique (see Hall 1997). However, with the more recent rise in practices and theories of simulation this old-fashioned concept of representation has been newly foregrounded. This then enables the contrast: 'simulation' produces and constructs while 'representation' mimics something pre-existing. A simulation 'models' or 'constructs' dynamic and systematic worlds while representations (passively) 'copy' things that pre-date them. The problem with this contrast is the reduction of the force of the concept of representation to 'mimesis'.

The success of a mimetic representation must lie in its resemblance to the thing represented. However, even the most optically 'realistic' of images are very different things from the objects they represent or depict. For example, the most realistic and 'straightest' (least manipulated) photograph differs from what it represents in obvious ways as a rectangular, fragile, silent, 2-D object that represents a spatially infinite, complex, multi-dimensional, noisy 3-D world. In the case of film or video, sound and movement may be added, but the distance of the image from what it represents is still great. An image of a horse resembles an image of a boat more than either image resembles real horses or boats. (For a detailed critique of imitation as a theory of representation see Goodman 1976: 3–40.)

The lack of an original

One definition of a simulation (as we use it above, in **2.3** 'The digital virtual') is that it is an artefact that can be experienced as if it were real, even when no corresponding thing exists outside of the simulation itself (see page 114). In such a case the simulation cannot be a copy of an original. In an early study of the impact of electronic reproduction on social life, written while digital media were in their infancy (Poster 1990), the production and reproduction of musical performances was used to explain the nature of simulation. It was becoming common for recordings of rock music to be produced from many 'tracks' recorded separately, at different times and even in different places. These tracks were then assembled, changed, and enhanced by a recording engineer into a master tape. Part of the engineer's work would be to position or reposition the 'instruments' (themselves often synthetic) in space, in the stereophonic 'soundfield'. As Poster observes, in such cases, 'The performance that the consumer hears when the recording is played is not a copy of an original but a simulacrum, a copy that has no original' (1990: 9). In other cases, where an original classical musical performance was recorded, 'audiophiles' invested immense effort and money in extracting the most musical information and quality from the resulting vinyl records and tapes using sophisticated high fidelity equipment. In some cases even the size and insulation qualities of the room in which the equipment was used were specially designed. In these cases it was quite possible that the audiophile heard more than someone present at the original performance. He notes:

> While the aim of choruses, for example, is to blend voices into unified waves of sound, the audiophile, aided by expensive stereo gear that resolves complex sounds into their discrete parts, claims to discern individual voices within the ensemble, hearing through electronic mediation, more 'information' than was audible to a listener at the original performance.
>
> (1990: 10).

In this latter case, we may not have a simulacrum in quite the same way as synthetic rock concerts (performances that exist 'only in their reproduction', (p. 9), but it is difficult to decide whether we have simulated elements (a partial simulacra) or a high degree of mediation (a quality of representations).

We should also recognise that there is a large class of visual representations for which nothing corresponding exists (depending upon belief) outside of the representational artefact itself – take the baroque ceiling (Fig 18) which represents a certain vision of 'heaven' as an example. Neither are all pictures 'representations of . . .' in the sense of having as their purpose the re-presentation or mimicking of empirically existing worlds. Consider for example John Martin's 1820 painting of 'Macbeth'; a stunning but imaginary image of fictional characters in a constructed landscape. This image does not represent 'Macbeth' (how could we know if it did?). But we might (with Nelson Goodman) call it a 'Macbeth-picture', a class of images (1976: 21-26) with a theme or subject which we group together as we may sort furniture into tables here and chairs there.

2.22 John Martin (1789–1854), 'Macbeth' © National Gallery of Scotland, Edinburgh, Scotland/The Bridgeman Art Library

Here then, the whole issue begins to hinge on more subtle distinctions than those existing between simulation and representation. It begins to involve us in constructions, engineerings, mediations, fictions, visions and imaginings that cross the two terms. Even 'illusion' (of a performance that didn't take place or of heaven), the very term we warned against earlier, returns again. Maybe what we gain from this discussion is that 'simulation' can only really be contrasted with representation when (a) the simulation models a world in time or (b) one that does not exist outside of itself, and when the representation is of the kind that aims to *refer*, through mimesis, to real things beyond itself. This is not an absolute distinction between the two activities but one between certain of the things we do with them.

2.6.4 From representation to simulation (and back again)

If we want to go further, being dissatisfied with a distinction that has returned us to thinking about the different uses or kinds of simulation and representation that we can find, a better approach might be to return to the history we traced in **2.4**. This was, after all, a history of a certain kind of visual representation which we can now see as antecedent to contemporary simulation and virtualising technologies. In doing this, we may glimpse how representations can tip into simulations and the degree to which simulations may sometimes depend upon representations.

A genre of painting known as 'trompe l'oeil' (tricking the eye) will help us do this. This genre of images strove hard to close the gap between the picture and the thing depicted. To do this, the 'trompe l'oeil' artist would choose subjects which provided the best conditions for success – flat or almost flat, real world displays with framed or distinct edges, for example (see **Fig 2.23**) which in that respect at least did not differ greatly from the bounded, two-dimensional nature of the painting itself. Here, literally as well as figuratively, there was a narrow space between the image and its referent in which to counterfeit the information presented to the eye. Frequently, 'trompe l'oeil' artists painted their images in places where we might expect the real thing to be, a door in a wall for example, or a key hanging on a hook.

2.23 'Quod Libet', Edward Collier (1701). Victoria and Albert Museum, London

Part of the success of a trompe l'oeil image, to trick the eye into momentarily believing that the depiction was the reality, was also to trigger our haptic sense – to imagine that we might almost feel the surface texture or the material quality – the brittleness or suppleness – of the objects depicted. Part of the pleasure of looking at trompe l'oeil images lay precisely in knowing that they were not 'real' but seemed so. The viewer oscillates, as it were, between awareness of the image itself and of the means by which it was produced.

Unlike perhaps the majority of images, including many photographs, movies, TV, and computer-generated images, which tend to function as 'windows on the world' and which dissolve the surfaces which carry them so that we look through the surface or screen to the 'thing itself', these trompe l'oeil images have a different representational tactic. Rather than framing and then opening onto the real; they supplant the real, they claim to take its place. They sit on its surface and pretend to be part of it.

If we insist on thinking about these images as 'signs' or as language-like collections of signs which represent things, then we would have to say that as representations, they are at the end of the spectrum where maximum resemblance is sought between the sign and the object signified. They are low on symbolic abstraction. In this sense the room for 're-presentation' and 'mediation' (in the media studies sense of importing meanings into things) is low. Their real success seems to lie in the attempt to duplicate the conditions in which we would have looked at the objects they represent (as well as their surfaces and appearance). In this way, trompe l'oeil images constitute a kind of degree zero of 'style', of evident artifice. For this reason the artists who made them were, as were those who painted Panoramas, given low status in the hierarchy of artistic production and there was doubt as to whether they would be allowed to become members of art Academies (Grau 2003: 68).

While these trompe l'oeil images do not themselves offer or afford the viewer immersion in the virtual picture space (as we noted, they sit on material reality's surface), they share with, and point strongly toward, the strategies of immersion employed by the producers of immersive architectural schemes, Baroque ceilings, and Panoramas. These are strategies to *remove or disguise the overt conditions of visual or pictorial representation*, the frame and the surface, and the point of difference – the edge – between the actual (the architecture, the Panorama's rotunda) and the virtual (the painted vistas seamlessly and credibly placed within these buildings' apertures). To put this another way, they carefully articulate the relationship and movement between the actual and the virtual. This is achieved as we move progressively from the early Renaissance fresco cycles which employed the new perspective technology, or the buildings that were conceived and designed from the outset to combine actual and virtual space, through the technique which underpins the Panorama (the rendering of continuous perspectival images on a 360 degree surface) and the hiding of the edges of the images by the design of the viewing station and the 'faux terrain', to the moving of the image and the reinforcement of the visual experience by light, wind and sound.

On this basis another way of understanding a simulation emerges. It is the digital forms of immersive images (our virtual realities and environments) which we now understand as simulations. It may be the complexity (and 'black-boxed' invisibility) of the visual and informational technologies employed, on the one hand; at times the interactive relationship with the image, at others the sheer optical verisimilitude of effect, that push us to want to distinguish these virtual spaces from mere 'representations'. Yet, in a final twist, where visual or image culture is concerned (if not game culture), even when no corresponding reality exists for what is simulated, a degree of optical realism is required, the resources for which are still now found in photo-realist representations. As we have seen, 'realistic representations' are not realistic simply because they are 'like' what they represent. Mimesis is not an adequate theory of representation. They must employ visual codes (of which photo-realism is one) that we accept as the signs of the real.

'Faux terrain' refers to the way the seam or edge between architectural and painted space in Renaissance and Baroque 'spaces of illusion', and later in Panoramas, was disguised or hidden by a transitional area of three-dimensional 'props' such as faked grass, earth, bushes, fences etc.

2.7 Digital cinema

Questions of simulation and photo-realism are key to understanding recent developments in popular cinema. Computer-generated imagery (CGI), from its early experimental and explicit uses in special effects in films such as *Tron* in 1982 or Pixar's short animated films (e.g. *Luxo Jr.* 1986) to blockbusters such as *Terminator 2: Judgement Day*, *Jurassic Park* and *Toy Story* in the mid-1990s, is now a feature of many mainstream popular films, is usually key to big budget blockbusters, and has virtually elimated hand-drawn and cel animation in animated feature films. While it is widely used in postproduction to generate hard-to-shoot backgrounds or lighting effects, it is in its explicit application as spectacular special effects that it has generated intense excitement, anxiety, and popular and critical debate.

In this section we will consider the popularisation of **CGI** (computer-generated imagery), and its use in special effects and computer animation. These forms will be considered, on the one hand, as materially and historically situated technologies and media, and on the other as informing a **technological imaginary** in which the impact of digital technology on cinema is presented as either symptomatic of, or a causal factor in, the 'virtualisation' of the modern world. We will consider the implications of CGI's shifting of animation from the margins of cinematic culture back to its centre, and ask what happens to the audiences of digital cinema.

Cinema and VR

> [Virtual reality] is frequently seen as part of a teleology of the cinema – a progressive technological fulfilment of the cinema's illusionistic power.
>
> (Lister 1995: 15)

Popular ideas about, and expectations of, the potential of VR are inseparable from the cinema as an aesthetic form. While the ubiquity and simultaneity of broadcast television, or the communication 'spaces' of the telephone or Internet are in many ways more significant to the development of VR technologies and applications, it is the clarity and seduction of cinema's visual imagery and the 'immersion' of its viewers against which emerging (and potential) VR experiences are measured. As we will see, cinema is a key factor in VR's 'remediations'.

Conversely, cinema has developed and disseminated images, ideas and dreams of VR and the virtual particularly in recent science fiction films. Moreover, the design of certain VR systems draws heavily on cinematic imagery, forms, and conventions. And, significantly, if we take the term 'cinema' to mean a broad field of moving image technologies and cultures rather than the narrow industrial and ideological establishment of the dramatic, live action, feature film, then the hugely popular medium of the videogame must be seen as central to developments in, and ideas about, digital cinema. The videogame has been integral to the development of a technological imaginary of cyberspace and VR (see Parts 4 and 5) and has opened up virtual worlds, artificial intelligences and computer-generated characters for popular play and consumption.

To the distinction between immersive and metaphorical VR we could here add one more, what Ellen Strain calls 'virtual VR' (Strain 1999: 10). On one level this is simply the representation of speculative forms of VR and cyberspace in science fiction films such as *Lawnmower Man* (1992), *Strange Days* (1995), *Johnny Mnemonic* (1995) (as well as subsequent films including David Cronenberg's *eXistenZ* 1999). On another level Strain refers to the phenomenon of fictional and speculative images of VR becoming blurred with actual existing forms and uses of VR technologies. Given the point made in **2.6**, that VR is in fact a rather exclusive experience and not a mass medium, it is not surprising that films have projected fantasies of digital worlds that have generated a misleading sense of the current state, or putative soon-to-be-realised future, of VR.

See special issues of *Screen* 40.2 (Summer 1998), and *Convergence* 5.2 (1999)

See **1.2.5**, **1.2.6**, **2.1**, **2.6**, **5.4.2** for more considered discussion of 'the virtual'

1.2.5 Virtual

2.1–2.6

5.4.2 Cybernetics and the virtual

Key text: Philip Hayward, 'Situating cyberspace: the popularisation of virtual reality', in Philip Hayward and Tana Wollen (eds) *Future Visions: new technologies of the screen*, London: BFI, pp. 180–204. See Part 4 for further discussion of the relationships between popular culture and the development of computer media

> Both VR researchers and cultural theorists have drawn heavily on popular science fiction literature and film as points of reference and as resources for speculation and possibility. Philip Hayward lists the subcultural and popular cultural points of reference of the early VR enthusiasts: to science fiction he adds New Age mysticism, psychedelia and rock culture. This promotion of the possibilities of VR through popular cultural discourses not only shapes public expectations but may even affect VR research itself:
>
> > These discourses are significant because they have shaped both consumer desire and the perceptions and agenda of the medium's developers. In a particularly ironic twist . . . they have created a simulacrum of the medium in advance (against which its products will be compared).
> >
> > (Hayward 1993: 182)
>
> It is important to note that this is not necessarily naive; there are instances where this is a particular strategy: reading (science) fictions as one would read any other document or source of data. (See David Tomas, 'The technophiliac body: on technicity in William Gibson's cyborg culture', in David Bell and Barbara M. Kennedy (eds) *The Cybercultures Reader*, London: Routledge, 2000, pp. 175–189.) Thomas there reads William Gibson's fictional worlds as straight sociological data, from which informative results are gathered (see **5.1**).

2.7.1 Virtual realism

There is great excitement about the future possibilities of immersive or interactive entertainment, but also fear that digital technologies are leading film into a descending spiral of spectacular superficiality. Such fears are evident in both popular film criticism and academic, **postmodernist** discourses. They are evident in the critique and conceptualisation of digital images specifically – images which threaten our understanding of the world as they present themselves with the look of photography, an illusion of photography's 'indexicality'. They seem to speak to us of the real world but are synthetic and fabricated. This troubled relationship between images and the world they claim to represent is also applied more generally to Western culture as a whole, now characterised, it is argued, by a waning of 'meaning', becoming (and the metaphors are telling) simulated and flattened, screen-like.

Film theory and media studies are centrally concerned with the relationship between popular representations and the real world. The term '**realism**' is therefore a useful one in this context, not least because it highlights the argument that any representation, however technologically advanced, is a cultural construction and not the 'real' itself. That is to say, a critical notion of realism foregrounds not the 'capture' of the real but its articulation or constitution in representations. However, as we will see, an emphasis on realism and representation can carry assumptions about the reality of images themselves, about illusions etc.

> [T]there is no realism, but there are realisms.
>
> (Ellis 1982: 8)

John Ellis identifies a number of realist conventions in cinema and television. They include:

- common-sense notions and expectations, such as correct historical details in costume drama, or racial stereotypes in war films;

- adequate explanations of apparently confusing events, establishing logical relationships between cause and effect in events;

- coherent psychological motivations for characters.

Some of these are contradictory, they often co-exist within the same film or television programme. We could add others: the assumption of truth in documentaries, or the social realism of politically motivated film-makers such as Ken Loach.

Film theory has extensively explored the ideological workings of realisms in cinema. Debates in the French journal *Cahiers du Cinéma* and the British journal *Screen*, in the late 1960s and 1970s, though diverse and at times antagonistic, shared the premiss that dominant cinematic realist codes construct a fundamentally conservative view of reality. In establishing a coherent 'real world' within the film, this critique argues, Hollywood films deny the contradictions of a reality characterised by class conflict, gender inequalities and hidden power structures. Realist codes ensure that conflicting points of view and power relationships within the film's fictional world are always resolved or reconciled. A world riven by contradiction is always, by the end of the last reel, whole, coherent – if the ending is not always entirely happy, it does at least provide narrative 'closure' (McCabe 1974). These debates argue, then, that Hollywood film production and reception do not present the real world; quite the opposite, they mask or mediate the real world and real social relations. Different realisms are not mere aesthetic choices, but each correlate with a particular ideology of what constitutes the 'real world' in the first place.

There are a number of ways in which these debates relate to our discussion of digital cinema. They represent a sustained and influential enquiry into the relationships between representations and the real. They raise questions of the meanings of popular visual culture in terms of ideology, and of audience. However, it is significant that of the various realisms discussed so far most do not rely for their effects on the photographic image as an index of reality, or even on visual communication at all. Some would apply equally well to radio as to television and cinema. Similarly, while the technological apparatus of cinema and television is sometimes discussed in these debates, it is rarely identified as a key factor in the construction of the ideological effects of these realisms. The following quotes give an indication of a significant shift in the critical consideration of realism when applied to recent technological change in cinema:

> The drive behind much of the technical development in cinema since 1950 has been towards both a greater or heightened sense of 'realism' and a bigger, more breathtaking realization of spectacle. Both of these impetuses have been realized through the development of larger, clearer, more enveloping images; louder, more multi-layered, more accurately directional sound; and more subtle, 'truer-to-life' colour. The intention of all technical systems developed since the beginning of the 1950s has been towards reducing the spectators' sense of their 'real' world, and replacing it with a fully believable artificial one.
>
> (Allen 1998: 127)

For Allen, in the context of a discussion of CGI special effects, realism is no longer film theory's set of ideological and formal conventions of narrative, character, plot and hierarchies, but rather technical and aesthetic qualities of sound and image. Realism now operates between the image and its qualities and the technological apparatus that generates it. What we see here is an uncomfortable conflation of three distinct notions of realism: first,

Ellis points out that forms not generally seen as 'realist', such as horror and comedy, are made coherent by these conventions (Ellis 1982: 6–9)

See MacCabe (1974). For an introduction to theories of realism in film, see Lapsley and Westlake (1988: 156–180)

photographic or cinematographic verisimilitude or indexicality (i.e. the photographic image is seen to be privileged among all other representations in its grasping of the real world); second, the spectacular or illusionistic; and third, the 'immediate' grasping of reality in which the medium itself seems to flicker out of the picture. Thus the more visually 'realistic' (or in Bolter and Grusin's terms 'immediate') a film or special effects sequence is, the more artificial or illusionistic it is. So, as Bolter and Grusin, discussing special effects-driven films like *Jurassic Park* point out:

> We go to such films in large part to experience the oscillations between immediacy and hypermediacy produced by the special effects . . . the amazement or wonder requires an awareness of the medium. If the medium really disappeared, as is the apparent goal of the logic of transparency, the viewer would not be amazed because she would not know of the medium's presence.
>
> (Bolter and Grusin 1999: 157)

These apparent paradoxes – that heightened realism is sophisticated illusion; and that audiences are both taken in by spectacle yet understand its artifice – run through much of the critical commentary on popular CGI cinema. To explore these apparent paradoxes and to suggest how CGI in popular film might be critically examined as spectacular imagery and technological advance, we will define four key terms: verisimilitude, photorealism, indexicality and simulation/**hyperrealism**.

Verisimilitude

As we have seen, discussions of the application of digital imaging to cinema generally centre around the realism of the image, or verisimilitude. Verisimilitude, as a type of representation, claims to capture the visual appearance of the world, people and objects, as they appear to the human eye. The trompe l'oeil genre of painting is a good example (see **Fig 2.23**). Special effects and computer animation are measured by their proximity to an 'unmediated' view of the real world. Verisimilitude is by and large taken for granted in conventional cinematography, given the photographic image's cultural status and technical characteristics, but in computer-generated imagery it becomes an object of interest to both producers and spectators. In *Toy Story* (1995), for example, the toy soldiers are lovingly rendered complete with the imperfections and tags of excess plastic characteristic of cheap moulded toys. This detail is offered to the audience as visually pleasurable – a knowing reference to the minutiae of childhood experience, and an invitation to acknowledge the animators' wit and attention to detail.

Indexicality

From its inception, photography has claimed for itself a more direct, less mediated relationship with the world than other forms of picture making. For Fox-Talbot photography was the 'pencil of nature', whereas more recently Susan Sontag related the photograph to footprints or deathmasks – images created through a direct physical relationship with their referent, in photography's case through light reflected from objects and environments striking photosensitive emulsion. Current anxieties about the synthetic (yet photo-real) moving image were prefigured in the arrival of digital photography. The ideological and artefactual nature of the photograph was forgotten in fears about how we would know the world once its priviledged recording medium could be so easily manipulated.

See Lister (ed.) 1995

Photorealism

> In cases where a real-life equivalent is clearly impossible, such as the morphing effects in Terminator 2, the pictorial quality of the effect must be sophisticated and 'photorealistic' enough to persuade the audience that if, for example, a tiled floor transformed into a human figure in real life, it would look exactly like its screen depiction does.
>
> (Allen 1998: 127)

Here we see verisimilitude again, but with an important difference. These CGI sequences are not so much capturing external reality as simulating another medium: in Bolter and Grusin's terms, 'remediation' – the visual replication of photography and cinematography. Indeed photo-realism is measured more by its figuration of these other media than by any capture of the look of the real itself. The quote from Allen (1998) demonstrates that this distinction is not always a clear one. Confusion and slippages between the 'real' and 'representation as realist' characterises much recent criticism of the digital moving image. A number of important issues relate to this confusion. The term photo-realistic implies a representation that has not been produced by photographic techniques, but looks as though it has. What does 'photo-realistic' mean when applied to an event or effect that couldn't be photographed? Some special effects construct real world events which are difficult or expensive to film conventionally (explosions, ships sinking, etc.), whilst others, as in the *Terminator 2* sequence or in *The Matrix*, depict events that could never be photographed and hence have no referent against which their effectiveness can be measured. Thus photography here functions not as some kind of mechanically neutral verisimilitude but as a mode of representation that creates a 'reality effect'; that is to say, the onscreen event is accepted because it conforms to prevailing or emergent realist notions of screen spectacle and fantasy, not the 'real world'. Thus, as Lev Manovich argues, again in relation to *Terminator 2*:

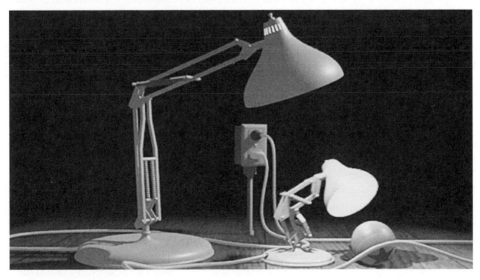

2.24 Luxor Junior. © Pixar

For what is faked, of course, is not reality but photographic reality, reality as seen by the camera lens. In other words, what digital simulation has (almost) achieved is not realism, but only photorealism . . . It is only this film-based image which digital technology has learned to simulate. And the reason we think that this technology has succeeded in faking reality is that cinema, over the course of the last hundred years, has taught us to accept its particular representational form as reality.

(Manovich 1996)

Hyperrealism

The use of terms such as 'simulation', 'virtual reality' and '**hyperrealism**' in the criticism of popular new media is often confused and imprecise. Hyperreality is used by Jean Baudrillard and Umberto Eco, though with different implications. Both take the theme park Disneyland as an example. For Eco, Disneyland is the ultimate example of what he sees as an emergent postmodernist culture characterised by the 'fake' (others include waxwork museums and animatronic displays), whereas for Baudrillard our enjoyment of the theme park's emphasis on its own spectacular 'hyperreality' serves to distract us from the fact that the real world as a whole is now hyperreal: there is no real left to 'fake'. For Baudrillard hyperreality is synonymous with simulation (Eco 1986; Baudrillard 1983).

The term 'hyperrealism' however, is ostensibly quite different. It is used to identify a distinct and dominant aesthetic in popular animation, developed by The Walt Disney Company in their animated feature films, beginning with *Snow White and the Seven Dwarves* in 1937. Disney's hyperrealist aesthetic is pertinent to the study of digital cinema. Disney animation presents its characters and environments as broadly conforming to the physics of the real world. For example, Felix the Cat or even the early Mickey Mouse were never constrained by gravity or immutability as Snow White or Pocahontas are. They were characterised by what Eisenstein called 'plasmaticness', the quality of early cartoon characters and environments to stretch, squash and transform themselves (Leyda 1988). Hyperrealism also covers the Disney Studio's application of realist conventions of narrative, logical causality and character motivations – breaking with the largely non-realist and anarchic dynamics of the cartoon form. Here, then, hyperrealism is a measure not so much of the proximity of the representation to its referent but of the remediation of the codes (and attendant ideologies) of live action cinema.

However, given the important role of Disney in the development of popular spectacular culture in general (theme parks as well as movies), and in the pioneering of new cinematic technologies (from sound and colour in cartoons, the Multiplane camera in *Snow White and the Seven Dwarves*, through to the CGI innovations of *Tron* and the corporation's collaborations with the computer animation studio Pixar in the 1990s), it could be argued that the concept of hyperreality and the animation aesthetics of hyperrealism are closely connected.

However, hyperrealism in the context of animation, as its 'hyper-' prefix suggests, is not wholly constrained by live action conventions. Disney hyperrealist animation never fully remediated the live action film – it always exceeded verisimilitude. This is evident in the graphic conventions of caricature in character design, as well as in the exaggeration of the forces of the physical world. The verisimilitude of these films always operates in tension with the graphic limitations and possibilities of drawn animation, the vestiges of plasmaticness in conventions of 'squash and stretch', metamorphosis, as well as the often fantastic subject matter (talking animals, magic, fairy tales and monsters).

Thus 'hyperrealism' can conflate the 'remediation' of live action film within animation (and photo-realism in CGI) with a rather indistinct notion of contemporary culture as increasingly

This distinction between 'simulation' and 'imitation' or representation is discussed further in **1.2.6** Simulated; **2.6.3** and **5.3.1** (see also Glossary)

5.3.1 Automata: the basics

2.25 Disney animation from Silly Symphonies to hyperrealism: The Skeleton Dance, Flowers and Trees, Snow White and the Seven Dwarfs. © Disney Enterprises, Inc.

Cel animation is the use of layers of transparent sheets (cels), each painted with elements of the image which are to move independently. For example, a figure's torso might be painted on one cel, each leg on separate layers of cels. This removes the need for a separate drawing for each frame of animation

Disney's hyperrealist aesthetic has also been interpreted as motivated by moral and ideological concerns. See Forgacs (1992), Giroux (1995), Giddings (1999/2000)

virtual. These two senses come together in a more concrete way in recent computer-animated films, notably the collaborations between Pixar and Disney on feature films such as *Toy Story* (1995) and *A Bug's Life* (1998), or in DreamWorks' *Antz* (1998) and *Shrek* (2001).

2.7.2 Reality effects

Photorealism in CGI and the hyperrealist imagery and narrative structures of Disney, Pixar and DreamWorks animated features are all examples of what Jean-Louis Comolli calls 'reality effects'. They are understood as, or are claimed to be, in different ways, offering a more real-istic experience, a less mediated grasp of the world and experience. Each of these reality effects references not the actual external world directly, but rather other cinematic and media conventions. Photo-realism is the accurate depiction of photography, not an index of the world.

Jean-Louis Comolli's essay 'Machines of the Visible' (1980) foregrounds the reality or materiality of cinema and its technologies within the contexts of economic, ideological and historical change. He argues that any particular realism is determined not by any linear or tele-ological technological, or aesthetic development but by competing and historically contingent aesthetic conventions, technical developments and economic and social forces. The Hollywood film industry often presents an idealist view of cinematic technological progress to

See Wells (1998: 25–26)

Materialist approaches implicitly or explicitly oppose themselves to 'idealist' film criticism. The French critic André Bazin (1918–1958) is the key figure here. For Bazin, 'cinematic technology and style move toward a "total and complete representation of reality"' (Manovich 1997: 6). He sees cinema as the culmination of art's mimetic function, evidence of which can be seen in ancient cultures (see **1.4.1** for discussion of teleological accounts of technological change). Cinematic realism, moreover, should also 'approximate the perceptual and cognitive dynamics of natural vision' (ibid.). Hence Bazin's particular interest in techniques of photography generating depth of field, within which 'the viewer can freely explore the space of film image' (ibid.). See Bazin (1967). For a reassessment of Bazin's work, see Matthews (n.d.)

1.4.1 Teleological accounts of new media

ever-greater realism and immersion for its audiences. What is perhaps more surprising, as we will see, is that this idealism, reanimated by the novelty and excitement of digital technologies, has re-emerged within critical studies of digital cinema.

Though written before the advent of digital technology, Comolli's argument – that the history of technological change and realist forms is fundamentally discontinuous, not a linear path to mimetic perfection – is entirely relevant to current developments in film technology and aesthetics. For Comolli, this discontinuous history of cinema is not merely the product of competing technologies, studios and institutions, but of cinema as a 'social machine' – a form through which the dominant social configuration (class relationships within capitalism) attempts to represent itself. From this perspective verisimilitude is seen to be ideological, a set of realist codes, not the product of inevitable technological and aesthetic evolution. 'Realism' in general, and verisimilitude in particular, cannot be understood without considering determinations that are not exclusively technical but economic and ideological: determinations which go beyond the simple realm of the cinematic . . . which shatter the fiction of an autonomous history of the cinema (of its 'styles and techniques'). Which effect the complex articulation of this field and this history with other fields, other histories.

Jean Louis Comolli's (1980) essay is directly brought to bear on debates around new media in Timothy Druckrey (ed.) *Electronic Culture: Technology and Visual Representation*, New York: Aperture, 1996. See also Lev Manovich's application of Comolli's ideas to digital cinema (Manovich 1996).

We will look at three examples, the first from Comolli, the second relating to the historical development of animation, and the third a more recent example of the technology of cinematic realism.

Realism and film stock in the 1920s

From an idealist position the introduction, around 1925, of panchromatic film stock (black-and-white film which renders the colour spectrum into shades of grey more sensitively than previously) would be evidence of cinema's inevitable progress towards greater verisimilitude. However, Comolli argues that this 'progress' is as ideological as it is technical. A key determinant for the adoption of panchromatic stock lay outside cinema. It was a response to developments in the realist aesthetics of another popular medium: photography. 'The hard, contrasty image of the early cinema no longer satisfied the codes of photographic realism developed and sharpened by the spread of photography.' Significantly, this technical development entailed the decline of a previously accepted standard of visual realism: depth of field. Thus codes of shade, range and colour overthrow perspective and depth as the dominant 'reality effects' (Comolli 1980: 131).

Animation, hyperrealism and anti-realism

For Bazin, cinematic realism was predicated on the photographic image's indexicality and the assumption that it 'captures' the real world in a way that no other medium can. The privileged status of photography as a medium of verisimilitude accounts for much of the confusion around CGI. We have touched on this already in our definition of 'photo-realism'. The often-stated aim of CGI is to replicate the live action cinematographic image convincingly. Yet the hyperrealism of early animated feature films and shorts in the 1930s was introduced for reasons that were economic as much as aesthetic. Techniques such as the line test were established to industrialise this relatively expensive mode of production, allowing divisions and hierarchies of labour and restricting the independence of individual animators.

In an analysis of the introduction of cel techniques to Hollywood cartoons such as those by Warner Brothers, Kristin Thompson explores the complex relationships between changes in technique, relations between different cinematic forms (live action and animation) and dominant ideologies in the Hollywood system. As in Disney's feature films, the cel animation techniques in cartoons served to industrialise cartoon production, but also offered new techniques of experimentation with, and disruption of, visual realist codes. The aesthetics of the cartoon and its position within Hollywood was the result of a struggle between two opposing forces:

> We have seen how cartoons use some devices which are potentially very disruptive (for example, mixtures of perspective systems, anti-naturalistic speed cues). As we might expect within the classical Hollywood system, however, narrative and comic motivations smooth over these disruptions . . . The fact that cel animation lends itself so readily to disruptive formal strategies suggests one reason why the conservative Hollywood ideology of cartoons developed as it did . . . Since disruption unmotivated by narrative is unwelcome in the classical system, Hollywood needed to tame the technology. Trivialisation provided the means.
>
> (Thompson 1980: 119)

> The line test or pencil test is a method by which an animated sequence is roughly sketched out on sheets of paper to establish timing, continuity and control over characters' movement, before the cels are painted. See Wells (1998: 21–28) for a materialist study of Disney hyperrealism.

IMAX and the immersive experience

The attraction of IMAX cinema lies primarily in its technology of spectacle. The 70-mm IMAX film is projected onto a 60-foot high screen, immersing the audience's field of vision with high-resolution images. Yet the technology that delivers this visually immersive experience at the same time rules out other well-established realist codes. Due to the practical difficulties of close framing, IMAX films tend not to use the shot–reverse shot conventions for depicting dialogue central to audience identification with character-driven narrative (Allen 1998: 115). IMAX films have to draw on alternative realist codes, for example natural history documentary or the 'hyperrealism' of computer animation. We will now ask how these contradictory discourses of realism help us to understand the impact of digital media on popular cinema.

2.26 Stepping out of Alberti's window? IMAX. Deep Sea 3D, 2006. © Warner Bros

2.7.3 Spectacular realism?

With the advent of popular CGI cinema we are left with an apparently paradoxical notion of realism, one that refers both to a perceived immediacy but also to a heightened illusion and spectacle. It is a visual realism, a verisimilitude, premissed not on the indexicality of photography, but on the 'wizardry' of digital synthetic imagery and its designers, that re-introduces that least realist cinematic form, animation, back into the mainstream. This paradox serves to foreground two further important factors:

1   the identification by a number of critics of significant continuities with earlier spectacular visual media forms – not only in cinema, or even twentieth-century popular culture more generally, but even further back – to the nineteenth or even the seventeenth century;

2   the critical concern with the visual image over other aspects of cinema.

In addressing the latter point – the dominance of the visual – it should be noted that the term 'spectacle' has two main connotations here. In everyday usage it refers to the visual seductions of cinema (special effects, stunts, song-and-dance routines, and so on) that apparently oppose, temporarily halt, or distract the spectator's attention from narrative and character development. The other connotation of spectacle is drawn from Guy Debord's book *The Society of the Spectacle*. Debord, a leading figure in the radical art/political group the Situationist International in the 1950s and 1960s, has been influential on both cyberculture and postmodernist thought. In a series of epigrammatic paragraphs *The Society of the Spectacle* asserts that postwar capitalism has reinforced its control over the masses through the transformation of culture as a whole into a commodity. Thus the spectacle is not so much a set of particular cultural or media events and images, but characterises the entire social world today as an illusion, a separation from, or masking of, real life:

> The spectacle is the moment when the commodity has attained the total occupation of social life. Not only is the relation to the commodity visible but it is all one sees: the world one sees is its world.
>
> (Debord 1983: 42)

Debord's spectacle is profoundly, though negatively, influential on Baudrillard's notion of simulation

This suspicion of the illusory potential of visual (especially photographic) images is evident in film theory. Because the photographic image, it is argued, captures the surface appearance of things, rather than underlying (and invisible) economic and social relationships, it is always, by its very nature, ideological. For example, in a lengthy footnote Comolli relates photographic realism in Hollywood (and bourgeois society as a whole) to gold, or money. Its illusions are those of commodity fetishism: [that] the photo is the money of the 'real' (of 'life') assures its convenient circulation and appropriation. Thereby, the photo is unanimously consecrated as a general equivalent for, standard of, all 'realism': 'the cinematic image could not, without losing its "power" (the power of its "credibility"), *not* align itself with the photographic norms' (Comolli 1980: 142).

But if these images are realism as illusion and artifice what do they tell us, if anything, of our 'real world' today? If we are sceptical about the ability of these, or any, images to speak the truth in any straightforward way, what might these images mean, what might they tell us (if anything) about our world (and their place within it)?

Special effects and hyperreality

The Mask (1994) is a good example of a film the form and popularity of which were predicated on its advanced use of computer-generated special effects. Special effects in films have often been regarded as at best distractions from, and at worst, deleterious to, the creative or artistic in cinema:

> *The Mask* underscores the shrinking importance of conventional story-telling in special-effects-minded movies, which are happy to overshadow quaint ideas about plot and character with flashy up-to-the-minute gimmickry.
>
> (Janet Maslin, *New York Times*, quoted in Klein 1998: 217)

Evident in genres preferred by the young – science fiction, horror, fantasy, action films – special effects-driven films are commonly seen as illusory, juvenile and superficial, diametrically opposed to more respectable aspects of popular film such as character psychology, subtleties of plot and *mise-en-scène*. They are often associated more with the technology, rather than the 'art' of cinema.

2.27 *The Mask*, 1994. © New Line/Dark Horse/The Kobal Collection

Claims that blockbuster films are symptomatic of, or are bringing about, the 'dumbing-down' of culture are a familiar feature of popular film criticism. These fears find a resonance in certain theoretical discourses on the relationships between digital and/or electronic technologies, popular culture and culture as a whole. In an essay in *Screen*, Michele Pierson identifies a fusion, in the work of critics such as Sobchack and Landon, of established pessimistic attitudes to spectacle in cinema with more recent 'cyberculture' discourses. Thus, it is argued,

> the popularization and pervasiveness of electronic technology has profoundly altered our spatial and temporal sense of the world. [Sobchack and Landon] agree that the hyperreal

space of electronic simulation – whether it be the space of computer generated special effects, video games, or virtual reality – is characterized by a new depthlessness.

(Pierson 1999: 167)

We can identify, then, a set of overlapping discourses, some mourning the loss of 'earlier' realist aesthetics as 'meaningful', some celebrating developments in the technologies of verisimilitude. These discourses can be broken down as follows:

1   The forms and aesthetics of CGI are the latest in an evolutionary process of ever-increasing verisimilitude in visual culture; for example, regarding the dinosaurs in Jurassic Park as the technical perfection of the pioneering stop motion special effects of Willis O'Brien and Ray Harryhausen in films like *The Lost World* (1925) and *One Million Years BC* (1966).

2   A pessimistic version of 1, characterised by a suspicion of special effects and image manipulation as illusory, superficial and vulgar. The spectacular is posited as in binary opposition to the 'true' creative qualities of film as a medium. Here, the significance of digital effects lies not in any sense of virtuality *per se* but rather in their popular appeal (perceived as taking over 'traditional' cinema) and the technical virtuosity they bring.

3   A cybercultural perspective, from which this digitally generated verisimilitude marks a new, distinct phase in Western culture. 'Simulation' and the 'hyperreal' are key terms here; the computer modelling of '3-D', 'photo-realistic' environments and characters is seen as ontologically distinct from photographic representation.

4   An inversion of this cyberculture perspective, in which cinematic technology is symptomatic of technological change more generally, but which sees this change as one of a slide into digital illusion and depthlessness rather than the creation of new 'realities'.

Position 4 is evident in a number of postmodernist accounts of developments in media. For example, Andrew Darley (2000) places computer-generated special effects as an important cultural form within an emergent 'digital visual culture', alongside video games, pop videos, digital imaging in advertising and computer animation. Drawing on Jean Baudrillard and Fredric Jameson, he argues that these visual digital forms

lack the symbolic depth and representational complexity of earlier forms, appearing by contrast to operate within a drastically reduced field of meaning. They are direct and one-dimensional, about little, other than their ability to commandeer the sight and the senses. Popular forms of diversion and amusement, these new technological entertainments are, perhaps, the clearest manifestation of the advance of the culture of the 'depthless image'.

(Darley 2000: 76)

Key text: Andrew Darley, *Visual Digital Culture: surface play and spectacle in new media genres*, London: Routledge (2000)

In this account, mass culture is not yet entirely dominated by this 'neo-spectacle', but it occupies 'a significant aesthetic space . . . within mainstream visual culture', a space that is 'largely given over to surface play and the production of imagery that lacks traditional depth cues. Imagery that at the aesthetic level at least is only as deep as its quotations, star images and dazzling or thrilling effects' (Darley 2000: 124).

Though he establishes important precedents for, or continuities with, contemporary spectacular visual culture (early cinema, Hales's Tours, amusement parks, for example), this 'depthlessness' is new, the product of technological developments. Darley argues that there is a qualitative difference from earlier, pre-digital effects: 'it is the digital element that is introducing an important new register of illusionist spectacle into such films' (Darley 2000: 107).

Critique of the depthless model: inverted idealism?

In the contemporary critique of 'meaningless', 'depthless' digital popular culture and its implication in the 'loss of the real', there is the implication, never fully spelt out, that it is exactly the characteristics of the classic realist text criticised by film theory (character psychology depth, narrative coherence, and so on) that embody the 'meaning' now lost in postmodernist digital culture. Classical realist narrative and photography, whilst perhaps not telling the truth, had 'meaning' and depth. The much-critiqued notion of photography's indexicality is resurrected (see for example Barbara Creed's discussion of the 'synthespian', Creed 2000, or Stephen Prince's notion of perceptual realism, Prince 1996). If any given 'realism' assumes and articulates its own particular model of the 'real world' then it is not surprising that in postmodernist theories the 'hyperrealism' of computer graphics has been interpreted not as presenting a more analogous image of the real world, but rather as heralding its disappearance.

A number of questions are raised for a materialist study of digital cinema:

- How new is neo-spectacle? While digital technologies clearly generate a great deal of interest and facilitate new, spectacular images, even new ways of making films, it isn't clear exactly what the distinction is between the 'second-order' realism of digitally produced special effects and, for example, the stop motion animation of Ray Harryhausen's famous skeleton army in *Jason and the Argonauts* (1963). Or, for that matter, the distinction between pre-digital and digital animation, neither of which rely on the photographic capture of external reality.

- Concomitantly, we could ask again the question posed throughout this book: in what ways are digital media themselves new? According to Baudrillard, for example, simulation has its roots in the Renaissance and contemporary hyperrealism had already arrived with television and other electronic media.

- What about the films themselves: are spectacular images necessarily meaningless? Action sequences and effects in films, along with song-and-dance numbers and the gendered visual pleasures of the display of bodies, are distinct from narrative – but is meaning only to be found in narrative and character?

- If films such as *Jurassic Park* and *Terminator 2* are evidence of an emergent postmodernism, do they escape the historical, economic and ideological contexts of earlier moments in cinema's history?

These last two points raise questions of audience – are the people who enjoy the spectacular realism of CGI merely dupes; seduced and exhilarated?

2.7.4 Thoroughly (post)modern Méliès, or the return of the repressed in digital cinema

> [D]igital media returns to us the repressed of cinema.
>
> (Manovich 1999: 192)

Critical studies of digital cinema often establish histories: either an implicit and more or less idealist history of technological evolution towards verisimilitude or immersion, or, more interestingly, a discontinuous history in which early cinematic (and pre-cinematic) technologies return at the end of the twentieth century.

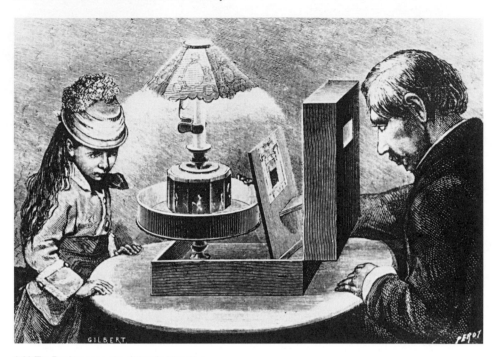

2.28 The Praxinoscope: pre-cinematic apparatus.

Early cinema to digital culture

> What happened with the invention of cinema? It was not sufficient that it be technically feasible, it was not sufficient that a camera, a projector, a strip of images be technically ready. Moreover, they were already there, more or less ready, more or less invented, a long time before the formal invention of the cinema, fifty years before Edison and the Lumière brothers. It was necessary that something else be constituted, that something else be formed: the cinema machine, which is not essentially the camera, the film, the apparatuses, the techniques.
>
> (Comolli 1980: 121–122)

Key text: Tom Gunning (1990a) 'The Cinema of Attractions: early film, its spectator and the avant-garde', in Thomas Elsaesser (ed.) *Early Cinema: space, frame, narrative*, London: BFI

See also **1.4** What kind of history?

As we have seen, this 'cinema machine' is the product of social and economic forces, drawing from the diverse range of photographic and other technologies for the presentation of moving images. Recent research into the early years of cinema has explored this 'cinema machine' as the reining in of early cinema's many competing technologies and modes of presentation and representation, undermining any notion that the emergence of the feature film was somehow inevitable, evolutionary (Gunning 1990a: 61).

Parallels are drawn between this 'radical heterogeneity' and the multifarious, yet interlinked, digital technologies today – technologies which operate across the boundaries between entertainment, art, science, governments and the military – seeming to offer an analogous cultural, historical and technological moment. A moment of flux in which future directions are up for grabs. Of course, unlike cinema, digital technologies emerge into a world already familiar with a century's development of mass media. We have already seen how VR and CGI are being shaped discursively and actually by the codes and institutions of dominant entertainment media. On the other hand, this revisiting of cinema's 'prehistory' also highlights alternative cinematic forms that appeared to have fallen victim to the dominance of the feature film, but continued, marginalised, repressed or channelled into other media (and may now themselves be poised to take over). Animation is one such form, special effects are another, as we shall see.

Lev Manovich argues that with the advent of digital media we are seeing not so much the end of cinema as the end of cinema's privileged status as recorder of reality and the dominance of the fiction film (he calls this the 'super-genre', after the film theorist Christian Metz). At the end of the twentieth century, he argues, this super-genre is revealed as an 'isolated accident', a diversion from which cinema has now returned (Manovich 1999). The return of repressed alternatives to the super-genre displaces cinematic realism to being just the 'default option', one among many others.

This is one of Andrew Darley's key arguments – that digital visual culture, though 'new' in important ways, is at the same time continuous with a 'tradition' of spectacular entertainment that runs throughout the twentieth century (from vaudeville and 'trick' films at the turn of the century, through theme park rides, musicals to music video, CGI, IMAX, motion simulators, etc.), but with its origins much earlier in the magic lantern shows, phantasmagoria and dioramas of the eighteenth and nineteenth centuries. Some cultural theorists reach further back, to the seventeenth century, seeing the intricacy and illusionism of baroque art and architecture as prefiguring the forms and aesthetics of digital entertainment (Cubitt 1999; Klein 1998; Ndalianis 1999).

Despite their diversity all these forms share, it is argued, an invitation to their audiences to engage with the visual or kinaesthetic stimulation of these spectacles, and to be fascinated by their technical ingenuity, by entertainment technology itself as spectacle. The classic realist codes (character motivation and psychological depth, logical causality and narrative complexity), if present at all, function merely as devices to link together these dynamic sequences.

'Cinema of attractions'

The film historian and theorist Tom Gunning has established the year 1906 as pivotal to the establishment of narrative cinema. Before then narrative, where it had existed, was used very differently, primarily as a pretext for sequences of tricks, effects or 'attractions'. The films of George Méliès are paradigmatic here. Méliès' career began in fairground magic and illusionism, and his innovations in cinema continued this non-realist mode. His studio, Méliès said, 'was the coming together of a gigantic photographic studio and a theatrical stage' (Méliès 1897, in Comolli 1980: 130). The actualities films (records of trains entering stations, people disembarking from boats, etc.) of the Lumière brothers, though today more commonly regarded as pioneering a documentary – rather than spectacular – realism, are included by Gunning in this 'cinema of attractions'. Ian Christie points out that the first presentations of the Lumière projector began with a still image, which then 'magically' started to move. Similarly, films could be projected at varying speeds or even backwards (Christie 1994: 10). It was as much the spectacle of the cinematic technology and images in motion as the scenes and events depicted that drew the attention of audiences. This is evident in the fact that publicity for the films more often used the names of the projection machines, rather than the titles of the films. Films would often be presented as one item on a vaudeville bill, one attraction within the discontinuous sequence of sketches, songs and acts (Gunning 1990a).

Animation, in both its popular and avant-garde contexts, has very often explored its own status as a form not predicated on the photographic analogue, revelling in the artificial, the fantastic, the illusionistic, or indeed its own apparatus

The cinema of attractions was by no means entirely removed from the feature film. It persists as spectacle within narrative, whether sweeping landscape, show-stopping *femme fatale* or breathtaking stunts, emerging more forcefully in genres such as the musical (Gunning 1990a: 57)

2.29 Ladislav Starewicz, 'The Cameraman's Revenge', 1911.

2.30 *Antz*, 1998. Courtesy of the Ronald Grant Archive

Theatrical display dominates over narrative absorption, emphasizing the direct stimulation of shock or surprise at the expense of unfolding a story or creating a diegetic universe. The cinema of attractions expends little energy creating characters with psychological motivations or individual personality . . . its energy moves outward towards an acknowledged spectator rather than inward towards the character-based situations essential to classical narrative.

(Gunning 1990a: 59)

Thus, the 'realism' of the photographic capture of movement was not originally allied to the 'realism' of the classical realist text.

Rooted in magic and vaudeville, but also in a long tradition of scientific presentations and display, the spectacular possibilities of science, technology and magic run throughout the prehistory and history of cinema:

although today's film technology may be transforming at a dramatic rate and is radically different from that of early cinema, its fundamental concern with constructing magical illusions out of the more rational and scientific realms associated with the technological remains similar.

(Ndalianis 1999: 260)

This 'cinema of attractions' did not disappear after 1907, but continued in other moving image forms. Animation, for example, has remained a cinema of theatrical display and technical virtuosity. Thompson implies that cartoons, while marginalised and trivialised, were not repressed so much as positioned in a dialectical relationship with classical live action films. The anti-realist and disruptive potential of animated attractions, though tamed, sustain a sense of wonder in Hollywood films; 'they brought the mystery of movie technology to the fore, impressing people with the "magic" of cinema. Animation made cinema a perpetual novelty' (Thompson 1980: 111).

But what does it mean to identify these aesthetic and technical connections across the history of cinema? Critics like Bolter, Grusin and Darley have identified important areas of continuity and rupture within the technological development of visual culture, rejecting any utopian 'newness'. However, their histories are largely chronological or associative: questions of determination, beyond the immediate circumstances and characteristics of the media in question, are largely absent. We see, then, a critically productive set of analogies and continuities between the 'old' and the 'new' in cinema, but crucial questions of history and change remain. Without the explicit development of a materialist analysis of technological and cultural change we are left with either 'remediation' as an idealist logic of media themselves, or a postmodernist 'end of history' in which earlier cultural forms are reanimated, zombie-like, to dazzle, excite or terrify their audience into some sub-Baudrillardian ecstasy of communication.

If the dialectical relationship between dominant fictional film and the cinema of attractions is comparable with contemporary developments in digital visual culture, then the assumption within VR discourses of a disembodied experience – the rediscovery of the Cartesian divide – could be seen as analogous to the ideal audience of film in both popular and theoretical accounts (see Strain 1999). CGI, as the popular and vulgar repressed of VR, assumes, like its spectacular forebears, a nervous, sensual audience – we see the return of the body.

CASE STUDY 2.2 The digital cinema of attractions

2.31 *Cyberworld 3D*, 2000 Imax Ltd.

The film *Cyberworld 3D* (2000) is an encyclopaedia of the contemporary cinema of attractions: made for IMAX, and in 3-D, it immerses the spectator in visual excess and visceral kinaesthesia, and revels in the spectacular presentation of its own virtuosity. Images reach out from the vast screen as if to pull the polarised glasses from the face of the spectator, and recede back into a fantastically deep focus in which the eye is wrenched from impossible perspectives and pushed up against gleaming surfaces, animated characters, or, in one sequence, the gleefully rendered squalor of peeling paint and refuse.

It is a film made up of other films, linked by a VR conceit: a gallery of animated short films through which the spectator is guided by a computer-generated 'host' – a cross between Lara Croft and the avatar in the AOL advertisements. The films within films range from a special episode of *The Simpsons*, to extended advertisements for the skills and services of software media houses and animation studios. Overall it is a commercialised vaudeville: a digital phantasmagoria of baroque fantasy, of generic promiscuity: science fiction, music video, fantasy, horror, whimsy, Victoriana, monsters, and chases.

2.7.5 Audiences and effects

What then are the implications of the fact that 'depthless' digital cinema has a history as well as a future? Does the shift to centre-stage of the cinema of attractions and animation reinforce or undermine discourses of postmodernist depthlessness? What does the 'acknowledged spectator' make of it all? Gunning's research highlights the active role the audience of the cinema of attractions plays in making sense of these spectacles, as well as the moral anxieties these attractions (and their audiences) provoked:

> The Russell Sage Survey [commissioned by a middle-class reform group in the 1910s] of popular entertainments found vaudeville 'depends upon an artificial rather than a natural human and developing interest, these acts having no necessary and as a rule, no actual

connection'... A night at the variety theatre was like a ride on a streetcar or an active day in a crowded city . . . stimulating an unhealthy nervousness.

(Gunning 1990a: 60)

Whatever these attractions mean, their significance does not lie solely in the 'artificial acts' themselves, but in their effect on the audience. This is not the ideal, non-specific and disembodied audience of 1970s film theory. This audience is addressed physically as much as intellectually, the 'nervous', embodied spectators experiencing kinaesthetic 'rides'.

Terry Lovell has questioned 1970s film theory precisely because of its assumption of naive audiences 'petrified' in their subject-positions. Lovell argued that audiences 'are . . . much more aware than conventionalist critics suppose, or than they themselves can articulate, of the rules which govern this type of representation' (Lovell 1980: 80). Notions of a depthless 'neo-spectacle', like earlier film theory, also assume popular cinematic forms to be dangerous (though perhaps distracting and superficial rather than ideological). Audiences may recognise the illusions, but there is no meaning beyond a play with expectations.

So, if the audiences for digital spectacular realism (or popular film in general for that matter) are not deluded or tricked, we could ask whether the notion of depthlessness is adequate to the analysis of popular understanding of, and pleasure in, special effects. Indeed a knowledge and appreciation of special effects as effects is a necessary part of the pleasure of spectatorship. The familiar notion of 'suspending disbelief' is not enough: the spectator is never completely immersed in or 'fooled' by the spectacle, and it is important that they are not – spectacular special effects are there to be noticed. There is then a play between the audience's willing acceptance of illusory events and images and their pleasure in recognising the sophistication of the artifice (see Darley 2000: 105). Here we are back with the notion of spectacular realism as simultaneously immediate and hypermediate. Without a sense of the immediate, the effects would lose their thrilling plausibility and 'reality effect', but the pleasure is equally in the implicit recognition of their hypermediacy – as technical wizardry or as an example of cutting-edge technology.

Michele Pierson has argued that this pleasurable awareness of cinematic artifice is key to the popular reception of special effects-driven blockbusters. Her analysis is historically located and sensitive to distinct categories of special effects. The late 1980s and early 1990s, then, were a 'golden age' for these films, films in which the main selling point and attraction was their innovative and spectacular use of computer-generated special effects. This period includes *The Abyss* (1989), *The Mask* (1994), *Terminator 2: Judgement Day* (1991). The release and theatrical presentations of these blockbusters were cultural events in their own right, centring on the presentation of digital spectacle as entertainment.

For Pierson the CGIs in these particular science fiction films both represent futuristic technology (for example the liquid robot in *Terminator 2*) and present themselves as cutting-edge technology (the CGI that rendered the liquid robot). The special effects in and of themselves marked 'the emergence of a popular, techno-futurist aesthetic that foregrounds the synthetic properties of electronic imagery' (Pierson 1999: 158). Science fiction special effects (or indeed, any 'cinema of attractions') could then be seen as a particular kind of realism: though they may represent the fantastical and the speculative, they present actual cinematic technological developments. In this context the terms 'presentation' and 'representation', as used by Gunning and Pierson, are roughly equivalent to Bolter and Grusin's 'hypermediacy' and 'immediacy'.

Key text: Michele Pierson, 'CGI effects in Hollywood science-fiction cinema 1989–95: the wonder years', *Screen* 40.2 (1999): 158–176

Pierson's study highlights the importance of not treating special effects as a homogeneous set of spectacular images, or indeed a teleological trajectory towards either

CASE STUDY 2.3: What is Bullet Time?

Audiences for CGI special-effects-driven films are also addressed through supplementary books, magazines and films, detailing 'The Making of . . .' the effects and spectacle, profiling key figures in the industry, offering explanations of how the effects were achieved, etc. In recent years, VHS and DVD releases of some such films have included documentaries on the making of the effects.

If in *The Matrix*, as in other special-effects-led films, the pleasures of viewing lie in the tension between immediacy and hypermediacy, then *What is Bullet Time?* (a short documentary included on *The Matrix* VHS and DVD [1999]) is positively orgiastic. It explains how the effects were achieved, and presents the stages of the construction of the illusion: from wireframe computer simulations of the positioning of cameras and actors, to actors suspended from wires against green screens bounded by a sweeping arc of still cameras, and so on through digital compositing and layering of backgrounds and the effects of bullets in flight.

The 'timeslice' technique (now much replicated, and parodied) is a striking example of parallels between the technologies of early and late cinema. A sweeping arc of cameras surround an actor suspended by wires, and simultaneously shoot a single frame. A movie camera at each end of the arc records motion up to and after the 'snapshots'. By editing all the single frames together the director can then generate the illusion of the freezing of movement and action – a frozen image around which the 'camera' appears to roam. The comparison with Eadweard Muybridge's experiments with sequences of still cameras to capture movement in the 1880s and 1890s is striking (see Coe 1992).

What is Bullet Time? carefully explains that to all intents and purposes the bullet time and timeslice sequences in *The Matrix* are animation. Indeed animation is needed 'inbetween' the extra frames to manipulate the timespan of slow motion scenes without losing clarity. We could add that the physical abilities of the film's protagonists are informed by animation's hyperrealist codes (the film was originally proposed as an animated film) fused with other spectacular forms, such as Hollywood action films and Hong Kong martial arts cinema.

We should be careful here to distinguish between postmodernist notions of simulation and the realist definition set out in **1.2.6**. Photo-realist CGI is a good example of simulation: a copy without an original, it is artificial and yet as such it exists, and is experienced in, the real world. It is an addition to the real world, not a step away from it

postmodernist simulation or verisimilitude. Special effects aesthetics and meanings are discontinuous and historically contingent. Each category of effects entails a specific relationship with the film's narrative on the one hand, and with its audience on the other. Indeed, we could begin to categorise the functions of distinct types of digital effects in films:

- Most Hollywood feature film production now features digital effects, but they are not always presented as such to the audience. Here, digital imaging is used to generate backdrops or climatic conditions that prove difficult or expensive to film conventionally.

- Some effects are designed not to simulate ostensibly normal events (or at least events not characterised by the supernatural or alien). An example here would be James Cameron's *Titanic* (1997). Effects were used to depict a real historical event, but still aimed to inspire awe in the technological spectacle.

- Special effects may play with other registers of filmic realism. For example, in *Forrest Gump* (1994), the protagonist is depicted meeting historical figures such as John Lennon and John F. Kennedy. The effects place Tom Hanks's character 'within' news footage of these figures. Here the technological trickery impacts on the documentary status of film.

- In *Who Framed Roger Rabbit* (1988) and *The Mask* (1994) the effects mark the irruption of other media (animation) as disruptive force. In fact the computer animation disrupts the form of these films, just as the animated characters disrupt the fictional worlds of the films.

We have seen that audiences respond to spectacular cinema as shared cultural event and as object of specialist 'fan' knowledges and practices. Steve Neale, in an essay on John Carpenter's remake of *The Thing* (1982), analyses the complex relays of signification between the 'acknowledged spectator' and the film text itself. Drawing on work by Philip Brophy, Neale bases his argument on a specific line in the film. The line is uttered at the end of a scene characterised by a series of particularly gruesome and spectacular metamorphoses in which the 'thing' itself (an alien which assumes the appearance of its victims) eventually transforms into a spider-like creature, legs sprouting from a 'body' formed from the severed head of one of its human victims: 'As it "walks" out the door, a crew member says the line of the film: "You've got to be fucking kidding!"'(Brophy, quoted in Neale 1990: 160). As Neale summarises Brophy's argument, this line exists as an event within the diegesis of the film, but it is also an 'institutional' event,

> a remark addressed to the spectator by the film, and by the cinematic apparatus, about the nature of its special effects. The scene, in its macabre excess, pushes the audience's acceptance of spectacular events within the codes of the science fiction–horror film beyond conventional limits, a transgression negotiated and accepted because of the film's ironic and reflexive acknowledgement of the transgression. Not only is the film 'violently self-conscious', but 'It is a sign also of an awareness on the part of the spectator (an awareness often marked at this point by laughter): the spectator knows that the Thing is a fiction, a collocation of special effects; and the spectator knows that the film knows too. Despite this awareness, the special effects have had an effect. The spectator has been, like the fictional character, astonished and horrified.'
>
> (Neale 1990: 161–162)

The persistence of particular images and spectacles from pre-cinema to the contemporary cinema of attractions has been noted. We do not have the space to suggest why such images and figures resonate in popular culture, but refer the reader to some excellent work done in this field in recent years, particularly in terms of gender in popular genres. See for example Kuhn (1990), Creed (1993) on science fiction and horror, and Tasker (1993) on action films. Carol Clover (1992) has an exemplary discussion of slasher films and their audiences. Here, then, special effects are not 'meaningless', rather they often develop a complex relationship with the audience's expectations and pleasures.

Could this merely mean that the spectator has a sophisticated relationship with a meaningless text? Judith Williamson shares Lovell's assertion of the more epistemologically 'active' nature of popular audiences, as well as arguing that popular films themselves are neither meaningless nor exhaustively ideological. As popular products they must find resonances, however contradictory, with collectively felt sentiments:

> Popular films always address – however indirectly – wishes, fears and anxieties current in society at any given moment . . . Anyone interested in the fantasies and fears of our culture should pay close attention to successful films, for their success means precisely that they have touched on the fantasies and fears of a great many people.
>
> (Williamson 1993: 27)

As we have seen, Pierson argues that part of the pleasure of science fiction special effects of this period is that they not only represent the future, but are the future, or, at least, the most up-to-date technological developments. For her, 'techno-futurism' is progressive in that it encourages its audiences to imagine and speculate about possible futures. So popular spectacular genres are not necessarily empty of meaning; indeed the opposite could be argued. As Judith Williamson points out: 'Through use of genre conventions an apparently

2.32 and 2.33 Phantasmagoria to *Resident Evil*:
body horror before and after cinema.

run-of-the-mill horror movie may speak eloquently about sexuality and the body, or a
"second-rate" thriller articulate widespread fears about knowledge and secrecy' (Williamson
1993: 29).

Animation has never been entirely separated off from the 'super-genre' of the fictional feature film; most notably it has maintained its presence through the techniques of the production
of special effects. Animation has provided a means of imaging that which cannot be conventionally photographed (for example, dinosaurs, from McCay to Harryhausen to Spielberg), and
also functions, as we have said, as spectacular realism, simultaneously figuring magic, dreams

CASE STUDY 2.4: Computer animation

If, as has been argued, cinema's presentation of its own technological (yet 'magical') attractions was channelled into animation, digital cinema welcomes this marginalised form back to the centre of moving image culture. Once prevalent assumptions that computer animation will achieve full photo-realism (generating characters and environments indistinguishable from those filmed conventionally) have been set back in recent years however. The materialist analysis of competing codes of verisimilitude is instructive here. For example, the *Toy Story* films made by Pixar (also a software developer) and Disney are characterised by a play between spectacular realism (sophisticated rendering of depth, lighting, texture, and so on) and cartoon-derived codes of character design, action, humour and movement. Indeed, it becomes evident that computer animation in *Toy Story* brings together Disney with the Disney hyperrealist aesthetics that have often been placed as the yardstick of digital spectacular realisms. Yet subsequent Disney/Pixar features such as *The Incredibles* and *Cars* have played up the graphic stylisation of animation's graphic heritage within photorealistic and 3-D-rendered environments. The first attempt at a fully photo-realist CGI feature, *Final Fantasy: the spirits within*, was a critical and commercial flop.

Note: For histories of computer animation, see Allen (1998), Binkley (1993), Darley (1991), Manovich (1996)

2.34 *Final Fantasy: The Spirits Within*, 2001

2.35 Monsters Inc, 2001. © Disney Enterprises, Inc. Courtesy of The Movie Store Collection

Thus, the specific material limitations and characteristics of computer animation, and animation's centuries-long history of synthetic moving image making, help to determine the modes of spectacular realism developed today. On the one hand there are technical and economic obstacles to the digital rendering of complex textures and shapes. Toys, and the insects of *A Bug's Life* and *Antz*, because of their stylised shapes and generally smooth surfaces, suit the medium perfectly; organic, complex structures like human bodies and hair, or atmospheric effects do not. Hence the human characters in *Toy Story* ironically appear as cartoon-like, less 'realistic' than the toys themselves. Of course, toys also perfectly suit the industrial strategies and structures, the tried and tested language of children's moving image culture that established Disney as a global media conglomeration, generating new child-oriented characters for merchandising, licensing of images, new theme park attractions. When the Disney/Pixar feature *Monsters Inc.* was released particular attention was paid in its publicity material, and in sequences in the film itself, to the sophistication of the rendering of the monsters' fur: a reality effect celebrating new developments in computer imaging and processing power.

Key text: Norman M. Klein, 'Hybrid cinema: the mask, masques and Tex Avery', in Kevin S. Sandler (ed.) *Reading the Rabbit: explorations in Warner Bros. animation*, New Brunswick, N.J.: Rutgers University Press (1998), pp. 209–220

and illusion in films, and fulfilling Hollywood's ideological need for a tamed presentation of technological 'magic' and illusion. What is new about contemporary developments in spectacular film is the increasingly sophisticated integration of animation and live action. This integration is not adequately described by the term 'remediation'; this is not so much the re-presenting of one medium by another as the emergence of a new hybrid cinema (Klein 1998).

Klein argues that *The Mask*, for example, not only makes direct references to the imagery of 1940s cartoons (in particular Tex Avery's *Red Hot Riding Hood* [1943]), but also draws closely on the form of this mode of animation: the extremely rapid editing and precision of timing developed in the chase cartoon. This type of cartoon timing is now widely used in conventional action scenes as well as in digital special effects. 'Today, essentially everyone working in special effects is expected to understand techniques from the chase cartoon. Knowing cartoon cycles and extremes helps the artist time an action sequence or splice in mid action: the offbeat aside, the wink to the audience' (Klein 1998: 210). We have already noted that the innovative special effects of *The Matrix* mark a fusion of live action cinematography and frame-by-frame manipulation that cannot easily be described as either live action or animation.

'Photorealism' may not be a fully adequate term here – see earlier sections on pictorial space (pages 115–120) – one of the features of *Toy Story* that captured audiences' imaginations in the mid-1990s was not only its sophisticated photorealist rendering of three-dimensional characters and their surface textures but also the capacity for these objects to move effortlessly through their three-dimensional environments from Andy's bedroom to pizza parlours, streets and vehicles. This is clear in films such as *Toy Story*'s precursor, Pixar's short film *Tin Toy* (1988): Images such as these are now the norm for mainstream animated films, but *Tin Toy* marked an early break from the various long-established aesthetic and economic strategies of animation, all of which (as we have seen) struggled with (or blithely rejected) the sheer time and effort in producing the impression of fully inhabited three-dimensional space. As we saw early in Part 2, this aesthetic is rooted not only in cinematic photography but in the scopic regimes of the Renaissance of which photography is but one descendant.

Meanwhile some technically experimental but industrially mainstream films have more thoroughly woven together live action footage and pictorial conventions with the graphic possibilities afforded by digital postproduction. Richard Linklater's films *Waking Life* (2001) and *A Scanner Darkly* (2006) for example process live action footage with the kind of vector animation familiar from web-based Flash animation to produce films that play with ideas of reality both aesthetically and diegetically. Other recent examples of this extension to Klein's hybrid cinema include *300* (2006) and *Sin City* (2005), the latter explicitly remediating its comic book origins.

We could therefore invert Manovich's argument – that the live action feature film is only the default option in a wide spectrum of moving image forms – and argue that animation is the default option of cinema and moving images. Most computerised moving images are constructed by graphic manipulation rather than cinematographic recording, by default animation as 'frame by frame manipulation'. So, if we look beyond the theatrical film and to moving image culture at large, new animated forms predominate, developing through the material possibilities and restrictions of digital technologies and networks.

2.36 *Waking Life*, 2001. © Detour/Independent Film/Line Research/The Kobal Collection

2.37 *Sin City*, 2005. © Dimensional Films/The Kobal Collection

Bibliography

Alberti, L.B. *On Painting*, New Haven, Conn.: Yale University Press, 1966.

Allen, Michael 'From Bwana Devil to Batman Forever: technology in contemporary Hollywood cinema', in *Contemporary Hollywood Cinema*, eds Steve Neale and Murray Smith, London: Routledge, 1998.

Ascott, Roy http://www.artmuseum.net/w2vr/timeline/Ascott.html, 2000.

Balio, Tino 'A major presence in all of the world's important markets. The globalization of Hollywood in the 1990s', in *Contemporary Hollywood Cinema*, eds Steve Neale and Murray Smith, London: Routledge, 1998.

Batchen, Geoffrey 'Spectres of cyberspace', in *The Visual Culture Reader*, ed. Nicholas Mirzoeff, London and New York: Routledge, 1998.

Baudrillard, Jean *Simulations*, New York: Semiotext(e), 1983.

Baudrillard, J. 'Simulacra and simulations', in *Jean Baudrillard: Selected Writings*, ed. Mark Poster, Cambridge: Polity Press, 1988.

Baudry, Jean-Louis 'Ideological effects of the basic cinematic apparatus', in *Narrative, Apparatus, Ideology,* ed. Philip Rosen, New York: Columbia University Press, 1986.

Baxandall, Michael *Painting and Experience in Fifteenth Century Italy: A Primer in the Social History of Pictorial Style*, Oxford: Clarendon Press, 1972.

Bazin, Andre *What is Cinema?,* Berkeley: University of California Press, 1967.

Benjamin, Walter 'The work of art in the age of mechanical reproduction' [1935], in *Illuminations*, ed. Hannah Arendt, revised edn, Glasgow: Fontana, 1970.

Berger, John *Ways of Seeing*, London: Penguin, 1972.

Besser, Howard 'Longevitiy of electronic art' (2001) http://www.gseis.ucla.edu/~howard/Papers/elect-art-longevity.html (accessed 15.08.06).

Binkley, Timothy 'Refiguring culture', in *Future Visions: new technologies of the screen*, eds Philip Hayward and Tana Wollen, London: BFI, 1993, pp. 90–122.

Bolter, Jay David and Grusin, Richard *Remediation: understanding new media*, Cambridge, Mass: MIT, 1999.

Brooker, Peter and Brooker, Will *Postmodern After-Images: a reader in film, television and video*, London: Arnold, 1997.

Buck-Morss, Susan 'Aesthetics and Anaesthetics: Walter Benjamin's Artwork essay reconsidered', *October* 62, MIT Press, 1992.

Buckland, Warren 'A close encounter with Raiders of the Lost Ark: notes on narrative aspects of the New Hollywood blockbuster', in *Contemporary Hollywood Cinema*, eds Steve Neale and Murray Smith, London: Routledge, 1998.

Buckland, Warren 'Between science fact and science fiction: Spielberg's digital dinosaurs, possible worlds, and the new aesthetic realism', *Screen* 40.2 Summer (1999): 177–192.

Bukatman, Scott 'There's always tomorrowland: Disney and the hypercinematic experience', *October* 57, Summer (1991): 55–70.

Cameron, Andy 'Dissimulations', *Mute, Digital Art Critique*, no. 1 (Spring), 1995: p. X.

Cholodenko, Alan 'Who Framed Roger Rabbit, or the framing of animation', in *The Illusion of Life: essays on animation*, ed. Alan Cholodenko, Sydney: Power Publications, 1991, pp. 209–242.

Christie, Ian *The Last Machine – early cinema and the birth of the modern world*, London: BFI, 1994.

Clover, Carol J. *Men, Women and Chainsaws: gender in the modern horror film*, London: BFI, 1992.

Coe, Brian *Muybridge and the Chronophotographers*, London: Museum of the Moving Image, 1992.

Comolli, Jean-Louis 'Machines of the Visible', in *The Cinematic Apparatus*, eds Teresa de Lauretis and Stephen Heath, London: Macmillan, 1980, pp. 121–142.

Cotton, Bob and Oliver, Richard *Understanding Hypermedia from Multimedia to Virtual Reality*, Oxford: Phaidon, 1993.

Cotton, Bob *The Cyberspace Lexicon: an illustrated dictionary of terms from multimedia to virtual reality*, Oxford: Phaidon, 1994.

Coyle, Rebecca 'The genesis of virtual reality', in *Future Visions: new technologies of the screen*, eds Philip Hayward and Tana Wollen, London: BFI, 1993.

Crary, Jonathan *Techniques of the Observer: on vision and modernity in the nineteenth century,* Cambridge, Mass. and London: MIT, 1993.

Creed, Barbara *The Monstrous Feminine – film, feminism, psychoanalysis*, London: Routledge, 1993.

Creed, Barbara 'The Cyberstar: Digital Pleasures and the End of the Unconscious', *Screen* 41(1) (2000): 79–86.

Cubitt, Sean 'Introduction: Le réel, c'est l'impossible: the sublime time of the special effects', *Screen* 40.2 Summer (1999): 123–130.

Cubitt, Sean 'Introduction: the technological relation', *Screen* 29.2 (1988): 2–7.

Darley, Andy 'Big screen, little screen: the archeology of technology', *Digital Dialogues*. *Ten-8* 2.2. (1991): 78–87.

Darley, Andrew *Visual Digital Culture: surface play and spectacle in new media genres*, London and New York: Routledge, 2000.

Davies, Char 'Osmose: notes in being in immersive virtual space', *Digital Creativity* 9.2 (1998): 65–74.

Debord, Guy *The Society of the Spectacle*, Detroit: Black and Red, 1983.

De Lauretis, Teresa and Heath, Stephen eds *The Cinematic Apparatus*, London: Macmillan, 1980.

Dery, Mark *Culture Jamming: hacking, slashing, and sniping in the empire of signs*, Westfield: Open Media, 1993.

Dovey, Jon ed. *Fractal Dreams: new media in social context*, London: Lawrence and Wishart, 1996.

Druckrey, Timothy ed. *Electronic Culture: Technology and Visual Representation*, New York: Aperture, 1996.

Eco, Umberto *Faith in Fakes: travels in hyperreality*, London: Minerva, 1986.

Ellis, John *Visible Fictions*, London: Routledge, 1982.

Elsaesser, Thomas *Early Cinema: space, frame, narrative*, London: BFI, 1990.

Evans, Jessica and Hall, Stuart 'Cultures of the visual: rhetorics of the image', in *Visual Culture: the reader*, London: Sage, 1990.

Featherstone, Mike and Burrows, Roger *Cyberspace, Cyberbodies, Cyberpunk: cultures of technological embodiment,* London: Sage, 1995.

Flanagan, Mary 'Digital stars are here to stay', *Convergence: the journal of research into new media technologies*, 5.2 Summer (1999): 16–21.

Forgacs, David 'Disney animation and the business of childhood', *Screen* 53, Winter (1992): 361–374.

Foucault, M. *Discipline and Punish: the birth of the prison*, Harmondsworth: Penguin, 1977.

Gibson, William *Neuromancer*, London: Grafton, 1984.

Gibson, William *Burning Chrome*, London: Grafton, 1986.

Gibson, William *Spook Country*, London: Viking, Penguin, 2007

Giddings, Seth 'The circle of life: nature and representation in Disney's *The Lion King*', *Third Text* 49 Winter (1999/2000): 83–92.

Giroux, Henry A. 'Animating youth: the Disnification of children's culture', (1995). http://www.gseis.ucla.edu/courses/ed253a/Giroux/Giroux2.html.

Goodman, Nelson *Languages of Art: an approach to a theory of symbols*, Indianapolis, Cambridge: Hackett, 1976.

Grau, Oliver *Virtual Art: from illusion to immersion*, Cambridge, Mass.: MIT Press, 2003.

Gunning, Tom 'An aesthetics of astonishment: early film and the (in)credulous spectator', *Art and Text* 34 Spring (1989): 31.

Gunning, Tom 'The cinema of attractions: early film, its spectator and the avant-garde', in *Early Cinema: space, frame, narrative*, ed. Thomas Elsaesser, London: BFI, 1990a.

Gunning, Tom '"Primitive" cinema: a frame-up? Or the trick's on us', in *Early Cinema: space, frame, narrative,* ed. Thomas Elsaesser, London: BFI, 1990b.

Hall, Stuart 'The work of representation', in *Cultural Representations and Signifying Practices*, ed. Stuart Hall, London: Sage, 1997.

Harvey, Silvia 'What is cinema? The sensuous, the abstract and the political', in *Cinema: the beginnings and the future,* ed. Christopher Williams, London: University of Westminster Press, 1996.

Hayles, N. Katherine *How We Became Posthuman: virtual bodies in cybernetics, literature, and informatics*, Chicago and London: University of Chicago Press, 1999.

Hayward, Philip *Culture, Technology and Creativity in the late Twentieth Century*, London: John Libbey, 1990.

Hayward, Philip 'Situating cyberspace: the popularisation of virtual reality', in *Future Visions: new technologies of the screen*, eds Philip Hayward and Tana Wollen, London: BFI, 1993, pp. 180–204.

Hayward, Philip and Wollen, Tana eds *Future Visions: new technologies of the screen*, London: BFI, 1993.

Heim, Michael *The Metaphysics of Virtual Reality*, New York, Oxford: Oxford University Press, 1994.

Heim, Michael 'The Design of Virtual Reality', in *Cyberspace, Cyberbodies, Cyberpunk: Cultures of Technological Embodiment*, eds M. Featherstone and R. Burrows, London, Thousand Oaks (Calif.) and New Delhi: Sage, 1996.

Hillis, Ken 'A geography for the eye: the technologies of virtual reality', in *Cultures of the Internet*, ed. R. Shields, London, Thousand Oaks (Calif.), New Delhi: Sage, 1996.

Holmes, David *Virtual Politics*, London, Thousand Oaks (Calif.), New Delhi: Sage, 1997: 27–35.

Hulsbus, Monica 'Virtual bodies, chaotic practices: theorising cyberspace', *Convergence* 3.2, 1997: 27–35.

Jameson, Fredric *Postmodernism, or the Cultural Logic of Late Capitalism*, London: Verso, 1991.

Jay, Martin 'Scopic regimes of modernity', in *Vision and Visuality*, ed. Hal Foster, Seattle: Bay Press, 1988.

Kember, Sarah 'Medicine's new vision', in *The Photographic Image in Digital Culture*, ed. Martin Lister, London and New York: Routledge, 1995.

Kipris, Laura 'Film and changing technologies', in *The Oxford Guide to Film Studies*, eds John Hill and Pamela Church, Oxford: Oxford University Press, 1998, pp. 595–604.

Klein, Norman M. 'Hybrid cinema: The Mask, Masques and Tex Avery', in *Reading the Rabbit: explorations in Warner Bros. animation*, ed. Kevin S. Sandler, New Brunswick, N.J.: Rutgers University Press, 1998, pp. 209–220.

Kline, Steven *Out of the Garden: toys and children's culture in the age of TV marketing*, London: Verso, 1994.

Kubovy, Michael *The Psychology of Perspective and Renaissance Art*, Cambridge, New York, New Rochelle, Melbourne, Sydney: Cambridge University Press, 1986.

Kuhn, Annette ed. *Alien Zone – cultural theory and contemporary science fiction cinema*, London: Verso, 1990.

Langer, Mark 'The Disney–Fleischer dilemma: product differentiation and technological innovation', *Screen* 53, Winter (1992): 343–360.

Lapsley, Robert and Westlake, Michael *Film Theory: an introduction*, Manchester: Manchester University Press, 1988.

Lévy, Pierre *Becoming Virtual: reality in the digital age*, New York and London: Plenum Trade, 1998.

Leyda, Jay ed. *Eisenstein on Disney*, London: Methuen, 1988.

Lister, Martin ed. *The Photographic Image in Digital Culture*, London and New York: Routledge, 1995.

Lister, Martin, Dovy, Jon, Giddings, Seth, Grant, Iain and Kelly, Kieran *New Media: a critical introduction*, 1st edn, London: Routledge, 2003.

Lister, Martin and Wells, Liz 'Cultural studies as an approach to analysing the visual', in *The Handbook of Visual Analysis*, eds van Leewun and Jewitt, London: Sage, 2000.

Lovell, Terry *Pictures of Reality: aesthetics, politics and pleasure*, London: BFI, 1980.

Lunenfeld, Peter *The Digital Dialectic: new essays on new media*, Cambridge, Mass.: MIT, 1999.

MacCabe, Colin 'Realism and the cinema: notes on some Brechtian theses', *Screen* 15.2 Summer (1974): 7–27.

MacCabe, Colin *Theoretical Essays: film, linguistics, literature*, Manchester: Manchester University Press, 1985.

Manovich, Lev 'Cinema and digital media', in *Perspectives of Media Art*, eds Jeffrey Shaw and Hans Peter Schwarz, Ostfildern, Germany: Cantz Verlag, 1996.

Manovich, Lev 'Reality effects in computer animation', in *A Reader in Animation Studies*, ed. Jayne Pilling, London: John Libbey, 1997, pp. 5–15.

Manovich, Lev http://jupiter.ucsd.edu/~culture/main.html, 1997.

Manovich, Lev 'What is digital cinema?', in *The Digital Dialectic: new essays on new media*, ed. Peter Lunenfeld, Cambridge, Mass.: MIT, 1999.

Manovich, Lev 'Database as symbolic form', *Convergence* 5.2 (1999): 172–192.

Marchessault, Janine 'Spectatorship in cyberspace: the global embrace', in *Theory Rules*, eds Jody Berland, David Tomas and Will Straw, Toronto: YYZ Books, 1996.

Matthews, Peter 'Andre Bazin: divining the real', http://www.bfi.org.uk/sightandsound/archive/innovators/bazin.html [n.d.]

Mayer, P. *Computer Media and Communication: a reader*, Oxford: Oxford University Press, 1999.

Metz, Christian 'The imaginary signifier', *Screen* 16.3 (1975): 14–76

Mirzoeff, Nicolas ed. *The Visual Culture Reader*, London and New York: Routledge, 1998.

Mitchell, William J. 'The reconfigured eye: visual truth', in *Photographic Era*, Cambridge, Mass.: London: MIT, 1992.

Morse, Margaret *Virtualities: television, media art, and cyberculture*, Bloomington, Ind.: Indiana University Press, 1998.

Moser, M.A. and MacLeod, D. *Immersed in Technology: art and virtual environments*, Cambridge, Mass. and London: MIT Press, 1996.

Mulvey, Laura 'Visual pleasure and narrative cinema', *Screen* 16.3 (1973): 6–18.

Murray, Janet H. *Hamlet on the Holodeck: the future of narrative in cyberspace*, Cambridge, Mass.: MIT Press, 1997.

Ndalianis, Angela 'Architectures of vision: neo-baroque optical regimes and contemporary entertainment media', *Media in Transition* conference at MIT on 8 October 1999. http://media-in-transition.mit.edu/articles/ndalianis.html.

Neale, Steve *Cinema and Technology: images, sound, colour*, London: Macmillan, 1985.

Neale, Steve 'You've got to be fucking kidding! Knowledge, belief and judgement in science fiction' in *Alien Zone – cultural theory and contemporary science fiction cinema*, ed. Annette Kuhn, London: Verso, 1990, pp. 160–168.

Neale, Steve 'Widescreen composition in the age of television', in *Contemporary Hollywood Cinema,* eds Steve Neale and Murray Smith, London: Routledge, 1998, pp. 130–141.

Neale, Steve and Smith, Murray *Contemporary Hollywood Cinema*, London: Routledge, 1998.

Nichols, Bill 'The work of culture in the age of cybernetic systems', *Screen* 29.1 (1988): 22–46.

Nichols, B. *Blurred Boundaries*, Bloomington and Indianapolis: Indiana University Press, 1994, pp. 17–42.

Nunes, M. 'What space is cyberspace: the Internet and Virtual Reality' in *Virtual Politics*, ed. D. Holmes, London, Thousand (Calif.), New Delhi: Sage, 1997.

Panofsky, Erwin *Perspective as Symbolic Form*, New York: Zone Books, 1997.

Penny, S. 'Virtual reality as the end of the Enlightenment project', in *Culture on the Brink*, eds G. Bender and T. Drucken, San Francisco: Bay Press, 1994

Penny, S. *Critical Issues in Electronic Media*, New York: State University of New York Press, 1995.

Pierson, Michele 'CGI effects in Hollywood science-fiction cinema 1989–95: the wonder years', *Screen* 40.2 Summer (1999): 158–176.

Pilling, Jayne ed. *A Reader in Animation Studies*, London: John Libbey, 1997.

Poster, Mark, *The Mode of Information: poststructuralism and social context*, Chicago: University of Chicago Press, 1990

Prince, Stephen, 'True lies: perceptual realism, digital images, and film theory', *Film Quarterly*, 49(3), Spring (1996): 27–37.

Rheingold, Howard *Virtual Reality*, London: Secker and Warburg, 1991.

Robins, Kevin *Into the Image: culture and politics in the field of vision*, London and New York: Routledge, 1996.

Rogoff, I. 'Studying visual culture', in *The Visual Culture Reader*, ed. Nicolas Mirzoeff, London and New York Routledge, 1998.

Shields, Rob *The Virtual*, London: Routledge, 2003

Silverman, Kaja *The Subject of Semiotics*, Oxford: Oxford University Press, 1983.

Sontag, Susan *On Photography*, London: Penguin, 1977.

Spielmann, Yvonne 'Expanding film into digital media', *Screen* 40.2 Summer (1999): 131–145.

Strain, Ellen 'Virtual VR', *Convergence: the journal of research into new media technologies* 5.2 Summer (1999): 10–15.

Sutherland, I. 'A head-mounted three dimensional display', *Joint Computer Conference, AFIPS Conference Proceedings* 33 (1968): 757–764.

Tagg, John *The Burden of Representation*, London: Macmillan, 1988.

Tasker, Yvonne *Spectacular Bodies: gender, genre and the action cinema*, London: Routledge, 1993.

Thompson, Kristin 'Implications of the Cel animation technique', in *The Cinematic Apparatus*, eds Teresa de Lauretis and Stephen Heath, London: Macmillan, 1980.

Tomas, David 'The technophiliac body: on technicity in William Gibson's cyborg culture', in David Bell and Barbara M. Kennedy (eds) *The Cybercultures Reader*, London: Routledge, 2000.

Virilio, Paul 'Cataract surgery: cinema in the year 2000', in *Alien Zone: cultural theory and contemporary science fiction cinema*, ed. Annette Kuhn, London: Verso, 1990, pp. 168-174

Walsh, J. 'Virtual reality: almost here, almost there, nowhere yet', *Convergence* 1.1 (1995): 113–119.

Wasko, Janet *Hollywood in the Information Age*, Cambridge: Polity Press, 1994.

Wells, Paul *Understanding Animation*, London: Routledge, 1998.

Willemen, Paul 'On realism in the cinema', *Screen Reader 1: cinema/ideology/politics*, London: SEFT, 1971, pp. 47–54.

Williams, Christopher ed. *Cinema: the beginnings of the future*, London: University of Westminster Press, 1996.

Williams, L. *Viewing Positions*, New Brunswick, N.J.: Rutgers University Press, 1995.

Williamson, Judith *Deadline at Dawn: film criticism 1980–1990*, London: Marion Boyars, 1993.

Winston, B. *Media, Technology and Society: A History: From the Telegraph to the Internet*, London and New York: Routledge, 1999.

Wollen, Peter 'Cinema and technology: a historical overview', in *The Cinematic Apparatus*, eds Teresa de Lauretis and Stephen Heath, New York: St Martins Press, 1980.

Wood, Christopher 'Questionnaire on visual culture', *October* 77 Summer (1996): 68–70.

Woolley, B. *Virtual Worlds: a journey in hype and hyperreality*, Oxford: Blackwell, 1992.

3 Networks, Users and Economics

3.1 Introduction

What we now understand to be the Internet in general and the web in the specific is the product of a number of factors. Its method of development has not been by design, like a state broadcasting institution such as the BBC. Instead its protean identity is reproduced by a mix of fandom, community, commerce and business, linked by technologies that are both private and publicly owned and variously regulated. In other words the Internet came into existence as the result of numerous factors, accidents, passions, collisions and tensions. Its ongoing development must therefore be seen as the product of those tensions; tensions which can be seen in this section between economic and regulatory factors and the communicative practices discussed further on in the section. Once this book is a few years old we think that you should be able to take some of the approaches to its study delineated in this text and be able to make sense of the direction of development. Given the dynamics of permanent upgrade culture this is a tall order but one we think worthwhile.

If you were to compare this section with that in the first edition you will find a number of similar themes; however we think that the processes that we began to explore in the first edition have now come much more to the fore and their outcomes are easier to identify. In particular we note the ways in which the desire for communication and the pressures of commercialisation have interacted to bring us Web 2.0 and its expression in the form of social networking sites (SNS). We also note the ways in which the interaction between the culture of open-source and commercially produced and protected software gives the development of networked digital media a distinctive character. We can note the way in which the development of the Internet has not only given rise to new cultural practices that have actually become a threat to the interests and business practices of huge corporations but *at the same time* given rise to new media behemoths in online distribution, retailing and services. An obvious example is the way in which the ownership of intellectual property in media and the desire to protect that ownership competes with the ongoing enthusiasm of users to swap files via a myriad of technologies, some of them having developed in a particular way directly as a result of need to get round legal prohibitions on earlier methods. It is precisely this type of interaction between enthusiasm, politics, commerce and technology that we wish to explore across the myriad forms of geeks and businessmen, college students and housewives, children and adults, gamers and gardeners that make up the web. To put it simply we think that to understand networked media it is necessary to understand their development as an ongoing product of the tension between culture and commerce. The history that we offer in these pages is the history of that tension.

In this section we use the tools of traditional political economies of the media in order to understand how the potential for the development of networked new media has been influenced by commercial interests. We are concerned with the characteristics of networks and how they have consequently been considered to have an important (some say revolutionary) impact both on the ways in which we live our lives and on the economic organisation of society. The pace of technological development and cultural change associated with the net make any fine-grained book-based analysis of it impossible. To understand contemporary net based media one must spend time online, not reading books. However a book like this *can* help us to shape the right kind of questions by putting the 'new' into an historical and economic framework and by assessing the kinds of research that have contributed to the formation of net studies.

In this section we have developed a form of writing which tries to be faithful to the complexity of web studies by trying to attend to macro economic drivers and at the same time be sensitive to the daily experiences of online media users. Just as, we have argued above, networked media are the product of the relationship between culture and commerce so this writing embodies a tension between Cultural Studies and Political Economy. The method calls upon the reader to be able to reframe as we move from the global or corporate to the daily practice of online media and back again. The ecology of networked media call for juxtapositions that suggest the rhizomatic connections between, for instance, intellectual property (IP) rights and viral media, or neo-liberalism and social network sites (SNS).

3.2 What is the Internet?

The Internet simply describes the collection of networks that link computers and servers together. An official definition was made by the Federal Networking Council in the US in 1995

See the Internet Society site for definitions and technical development http://www.isoc.org/ Internet/history/brief. shtml

> The Federal Networking Council agrees that the following language reflects our definition of the term 'Internet'. 'Internet' refers to the global information system that (i) is logically linked together by a globally unique address space based in the Internet Protocol (IP) or its subsequent extensions/follow-ons; (ii) is able to support communications using the Transmission Control Protocol/Internet Protocol (TCP/IP) suite or its subsequent extensions/follow-ons, and/or other IP-compatible protocols; and (iii) provides, uses or makes accessible, either publicly or privately, high level services layered on the communications and related infrastructure described herein.

This primarily technical definition argues for an Internet defined by the ways in which computers are able to send and receive data through the globally agreed protocols that permit computers to link together. The important aspect of such a definition is how minimal it is – the Internet is here simply a means for computers to communicate in order to provide (undefined) 'high level services'. The definition is intended to facilitate flow and exchange of data. Built into such a definition is the concept of 'open architecture' – there is no attempt here to prescribe how or where such data flows. Previous 'mass media', e.g. newspapers, film or TV, were designed as systems to send messages from a centre to a periphery; here is a system designed from the outset to provide for the circulation of information. This 'open architecture' model was envisioned as early as 1962 by the visionary J. C. R. Licklider who wrote a series of memos at MIT describing his 'Galactic Network' concept. Licklider became the first head of computer research for the Defense Advanced Research Projects Agency (DARPA) in the US, and it was this Pentagon-funded agency that eventually developed the protocols referred to above in order to allow computers to form networks that could send small packets of data to one another. The Internet Society records the astonishing growth of computer-based communications from a system based round four hosts/servers in 1969 to 200,000,000 hosts by 2002. (William Slater III, *Internet History and Growth* Chicago; Chapter of the Internet Society http://www.isoc.org/Internet/history/.) These hosts supported an enormous variety of networks, all of which developed from the initial scientific and defence oriented networks of the original Internet. These computer engineering histories determine much of the character of the Internet as we experience it today – especially the idea of an open architecture.

The question 'What is the Internet?' becomes problematic as soon as we move away from the protocols that facilitate data transfer and into the realm of the 'high level services' that they make possible. In what follows we will attempt to map the central critical debates that arise from users' engagement with the astonishing multiplicity of the Internet.

3.3 Historicising net studies

The rapid spread of networked communication through PCs and servers has attracted enormous quantities of popular excitement, critical attention and commercial interest. In truth, the growth of the Internet since the invention of World Wide Web software ranks as a truly remarkable *cultural* achievement. The quantity of human labour and ingenuity that has gone into building net-based communication systems in a very short space of time is unprecedented. It is impossible to contemplate the mass of data that has been written into web based software without experiencing a vertiginous sense of cultural endeavour. Clearly the growth of the Internet has been the site for major investments of the 'technological imaginary' (see **1.5.2** for definitions); successive waves of visionary speculation have accompanied its growth from a very limited enthusiasts' network to its current status as a popular and widely distributed form of media and communications. This investment in the technological imaginary can be seen at work, *literally,* in the rise and fall of the 'dot.com bubble' between 1995 and 2001 in which share prices for any company associated with digital technology and the Internet were inflated by excitable demand beyond their real value. Investors, seduced by techno-hyperbole, rushed to put money into companies with no proven revenue streams. The crash that followed the March 2000 peak share price has often been credited with triggering a global economic recession. The technological imaginary is powerful indeed.

In this section we will be looking at uses of the Internet and some of the dominant ways in which media and communication scholars have sought to conceptualise these developments. Although our day-to-day experience of the Internet is suffused with novelty, with a sense of immediacy and up to the minute communications, it has a history that stretches back to the Second World War. The discursive, technological and economic developments of the Internet all serve to shape our experience today.

The critical history of the Internet draws upon a wide range of approaches some of which are synthesised as the study of Computer Mediated Communication (CMC). The study of CMC has primarily developed as a socio-linguistic discipline based in Communications Theory and Sociology. Whilst there is some overlap with Media Studies in a common concern for understanding forms of technologically mediated communication it was for many years by no means clear how 'the Internet' was a medium in the same way as TV, Film or Photography were distinct media (**Case study 1.9**). It has become increasingly clear however that, following Boulter and Grusin's model of remediation, as existing media, e.g. TV, photography, find new distribution channels online they in turn *change* their cultural form. Hybridising forms of new media emerge through the interaction between existing forms and the new distribution technologies of the net. All media producers now have to consider what TV executives call '360-degree programming', i.e. how a TV text will have an online life, how audiences will be offered additional interactive experiences, how a media product might become 'trans-medial' by generating revenue across a range of audiences and platforms linked by Internet marketing and distribution. Just as the 100-minute feature emerged as the ideal length for the dream palace cinemas of the 1930s so the 5-minute video clip becomes a standard for the early days of broadband. However when these processes of remediation occur online they are often accompanied by particular kinds of claims associated with rhetorics of Internet enthusiasts.

Writing in 1995 leading net scholar Steven Jones (1994: 26) summed up the inflated claims for the impact of what was then termed 'Computer Mediated Communications' (CMC). He observed that popular and critical writing claimed that the net would:

• create opportunities for education and learning

• create new opportunities for participatory democracy

• establish countercultures on an unprecedented scale

• ensnarl already difficult legal matters concerning privacy, copyright and ethics

• restructure man/machine interaction.

These themes have continued to interest students of the net in its fully 'post web' era. Publishing nine years later David Gauntlett's review of 'some of the main issues' (2004: 14–20) are surprising insofar as they display strong continuities with the fundamental issues identified by a previous generation of CMC research. Gauntlett summarises the research areas in the field as:

1 *The Web allows people to express themselves* – through putting up their own sites, though Social Networks and peer-to-peer media sharing, through blogging and YouTube posting, 'The Web . . . offers an extraordinary explosion of opportunity for creativity and expression' (2004: 16).

2 *Anonymity and play in cyberspace* – Gauntlett extends the earlier CMC based work that seized on the possible anonymities of net based communications as a living embodiment of post-structuralist identity theory and asserts that it is where queer theory can 'really come to life . . . because the Internet breaks the connection between outward expressions of identity and the physical body' (2004: 19). However he goes on to say that this is now perhaps of less interest than thinking about expressions of identity *between* people's sites. This prefigures the growth of interest in social network sites which, as we will see below, in some ways reverses the previous focus on anonymity.

3 *The Web and Big Business* – Here Gauntlett makes the excellent point that throughout the early phase of net development the dominant discourse on the economics of the web was that business interests would destroy the culture of the web but that 'Nowadays, the bigger panics run in the opposite direction – big business are scared that the Internet will ruin them' (2004: 19). Since this publication we have seen the rise of 'open innovation' and 'wikinomics' in which the culture of co-creativity articulated through the net is becoming the basis for corporate business practice.

4 *The Web is changing politics and international relations* – This continues the arguments made by the first generation of net researchers that the Internet had the potential to revive

the public sphere through providing for multiple lateral public conversations. These trends clearly continue both in the use of web publication by 'subaltern' or outsider groups as well as through the impact of the blog explosion on the fourth estate functions of journalism.

The educational potentials of the web are now more or less taken for granted with enormous investment in IT in education and training sectors. However the emancipatory aspects of knowledge production and circulation envisaged by the first scholars of CMC are more truly apparent in the development of Wikipedia – an online encyclopaedia produced by the hive mind of its many users. The enormous success of Wikipedia has prompted all kinds of other 'Wiki' based knowledge generating and sharing processes, such that 'Wiki' has become a noun referring to a shared knowledge site just as 'Google' has become a verb meaning to find information. The academic production of knowledge has started to acknowledge that open processes of peer review are a useful way to 'guarantee' knowledge (the *British Medical Journal* began an open peer review experiment in 1999 and was followed by the prestigious journal *Nature* in 2006) and business has adopted the idea of 'open innovation' represented in the publication of books like Tapscott and Williams *Wikinomics: How Mass Collaboration Changes Everything* (2006).

On the other hand the claim that CMC would create a democratic dividend looks a little pale in a post 9/11 global environment where democratic rights of all kinds are sacrificed to the 'war on terror' and the intimate weave of communications technologies into the fabric of everyday life offers unprecedented opportunities for consumer and political surveillance. Nevertheless this apparent intensification of global control has been accompanied by extraordinary renewals of the public sphere whether by bloggers working outside the discourses of the 'embedded' journalist or by soldiers posting YouTube videos from the frontlines of Afghanistan and Iraq. Here the continuing public sphere functions of the net can be seen to afford increased levels of participation in democratic debate.

This renewal of the public sphere of course also overlaps with Jones's third point above that the net, it was alleged, would establish countercultures on an unprecedented scale. It is certainly the case that the net has facilitated the communication and consolidation of every kind of cultural community imaginable – how many of these are genuinely 'countercultural', or what this term might even mean ten years on is less clear. To be 'counter' is to be in opposition, to something, some 'mainstream'. The sheer profusion of net based affinity groups with whom users might ally themselves make the political 'edge' of the term 'countercultural' increasingly irrelevant.

Clearly Jones's fourth claim of CMC studies is all too accurate. The twentieth-century laws of Intellectual Property have been thrown into all kinds of disarray. The technological affordances of digital net based communication to illegally copy and distribute IP in the form of music and movies through peer-to-peer networks like Napster, Kazaa and BitTorrent are transforming not only IP law but also media distribution. The affordances of the net, combined with the 'open innovation' trend described above, both tied to the historical force of the open source 'information wants to be free' movement, combine in the development of the 'copyright commons'. This is a way of licensing copyright that makes work freely available: 'A protocol enabling people to ASSERT that a work has no copyright or WAIVE any rights associated with a work.'

http://creative commons.org/

Finally Jones summarises the claim that CMC will 'restructure man/machine interaction'. This prediction can certainly be seen to be true as far as the imbrication of technologies of communication into everyday life is concerned. Whether that could be said to represent a total 'restructuring' is debatable. What is clear is that the increasingly intimate relationships we have with technologies of communication continue to call into question the autonomous embodied subject. Understanding the self as a networked presence has almost become a commonplace – consciousness is increasingly understood as an 'assemblage' in which technologically mediated communications systems are as much part of our consciousness as 'nature' or the body.

In looking at the evolution of web studies as broadly summed up by Jones and Gauntlett there are, then, clear questions that continue to drive our inquiries into net based communications systems. Questions of identity performance, the influence of the net on the public and business spheres, and questions of IP continue to be the focus of the critical questions which new media scholarship attempts ask.

However in bringing these questions to bear we should be conscious that some of the research methods underpinning these inquiries are the province of other disciplinary fields such as psychology, sociology and law. This signifies a tension in new media studies itself – as the media objects of our attention transform and mutate in conditions of digital interconnectedness we need to call upon other disciplines to explain what is occurring. In these circumstances it may be beyond the scope of this book to cover all the psychological or sociological ramifications of the net. Our focus has to be on the impact of these ramifications on *media* practices. Recent developments in user-generated content (UGC), Web 2.0, co-creative practices and so called 'Long Tail' economics all suggest a distinctively new phase in the impact of the web on media production and use.

In part these 'new' developments online of the early years of the century are developments of existing Internet affordances made possible through increased bandwidth and information processing speed. This is especially true of the growth of moving image services online in sites like YouTube or online TV services such as *Joost, Babelgum* and *Current TV* because moving image is very processor and bandwidth 'hungry'. In yet other cases the development of particular net based platforms is more explicable through thinking about the complex ecologies of users, technologies and cultural forms that net applications have to survive within. For instance the first true Social Network Site *Six Degrees.com* was founded as early as 1997 but failed to thrive in the way that later SNS were able to – the 'media ecology' into which the software was introduced was not yet suitable.

Apart from the increase in bandwidth and speed of processors there is a second major new factor in the contemporary web landscape compared to its historic structure – the web is now more commercially viable, and therefore, sustainable. Web generated revenue still depends on two very traditional sources of income, advertising and retail. However retail operations are now more careful, better run and have better security than in their early days. Web retailers have also embraced the economics of 'the Long Tail', exploiting the global reach of the web to turn many tiny regional markets into one big worldwide market for many different products (see **3.13** for discussion of the Long Tail). As we will see the economic viability of the Long Tail is having significant impacts not only on the retailing of music or DVDs but also on the size of moving image audiences. This is linked to what we would argue is the most significant aspect of web media development in recent history – its establishment as a reliable advertising market. Advertising and sponsorship of web sites has also grown very fast in the first years of the century and can now offer a reliable income stream for some web based media aggregators. Figures for Internet ad spend are often provided by the industries with most interest in boosting their credibility so need to be interpreted accordingly – however most estimates point to a current (2008) ad share of around 8 percent of total advertising spend, in the UK bigger than the radio advertising sector. Moreover the trend in these figures over the past five years shows very high growth of 30–40 percent p.a. therefore attracting high investment. Market specialists predict that the Web will account for more than 10 percent of total advertising spend from 2009 onward.

Since the first edition of this book was published models of advertising online have evolved into forms more suited to the particular ecology of the web. Media production such as TV, Radio and the Press have always relied in various ways on advertising revenue for their survival. However in the age of mass media advertising revenue was measured by number of 'eyeballs' exposed to a particular ad – the *quality* of attention paid to the ad was of a considerably lower importance than the *size* of the audience. Net advertising is evolving away from that model. New forms of online advertising are emerging such as viral marketing and brand advocacy programmes using social networks, bloggers and forum moderators.

These forms of advertising are designed to cultivate 'engagement', investment in brand identities rather than merely exposure. Advertising that achieves this aim can be sold at a much higher premium than Google ads, banners or pop ups. This is key because it means that a high quality, engaged audience of a few hundred thousand can now earn as much revenue as much larger audiences in the mass media era. The consolidation of a properly founded online advertising market releases revenue streams for media production. This advertising market had not developed at the time of the first dot.com boom and crash – Internet based media practices, although still in their infancy, can have confidence in the future whilst they continue to take advertising share from the traditional media forms.

> In late 2007 *The Times* reported that Google was reporting a greater ad revenue from UK sources than ITV 1, the principal and oldest commercial channel in the United Kingdom. http://business.times online.co.uk/tol/ business/industry_ sectors/media/article 2767087.ece. Also see http://www.imedia connection.com/ content/17021.asp

3.4 Economics and networked media culture

This understanding of the economic power of the newly confident, post dot.com crash Internet media sectors prompts us to ask how its uses might interact with issues of power and control that are central to networks and consequent upon issues of ownership and investment associated with them. Here we will be concerned with the characteristics of networks and how they have consequently been considered to have an important (some say revolutionary) impact, both on the ways in which we live our lives and on the economic organisation of society. In this section we survey the development of the Internet as communications using the tools of political economy, and we look at how the development of interactive new media has been influenced by the introduction of commercial interests.

In asking these kinds of questions we will have recourse to the arguments of Williams (1974) for a model of thinking about the outcomes of communication technologies that are shaped by, on one the hand, what he refers to as social investment, and, on the other, by 'community needs' (see **1.6.3**). Social investment includes both state and private capital investment in the development and manufacture of new technologies, for reasons of both profit and social value. For example, email has been the reason for the sale of many computers because it has allowed people to keep in touch at home as well as in business. 'Community need' includes both the market, in the sense of a collection of potential purchasers with the ability to pay, and also a more generalised sense of what communicative needs different kinds of societies and cultures might have. So, for instance, the communication needs of a feudal village are different from the communication needs of a twenty-first-century house dweller, not just in terms of the kinds of information in use but also in terms of methods of delivery. The village can survive with one-to-one communications; the increased complexity of the urban setting requires systems that can deal with a mass audience. Here then we assume, for a moment, that which of the many possible affordances of web media become dominant is determined by the interaction between the communicative needs of the mode of early twenty-first-century Western societies and the ways in which commercial interests can profitably sustain them.

One of the factors determining the use of technologies of communication will be the kinds of investments made in equipment and personnel; who makes them, and what they expect in return. There is no guarantee that the investment will necessarily be in forms of communication that are most appropriate for the majority of people. Because the ownership of investment funds tends to be in the hands of commercial organisations, the modernisation of communications infrastructure only takes place on the basis of potential profitability. Take, for example, the installation of fibre-optic communications cable across the African continent. A number of African nations are involved in the development but its operational structures will be oriented to those who can pay for access. Many states that might wish to use it for education and information may not only find it too expensive but also simply unavailable to them (McChesney *et al*. 1998: 79; hyperlink: http://www.unicttaskforce.org/thirdmeeting/documents/ jensen percent20v6.htm). There can be no doubt that the development has been led by investment opportunity rather than community demand. It will undoubtedly provide much-needed communications facilities, but their actual availability is clearly not being pursued primarily for the public good. The consequences of the uneven access that will flow from such an investment are not always possible to predict.

The uses to which media technologies are put, including attempts to mobilise them for practices resistant to their commercial ethos, will also have an impact upon the social form they come to assume. Throughout the period in which economic imperatives were positioning new media of communications as central to the global economy (the 1980s) a worldwide community of users and developers was growing whose direct material communicative aims had far more in common with pleasure and entertainment, such as music, dating and photography, than with competitive advantage, profitability and commercial use.

Because we are concerned with economic development, cultural uses and their interaction we draw on a theory of base and superstructure, particularly as developed by Raymond Williams. For Williams this is not simply a case of the economic base of society defining the kinds of cultural and social formations that might exist – rather the notion of the relationship between base and superstructure is an interactive one and primarily about determination. The relationship is one by which each aspect both enables and limits the other. In other words, the development of communicative and information technologies is both about possible technical uses and about the social and economic circumstances within which they develop. It is, as Garnham has argued, about the way in which production takes place and is associated with particular social practices (Garnham 1997). To put it simply: where a free and open system of communicative networks (the Internet) has developed within an economic system based on property and profits (capitalism) one has to come to an accommodation with the other. It is important to emphasise that in the middle of this interaction lie real people who make real decisions, to paraphrase Marx: people make culture but not necessarily under conditions of their own choosing. Theories of base and superstructure need to be understood as ways of understanding those factors constraining and enabling the implementation of decisions made by people not simply as economic concerns bulldozing everything and everyone before them.

Williams expressed this as a direction of travel rather than an inevitable conclusion. 'Much of the advanced technology is being developed within firmly capitalist social relations, and investment, though variably, is directed within a perspective of capitalist reproduction, in immediate and in more general terms' (Williams 1980: 59)

It is certainly true that commercial pressures have significantly influenced the development

See 'Base and superstructure in Marxist cultural theory' in Williams (1980) for this discussion of new media; this was not an inevitable outcome of the technology but rather a product of the relationship between a range of factors that we explore in this section. Williams saw that the appropriation of new means of communication for a range of democratic uses was a possibility, whereas the dominance of neo-liberalism in the economic sphere has impacted on the character of these potential uses in particular ways. There are many, many examples of the 'democratic dividend' of networked media (for an example see Kahn and Kellner 2004). However it is also true that even a high profile ecologically based radical channel like *Current TV* becomes a site of lifestyle consumption and branding in its identification between ecology, human rights, skateboarding and extreme sports. In these circumstances the old European idea that public communication was a public good like healthcare or education has been swept away. It is also worth noting that the hostility to regulation contained within that ideology has, at least in the Western democracies, prevented the imposition of censorious regimes of control. However in China the 'Great Firewall' has combined growth of the Internet with control of access to external sites and limited what people have been prepared to produce in important fields of political and social debate. All in all, we want to avoid any sense of inevitability, either that the technology leads to particular outcomes or that the use of new media as a broadcast technology inevitably supersedes its communicative capability. It would appear that the popularity of social networking sites such as Facebook, Bebo and others have confirmed in the most recent period of web use that the communicative capability of new media have again come to the fore (www.facebook.com; www.bebo.com; www.myspace.com).

> See 'Means of communication as means of production' (Williams 1980: 62)

One of the central problems in studying media has been the question of control and the sheer scale of the capital investment required to develop communications technology. On the one hand a server can be set up in a bedroom for a thousand pounds, use free software and cost just a few pounds a month for an Internet connection. On the other hand Google deploys in the UK alone a huge amount of money which may help or hamper users and producers to put their ideas into practice. The question therefore remains: is the Internet actually meeting the hopes and aspirations of many of its early users? We can discuss this in terms not only of cash and costs but also within the dynamics of a capitalist economic system. More than that we also need to be aware of the political and social pressures that constrain the development of technology (other ways of thinking about that are offered in Part 5) and the ways in which their use is directed and determined. Some of that work is also done in Part 4, particularly in the domestic domain. In this section we want to concentrate on how commercial, social, legal and political factors impinge on the communicative potential of the new technologies, as well as their uses. One of the approaches we have found useful when considering the production of cultural practices and industrial outputs that constitute the Internet has been in that of David Hesmondhalgh, particularly in *The Cultural Industries* (2007).

It is not enough simply to deal in abstract categories. Williams himself continually differentiates between abstraction and the actual experience of culture. Rather, we need to survey the dynamics of the processes underway and consider them in relation to the theoretical approaches being used. This is particularly important with the work of Williams who, although within sight of the oncoming tide of market dominance, frequently wrote hopefully of the potential of new technologies to enable alternative modes of communication less reliant on the control of significant sums of capital. Williams argued that the amplificatory and durative aspects of media (the ability to broadcast and to store material) due to their dependence on capital investment, were much less readily available outside of the control of the state and industry (Williams 1974). In fact it has been these elements which have become more widely available.

> Williams identifies three forms of communication technology: the amplificatory, that allows the spread of speech over distance; the durative, that allows its storage; and the alternative which is made up of the use of signs – that is, methods alternative to the use of speech to convey meaning (e.g. writing, graphics etc.) (Williams 1980: 55–57)

We can see this in the way in which it is possible to easily run a blog or store a film but to mobilise a commercial peer-to-peer network like the BBC's iPlayer requires the mobilisation of millions of pounds of investment. Williams was right in that control of capital remains important, however within the communications systems he discussed the location of control has moved; primarily as a result of other decisions made about the investment of productive resources in one form of technology rather than another. To put it more simply, the expression of the ideology of neo-liberalism has been that you can do what you want with the networks available on condition that you can pay for access and use. How you find an audience is another matter!

It is clear that many of the initial barriers to entry into the web media market are far lower than they would have been for analogue media production; a lot more designers, software engineers, artisans and craftspeople can have a bright idea and develop it as the intellectual property that underpins a platform or application. However the platform only becomes a viable product when it can be shown to attract an income stream – for most web media purposes this income will derive from advertising. The Web is just as much a system for delivering eyeballs (and hearts and minds) to advertisers as the early studies of TV economics demonstrated (Smythe 1981). But the new platform or application cannot become a significant new media object until it finds an audience and to find an audience online it is necessary to develop a profile, to do marketing, to push your site. It is of course possible to take what we might call the Long Tail grassroots method to achieve this goal – i.e. invest a great deal of unpaid time and labour till someone decides to invest in it. (See **Case study 3.4**: Kate Modern – Web Drama.) However to set up a YouTube or other Content Delivery Network (see **3.23**, YouTube and post television) requires millions of dollars of investment. The venture capitalists who put money into such an enterprise do so because they expect a big return – profits certainly but more importantly the prospect of flotation on NASDAQ or in the UK AIM, or even better the prospect of a takeover by one of the big fish, Google (YouTube) or Fox (MySpace).

This kind of investment is only possible if the IP owner can prove the site or platform will attract the right kind of audience and attention, and because of the way the net affords Long Tail market reach, that audience may be much smaller than in the era of mass media. Production costs are lower and charge to advertisers per eyeball (or page impression) may be higher because – it is argued – the quality of attention brought to bear by a web ad user is higher; it can be targeted; or it requires the click that signifies brand assent. Value is also created by the pattern of user behaviour itself which provides brands with sophisticated consumer information. This new economy of web advertising has spawned a whole new method of audience analysis in the dark art of user metrics – measuring user behaviour and engagements. The affordances of the net enable advertisers to collect information about how long a user hovers over an ad, whether they click, how long they spend on a page, if they 'click through' to further brand information. All of this information can be totalised and sold to advertisers on a whole new range of packages that are far more sophisticated than previous forms of TV or Press advertising.

To summarise, lower barriers to entry mean an exponentially widening field of availability of media services all competing with each other for the capitalisation to reach profitability. Once capitalised these enterprises are competing heavily for users, therefore marketing and promotion are key. These economic conditions have a direct effect upon our user experience. The web media user constantly finds herself hailed, solicited, invited to connect. Community management has become the starting point for web marketing – web media invite the user to join, to create a profile, to post blogs or other announcements, to make links, to invite other friends and so on. This is not because the advertising and media industries just want us all to play nice and have lots of warm friendships. It is because they are seeking, in a crowded, transient marketplace characterised by a nomadic audience to create brand engagement. For users this means that our web media experiences are interrupted by, suffused with, and sometimes nearly drown in, a sea of advertising and sponsorship content. Pop-ups, banners, sponsorships, product placements, interactives and virals that pretend not to be ads are all characteristic of this media ecology. Web media are supported by an explosion of innovative forms of advertising that make our web experiences anything but the seamless flow of, for example, television. If TV, as Williams argued, was characterised by flow, then web media are characterised by interruption. A final consequence for web media users of this economic context is that our behaviours become data that can be sold on without our understanding and then used to maintain consumption in whatever segment of the Long Tail our habitus is identified with.

In a more global sense the consequence for users is that our media liberation is even more powerfully tied to a global system of production that is clearly unsustainable. The apparent liberation of the nomadic web media surfer in this light is more like the confinement of the force-fed goose engorged on a diet of virtual consumption sufficient to ensure that a steady flow of actual spend is produced.

However for most of us the consequences of the economic base become invisible through their ubiquity or even bearable – to be part of a community, to have to close down lots of ads, many of them mildly entertaining, to have our very specific modes of consumption facilitated – these all seem like small or negligible prices to pay for 24/7 on demand media.

It is also true that new media, in its networked form, has been closely identified with processes of globalisation and there are fundamental disagreements about the nature of this relationship. Many working in the tradition of political economy would claim that it is an extension of the 'universalist' tendencies present in capitalism from its early origins (Meiksins Wood 1998). More importantly, particularly in relation to the arguments about the compression of time and space (Giddens 1990), we must consider the ways in which the global and local are interlinked and whether this is peculiar to the Internet. In fact we find that the relationship is a common one and part of a widespread practice in commerce that depends on fairly conventional practices of investment and control of intellectual property.

In the rest of this section we will be dealing with some of the most important claims for the social impact of new media, particularly in relation to their new networked formation. This can be found at its most robust in the work of Manuel Castells who goes so far as to state, 'The internet is the fabric of our lives' (2000: 1). For those of us who are regular users it is certainly an important place of work, entertainment, or source of useful information. Such a claim raises more questions than it answers: in what way are our lives infiltrated by a net based experience and how is that experience influenced by the social, political and economic shaping of the technologies involved? Within this discussion we must be careful to hold onto the central idea of Williams that 'culture is material'; that is, culture is not simply an influence on the way that we live our lives – it is our lives (see **1.6.3**).

The opening line in *The Internet Galaxy*, Manuel Castells's book of reflections on the Internet, business and society. At the heart of Castells's position lies a belief that the impact of the Internet is as great as that of electricity distribution or the development of the modern corporation

3.5 Political economy

Although there is a long tradition of paying attention to the variety of contexts within which cultural production takes place, political economy differs from much of media studies in that it places the focus of research on the circumstances of production. First, it asks the question to what extent is the production of culture a practice of material production? This is not to say that Media Studies has not been concerned with the circumstances of the production of texts as well as with their content. In the 1980s and 1990s there was, however, a turn to a greater concern with the text, to audience interpretation and the reception of media texts. Work by Ien Ang on how the audience of the glossy American series *Dallas* related to the programme and David Morley's work on viewers' relationships with the UK current affairs programme *Nationwide* are good early examples of this approach (Ang 1985; Morley 1980). Earlier work, for example the Glasgow Media Group's study of news media, was much more concerned with the ways in which content maintained and replicated existing relationships of ownership and power in society. The move away from the use of political economy intensified, with theorists such as McRobbie and Radway using studies of female experience to argue that economics did not necessarily determine cultural experience (see Tulloch 2000). There have been attempts by proponents of the application of Political Economy to the study of communication to reach a rapprochement with Cultural and Media Studies, including a substantial essay by Nicholas Garnham (Garnham 1995). Others such as James Curran have argued for a need to move back towards the study of the contexts of production of media texts, but without losing the insight generated by more recent work (Curran 2000: 9–11). Perhaps two of the most significant contributions along these lines have been made by Henry Jenkins (Jenkins 2004) and Toby Miller (Miller 2004). The latter has argued that any analysis of media must pay attention to economic social and political issues whereas Jenkins has identified these issues as lying in the province of business as well as cultural practice. More typical of the divide has been Vincent Mosco's contribution which analyses, the myths, as he puts it, associated with the development of New Media (Mosco 2004). However there is some irony in that Mosco's concern with how myths influence discussion of the web is rather less useful in analysing the political and economic phenomenon that is the web itself.

McChesney *et al.* (1998) state the theoretical basis of the political economy of communication as follows:

> The scholarly study of the political economy of communication entails two main dimensions. First, it addresses the nature of the relationship of media and communications systems to the broader structure of society. In other words, it examines how media (and communication) systems and content reinforce, challenge, or influence existing class and social relations. Second . . . looks specifically at how ownership support mechanisms (e.g. advertising), and government policies influence media behaviour and content. This line of inquiry emphasizes structural factors and the labor process in the production, distribution and consumption of communication.
>
> (McChesney *et al.* 1998: 3)

Our understanding of political economy in this context is very broad, but central to what follows is a materialist grasp of the circumstances of new media production and consumption. This means we are concerned with ownership, the economics of production and consumption, competition and the role of the state, law and regulation in determining both how we experience new media and how they in turn shape our world. In other words, the central questions in this section echo those encountered elsewhere in this volume; namely, how far do our existing methods and analyses continue to be useful for understanding new media and how far do we need to reinvent them for networked media, a newly emergent object of study? We have attempted in what follows to outline some of what have become 'orthodox' ideas about the economic significance of new media, while at the same time

See 'Culture is ordinary' in N. McKenzie (ed.) *Conviction*, London: Monthly Review Press (1959), pp. 74–92 providing enough critical analysis to open up the debate. If we apply this tradition of political economy to new media, we might develop a number of central areas of research including considering the patterns of ownership of new media; how regulation and the policies of state and supra-state organisations influence the 'social form' of new media. We might also investigate the conditions of access to new media including the impact of associated costs on social distribution

Because the very forms of new media that are made available for use depend on the interaction of these forces with the activities and interests of users we also consider the early practices in the use of new media and information and communications technologies (ICT) and the potential for new types of media activities and interactions. As Graham Murdock has argued, in this way we can move towards an understanding of cultural practices and the conditions in which they take place: situations that include the process of political and economic development (Murdock 1997).

Production in a capitalist society is primarily, but not exclusively, organised around the production of goods and services (i.e. commodities) for profit. In media production, a capitalist model of production therefore leads to the creation of cultural commodities such as books, television programmes, music CDs, websites, CD-ROMs, DVDs, computer software and so on. With these types of commodity, the ways in which profitable distribution can be achieved can be quite complex. For instance, in commercial television this happens primarily through securing audiences so that advertising space can be sold. Indeed, Dallas Smythe has argued that it is the audience viewing figures or 'ratings' that are actually for sale (Smythe 1981). In fact we can see this very clearly in the way in which Google's business model actually functions on the basis of the number of clicks that an entry provides (Van Couvering 2004).

Production also increasingly takes place for the purposes of programme or programme format sales. In the US, the major studios have long been directly involved in programme production for sale to an international array of customers. In all of these cases, there is the production of a commodity that has real monetary value in the marketplace. The production

> Vincent Mosco provides a useful overview of the political economy of the cultural industries in his book *The Political Economy of Communications: dynamic rethinking and renewal*, London: Sage (1996)

Google.com

The success of Google has been built on providing a mechanism for automatically providing a ranking on the returns from searches. Most search engines use a web crawler (otherwise known as a web spider) to locate web pages. These are software applications that visit Internet servers and note the contents and links in web formatted pages. The pages are subsequently retrieved for indexing. Such crawlers provided the earliest search engines but were unable to indicate how useful the page might be. The founders of Google went a stage further and developed an algorithm (a series of steps and calculations) to weight the number of links made to a particular page. In this way a measure can be made of how useful the page might be considering how many others have links to it. Put simply the more links the higher the ranking. Google Corporation stores all the original pages on 'server farms' made up of linked PCs. Subsequent development has focused on providing mechanisms to include links to what might be considered to be appropriate adverts. Google now offers a variety of ways in which advertising strategies are sold to a wide range of small, medium, national and global enterprises. Google has accumulated considerable cash reserves and is cautiously expanding into related net based services such as mail and mapping.

(Vise 2005; Sherman 2005)

of culture also requires the development of studios, the purchase of kit and the utilisation of the labour of real people. Into this process of cultural production also enter less tangible factors of taste, aesthetics, audience desire, novelty, and so on, which are difficult to predict but nonetheless are important arbiters of commercial success. In all these ways, and no less in the case of new media, there is an actual process of production underway. The problem is to explain how cultural commodities are both part of the economic base of society but also function symbolically or ideologically as cultural artefacts and texts. For example, regulations claiming to ensure taste and decency in television exist in the US and the UK and are increasingly being sought for new media as well. Breaching social mores might increase profitability in one area but cause considerable difficulty in terms of public opprobrium. Precisely this process was seen in the use of video cassettes in the 1980s for the distribution of horror films that had a limited and controlled distribution within film distribution networks (Barker 1992). Political economy tells us there is a balance to be discovered between how the power relationships in society, corporate and state, interact with social attitudes and audience taste to determine what is possible in a particular media arena. It is necessary therefore to look at the ways in which the actions of users, the development process and the re-articulation of those uses can impact on the intentions of the original developers to bring new uses and practices into existence. The process has been identified as comprising the social forms of media and it is to this that we now turn.

3.6 The social form of new media

The process of 'social shaping' (**1.6.3**) leaves a medium with a social form, an identity, which influences the way it is used and its impact on the world; it is never quite shaken off. In this way we can see that new media are as much the product of social, political and economic forces as they are of technological endeavour. Media not only influence the way in which we see and experience our world but are products of the world in which we live. As we discussed earlier (see **1.1**) our contemporary experience of intense change is not only associated with new media but also with other wider kinds of social, economic and political experience. It is also true that the very intensity of change is something we associate with the capitalist economic system. So it is that in a modern economy the development and use of media are deeply imprinted by the circumstances of their creation. Williams pointed out in theoretical terms how the 'social significance' of a technical invention only came about once it had been selected for investment and production, 'processes which are of a general social and economic kind, within existing social and economic relations, and in a specific social order' (Williams 1989: 120). The spread of the Internet and its colonisation by commercial forces, particularly in retail sales is an excellent demonstration of this process in action.

See Brian Winston, *Media Technology and Society: a history from the telegraph to the Internet*, London: Routledge (1998), for more on the operation of these forces on technological development

To understand this process better we will look at three examples, starting with the personal computer, the machine that plays such an extremely important role in the growth of new media (see **4.2.1**).

The IBM PC originated in the company's research labs in the 1980s because of the pressure on its traditional business from the new desktop computers. To get the new IBM machines onto the market as rapidly as possible they were assembled from readily available components. They were, therefore, always going to be easy to replicate. The operating system, Microsoft's Disk Operating System (MS-DOS), used on the new PCs was also sold as PC-DOS. It was widely available and easily distributed on cheap floppy disks. Overall the very origins of the IBM PC made it very difficult to protect it from copying, since almost everything that made it work was already widely available. The fact that it was assembled from all sorts of bits and pieces also meant that it was impossible to use patent law to protect the design of the hardware. The IBM PC may have been clunky and inelegant but anyone could make one, and they did. To make matters worse (for IBM), because of a commercial miscalculation Microsoft were left with the rights to the operating system, which was where the new monopoly in software was eventually to flower.

In the origins of the World Wide Web, we can see how the idea of social form applies not only to hardware and commercial objects but also to forms of knowledge. The origin of the web lay in a widely readable computer code, **HTML** (HyperText Markup Language), first published in 1990. It was developed in the scientific academic world to transfer images and text within the international user community associated with CERN (Organisation Européenne pour la Recherche Nucléaire).

Since that community was using a variety of types of computers and associated software, many with their own ways of handling text and images, the challenge was to develop a code that would work equally well on all of them. Rather than try to develop yet another set of international standards for files, the new code simply told a wide range of computer systems what to do with the files they were receiving. To make the new code even easier to use web browsers were developed at the university-based National Centre for Supercomputer Applications (NCSA). The code was made publicly available and is still the basis of both Netscape and Internet Explorer. Once web browsers became items of commercial interest, extra gimmicks and capabilities gave a business advantage and meant that there was good reason for private companies to keep some code developments to themselves. In consequence, business organisations were now creating new standards that only their own products could interpret. Commercial investment building on academic research has thus given the web browser a new social form. In other words, the form and distribution and capabilities of a web browser are as much a product of the ownership of the code as of technical potential. Moreover the fact that this code was first developed in the public sector, as part of an attempt to promote co-operation and exchange, has a legacy within the social form of the web browser despite its subsequent development within a market framework. The roots of the Internet in the publicly funded uses and the PC in the private sector are both integral to the way in which the Web and its communicative capabilities have remained in play. It is notable that the power of this public root of Internet use is such that the control of specifications for HTML and it offshoots such as XML remain important methods for determining the actions and locations of other software within browsers. For example Microsoft's latest application for delivering media, Limelight, still depends on some very traditional HTML as well as a variety of proprietary software.

We have seen in these examples that the form of a medium is a product not only of what is technically possible, but also of the material and economic circumstances of its creation. These circumstances may be commercial or intellectual, or a mixture of these and other factors, but they leave the medium with a social form that cannot be ignored. The outcome of these three vital developments is hardly determined any more by the technology that they contain than by the social circumstance of their development. But the 'social form' which they take, along with other developments, and investment in communications combine to give us the Internet.

We can see that new media, how they are represented, how they are sold and the commercial interests underlying them, are the complex outcomes of the interaction between our existing culture, business interests, and major investments in telecommunications. All are underpinned by the availability of computing power in an average home that far exceeds that which put a man on the moon in 1969. But on its own this is not enough to explain the

See **4.2.1** for a discussion of the social form of the PC as a domestic commodity

See Robert X. Cringely, *Accidental Empires: how the boys of Silicon Valley make their millions, battle foreign competition and still can't get a date*, London: Penguin (1996b), for a well-informed and entertaining description of the ups and downs of the invention of the Personal Computer particular form that information and communications technologies have taken. At this point it is important to note that the interaction under discussion is actually implemented by real people who also require an ideological structure in order to negotiate the range of meanings and practices that will construct the media regime under discussion. We will see how terms such as information economy both express and construct ways of thinking and consequent action.

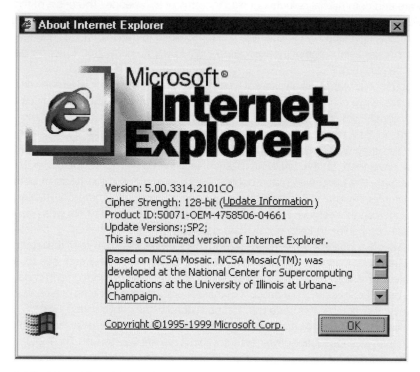

3.1 The history of the web browser in an earlier version of Internet Explorer Browser. Courtesy of Microsoft

3.7 Limits on commercial influence

We have argued that it is important to note the influence of commercial interests on the development of the Internet; however it would be a mistake to see business and corporations as always successful in their attempts to dominate new media. As we can see in the discussion of the music industry and the control of the distribution of music the existing structures and practices can make it difficult for them to switch operations to new potentially profitable investments (see **3.12**).

For example the big Internet service providers in the US, Prodigy and CompuServe, completely misinterpreted the demands that users would begin to make of the Internet in the 1980s (Stone 1995). They assumed they would be able to market information on a broadcast model such as booking services, weather forecasts, news services, etc. It transpired that the subscribers who formed their early users were more interested in connectivity, in chat, bulletin boards and email – in new collaborative or intimate communication experiences. In fact as the development of Web 2.0 has shown besides retail provision, communications has remained a number one use (see **3.16**).

New media can carry a sense of being the technological correlative of postmodern thought. Speed, flexibility, digitality, hypertextuality have all been posited as characteristic both of new media and of postmodernity. If this is the case, can political economy explain these apparently radically innovative technological and social forms? It could be argued that post-modernism, with its emphasis on fluidity, the immediate, and the constant re-referencing of texts, sits uneasily alongside the more materialist approach of political economy. However, it is equally true that to attempt to develop a critical method for thinking about cyberculture without recourse to its material history is to operate entirely from within its own discourse. To allow history to be dematerialised or production to masquerade as entirely virtualised is to lose an important critical perspective. Therefore, we must now turn to some economic history in order to offer a broad context within which to understand the relationships between networked communication and economic development.

3.8 Globalisation, neo-liberalism and the Internet

Strong claims were made for the apparently obvious association of information processing technologies with new economic structures (see Castells 1996, or the UK Government White Paper quotation below). To understand more about this relationship we have to go back to an economic history of increased flexibility, mobility of finance, and free markets described by theories of globalisation and experienced at precisely the time the Internet was going through a huge expansion.

During the 1970s Western capitalism experienced a crisis. Increases in unemployment, the closure of production plants and the slashing of public expenditure and welfare budgets all ensued. It is with this crisis that accounts of the post-industrial economy begin. Variations of **Keynesian** economic models had been adopted within social democratic frameworks in the West during the postwar years as a way of managing and stabilising the capitalist indus-trial economies. Keynesianism, which had involved the government increasing public investment at times of low private investment, had been intended to smooth over the booms and slumps associated with the great depression of the 1930s and earlier periods of eco-nomic difficulty. However, during the 1970s low economic growth rates combined with high inflation in ways that began to demonstrate the limits of the Keynesian economic model. In particular growth prompted by government spending came to be perceived as a significant cause of inflation, which itself then undermined the value of savings and purchasing power. This underlying problem was exacerbated and elevated to crisis by sudden sharp increases in the price of oil.

The policy involved the state divesting itself of publicly owned enterprises such as gas, electricity and telecommunications. This was allied with a reduction in public sector invest-ment and tax cuts that primarily benefited the wealthy. In addition, there was a considerable reduction in the power of organised labour achieved partly by the imposition of legal fetters on the right to strike. Overall, it involved a further intensification of the uneven distribution of wealth across society. Justified by pointing to a 'trickle down' effect, it was argued that the concentration of wealth in fewer hands would overcome poverty as it was reinvested in new firms and jobs. Because of its impact on public services it was characterised in a term first used by the American economist J. K. Galbraith as 'private wealth, public squalor'. It repre-sented a repudiation of social responsibility for every member of society.

See J.K. Galbraith, *The Affluent Society*, London: Hamilton (1958)

The response of owners of investment capital to the limits of growth that this crisis seemed to represent was to devise three new strategies. First was to seek to reduce the costs of production and to cultivate new markets. This was followed by the generation of a demand for the release of resources controlled by the state (e.g. energy, telecommunications, transport) into the marketplace. The third strategy was to produce an intensified search for cheaper sites of production as well as new markets across national borders. These developments were represented politically by the rise of a newly militant right-wing politics, based on economic **monetarism**, represented most clearly in the West by the Reagan–Thatcher axis of the 1980s.

This first strategy led to large-scale programmes of deregulation as part of what we might now call the ideology of **neo-liberalism**; that is to say, the belief that the commodity market is the best way of distributing resources, and to that end as many goods and services must be available for trading, and at as many sites and in as many markets as possible. Hence markets that had been 'regulated', managed or protected by state legislation were thrown open to competition, leading to large-scale transfers of capital from state to private sectors and to increases in profitability. Equally, production processes such as steel or coal that had been 'regulated' (i.e. protected through subsidy) were thrown open to an allegedly free market.

The second of these strategies led to what was labelled as globalisation – the rate of annual increase in investment from abroad in individual economies soared from 4 percent from 1981–1985 to 24 percent in the period 1986–1990 (Castells 1996: 84). One of the outcomes of this process it was claimed was an economy largely freed from the constraints of national borders and local time. It was argued that this was something different, 'an economy with the capacity to work as a unit in real time on a planetary scale' (Castells 1996: 92). A flavour of the period can be deduced from the claims that distinctively different, but not wholly new, forms of economic production were established in the last quarter of the twentieth century. These have been variously described as 'late capitalism' (Jameson 1991), 'post-Fordism' (Coriat 1990), or earlier formulations such as 'post-industrialism' (Touraine 1969; Bell 1976), and by Castells as 'the network society'.

Castells summarised the shift:

> In the industrial mode of development, the main source of productivity lies in the introduction of new energy sources, and the ability to decentralise the use of energy throughout the production and circulation process. In the new, informational mode of development the source of productivity lies in the technology of knowledge generation, information processing, and symbol communication.

> (Castells 1996: 17)

US policy combined a very particular libertarian approach with the needs of business and community:

> We are on the verge of a revolution that is just as profound as the change in the economy that came with the industrial revolution. Soon electronic networks will allow people to transcend the barriers of time and distance and take advantage of global markets and business opportunities not even imaginable today, opening up a new world of economic possibility and progress.

> Vice President Albert Gore, Jr., in Clinton and Gore, 1997

In the United Kingdom the techno utopian tone even appeared in normally somewhat staid parliamentary papers:

Our world is changing, and communications are central to this change. Digital media have revolutionised the information society. Multi-channel television will soon be available to all. More and more people can gain access to the Internet, through personal computers, televisions, mobile phones, and now even games consoles. The choice of services available is greater than ever before. High-speed telephone lines give households access to a whole new range of communications services and experiences. Using their TV sets people are able to email, shop from home, and devise their own personal viewing schedules. The communications revolution has arrived.

Foreword to A New Future for Communications
UK Government White Paper (Policy Proposal)
DTI/DCMS, December 2000 [www.dti.gov.uk]

At the beginning of the twenty-first century for large swathes of the population in the advanced countries of the world what is described is simply commonplace and at the same time for many billions more simply unattainable.

3.9 The digital divide

One of the implications of the account above is that the internationalisation of the world economy could only have happened with high-speed digital communications. These concurrent developments need to be examined carefully to disentangle those elements that are genuinely novel from those that are simply the intensification of existing tendencies. For example, capitalism has always been associated with international trade and that trade has always been associated with social upheaval. The earliest capitalist epoch, that of mercantilism, generated the largest migration in human history when some 11 million slaves were transported from Africa to the Americas, a cultural impact that has probably never been equalled. It can also be shown as Rediker does in his study *The Slave Ship* that it was the capacity of a new machine, in this case the slave ship itself that enabled a new form of trade and empire to flourish (Rediker 2007).

The period of modern industrial development since the mid-eighteenth century introduced the most rapid and unrelenting social change (Hobsbawm 1987). Once the demise of peasant and artisanal production was complete the speed of development of new technologies, from steam to petrol to fission, was only equalled by their spread across the face of the world. However, there are still major inconsistencies in access to even the basics of existence, as is indicated by the term 'least-developed countries' that now describes the Third World. The promise of industrial capitalism, enjoyed so deeply by some, is still to reach many.

This inconsistency is a part of the industrial character of our world and can be seen in its very origins. The Industrial Revolution uprooted traditional small-scale communities, set large-scale migrations of workers in process, destroyed traditional craft skills and ways of life, introduced new patterns of work and rhythms of daily life, reconstituted the nature of the family unit and, above all, brought all kinds of production, including cultural production, face to face with the demands of the marketplace. Populations increased rapidly and were concentrated in new urban industrial centres – traditional institutions of communication and education (church, word of mouth, broadsheets, basic literacy) were outstripped by newer mass media. The scale of the changes begs the question of whether we can really compare the digital revolution with the almighty upheaval of the relatively recent past.

To see globalisation as purely a product of a technological push into digital media is to succumb to a form of technological determinism. As was discussed at **1.6**, a more complex

Hobsbawm (1987) brings together the history of economic and political change consequent upon the development of industrial production in the UK in the period 1750–1960. Although published some years ago it is still a vibrant study of the relationship between industry, politics and international economy

view offers technology as a cultural construct as well as an influence on culture and human development. For instance, it has been argued that the increased global interconnections facilitated by ICTs offer great potential progress for social change (Featherstone 1990). That this view of the interconnectedness of globalisation and the advent of ICTs should gain widespread support is hardly surprising if we consider the major changes in international relations that have taken place at the same time as the growth of the digital technologies. The 'new era' of global geopolitics is contemporaneous with the development of networked communications media.

In contrast McChesney *et al*. (1998) argued that much of what has been called globalisation is rather another version of neo-liberalism (i.e. the opening up of markets to international investment). This local/global relationship is also extremely important in the media industry. Local companies owned by global media businesses such as Sony Bertelsmann Music Group frequently source local products to fit with particular musical styles and tastes.

It has also been argued that the possibility of a genuinely global economy is limited by the inability of capitalism to provide the required material resources (Amin 1997). In other words, that far from delivering social and economic development the very spread of digital media is handicapped by the capitalist economic system within which it came into existence. The disparity between the claims for world dominance of the Internet and its actual spread around the world needs to be kept in mind if we are to develop a more sophisticated and open model of globalisation. Similarly, while corporations and world bodies such as the World Trade Organisation are increasingly important, individual states have considerable power to develop or inhibit the growth of new systems of communications. For example, the reluctance of the Chinese government to allow free access to the Internet is an inhibitory factor just as the enthusiasm of the US government plays a role in its growth.

Globalisation, in the preceding account of the development of the post-industrial information economy, has become its own 'meta-narrative', implying an unrealistic degree of homogenisation and inevitability. Well-known global processes such as McDonald's or Coca-Cola already have regional difference built into their global reach; there is no reason to suppose ICT use should be any different.

In addition, unequal patterns of access are likely to be the dominant shaping factor of the global character of ICT use. Dan Schiller (1999) went further and argued that, if anything, the Internet is likely to exacerbate existing social inequalities. Certainly, access to networked communication is not a global enveloping phenomenon. Servers, despite their rapid spread are still overwhelmingly concentrated in the advanced and developed nations. We will return to these questions of access again.

Overall these changes in the ways in which capitalism operates work primarily at the level of intensity rather than signifying any significant change in the underlying principles. They make it easier for investors to operate in parts of the economy (or the globe) from which they were previously excluded. However, such changes cannot be simply dismissed as 'more of the same' (Garnham 1997). It is vital (and we pay a lot of attention to this subject below) that we hang on to this sense of the way in which the intensification of the practices associated with capitalism has also led to people trying to find ways to maintain community, to keep friendship networks alive, to entertain themselves and to educate themselves and how many of these practices now take place via electronic communications systems, powered by electricity, mobilised via screens and paid for by subscription to incredibly extensive communications networks.

In addition to the drive to seek new markets outside national boundaries, enterprises also began to export their manufacturing bases to other countries, especially those of the Pacific

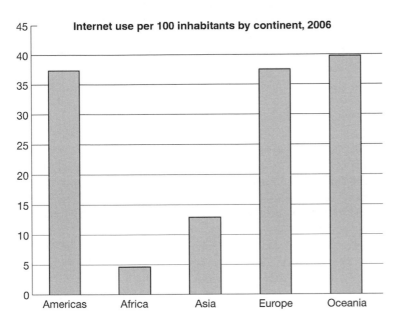

3.2 Internet users by continent, 2006.
Source International Telecommunications Union http://www.itu.int/ITU-D/ict/statistics/ict/index.html
Viewed 3 April 2008

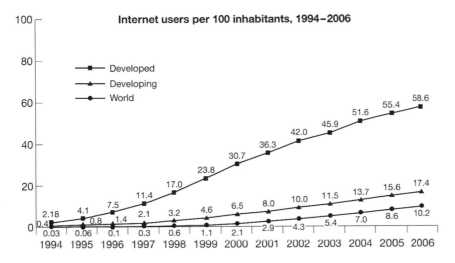

3.3 Internet users per 100 inhabitants.
Source: International Telecommunications Union; http://www.itu.int/ITU-D/ict/statistics/ict/index.html

Rim, in an effort to find cheaper production based on lower wages, lower taxes and fewer social obligations: hence the widespread relocation of smokestack industries from the rich Northern Hemisphere countries to the poorer countries of the South and East. This development required increased use of subcontractors and their plants, and increased global information flow to manage such mobility. To this picture was added a new factor when in the 1990s the deregulation of international financial markets combined with the deregulation of telecommunications to generate an important new opportunity for investment in ICTs (Baran 1998). This was not a 'natural' occurrence; in 1997, sixty-five companies signed an agreement under the aegis of the World Trade Organisation to transfer all state-owned telecommunications enterprises into private hands. The process had started in the UK with British Telecom in 1984 and in the US through the breakup of telecom corporation AT&T in 1984. Deregulation of telecoms generally refers to the removal of public service obligations from telecommunications companies. The role of bodies such as the Federal Communications Commission in the USA is now primarily in the preservation of a number of providers and to maintain competition in a system prone to the development of monopoly. Privatisation was a way of divesting the state of ownership of industries and transferring considerable resources into the private sector at a low cost to it. The acceptability of both approaches depends on an acceptance by society as a whole that the market is the most efficient method for the allocation of resources (Baran 1998). In the United Kingdom the establishment of the Office for Communications Regulation (Ofcom) saw the introduction of a neo-liberal approach to the management of broadcast media and telecommunications. The result was the development of an approach which saw the market as the arbiter of behaviour rather than any need for legal and political oversight of content by regulators.

The development of a global economy required the deregulation of international financial markets, characterised in the UK as the Stock Exchange Big Bang of 1988. An international deregulated financial market was more easily achievable because of computer networking and the increasing capacity of such networks to handle complex data. The result was a large inflow of capital into the telecom industries and the loosening of laws governing cross-media ownership (e.g. of newspapers and television broadcasters) that had previously been designed to maintain a certain diversity of view in public debate. The recognition that networked communications held the key to the success of newly globalised systems of production together with the deregulation of telecommunications combined to produce very high levels of investment and attendant euphoria around the emergent digital media industries. The economic changes that determined the development of networked communications were accompanied by political arguments for the importance of the information economy as the saviour of capitalism. The widespread exaggeration of the efficacy of digital communications that characterised the early 1990s (see Dovey 1996: xi–xvi) had been prefigured during the previous decade by politicians and futurologists keen to embrace the technological implications of the new global economies of neo-liberalism. It is during the mid-1980s that we begin to see the rhetoric surrounding the emergence of computer communications shift from a kind of pan-educational enthusiasm for civic revival to a rhetoric of economic regeneration.

As we have discussed above many early predictors of the information economy foresaw utopian humanist possibilities in the technology. However, as Roszak pointed out (1986: 23–30) by the middle of the 1980s hi-tech had been identified by politicians of the new radical Right as the economic engine of change. The aim of this enthusiasm for hi-tech was, argues Roszak, 'to design a flashy, updated style of conservatism that borrows heavily upon the futurologists to create a sense of forward looking confidence' (Roszak 1986: 24).

The idea of the information economy was being promoted as a political future at the same time as the economic conditions (of neo-liberalism) that would bring it about were being established; it was promoted incessantly as the alternative to the dirty, worn-out, politically intransigent industrial economy. With remarkable prescience, Roszak poses the question as early as 1986:

[C]an the latest generation of micro and mini computers be merchandised on a larger scale as mass communication items? Can the general public be persuaded to see information as a necessity of modern life in the same way it has come to see the refrigerator, the automobile, the television as necessities? The computer makers are wagering billions that it can. Their gamble has paid handsomely and lost disastrously with each turn of the business cycle. Yet it is primarily from their advertising and merchandising efforts that information has come to acquire a cult-like following in society.

(Roszak 1986: 30)

In the first half of the 1990s we saw these two strands, economic determinations and the discourse of marketing, combine to produce the all-pervasive idea of 'the information economy'. This dynamic historical interaction between technology, economics and politics has been described as 'the old society's attempt to retool itself by using the power of technology to serve the technology of power' (Castells 1996: 52). It has been argued by Garnham that the use of terms such as 'knowledge' or 'information' economy are in this sense ideological; that is, that they are used to fix critics of these processes as old fashioned and unprepared to modernise (Garnham 2000). More importantly, the central claim that we all live in an 'information age' is also open to question on the basis of the actual spread of the technologies and access to them and the nature of the content of new media. We now therefore turn to an examination of the digital divide between the haves and the have-nots.

We can see particularly if we pay attention to the data in **Figures 3.2** and **3.3** that the dissemination of communications technologies has still not reached the level of penetration that would suppose the globe is encompassed in a complete web of interconnectedness. It is also true to say that in many parts of the world significant numbers of people do not have sufficient funds to pay for an international telephone call much less subscribe to, or make use of, more sophisticated communications technologies. It may well be more appropriate to say that for a layer of society, a thinner or thicker layer depending upon the level of economic development, the world is actually globalised in terms of access to and investment in the world's resources.

Not only is access to online resources globally uneven, it has also been shown that the digital divide mirrors income inequality in Western countries. It is therefore not possible to talk about simple, universal, levels of involvement with, and experience of, new media. The raw data about the distribution of servers and PCs tells as much about internal difference within nation-states as it does about the division between countries. The lines of the divide within states has been considered in a number of ways and identified as consisting of as many as eight different elements across class, access, gender, physical location, as well as skills and the ability to contribute content or locate useful content (Wilson 2003; Castells et al. 2006). In 2007 the US Department of Commerce reported that urban households with incomes of $150,000 and higher were three times as likely to have access to the broadband Internet as those with incomes less than $25,000. Whites are more likely to have access to the Internet from home than Blacks or Hispanics have from any location. Almost half of households with an income of less than $50,000 are without broadband Internet access at home.

http://www.ntia.doc.gov /reports/2008/Table_Ho useholdInternet2001.pdf More detail can be found on The National Telecommunications And Information Administration website at http://www.ntia.doc.gov

Up-to-date figures on US computer use and Internet access can be obtained from http://www.ntia.doc. gov/ntiahome /fttn00/chartscontents. html

On-Line Content for Low Income and Underserved Americans: http://www.childrens partnership.org/ pub/low_income/index .html

Pierre Bourdieu identifies the non-economic forces such as family background, social class, varying investments in, and commitments to, education, different resources, etc. which influence academic success as 'cultural capital': a form of non-financial advantage. Pierre Bourdieu, 'The forms of capital', in John Richardson (ed.) *Handbook of Theory and Research for the Sociology of Education*, New York: Greenwood Press (1986), pp. 241–258

In other words, across the richest country in the world access to new media remains differentiated by income and ethnicity (but at least in the US the gap between men and women is narrowing). The report also indicated that there was little or no difference on an ethnic basis; the ethnic disparities in access referred to above simply mirror economic inequalities. Back in 1998 Novack and Hoffman also argued that differential access to online resources is a function of income. They also discovered more specific instances of 'unevenness' in their study; for example, African Americans were more likely to have access at work and black students had less likelihood of having a computer and Internet connection at home. These differences are clearly important in considering the ways in which the places from which we access online affect what we can do when we go there. A report on attempts to provide alternative ways to access the Internet in two US cities demonstrated that free use alone is not enough (Kvasny and Keil 2006).

When it comes to the question of gender there is a similar picture of differentiated access on the basis of income. But the question of access to digital information is not restricted to questions of hardware and telecommunications links. There is also a problem in what is actually provided over the net and what uses can be made of it. The emphasis during the dotcom explosion was on the provision of services and purchasing opportunities, the important factor being the extraction of surplus cash by variations of a retail market. By contrast, for low-income families net use concentrated on improving educational opportunities for children. At its heart the question of content, the purpose of content and what it might be used for is also differentiated according to income and even to other uses, such as to keep in touch with dispersed families. Unfortunately the costs in simply gaining access to such opportunities in the first place remain prohibitive for many.

Interviews with those on low incomes in the US indicated that their desire to use the Internet is informed by a wish to overcome just those factors that impeded their access to it. People want access to job listings, community services, housing, and so on. The coincidence of low incomes and recent immigration status and widespread problems with literacy also adds another dimension to people's information requirements, raising questions of the level of content, as well as opportunities to overcome poor education. In other words, the much-lauded capabilities of the Internet, the ability to connect communities and to provide access to social resources are unavailable to precisely those people who would benefit most. This is not an insuperable problem, but the ideology of neo-liberalism, so closely associated with the digital revolution, is inimical to those without the cultural capital or economic wherewithal to get past the first hurdle of affordable access.

The response of government, both in the UK and in the US, had been to see computer use as primarily about the acquisition of computer skills. Once these skills are acquired employment should follow and then income will resolve any other questions about access. Of course this might be the case for those who are excluded from the labour market for the sole reason of poor employability. The problem remains that those who are excluded for other non-employment related reasons (e.g. language, caring responsibilities, lack of 'cultural capital') may remain cut off from an increasingly important part of our society.

The report of the Children's Partnership made nineteen recommendations to overcome these problems, and some of them, such as availability of public information in appropriate languages, are well within the capabilities of many government departments. However, it is the delivery of skills, the creation of practically useful community based resources, and ongoing research and development that are difficult to supply in a commercial environment. Where it has been argued (Callanan 2004) that an important element in delivering access to many lay through the national broadcasters, the extension of privately owned broadcasting and the decline in protection for public service in the UK at least, has weakened the ability of the public sector to provide such resources.

In other words, the digital divide reproduces other kinds of inequalities in the society at large and has become a key site for debates about social inclusion. However, the outcome of these debates has been determined by precisely the kind of complex interactions between ownership, regulation, technology and ideology previously referred to. In particular the resolution of the 'digital divide' will depend upon whether any notion of public service media can be maintained in the face of a context dominated by neo-liberalism's antipathy toward regulation and state intervention. In the absence of regulation and an increased role for markets the volatile nature of a capitalist economy, with its tendency to expansion and slump must also be factored into the development of media.

3.10 Boom and bust in the information economy

Nobel laureate Joseph Stiglitz, former chair of the President's Council of Economic Advisors and chief economist at the World Bank, has stated that the recession of 2001 illustrated that the 'New Economy rhetoric contained more than a little hype' (2002) via the biggest bankruptcy in history (WorldCom), the largest stock market slide since the Depression (Wall Street), the most profound exposure ever of fictive capital (Enron) and unprecedented bank failures and the associated credit crunch of 2008. Stiglitz memorably perorates that the new economy came at a time when:

> Money that could have gone into basic research, to improve the country's long term prospects; money that could have been spent to improve the deteriorating infrastructure; money that could have been invested in improving both dilapidated inner-city schools and rich suburban ones, instead went into useless software, mindless dot-coms, and unused fibre-optic lines.

> (Miller 2004)

By the mid-1990s, the idea of information as *the* commodity of the post-industrial economy had become firmly established. The centrality of computing and of networked communication had become clear. However, during the final years of the century there was an increased awareness that new media, particularly information (rather than entertainment) had a specific economic identity and value of its own. This expressed itself in two related ways and represents another point at which we start to bring ICTs and the global economy back together in our analysis. First, massive amounts of capital have been invested in hi-tech industries themselves, especially communications networks and the associated computers. Here we see the technology that had previously played only a propaganda role in the ideas of neo-liberalism become the object of real investment in the new liberated market economy. Investment funds, unable to find a profitable home in more traditional industries, were sucked into the seemingly undeniable promise of hi-tech stocks which found their own market on the NASDAQ (National Association of Securities Dealers Automated Quotation).

Second, the speculative market in hi-tech stocks on the NASDAQ was fuelled at least in part by the second aspect of the intensification of the economic character of new media. By the end of the century, the idea of the 'information society' as representing the dissemination of humanist educational value, an arguable conception as Garnham has pointed out, had all but withered in the face of a neo-liberal reconstruction of the idea of cyberspace itself. The innovative informational spaces, interactive, information-rich and largely free, opened up by

See http://www.childrens partnership.org /pub/ low_income/index.html

See 'Statutory Duties and Regulatory Principles' on the Government regulator, Ofcom's website for an indication of a preference for a 'light touch' regulation of markets rather than prescription of services or content http://www.ofcom.org. uk/about/sdrp/

The NASDAQ was formed to provide a home for the dealing in shares of companies too small for the New York Stock Exchange. It went live on 8 February 1971. It later became a home for fledgling computer companies and many of them have kept their listing on the computer-based system. In 1994, it overtook the NYSE in volumes of shares dealt. See http://www.nasdaq.com /about/ timeline.stm and for a more critical view http://slate.msn.com/ Assess ment/ 00–04–21/Assessment. asp new media, and discussed in greater detail above, were transformed from open fields of human potential to marketplaces pure and simple.

Here we come to another clear point of intersection between economic determination and media form. We would argue that the website, as a form, has changed in quality over the past few years as a direct result of economic context. The owners of investment capital placed in NASDAQ-listed companies also saw cyberspace as a marketing and consumption opportunity. Despite the difficulties of actually trading over the net innumerable businesses were set up in order either to sell directly – web based mail order – or to sell site users to advertisers and hence create profit through advertising revenue. The website was redefined on a broadcast economic model in which 'page impressions' became the measure of 'eyeballs' delivered to advertisers and therefore the determinant of the rate at which ads on a site can be charged. Interactivity is here limited to the expressions of willingness and ability to purchase

However, the dotcom businesses proved to be another example of one of finance capital's oldest experiences, the speculative boom. Common to many periods, from the eighteenth-century South Sea Bubble to tulipomania, through railways to the Wall Street crash, each spectacular explosion of speculative investment has risen like a rocket and come down again like the stick.

Through 1999 and early 2000 the rush to invest in dotcoms reached a frenzy, with investment funds offering returns of more than 100 per cent in less than a year. This promise was based on little more than enthusiasm and technophilic passion – very few direct consumer service providers were able to demonstrate that their sites could actually maintain secure income streams. Continuing security and cryptography problems disadvantaged the Internet as a site of consumption. Dotcom entrepreneurs chose to overlook the fact that many consumers actually enjoy the physical as opposed to virtual aspect of shopping. When it became clear that the new dotcom businesses could not deliver the promised rates of investment share prices began to fall. Between the end of 1999 and mid-2000, NASDAQ shares fell by 40 percent, proving that the new information economy was subordinate to at least some of the laws of capitalist economics.

Our experience of new media is likely to be directly affected in conditions of such high market volatility, not only by the disappearance of favourite sites or other services but also by the way in which the structuring of the website as a commodity within a capitalist regime will determine something of its character. For instance, there are a wide variety of travel sites on the web, offering advice to travellers and the possibility for them to plan their own journeys directly and outside of the markets of the big tour operators. Many of these sites are simply a marketing operation of existing destinations, electronic brochures that offer the benefit of direct contact with service providers at a distance. However, there are also sites such as last-minute.com, one of the best known of UK dotcom businesses, offering cheap travel deals. Lastminute lost £15.3 million in the last quarter of 2000 – they then announced a joint venture with the oldest travel operator in the world, Thomas Cook. The potential for 'new' patterns of travel consumption (i.e. more individualised, less pre-packaged) here takes a blow as the newest operator in the sector makes alliance with the oldest in order to survive economically. The survival of even relatively innovative sites such as FaceBook and YouTube depends on relations with computer companies both new and old. The acquisition of YouTube in 2006 by Google also brought attention to bear, not least because the latter company is now one of the most significant web presences. YouTube was founded in 2005 and therefore bypassed one of the more common aspects of Internet development – relying on venture capital – as it was initially funded by individuals who had made their money with

Peter Fearon, *The Origins and Nature of the Great Slump 1929–1932*, London: Macmillan, (1979)

See www.nasdaq.com for the data and John Cassidy's *dot.con: The Greatest Story Ever Sold*, London: Allen Lane, 2002 for the details

PayPal, the Internet payment system, itself an offshoot of eBay (*Financial Times*, 7 December 2008). FaceBook was also financed via venture capital in two tranches in 2005 and 2006; it has continued to provide social networking facilities for students and graduates while having Microsoft own 1.6 percent of the company since 2007.

Our experiences and choices are directly subject to financial and market conditions. The consequence of this discussion is that we cannot simply deduce the shape of new media from their technological capability – their economic context, investment strategies and methods of return will profoundly affect our experience and use of networked media.

These uses of ICTs had not been predicted by commercial investors, nor had the fact that they opened up a communicative realm of participation that took users into direct conflict with the owners of commodified artefacts. So, for instance, the producers of Star Trek fan sites or online 'slash' movies in which well-known characters are re-edited into subversively sexualised parodies of themselves, posed direct problems to the owners of the rights in Star Trek. The 'consumer as producer', together with the ease of reproduction offered by digital technologies, has created a fundamental challenge to existing laws of intellectual property ownership. Ownership of copyright, regulation and the law had already been determined in relation to older media forms and practices. The exploitation of intellectual property rights is an extremely important source of income for traditional media producers. We now turn to this area of the law and its impact on new media.

3.11 Intellectual property rights, determined and determining

The development of New Media have also been constrained (and encouraged) by the legal and social practices associated with the preservation and extension of Intellectual Property Rights, or in common parlance copyright and patents. In fact it may be possible to argue that it is difficult to understand how some uses of new media such as peer to peer in its non-commercial forms such as Limewire and Gnutella have developed without considering their attempts to evade the implications of copyright legislation. The transfer of music and movies between users has become so commonplace that many colleges ban the software from their systems as it is such a heavy user of bandwidth.

As Dean and Kretschmer have argued, the existence of intellectual property is rooted in capitalist modes of organisation of the economic basis of society. After all it can be said that if reproduction of books depends on pen and ink there is unlikely to be a problem with the appropriation of texts for distribution of profit (Dean and Kretschmer 2007). In fact copyright, i.e. the right of property in a text, or performance, music or other media representation such as a film or TV programme can only be said to be necessary where it is possible for non-owners to reproduce such a text without incurring some of the original costs. So it is easy to understand copyright in texts where the original author may miss out on royalties when the text is appropriated by another printer. In the case of films it was difficult for piracy to occur in the unauthorised reproduction and circulation of a film via an alternative network of cinemas and film laboratories. For these reasons copyright and the related laws covering patents and trade marks were generally the subject of dispute between corporations. Even with the advent of video piracy following on from the availability of cheap tape copying the legal struggles were largely between large companies and small entrepreneurs avoiding the payment of royalties. It has only been the advent of home-copying and mass distribution via the Internet that has seen corporations interact in the realm of the law with individual consumers. It is worth noting that even so the Recording Industry Association of America (RIAA), which has led the attempt to preserve copyright, tends to pursue large-scale operators and bodies with commercial potential, although it has been known to take legal action against private individuals. It is worth considering whether the opprobrium such cases attract is worth the deterrent effect of such actions.

One of the great promises of digital media is the ease with which material can be copied again and again without any degradation in quality. However, scarcity of copies, and access to them, has been one of the ways in which the owners of cultural objects have ensured that they received an income. For example, cinemas, as the only place one can easily see a film on a large screen, also meant that they were convenient places to charge for its use. To explain this requires a short diversion. Since political economy holds that the organising principal of a capitalist economy is the production of commodities (i.e. objects which are both useful and exchangeable) it is important to know whether this is true for cultural products such as music, art, web pages and so on. When an object is made it usually has certain usefulness and a price in the market. In the case of a personal computer, for example, this is easy to understand, how much is it worth, the cost of the expertise, metals, plastics, distribution and labour that went into it, along with what it will do, word-processing, image manipulation, making an Internet connection, and so on. When it comes to a cultural commodity, for example say a web page, what exactly is its value? In the past this question has created some difficulties for the discussion of broadcast media. How was the price established and how do you characterise the process by which it was turned into income? For some such as Dallas Smythe, the process in terrestrial commercial television involved turning the audience into a commodity, which was then sold to advertisers. The question of how to disseminate material that people want and obtain a payment for its use lies at the heart of the current developments of new media by business.

The essential characteristic of the capitalist economy is the way that it uses systems of property, particularly the ownership of commodities. The right to ownership demands the acceptance of all parties that it is 'common sense' and also supported by the courts where necessary. In this way television broadcasters, for example, are able to disseminate their material as widely as possible without fear of copying and re-broadcasting on a commercial basis. The acceptance that it is impossible without legal retribution means that it is rarely attempted. However, social practice imposes limits on the extent to which copying can be prevented and although home copying is an everyday occurrence and is, strictly speaking, an infringement of the law, its prosecution would be unacceptable to most people.

This is just the beginning of the story since the wholesale reproduction of material, particularly in analogue forms, also had problems with degradation of the image, increasingly poor sound, and so on. In contrast digital material is much more easily copied, altered and integrated. This potential for infinite reproduction was first explored in law in 1999 and 2000 around the Napster organisation and the way its software facilitated the free distribution of music files between Internet users. (See Napster **Case study 3.1**.)

A different kind of attempt to determine property rights in new media had previously been explored in a landmark case between Microsoft and Apple corporations over issues of 'look and feel'. 'Look and feel' primarily related to the way in which graphical user interfaces developed by Microsoft out of its relationship with Apple brought about infringement of copyright in the digital age. The case was mainly concerned with the integration of known and unprotectable elements (e.g. icons, simple images and screen layouts) which when brought together constituted an overall similarity to an existing interface. Although the case was settled out of court, with Microsoft preserving its right to use a graphical user interface originated by Apple (who incidentally had obtained the idea from Rank Xerox), it established a set of tests for the identification of a property right in a screen representation.

The significance of the 'look and feel' case was that it took notice of the ease of replicability enshrined in digital media. Most importantly, it was the first signal that the new media was not to be left to its own devices in this key aspect of commercial use just as television and film had been brought under firm regulatory control.

Digital reproduction has again become a major problem with the continued development of the web. The control of distribution has always been a big concern for the owners of cultural commodities. When such commodities could only be distributed by printed page, the pressing of vinyl or by controlled access to the cinema, the difficulty of high capital requirements for the equipment or venue prevented much effective piracy. However, the development of the law in relation to trading in commodities came second to the problems of the protection of ideas that form the property of corporations. The most important location for this debate has been in the domain of music.

> Gaines's (1991) work makes it clear that the priority remained the prevention of theft between capitalist organisations rather than by consumers

3.12 Music as new media

It is almost impossible to talk about music without almost immediately considering the means by which it is consumed. To consider the difference between live performance and a CD is to immediately discuss different experiences of music. Whether in a concert hall, a stadium, in the car, or with headphones plugged in, the experience of music is as much defined by its form of consumption as by the music itself. There is another sphere in which the interactions of music with circumstance are also inseparable: the appropriation of music as a mode of representation of identity. In youth culture, particularly in the West, whether one is an emo, or a rocker, a follower of hip hop or R' n' B all indicate a relationship to the rest of one's cultural world. At times these affiliations, such as to punk or rave music have entered into the larger social discourse about the very nature of legal cultural practices involved in using music.

For these reasons the discussion of music and its relationship to new media is necessarily a partial one. It is impossible to comprehend the richness and diversity of the cultural forms of pop, classical, reggae, non-Western, religious and secular music in these few pages. It is for this reason that we concentrate mainly on the areas where the interaction of music and technology are most closely experienced. Even then we will comment on radio distribution of music only in passing. It is for this reason also that the discussion concentrates on a range of practices primarily associated with Western music, because this field contains much of the material on the relationship between music and technology; also it dominates music production by US and European companies.

> In the UK the Conservative government of John Major introduced a law (Criminal Justice and Public Order Act 1994) that outlawed the unlicensed public performance of music characterised by the 'emission of a succession of repetitive beats'

It is important to note that there has undoubtedly been a great gain from the mechanical reproduction of music. The ability to use music at any time and any place refers as much as to Beethoven's Ninth Symphony performed by a full Western classical orchestra as much as it does to the latest chart hit. It should also be noted that mechanical reproduction has enabled the spread of the music of the streets of industrial Detroit and the sounds of rural Islam. However the main direction of travel of recorded music in the US and Europe can be located in the dominance of the global music scene by a small number of Western based and /or active corporations. It is the interaction between corporate dominance, music technology and the superstructural elements, particularly law, to which we therefore turn.

The global music industry is dominated by just four corporations; EMI, Warner Music, Sony BMG and Universal. Each of these is the product of the process of concentration, an ongoing theme in the capitalist mode of production, with Sony BMG being the outcome of the merger of Sony (based in Japan) and Bertelsmann of Germany.

One of the key factors in domination of the music industry has been the need to invest significant amounts of capital across a number of areas. The industry needs to be understood as both vertically integrated, from musicians and performers, through production, into marketing and distribution. It also needs to be understood as horizontally integrated with marketing, sales of rights to use music in films, TV and radio. All of these are linked by legal ownership enshrined in contracts and law, particularly those relating to Intellectual Property.

In a simple schematic of the industry, record companies locate talent. The performers and their managers sign up with a record company and in return for a share of the profit, the company takes unto itself the copyright in the music and the neighbouring rights to control distribution through a range of formats as well as the control of the uses to which the music is then put, such as radio, advertising, movies and so on. The company, operating through a label, will market and manage the entry of the material into the public domain. There are innumerable variations on this theme but even where, as in the UK, there is an Indie scene (i.e. labels not owned by the major corporations) they work closely with major companies who control much production and marketing. Although this sounds like a clinical description, one of the most important characteristics of the industry is the way in which it has relied on the expertise of agents to locate music that is likely to be popular and part of burgeoning trends. The creative aspect of the industry cannot be ignored; one way of selecting which artists to support is simply by giving out a large number of contracts and continuing with those that show commercial potential. It should be noted that while this volume was in preparation one of the great names in recorded music, EMI, following its transfer into the hands of a private equity firm with little interest in original product, was in the process of discontinuing these practices and switching to exploiting its existing catalogue.

It is not difficult to see how this model of music ownership and distribution, legal rights and capital investment has come into conflict with the tremendous capabilities of new media technology to distribute music at little cost. The music industry has coped with major technological change in the past. In the 1960s the development of the compact cassette by the European electronics firm Philips enabled the distribution of prepared music that could be enjoyed while on the move, particularly in cars and via devices such as the Sony Walkman. The cassette tape also had the advantage that vinyl records could be copied to tape and copies of tapes could be run off easily, but since most recording had to be done in real time an overly massive expansion of home copying was avoided with probably a few albums being taped a lot and most not at all.

> A tape system, 'eight-track' with higher quality but without the home-copying capability of compact cassettes was also offered at around the same time but did not match the take-up of the cassette

The second significant technological innovation was the Compact Disc (CD). This was more important in that although the cassette had established a number of cultural practices (sharing music, home-copying, mobile use) the Compact Disc, with its digital format, offered the opportunity to copy at rates faster than real time with no degradation in quality compared with the original.

The technological innovations discussed throughout this chapter converged with the popularity of recorded music to bring into existence a new form of social interaction via networks, as we see in the discussion of Computer Mediated Communications. The social networks fostered by the exchange of music are the product of more than just technology. In the case of MySpace the linking and social networking capabilities developed through the history of the Internet combined with the commercial and non-commercial music scenes to offer media for the distribution of music. However as we saw in the case of Napster the legal forms of control of intellectual property imposed limits on the extent to which commercial music could be distributed via MySpace. Rather those sites have become mechanisms for floating new music, fandom and the viral marketing of commercial music marketing.

The alternative modes of distribution from Napster, through Limewire, Gnutella, e-donkey and BitTorrent have tended to concentrate on the distribution of commercial music. In other words control of the capital necessary to select and develop musical output has remained in the hands of the industry majors with some of the sources of income removed. Since the overt purpose of music industry majors is to secure a profit and return it to their shareholders it is not surprising that this is considered to be something of a problem.

It is at this point that we turn to the ongoing tension that exists in the development of new media and of which music is one of the sharpest examples. The form of the technology and the media uses to which it is put are 'socially formed'. It is worthwhile taking a short diversion at this point to consider the origins of the ubiquitous format; the MP3 file. These have become so commonplace that the term MP3 now has the same level of usage as the '45' or LP when referring to vinyl, or the CD has for the still dominant medium format used for the distribution of the majority of music. In essence the MP3 or Moving Picture Expert Group Layer 3 (to give it its full title) represents an industry standard algorithm for the 'lossy' compression of digitally recorded music. It works by losing parts of the range of sound that are considered to be less important for enjoying music. It may also be the case that since they were originally played via personal computers rather than sophisticated music systems the losses were difficult to notice. In any case the file format has become the standard alongside the AAC format preferred by Apple, developers of one of the most popular portable music player known as the iPod which is frequently known as an MP3 player (although it usually bears AAC files).

3.4 Earlier forms of media distribution: the vinyl disc and the compact cassette. Courtesy of iStock Photo

The response of the music industry to Internet distribution, social networking sites, home-copying and the creation of non-commercial distribution mechanisms has been complex and even chaotic. It is an excellent example of the ways in which the technological capabilities of the New Media have been limited and determined by existing social relations and also of how the inherent technical capacities of New Media have simply adapted to changed circumstances.

These difficulties were first seen with the development of home taping. In the US they gave rise to specific legislation that allowed recording in digital or analogue media for personal non-commercial use. The response was to make home taping legal, and to ensure that

Audio Home
Recording Act of 1992,
Pub. L. No. 102–563,
106 Stat. 4237
amending title 17 of the
United States Code by
adding a new chapter
10, enacted 28 October

businesses that made their profits from selling domestic recording equipment gave some of their income to those that depended on the enforcement of copyright (i.e. the software or content producers). The way the law developed cannot be seen as purely the result of right or justice; it was also the way a balance of influence and power was exerted on the US legislative process. It is no accident that the owners of copyright, such as major music companies and film and television businesses, reside mainly in the US and recording equipment is primarily an import. There is no similar law in the UK. Now with the advantages of digital reproduction the infringement of copyright presented itself in a new and potentially virulent form.

The Internet, allied with digital reproduction, has generated a new problem for the owners of copyright because the ability to record is allied with the ability to distribute. At the same time the availability of powerful computing capabilities in the home stimulated the development of new preventive measures in the form of cryptography, or secret codes. Cryptography works by encoding the data involved in reproducing a media text and requiring the user to have another piece of data, a 'key', that will allow the user's computer to make sense of the information sent by the provider. The speed of modern methods of computer encoding means that a new 'lock' and 'key' can be made and sold every time the text is sent. The incorporation of these measures in the Digital Millennium Copyright Act was a reflection of an important new direction in the distribution of cultural commodities. The intention was undoubtedly to control the use of commodities on a pay-per-use basis. The new law, at least in the USA, made it illegal to try to circumvent the techniques used for the encryption of the material. In other words, a piece of music sold to you over the web may only be decrypted with the key supplied. Any attempt to decode it is against the law, as would be the distribution of a machine with such a capability. The control over intellectual property is not only a commercial question, it also influences the development of cultural practices, of reuses and revisits to material. The great potential for the cheap and easy distribution of our cultural heritage and shared cultural life is actively limited by these legal pressures as was noted by the US Supreme Court in Eldred v. Ashcroft Attorney General (537 US (2003) S.Ct. 01-6180). This is one way in which the potential of new media is greatly foreshortened.

Digital Millennium
Copyright Act:
http://lcweb.loc.gov/
copyright/
legislation/hr2281.pdf

It was thought that the US legislation would bring about the ultimate in commodification of cultural objects. That by integrating technological capability with powerful systems for encrypting and then decrypting in the home, it would enable 'pay per use'; each use of the cultural commodity being paid for. Nor would you have necessarily purchased a book, a magazine, film or the new media variation; what you would have purchased was the single use of that item. This would have been a new phenomenon; the temporary nature of the newspaper is known to us all, as is the one-off visit to the cinema, the single viewing of a television programme, or the rental of a video. What is different here is that the technology exists to make it possible to view, store and reuse cultural commodities, and makes it cheap to reproduce them infinitely. Instead of this, powerful technology was to be developed to inhibit all of these potentials. Cultural production would have become organised around impeding the very gains that new technology was assumed to provide. However it is also true that the establishment of corporate control is not to be assumed to be an easy matter, and the development of a new media industry has not been without its problems for such interests.

In contrast what happened despite the best intentions of the promoters of the Digital Millennium Copyright Act was in fact something completely different. What owners of copyright have had to cope with has been the establishment of alternative methods of distribution outside their control. This is most obvious in music, but is increasingly a concern in television and film. The Napster case demonstrated one response to the problem (see **Case Study**

3.1). The intention was to simply put this alternative out of business using existing legal principles. However the response of Internet users was to exploit the approaches deep-rooted
in the architecture of the Internet – its distributed nature. It was the actions of the music corporations that stimulated the development of distribution methods that draw on the
distributed nature of the Internet itself, in particular Peer to Peer (P2P) which used servers
holding addresses of the locations of files rather than the files themselves. It had been the
exact duplication of files on Napster servers that had left them open to attack under the traditional prohibitions on direct copying. Where it was only the location of the file that was held
on the server then it was argued that no such an offence had been committed. The survival
of peer to peer networks, Limewire and Gnutella being two of the best known has depended
upon this distinction. A further development in the form of BitTorrent does not actually need
a whole file to be kept on any server and allows the building of complete files from any
number of parts. Two responses have since been developed to these activities. The
Recording Industry Association of America decided to pursue file-sharers through the courts
for damages, although whether suing people who are also your customers is a good idea is
perhaps debatable. The consequence of these manoeuvres, it has been argued, has been
that far from defending the profits of record companies they have failed to adapt to the new
world of digital distribution with sufficient alacrity (Curien and Moreau 2005).

The alternative approach was that pursued by an outsider to the music industry, Apple
Corporation, producers of the Apple Mac, which was to offer a controlled paying method of
distribution using bought and paid for licensed copies. The integration of the iPod and the
iTunes music store is dealt with in more detail below.

Particular problems have been how to secure an income stream in the absence of control over distribution, an expectation by users that the web is free, and the high costs involved
in establishing a new business dependent on scarce skills and powerful computers. In view
of the accessibility of the web it is also necessary to consider other non-technical aspects of
media distribution. One of the promises of new media is ease of access and distribution, but
this is to ignore the control over resources enjoyed by large media corporations. New media
will allow the distribution of huge amounts of material, but the filtering role, the exercise of
taste and judgement, may still have to be paid for. One of the reasons that corporations can
charge for access to their commodities is that they control the resources required to produce
particular kinds of content. Put simply, control of distribution is the way in which corporations
achieve a return on the investment in resources used to select and create media content.
Until media corporations can solve the problems of distribution and the consequence of
security of income streams the spread and utilisation of new media may be somewhat inhib-
ited. In this way we can see how new media has entered into a world of law, economic
organisation and regulation that has been developing since the eighteenth century and will
upset many practices and accepted interests.

Issues associated with intellectual property are not only influential on the forms of media
or software, or even web presence; they have also come to have a bearing on the direction
of development of new media across hardware and software as well as the media. One successful attempt to solve this problem can be seen in the form of the Apple iPod. The only way
to understand the particular character of its development is by analysing social, legal and
economic factors. It can be argued that it is probably the only genuine innovation linking the
Internet, the PC and old media that has become a commodity with mass popular take-up
since the Personal Computer itself. The iPod had the advantage of linking the capability of the
Internet to distribute small music files with great rapidity. It coincided with the demise of the
tape cassette that had previously dominated mobile audio in the form of the Sony Walkman.

CASE STUDY 3.1: Napster: from community to commerce

In July 2000 the Recording Industry Association of America (RIAA) attempted to have Napster Inc. closed down. Napster used software to facilitate the sharing of music files between personal computers across the net. The RIAA argued that the copyright in music belonging to record companies was being infringed and that Napster was responsible. The initial injunction was quashed on the grounds that similar software was widely available across the Internet and that it was a simple technical question. This court case and others like it will be one of the factors determining the character of new media, just as was the case with old media, just because something is technically possible does not mean that it can be freely implemented.

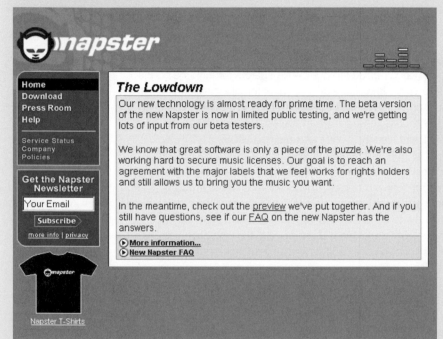

3.5 Napster seeks a legal way to make money offering licensed music.

One of the great claims for the Internet has been that it would enable people to share digital media with great ease. It may be the case that this is technically possible since one of the great advantages of digital media is its ease of duplication. However, in a system within which property rights and network protocols play such an important role the question of ownership of cultural commodities in digital formats was always certain to become significant. Once the Internet provided an alternative to the extremely expensive distribution systems of old, primarily capital investment in presses, cinema chains and so on, the law had to adapt to new circumstances.

The importance of adaptability in commercial law is demonstrated clearly in the Napster case. Its response was to identify its distribution of MP3 files over the Internet as just another form of home recording. The core of the case revolved around legal detail about the difference between copying sound and copying file information. To concentrate on the detail, however, would be to ignore the underlying principle, which is that the law is as important a determinant of the form of new media as is the technology.

It is in the laws covering commerce that much of the content and the relationship between the users of cultural commodities and their producers will be decided; that is, who can buy, own and distribute material.

An important twist occurred when the German-owned Bertelsmann Corporation announced that rather than support the case against Napster it had negotiated an agreement with the company to work on subscription models of distribution. This shows, in a particularly acute way, how the technical capabilities of the technology, for free and easy distribution of infinitely copyable music, can be subordinated to corporate interests.

It also had a promoter in the form of Steve Jobs who understands the importance of matters such as design and marketing in securing market share. Most importantly however the iPod overcame the opposition of the music industry in that it offered a measure of security with some Digital Rights Management and a return in cash via the tunes store through which further music could be bought. However Apple had the good sense to not make the DRM too restrictive and continued to allow users to rip music from CDs to the PC and to the device itself. From the point of view of the user the imprint of Apple meant that there was no question of being involved in the kind of 'piracy' associated with Napster, Limewire and the rest of the P2P networks.

If we return to the way we argued we should understand the development of New Media at the beginning of this chapter, it would be a mistake to see it as only re-adjusting the dissemination methods of existing formats such as the three-minute pop song. Rather just as Google developed out of the need to secure income in a distributed medium so new media forms can bring out new media practices. One of these is an economic change which EMI, as mentioned above, is putting into effect: the translation of the existing catalogue into an object for sale and distribution via a new medium. It is this practice that may lead to Long Tail economics.

3.13 The Long Tail

One of the ways that the new dynamics of global economics both shapes and reflects the tension between economic determination and media cultures can be seen in the theory of Long Tail economics.

Originally argued in *Wired* in October 2004 and then developed as a book (2006) Chris Andersons' work on the Long Tail is one the most compelling accounts of the ways in which conventional media economics have changed in the post network cultures of the broadband world. The implications of the Long Tail analysis are far reaching, arguing that the economic basis of production is changing in ways that unlock market diversity on an unprecedented scale. Anderson argues that the capacity of networked communications to connect with a multiplicity of niche markets ensures that lower volume products can attain a sustainable margin of profitability. 'Our culture and economy are increasingly shifting away from a focus on a relatively small number of hits (mainstream products and markets) at the head of the demand curve, and moving toward a huge number of niches in the tail' (Anderson 2006: 52).

Existing economics of the media have had two major characteristics. One is the 'hit driven' economy – producers of e.g. TV, music, film have to produce several flops or mid-ranking products to achieve the one hit that will sustain the enterprise. The other is the 'first copy' cost principle – that actually getting to produce the first copy of a newspaper or film is a very expensive part of the operation, the costs of production are very high but thereafter margins of profits depend on the costs of distribution; in newspapers this has traditionally been good, each paper is cheap to print; in film each film print is expensive to make. Successful mass media economics depended upon highly capitalised businesses able to spread the risk of the hit seeking market as well as mass produce products and get them to the right kinds of consumers. These conditions have had the effect of making media production a high cost, high volume business – high cost, low volume products were unlikely to get made since they lingered relatively invisible in the 'long tail' of the demand curve. These market conditions led to a situation where a very small proportion of the possible media 'inventory' (or products) was commanding a very high percentage of the overall sales – the hits – and that retailers, TV channels and cinema chains were unable to carry products from

See Gaines (1991) for more on the relationship between media, meaning and the law

See du Gay *et al.*, *Doing Cultural Studies* for an interesting if flawed account of the development of the Walkman

The development of the iPod is explored in more depth in Kieran Kelly, 'How the iPod Got its Dial', in Seaton, J., *Music Sound and Multimedia*, Edinburgh, 2007 further down the demand curve because the revenues they could achieve would be too small. There would not be enough customers in any particular geographical region to justify giving obscure titles shelf space. Long Tail theorists argue that these conditions have changed forever,

> For most of the past century, companies of all types strove to introduce products and services that were blockbuster hits and could capture the mass market. Bigger was better. But now dozens of markets, from beer to books, music to movies, and software to services of all types are in the early stages of a revolution as the Internet and related technologies vastly expand the variety of products that can be produced, promoted, and purchased. Though based on a simple set of economic and technological drivers, the implications of this are far-reaching, for managers, consumers, and the economy as a whole.
>
> (Brynjolfsson, Hu and Smith 2006)

Chris Anderson is more succinct 'A Long Tail is just culture unfiltered by economic scarcity' (Anderson 2006: 53). This has been brought about by two factors. The first is the lowering of the costs of production as digital media tools have become more widespread and cheaper – the barriers to entry into the marketplace are much lower, we can produce work a lot more cheaply. A blog costs a fraction of a newspaper, a YouTube viral hit a tiny fraction of a TV ad. The second factor is the effect of search technologies and recommendation networks on distribution and marketing. Search technologies place the most obscure product at your fingertips; automated recommendation, reviewing and rating processes make it possible for the consumer to make purchase decisions in the jungle of the Long Tail marketplace. Search and recommendation make it possible for us to consume with confidence, to make often very highly individualised choices from the vast array of media choices that lower barriers to entry produce.

Anderson argues that in most markets 'there are for more niche goods than hits' and that the cost of reaching them is falling; there are, he suggests, 'so many niche products that collectively they can comprise a market rivalling the hits'. These conditions have the effect of flattening the demand curve, consumers buy fewer hits and more obscure 'niche' material,

> the natural shape of demand is revealed, undistorted by distribution bottlenecks, scarcity of information, and limited choice of shelf space. What is more, that shape is far less hit driven than we have been led to believe. Instead it is as diverse as the population itself.
>
> (Anderson 2006: 53)

This rhetoric is seductive and Anderson's analysis certainly appears to describe accurately a shift in media economics. However we should beware conflating diversity of consumer choice with diversity of political or economic power. The economic freedom to take advantage of the unlimited choices of the Long Tail is enjoyed by a minority even in the broadband world. The neo-liberal mantra of choice is usually at the expense of the denial of economic, political or ecological choice elsewhere. Moreover in advancing his case for the Long Tail Anderson never claims that the hit, the high volume end of the demand curve, is ever going to die away. Although he talks about the democratisation of the means of production he hardly implies that Fox, Virgin or Warner Bros are about to wither in the face of camcorder wielding armies of the night.

What his analysis does do is draw our attention to the way that our own media experiences are shaped by technologically produced opportunities and shifting economic conditions. On the production side the possibility of being able to reach Long Tail niche audiences changes the terms of production, Brynjolfsson, Hu and Smith (2006) allege, 'The music industry has seen a similar effect owing to changes in the cost to produce, market, and distribute music. Niche bands can reportedly turn a profit with sales of 25,000 albums, compared to break-even points of 500,000 through major labels.' The figures for online video production appear to be going in the same direction; audience numbers and advertising revenue for web dramas like My Space's *Quarterlife* and Bebo's *Kate Modern* suggest that whilst traditional advertising remains sceptical about the value of the Long Tail viral TV market it is only a matter of time before niche viewing communities deliver economically sustainable margins. Although total volumes might be low, high margins make businesses very profitable. Anderson himself cites the example of *Rocketboom*, a comedy news revue produced online for next to nothing by just two clever creatives that attracted 200,000 viewers a week and made $40,000 ad revenue in its first week of commercial sales (Anderson 2006: 193). Blogging is perhaps the most obvious phenomenon illustrating the impact of lower barriers to entry into the media publishing arena; Anderson claims, 'The decline of newspapers, which are down more than a third from their mid eighties peak, is the most concrete evidence of the disruptive effect of Long Tail can have on entrenched industries' (Anderson 2006: 185). This isn't only because we all read our news from blogs since we also get our news from traditional papers' online publications – however the astonishing popularity of many thousands of blogs where specialist interests, gossip, investigation, and geek cultures can all be accessed is evidence of the Long Tail in action. The incredible diversity of blog culture has of course generated its own 'short head' in the demand curve, in which a small number of blogs command a very large amount of attention and advertising revenue. It is clear that the Long Tail is creating new opportunities for a wider variety of media producers to produce work, to express themselves and to publish. More importantly niche markets and high margins make more of these enterprises economically sustainable than would previously have been the case.

From the point of view of the consumer or user the economic reality of the Long Tail clearly has all kinds of effects upon our online media experience. The remote control is replaced by the search engine. Our ability to control and to choose our media consumption depends increasingly upon our skill at working with the logic of search technologies. Brynjolfsson, Hu and Smith (2006) defined 'Active' and 'Passive' media locating experiences:

> Active search tools allow consumers to easily locate products they know they are interested in. Sampling tools, such as Amazon.com's samples of book pages and CD tracks, on the other hand, allow consumers to learn more about products they might be interested in . . .
>
> Passive tools, such as most recommender systems, use the consumer's revealed preferences from past purchases or even page views to identify new products they might be interested in. Consumer search is also facilitated by tools combining both active and passive search such as customer product reviews, online communities, or the readership of product-focused blogs.

Searching, signing up, registering, recommending, rating, are all central activities that the user of online media must submit to. These practices go on to create value by providing consumer behaviour data which then feeds back into search algorithms making even more targeted advertising possible to facilitate the operation of the Long Tail (see **3.15**, **3.16**).

3.14 Going viral

The explosion of content created by lower barriers to entry into the media marketplace makes it possible for many more of us to become niche consumers. In the past some of these behaviours may have been accounted for in Cultural Studies by recourse to subculture theory and fan studies. Subcultures and fans have always inhabited 'niche' cultural zones or created informal communication networks, the zine, the slash movie, to create community and identity. In this sense we can understand the work of theorists like Matt Hils and Henry Jenkins as providing us with a kind of primer in Long Tail cultural consumption. We are all fans now. Anderson describes certain kinds of net based catchphrases and trends as 'viral memes', Internet phenomena that somehow 'catch on' in a particular subculture and spread round the world driven by fans' excitement and pleasure (e.g. 'All Your Base Belong to Us' or 'The Star Wars Kid' or 'Chocolate Rain', the 2007 YouTube hit). However Anderson argues that although many of us know some of these memes none of us know them all – each social grouping and subculture has its own favourites, which, he argues, 'shows that my tribe is not always your tribe, even if we work together, play together, and otherwise live in the same world' (Anderson 2006: 183).

The idea of the virus can help us to understand how culture is reproduced in Long Tail market conditions. We argue that the virus is the communicative logic of the Long Tail. In the moment of media abundance, where the traditional filters and gatekeepers of mass media have been replaced by *us*, we depend more and more on personal or network recommendation. These networks of recommendation are processes that the direct advertising of the mass media found hard to understand or control. Clearly word of mouth has always been important. Marketers sought, as it were, to prime word of mouth through direct advertising but they did not attempt to intervene in the process directly. This situation has changed with the rise of the virus as a metaphor for understanding the transmission of online media in Long Tail conditions.

The idea of the virus as a way of understanding online media transmission networks has been around since the mid-1990s (see Rushkoff 1994, *Media Virus*). The biological reality of the virus as organism was first used as a metaphor to describe the behaviour of computer programs that would spread themselves through computer systems, fulfilling the criteria set by epidemiologists for viral contamination that the virus should always infect more than one subject, creating the epidemic growth curve. From the computer virus that, once created, had an autonomous life it was a short step for consumers to become the agents of viral marketing. Perhaps the first and most often cited example is the way in which the Hotmail program was spread, for free, by its users, as every mail sent from a Hotmail account included an invitation to sign up – Hotmail spent a mere $50,000 on traditional marketing and still grew from zero to 12 million users in 18 months (see Jurvetson and Draper 1997). This phenomenal growth of course drew the attention of the marketing community and soon consumers were being understood for their 'social networking potential', the likelihood that we would pass on a recommendation to other potential consumers. Thus consumers are no longer classified just by their spending power but by their influence – hence advertising to a group with high social network potential such as young people who spend a lot of time on social network sites, will attract a premium rate. New entrants to the online media market now need to plan how to take advantage of the potential for viral transmission which will drive their use figures up to a worthwhile acceptable audience or a commercially viable proposition to advertisers. Viral transmission can carry an item from a blog read by three close friends to a profitable business (see e.g. www.boingboing.net or www.dooce.com) read by hundreds of thousands. When there is so much content available and the gatekeepers have been ejected from their posts we may find ourselves increasingly dependent on viral logics.

However try as they might advertisers find controlling the logics of viral transmission very difficult. The very pleasure of the viral communication for the user is that it needs to feel 'discovered', 'original', 'fresh' – it needs to arrive with the serendipitous feel of the spontaneous and the authentic. This is very hard to manufacture – a viral video that turns out to be an ad is invariably a disappointing experience. On the other hand a mainstream ad that looks like a viral has more chance of finding crossover YouTube success and enhancing brand awareness. In the UK the chocolate manufacturer Cadbury recovered damage to their market position caused by a salmonella scare at least in part through the stunning success of their gorilla drumming ad run in May 2007 (www.YouTube.com/watch?v=iKdQC-hbY7k). The ad featured a gorilla appearing to drum the Phil Collins part to the hit tune 'In the Air Tonight' – no mention of the product was made at any point till a strapline at the very end. It was weird; it was a viral success on YouTube and phone download, re-establishing the Cadbury's Dairy Milk as a cool brand. Viral networks are a key component in building brand identity. Laurence Green, planning director of Fallon, the advertising agency behind the ad was reported at the time as observing

> Advertising can be effective without a traditional 'message', 'proposition' or 'benefits'. Indeed, some of the latest advertising thinking suggests that attempts to impose them can actually reduce effectiveness. We are trading our traditional focus on proposition and persuasion in favour of deepening a relationship.
>
> (The *Independent* 2007)

Understanding viral communications patterns has become a major new field of study for social scientists and communications researchers who are developing new ways of measuring and visualising the topology of networks. Researchers Leskovec, Adamic and Huberman (2007), for instance, conducted an exhaustive survey of links and recommendation behaviours on a major retail site. One of their conclusions was that

> Firstly, it is frequently assumed in epidemic models . . . that individuals have equal probability of being infected every time they interact. Contrary to this we observe that the probability of infection decreases with repeated interaction. Marketers should take heed that providing excessive incentives for customers to recommend products could backfire by weakening the credibility of the very same links they are trying to take advantage of.
>
> Traditional epidemic and innovation diffusion models also often assume that individuals either have a constant probability of 'converting' every time they interact with an infected individual, or that they convert once the fraction of their contacts who are infected exceeds a threshold. In both cases, an increasing number of infected contacts results in an increased likelihood of infection. Instead, we find that the probability of purchasing a product increases with the number of recommendations received, but quickly saturates to a constant and relatively low probability.
>
> (Leskovic *et al.* 2007)

In other words the dynamics of viral transmission in consumer behaviour are particular and unpredictable. Consumers rapidly develop immunity – the viral has to come as a surprise.

Despite the compelling evidence for the effects of the Long Tail on networked media we would want argue for the historical continuity as well as change in the economics of online media as they relate to mainstream or mass media of TV, Hollywood or publishing. As Anderson himself concedes we are not witnessing a revolutionary break so much as an evolutionary gradualism in which the institutions of mass media are adapting to new conditions and a few new entrants to the market can gain an economically sustainable foothold. The demand curve for media products and services is flattening out – but it remains a pretty steep curve. In macro-economic terms the really big money is being made by enterprises that can aggregate all the nodes of influence in a social network and either direct them to consumption opportunities or harvest their data traces to use in enhancing marketing. eBay, Google, MySpace have all, for instance, become highly profitable through this combination of aggregation activities. For many small producers struggling to find an audience there is no magic bullet or viral miracle cure that substitutes for the usual combination of talent, graft and luck, as Anderson himself observes,

> For the individual producer who's way down there in the weeds, the forces that created the Long Tail market in the first place – democratized access to market and powerful filters that can drive demand to niches – certainly help, but even doubling a small number still leaves a pretty small number. Good thing there are all those non-monetary rewards, such as attention and reputation, huh? How to convert them to real money is up to you. Have you considered playing a concert?
>
> (http://www.thelongtail.com/the_long_tail/2007/01/the_beginners_g.html)

3.15 Fragmentation and convergence

This experience of an explosion of media products, distributed virally to our particular segment of the Long Tail often feels like a substantial fragmentation of the media landscape compared to its pattern of organisation in the twentieth century. Fragmentation seems in some way to be one of the important features of new media. Yet at the same time one of the buzzwords of the new media explosion has been 'convergence' – the idea that at some point the technologies of media would all come together. Television, online video delivery, Internet communications and telecommunications combined in one 'black box' that will look something like a phone. However this vision has been widely challenged as devices and platforms have proliferated and instead *content* has converged (see Jenkins 2006: 15). Convergence however has at least two other meanings in this context. The first is the merger of media corporations in an attempt to provide a horizontal integration of different media products across a range of platforms. Thus the acquisition of MySpace by Rupert Murdoch's Fox Interactive in 2005 means not only that Fox have a foothold in the social networking market but that they can find new markets for the Fox back catalogue online as well as using the social network as a site for the development of new media products which may have a life in TV and cinema. 'Win / win' situations. The final meaning of the idea of convergence is the one used by Henry Jenkins in his 2006 book of the same name in which he argues that the convergence is most importantly occurring *not* in the labs of technologists or the boardrooms of corporations but in the minds of the audience. It is we who are convergent – moving freely across a range of media platforms making connections between storyworlds where the convergent activity has to do with the ways we make meaning of a fragmented media landscape, 'convergence represents a cultural shift as consumers are encouraged to seek out new information and make connections among dispersed media content' (2006: 3). This is all very contradictory – we seem to be living through a period where the conflicts and opportunistic alliances of business interests produce a very dynamic system in which we experience fragmentation *and* convergence occurring concurrently. It is as if we are experiencing centripetal *and* centrifugal forces as outcomes of the same rapidly spinning wheel of media business and innovation.

We can explain this in part by reference back to Anderson's Long Tail idea. The big media businesses who produce the 20 percent of products commanding 80 percent of sales at the head of the demand curve are not going away. However Sony, Disney, Warner, Bertelsmann and the rest will either consolidate or make way for newer global businesses depending on what kind of adaptations they are able to make to the convergent media landscape described by Jenkins above. In this sense many of the same methods of economic analysis work now as they did before. Some mergers make good sense, others may create behemoths that crucially fail to understand the new market circumstances. What is clear is that although the odds in favour of the dominance of global media markets by a very small number of big players are very good they are by no means certain. The challenges of rapid change and dynamic innovation will produce winners and losers.

At the end of the last century Cornford and Robins (1999) showed how the major Internet service providers' search for exclusive content led them into alliances with already existing producers of media content. They argued that the UK market for subscription-based content was dominated by six corporations: AOL, CompuServe, Microsoft, News International, Virgin and British Telecom (Stokes and Reading 1999: 119–120). They argued that the level of capitalisation required to sustain production in the fields of new media is just as high as it was for the existing media. Hence the fact that the emergent dominant players in the field of new media are either extensions of existing media concerns or are in alliance with existing content providers. The merger between Time-Warner and AOL in 2001 appeared to be a case in point.

This new business organisation brought together the media content provider, rooted in cinema and print, with the Internet Service Provider. The Holy Grail of the digital entertainment revolution. The £130-billion value of this new company represented the ownership of newspapers, magazines, cinema, video distribution, television networks, programme makers and cable companies allied to the subscription model of interactive connection.

In this case, far from the intense freedom of the digital world, the corporate economy increased concentration, and the once claimed benefit of competition – diversity of provision – disappeared, to be replaced by homogeneous products from a narrow range of suppliers. In the absence of competition, the responsibility for the preservation of access to the culture of society has to be guaranteed by the state, in this case the FCC in the US and the European Commission. The state organisations were concerned that the new organisation would, through its ownership of cables, prevent other providers offering alternative services. They were also concerned that the 25 million subscribers to AOL would be so locked into particular software for music and video that no one else would be able to distribute their material. The Disney Corporation used just this comparison in its attempts to scupper the deal before the FCC hearings. In the end, TWOL demonstrated their commitment to open access to the 12.6 million households connected to cable by signing a deal with an independent by the name of Imius.

In all of the to-ing and fro-ing, the role of the state as regulator of communications media had undergone an important change. The FCC had no interest in the regulation of the content to be provided within the new arrangements. The strictures about bad language, sex and violence that apply to TV and other media played no role in the discussion. That argument had been settled with the demise of the Communications Decency Bill in 1999. The net is free. Instead, the state and its agencies had reverted to the role of holding the ring for the competing commercial bodies involved in commercial production. The regulatory bodies do have real powers to control the structure of the media industry. The only basis, therefore, for the regulation of the merger of AOL and TW is its overall impact on the general health of the economic system, as interpreted by the proponents of the free market. Ironically, the tendency of the free market is to foster monopoly, particularly where there are, as in the media industry, considerable advantages in concentrated ownership.

Unfortunately, and this is an important lesson for those interested in the interaction between commerce and communication, the model of convergence envisioned by the owners and managers of Time Warner and America On-line was driven by the manoeuvres of the financial markets rather than by the actual demands of customers for the proposed services. By 2003 the company was largely regarded as having made a disastrous decision. The dominance of the market in cultural commodities that was envisioned by TWOL and its merged successor did not allow it to escape from the particularities of cultural production. The difficulties in predicting aesthetic choices, the expense of prototyping and the need to create and maintain markets all remained important factors. Despite looking like the Holy Grail this particular example of corporate convergence became more of a poisoned chalice – falling victim at least in part to the disillusion with digital media that followed the dotcom crash.

> http:
> //www.redherring.com
>
> www.ft.com
>
> www.ft.com
> 11 December 2003

3.16 Wiki worlds and Web 2.0

One of the responses to the dotcom crash and the widespread sense that the traditional media behemoth may no longer be suited to the dynamic conditions of the twenty-first-century media market was the important idea of 'Web 2.0'. This is a term coined in 2003 and popularised by the media consultant Tim O'Reilly. The idea of Web 2.0 is that a particular assemblage of software, hardware and sociality have brought about 'the widespread sense that there's something qualitatively different about today's web' (O'Reilly 2005a). This shift is allegedly characterised by co-creativity, participation and openness, represented by softwares that support, for example, wiki based ways of creating and accessing knowledge, social networking sites, blogging, tagging and 'mash ups'. O'Reilly envisions the shift from Web 1.0 to Web 2.0 as a series of technological shifts and new practices in his influential article.

Web 1.0	Web 2.0
DoubleClick	Google AdSense
Ofoto	Flickr
Akamai	BitTorrent
mp3.com	Napster
Britannica Online	Wikipedia
personal websites	blogging
page views	cost per click
screen scraping	web services
publishing	participation
content management systems	wikis
directories (taxonomy)	tagging ('folksonomy')
stickiness	syndication

3.6 The shift from Web 1.0 to Web 2.0.

We will spend a short time analysing the discursive formation of Web 2.0 since it provides us with an excellent site through which to understand the tensions that have run throughout this section of the book – tensions between the creative, open source practices of web media and the economic and commercial forces with which they react.

The idea of Web 2.0 was formulated by O'Reilly with Media Live International, a company organising media trade conferences. It was a marketing slogan from its inception. It also has a clear economic goal; O'Reilly introduces the idea as a phoenix to resurrect the internet economy from the still smouldering ashes of the dotcom crash of 2000,

> far from having 'crashed', the web was more important than ever, with exciting new applications and sites popping up with surprising regularity. What's more, the companies that had survived the collapse seemed to have some things in common. Could it be that the dot-com collapse marked some kind of turning point for the web, such that a call to action such as 'Web 2.0' might make sense?
>
> (O'Reilly 2005a)

In the section 'Web 2.0 Design Patterns', he sketches a kind of Web 2.0 manifesto that might also be read as a primer in the economics of web media. He begins with 'The Long Tail', as we have seen above an important feature of the web media marketplace, 'narrow niches make up the bulk of the Internet's possible applications'. Service providers should, he urges, 'leverage customer-self service and algorithmic data management to reach out to the entire web, to the edges'. Producers need to use customer behaviour in order to reach all the 'narrow niches' of the Long Tail and find all the possible trading spaces in the online souk. The next three statements all follow on from this position, 'Data is the next Intel inside', 'Users Add Value' and 'Network Effects by Default', all argue in different ways that user behaviour itself at your site itself creates a commodity (market data and audience as community) that has value. By archiving and analysing user behaviour the service provider learns more and more about how to connect with those long narrow niches where consumers lurk. 'Unique hard to create' data is, O'Reilly argues, the next significant component of the assemblage, not a faster chip, but data that we will pay to access. Moreover 'users add value', we will enhance the service through the traces of ourselves that we leave behind when we add data to the service. These effects should be designed into the experience 'by default'; most of us will not want to actively add data but just by using a site information can be collected, as a side effect of our use of the application. He further goes on to suggest that in order to facilitate this understanding of 'collaboration as data collection' applications should only have 'some rights reserved'; licences should be as unrestrictive as possible designed to afford 'hackability' and 'remixability'. This reflects the general understanding of user-generated content and participatory culture in media by arguing that ease of use and 'remixability' actually increases market share.

As we have suggested above this is a major change in the way that IP has been understood in mass media practice. 'Co-operate don't control' echoes this principle – software services have to be able to link easily to further systems, that is the nature of networked media; there is no point in trying to enclose areas of online experience with hard fences – applications should be porous to other systems and should be 'loosely coupled', co-operating with other data services. So social network software has begun to make itself amenable to third party applications affording users the opportunity to mix and match content on their sites. The Web 2.0 prescription next urges 'The Perpetual Beta', the idea that software should be in a permanent stage of being upgraded and improved compared to the traditional pattern of repeated iterations released at long intervals. This ensures that applications stay fluid, open to being 'loosely coupled' and not too 'hard wired' into their own domains. Finally O'Reilly draws our attention to the idea that software should not be designed for a 'single device' like the phone or PC but should be designed to operate across a range of handheld devices, GPS, or set top boxes. Interoperability is key.

The O'Reilly Web 2.0 manifesto can be read as a sharp abstraction of the net based communication practices taking off at the time of its conception. The success of SNS, blogging and Wikipedia all provided the evidential context for the Web 2.0 proposition. Simultaneously new services were being developed which appear to confirm O'Reilly's analysis. Services like Flickr and del.icio.us use the idea of the 'folksonomy', user classification of knowledge or data. del.icio.us makes it possible for users to share their bookmarked pages; each 'entry' is given a series of tags, search engine-recognisable words, to make it searchable by other users. The effect of this is the ability to follow interest trails via the research online that other people have already done in a manner very close to Vannevar Bush and Ted Nelson's visions of the hypertext data base (see **1.2.3**). The important Web 2.0 difference here is that the generation and classification of that knowledge or data is not controlled by any external authority but by the users themselves. So the patterns of knowledge association and linkage are permanently re-forming on the basis of users' tagging activities. Flickr allows users to create a huge online image database tagged by its users. 'Folksonomy' is thus defined here as a people-led practice of knowledge classification in contradistinction to the traditional expert led taxonomy of knowledge.

The growth of Wikipedia since its inception in 2001 is an even more forceful demonstration of the way that users create value – except, crucially, in this case the value created is knowledge pure and simple since Wikipedia operates as a trust – there is no business model or commercial exploitation. As a collectively authored encyclopaedia Wikipedia is the prototypical model of an open source user-generated knowledge world. The development of wiki based forms of knowledge production appears to be the precise technological correlative of Pierre Lévy's influential Utopian writing on collective intelligence (1997), in which he asserts that 'networks promote the construction of intelligent communities in which our social and cognitive potential can be mutually developed and enhanced' (1997: 17). This notion reflects the enthusiasms of early cybertheorists and can also be seen to be very influential in the work of Henry Jenkins (2002) and Jane McGonigal (2007).

While Wikipedia has been hit by the occasional scandal as information is revealed to be unreliable, its reputation as a 'trustworthy enough' source has grown steadily. This trust of course depends on the unpaid work of the wiki community to edit and check entries – however this self policing community regulating environment is an important feature of this type of knowledge production environment. It places responsibility on all of us to check information (if we know it) or 'tag as inappropriate' offensive online content.

The 'democratic' claim that appears to be foundational to Wikipedia was in fact challenged during the early days of its success by Jimmy Wales, one of its founders. Blogger Aaron Swartz reports Wales's investigations into who actually writes Wikipedia:

> I expected to find something like an 80–20 rule: 80% of the work being done by 20% of the users, just because that seems to come up a lot. But it's actually much, much tighter than that: it turns out over 50% of all the edits are done by just .7% of the users . . . 524 people . . . And in fact the most active 2%, which is 1400 people, have done 73.4% of all the edits.

The remaining 25 percent of edits, he said, were from 'people who [are] contributing . . . a minor change of a fact or a minor spelling fix . . . or something like that'.

Swartz then undertook further research of his own that measured not the edits made but the letters posted; this appeared to contradict Wales's own findings. Swartz concluded that there was a small community of dedicated users who make a lot of edits while maintaining the Wikipedia environment by working on typos, designing formats and so on. However original page content was from a far wider community often posted by very irregular users with specialist knowledge. 'As a result, insiders account for the vast majority of the edits. But it's the outsiders who provide nearly all of the content' (Swartz 2006).

The knowledge produced through this process is transparent insofar as its history can be traced. Anyone can register to track the evolution of a wiki page through its different stages and edits to see how the statements have been arrived at. The process of knowledge production thus becomes differently transparent – its dialogic nature is manifest. Rather than the final authoritative text of the conventional encyclopaedia presenting knowledge as 'fact' the wiki process offers knowledge that is part of an ongoing conversation.

In assessing the claims of Web 2.0 we will have recourse to a number of familiar questions – first of all how new are the softwares and practices that together have been identified with Web 2.0? As we argued above O'Reilly's description was inspired by applications like SNS, blogs and Wikipedia that were already succeeding, each of which had their own technological and cultural antecedents (friends' lists, homepages, Usenet groups etc.). Moreover as we have observed the collective intelligence thrust of cyber enthusiasm informs all kinds of writing about the Internet from the 1970s onward. The historical accuracy of the idea of Web 2.0 is further problematised at the software level – although XML as an upgrade to HTML is often considered a Web 2.0 innovation because it allows users to more easily upload to a site and because of its flexible potential to link applications, it can be argued that XML itself relies heavily on already existing Java script applications. Despite these questions over what exactly has changed from Web 1.0 to Web 2.0 it is clearly an idea whose time has come. The public and market awareness of the enormous amount of creative enterprise expended by ordinary people online has become an established part of mainstream cultural debate. These practices are no longer geeky subcultures but have become the engine of early twenty-first-century capitalism with the spread of ideas like 'crowdsourcing' (Howe 2006) and 'wikinomics' (Tapscott and Williams 2006). Here we can see the affordances of net based communication having effects far beyond its own domain rather in the way that the first flush of digital communications was demanded by and built into globalisation in the 1980s and 1990s. However these effects on the organisation of production and marketing products have to be understood in their economic and material context. The discourse of Web 2.0 has a tendency to elide the material world, to assume that we all have equal access, skill and time; 'the user' becomes a subject category that all too easily transcends material context.

We are currently in the midst of a second, better balanced, dotcom boom in which the persuasive technophilic enthusiasm for the idea of Web 2.0 is nevertheless driving great waves of corporate investment. This is Bill Gates in March of 2006 at the Microsoft CEOs conference:

In 1997, the theme of CEO Summit was 'Corporate Transformation for Friction Free Capitalism.' Today, in a world where we have access to virtually unlimited information at our fingertips, global supply chains, international markets that operate 24 hours a day and communication tools that enable us to move data around the world instantly have brought us a lot closer to a world of friction free capitalism than many people thought possible back then.

The idea of the friction free world derives from Ted Lewis's 1997 book *The Friction Free Economy.* The whole idea of the friction free economy is that somehow digital rationalisation replaces Newtonian physics and Keynesian economics with the seamless mathematical abstraction of chaos theory. The shiny promise of Web 2.0 (O'Reilly 2005a) is once again conjuring a friction free future. Operations like Wikipedia, MySpace, Flickr, YouTube, Technorati and Digg are the poster stars for the new media era of user-generated content when we will *all* be enjoined to be creatives in order to have a voice, a place and space in the new knowledge based digital economies. Web 2.0 is defined by co-creativity and the idea of an equivalence or mutuality in the power relationship in the generative process that allegedly erases the old divisions between 'producers' and 'consumers'. The following remarks from Web 2.0 gurus indicate how far technology is expected to embed itself into daily experience as expressive practice. Wikipedia founder Jimmy Wales forecasts 'It's going to be a part of everyday life – creating and sharing media will be a thing that normal people will do all the time, every day, and it doesn't seem strange.' Matt Mullenweg of blog engine WordPress observes 'Now you see people *with no technical ability* creating really amazing sites reaching audiences they would never have imagined reaching' (our italics). Caterina Fake and Stewart Butterfield of photo share site Flickr emphasise the same combination of expression and universality. 'What's changed is expanding on that theme of communication and personal publishing and making it available to millions of people *who don't have technical skills*' (all from Lanchester 2006).

Here the technology becomes invisible in the new era of technologically mediated self expression. Content will be delivered by us, by 'people who don't have technical skills', 'by people with no technical ability'. As usual technophilia strives to make techniques, technologies and interfaces invisible, that is to say the actual flesh/computer interface somehow becomes a transparent two-way membrane rather than an experience structured through scarce resources, economics and power. While we too are excited by the creative and expressive potentials of web media we insist on their economic and material basis. Web 2.0 shows how our creative expression becomes commodified and sold back to us. This process was clearly theorised before Web 2.0 by Tiziana Terranova (2003):

> In this essay I understand this relationship as a provision of 'free labor,' a trait of the cultural economy at large, and an important, and yet undervalued, force in advanced capitalist societies. By looking at the Internet as a specific instance of the fundamental role played by free labor, this essay also tries to highlight the connections between the 'digital economy' and what the Italian autonomists have called the 'social factory.' The 'social factory' describes a process whereby 'work processes have shifted from the factory to society, thereby setting in motion a truly complex machine.' Simultaneously voluntarily given and unwaged, enjoyed and exploited, free labor on the Net includes the activity of building Web sites, modifying software packages, reading and participating in mailing lists, and building virtual spaces on MUDs and MOOs. Far from being an 'unreal,' empty space, the Internet is animated by cultural and technical labor through and through, a continuous production of value that is completely immanent to the flows of the network society at large.

Terranova's position here can be read as one of the most sophisticated attempts to apply the traditional methodologies of the study of the political economy of the media to their newly networked, web based formations. For Terranova, developing Barbrook's essay on the 'Hi Tech Gift Economy', the enthusiasms and passions of millions of web users need to be understood as 'cultural and technical labor' – as work that produces economic value. However this analysis reduces the human creativity and passion that has built the Internet to an economic function. The tension between a view of web media that understands it as free labour and one that understands it as vibrant culture exactly mirrors the dialectic that determines the nature of web based media. The potential of our experiences as either users or producers of web media is realised through the negotiation between the creative modes of communication, and the constraints of the neo-liberal market. Therefore we now shift our emphasis from a concentration on the economic and regulatory contexts of web media to a focus on the human investments made by millions of internet users into new forms of identity expression and new forms of online community. These expressions of self and sociality afforded by the net have a long history which also shapes the contemporary landscape of the possible, underpinning our analyses of Web 2.0, the blogosphere or YouTube.

3.17 Identities and communities online

In order to grasp the significance of online culture in shaping the contemporary media landscape we will once again have recourse to the history of new media studies. The fact that the Internet has afforded new ways of experiencing the self and new ways of relating to groups in society has driven a significant body of net scholarship. This work has sought critically to tease out the nature of the communicative practices that network computing facilitate and to define the precise nature of those forms of interaction where the participants are there but not there, in touch but never touching, as deeply connected as they are profoundly alienated.

This research has had a number of clear threads that will guide our review of approaches and questions. The first is the idea of anonymity and the effects that it has on communication. A focus on anonymous communication was a primary site of early investigations into CMC and continues now in research into avatar based communication environments such as MMOGs or 'Second Life'. Research based in this tradition has emphasised ideas about identity, masquerade, performance and performativity. A second overlapping tradition has been with the idea of the self in relation to others, to a community or network. This work that begins with investigation of community online, continues through research into people's use of the home page, and now focuses on Social Network Sites. Here the focus is not on anonymity but on its opposite – self publication. An SNS affords its users the opportunity not only to publish themselves but also, and crucially, to publish their network. The third strand that runs through the history of net research has to do with resolving the alleged dichotomy or difference between 'real' and 'virtual' experiences. It has become increasingly clear that we are in need of an epistemological framework that enables us to speak about the complex interplay between our experiences of the 'virtual' and the 'real', since daily life demands constant interaction between them.

3.18 Being anonymous

Different mediations afford the expression of different aspects of our identity. At the primary level of our own experience we know that different forms of communication will inflect how we present ourselves and therefore how we experience ourselves (see e.g. Baym, Zhang, Lin, M.-C., Kunkel, Lin, M. and Ledbetter 2007). Talking on the phone to family is a different experience to chatting online to friends or texting one's lover. Our email 'identity' is different to our letter writing self. Pre web based research into the chat room, MUD, or bulletin board observed that users took on a nickname or handle that allowed them to participate in a carnival like masquerade of online identity play. CMC researchers in this tradition argued that wearing the mask of a 'handle' in communication without physical or verbal cues appeared to produce a particularly playful 'wavelength' for communications. Many of these observations could now be made of avatar based interactions. We can experiment with other parts of ourselves, take risks or express aspects of self that we find impossible to live out in day-to-day 'meatspace'. As Boulter and Grusin observe, 'MUDs and chatrooms serve almost no other cultural function than the remediation of the self' (Bolter and Grusin 2000: 285). This presumption of the pleasures of anonymity online was foundational to the kinds of questions that early CMC researchers asked about online communications (see Kennedy 2006). In particular it was a problematic that chimed with particular constructions of the self current in critical theory of the 1990s.

These constructions of the self in CMC all had a common post-structuralist history. Within this theoretical framework, identity is seen as anything but essential or fixed, on the contrary identity is understood as a fluid process in which 'self' and environment are constantly interacting. This idea rests upon the proposition that identity is constructed through discourse. (Or conversely since identity cannot be expressed as anything but discourse it must therefore exist as discourse.) Similarly arguments have long been advanced in sociology that social reality is created through discursive activity.

The way we talk about (and represent) our experiences somehow creates the possibility for the conditions of those experiences. This convention of thinking about identity as an anti-essentialist, disembodied and discursive *process* derives more recently from Deleuze's idea of identity as a 'becoming' filtered through authors such as Rosi Braidotti who discussed 'nomadic identity' in 1994 as a practice involving 'the affirmation of fluid boundaries, a practice of the intervals, of the interfaces, and the interstices' (1994: 7).

Much of the early critical enthusiasm for new online forms of communication stemmed from its construction as in some way the technological embodiment of the then current ideas about fragmented, decentred identities. (This is just like the excitement experienced by literary scholars when they first began to understand hypertext as the technological manifestation of post-structuralist literary theory that we saw in **1.2.3**.) Here was a text-based form of communication that actually builds worlds (e.g. MUDS). A form of speech that actually leads the speaker to become other than themselves, to transform, to be formed by the acts of speaking (e.g. chat rooms). 'Internet discourse constitutes the subject as the subject fashions him or herself' (Poster 1997: 222).

The central question that emerged from this position was 'Who are we when we are online?'. It was argued by, for instance, Allucquere Roseanne Stone (1995: 18-20) that in previous ages identity was in part guaranteed through embodiment, the body and identity were coterminous. The King guaranteed his signature by a seal carried on his finger; the signature is a token of physical presence. Increasingly however, using a McLuhanite argument based in the idea of technology as human extension, we have used technology to communicate our selves over distance. Through the telegraph, the telephone, mass media and now online communications we have learnt that the self does not subsist only as an embodied presence but also as a networked presence. It is these shifts in the status and experience of identity that are at the heart of Stone's understanding of what she called the virtual age:

> By the virtual age I don't mean the hype of virtual reality technology, which is certainly interesting enough it its own ways. Rather, I refer to the gradual change that has come over the

relationship between sense of self and body, and the relationship between individual and group, during a particular span of time. I characterise this relationship as virtual because the accustomed grounding of social interaction in the physical facticity of human bodies is changing.

(Stone 1995: 17)

The retreat from 'physical facticity' in our experience of identity was key to understanding the debates that constituted the study of CMC in its initial responses to the development of the Internet. The fact that text based online communication was 'cues filtered out' interaction with no physical codes to locate gender, race or class formed the basis for arguing that the Internet facilitates the development of different experiences of identity and different experiences of group belonging.

In *Life on the Screen* (1995) Sherry Turkle also explored at length the possibilities that online communications offer for identity re-construction work. Both Stone and Turkle in different ways also made connections between these new experiments with individual identity and our sense of group or community identity. Turkle argued, for instance,

> The networked computer serves as an 'evocative object' for thinking about community. Additionally, people playing in the MUDs struggle toward a new, still tentative, discourse about the nature of community that is populated both by people and by programs that are social actors. In this, life in the MUD may serve as a harbinger of what is to come in the social spaces that we still contrast with the virtual by calling them 'real'.

(Turkle 1996: 357)

Many of the themes arising out of this thread of inquiry into anonymity have continued to circulate since the online worlds became avatar based rather than merely limited to text only interactions. Virtual worlds like *Second Life* and Massive Multi Player Online Games (MMOGs) like *Lineage, Everquest, World of Warcraft* and *The Sims* all function through users interacting through the control functions represented by an avatar. (Castranova (2006) claimed that 20 million people subscribed worldwide to online environments.) Different sites allow different levels of avatar design and have different gestural repertoires. These online environments have been compared to the science fiction visions of cyberspace in William Gibson's *Neuromancer* (1986) or the Metaverse of Neal Stephenson's *Snow Crash* (1992). Researchers into virtual worlds have pointed out for instance the intensity of relationship engagements made through the limited 'bandwidth' of the 'cues filtered out' communications where a limited menu of movement supplemented by text based interaction occurs. These observations on the powerful *immersion* afforded by online environments recall Stone's (1995) original work on phone sex workers in which she analysed the powerful physical and emotional affect constituted through the highly limited range of voice only communications over a phone line. In South Korea, which has one of the highest percentage uses of broadband in the world, nearly 40 percent of the population plays the online game *Lineage*; Seoul has its own 'cyber crime unit' which reports at least 100 real life attacks a month that result from game world interactions. Passions in this game are sufficiently aroused for real world pain to be inflicted.

Similarly analyses of how users' text communication styles become an expressive means to the formation of relationships and community recall Andrea Baker's (1998) work on CMC communications in which she observed that couples who met in cyberspace were initially attracted both by the usual kinds of cues ('good sense of humour', 'having something in common') and also by medium-specific qualities such as 'response time' and 'style of writing'. This suggests that there are medium-specific qualities to the communication. Despite being masked by the avatar users report a high level of physical identification with the non space of cyberspace. Users describe their activities in an online environment in the first person: 'I went to the bar', 'I levelled up', 'I went on a guild raid'; they never say 'My avatar went to a bar' and so on. This is a very similar process to the one through which we routinely mistake the representation of an object for the object itself. Asked to describe a photograph of a chair most respondents will say 'That's a chair' not, 'That's a photograph of a chair'. Avatar relations carry this level of misidentification to another level, mobilising the invisible body and identity of the user as part of the apparatus of virtual world representation. It seems that users bring many of the spatial and social cultures of real life into online environments while at the same time using the affordances of anonymity to experiment, to take risks, to find connection in ways that they would find difficult or impossible in real life.

T. L. Taylor (2003) reminds us however that these worlds are hardly transparent media for free expression – they are coded, created by particular designers in particular industrial contexts within particular economic constraints. Nevertheless she argues, in a manner that looks forward to our discussion of user-generated content below, that the whole enterprise of creating a virtual world is not a process designers can have total control over:

> As one designer remarked, 'Once it (the world) starts going . . . it won't stop. It will go its own direction. You can kind of, you can knock it one way, you can guide it a little, you cannot change its direction. The best you can hope for is maybe it should go this way, maybe it should go that way and then you find out whether it does or not. And that's it, so absolutely it's a thing in and of itself. In fact it's more than it originally was because there's so much input from so many people.'
>
> (Taylor 2003: 32)

The shifting balance of power between authors and users in online environments can be seen having its first major impact in the 'revolt' of players against Origin, the developers of Richard Garriot's 'Ultima IV' (Kushner 2003: 169). This was the most sophisticated iteration of Richard Garriot's Ultima world in which the virtues of compassion, valour, honesty and justice were championed. The online game world however was quickly overrun by gamers more used to the worlds of Doom and Quake where player-kills were a more reliable measure of success. An online revolt of Ultima subscribers eventually spilled over into real life when players organised a class action against the producers on the basis of poor software and poor support for players. The case was thrown out by a judge who stated that its success 'would kill online gaming if consumers were allowed this power' (Kline *et al.* 2003: 162–163). The avatar itself has also become the site for contestations that challenge the culture of online environments. H. W. Kennedy reports how women *Quake* players formed clans distinguished by their own customised avatar designs made through the process of 'skinning', in which skilled users can apply their own customised 'skins' to a pre-built avatar skeleton:

> The imagery used draws heavily from fantasy/science fiction as well as closely resembling the types of female subjects that have featured in feminist cyberpunk literature. These fantasy constructions of identity offer exploration of alternative subjectivities in which being feminine doesn't necessarily equal being technically incompetent, in need of rescue or

simply the object of male desire. The ability to play in this masculine context with an avatar/persona entirely created out of their own fantasies of empowerment, mastery and conquest appears significant in this transition from consumption to production.

(Dovey and Kennedy 2006a: 129)

Although the theme of anonymity has dominated a good deal of CMC research pre and post web it often features as a starting point for research rather than a conclusion. More and more researchers find that while anonymity encourages experiment and play these processes are rooted in the real life personae of the participants. That, as we will argue below, real life is always in cyberspace and vice versa.

3.19 Belonging

If the development of CMC interested researchers from the point of the view of the possibilities it created for individual acts of anonymity-inspired expression its potential for new forms of group identity prompted similar levels of research interest. This section will look at some of the early critical responses occasioned by the formation of such groups. These responses in the main centred round the idea of 'community'.

Popular understandings of group identities in CMC ranged from the idea of the online community as an antidote to the social fragmentation of contemporary life, envisaged as a particularly American edenic moment as the online 'frontier homestead' (Rheingold 1993) to an idea of online groups as the heart of a newly revived Public Sphere (Kellner 2001; Poster 1997). Academic inquiry focused around attempting to define the new kinds of belonging brought about by online communities. It asked a number of key questions; can communities be separate from physical location? What kinds of discursive or behavioural strategies define communities? What value or significance might such communities have to the polity at large? What social policy frameworks might be necessary both to take advantage of the potential for online communities as well as to limit the 'digital divide' that they create?

These critical inquiries were driven in part as a reaction to the visionary speculations about 'community' and 'belonging' that sprang from particular claims arising from the online practices of a few hundred West Coast computer visionaries in the 1980s. The Bulletin Board System known as The Well for instance was widely cited (Smith 1992; Rheingold 1993; Hafner 1997) as an example of the potential for Utopian online communal interaction. This system, built by individuals based in the San Francisco region, seemed to embody the libertarian aspirations of the early 1970s for a less alienated and more communal way of life.

> There's always another mind out there. Its like having a corner bar complete with old buddies and delightful newcomers and new tools waiting to take home and fresh graffiti and letters, except instead of putting on my coat, shutting down the computer and walking down to the corner, I just invoke my telecom programme and there they are. Its a place.
>
> (Rheingold 1995: 62)

Rheingold's description of his cyber community recalls the fictional locales of soap operas – in which the audience are witness to simulated community. However this Utopianism was subject to criticism from its own community. John Perry Barlow, a scion of online community and the author of a 'Declaration of Independence for Cyberspace', pointed out there are many differences between such communications and belonging to a community. There was a lack of diversity of age, ethnicity and social class. The communication was disembodied,

See e.g. Steven G. Jones (ed.) *Cybersociety 2.0,* Sage, 1998. Steven G. Jones (ed.) *Cybersociety* Sage, 1994. David Holmes ed. *Virtual Politics,* Sage, 1997 manufactured, inorganic. The group has no common bonds of shared adversity. His analysis foreshadows debates about the digital divide and about the ways in which particular community practices are anything but inclusive (Barlow 1995).

The circulation of visionary claims about online communities in popular culture prompted scholarly attempts to define what might constitute an 'online community'. These attempts emanated primarily from the study of computer-mediated communications. This project was in part determined by its intellectual history in Sociology which has made community and group belonging a central object of study – in particular a sociological tradition derived from Durkheim in which group identity is identified through shared values and norms. This idea in turn overlaps with an idea of community based in ties of family, work and economic relations that may often be associated or represented through physical location. In thinking about the meaning of new forms of online communication scholars have used this analytic triad of *common relationships, shared values and shared spaces* through which to begin to define online community. This sociological trajectory meets politics at the point at which we begin to think about how our sense of group belonging is either empowering or disempowering, how new communities might presage new formations of power and how new (online) communities might reconstitute the public sphere of political and cultural debate. The focus of this research has continued relevance to media through the increasing requirement for producers to think about how their texts are in a co-creative relationship with users which occur in the 'community' created round a particular programme, film or game. 'Community management', through which users are encouraged to feel that they have a participatory role in media processes, is an increasingly recognised role within media production (see **3.22** below on UGC).

Many of the early attempts to analyse community online proceeded from the assumption that community could be identified through its own internal discursive practices. If it is assumed that discourse shapes social reality then particular discursive practices shared by a group may be said to construct a social reality and that reality, it can be argued, would constitute a community. Since any online community exists as just text and code (unless the participants choose to meet 'IRL' – in real life) we can see that there is an apparent 'fit' between 'discourse is social reality' and 'text as virtual social reality'.

Within this model, it is therefore possible to argue that one indicator of community might be common discursive practices represented in textual norms and behaviours. The simplest form here are the numerous abbreviations (LOL, BTW etc.) and emoticons (:-) = smile) developed as specialised language to communicate in conditions of bandwidth scarcity (i.e. online) – these conventions have now of course been massively popularised through mobile phone text messaging. McLaughlin, Osborne and Smith (1994) argued that the evolution of codified forms of acceptable communicative behaviours in Usenet groups similarly begins to constitute a group identifiable through communication patterns. They identified for instance that Usenet users would be criticised for 'incorrect novice use of technology', 'bandwidth waste' or violation of existing networking or news group conventions. Similarly the creation of language norms and pragmatic communication tactics had also led to the generation of ethical codes (identifiable through their violation) and a shared awareness of appropriate language.

Baym (1998) argued that more substantive shared bonds develop online through her study of the rec.arts.tv.soaps Usenet group. These bonds emerged out of the work of creating a functional communicative space. In her carefully measured conclusion Baym finally sidestepped some of the questions around whether or not these interactions constitute community, and if so what implications for the polity at large this might have:

The social and cultural forces I've examined here often emerge into stable patterns within a group. It is these stable patterns of social meanings, manifested through a group's ongoing discourse that enable participants to imagine themselves part of a community.

(Baym 1998: 62)

However Baym's research also revealed a very important principle that would be borne out in the development of Social Network Sites shortly after the publication of her study, namely that many participants in online community *seek* ways of integrating their on and offline experiences.

The research I have reviewed and the model I have proposed suggest that online groups are often woven into the fabric of off-line life rather than set in opposition to it. The evidence includes the pervasiveness of off-line contexts in online interaction and the movement of online relationships off line.

(ibid.: 63)

One of the reasons that Social Network Sites have taken off so remarkably is that they afford their users the opportunity to *articulate their existing communities* through the links made.

This practice is hardly about anonymity – although it is possible to be a 'faker' in an SNS the norm here is self publication rather than masquerade. This use of the social network has more in common with the history of the 'homepage' – an online space where, far from seeking 'disguise' or 'masquerade' designers base their online self in their offline world; Helen Kennedy observed of the women from the East End of London involved in her study

> Penetration of SNS in a short space of time has been remarkable – the Pew Centre for Internet Research claimed a 22 percent use by Americans in December 2007 (Internet's Broader Role in Campaign 2008 http://people-press.org/reports/display.php3?ReportID=384) which translates to a figure of a little under 65 million people

More importantly, it was found that the students showed no sign of wanting to hide their gender and ethnicity and so 'benefit' from the possibility of anonymity that cyberspace offered them. Rather, they made explicit and implicit references to their gender and ethnicity in their homepages. Many of the Her@students made their ethnicity central to their homepages, just as it is central to their identity.

(Kennedy 2006)

Boyd and Ellison in their article (2007) on the history of Social Network Sites argue that 'On many of the large SNSs, participants are not necessarily "networking" or looking to meet new people; instead, they are primarily communicating with people who are already a part of their extended social network.' They define SNS as:

web-based services that allow individuals to (1) construct a public or semi-public profile within a bounded system, (2) articulate a list of other users with whom they share a connection, and (3) view and traverse their list of connections and those made by others within the system.

Boyd and Ellison's work also illustrates some of the continuity in CMC research over the past two decades, when they talk about how the profile page is a space where the user can 'type oneself into being' (Sundén 2003: 3). SNS, like MUDs and Usenet groups before them, can be understood as sites affording discursive opportunities for the re-engineering of the self in ways that correlate with post-structuralist frameworks for thinking about identity. They also point out that though SNSs appear to have exploded into public consciousness in a very short space of time following the launches of MySpace (2003), Facebook (2004), and Bebo

(2005) there is in fact a much longer history to the development of the applications that have been combined in the most popular SNSs. They point out for instance that profiles had always been a feature of dating sites and that instant messaging and chat applications also facilitated 'buddy lists'. They date the first SNS as 1997 with SixDegrees.com which failed to take off in the manner of its later imitators. Despite these continuities with earlier research into social uses of the net they argue that the distinctive feature of SNSs is that they are 'ego centric' not 'topic centric':

> The rise of SNSs indicates a shift in the organization of online communities. While websites dedicated to communities of interest still exist and prosper, SNS are primarily organized around people, not interests. Early public online communities such as Usenet and public discussion forums were structured by topics or according to topical hierarchies, but social network sites are structured as personal (or 'egocentric') networks, with the individual at the center of their own community.
>
> (Boyd and Ellison 2007)

Boyd and Ellison highlight the most significant and popular areas of research into SNS as:

- Impression Management and Friendship Performance i.e. how we 'manage' our self presentation online

- Bridging Online and Offline Social Networks i.e. investigating the relationships between IRL and online communities

- Networks and Network Structure i.e. using data from SNS to map or visualise the dynamics of network based communications

- Privacy i.e. availability of SNS data for other uses in marketing or consumer surveillance; linked to other research on trust, the reliability of SNS information and the safety of users.

The first two of these areas seems familiar enough from the traditions of CMC that we have identified above. The last two however are more recent. They are both based on the richness of the data traces of our lives that we leave online in our SNS interactions. This data can be used by researchers to think about the way that networks of contact communication and culture function in contemporary techno-capitalist societies. However, it can also be used by corporations, states and deviants to manipulate or damage the interests of its originators. This concern with the possible 'dark sides' of net use is a new departure from the ebullient and by and large enthusiastic embrace of networked communications by earlier researchers. The threats to privacy and safety and the new idea of addictive online behaviours are all now the subject of research in a variety of disciplines.

3.20 Living in the interface

Another dominant thread in the study of Computer Mediated Communications has been to understand the *nature* of the relationship between offline and online experiences. A good deal of this work in the early days of CMC study was underpinned by the idea that in some way these identity experiments in Cyberspace represented a retreat from, or an alternative to, social reality. This view could be seen as consistent with the idea that the spread of 'the virtual' (as identity, as media, as reality) is a radical epistemic break with all that we have known. However when we go out and talk to users of CMC we discover that their cyberlives are thoroughly enmeshed in their real lives and vice versa: online experiences are determined by social reality, by material resources, by gender, sexuality, and race. In short by material, economic and political structures. As media have become more and more ubiquitous through various forms of wireless communication this integration of mediation and everyday life has become even more pronounced. We no longer have to go to a stationary screen to access a data world of interlocutors – the mobile phone, laptop or PDA can all allow our online lives to continue to function as part of our 'nomadic' and intimate daily rhythms. We want to explore two different illustrations to underline the ways in which critical thinking about 'cyberspace' should begin with the assumption that it is no more separate from the material world than any other kind of mediated experience and indeed precisely because of its ubiquity may in fact be more seamlessly and intimately stitched into everyday life.

The first concerns the way in which online worlds have become subject to the real world laws of property and real estate. In 2001 economist Edward Castranova hit the headlines with his research that the value of work calculated by sales of virtual objects of the Sony online game *Everquest* was the equivalent of the Bulgarian GNP. An entirely *immaterial* environment was producing as much wealth as a large European state. How? Through labour, through person hours. Gamers were able to build up costumes, uniforms, weapons and property in game through extensive and often skilled endeavour. They were then able to sell these prizes online at eBay to enable other players to acquire them without the hard graft. In 2006 Castranova estimated that the value of real money trading (RMT) in what he calls 'synthetic worlds' was $100m (Castranova 2006). This economy has also produced an industry of game farms in which players are paid to generate valuable in-game items which can be sold on to the cash rich time poor. Despite the fact that eBay banned the sale of goods made in game in January 2007 the RMT business thrives in specialised sites now set up just to take a percentage from this very lucrative market. (The eBay ban did not extend to *Second Life* where the End User Licence Agreement (EULA) gives rights to the creator of the goods.) This commodification of the game world of course completely blurs the 'magic circle' of play described in Huizinga's classic analysis by bringing the 'real' world into the play space. In May 2007 the Korean government passed the 'Advancement of Gaming Industry Act' which proscribed RMT. When the synthetic world falls under the orbit of the state in this way it can hardly be constructed as a self organising 'virtual realm'.

There are numerous other examples of online/offline interaction. For instance Andrea Baker (1998) has shown from a study of eighteen couples who first met online that these relationships are every bit as actual as those formed IRL (in real life). Six of her sample couples were married, with a further four either engaged or cohabiting. The couples in her sample met in a variety of locations, the majority not in chat spaces designed for pick-ups or sex but in topic-based conversations of mutual interest. The interaction formed in the supposedly 'virtual' environment has profoundly 'real world' consequences for those concerned. These are real human fleshly relationships formed in the space between the 'actual' and the 'virtual' – again perhaps suggesting that this may be a false dichotomy, that our engagements with CMC are every bit as embodied and embedded in social reality as our engagement with any other media. The problematic dichotomy only arises when identity and social reality are assumed to be entirely material as opposed to discursive, and when 'cyberspace' is assumed to be entirely discursive rather than material. Kennedy (2006) argued that

> online identities are often continuous with offline selves, not reconfigured versions of subjectivities in real life; for this reason it is necessary to go beyond Internet identities, to look at offline contexts of online selves, in order to comprehend virtual life fully.

The developing field of Ubiquitous Computing and Pervasive Media offers a different kind of illustration of the relationships between physical and virtual environments. Here the constantly shifting mappings of one onto the other argue for an understanding of their necessary co-relation rather than separation. Wireless applications make physical locations available for data downloads which alter their meaning and change the way users experience them. In a way these applications extend the effects of the walkman or iPod on our everyday environments by providing a media 'overlay' to them. Hewlett Packard for instance have developed a software called Mscape that allows users to map sounds and images onto specific locations which can be downloaded using a PDA and headphones, the strapline on their site (http://www.mscapers.com/home) expresses the situation 'Mediascapes are all around you'. Research by Dovey and Fleuriot (2005) into user experiences for mobile gaming and pervasive media applications found that users take real pleasure in the interplay between actual locations and data inputs, leading to a consideration of the aesthetics of these augmented realities. Users expressed pleasure in the feelings of deep concentration that location based audio applications offered them. They were fascinated by the new ways of navigating actual spaces unlocked by audio and image based augmentations of their actual space. In particular they reported delight in special moments when the sounds in their headphones appeared to be in accord with the physical location or when 'real world' sounds seemed to fit in with the data mix. Artists and designers working in this field have been able to produce heritage applications, mobile games and educational work that exploits these properties. However the point in this context is that users naturally and pleasurably moved 'between worlds'; the separation of virtual and material is undermined as computing goes wireless.

Identity, belonging and real/virtual relations have all been continuing threads in the study of the Internet. The pleasures afforded to users through these activities are at the heart of understanding what drives Web 2.0 or YouTube. These pleasures have also contributed to debates about the way in which the Internet has the potential to revive the public sphere.

3.21 The Internet and the public sphere

The contemporary stress on *participatory culture* driven by web media suggests that we are living through both an extraordinary enlargement of the possibilities of the public sphere at the same time as its commodification through user surveillance. Indeed in the rhetoric of Web 2.0 public sphere participation via the web and self commodification through voluntary surveillance are *one and the same thing*.

The claim that the Internet has revived the Public Sphere is a deep running theme in net scholarship and public net discourse. The essentially participatory and interactive elements of the pre-Web Internet clearly suggested attractive homologies with Habermas's description of the idealised public sphere. News groups, bulletin boards and email groups all have the facilitation of group communications as their technological *raison d'être*. Many of them were devoted to discussion of 'affairs of the day' and culture of all kinds (including culture that Habermas would certainly consign to the outer limits of the public sphere!). The pre-Web Internet was essentially about dialogue, a fundamental basis for democratic political systems and culture – hence some of the excited political pronouncements associated with the Internet right from the 1970s

> Community memory is convivial and participatory. A CM system is an actively open 'free' information system, enabling direct communications among its users, with no centralised editing of or control over the information exchanged. Such a system represents the

precise antitheses to the dominant uses both of electronic communications media which broadcast centrally determined messages to mass passive audiences, and of cybernetic technology, which involves centralised processing of and control over data drawn from or furnished to direct and indirect users. The payoff is efficient, unmediated (or rather self mediated) interaction, eliminating roles and problems that develop when one party has control over what information passes between two or many others. This freedom is complemented by the way the system democratises information – power, for no group of its users has more access to its main information than the least user has.
(Michael Rossman, 'What is community memory?', mimeograph, 1979 cited by Roszak [1985: 140])

This strand of emphasis on participatory culture produced through the Internet has a continuous forty-year history. Where Habermas originally criticised electronic media for simulating a face to face public sphere it was widely argued that the Internet does the essential work of the public sphere.

The age of the public sphere as face to face talk is clearly over; the question of democracy must henceforth take into account new forms of electronically mediated discourse
(Poster 1997: 220)

The Internet appears to do the trick of giving the concept of the public sphere a new lease of life by reformulating it in a way that answers some of the major defects that critics have pointed out since its original formulation by Habermas (1989). These are well summarised by Garnham (1992) – the public sphere described by Habermas was far from democratic or even public. It was public only in the sense that a British public school is public, i.e. exclusive to all but white bourgeois males. Predicated on exclusion it could only ever be the basis for a partial version of democracy that would inevitably exclude other genders, sexualities, ethnicities and classes. Moreover the Habermas version of the public sphere and particularly his account of the role of the mass media are resolutely serious; pleasure and desire are denied space in a culture determined by 'critical reasoning'. The whole idea of universal enlightenment values ('We hold these truths to be self-evident . . .') is undermined by postmodern critics who, after Foucault, perceive in them new structures of power and authority. In its place the postmodern critical theorist argues for specificity and particularity,

For a number of post modern theorists – Foucault, Rorty, Lyotard, Laclau and Mouffe etc. – macropolitics that goes after big institutions like the state or capital is to be replaced by micropolitics, with specific intellectuals intervening in spheres like the university, the prison, the hospital or for the rights of specific oppressed groups like sexual or ethnic minorities.
(Kellner 2001: 3)

As a 'public' communicative space the Internet does indeed appear to offer highly specific and limited engagements – whatever your politics, whatever your fetish, a corresponding website and 'sense of community' can be found online. The Internet as postmodern communication space has almost become a 'given' of cyberculture studies. No grand narratives here, micro fragments encountered through an aleatory hypertext reading; 'critical reasoning' here replaced by opinion and subjective comment.

Kellner argues that the pluralism of the Internet as mediated communication offers uniquely new opportunities for dissident marginal and critical points of view to circulate:

Democracy involves democratic participation and debate as well as voting. In the Big Media Age, most people were kept out of democratic discussion and were rendered by broadcast technologies passive consumers of infotainment. Access to media was controlled by big corporations and a limited range of voices and views were allowed to circulate. In the Internet age, everyone with access to a computer, modem, and Internet service can participate in discussion and debate, empowering large numbers of individuals and groups kept out of the democratic dialogue during the Big Media Age.

(Kellner 2001: 6)

Kellner goes on to cite the Zapatistas and anti-capitalist movements' use of internet communications as examples of how the new media offer new spaces and mechanisms for radical political organisation. However, such specific engagements and campaigns, though certainly based in Enlightenment meta-narratives of humanism, e.g. freedom, equality, dignity, appear online as a series of fragmented, single-issue information clusters. Nowhere is there any necessary or prescribed causal or dialectical linkage between them, only the hyperlinkage of network media.

For Mark Poster (1997) the postmodern public sphere is based on the idea that it is a mediated and mediating space, not a technology. The space of communications flows is a space in which our subjectivities cannot remain fixed but both engage and are engaged by the network. This is a space characterised most of all by expressions of post-structuralist subjectivity grounded in a critique of Habermas that questioned the autonomous rational subject at the heart of his idealised public sphere.

Poster is quite specific about which parts of the Internet might build such a new public sphere; his 'margin of novelty', the genuinely new, are virtual communities, MOOs and (at the time of this comment purely fantasy) 'synthesis of virtual reality technology with the Internet'. 'Internet technology imposes . . . a dematerialization of communication and, in many of its aspects, a transformation of the subject position of the individual who engages with it' (Poster 1997: 215). Poster's new Public Sphere is predicated on this alleged new fluidity of subject position that online communication calls into play: 'the salient characteristics of Internet community is the diminution in prevailing hierarchies of race, class, age, status and especially gender' (1997: 224).

Given that Habermas's account of the public sphere has been fatally undermined by criticism based on its exclusions, this new communicative forum in which the signifiers of 'otherness' no longer operate is assumed to be automatically emancipatory and democratic. However as Poster himself makes clear we can only call this a Public Sphere by redefining its original formulation.

In a sense, they (MOOs) serve the function of a Habermasian public sphere, however reconfigured, without intentionally or even actually being one. They are places not of validity-claims or the actuality of critical reason, but of the inscription of new assemblages of self-constitution.

(Poster 1997: 224)

In the sections immediately below we will bring these discussions about the Public Sphere to bear upon the most recent claims for Internet based media.

3.22 User-generated content: we are all fans now

One of the ways in which the Internet has become so central to contemporary media is through the way in which its symbiotic relationship with media culture has offered audiences participatory opportunities. The history of the take-up of these opportunities shows how the marginal possibilities offered by the net for audiences to interact with media is now refashioning the whole enterprise of what Kellner above terms 'Big Media'. As audiences have become 'users' and user-generated content has started to become a real competitor to traditional media the impact of the Internet on traditional media institutions is stronger than even Poster and Kellner above might have predicted ten years ago. As we will see below these developments dovetail with the claims and practices of 'Web 2.0' in ways that suggest that contemporary developments in media are at the heart of powerful forces for change across state and corporate sectors.

The growth of the blogosphere, the impact of peer to peer music distribution and the explosion of YouTube in 2006 have all challenged the foundations of mass media industries. The traditional gatekeepers of culture, the filters of news and guardians of quality have all had to adjust to the realities of participatory culture. Examples are almost too numerous to cite; the American Press Institute published Bowman and Willis's *We Media; How Audiences are shaping the future of news and information* in 2003. In the UK the BBC has been tying itself in knots trying to accommodate 360-degree programming and user participation – see e.g. Peter Horrocks *The Future of News* http://www.bbc.co.uk/blogs/theeditors/2006/11/the_future_of_news.html. In the US the Gannet Publishing Group, responsible for *USA Today* and ninety other US dailies, jumped onto the same UGC bandwagon announcing in November of that year that they would be 'crowdsourcing' parts of their news operations, 'to put readers to work as watchdogs, whistle-blowers and researchers in large, investigative features' (Howe 2006). In the UK in November 2007 Channel Four TV could be found running a seminar on 'The Power of Collaboration' claiming, 'The next generation of customers will be more active and creative in building content' and asking, 'Can this be harnessed to build new business models to benefit both? . . . [H]ow does this work and what benefit is it for the customer to contribute to design?' This incursion of the 'ordinary person' into the bastions of media privilege is experienced as both opportunity and threat by the industries themselves and has been understood by academic researchers primarily through the history of active audience studies.

Studies of fans and fan cultures have spearheaded the theoretical construction of this shift from 'audience' to 'user' in media studies. 'Fans' were the first groups to avail themselves of the mass of website material that exists in a symbiotic relationship with other media. On the one hand this seamless lattice of mediation can be seen as the extension of mass mediation into more and more of our time, more and more of our space. On the other, it also brings within our reach the possibility of becoming producers in our own right. Every SNS post, or conversation in a chat room, every home page and downloaded MP3 playlist facilitates the individual communicating in a pseudo public mode of address. What is clear is that a great deal of web use facilitates a feeling of participation in media space. Senft (2000) offered an analysis of web use around celebrity scandal sites such as those based on the Lady Diana and OJ Simpson sites. She suggested this model of a participatory (rather than interactive) media zone had become not a 'court of public opinion' but a 'cult of public opinion'. Users are here able to participate in the space of media representation. The conversations, interactions and arguments about TV that active audience researchers have studied are here enacted in numerous interactive chat rooms linked to the primary information based parts of the site. For instance in the UK in 2000 Channel Four's biggest hit programme was the formatted Reality Gameshow *Big Brother*. Demand for access to the chat rooms to talk to the recently evicted member of the household far outstripped the ability of the servers to keep track. 'Overflow rooms' were filled with viewers eager to discuss the latest episode with one another. Significantly the climactic moment of the entire first UK series occurred in the daytime and was therefore seen first by viewers to the programme's live webcams in a moment already spoken of as a breakthrough for UK web use. This desire to 'be part of it', to continue the moment of the text through its constant reiteration and circulation has a great deal in common with a tradition of work in media and cultural studies around fan cultures (Tulloch and Alvarado 1983; Barker 1989; Jenkins 1992). Certainly the web is the place to go to find any aspect of fan culture it is possible to imagine, the sites are out there.

This focus on the 'fan' as New Media co-creator has been particularly compelling in the recent work of Henry Jenkins (2006). Jenkins has traced the relationships between active fan communities and media producers to analyse the radical shifts between producers and consumers that underpin twenty-first-century media markets. In an essay (2002) based on Pierre Lévy's avowedly Utopian ideal of 'collective intelligence' Jenkins argued that new media offered 'new tools and technologies that enable consumers to archive, annotate, appropriate, and recirculate media content', and that these tools led to 'a range of subcultures that promote Do-It-Yourself media production'. The affordances of the web to fans and DIY culture enthusiasts all coincide with the era of 'transmediality', 'economic trends encouraging the flow of images, ideas, and narratives across multiple media channels and demanding more active modes of spectatorship'. As media markets fragment producers seek to maximise audiences and revenue by repurposing texts across as many platforms as possible. This distributed form of storytelling and media production demands 'more active modes of spectatorship' argues Jenkins, as we navigate between e.g. movie, DVD, online mash ups and computer games. Jenkins suggests that these trends are altering 'the way media consumers relate to each other, to media texts, and to media producers' (Jenkins 2002). As we have seen above (**3.5**, Fragmentation and convergence) in his book *Convergence Culture* (2006) Jenkins develops these arguments suggesting that 'convergence' is not a technological process but a feature of audience behaviour – it is us who are 'converging'. In turn these processes are reflected in the kind of texts that facilitate an ongoing involvement with the storyworld; Jenkins cites *The Matrix* trilogy as the prototypical transmedial text inviting audiences into engagements that require puzzling out ambiguities, sharing readings and comparing notes across film, game, animation and web. Jenkins argues that:

> it is clear that new media technologies have profoundly altered the relations between media producers and consumers. Both culture jammers and fans have gained greater visibility as they have deployed the web for community building, intellectual exchange, cultural distribution, and media activism. Some sectors of the media industries have embraced active audiences as an extension of their marketing power, have sought greater feedback from their fans, and have incorporated viewer generated content into their design processes. Other sectors have sought to contain or silence the emerging knowledge culture. The new technologies broke down old barriers between media consumption and media production. The old rhetoric of opposition and cooptation assumed a world where consumers had little direct power to shape media content and where there were enormous barriers to entry into the marketplace, whereas the new digital environment expands their power to archive, annotate, appropriate, and recirculate media products.
>
> (Jenkins 2002)

CASE STUDY 3.2: Transmedial textualities

Global media enterprises now seek the active engagement of audiences using their products across a range of platforms. Blockbuster budgets in a globalised market require the maximisation of revenue streams across as many media outlets as possible. The *Return of the King* (Electronic Arts 2003) console game has significant markers of transmediality; within the 'text' itself, the user is invited to enter into the *Lord of the Rings* storyworld bringing with them whatever knowledge they have from the novels, the films or the films' marketing. The design, packaging and *mis en scène* of the game are all designed to evoke numerous associations with *Lord of the Rings* brand created by New Line cinema.

The introductory notes claim, 'In this final chapter of *The Lord of the Rings* the fate of Middle Earth is in your hands' (EA /New Line 2003). The game is structured through fifteen levels which represent the narrative timescale of the *Return of the King* film; each level notionally represents an episode in one of the film's three journey narratives. For instance a single player enters the story as Gandalf arriving at the critical moment at *Helm's Deep,* but in co-operative mode the players begin as Aragorn, Gimli or Legolas on the *Paths of the Dead* through the mountain, and are required to defeat the King of the Dead before progressing. The remainder of the game levels are divided between *The Path of the King*, *The Southern Gate* through *The Black Gate, Pelennor Fields* to Mordor's *Crack of Doom*. At different levels the player may chose to play as key members of the fellowship, namely Gandalf, Aragorn, Legolas, Gimli, Frodo or Sam. The game genre is action adventure, 'hack 'n slash', with the gameplay emphasis on navigation and enemy slaying – each character has different fighting characteristics which can be amended through the use of experience points accumulated through fighting. Players are required to remember and to master particular control combinations in order to dispatch the endlessly respawning followers of Sauron in the shape of ghosts, orcs and so on.

This series of computer games goes to great lengths to emphasise its relationship with its cinematic forebear. Levels in a computer game often begin with a 'cut scene', a short full-motion video non-playable sequence which sets the scene for the subsequent gameplay. In the *Return of the King* game these cut scenes are re-edited sequences from the original movie; cut and narrated like cinema trailers they offer a powerful evocation of the cinematic spectacle of the film. Compared to the cut scenes in other action adventure computer games these sequences are long and very lavish. On first and second encounter they are genuinely forceful in offering the player an anticipatory sense of *participation* in the cinematic spectacle.

Moreover enormous care has been taken in the cut sequences to make the move from non-playable to playable sequence almost invisible; the designers have elected to dissolve from cinema image to graphic render in the 'smoothest' ways possible so that the player has the sense of suddenly finding oneself *in* the scene as the avatar becomes playable. The dissolve from film image to graphic rendered image is often made on sweeping camera moves thus disguising itself in the dynamic of the changing screen space. The original film dialogue or narration also continues *over* the transition further reinforcing a sense of flow *into* the filmic space. Once in playable mode the avatars have lines from their film dialogue mixed into the game soundtrack. The flow of the gameplay itself is often disrupted by the designers' insistence on our participation in the cinematic storyworld. The graphic action often dissolves back out to the cinematic image for a few moments for a character to comment as the game moves us on to another location. Virtual camera angles too have been designed with cinematic point of view rather than gameplay fluency in mind. The convention of most avatar control in third person computer games has been that we push the avatar away from us with the console controller as we navigate the game environment. Here however we are often required to reverse this procedure, 'pulling' the avatar towards us and the virtual camera lens in ways that insist on the game's remediation of the film rather than ease of gameplay. Many aspects of the *design* of the game reinforce the transmedial experience of immersion in a storyworld that has less to do with the user's pleasure in a particular narrative sequence but in a sense of inhabiting a storyworld where different experiences can unfold.

In this account of the enhanced role of audiences in new media environments the increasingly 'interactive' user is constructed as being part of an ever more intimate feedback loop with media producers. Just as the interactive author has to give away complete textual control to the interactor so media industries at large recognise that consumers' participation in the 'transmedial' landscape must inform their own production processes in ways that are distinctive from the old reliance on ratings or box office. The understanding of media audiences as having a 'configurative' relationship with media texts of all kinds developed by

See Dovey and Kennedy, 'Playing the Ring', in *Branding the Ring*, ed. E. Mathijs Wallflower Press/ Columbia (2006b)

Moulthrop (2004) and others is a *claim* that is fast becoming a central quality of the discourse of new media.

Computer game playing consumers are exemplary in this move from audience to producer. Active play with the 'text' inevitably produces a tendency for the player to refashion the text in her struggle to gain mastery over it. Equally the computer game playing subculture provides a supportive and appreciative context for players wishing to share their own productive game activities. Strong subcultural aspects of computer gameplay produced powerful communities where fan production could find an immediately appreciative audience.

Computer game cultures are characterised by high levels of productive audience behaviours from walkthroughs, fan art, modifications and hacks. The designers of the game *Doom* (1993) were the first to realise the potential of this activity for a different kind of relationship with media consumers. They released a 'freeware' version of the game on the Internet and requested that 'modders' only work with the editing tools available with the purchased licensed version in their creation of new characters and new level scenarios. The modding community can now help to secure the success of a game – '[d]isappointment tinged reviews of *Quake III*, while often nonplussed with the actual content of the game proper, insisted it was worth buying for the support it would inevitably receive from the mod community' (*Edge* Magazine 2003). Valve's *Quake* appeared in 1996 followed shortly by level editors, software provided by the publishers to allow players to make their own versions of the game, and in 1997 i.d. made *all* the *Doom* source code available online. In a paper analysing the role of non-professional agents in first person shooters (FPS) game researcher Sue Morris wrote,

> In a multiplayer FPS game such as *Quake III Arena,* the 'game' is not just a commercially released program that players use, but an assemblage created by a complex fusion of the creative efforts of a large number of individuals, both professional and amateur, facilitated by communication and distribution systems that have developed out of the gaming community itself. As a cocreative media form, multiplayer FPS gaming has introduced new forms of participation, which have led to the formation of community structures and practices that are changing the way in which these games are developed and played.
>
> (Morris 2003)

CASE STUDY 3.3: Players as producers

The game *Counterstrike* (Sierra 2000) has sold over a million copies and despite always being available as a legally free download, it has spawned a huge online user community since its release in 2000 (see Boria *et al*. 2002). *Counterstrike* is a team based terrorist/counter terrorist game based in the realities of post 9/11 military action. *Counterstrike* is one of the first major commercial successes of 'user-generated content'. It was produced by a group of 'player creators' led by Canadian student Minh 'Gooseman' Le. They created *Counterstrike* from the *Half Life* game engine, it is a 'total conversion mod', a modification of the original artefact in which an entirely new and different game is created; in this case from software written by Valve's programmers for their 1998 'Half Life'. Minh Le and his team were anything but a group of lucky or talented amateurs; the development process was a well organised collective effort aiming at producing the best game they could. They were player enthusiasts, expert users, and *Half Life* fans participating in the culture of shareware which has been such a significant driver in the development of digital technologies. The production company Valve recognised the developmental value of these expert user fans when they established the 'Half Life Mod Expo', to showcase the best and most interesting modifications of their game being made by these 'player creators'. It was through this expo that Minh Le's team were signed up by Valve.

In 2002 Valve launched the 'Steam' broadband network exclusively devoted to distribution of Valve titles and the support of the Valve consumer as part of a community. One of the founders of Valve, Gabe Newell, argued that the new network would provide 'a smoother transition between the amateur world and the professional world' (Au 2002). Will Wright, the designer behind the *Sims* series, also suggests that the Internet blurs the distinction between the amateur and the professional media producer:

> I think the Internet's probably the prime example of that. I think there are going to be certain types of new media where this is the natural form of interaction, a smooth ramp from consumer to producer . . . I think right now, it comes down to how steep maybe the ramp is. Because I think you have this kind of natural progression in all media between a consumer and an author, a producer, a designer . . . That possibility exists more now than it did twenty years ago.
>
> (Pearce 2002)

This optimism at the potential for personal expression and product development by game fans should be tempered by an understanding that rather than fundamentally changing the relationship between the media owners of intellectual property and their consumers these developments can also be understood as the exploitation of free labour that intensifies brand engagement as well as developing new products. Andrew MacTavish argued in his study of game mods that in fact they are already a highly restricted and regulated practice; first by the way the necessary high end computer skills restrict access to a particular kind of player creator and second through the ways in which End User Licence Agreements function. These agreements, signed by us all by clicking the 'accept' button when we open new software, contain clauses that restrict the circulation of mods to non-profit networks, i.e. modders wishing to charge for use of their mods are prohibited or instructed to contact the copyright owner. In other words, the point at which modding becomes competition rather than brand development and viral marketing is very carefully policed (Mactavish 2003). Game modders provide the industry with free research and development of new ideas and sometimes whole new titles; the work of creating mods, maps and skins also extends the life of a game, and this life becomes revenue when the tools to do it are only available with licensed versions. As Morris's example above shows the productive activities of gamers lie at the heart of player communities facilitating the use of the game – these communities provide beta testing for publishers, as well as reflecting user tastes and aspirations. These processes are not confined to the games business – Lucas Arts, having once been enthusiastic dispatchers of 'cease and desist' letters to fan producers of video parodies, now use the web to co-operate with fans to work out scenarios for the online multiplayer version of the *Star Wars* franchise (Jenkins 2003).

In this context we argue that the relationship between game industry and game players is prototypical of the new relations between media and media audiences in the era of user-generated content. Web distributed media have refined the mechanism by which audience engagements become part of a community of expert consumers to be managed by brands to consolidate their market position.

See Dovey and Kennedy 2007 for a fuller discussion of this material

3.23 YouTube and post television?

The growth of YouTube is one of the most astonishing and characteristic developments of networked new media. YouTube was developed by three ex-employees of the net banking system Pay Pal. Jawed Karim, Chad Hurley and Steve Chen were discussing in 2004 how hard it was to find footage of TV items that they wanted to see again such as Janet Jackson's Superbowl breast flash or tourist shot tsunami footage from the recent South East Asian disaster. They decided to build a video sharing site which launched as a venture capital start-up in November 2005. Its success was immediate, serving millions of short videos to viewers worldwide everyday. Within a year it was bought by Google for $1.6 billion.

YouTube is the paradigmatic new media start-up story – three bright young guys, some venture capital and an idea whose time has come. The most recent figures at time of writing show that watching video on the Internet is one of the fastest growing areas of media activity. The Pew Internet and American Life research survey published in January 2008 found that 48 percent of Internet users said they had ever visited a video-sharing site such as YouTube which represented a growth of more than 45 percent from the previous year. They found that on an average day, the number of users of video sites nearly doubled from the end of 2006 to the end of 2007. The same Pew survey found that 22 percent of Americans shoot their own videos and that 14 percent of them post some of that video online. This was a 300 percent increase on the previous year, though notably this 14 percent represents a little less than 3 percent of all possible contributors in the population (Pew Internet and American Life 2008).

Successful new media platforms rarely spring unforeseen out of the blue. As we saw above, the elements that were brought together in successful social network sites had been present on the net for ten years. The development of YouTube as a moving image delivery platform needs to be understood as part of the long history of the fragmentation of television which began with the development of timeshift use of VCRs in the 1980s and continued with the penetration of cable and satellite channels through the 1990s. Where the twentieth-century age of mass media had understood television as means to communicate from the centre to the mass and as a commercially protected environment, twenty-first-century tele-visual image systems are developed through the economic determinations of neo-liberalism where televisual systems are primarily understood as sites for commercial exploitation. This has had the effect of massively multiplying the sites of the televisual.

Online video started to appear regularly ten years before the formation of YouTube; however its widespread adoption was slow due to slow connection speeds and bandwidths too narrow for fast moving image delivery. By 2003 video had been combined with blogging to create the video blog or Vlog. A vlog is what happens when people add video into the blog format, so typically a vlog site consisted in a series of short movie posts which were datelined like a diary, and often also have some text introduction. Vlogs were originally living diaries written as we watched day by day. Moreover like the blog the vlog was a networked platform which invited other vloggers to respond by video and thereby constructed global conversations on video. By 2004 the business community was beginning to take note,

> The grassroots movement to post visual blogs makes astonishing viewing, and vlogs' rising audiences may give them an increasing impact. Following in the footsteps of text blogs, video blogs are starting to take off on the Internet. This new form of grassroots digital media is being shepherded along by groups of film makers and video buffs who started pooling publishing tips and linking to each other in earnest this year.
>
> (*Business Weekly* 29 December 2004)

By now pioneer vloggers like Michael Verdi (http://michaelverdi.com/) have four years of continuous video blogging archived online. The media academic and vlogger Adrian Miles coined the term 'softvideo' to describe these developments; 'softvideo' refers to a new kind of audio

See e.g. plugincinema.com who published a manifesto for online cinema in 1998 which argued for production that worked with the constraints of bandwidth and compression visual practice that should be understood not by its previous material form as broadcast, disk or tape, but by its being authored and watched all within the digital domain: so soft video is to hard video what soft (text) copy is to hard copy.

A first step towards softvideo is to no longer regard digital video as just a publication or delivery format, which is the current digital video as desktop video paradigm (which is of course the same as the desktop publishing model) but to treat it as an *authoring* and publication environment. This suggests that a major theme for a softvideo poetics to explore is the description or development of a videographic writing practice within video itself, that is to use digital video as a medium in which we write.

(Miles 2002)

YouTube was developed as a response to this growing ecology of online video. Technically YouTube has three major characteristic features; bandwidth and memory restrict video length to 10 minutes; the url code for any clip can easily be embedded in other sites so that access to the clip can be from any online location; thirdly it is officially not possible to download YouTube videos to your own hard drive. Other technical features include standard search capabilities and some social network functions through the ability to set up your own channels and contact networks. These design functions of course have commercial and aesthetic consequences.

The YouTube clip has become the dominant form of early twenty-first-century videography – previously remediating televisual and cinematic forms of video had also become associated with the short form through the music promo. All these histories are represented in the endlessly creative worlds of the YouTube posting communities. However we are also able witness the return of the primitive 'cinema of attractions' one shot film – the clip that captures in a continuous shot a memorable event or striking moment. Video has by now become so ubiquitous through the mobile phone, the digital stills camera and the webcam that we are experiencing an explosion of point and shoot videography that uses little or no postproduction. Thus the quality of the footage depends on the momentary, the live, the direct address of speakers and social actors to the recording device.

The ease with which the address of any clip can be made available at other online locations recognises the viral nature of networked media. Where the gatekeepers of media content – in this case the TV schedulers – have been bypassed, users discover content through other means, often the recommendation of their friends or online social network. Hence the importance of the idea of the virus for network based media production – all online media are looking for ways to 'go viral', to set up that illusive process whereby users want to share their discovery of a particularly thrilling, amusing or shocking piece of media content with *all* their friends – *immediately*. Before YouTube moving image content like this was either accessed by being sent as a file person to person or phone to phone or else it was downloaded from sites that required more mouse clicks and more time than the quality of the media experience actually warranted. We don't want to have to negotiate Windows Media Player update messages or download times just to see our friend on the dance floor last night or some random person doing extraordinary things with their tongue. YouTube just works – ease of use is its major u.s.p. – no need to download media players or wait endlessly for files to get through on email or phone message. The content is very portable and therefore designed for viral distribution patterns.

Finally the fact that it is hard (but not impossible) to download YouTube content has the effect of always driving the user back to the YouTube site – we cannot easily repurpose or relocate the material. Wherever content appears it will always be YouTube branded. This is a strategy designed for powerful brand building. If video clips simply circulate as viral across online and mobile formats they have no 'branding affiliation' – YouTube videos are always branded as such.

The sheer profusion of video clips available make classification and genre typology seem a daunting task. The software itself offers its own genre classification in the category choices offered for uploaded clips. They are:

- Autos and Vehicles
- Comedy
- Education
- Entertainment
- Film and Animation
- How to and Style
- Music

- News and Politics
- Non Profit and Activism
- People and Blogs
- Pets and Animals
- Science and Technology
- Sports
- Travel and Events

This looks rather like a TV scheduler's list of programme genres. The categories for the user voted YouTube Awards 2007 offer a genre classification that comes somewhat closer to describing the feel of YouTube content, the Awards are classified as:

- Adorable
- Commentary
- Eyewitness
- Instructional
- Politics
- Short Film

- Comedy
- Creative
- Inspirational
- Music
- Series
- Sports

However to understand what is actually innovative about this work we need to realise that even these genres may mean something entirely different in the world of User Generated Content. Sports for instance has nothing to do with its televisual equivalent, here sport is speed Rubik's cube, skateboarding and etch a sketch virtuosity – deliberately playful pursuits that implicitly subvert conventional sporting prowess and big business. 'Eyewitness' nominations are two extreme weather clips, wildlife (the famous Crocodiles at Kruger), one sequence of monks being shot at in Burma and a student being tasered by police. These are a range of events that the Lumière Brothers might have shot if there had been enough of their cameras in the world to be present when something dramatic actually happened! They concern the wonders and amazements of human life and the natural planet. They are memorable and shocking. 'Commentary' is about as far from its journalistic equivalent that it is possible to imagine – rants, witty and profane, heartfelt, hilarious or acute – pure first person opinion. 'Instructional' represents one of the surprise hit genres of web TV – akin to science programmes for children they show how to undertake odd little popular science projects like 'How to Charge an iPod using electrolytes' (an onion and some energy drink), or how to follow a dance routine, or how to use a Wii remote to make a desktop VR display. All of the genres are at once similar to the genres we are familiar with from TV culture but at the same time entirely unexpected and unpredictable, fresh with the imprint of living breathing individuals rather then the seamless patina of corporate product.

Contemporaneously with the success of YouTube we have also seen the development of many other Content Delivery Networks (CDNs) that offer an enormous range of often poor quality televisual content in the hope of attracting enough viewers to sustain online advertising revenues. CDNs are based in specific networking technologies that maximise ease of access to data heavy content like moving image by making it available in distributed server caches so that traffic is directed to the fastest point for the user. There are now literally thousands of TV channels available online, however most carry free to use content produced as promotional material originating in the music, film and leisure industries. Nevertheless CDNs have been massively capitalised through 2007–2008 with millions of dollars invested in for instance the CDNetworks and Highwinds Network Group. Of the many channels available *Current TV* (http://current.com/) is notable for its commitment to user-generated content that covers a range of political and ecological news as well as action sport, fashion and lifestyle segments all designed to appeal to a particular under-35 socially aware demographic. This profusion of TV online is accompanied by the availability of broadcast TV on the Internet through watch again TV on demand sites like the BBC's iPlayer platform. The iPlayer has been an unprecedented success with 17.2 million programmes served in March 2008.

These rapid developments all raise critical questions about how we understand what television is. One way that Television Studies has defined the medium is for instance through the development of Raymond Williams's idea of 'flow' – that in contradistinction to cinema as a moving image experience television was characterised by the unending relationships of one programme segment to another. This in turn was highly influential on conceptions of televisual narration (see e.g. Ellis 1982) and through audience research in the ethnographic tradition that followed on from David Morley's work on *The Nationwide Audience* (1980). This tradition clearly identifies the importance of the schedule in determining and reflecting the rhythms of daily family life as well as the importance of the television as a material technology situated in specific domestic spaces used by particular peoples at different times. According to traditional TV studies this assemblage of institutions, peoples, spaces and technologies produced particular regimes of ideological reproduction and commercial exploitation.

However these medium specific qualities are mutating as TV hybridises itself. Televisual content can now be experienced not just in the domestic living room, but in every room of the house on PCs and laptops and other TVs, on mobile phones whilst waiting for a bus, on the train, in clubs, pubs, shopping malls and airport lounges. The televisual has overflowed its twentieth-century channels and is dissolving into the material textures of the everyday. If the ways in which television was defined no longer apply then the critical question becomes what is television now? If television was defined by technological scarcity (Ellis 2000), flow, and the schedule and the televisual now is experienced as plentiful, fragmented, sometimes individualised and sometimes very public then is it still in fact television at all? As Max Dawson observes, 'television today more accurately refers to an ensemble of *site-unspecific* screens that interact with one another as viewers *and* forms traffic between them' (Dawson 2007: 250).

CASE STUDY 3.4: Kate Modern – Web Drama

The twin drives of changing technological possibility occasioned by broadband and the shifting revenue streams of television in the age of convergence are creating all kinds of new cultural forms that begin to define what it is to be 'web native'. To produce culture that does not simply use the web as another carrier for conventional content but could not exist without the web, to be web native is to create from and for the affordances of the Internet. The Web Drama is typical – short regular narrative based episodes that emulate or remediate TV drama forms but also address the particular possibilities of the web by creating communities of fans who can spend time online interacting with one another and with the storyworld. These interactions might involve chatting with other fans, voting on casting or story outcomes, helping to write the script, discussing characters, or participating in spin-off Alternate Reality Games (ARG) that require the 'hive mind' of the participants to solve narrative based puzzles. The Web Drama is an excellent example of the way screen media enterprises are adapting to new online markets and in the process creating innovative culture. In particular they demonstrate the so called 'Long Tail' in action where new forms of advertising can produce sustainable revenue streams from much smaller audiences than would previously have been the case.

Kate Modern launched in July 2007 on the Bebo social network and has to date run as two series totalling 240 episodes. Its producers claim that there were 25 million views of the first series with an average of 150,000 views per episode. Each episode runs as an exclusive for 24 hours on Bebo and is then made available on other networks such as Veoh and YouTube. Although the work can therefore circulate virally Bebo hopes that all those users who want to know more or to participate in the community will be driven back to the original Bebo pages.

Kate Modern follows the story of Kate, an East London art student whose life takes a turn for the dark and mysterious when she becomes the victim of a shadowy organisation who want her 'trait positive' blood supply. The narrative follows events as her friends get drawn into the mystery plot and Kate is kidnapped and eventually found dead in the series one climax. The second series followed Charlie, Kate's best friend as the group attempt to solve the murder mystery only to discover that their group is harbouring a gruesome serial killer who is also at odds with the original suspects, 'The Order'.

The story is set in the *Friends* type 20–30-year-old social network that is the inspirational generation for the Bebo 1–24 demographic. Its storyline is actually an extension of *Lonely Girl 15* produced by the same team in 2006 which really put web native narrative on the map. *Lonely Girl 15* achieved a level of web notoriety on its launch by appearing to be the real video blog of a 'Lonely Girl' which gradually become a more and more compelling story, becoming a YouTube hit and gathering an active and speculative fan base. The Lonely Girl was eventually exposed as an actress by journalists and the whole project revealed as a brilliantly staged promotion by a group of aspiring film makers and producers. The ambiguous status of the reality of *Lonely Girl 15* is typical of web aesthetics. The webcam blog carries the feel of authenticity and one to one communication that makes a strong dramatic 'proposition' to the viewer sitting at home on their own in front of the computer screen. The question 'is this real or is it fiction' is at the heart of the Alternate Reality Gaming experiences that are an equally significant web native cultural form and which often spin off from web dramas offering additional potential for audiences and advertisers.

This reality effect also poses dramatic problems. The webcam is self-evidently present as part of the diary confession scene – however there then has to be a reason for a camera to be present in all other kinds of scenes. If there are some people in a story who are choosing to communicate directly with us (the audience) in this manner then cutting to a conventional diegesis will be anomalous unless the communication is explained as part of the story in some way. In conventional film and TV we 'ignore' the presence of camera technologies and crew – we never need to worry about why the camera is there, it just is as part of the conventions of cinema that saw the camera and tripod replace the point of view of the theatre audience. However here the camera has to be a reflexive part of the action – so webcams, mobile phones, handheld cameras are all made part of the diegetic world of the story which can then be told through the data fragments that any digitally active group of chums could conceivably accumulate.

Kate Modern aims to promote user engagement by being of and from the digital world of its target audiences. Once you become a fan it's possible to comment on episodes and discuss characters and storylines. This permanent user testing feeds back into the writing process, for instance although series 1 was a success the producers discovered that the fans did not much like the lead character – so she disappeared, kidnapped and eventually killed off as Charlie, her more popular best mate, took centre stage. The mystery storyline of *Kate Modern* is a typical mix of teen soap with *Buffy* or *Lost* type conspiracy plotlines that appeal to the active fan who likes to decipher narrative mysteries. This sensibility is catered for by the 'this is not a game' ARG-like structure erected in and around the story.

The characters all appear to be constantly posting video 'for real' and all the main characters had Bebo profiles with which fans could interact. *Lonely Girl 15* actually had its own ARG for a period called OpAphid. The UK based web drama 'Where Are the Joneses?' set up a wiki site for fans to create scenarios and write scenes; each episode's wiki was locked off before the episode was shot, cut and uploaded. The key drive is to promote user engagement through creating as many points of contact with the story experience as possible – these may be with other fans or direct with the producers.

The goal of user engagement has economic drivers. Bebo announced in May 2007 that it was setting up the 'Bebo Open Media Platform' to make it possible for content providers to set up their own channels on the Bebo network. This would allow users in the Bebo community the chance to enhance their own profiles by linking to particular kinds of channel that would indicate their tastes as much as favourite music or choice of page skin. The Bebo launch announcement proclaimed

> Our goal in creating the Open Media Platform is to allow you, our media partners, to take advantage of the unique environment of Bebo's social network to reach, engage and cultivate your fans. Within Bebo, you can use our built in social networking architecture to develop community around your content brands and to drive wide spread usage through the magic of viral distribution.

This understanding of the audience as fan, to be cultivated, is underpinned in turn by changes in the advertising industry that seek brand identification rather than direct hard sell advertising. These changes in turn are reflected in the online advertising campaigns that monetise web dramas like *Kate Modern*. LG 15 Studio, the team behind *Lonely Girl*, had experimented with product placement in that series, even polling their users to see if it would be acceptable to them. (Results suggested over 90 percent approval.) These techniques were carried forward in *Kate Modern* which was funded through product integration and sponsorship deals all negotiated by the Bebo sales team – Bebo then commissioned the production just like a TV broadcaster. *Kate Modern* brought on board major sponsors like Microsoft, Orange, Disney and Paramount as well as a very long list of smaller product views or mentions that were paid for e.g. Kraft Foods, Procter & Gamble, and New Balance (see http://www.lg15.com/lgpedia/index.php?title=Product_placement for exhaustive listing). These sponsorship packages are not cheap – aiming at a 150,000 views per episode advertisers were asked to pay anything between £10,000 and £40,000 for packages of sponsorship broken down into specific numbers of plot line integrations or product placements. Other packages are available in smaller sums returning shorter exposure times.

This combination of semi-interactive user-oriented storytelling in a web native form together with these new revenue models generated a mass of positive PR for both Bebo and LG 15 Studios throughout 2007. After press stories speculated throughout 2007 that Bebo might be worth a billion dollars it was sold to AOL for $850 million dollars cash on 13 March 2008. One month later the Lonely Girl team announced a £5m investment from venture capitalists to form a new company called EQAL to become an independent 'social entertainment' company that will be equal parts TV studio and social networking site.

3.24 Conclusion

Networked media are produced within a system where technology is never stable, what Kline *et al.* (2003: 73) call a state of 'perpetual innovation'. This is not a teleological dynamic; there is no end point in sight. New media technologies will never stabilise in these conditions of permanent upgrade culture (Dovey and Kennedy 2006a: 52). In these conditions media will always be novel. In this section we have attempted to discuss some of the most important aspects of what those novel practices look like at the point of writing, not as an end in themselves but as a way of exemplifying methodologies for dealing with New Media. We have tried to demonstrate how human creativity, technological affordance and economic advantage each contribute to shaping our own individual networked media experiences – as both producers and consumers. The outcomes of this triangulation are necessarily dynamic and unpredictable. However we are certain that a taking into account of all three of these processes is a necessary part of understanding networked media ecologies and the media mutations that thrive or die within them.

Moreover we have stressed economic advantage as driver of this dynamic as a response to the ways in which it has often been disregarded in those technophilic accounts of web media that celebrate human creativity and technological potential as if it existed in a post scarcity void where competition for material resources had somehow been transcended. This tendency in the discourse of New Media has to do with the complex ways in which net culture somehow feels as though it comes to us as free. Forgetting the economic reality of our burgeoning monthly utility bills and focusing instead on the feeling of an infinite database at our fingertips we all tend to get caught up in the *immateriality* and explosive potential of web media. As we hope to have shown above this potential is real and is profoundly transforming mass media. However the nature of these transformations will only be grasped by students of the field if they are able to understand the continuing relevance of the contexts of political economy as well as technology and creativity.

Bibliography

Amin, Samir *Capitalism in the Age of Globalization*, London and Atlantic Highlands, N.J.: Zed Books, 1997.

Anderson, Chris *The Long Tail: Why the Future of Business is Selling Less of More*, London: Hyperion, 2006.

Ang, Ien *Watching Dallas*, London: Methuen, 1985.

Au, J. W. *The Triumph of the Mod* (16 April 2002) Salon.com www.salon.com/tech/eature/2002/04/16/modding.

Auletta, Ken *World War 3.0: Microsoft and its Enemies,* New York: Profile Books, 2001.

Baker, Andrea 'Cyberspace couples finding romance online then meeting for the first time in real life', *CMC Magazine* (1 July 1998). http://www.december.com/cmc/mag/1998.

Baran, Nicholas 'Privatisation of telecommunications', in *Capitalism and the Information Age: the political economy of the global communication revolution*, eds Robert McChesney, Ellen Meiksin Wood and John Bellamy Foster, New York: Monthly Review Press, 1998.

Barbrook, Richard 'The hi-tech gift economy', in *Communicating for development: experience in the urban environment*, ed. Catalina Gandelsonas, Urban management series, Rugby, UK: Practical Action Publishing, 2000, pp. 45–51.

Barker, Martin *The Video Nasties: freedom and censorship in the media*, London: Pluto, 1984.

Barker, M. *Comics: Ideology, Power and the Critics*, Manchester: Manchester University Press, 1989.

Barker, M. *A Haunt of Fears: The Strange History of the British Horror Comics Campaign*, Jackson, Miss.: University Press of Mississippi, 1992.

Barlow, J. P. 'A Declaration of the Independence of Cyberspace' http://homes.eff.org/~barlow/Declaration-Final.html see also 'Cyberhood vs. Neighbourhood' *UTNE Reader* Mar–Apr 1995 pp. 53–56 http://dana.ucc.nau.edu/~ksf39/Barlo-CyberhoodVSNeighborhood.pdf 1995.

Baym, Nancy 'The emergence of online community', in *Cybersociety 2.0*, ed. Steven G. Jones, Thousand Oaks, Calif.: Sage, 1998.

Baym, N.K., Zhang, Y.B., Lin, M.-C., Kunkel, A., Lin, M. and Ledbetter, A. 'Relational Quality and Media Use', *New Media & Society*, 9(5) (2007): 735–752.

Bell, Daniel *The Coming of Post Industrial Society*, New York: Basic Books, 1976.

Bettig, R. 'The enclosure of cyberspace', *Critical Studies in Mass Communication* 14 (1997): 138–157.

BFI Industry Tracking Survey, London: BFI, 1999.

Bolter, J. and Grusin, R. *Remediation,* Cambridge, Mass.: MIT, 2000.

Boria, E., Breidenbach, P. and Wright, T. 'Creative Player Actions in FPS Online Video Games – Playing Counter-Strike', *Game Studies*, vol. 2, issue 2 (Dec. 2002) www.gamestudies.org.

Bourdieu, Pierre 'The forms of capital', in John Richardson (ed.) *Handbook of Theory and Research for the Sociology of Education*, New York: Greenwood Press, 1986.

Bowman, S. and Willis, C. *We Media; How Audiences are shaping the future of news and information*, American Press Institute (2003) http://www.hypergene.net/wemedia/download/we_media.pdf.

Boyd, D. M. and Ellison, N. B. 'Social network sites: Definition, history, and scholarship', *Journal of Computer-Mediated Communication*, 13(1), article 11 (2007) http://jcmc.indiana.edu/vol13/issue1/boyd.ellison.html.

Braidotti, R. *Nomadic Subjects. Embodiment and Sexual Difference in Contemporary Feminist Theory*, New York: Columbia University Press, 1994.

Brynjolfsson, Erik, Hu, Jeffrey Yu and Smith, Michael D. 'From Niches to Riches: Anatomy of the Long Tail', *Sloan Management Review,* vol. 47, no. 4 (Summer 2006): 67–71.

Business Weekly Online Video: The Sequel (29 December 2004) http://www.businessweek.com/bwdaily/dnflash/dec2004/nf20041229_6207_db016.htm.

Callanan, R. 'The Changing Role of Broadcasters within Digital Communications Networks Convergence', *The International Journal of Research into New Media Technologies,* vol. 10, no. 3 (2004): 28–38.

Cassidy, John *dot.con: The Greatest Story Ever Sold*, London: Allen Lane, 2002.

Castells, Manuel *The Rise of the Network Society*, Oxford: Blackwell, 1996.

Castells, Manuel *The Internet Galaxy*, Oxford: Oxford University Press, 2000.

Castells, M., Fernandez-Ardevol, M., Qiu, J. and Sey, A. *Mobile Communication and Society: A Global Perspective*, Boston: MIT Press, 2006.

Castranova, Edward 'Virtual Worlds: A First-Hand Account of Market and Society on the Cyberian Frontier' *CESifo Working Paper Series No. 618* (December 2001) http://ssrn.com/abstract=294828.

Castranova, E. A. 'Cost-Benefit Analysis of Real-Money Trade', in The Products of Synthetic Economies *Info*, 8(6) (2006).

Cave, Martin 'Franchise auctions in network infrastructure industries', in *Report to the OECD Conference on Competition and Regulation in Network Infrastructure Industries*, Budapest, 9–12 May 1995. http://www.oecd.org/daf/clp/non-member_activities/BDPT206.HTM.

Christian Science Monitor, Wednesday, 15 October 1997.

Clinton, William J. and Gore Jr., Albert 'A Framework for Global Electronic Commerce' (1997), http://clinton4.nara.gov/WH/New/Commerce/summary.html.

Coriat, Benjamin ed. *L'Atelier et le Robot*, Paris: Christian Bourgeois, 1990.

Cornford, James and Robins, Kevin 'New media', in *The Media in Britain*, eds Jane Stokes and Anna Reading, London: Palgrave, 1999.

Cringely, Robert X. *Triumph of the Nerds*, Harmondsworth: Penguin, 1996a.

Cringely, Robert X. *Accidental Empires: how the boys of Silicon Valley make their millions, battle foreign competition and still can't get a date*, London: Penguin, 1996b.

Curran, J. *Media Organisations in Society*, London: Arnold, 2000.

Curien, N. and Moreau, F. *The Music Industry in the Digital Era: Towards New Business Frontiers?* 2005 http://www.cnam-econometrie.com/upload/CurienMoreauMusic2(2).pdf.

Danet, Brenda 'Text as mask: gender, play and performance on the internet', in *Cybersociety 2.0,* ed. Steven G. Jones, Thousand Oaks, Calif.: Sage, 1998.

Davis, Jim, Hirschl, Thomas and Stack, Michael *Cutting Edge Technology, Information, Capitalism and Social Revolution,* London: Verso, 1997.

Dawson, M. 'Little Players, Big Shows: Format, Narration and Style on Television's New Smaller Screens' *Convergence* 13:3 (2007): 231–250.

Dean, Jodi 'Webs of conspiracy', in *The World Wide Web and Contemporary Cultural Theory,* ed. A. Herman and T. Swiss, London: Routledge, 2000.

Dean, Alison A. and Kretschmer, M. 'Can Ideas Be Capital? Factors Of Production In The Post-Industrial Economy: A Review And Critique', *Academy of Management Review,* April 2007: 573–594.

Department for Culture Media and Sport. The Report of the Creative Industries Task Force Inquiry into Television Exports, London (2000). http://www.culture.gov.uk/pdf/dcmstv.pdf.

Dibbell, Julian *Independent On Sunday*: extract from *My Tiny Life: crime and passion in a virtual world*, 24 January 1999: 14–24 (Published by Fourth Estate, London, 1999.)

Dickinson, R., Linne, O. and Harindrinath, R. eds *Approaches to Audiences*, London: Arnold, 1998.

Dolfsma, Wilfred *Institutional Economics and the Formation of Preferences. The Advent of Pop Music*, Cheltenham, UK and Northampton, Mass.: Edward Elgar, 2004.

Dovey, Jon ed. *Fractal Dreams,* London: Lawrence and Wishart, 1996.

Dovey, J. and Fleuriot, C. 'Experiencing Mobile & Located Media Developing a Descriptive Language', *New Media Knowledge* (2005) http://161.74.14.141/article/2005/4/22/locative-media-common-language.

Dovey, J. and Kennedy, H. W. *Game Cultures*, London and New York: McGraw Hill, 2006a.

Dovey, J. and Kennedy, H. W. 'Playing the Ring', *'Branding the Ring'* ed. E. Mathijs, Columbia: Wallflower Press 2006b.

Dovey, J. and Kennedy, H. W. 'From Margin to Center: Biographies of Technicity and the Construction of Hegemonic Games Culture', in *Players' Realm: Studies on the Culture of Videogames and Gaming*, ed. P. Williams and J. Heide Smith, McFarlane Press, 2007: pp. 131–153.

du Gay, P., Hall, S., Janes, L. and Mackay, H. *Doing Cultural Studies: The Story of the Sony Walkman*, London: Sage, 2003.

Electronic Freedom Foundation. http://www.eff.org/pub/Censorship/Exon_bill/.

Edge Magazine 2003 26: 58.

Ellis, J. *Visible Fictions: Cinema Television Video,* London: Routledge & Kegan Paul, 1982.

Ellis, J. *Seeing Things: Television in the Age of Uncertainty,* London: I. B. Tauris, 2000.

Ellison, B., Steinfield, C. and Lampe, C. 'The Benefits of Facebook "Friends": Social Capital and College Students' Use of Online Social Network Sites', *Journal of Computer-Mediated Communication* 12 (4) (2007): 1143–1168.

Facer, K. L., Furlong, V. J., Sutherland, R. J. and Furlong, R. 'Home is where the hardware is: young people, the domestic environment and access to new technologies', in *Children, Technology and Culture,* eds I. Hutchby and J. Moran Ellis, London: Routledge/Falmer, 2000.

Farber, David J. http: //www.usdoj.gov/atr/cases/f2000/2059.htm.

Fearon, Peter *The Origins and Nature of the Great Slump 1929–1932*, London: Macmillan, 1979.

Featherstone, M. ed. *Global Culture: nationalism, globalization and modernity*, London: Sage, 1990.

Fuchs, C. and Horak, E. 'Africa and the digital divide', *Telematics and Informatics* 25 (2008): 99–116.

Gaines, Jane M. *Contested Cultures: the image, the voice and the law*, Chapel Hill: University of North Carolina Press, 1991.

Galbraith, J. K. *The Affluent Society*, London: Hamilton, 1958.

Garnham, Nicholas *Capitalism and Communication: Global Culture and the Economics of Information*, ed. F. Inglis, London: Sage, 1990.

Garnham, Nicholas 'The media and the public sphere', in *Habermas and the Public Sphere,* ed. Craig Calhoun, London: MIT, 1992.

Garnham, Nicholas, 'Political Economy and Cultural Studies: Reconciliation or Divorce?', *Critical Studies in Mass Communication*, vol. 12 no. 1 (Mar 1995): 62–71.

Garnham, Nicholas 'Political economy and the practices of cultural studies', in *Cultural Studies in Question,* eds Marjorie Ferguson and Peter Golding, London: Sage, 1997.

Garnham, Nicholas 'Information society as theory or ideology: a critical perspective on technology, education and employment in the information age', *ICS* 3.2 Summer (2000): Feature article. http: //www.infosoc.co.uk/ 00110/feature.htm.

Gates, Bill, *The Road Ahead,* London: Penguin, 1996.

Gauntlett, David 'Web Studies: What's New', in *Web Studies*, eds David Gauntlett and Ross Horsley (2nd edition), London: Arnold, 2004. Also available at http://www.newmediastudies.com/intro2004.htm.

Giddens, A. *The Consequences of Modernity,* Cambridge: Polity Press, 1990.

Goodwin, Pete *Television Under The Tories: broadcasting policy, 1979–1997*, London: BFI, 1998.

Habermas, Jürgen *The Structural Transformation of the Public Sphere*, Cambridge: Polity Press, 1989.

Hafner, K. 'The epic saga of the Well', *Wired* (May 1997).

Hagel, John and Armstrong, Arthur G. *Net Gain*, Watertown, Mass.: Harvard Business School Press, 1997.

Hesmondhalgh, D. *The Cultural Industries*, 2nd edn, London, Los Angeles and New Delhi: Sage, 2007.

Hobsbawm, E. J. *Industry and Empire*, London: Pelican, 1987.

Hoffman, D. L. and Novak, T. P. 'Bridging the Racial Divide on the Internet', *Science*, 280 (April 1998): 390–391.

Holmes, David ed. *Virtual Politics*, Thousand Oaks, Calif.: Sage, 1997.

Howe, J. 'The Rise of Crowdsourcing', in *Wired* (June 2006), http://www.wired.com/wired/archive/ 14.06/crowds.html.

Huizinga, Johan *Homo Ludens: a study of the play element in culture*, Boston: Beacon Press, 1986.

ILO *Globalizing Europe. Decent Work in the Information Economy*, Geneva: International Labour Organisation, 2000.

Independent 14 May 2007, http://www.independent.co.uk/news/media/advertising-spot-the-link-between-a-gorilla-and-chocolate-448699.html.

Jameson, Fredric *Postmodernism, or the Cultural Logic of Late Capitalism*, London: Verso, 1991.

Jenkins, H. *Textual Poachers: television fans and participatory culture*, London: Routledge, 1992.

Jenkins, H. *Interactive Audiences? The 'Collective Intelligence' Of Media Fans* (2002) http://web.mit.edu/ cms/People/henry3/collective percent20intelligence.html.

Jenkins, H. 'The Cultural Logic of Media Convergence', *International Journal of Cultural Studies*; 7 (2004): 33–43.

Jenkins, H. *Convergence Culture*, New York and London: New York University Press, 2006.

Jenkins, J. *Quentin Tarantino's Star Wars?: Digital Cinema, Media Convergence, and Participatory Culture* (2003) http://web.mit.edu/21fms/www/faculty/henry3/starwars.html.

Jensen, Jens F. 'Interactivity – tracking a new concept in media and communication studies', in *Computer Media and Communication*, ed. Paul Mayer, Oxford: Oxford University Press, 1999.

Jensen, M. 'Information and Communication Technologies (ICTs) in Africa – A Status Report' (2002) http://www. unicttaskforce.org/thirdmeeting/documents/jensen percent20v6.htm.

Jones, Quentin 'Virtual communities, virtual settlements and cyber-archaeology: a theoretical outline', *Journal of Computer Mediated Communications* (3) (1997) www.ascusc.org/jcmc/vol3/issue 3/jones.html.

Jones, Steven, G. ed. *Cybersociety,* Thousand Oaks, Calif.: Sage,1994.

Jones, Steven, G. ed. *Cybersociety 2.0*, Thousand Oaks, Calif.: Sage, 1998.

Jones, Steven G. 'The bias of the web', in *The World Wide Web and Contemporary Cultural Theory,* eds A. Herman and T. Swiss, London: Routledge, 2000.

Jurvetson, S. and Draper, T. *Viral Marketing*, 1 May, 1997. Original version published in the Netscape M-Files, 1997, edited version published in Business 2.0 (November 1998) http://www.dfj.com/cgi-bin/artman/publish/steve_tim_may97.shtml.

Kahn, R. and Kellner, D. 'New Media And Internet Activism: From The "Battle Of Seattle" To Blogging', *New Media & Society* 6(1) (2004): 87–95.

Kapoor, Mitch 'Where is the digital highway really heading?', *Wired* (August 1993).

Kellner, Douglas 'Techno-politics, new technologies, and the new public spheres', in *Illuminations* (January 2001) http://www.uta/edu/huma/illuminations/kell32.htm.

Kelly, K. 'How the iPod Got its Dial' in J. Seaton *Music Sound and Multimedia*, Edinburgh, 2007.

Kendall, Lori 'MUDder? I Hardly Know 'er! Adventures of a feminist MUDder' *in Wired Women: gender and new realities in cyberspace,* eds L. Cherny and E. R. Weise, Washington, DC: Seal Press, 1996, pp. 207–223.

Kennedy, Helen 'Beyond anonymity, or future directions for Internet identity research', *New Media and Society* vol. 8, no. 6 (2006): 859-876.

Kline, S., Dyer-Witherford, N. and de Peuter, G. *Digital Play: The Interaction of Technology Culture and Marketing*, Montreal and Kingston: McGill Quarry University Press, 2003.

Kramarae, Cheris 'Feminist fictions of future technology', in *Cybersociety 2.0*, ed. S. Jones, Thousand Oaks, Calif.: Sage, 1998

Kushner, David *Masters of Doom: How Two Guys Created an Empire and Transformed Pop Culture*, London: Piatkus, 2003.

Kvasny, L. and Keil, M. 'The challenges of redressing the digital divide: a tale of two US cities', *Information Systems Journal* 16(1) 2006: 25–53.

Lanchester, John 'A Bigger Bang', *The Guardian Weekend* (4.11.06): 17–36.

Leskovec, J., Adamic, L. A. and Huberman, B. A. *The dynamics of viral marketing,* http://www.hpl.hp.com/research/idl/papers/viral/viral.pdf (2007).

Lévy, Pierre *Collective Intelligence: Mankind's Emerging World in Cyberspace*, Cambridge: Perseus, 1997.

Lewis, T. G. *The Friction-Free Economy: Strategies for Success in a Wired World*, Harper Business: London and New York, 1997.

Mactavish, A. 'Game Mod(ifying) Theory: The Cultural Contradictions of Computer Game Modding' delivered at 'Power Up: Computer Games Ideology and Play' Bristol UK 14–15 July 2003.

McChesney, Robert W., Wood, Ellen Meiksins and Foster, John Bellamy eds *Capitalism and the Information Age: the political economy of the global communication revolution*, New York: Monthly Review Press, 1998.

McGonigal, Jane 'Why I Love Bees: A Case Study in Collective Intelligence Gaming' (2007) http://www.avantgame.com/McGonigal_WhyILoveBees_Feb2007.pdf.

McKenzie, N. ed. *Conviction*, London: Monthly Review Press, 1959.

McLaughlin, Margaret L., Osborne, Kerry K. and Smith, Christine, B. 'Standards of conduct on Usenet', in *Cybersociety*, ed. Steven G. Jones, Thousand Oaks, Calif.: Sage, 1994.

McRae, S. 'Coming apart at the seams: sex text and the virtual body', in *Wired Women: gender and new realities in cyberspace,* eds L. Cherny and E. R. Weise, Washington, DC: Seal Press, 1996, pp. 242–264.

Mayer, Paul *Computor Media and Communication*, Oxford: Oxford University Press, 1999.

Meiksins Wood, E. 'Modernity, postmodernism or capitalism', in *Capitalism and the Information Age*, eds R. McChesney *et al.*, New York: Monthly Review Press, 1998.

Miles, A. *Softvideography: Digital Video as Postliterate Practice* (2002) http://vogmae.net.au/drupal/files/digitalvideo-postliteratepractice.pdf.

Miller, T. 'A View from a Fossil The New Economy, Creativity and Consumption – Two or Three Things I Don't Believe', *International Journal of Cultural Studies*, 7/1 1 (2004): 55–65.

Morley, David *The Nationwide Audience*, London: BFI, 1980.

Morris, Sue 'Wads, Bots and Mots: Multiplayer FPS Games as Co Creative Media', *Level Up – Digital Games Research Conference Proceedings* 2003 University of Utrecht /DIGRA (CD ROM).

Mosco, V. *The Political Economy of Communications: dynamic rethinking and renewal*, London: Sage, 1996.

Mosco, V. *The Digital Sublime: Myth, Power, and Cyberspace,* Cambridge, Mass. and London: Sage, 2004.

Moulthrop, Stuart 'Error 404 doubting the web', in *The World Wide Web and Contemporary Cultural Theory*, eds A. Herman and T. Swiss, London: Routledge, 2000.

Moulthrop, S. 'From Work to Play: Molecular Culture in the Time of Deadly Games', in *First Person: New Media as Story, Performance and Game*, Cambridge, Mass. and London: MIT Press, 2004.

Murdock, Graham 'Base notes: the conditions of cultural practice', in *Cultural Studies in Question,* eds Marjorie Ferguson and Peter Golding, London: Sage, 1997.

O'Reilly, T. *What Is Web 2.0_Design Patterns and Business Models for the Next Generation of Software* (2005a) http://www.oreilly.com/pub/a/oreilly/tim/news/2005/09/30/what-is-web-20.html.

O'Reilly, Tim *Not 2.0?* (2005b) http://radar.oreilly.com/archives/2005/08/not_20.html.

Pearce, C. *Sims, BattleBots, Cellular Automata, God and Go A conversation with Will Wright* (2002) http://www.games-tudies.org/0102/2002.

Pew Internet and American Life *Increased Use of Video-sharing Sites* (2008) http://www.pewInternet.org/PPF/r/232/report_display.asp.

Poster, Mark 'Cyberdemocracy: the Internet and the public sphere' in *Virtual Politics*, ed. David Holmes, Thousand Oaks, Calif.: Sage, 1997.

Rafaeli, S. 'Interactivity from media to communication', in *Annual Review of Communication Research*, vol. 16 Advancing Communication Science, eds R. Hawkins, J. Wiemann and S. Pirgree (1988): 110–134.

Rediker, M. *The Slave Ship*: *A Human History*, London: John Murray, 2007.

Rheingold, H. *The Virtual Community – homesteading on the virtual frontier*, London: Secker and Warburg, 1993.

Rheingold, H. 'Cyberhood vs Neighbourhood', *UTNE Reader*, March–April 1995.

Ritzer, Martin *The McDonaldization of Society*, New York: Sage, 2000.

Robins, Kevin 'Cyberspace and the world we live', in *Fractal Dreams*, ed. J Dovey, London: Lawrence and Wishart, 1996.

Roszak, Theodore *The Cult of Information*, Cambridge: Lutterworth Press, 1986.

Rushkoff, D. *Media Virus*, New York: Ballantine Books, 1994.

Schiller, D. *Digital Capitalism: System, Networking The Global Market*, Cambridge, Mass.: MIT Press, 1999.

Schiller, H. *Culture Inc.: The Corporate Take-over of Cultural Expression*, New York: Oxford University Press, 1989.

Senft, Theresa 'Baud girls and cargo cults', in *The World Wide Web and Contemporary Cultural Theory*, eds A. Herman and T. Swiss, London: Routledge, 2000.

Sherman, Chris *Google Power: unleash the full potential of Google*, McGraw Hill: New York, 2005.

Shultz, Tanjev 'Mass media and the concept of interactivity: an exploratory study of online forums and reader email', *Media, Culture and Society* 22 (2000): 205–221.

Smith, M. 'Voices from the Well' (1992). http://netscan.sscnet.ucla.edu/csoc/papers.

Smythe, Dallas *Dependency Road, Communications, Capitalism Consciousness and Canada*, Norwood: Ablex Publishing, 1981.

Stokes, J. and Reading, A. eds *The Media in Britain: current debates and developments,* London: Palgrave, 1999.

Stone, Allucquere Rosanne The *War of Desire and Technology at the Close of the Mechanical Age,* Boston, Mass.: MIT Press, 1995.

Sundén, J. *Material Virtualities*, New York: Peter Lang, 2003.

Swartz, Aaron 'Who Writes Wikipedia?' (2006) http://www.aaronsw.com/weblog/wqhowriteswikipedia.

Tapscott, D. and Williams, A. *Wikinomics: How Mass Collaboration Changes Everything*, London: Penguin Books, 2006.

Taylor, T. L. 'Intentional Bodies: Virtual Environments and the Designers Who Shape Them', *International Journal of Engineering Education*, vol. 19, no. 1, 2003: 25–34.

Terranova, T. *Free Labor: Producing Culture for the Digital Economy* (2003). http://www.electronicbookreview.com/thread/technocapitalism/voluntary.

Touraine, Alain *La Société Post Industrielle*, Paris: Denoel, 1969.

Tulloch, J. *Watching Television Audiences: cultural theory and methods*, London: Arnold, 2000.

Tulloch, J. and Alvarado, M. *Doctor Who: the unfolding text*, Basingstoke: Palgrave, 1983.

Turkle, Sherry *Life on the Screen*, London: Weidenfeld and Nicolson, 1995.

Turkle, Sherry 'Constructions and reconstructions of the self in virtual reality', in *Electronic Culture: Technology and Visual Representation*, ed. T. Druckrey, New York: Aperture, 1996.

US Department of Justice. http://www.usdoj.gov/atr/cases/ms_index.htm.

Van Couvering, E. *New media? The political economy of Internet search engines*, Annual Conference of the International Association of Media, 2004. www.personal.lse.ac.uk.

Vise, David A., *The Google Story*, New York: Delacorte Press, 2005.

Williams, Raymond *Television, Technology and Cultural Form*, London: Fontana, 1974.

Williams, Raymond *Problems in Materialism and Culture*, London: Verso, 1980.

Williams, Raymond *The Politics of Modernism*, London: Verso, 1989.

Wilson, E. J. *The Information Revolution and Developing Countries*, Cambridge, Mass.: MIT Press, 2006.

Wilson. K., Wallin, J. and Reiser, C. 'Social Stratification and the Digital Divide', *Social Science Computer Review* 21(2) (2003): 133–143.

Winston, Brian *Media Technology and Society: a history from the telegraph to the Internet*, London: Routledge, 1998.

Wired March 2006, *Gannett to Crowdsource News.* www.wired.com/news/culture/media/0,72067-0.html.

World Bank Data, See Table 5.11 'The Information Age'. http://www.worldbank.org/data/wdi2000/pdfs/tab5_11.pdf.

4 New Media in Everyday Life

4.1 Everyday life in cyberspace

From clocks to telegraphs to radio and television, new media have always woven themselves into everyday life, interfering with existing patterns of spatiotemporal organisation, generating new rhythms and spaces. The migration of computer technology from industry and research laboratory to the home over the past thirty years or so has intensified these processes. The popular culture of new media began with videogames, a medium that brought with it a technological imaginary of an everyday future disappearing into the 'cyberian apartness' of virtual worlds. As, over time, some new digital media have become unremarkable due to their familiarity and ubiquity, and others have been refashioned or displaced, we can see not a Narnia or Matrix-like division of virtual and actual worlds, but rather a complicated interweaving of mediated, lived, time and space. For example, mobile devices such as cell phones, GPS/satnav, MP3 players, and handheld games consoles, draw bodies and communication across everyday and technological realms and temporalities. Attention, throughout the

4.1 Handheld virtual worlds

working or playing day jumps to the communicational polyrhythms of diverse digital media: from the Tetris-like deluge of the email Inbox; the rapid volleys of IM and SMS; the insistent realtime pull of the social network page; the bubbles of virtuality that pop into existence as a handheld games console is snapped open; the gravitational pull of persistent virtual worlds such as *Second Life* or *World of Warcraft* with their event horizons from which little or nothing may escape for hours.

Cultural and Media Studies offers vital tools, concepts and methods for the study of a mediated everyday life, and this Part will survey important research in this field. It will identify useful tools, concepts and methods for the study of everyday cultures of technologies and media technologies. This will be a critical survey however, as it will become clear that some of the underlying tenets and assumptions of Cultural and Media Studies (and the humanities and social sciences more generally) limit the possibilities of the study of technoculture. In particular three foundational, and interlinked, assumptions will be interrogated. These are:

1   that culture, everyday life, individuals and households are materially and conceptually distinct from technologies – that the former 'adopt' technologies for instance or suffer the 'impact' of new technologies, and hence that distinctions between subject and object are absolute

2   that technologies are socially shaped but that society is not technologically shaped

3   that human activity – in the form of social, historical or economic forces, or subjectivity and identity – is the sole motive force or agency in everyday life and culture.

This section will introduce, synthesise and deploy some key alternative ways of thinking about everyday technoculture drawn from the emerging field of new media studies, from the study of videogames and from cybercultural studies.

4.2 *The Sims*: everyday life as cyberspace. © 2002 Electronic Arts. All rights reserved

4.1.1 Everyday life

The concept of everyday life is central to work in Cultural Studies and Media Studies. It covers the family relationships, routines, cultural practices and spaces through which people make sense of the world. On the one hand then, everyday life is the site in which the popular meanings and uses of new media are negotiated and played out. On the other hand, nearly all of the discussions of new media to a greater or lesser degree make claims that they transform, or will soon transform (or transcend) day-to-day life, its spatio-temporal limits, its restrictions and power structures. The nature of this transformation is contentious; for some observers new media offer new creativities and possibilities, for others they reinforce and extend existing social constraints and power relationships.

Everyday life is a central concept within Cultural Studies' approach to technologies. It is studied and theorised as:

- the market for which companies develop consumer hardware and software

- the site of practices and relationships in which sense is made of new media

- the focal point of an interlocking set of convergences of consumer, media, educational and entertainment technologies and markets

- the social conditions which are, to a greater or lesser degree, transformed by the use and consumption of new media

- the absent or underplayed term in utopian visions of new knowledges and shifting identities in cyberspace – as alienation and routine to the connectivity and creativity emerging in Internet communication media

- the site of consumption of mediated popular culture, not least the images and dramas from comics, television and video that constitute a commercial technological imaginary.

From the perspective of Cultural Studies, the 'newness' of any new medium is always tempered by the longevity of the economic and social conditions from which it emerges and the domestic and cultural contexts – from the architecture and layout of the home to the relative stability of the nuclear family – into which it is inserted. In his study of an old medium that was once new, Raymond Williams argues that the arrival of television as a popular medium was bound up with historical and cultural processes originating in the Industrial Revolution. His notion of 'mobile privatisation' highlights, for example, a complex of developments linking the privatisation and domestication of screen media with television's usurpation of cinema, and the new mobilities of the privatised family afforded by technologies such as the motor car:

> Socially, this complex is characterised by the two apparently paradoxical yet deeply connected tendencies of modern urban living: on the one hand mobility, on the other hand the more apparently self-sufficient family home. The earlier period of public technology, best exemplified by the railways and city lighting, was being replaced by a kind of technology for which no satisfactory name has yet been found: that which served an at once mobile and home-centred way of living: a form of *mobile privatisation*. Broadcasting in its applied form was a social product of this distinctive tendency.
>
> (Williams 1990a [1975]: 26)

For accounts of everyday life in the study of media culture and technologies, see Silverstone (1994), Mackay (1997), and Highmore (2001)

Popular culture is here taken to mean both the commercially produced artefacts of entertainment culture (television and television programmes, toys, films, etc.) and the lived practices, experiences and contexts within which these artefacts are engaged with and consumed

However, whilst these longer historical trajectories have shaped the everyday world into which new media insinuate themselves, and indeed have shaped the design of, and intentions for, new media technologies, the new media and the cultural activities and uses to which they are put are by no means wholly determined by these contexts. In its review of research into, and theories of, technology and culture in everyday life this section will highlight how newness and continuity are identified and articulated, and signal the underlying conceptions of the relationships of determination between technologies, people and culture.

4.1.2 Cyberspace

Cultural Studies' concentration on everyday life would seem at first glance to be unhelpful in the study of new media and cyberculture. The former implies the mundane and quotidian, the routine and ordinary – all the features of daily existence from which the latter, in both their fictional and actual forms, promise to transform. Both celebrations and critiques of cyberspace tend to posit its separateness, its profound otherness to everyday life, embodiment, subjectivity. For Michael Heim, 'cyberspace is Platonism as a working concept', and 'the cybernaut seated before us, strapped into sensory-input devices, appears to be, and is indeed, lost to this world. Suspended in computer space, the cybernaut leaves the prison of the body and emerges in a world of digital sensation' (Heim 1993).

The intense excitement generated by new media forms such as the World Wide Web and Virtual Reality in the late 1980s and early 1990s has waned as such media have become part of a commonly experienced media world. However, the notion of 'cyberspace' as a separate, emancipatory (or more often, threatening) realm within, yet distinct from, everyday media culture persists. Journalists routinely affirm the apartness of Internet media such as chatrooms and social networking sites in articles on the ominous implications for children and young people. Here cyberspace is either an alienating, anti-social distraction from more authentic

4.3 Telewest brochure. Courtesy of Telewest

social and communicative activities, or a dangerous realm stalked by predators. Manufacturers of, and service providers for, new (or newly upgraded) digital communication media also invoke the transformation of daily routines and domestic space through the collision of actual and virtual space, albeit in an enthusiastic and celebratory tone.

Another persistent model of a more fully mediated everyday life is that of ubiquitous computing. Futurologists from Nicholas Negroponte to the US National Academy of Engineering's Ray Kurzweil have predicted personalised media, the transformation of everyday products and furniture into 'smart' objects through the minituarisation of computer chips and circuits, and recently, the possibilities of nanotechnology for both everyday life and the human body and mind's relationship with it:

> Intelligent nanobots will be deeply integrated in the environment, our bodies and our brains, providing vastly extended longevity, full-immersion virtual reality involving all of the senses . . . and enhanced human intelligence.
>
> (Ray Kurzweil, quoted in Jha 2008).

It is not our concern in this book to assess the likelihood of any particular prediction for new media cultures coming to pass. A glance at any past predictions for future everyday technologies from jetpacks to holographic television would remind us that predictions often tell us more about the immediate concerns and technological imaginary of the time they were made than about their future.

For example, Kevin Robins, in a widely anthologised essay 'Cyberspace and the worlds we live in', argued that the hyperbole that characterised early, and enthusiastic, cybercultural studies rendered cyberspace as little more than a rhetorical or ideological construction. William Gibson's articulation of cyberspace as a 'consensual hallucination' is, Robins argued, applicable to discourses of non-fictional cyberspace (i.e. actual VR or Internet applications and practices), at best perhaps representing a naive neophilia, a 'metaphysics of technological progress – whatever comes next must be better than what went before' (Robins 1996: 25). At worst (and it is clear Robins suspects the worst), it is an ideological construction, a faith in new technologies blinding its celebrants to the real, here-and-now, political and economic contexts from which the technologies spring and to the problems and contradictions of which they assert false solutions. This faith presents

> a common vision of a future that will be different from the present, of a space or reality that is more desirable than the mundane one that presently surrounds and contains us. It is a tunnel vision. It has turned a blind eye on the world we live in.
>
> (Robins 1996: 1)

Robins's critique of this particular cyber-rhetoric is convincing and amusing, yet misses an important point. Neither enthusiastic cyberculturalists nor their critics address the *reality* of cyberspace as a set of already existing industrial, entertainment and everyday technocultural phenomena. Robins's target is cybercultural discourse, he says nothing about actual, material, technologies of cyberspace. For these celebrants all is new, for their critics all is old – or an even worse upgrade of the old. The object of each is not lived technoculture but concepts and images, fictions and speculations. It becomes clear that on the one hand a more nuanced conception of the relationship between the 'new' and the 'old' in everyday digital culture is required; while on the other, that the materiality, the reality of new technologies and new technocultures must be addressed.

However, excitement about, and anticipation of, particular consumer technological trajectories (currently minituarisation, virtualisation, pervasiveness, etc.) does inform and shape producers' designs and research, and consumers' expectations and willingness to invest in new formats and devices

In their ethnographic study of Internet use in Trinidad, Daniel Miller and Don Slater question the assumption that the virtual and the everyday or material are distinct realms. They argue that the Internet *cannot* be explained in terms of a fictional or speculative cyberspace, 'a kind of placeless place'. Indeed we can only make sense of it as it is encountered in concrete places and through specific practices. For the individuals, families and groups studied, Internet media such as email and websites are experienced, they argue, not as virtual but as 'concrete and mundane enactments of belonging' (Miller and Slater 2000: 4). Just as new media in this case were not experienced as places apart from 'real life', so too the changes brought about through the interaction of new media and Trinidadian culture, while significant, were not experienced as revolutionary transformation, but as continuous with already existing social structures and senses of identity. Indeed the authors argue that new media quickly cease to represent exciting new futures and are incorporated into the fabric of everyday experience. Importantly though, this is not to argue that there is nothing new or revolutionary in the mediations of the Internet and everyday life (or that the widespread sense of 'space' that computer media produce is false). Rather it is to suggest that any progressive understanding of the potentialities of new media in everyday life is only possible by rejecting a notion of 'a self-enclosed cyberian apartness' (Miller and Slater 2000: 5) *and* recognising the materiality of these technologies and their place in everyday lived experience. We could instead think of a productive tension between the places and practices of new media: 'these spaces are important as part of everyday life, not apart from it' (Miller and Slater 2000: 7).

However in their emphasis on the rolling horizon of everyday media mundanity, Miller and Slater downplay aspects of new media that are genuinely novel. Everyday cyberspaces do exist, generated by telematic communication through networked and mobile digital media, and in the dynamic software worlds of videogames. Whilst they are thoroughly enmeshed in, and accessed from, everyday life, they generate new modes of communication, new games, new opportunities for identity play, and new relationships between the human and technological. The virtual and the actual are intertwined, and each is all the more interesting for it. This Part offers some productive theoretical resources for the study of the historical, social and cultural dynamics that shape, and are shaped by, everyday technoculture.

4.1.3 Consuming new media

The concept of consumption is central to Cultural and Media Studies' approach to technology in everyday life. It is a contested term: seen variously as the primary cultural practice in a passive, greedy consumer society; or as a potentially rich and creative way of making sense of individual identity in a complex world: 'Rather than being a passive, secondary, determined activity, consumption . . . is seen increasingly as an activity with its own practices, tempo, significance and determination' (Mackay 1997: 3–4). Though Cultural and Media Studies are characterised by a wide range of conceptual and methodological approaches, it is possible to generalise and assert that their analyses of technology and consumption tend to be based on certain premises. First, digital media technologies tend not to be seen as fundamentally distinct from 'old' electronic media, or even, in some studies, other domestic technologies, such as microwaves or freezers (Silverstone and Hirsch 1992). Second, there is a general reluctance to privilege either consumption or production in the generation of the meanings of a domestic technological device. That is to say, the meanings and uses of domestic technologies (and consumer goods and mediated images) are not fixed in either the moment of their production or in the act of their consumption. Rather, they are the always contingent product of the relationship between the constraint or 'encoding' of meaning through production and marketing, and the creative activities through which individuals and groups make sense of or 'decode' these meanings. Cultural and Media Studies' work on domestic media technologies is based on a political dynamic between 'constraint' and 'creativity' (Mackay 1997). Producers attempt to constrain the uses and meanings of their products, consumers negotiate these intended meanings more or less in accordance with the producers' desires, and Cultural Studies scholars attempt to identify creative or progressive trends within the consumers' negotiations.

The emphasis on the 'meanings' rather than, say, the 'uses' of media technologies here is significant. It draws our attention to the cultural nature of technologies, for instance the ways in which the acquisition of the latest mobile phone or MP3 player might be driven more by its owner's desire for status than by its functionality. Producers and advertisers operate by the long-established dynamic of differentiating essentially similar products through the generation of images and brand identities. In this regard, a phone is the same as any other commodity. However, the notion of 'meaning' by no means exhausts the cultural operation and circulation of media technologies, indeed concentrating only on their discursive construction detracts from their material nature as technologies, in actual lived moments of adoption and use. This tension between meaning and use will be explored further below. For now we will look at some ethnographic case studies that draw out some of the dynamics of the relationships between new media technologies and their domestic context.

4.2 Everyday life in a media home

In an influential Cultural and Media Studies textbook on consumption and everyday life, Hugh Mackay argues that '[t]o understand the consumption of technologies in households, we have to understand the practices of everyday life there – how new technologies are implicated in household routines and activities' (Mackay 1997: 277). To this end, and with particular reference to computer media (or information and communication technologies – ICTs), he identifies four key areas of enquiry:

- the significance of consumption of ICTs for domestic lives and relationships

- how ICTs are implicated in the establishment of individual and family identities

- the relationship between household members' public and private worlds; and

- how technology (as well as the household) is transformed in the process of domestication and incorporation (Mackay 1997: 278).

The emphasis here is on the shifting or negotiated meanings and implications of media technologies as they are adopted and consumed in the home, in everyday life. Shaun Moores' study of the 'domestication' of satellite television exemplifies Mackay's four areas of enquiry. In describing the 'embedding' of a new media technology in the home, he too draws a picture of domestic media technology adoption and consumption as dynamic and requiring negotiation between household members and their established consumption tastes, patterns and devices. Households are not static environments into which media technologies are straightforwardly 'inserted'. Often the purchase of new media technologies coincides with 'the redrawing of domestic boundaries and relationships' (Moores 1993a: 627). For example growing children may make new demands for educational and entertainment hardware. Also, households have their own dynamics and politics, not least along the lines of gender and generation. Such power relationships intersect and interact with producers' expectations of

Hugh Mackay, *Consumption and Everyday Life: culture, media and identities*, London (1997). See also Dewdney and Boyd (1995), du Gay *et al.* (1997), Silverstone and Hirsch (1992), Howard (1998)

the uses and meaning of new media products: 'Social divisions of gender or generation produce differential dispositions towards a technology like satellite TV' (Moores 1993a: 633).

4.2.1 Home computing

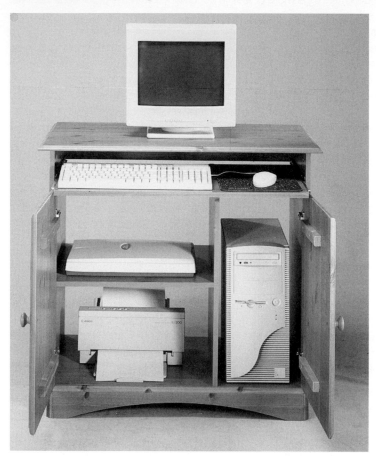

4.4 Tradition and newness. Courtesy of Argos

In a large-scale ethnographic study, the *Screen Play* project (based in the Graduate School of Education at Bristol University, and conducted from 1998 to 2000) researched children's 'techno-popular culture' and its implications for education. The project recently drew attention to issues of access to new media, first by recognising that many children do not have a PC in their home, and second by pointing out constraints on access to, and use of, ICTs, even in those households which did have computers. They found that physical as well as social or familial constraints had significant effects on the ways in which computers and networks are accessed. For instance, the families studied in the Screen Play research tended not to place PCs in the main communal spaces of the house – for example in the living room alongside the television – but rather in spare or 'dead' space: landings, spare bedrooms, under stairs, lofts:

> **Mrs H** Well because it's the other side of the house at the back so you don't have to hear it. So if you were in here watching television and we've got company then they're out the way.

Q Why did it go in the spare room? What was the reason. What was the thinking?

Mr D Because it was a spare room.

Mrs D Because its nobody's room in there and just let everybody else use it. It's a sort of spare room cum office.

Steven, 13 It's not as private as your bedroom.

(Facer, Furlong, Furlong and Sutherland 2001b: 18)

It is clear that the existing layout and use of space in the house affected the ways in which the new technologies were used. Computers were occasionally placed in children's bedrooms, though this was rarely the ideal, 'one child one computer' image of the instrumental fantasies of computer manufacturers or furniture catalogues. As Sara McNamee observes in her study of the domestic gender politics of video game playing, the location within the home of a computer or games console can lead to unequal use. This inequality is frequently structured around gender. She notes that girls *say* they like playing videogames as much as boys, but often *play* less. This is in part due to the fact that although consoles are often shared within the family, especially between siblings, they are usually kept in the boys' rooms, and hence, girls' access is controlled by their brothers: 'the machine becomes a symbolic focus around which gender relations are negotiated and expressed in domestic space' (McNamee

4.5 One child, one PC, and the domestic ergonomics of new media. Courtesy of Argos

1998: 197). So, it is argued, even where everyday consumption or use of digital networks is possible, it is constrained by socio-economic factors, established household politics and relationships of gender and age, and by material constraints of space and time.

Ironically, the same 'open' nature of computers that appears to free them from established media constraints can also entail complex negotiations around access. In households that can only afford one machine (i.e. most: 14 out of the 16 Screen Play case studies), new systems of 'time-sharing' have to be developed to allow different family members to perform different uses, 'managed around the temporal organisation . . . of the family':

> **Mum** . . . Steven normally gets in first you see, so he would always get the opportunity of going to the computer first. So we said 'that's not fair'. So Mondays and Thursdays Helen has first choice. She can decide whether she wants to go on the computer or watch television and on the other . . . I mean it tends to be just the Tuesday and Wednesday because Friday you're quite often not here or doing other things. – But we try and stick to only two hours on the computer each in any one day. – Generally speaking that's probably about enough. In terms of playing games. If they want to then go on and do some homework, then that's fine.
>
> (Facer *et al*. 2001b: 19).

This organisation is also partly determined by discourses of computer use that originate outside the home, in particular the conflict between the domestic computer as an educational resource and as a leisure/entertainment device (see **4.3.2**). This conflict is evident even at the level of the arrangement of the 'space' of the computer itself. In many families, for example, one person (often, but not always, an adult) takes responsibility for the set-up of file-management systems and 'parental control' systems, installing short-cuts, de-installing software and freeing up memory for authorised or 'preferred' practices, perhaps removing games from the hard drive.

Thus the different levels of knowledge and authority within the family in relation to the computer ensure a different relationship to its use. Facer *et al*. (2001b) draw on Michel de Certeau's concept of 'tactics' to analyse the various methods by which the 'less powerful' in this context attempt to use the computer in their own ways. For example, by disguising games playing as homework or the grasping of an opportunity to use the computer in the competitive game of access:

> **Helen, 10** And I was having a go at that and I couldn't get past this particular bit and I called Steven . . .
> **Steven, 13** I did it in 30 seconds.
> **Helen** He did it in 30 seconds.
> **Q** Right. So if Steven shows you something . . .
> **Steven** He normally does it.
> **Q** He normally does it and then you carry on.
> **Helen** And then I carry on. Or he normally does it. He pushes me off and he goes the rest of the game. He does that a lot of the time.
>
> (Facer *et al*. 2001b: 20)

Alternatively, the tactical 'occupation of the digital landscape', though 'only ever temporary and transient' (Facer *et al*. 2001b: 20) can also be effected through changing the computer's desktop and settings, adjusting screen savers, etc. Thus, the features that can in some circumstances be seen as making the computer 'personal' are here tactics within a struggle for ownership of a communal 'space'.

The open, multifunctional nature of domestic computer technology can be seen, then, as a site of conflict or self-assertion. Family members may try to establish their own 'black boxes' (see **4.3.1**), however partial and temporary: 'This poaching of the computer space, a temporal appropriation of technology . . . can also be seen as a negotiation to fix the meaning and, subsequently, function of a technology which has the potential for multiple purposes' (Facer *et al*. 2001b: 21).

The networked home

Domestic access to the Internet is shaped in part by the same everyday constraints of time, space, access and resources as stand-alone PC use, though in some ways online activity can face more restrictions. One factor commonly cited by parents interviewed by Screen Play for monitoring and restricting their children's access to the Internet is the cost of telephone calls for Internet access in the UK. Since this particular study was undertaken, the rise of broadband connections has been marked, and this in itself changes the character of Internet access significantly, enabling people to 'treat the Internet as a ubiquitous, "always-on" dimension of their lives, instead of a special place they visited occasionally' (Burkeman 2008). This said, many homes still rely on telephone connection (broadband overtook the phone line as most common domestic Internet access in the UK in 2005). Broadband connections have done nothing to allay widespread anxieties about the Internet as potentially dangerous, threatening intrusion of pornography or even – through chat rooms – paedophiles, into children's lives. There is an irony here: many parents bought computers for their children because of the perception of the increasing dangers of them playing outside. Now the Internet seems to bring a dangerous outside world directly into the hitherto safe private realm. These anxieties had led some of the parents either to not go online in the first place, or strictly to control access through passwords or adult supervision:

> As the permeable boundaries of domestic space are made apparent in the introduction of the Internet (and television before it) into the home, the space of the networked home computer becomes a site of surveillance in which children's activities are monitored in not dissimilar ways to those employed in the space outside the front door.
>
> (Facer *et al*. 2001b: 23)

So, even where everyday consumption or use of digital networks is possible, it is constrained by socio-economic factors, established household politics and relationships of gender and age, by material constraints of space and time and by anxieties about the relationships between everyday space and cyberspace.

4.2.2 Theories of media consumption

The terminology of constraint, creativity and consumption is used to study all manner of everyday cultural practices. Its use in the study of technocultural artefacts and activities however raises questions. If consumption is seen as a primarily symbolic activity, one of meaning-making, is there a significant difference between this meaning-making and *use*? What is the difference between *consuming* and *using* a media technological device? Or, if the consumption of a product is motivated by the consumer's identity construction, is this process different in the materially productive activities of technological use? When technologies are used to *do* or *make* things, are the opposing terms 'constraint' and 'creativity' the most productive start-ing point for analysing the dynamics and power relationships mobilised? Do technologies themselves have any influence over their uses or meanings or are these latter fully shaped through the human activities of production and consumption? Within the diverse debates around new media the concept of consumption may be configured differently, ignored or sub-stituted by terms with different connotations. We will now set out the key discursive positions on the everyday consumption of media technologies. This grouping of discourses is far from definitive, and each brackets together some quite divergent positions, but they do give an indication of the debates and issues.

Cybercultural studies

Though the term cyberculture may seem rather dated, evoking a late-twentieth-century tech-nological imaginary of immersive VR worlds, headsets and an SF aesthetic of black leather and mirror shades, it has been very influential in the development of the academic study of new media. Cybercultural studies brackets together a diverse range of theoretical approaches to new cultural technologies. They share a premiss that technology, especially computer technology, is instrumental in profound transformations in contemporary culture and beyond – primarily through new, intimate relationships between the human and the technological. The cybercultural tone is by and large optimistic about this change, sometimes falling into Utopian assumptions about the emancipatory possibilities of digital media such as virtual reality and certain Internet media.

The term 'consumption' itself is rarely used in this context, indeed its absence tells us something of cybercultural studies' understanding of digital media. In popular celebrations of the 'newness' of new media, consumption is browsing, surfing, using, 'viewsing', we do con-sume so much as we are 'immersed'. Digital media and virtual culture are generally seen to transcend, or render obsolete, mundane questions of commercial interests or already exist-ing practices of media use. Either new relationships with technology – from immersion in cyberspace to the various notions of the cyborg – are so intimate that any sense of 'con-suming' technology as a distinct set of devices and media becomes impossible, or 'consumption' as a mode of engaging in culture belongs to the bad 'old' pre-digital media. These electronic media are centralised and authoritarian whereas new information and com-munication media are interactive and decentralised. The pioneer of personal computing, Ted Nelson, talking about the potential of computer media, hoped that:

> Libertarian ideals of accessibility and excitement might unseat the video narcosis that now sits on our own land like a fog.
>
> (Nelson 1982, quoted in Mayer 1999: 128).

Cyberculture discourses may well be informed by progressive politics, however; indeed, cyberspace is seen as a realm in which social divisions based on bodily and material attrib-utes and positions (age, gender, class, race, etc.) can be transcended (see **4.4**).

'Business as (or even worse than) usual'

Here the role of economic production in determining the meanings and uses of new tech-nology in everyday life is emphasised. Drawing on a Marxist model of consumption as operating in the sphere of the cultural superstructure, determined and shaped by the eco-nomic base of capitalist production, consumer goods and mass media serve primarily to sustain and reproduce the existing economic and social order.

See for example, Robins (1996) again, Robins and Webster (1999) or Stephen Kline, Nick Dyer-Witheford and Greig de Peuter (2003). We might bracket these studies as a 'left pessimist' approach, in reference to an earlier critique of culture and cultural technology – that of the Frankfurt School in the 1920s and 1930s (Adorno 1991). See **1.5.4** The return of the Frankfurt School critique in the popularisation of new media

This approach holds that the development, dissemination and consumption of media technologies is instrumental in the commodification and reification of everyday life. Culture is made subservient to the interests of bureaucratic control and capitalist accumulation. Thus this 'left pessimist' position might be superficially similar to cybercultural studies in its analysis of 'old' broadcast media as hierarchical, stultifying, and serving commercial and state interests. The difference is of course that the pessimists do not see new media as any escape from this controlling logic; there is a fundamental continuity between the dynamics of digital technologies and the electronic and industrial technologies of the nineteenth and twentieth centuries. If anything, new media are seen as even worse than earlier media. On the one hand, the technologies of computer media are seen as lending themselves to the production of spectacular but empty images and narratives – addictive immersion that makes the television-viewing couch potato seem positively energetic – and on the other to new forms of political and commercial surveillance and domination of the time and space of everyday life.

Videogames in particular are a digital medium that have been seen to epitomise the acceleration of, and colonisation by, capitalist technoculture. From this perspective the computer game, far from offering new interactive possibilities, instead presents 'an ideal image of the market system'. Computer games' meanings are locked into their code, and consumption only realises their repressive potential:

> In their structure and content, computer games are a capitalist, deeply conservative form of culture, and their political content is prescribed by the options open to democracy under modern capitalism, from games with liberal pretensions to those with quasi-fascist overtones. All of them offer virtual consumption of empty forms in an ideal market.
>
> (Stallabrass 1993: 104)

For Kline, Dyer-Witheford and Peuter, the videogame is the ideal commodity for post-Fordism:

> It is a child of the computer technologies that lie at the heart of the post-Fordist reorganization of work. In production, game development, with its youthful workforce of digital artisans and netslaves, typifies the new forms of post-Fordist enterprise and labour. In consumption, the video game brilliantly exemplifies post-Fordism's tendency to fill domestic space and time with fluidified, experiential, and electronic commodities. Video and computer games, moreover, are perhaps the most compelling manifestation of the simulatory hyperreal postmodern ambience that [can be seen] as the cultural correlative to the post-Fordist economy. The interactive gaming business also powerfully demonstrates the increasingly intense advertising, promotional, and surveillance strategies practised by post-Fordist marketers in an era of niche markets. In all these aspects the interactive game industry displays the global logic of an increasingly transnational capitalism whose production capacities and market strategies are now incessantly calculated and recalculated on a planetary basis.
>
> (Kline, Dyer-Witheford and de Peuter 2003: 75)

From this 'business as usual' perspective certain connections between the progressive cyberculture position and a neo-liberal celebration of digital media become evident. Without an analysis of the persistence of social and economic power in, and through, the everyday consumption of new technologies, any analysis of a new media age would be a delusional and utopian projection of future possibilities into the here and now, eliding or ignoring current power relationships and struggles.

Populists and postmodernists

Most postmodernist theories of the meanings of new media technologies subscribe to the view that it is now consumption and leisure rather than production and work that determine the texture and experiences of everyday life. Consumer culture is now the dominant, if not the only, cultural sphere. Some theorists celebrate the pleasures and freedoms of consumption, of individuals and groups actively constructing their identities through their choices in media and consumer culture.

> Rather than being a passive, secondary, determined activity, consumption . . . is seen increasingly as an activity with its own practices, tempo, significance and determination.
>
> (Mackay 1997: 3–4)

There is some overlap with cybercultural theory here; indeed, cybercultural studies is some-times closely engaged with postmodernist ideas. Notions of a hyperreal and simulated media world of pure consumption often strike a chord with those attempting to theorise the apparently non-material, disembodied and textual characteristics of virtual reality, MUDs and the Internet. However, whereas for cybercultural studies it is specifically the digital age which promises cre-ative mediated pleasure, for postmodernists it is the media/consumer society as a whole.

Cultural and media studies

These discursive categories are not mutually exclusive, and any particular approach to the analysis of new media may entail one or more of them. The academic discipline most thor-oughly concerned with theorising everyday cultural consumption is Cultural and Media Studies. Its attitudes to consumption have been outlined already, but it is worth pointing out that it is itself characterised by a wide range of conceptual and methodological approaches, including its own versions of both postmodernist and left-pessimist discourses, and, when cultural and media technologies are explicitly addressed, the influence of cybercultural stud-ies becomes evident.

The divisions between cultural studies and postmodernist positions can be hard to main-tain. While downplaying the significance of production, notions of active consumption are not necessarily without an analysis of power. Paul Willis, for example, doesn't see consumption of commodities and popular media as transcending the class system of capitalist production; rather, he is celebrating working-class culture in the face of bourgeois arts funding and priv-ilege. Indeed he argues that working-class youth should be given access to the production of the media images they appropriate (Willis 1990).

Alternatively, the feminist analysis of cultural consumption is critical of arguments that eco-nomic structures (and the social formations of class they entail) are all-determining. Addressing the gendered structures of consumption highlights different constellations of power and resistance in the face of commodified (and technologised) everyday life. Feminist debates have also pointed out that the marginalisation of the study of media consumption is related to issues of gender, in which domestic consumption generally and communications media like television in particular have been commonly ascribed to the feminine.

Returning to the study of the technologies of media, then, we can see that a focus on consumption tends to foreground the conflictual nature of meaning generation – the struggle for meaning between production and consumption. Producers' attempts to build in mean-ings, and articulate them through promotion and advertising, can result in nothing more than 'preferred readings' of their products. They may have wished us to see the Betamax video format, laser discs, or HD DVD as the future of home entertainment, but they could not make them mean, or become, that. Early home computers in the 1980s were often sold as information technologies, but were widely consumed as games machines (**4.3.2**). In mainstream Cultural and Media Studies all commodities and media, then, are 'texts', 'encoded' products which may be 'decoded' in their consumption to reveal a quite different message (Mackay 1997: 10). So – and this assertion is a highly significant one – 'the effects of a technology . . . are *not determined by its production, its physical form or its capability*. Rather than being built into the technology, these depend on how they are consumed' (Mackay 1997: 263, our emphasis). Or, put more baldly by John Ellis in *Visible Fictions: cinema, television, video*: 'there is *nothing* in the technologies themselves that dictated how they would be used by societies that invented them' (Ellis 1982: 12, our emphasis).

See for instance: Cockburn and Furst Dilic (1994), Gray (1992), Green and Adam (2001), McNamee (1998) and Terry (1997)

Each of the fields of enquiry loosely sketched above is bound up in its own models of the relationship between technology and culture. Cybercultural Studies and Cultural and Media Studies for instance may cite Marshall McLuhan and Raymond Williams respectively as key influences and inspirations. Thus the discussion, earlier in this book (Part 1) of the differences between these two models of technoculture is directly relevant to our concern with everyday life here. Before we consider such questions of shaping and determination in the next section however, we will introduce another approach to understanding consumption and media technology that is generally (though not entirely) overlooked by each intellectual position.

4.2.3 Consumption and play

Between preferred readings – or uses – and resistance to or appropriation of media texts and technologies lies a more ambiguous and under-theorised mode of engagement: play. The rise of the videogame is only the most obvious example of the ludic (playful) nature of popular digital media and the increasingly game-like nature of significant aspects of more established media from television game-shows and reality TV to interactive games accompanying feature films on DVDs to online fan cultures and the amateur production of YouTube as they adopt, and are adapted by, digital communication technologies.

Attention to play in the study of everyday media culture has a number of significant implications.

- It draws us to alternative genealogies of media technologies and modes of consumption (for example, pinball and board games are as significant to the study of videogames as television and cinema).

- It questions media studies' emphasis on journalism and drama as privileged popular media forms and genres at the expense of game shows, comedy and audience participation, etc.

- Concomitantly, play troubles attempts to categorise media consumption in political terms: to play a game is to 'play by the rules' and hence the player may be seen as complicit with the values and machinations of the producer. Yet play is disruptive and generative as well as conservative and rule-bound.

- Playing with digital media (not only videogames, as we will see) offers a vivid and intense paradigm of the intimate relationship between the technological and the human (human bodies and identities) in everyday cyberculture.

The implications of these points will be explored more fully in the rest of this Part of the book; for now we will introduce them with a small screen, a keypad, and a charm.

CASE STUDY 4.1: The mobile phone: gadgets and play

4.6 Hello kitty!

Over the past decade the status of the mobile telephone (or cell phone) has shifted from that of a rather exclusive communication device to being the near universal augmentation of children's and adults' everyday existence in the developed world. For example in 2003, 88 percent of 15–34-year-olds in Britain owned a mobile, and by 2006 91 percent of 12-year-olds had their own phone (Oftel). By July 2007 there were nearly 100 million mobile phone users in Japan (Daliot-Bul 2007: 968). While these statistics apply to the post-industrial world, it should be noted that the mobile phone has been widely adopted in developing countries. For example in rural areas of some African countries mobile networks and mobile phone ownership far outstrips landline networks. In Kenya the number of mobile phones was one million in 2002 but grew to 6.5 million in 2007. The number of landlines (around 300,000) did not change in this period (Mason 2007).

The mobile has been 'decoded' by a generation of teenagers, who have at once bought into the producers' dreams (coveting particular brands for example) and generated new communication practices such as text messaging. The ways in which texting has been adopted, and the kinds of message sent, represent a genuinely new communication medium in everyday life. The technical limitations of the keypad have proved to be not so much a constraint on texting's potential as facilitating a new vernacular shorthand of everyday communication. The incessant development and sale of new ringtones, games, and display graphics is a familiar consumer capitalist strategy of selling us new commodities we never knew we needed, but at the same time seems inseparable from other new media practices such as the customising and personalising of computer desktops or online services.

Jean Baudrillard, taking an earlier mobile personal communication device, the Dictaphone, as an example, highlights the uneasy status of the technological in a consumer culture:

whisper your decisions, dictate your instructions, and proclaim your victories to it . . . Nothing could be more useful, and nothing more useless: when the technical process is given over to a magical type of mental practice or a fashionable social practice, then the technical object itself becomes a gadget.

(Baudrillard 1990: 77)

He is less interested in exploring what the nature of everyday experience might be with these gadgets, what sensual and aesthetic pleasures might attend ludic gadgets and the play with communication they encourage. In an article which documents the tremendous variety of playful and creative uses to which young Japanese people put their mobile phones (in Japan, *keitai*), Michal Daliot-Bul suggests ways in which attention to playful media consumption demands that we rethink the boundaries of and within everyday life:

> Hanging a Hello Kitty charm on one's keitai, playing a simple cell phone digital game or having an animated character hosting one's keitai mail room are all acts of 'deviation' from reality into a play-dimension [. . .] Keitai blurs the distinction between the private and the public, leisure and work, here and there, and virtual cyberspace and reality. As this happens, the boundaries of play as a framed act separated from real life blur as well.
>
> (Daliot-Bul 2007: 967)

If popular media technologies are only ever symbolic and 'textual' and never practical or instrumental, then they may well be these gadgets of Baudrillard's. For Baudrillard tools and machines in contemporary consumer culture lose their instrumental functions, their practical uses, their use value. They instead operate as signs, fashion, toys or games. Digital personal organisers, text messaging on mobile phones, mobile phones themselves, may be sold as useful tools – but all seem to invite us to play. After all, who felt the need to 'text', to change a PC desktop's wallpaper or nurture a Tamagotchi virtual pet until a consumer device suggested we might?

Baudrillard's assertions, on the one hand, illustrate the logical conclusion of the argument that popular technologies are 'textual' and, in themselves, have no causal or instrumental function in everyday use: we are only ever playing at doing things, at performing useful tasks. On the other, his definition of a gadget as a 'ludic' device, a technological artefact with which we play, is a suggestive one. It asks us to consider what the significance of playful technology might be. The mobile phone user's weaving of spoken and written communication through the spare moments of the day may not be 'instrumental', but neither is it reducible to 'fashionable practice', nor to the decoding of Nokia or T-Mobile's marketing strategies. It suggests that much everyday communication is non-instrumental, playful, about making connections and eliciting a response, regardless of the content of any particular message. For Daliot-Bul, texting is primarily phatic communication, 'used for maintaining social contact and conveying feelings rather than exchanging information or ideas. It creates a playful and emotional connectedness among friends. It is about *feeling* and *reaffirming* the connection' (Daliot-Bul 2007: 956).

As the charm of Hello Kitty suggests, the distinction between the consumption of technologies as instrumental use and as play is not always easily drawn.

4.2.4 Issues and questions: meanings and uses

The study of the consumption of new media in everyday life needs to draw on, and challenge, each of the theoretical approaches to consumption outlined above. Though many of the examples and case studies cited in this part of the book come from cultural and media studies, the study of technology in everyday life raises important questions for this discipline. As we have seen already, the meanings and uses of popular new media such as the web or video games are by no means fixed.

The distinction (or lack of distinction) between 'media' and 'technology' underlies these shifting meanings. The sense of excitement (or anxiety) generated by the introduction of a new media technology (such as the domestic PC) or software application (such as Facebook) is inseparable from the understanding that this new device or network is technological: it can be used to do things and make changes. Of course its uses, and even its survival as a consumer technology, are not predetermined, and its meanings will be constructed as much around its symbolic status as its actual uses and effects.

The challenge here is to recognise this dynamic of encoding and decoding, or (and these two pairs of terms are by no means interchangeable) design and use, without losing sight of,

Jean Baudrillard, 'The gadget and the ludic', in *The Revenge of the Crystal* (1990). 'Ludic' means playful on one level, the unique characteristics and possibilities for popular new media as both media and technologies, and more fundamentally, the materiality and reality of everyday technologies. To assert that a PC, for example, is a 'text' is a useful metaphor for exploring its multiple meanings in contemporary culture, but it begs important questions:

- How do we account for the *instrumental* nature of the PC and its uses in the home (spreadsheets, word processing, etc.)? After all, it is a machine which can be used to do and make things. The practices of computer-related media – programming, information processing, communication, games playing – are not adequately accounted for with these literary metaphors.

- If hardware is a 'text' do we need to distinguish it from software as text? If we accept that a games console, for example, is textual, then surely the game played on it must be seen as a different kind of text?

- What are the implications of a ludic technoculture?

Media technologies enable or invite certain uses, precisely by their status as machines and tools. The negotiation of meaning between producers, advertisers, retailers, government agencies and consumers may suggest and shape uses, but use – the actual operations in everyday life that these technologies facilitate – is not reducible to, or exhausted by, 'meaning'. Many commentators discuss the ways in which information and communication technologies facilitate new relationships between people in their local domestic circumstances and global networks (Moores 1993b; Silverstone and Hirsch 1992). Marilyn Strathern sees domestic information and communication technologies as 'enabling'. In terms which assign agency to these technologies themselves, she suggests that '[t]hey appear to amplify people's experiences, options, choices. But at the same time they also amplify people's experiences, options and choices in relation to themselves. These media for communication compel people to communicate with them' (Strathern 1992: xi).

4.3 The technological shaping of everyday life

As we have already seen, a focus on everyday life and consumption, particularly from Cultural and Media Studies assumptions and methods, tends to militate against conceptions of technological agency in the study of popular new media. Research in this area is underpinned explicitly or implicitly by the Social Shaping of Technology thesis (SST), in particular, first, the foregrounding of the agonistic nature of the production and consumption of technological devices and systems. And second, the explicit resistance to the notion that technologies and technological systems could have agency or effects in the human world. For example, in a book on television, Roger Silverstone argues that we must 'privilege the social', by which he means human agency in general: in its historical, economic, cultural and political manifestations: 'indeed one must do so, since the natural, the economic, and the technical, in their obduracy or their malleability, have no significance except through social action' (Silverstone 1994: 85). Before we address these positions in more detail, we will explore this social constructionist approach and its effectiveness in accounting for the shape and uses of everyday new media technologies.

So, from the 'social shaping of technology' viewpoint, it is not only the choice of particular technical features included in any new black box device that determine its commercial success, its symbolic status, what William Boddy calls 'instrumental fantasies', is also crucial:

CASE STUDY 4.2: The black XBox and the social shaping of videogame technology

More recently the black-boxing of videogame console and DVD player has had a powerful impact on new formats for domestic television media. Perhaps learning from its failure in the war between its Betamax video format and JVC's triumphant VHS in the 1980s, Sony used its latest console, the Playstation 3, to help it establish the dominance, by early 2008, of its own high definition DVD format, Blu-Ray, over Toshiba's HD DVD

4.7 XBox. Courtesy of Microsoft

The development of the first XBox videogame console is an example of the social shaping of a media device. The initial success of Microsoft's console depended as much on the nuances of its marketing strategy as on the console's technical specifications and the quality of its games. Learning from Sony's tremendously successful marketing strategies for the Playstation in the 1990s, Microsoft had to battle against its (and its founder Bill Gates's) staid image. The cosmetic design of the console was therefore very important, and was modelled on hi-fi components: 'People are really into the design, and they've said they weren't expecting something as cool or as sleek from Microsoft, and that they thought it captured the enthusiasm and excitement behind gaming' (*Edge* 2001: 71).

After interviewing 5,000 gamers and visiting 130 gamers' homes to research the design of the XBox, they went to great lengths to establish it as the antithesis of the desktop computer. Rather than the beige box located in the study and associated with work, the console was promoted as a sexy machine designed to look good in the living room

(Flynn 2003: 557).

One early strategy for convincing sceptical consumers of Microsoft's commitment to 'serious' game playing was to not allow the XBox to be used as a DVD player for films (distinguishing it from the recently released Playstation 2). Thus the drive towards producing a multifunctional consumer entertainment system, and a potential selling point, is balanced against the need to match the device's symbolic status to the attitudes and preferences of the target audience (Microsoft later changed this strategy and XBoxes were allowed to play DVDs).

Every electronic media product launch or network debut carries with it an implicit fantasy scenario of its domestic consumption, a polemical ontology of it as a medium, and an ideological rationale for its social function.

(Boddy 1999)

Science and Technology
Studies (see **4.3.3**
below), alluding to
consumer media devices
such as hi-fis and
televisions, use the term
'black box' to discuss
this only-ever-
temporary fixing of
components,
technologies and
functions in any
particular device or
system. The term is
used in cybernetics as
well, denoting a system
or device analysed in
terms of its effects rather
than its inner workings.
STS analyses aim to
'open the black box' and
reveal its contingency
and heterogeneity,
whereas cybernetics has
used the term to refer to
a system the workings of
which have either yet to
be analysed, or whose
workings are of less
immediate interest than
its input, output and
effects (Wiener 1961:
x–xi)

For a different account
of the significance of the
PC, see **3.6**

See Levy 1994 for an
entertaining account of
this important aspect of
new media history. It
should be noted that the
term 'hacker' did not
originally mean the
mischievous or
malicious figure familiar
today. See also **4.5.2**

The development of the XBox demonstrates that the creation of a commercially successful digital media technology is dependent at least as much on its social form, its symbolic status, as on its technological capabilities.

There are two further important points to raise here. One is that new media technologies are rarely, if ever, entirely new. The XBox is a particular assemblage of existing technologies (PC hardware, DVD player, etc.) just as television and cinema as we understand them today were not 'invented' as such, but rather were, as Raymond Williams says of television, a complex of inventions and developments, a complex which at all stages 'depended for parts of its realisation on inventions made with other ends primarily in view' (Williams 1990a: 15).

The sheer flexibility of digital technologies, and the convergences between different media forms that digitisation affords (for instance the promiscuities of USB) accentuate this complex nature of media technological development. Games consoles can also be DVD players or networked for online play and communication. A mobile phone can also be a games console, a text-based communication device, a camera, a web browser. A key task for manufacturers and retailers then, in the process of production, is to identify possible uses or practices for their technologies, and build these into the consumer device. This would seem to support the social shaping thesis. And yet, as we will argue in more detail later in this section, while the fantasies spun around the launch of any media device shape and the symbolic status it may accrue in its everyday usage, shape its meanings and uses, they by no means wholly determine these uses and meanings. The 'black-boxing' of heterogeneous technologies is driven by factors that are at once technological and social (economic, historical, political). All videogame consoles are effectively computers black-boxed as games machines rather than as more 'open' PCs (see **4.3.2** below). The XBox in particular is built on a PC architecture and Microsoft operating system and so became the target of attempts to reverse-engineer or hack it, freeing up other potential but restricted uses, from the long-established practice of console 'chipping' (inserting hardware to get around security measures, allowing the playing of copied or other region games), to use as a media centre (playing CDs, VCDs and MP3s for example), to unlocking something like full PC functionality. We see here activities that are in important ways distinct from established notions of consumption or decoding: the production of the XBox was shaped by, exploited (and attempted to limit) the physical nature and capabilities of its arrangements of technologies. Its 'consumption' then can be predicated more on freeing up its technical potential than challenging its 'meanings'.

4.3.1 The 'open' PC

The user is an unreliable creature though. It was not clear for example, despite the excitement that attended their production and sale, quite what the owners of early home computers in the 1980s would *do* with them. They were often sold as information technologies (bought by parents anxious to prepare their children for the 'information revolution'), but were widely consumed as games machines (once the children got their hands on them). As research by Haddon and Skinner shows, 'producers and consumers constantly searched for and tried to construct the "usefulness" of this mass market product after it had been developed and launched' (cited in Haddon 1992: 84). So despite the 'black box' intentions of PC manufacturers and retailers, the machine (or perhaps more accurately, grouping of computer-based information, communication and entertainment technologies) has been widely seen as a uniquely multifunctional 'open device' (Mackay 1997: 270–271), 'chameleonlike' in its applications and possibilities (Turkle 1984).

The multifunctionality, and playfulness, of the PC is rooted in the history of the development of computing. Ambiguity around its use can be traced back at least to its origins in the hacker culture of students at the US universities MIT and Stanford from the late 1950s. This culture has been seen as a struggle against the rigid rituals developed around the use of number-crunching mainframes in university research and business applications, by the hackers' celebration of experimentation and the free sharing of computer code and information. The hackers' development of real-time, interactive information processing led to the first commercially available domestic computers in the 1970s (Levy 1994). At first the hackers' 'do-it-yourself' ethic meant that the first domestic computer users had to build the machine themselves from a kit, and even when home computers became available as completed products they retained their hobbyist image and market for some time. To use a home computer in the late 1970s and early 1980s the owner had to learn programming. Indeed, if nothing else the purpose and pleasure of home computers lay in learning to program, exploring the machine and its system, not, initially at least, consuming commercially produced software and services.

See **4.5.2** for more on the playful pre-history of personal computing

These early users of home computers would seem closer to the hobbyist enthusiasts of early crystal radio than Ted Nelson's dream of Computer Lib activists espousing 'libertarian ideals of accessibility and excitement' (cited in Mayer 1999: 128). However, as Leslie Haddon pointed out in his research into the discourses of home computing in Britain in the early 1980s, the spare room tinkering with these new devices could not be separated from a sense of excitement about this machine as evidence of an unfolding information revolution. Through the exploration of these enigmatic machines, some users felt a sense of participation in the larger technological forces of a changing modern world (Haddon 1988b). As Klaus Bruhn Jensen puts it, 'The personal computer . . . offers both a symbol and a touchstone of the information society' (Jensen 1999: 192).

The migration of the Apple or IBM-compatible personal computer from office to home in the late 1980s served to establish dominant platforms over the multitude of home computer formats, and signalled the end of the hobbyist era. If the home computer fostered a new media cottage industry of hardware and software manufacturers, then the PC marked the beginning of the commercial development of this technology as a mass medium. The marketing of PCs through the existing channels of advertising and promotion added further levels of complexity to the polysemic machine. Jensen sees in the advertising of PCs in the 1980s a contradictory discourse of individual empowerment through technology and images of social revolution. He points to Apple's television advertisement inspired by George Orwell's *Nineteen Eighty-Four*, and to the print advertisement, in a *Newsweek* special election issue in 1984 under the headline 'One Person, One Computer'. Thus the PC fits into an established pattern of individualised domestic consumption, but, Jensen argues, the desires and anxieties surrounding PCs in the information revolution may still threaten this consumerist norm (Jensen 1999).

Whether toy or tool, the domestic computer has invited excitement and contemplation that mark it out as distinct from the average consumer electronic device. It has been seen as a device within which we could see or create artificial 'microworlds' (Sudnow 1983). On a prosaic level this may mean individual customisation of the computer: changing desktop 'wallpaper', adding distinctive screensavers or sounds. On a more profound level it has suggested some fundamental shifts in our relationship with technology. In particular it invites comparisons with the human brain and has inspired both popular ideas of artificial intelligence and popular, but actual, artificial life applications, for example the computer game *Creatures* (see Kember 2003). Sherry Turkle evokes these aspects in her study of the culture of programming. When programming, the computer is a 'projection of part of the self, a mirror of the mind' (Turkle 1984: 15). She quotes an interview with a schoolchild: 'you put a little piece of your mind into the computer's mind and now you can see it' (ibid.: 145).

> When you create a programmed world, you work in it, you experiment in it, you live in it. The computer's chameleonlike quality, the fact that when you program it, it becomes your creature, makes it an ideal medium for the construction of a wide variety of private worlds and through them, for self-exploration. Computers are more than screens onto which personality is projected. They have already become a part of how a new generation is growing up.
>
> (Turkle 1984: 6)

It is not only information and images that computer technology allows this generation to experiment with and manipulate, she argues, but also the users' personality, identity and sexuality (Turkle 1984: 15). Such experimentation offers us, the artist Sally Pryor asserts, a way of 'thinking of oneself as a computer' (Pryor 1991: 585).

Since its arrival as a popular new media form in the 1990s, the domestic PC has been embroiled in a struggle over developments in the media technology market. The arrival and popularisation of the World Wide Web introduced a new set of meanings and predictions, not least of the 'death' of the PC itself, through its proposed replacement by dumb terminals on networks to (more recently) distribution to smaller, mobile devices such as PDAs and mobile phones. Alternatively, new convergences of domestic media technologies have been developed around the PC and its functions; both unsuccessfully (digital television systems offering email and interactive service), and successfully (e.g. networked videogame consoles for online multiplayer games). However, the widespread adoption of broadband access in developed countries has transformed the domestic PC into a widely-owned domestic media centre, its use no longer predicated on programming, but rather on the accessing of online information and the acquisition, distribution and sharing of media files from music to television programmes, from blogs to social networking. Wireless technology has set the PC free from the back bedroom as laptops cluster around wifi oases in cafes and libraries.

4.3.2 Edutainment, edutainment, edutainment

As we have seen, the purchase and use of home computers and new media in the home was, until relatively recently, often for broadly educational reasons. Both optimistic cybercultural discourses and more cautious analyses of the effects of computers on everyday life share the view that digital technologies cannot be understood only at the local, domestic level but through their linking of individual use and global forces and relationships. So, if we take a concern with 'knowledge': on a local level the computer may invite comparisons with the human brain, while on the 'global' level a broader sense of information or networks is invoked to explain current economic and social transformation.

However, home computers, from micros in the early 1980s to contemporary PCs and laptops, have been caught up in conflicting interests and discourses about the proper use and meaning of domestic computing. The lines of this conflict are most clearly drawn between education and entertainment: are home computers educational machines (in educational parlance, ICTs) or games and toys? The dividing lines between ICTs and computer entertainment media – or between educational software and games – are not so much blurred as constantly renegotiated and re-established. Helen Nixon's study of Australian parent-consumer magazines on domestic software shows how a publishing genre has been

---

The association of the computer and the self can also be an anxious one however. See Andrew Ross (1991) on the popular association of AIDS and computer viruses, Turkle (1984: 14) on parents' fears about their children's intimate relationships with electronic toys, or Pryor's (1991) critique of the notion of 'disembodiment' in the association of computer and brain

---

See **4.4** for further discussion of identity and new media

CASE STUDY 4.3: Crystal Rainforest

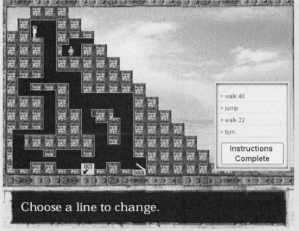

Choose a line to change.

The Azon rain forest is very important.
The trees make oxygen.   GO ON

Now the king is very ill.   GO ON

4.8 Images from *Crystal Rainforest 2000* reproduced by kind permission of Sherston Software Ltd.

An ecological drama unfolds in a multimedia story as the reader or player clicks on hot spots and navigational symbols. The king of an alien rain forest tribe is shot by a poisoned dart, fired by an agent of a logging company. While the king is in hospital, the player is directed to guide a small robot through a pyramid using simple strings of commands. The game reveals its secrets and stories through a collage of graphics, animated sequences, puzzles and photographs. The knowledge thus mediated is similarly eclectic – despite appearances this is not primarily a narrative about the environment; rather, the anthropological, ecological elements are laced with eco-friendly science fiction/fantasy. The game operates on two levels: the pleasures of the narrative, graphics and puzzles lure the player in, and frame the real pedagogical project – through playing with the robots the player learns the programming language Logo. There is a hierarchy of discourses here: the mathematical discourse of programming (and, inadvertently perhaps, popular fantasy genres) over the geographical or socio-political.

established largely on its promises to help parents differentiate between the educational and the entertaining. The kinds of educational software reviewed by these magazines represent a commercial strategy to reconcile this historic conflict in children's computing, a strategy sometimes referred to as 'edutainment', the use of entertainment, toys and games as a medium for learning.

The dual connotations of the term 'edutainment' illustrate the contradictory discourses around new media and education. On the one hand it is a derogatory term, a trivialising, 'dumbing down' or commercialisation of knowledge and learning. This fusion of popular media forms and learning is identified with other media offering hybrids of knowledge and information with commercial and/or fictional forms: the 'advertorial', 'infotainment' and 'docu-soap'. On the other hand edutainment has now been adopted, without irony, by the educational software industry itself. However it is used, 'edutainment' alludes to a broad belief that boundaries are dissolving between education and the consumption of commercial media. This phenomenon is not limited to new media, but it is the digital multimedia forms of CD-ROM encyclopaedias and learning games (and new technologies such as interactive whiteboards in schools) that seem to be of central significance.

The promotion of educational software for domestic PCs, and the ambitions of governments' policies, together attempt to reconstitute the home and time spent at home as no longer separate from school, but connected and interrelated. This is more than a simple technologising of traditional homework however: edutainment software is promoted by both manufacturers and governments' educational policies as central to an emerging 'knowledge economy' in which divisions between work and play, home and school are to be less and less important. These media technologies and texts are intended to transform young people's domestic leisure activities into 'more productive' and stimulating learning.

CASE STUDY 4.4: Visual Basic sucks!

The Screen Play researchers argue that the dominant discursive construction of young computer users as 'future workers' in the knowledge economy leaves little space for them to articulate their pleasure in using computers in non-authorised ways – primarily, though not exclusively, gameplaying. The following exchange, in which parents discussing their agenda for encouraging computer use at home are interrupted by their 'earwigging' teenage son, captures something of the ways in which these broader discourses and policies (and their contradictions) are struggled over in everyday family relationships:

Dad But we did get stuff for the kids to use on it.
Mum We got some educational software for the kids, at that point we were determined they weren't going to play games. [Laughter] I would like Steven to get involved in other things. I've tried a few times to interest him in various things and it's the games, definitely, that dominate his computer usage.
Q Right. And so that's a . . .
Mum Steven, what's the problem?
Steven I'm just saying that I'm going to bed now. And games rule!
Steven Visual Basic sucks!

(Facer *et al.* 2001a: 103)

Steven's outburst, like the immediate pleasures of computer gameplaying he refers to, disrupts the discourses of future rewards for 'educational' computer use.

4.3.3 Beyond social shaping

However 'open', domestic computer media technology is not infinitely flexible in use and meaning. For SST its 'openness' is always shaped by powerful discourses and practices. As we have seen, since computing became a 'family' rather than a hobbyist activity, both producers and consumers have struggled over the proper use of the home computer and PC as educational or entertainment device, providing the home computer with a dual heritage and identity (Haddon 1992: 91). However it is crucial to note that home computers and personal computers are *actual* information (and playful) technologies, not mere images of them; their openness and flexibility is inseparable from their technological nature, their materiality. The computer's polysemy is predicated in the range of uses to which it can be put, its *affordances*, as well as its symbolic circulation. Remember the assertions of Mackay and Ellis cited earlier: that the material form and capabilities of technologies have *no bearing* on their uses. This position is unsustainable: the XBox may be 'socially shaped' as a DVD player as well as a games console, but it plays games and DVDs because its physical form, design and capabilities allow it to do so. Its range of meanings is inseparable from this technical reality. It could conceivably be interpreted, and then deployed, as a rather expensive doorstop, but it could never be repurposed as a fridge or a tin opener.

Most research on technology and culture in the humanities and social sciences then, argues that technologies are never external to society, they are always already sociotechnical. And yet the necessary other side of this assertion is rarely acknowledged: that if technologies cannot be separated from the social and cultural forces that shape them, then social and cultural forces cannot be separated from the technological forces and forms that shape *them*. Just as human knowledge and actions shape machines, machines might shape human knowledge and actions. A critique of 'technological determinism' is more often than not included in any book on new media, but the rejection of naive technological determinism and the equally crude extolling of human agency often means that serious questions of how technological agency might be understood are not addressed. The materiality and agency of technologies are sidestepped and the 'meanings' or discursive construction of particular devices are assumed as the objects of research. The study of everyday media technological cultures tends to take as its object the 'insertion' of a particular technology (the PC, satellite TV, etc.) into households and lives, and its subsequent 'impact' on everyday life, space and identities. The emphasis is generally on how the social forces and contexts of production and consumption, households, generations and gender difference 'limit' technological possibilities; any notion that technologies shape their uses is resisted. The language of insertion and impact is symptomatic of an entrenched discursive opposition between the human and the everyday on one side and technologies on the other.

What follows then are two suggestions for re-thinking the complex relationships between technologies, media, people and social forces.

Science and Technology Studies and Actor-Network Theory

Science and Technology Studies (STS) and actor-network theory (ANT) offer ways of thinking about the relationships between technologies and everyday culture that avoid a priori assumptions about 'shaping' and agency, and argue for the conceptual and material inseparability of culture, nature, science and technology. Actor-network theory is concerned with 'the reciprocal relationship between artefacts and social groups' (Mackenzie and Wajcman 1999: 22). Or, as John Law puts it

> The term 'affordance' has recently been applied to such debates. As a concept it goes beyond the assumption that technologies in everyday life circulate primarily as 'meanings'. Technologies are symbolic, but they also allow us to do things, make things, change things. They facilitate. A device's affordances are the range of uses to which it can be put. See **1.2**

> See **1.6.6** A new focus for old debates: Science and Technology Studies

> If human beings form a social network it is not because they interact with other human beings. It is because they interact with human beings and endless other materials too [. . .] Machines, architectures, clothes, texts – all contribute to the patterning of the social.
>
> (Law 1992)

A study proceeding from an ANT hypothesis then would address the agency of both humans and non-humans (whether artefactual, scientific or natural), implicitly or explicitly rejecting the human-centred worldview of the humanities and social sciences. The implications of this are far-reaching and go beyond the nuances of the effects and determinations studied as the Social Shaping of Technology. It questions engrained conceptual distinctions between nature and culture, humans and artefacts, subjects and objects: '[b]oth society and technology, actor-network theory proposes, are made out of the same "stuff": networks linking human beings and non-human entities' (Mackenzie and Wajcman 1999: 24).

New media ecologies

> McLuhan has developed a theory that goes like this: The new technologies of the electronic age, notably television, radio, the telephone, and computers, make up a new environment. A new environment: they are not merely *added* to some basic human environment . . . They radically alter the entire way people use their five senses, the way they react to things, and therefore, their entire lives and the entire society.
>
> (Wolfe 1965)

As the novelist Tom Wolfe's contemporaneous commentary on Marshall McLuhan's theories of the environmental nature of everyday media demonstrates, the notion of 'media ecologies' is not particularly new. It has, however, been deployed by a number of contemporary media theorists to describe and account for the distinct characteristics of new media culture and everyday life.

Mizuko Ito contextualises her ethnographic studies of Japanese children and young people's playful engagement with the transmedial worlds of *Yu-Gi-Oh!* and *Hamtaro* in these ecological terms. The characters, dramas and worlds of *Yu-Gi-Oh!* and *Hamtaro*, like *Pokémon* before them, are distributed across videogames, trading cards, books, comics, toys, merchandising and television and cinema. Ito uses the popular Japanese term 'media mix' for these phenomena, a term synonymous with Henry Jenkins's 'transmediality' discussed in **3.22**. Her work echoes Jenkins's emphasis on the creative possibilities of these media ecologies, indeed she argues that their young consumers must engage with them productively, an 'activist mobilization of the imagination':

> New convergent media such as *Pokémon* require a reconfigured conceptual apparatus that takes productive and creative activity at the 'consumer' level as a given rather than as an addendum or an exception.
>
> (Ito, undated)

This approach suggests that media technologies have always generated changes in the everyday environment, but that with transmediality at the level of creative media production and digital convergence at the technological level, we are seeing a significant qualitative shift in the intensity and characteristics of connections between people, technologies,

4.9 A monstrous ecology

imaginations, and economies in lived popular technoculture. The Internet in particular mixes old and new media, develops geographically dispersed yet socially intense communicative and participatory networks, while from the establishment of common technical formats and standards in hardware (USB, flash memory) and software (MP3, AVI) has emerged a digital ecosystem of hybrid devices (cameraphones, MP3 sunglasses, USB powered and controlled toys) and chains of media reproduction, through sharing, manipulation and multiplication of digital images, sounds and sequences.

Whereas in the late 1990s Daniel Chandler could describe children's digital communication culture as the 'little hole in the wall' drilled through the construction of a home page, the current media environment in many children's lives in the developed world today is one in which the actual and the virtual worlds have thoroughly interpenetrated. Communicative and entertainment practices, activities and media such as MSN, texting, online games, blogging, social networking sites, etc. are not so much holes in everyday life as its cultural warp and weft, filling a few blank minutes at the bus stop, enlivening homework on the PC, forging and sustaining friendships and networks, playing and creating in the virtual worlds of videogames and media mixes. On the one hand this appears to make 'cyberspace' less exotic and more like the pre-digital communicative activities of (terrestrial) telephony, chat, letter-writing and socialising, yet on the other the sheer accessibility and ubiquity of these new media both through the home PC and broadband connection, and on the move via mobile phones, surely marks a qualitative difference from both pre-digital everyday communication and early Internet communication.

See **4.5.2** for more on *Pokémon* as playful media environment

4.10 Powering up

4.3.4 Technology and newness in everyday life

To differentiate between stages of children's everyday media culture both *within* the digital era as well as before it brings us again to the question of the newness of new media, of how it is understood and experienced.

CASE STUDY 4.5: Television, innovation and technocultural form

Raymond Williams, writing about the new generation of televisual communication technologies under development in the early 1970s, such as cable and satellite systems, observed that 'some of the new technical developments seem to open the way to institutions of a radically different kind from either "public service" or "commercial" broadcasting; indeed of a different kind, in some cases, from "broadcasting" itself' (Williams 1990a: 135). This section of his book *Television: technology and cultural form* is interesting on two counts. First it anticipates the undermining of long-established institutions of broadcasting through new technical and institutional developments. These include the advent of the multiple channels and niche markets of cable, the time-shifting of programme viewing made possible by VHS and later hard-disc video recording and on-demand services, all of which break down the synchronicity of television, and threaten commercial television's reliance on advertising. These developments have accelerated in the Internet era with peer-to-peer sharing of television programmes as digital files, and the fragmentation of such programmes into bite-size and manipulated clips on YouTube. The Internet also appears to have rendered obsolete attempts to use cable television for more participatory and democratic ends. Second, it is telling that Williams lets slip his usual careful resistance to any hint of technological determinism: here the technical developments *themselves* are opening the way to radical change. At times of rapid technological innovation it can be hard to maintain a purely culturalist position.

The sheer familiarity and mundanity of television as everyday media culture makes it a useful case study for examining the notion of the newness of new media as experienced in everyday life. It is common for media scholars to debunk excitement about new media technologies by pointing out how quickly these novelties become familiar to us and hence 'old'. Given the rapid adoption of, say, email or social networking sites, it could be argued that new media are already thoroughly assimilated into everday life and therefore no longer 'new', and therefore to attempt to analyse them as novel, revolutionary or transformational is mistaken.

Recent developments in television clearly illustrate this: flat screen LCD televisions and 'home cinema' sound systems are now common, and whereas particularly enormous or high definition screens are still remarkable, they may well not be for long. The challenge then is how to study something so thoroughly woven into the fabric of domestic time and space, to use Roger Silverstone's phrase in his book on television in everyday life (Silverstone 1994: 3). To pursue this textile metaphor, the fabric of everyday life is rapidly stitched back together after each new device or system tears it, and so to examine it we must unpick it again.

First, it is important to note that being familiar with something does not necessarily mean that it is understood. Asserting the mundanity of television overlooks the remarkable extent of its grasp of imagination, shared cultural understanding and communication, and its hold on the rhythms and spaces of everyday life. New media technologies lose their novelty but they don't disappear – it is perhaps precisely at the moment that they become banal and accepted that their full effects are realised (see for instance Miller and Slater 2000 on the 'naturalisation' of the Internet in Trinidad). In debunking wild futurological claims, we should be careful not to miss the very real, ongoing, yet hard to grasp, transformations of everyday life. We might instead try to imagine everyday life *without* media change. For example, in a line from the television sitcom *Friends*, Joey exclaims 'You don't have a TV? What do you point your furniture at?'

Second, it is useful to question the significance or value accorded to different kinds of change. Cybercultural studies is enthralled by paradigm shifts, new ages and near futures. Ethnographic research in everyday media culture is, at its best, sensitive to the microincrements of change. A good example of this is Bernadette Flynn's wry comparison of Playstation 2 advertisements – in which a living room and its furniture are devastated by the promised gameplay experience – and the actual lived negotiations between children, parents, domestic space and other media practices and routines (television viewing) she observes in her ethnographic studies. This latter is beautifully illustrated by a photograph from one of Flynn's field visits.

4.11 New media ergonomics
(Flynn 2003: 568)

The changes here are minute but significant:

During the play session recording, Jack lay on floor cushions in front of the lounge chairs operating the console handset whilst simultaneously chatting to friends on the telephone. Whilst the optimal distance for playing a video game is in between that for a television set and computer screen, the layout of [the living room] imposed the optimal distance for viewing television. Removed from the restraint of the lounge suite, Jack, like many players, adopted a position on floor cushions more suited to gameplay.

(Flynn 2003: 568)

Here is a complex relationship between established objects of cultural studies of everyday life and media studies of audiences: domestic media practices and social relationships (television viewing, telephone use); the cultural traditions of furniture and room layout and the ways of living they reflect; negotiations within household power relationships (who gets to play, or watch, where, and when), etc. There are other changes: the presence of the console in the living room brings 'an often disordered, temporary and flexible arrangement within the more traditional organization of the living room' (Flynn 2003: 571). Flynn notes a significant, gendered, trend in children's culture in which boys' play shifts from outside (the street, the arcade) to the bedroom and living room, transporting 'one system of sexually organized space – the arcade, into another – the more traditional female living-room space of domestic leisure' (Flynn 2003: 569, see also McNamee 1998, Jenkins 1998).

However (and this is our reading of Flynn's findings) more elusive objects are also in play: consumption/viewing/playing positions are established as much by the material affordances of different kinds of furniture, their ergonomic relationships with human bodies, and the capacities of the particular media device, as by cultural conventions or discourses. The point here is that the *materiality* of the furniture, the media technologies, and the human bodies is a crucial factor. These artefacts and bodies have effects on, and shape, social forms and relationships as well as being effects of, and shaped by, them. This shift of focus suggests a different attention to everyday life, an attention to the reciprocity between the social and the material, and suggests further that, from an altered conceptual point of view, the human and the non-human may not be fundamentally distinct: they at the very least share a materiality.

This discussion hints at some of the conceptual questions to come in this section, particularly those that arise in the rethinking of human and technological agency in everyday life. It also raises the question of how the significance and texture of everyday technoculture can be fruitfully traced and studied. We will now turn our attention to one area in which Cultural and Media Studies, along with other fields concerned with new media cultures, have felt more confident in their observations of technocultural change and newness: subjectivity and identity.

4.4 The everyday posthuman: new media and identity

In very general terms the various discourses of new media studies often concur that new media herald genuine change in relation to human identity or subjectivity. This may be in terms of an ever more thorough integration of everyday life and the mediasphere (Kinder 1991; Hutchby and Moran-Ellis 2001); shifting relationships between the public and private realms or between the individual (or local community) and the global reach of popular media and cultural forms (Mackay 1997; Moores 1993b); the claims for radical experimentation or play with identity in some Internet media (Stone 1995; Poster 1995a; Turkle 1996); or an increasing intimacy or hybridisation between the human and the technological figured in the cyborg (Haraway 1990; Gray 1995).

So questions of the relationship between the human and the technological in new media studies are generally addressed in relation to questions of identity and subjectivity. However, in research on media technologies and identity or subjectivity it is not always clear exactly what is meant by 'identity'. On the one hand it may indicate little more than the day-to-day choices about how an individual chooses to present him or herself to the world (choice of outfit for the day, preference in mobile phone model and ringtone, etc.), on the other a sense of identity 'under construction' implies more fundamental changes in the sense of self, closer

The following discussion should be seen as closely linked with, and complementary to, sections **3.16** through to **3.21**. In Part 3 we cover theories of identity and networks in relation to the constitution of communities. Evidently community and individual identity are inseparable; we separate them here in order to address the different overall concerns of Part 3 and this part of the book. Thus here we are concerned more with the local, domestic uses of new media, whilst Part 3 looks to the broader – though interrelated – public, political and economic spheres to the claims of cybercultural studies. The rest of this section will examine claims that identity and subjectivity have undergone, or are undergoing, profound changes in the age of new media, and suggest the implications of such claims for an understanding of contemporary lived experience.

4.4.1 From identity 'under construction' to social networks

The web is now the most widely accessed Internet medium and can be seen as both continuous with, and offering distinct new possibilities for, established relationships between public and private space, public and private selves. With the web's inception in the mid-1990s, the personal home page soon came to be a relatively accessible, and distinctly new, form of media 'production'. Designing and publishing a personal website was relatively easy and inexpensive, and allowed the designer to address a (potential) worldwide audience, or engage with a geographically distributed community of interest well beyond the scope of earlier DIY media production. The term 'home page' itself highlighted the relays between public and private space. Even in web browsers and large-scale commercial websites today this reassuringly domestic terminology offers the lost browser a return to a familiar page.

Daniel Chandler studied early individual websites and interviewed their designers. He linked their production with other forms of personal documentation, communication or samizdat publishing (diaries, newsletters, 'round robin' letters, fanzines), but pointed out that where home pages differed was precisely their potential for a global audience. The spare room or bedroom shift in their relationship with the outside world, becoming permeable:

> a home in the real world is, among other things, a way of keeping the world out . . . An online home, on the other hand, is a little hole you drill in the wall of your real home to let the world in.
>
> (John Seabrook, quoted in Chandler 1998).

Chandler's main interest, however, was in the ways in which individuals present themselves on websites. Borrowing a metaphor from the conventions of web page production, Chandler argues that just as incomplete web pages are often labelled as 'under construction', so too are the identities of their designers. He describes the aesthetics and construction methods of home page design as 'bricolage'. This term originates in anthropology, denoting the improvised use by pre-industrial peoples of everyday materials and objects to hand in the symbolic practices of art and rituals. The term has been adopted by Cultural Studies to describe the appropriation and manipulation – even subversion – of the meanings of commodities by youth subcultures:

> the extraordinary symbolic creativity of the multitude of ways in which young people use, humanize, decorate and invest with meanings their common and immediate life spaces and social practices – personal styles, and choice of clothes; selective and active use of music, TV, magazines; decoration of bedrooms.
>
> (Willis 1990: 2)

See also Hebdige (1979: 103–106)

Susanna Stern also makes the connection between the content and aesthetics of young people's public presentation and self-expression through web page production and the bricolage of the bedroom wall. Through her research into the home pages of adolescent girls, she argues that the construction and presentation of identity is mapped onto 'real world' gendered practices and spaces. Thus, Stern's research does not find 'fluid' identities as such, rather a more complex picture of self-presentation and construction of image: 'in this study, girls' home pages were ultimately regarded as texts that reflect in some way the selves girls think they are, the selves they wish to become, and most likely, the selves they wish others to see' (Stern 1999: 24).

There are distinct approaches to self-representation in the sites studied, which Stern summarises as 'spirited', 'sombre' and 'self-conscious' sites. Each of these develops new ways of making private practices of identity construction public, from light-hearted listings of likes and dislikes to the presentation of very personal, often painful, reflections or poetry, modes of writing previously confined to diaries and journals. Stern takes this further: the bedroom as a 'safe' if restricted social space for girls is transformed through the use of Internet media into a space for self-expression which is more public, but still safe:

> It seems likely that for some girls, the web presents the 'safe company' they need to 'speak their experience' and 'say what is true'. It also seems to grant some girls the freedom to 'develop their sense of possibility and to experience themselves as active agents in their own lives'.
>
> (Stern 1999: 38)

In recent years the weblog or blog has displaced the personal home page as the primary Internet medium for individual professional and non-professional self-expression. The key distinctions from the home page are that no knowledge of HTML editing software or FTP is required to set up a simple blog; the chronological journal or diary-like structure suggests and shapes a particular kind of engagement and content (a more or less frequent updating of thoughts, observations, comments and links to other blogs or sites of interest); and blog software facilitates and encourages other bloggers to link to and comment on the site. Thus the blog lends itself more to sustained and continuous communication than does the home page:

> the ability to archive blog posts creates a way to scaffold on previous impressions and expressions; thus, constructing identity can be a continuous process for adolescents, and one to which they can refer. Finally, when blog software offers ways to provide feedback or link to other bloggers, this can foster a sense of peer group relationships.
>
> (Huffaker and Calvert 2005)

Other Internet media and sites have developed their form and content in response to the particular technical format and cultural conventions of the blog, notably YouTube's support for the embedding of its video clips in blog posts, or facilities for linking to users' photograph albums on sites such as Flickr. Social networking sites such as MySpace and Facebook certainly build on the same long-established traditions of vanity publishing and journal-keeping; they often assume, or attempt to initiate, an ongoing communication network with their readers and viewers. They encourage the acquisition of online contacts ('friends'), providing all manner of channels of private and semi-public communication along the lines of email and messaging, but also with more playful modes such as quizzes, remediations of card and board games, virtual gifts, automated comparisons of tastes in literature and film, drawings and photographs, and games, such as Facebook's zombies, that exploit the interwoven networks of friends in a kind of ludic viral marketing.

If web home pages were sites of self-presentation or identity construction through the bricolage of interests, images and links, then personal blogs and social network profiles could be seen to add an ongoing identity *performance* both individually and collectively, driven by Web 2.0 technologies of multimedia, content management, network building and persistent communication.

4.4.2 Virtual identity

> Our interaction with the world around us is increasingly mediated by computer technology, and [thus] bit by digital bit, we are being 'Borged', as devotees of *Star Trek: The Next Generation* would have it – transformed into cyborgian hybrids of technology and biology through our ever-more-frequent interaction with machines, or with one another through technological interfaces.
>
> (Dery 1994: 6)

The language and concepts of cybercultural studies are shot through with science fiction and cyberpunk imagery, blurring distinctions between the human and machine in near-future worlds replete with media technologies, or riddled with gateways to virtual worlds. These discourses and their cyberpunk imaginary are widely critiqued in those strands of new media studies drawn from Cultural Studies, wary of assumptions of radical newness and the transcendence of historical and social divisions and conflicts via new technologies and their alternative, disembodied worlds. Feminist Cultural Studies in particular has questioned theories that assume a separation of mind (or consciousness or identity) from the body, evident in cybercultural studies (Bassett 1997; Kember 1998), cyberpunk fiction (Squires 1996) and computer sciences such as cybernetics and AI (Hayles 1999).

Yet there are resonances across this discursive divide. Cultural and Media Studies and Feminist Cultural and Media Studies make far-reaching claims for the mutability of the human subject in a heavily mediated culture, whether characterised by print and electronic media, or computer-based media. Moreover, important work on technoscience and technoculture emerges from both Cultural Studies and Feminist Cultural Studies, work that asks serious questions about the nature and volatility of the subject or of identity in a time of rapid technological change.

Theories of the virtual age responding to new computer media such as VR, the Internet and videogames in the 1980s and early 1990s promised the transformation of the everyday, or transport into realms far distant from the everyday. There was a tendency to define these new media and their users in opposition to the embodied and material: the virtual versus the real, play versus consumption, Utopia versus the mundane politics and contractions of the real world, cyberspace and VR versus commercial communications and information media, identity versus corporeality (and all the body's historical and cultural 'baggage'). To question some of the assumptions of the 'virtual age' thesis is not to argue that identities are not being constructed or transformed, or to deny that our increasingly intimate relationships with machines and networks challenge long-held conceptual oppositions between the local and global, public and private, or consumption and production. Indeed media technologies can be seen as implicated in a shifting sense of identity in numerous ways, including the following:

- through changes in mass media: we have seen, for example, how developments in television broadcasting can facilitate the presentation or performance of identity;

- through consumption as an active practice of bricolage, constructed through the images and consumer goods we 'choose', a process perhaps given new impetus by the interactive and reproductive power of digital software;

- identity can be 'constructed' in cyberspace or virtual worlds;

- as individuals within virtual communities;

- virtual reality and cyberspace are undermining (our understanding of) the real, within which we have constructed our identities;

- an ever more intimate relationship with technologies and media from the Internet to genetic engineering, raising questions of the boundaries between the human body and consciousness, machines and networks;

- that new media are only a part, however significant, of the impact of broader historical, economic and/or cultural change on identity.

As the excitement of the early 1990s and its assumptions of widespread entry (or upload) of human consciousness into virtual reality fades into cultural history, critiques of its naivety increasingly seem to have been misplaced, as attacks on straw men, running the risk of missing significant concepts and objects of study bound up in this technocultural idealism. If we put the fictional cyborgs in Dery's statement to one side (for now), the statement can be reread: it is clear that interaction with the world *is* increasingly mediated by computer technology, people *do* experience ever-more-frequent interaction with sophisticated machines – and with one another – through technological interfaces. Increasingly intimate relationships with machines and networks *do* challenge long-held conceptual and lived oppositions between the local and global, public and private, consumption and production, or as we shall see later, between the human and the non-human.

The discursive constitution of identity, subjectivity, and old and new media and technologies is thoroughly tangled. As we have noted, 'identity' and 'subjectivity' are rarely defined, are used differently in different discourses, and are often apparently interchangeable. Also, the term 'real world' should be read with caution. Virtual environments and media are no less real for being virtual – they exist as both data and lived experience. What follows is a short survey of how new media studies have constituted the relationship between identity, subjectivity, the body, technology and media.

What is new about networks?

New media studies generally concerns itself with networked new media, and the Internet media in particular. Much of the early excitement about the possibilities for users to present or perform alternative identities, to *play* with identity was predicated on the simple fact that Internet users were geographically remote from one another. Hence conventional markers of identity become irrelevant because users cannot see each other. This then, it has been argued, facilitates new online cultures based on meritocratic principles in which often marginalised people (the young, women, the disabled, black people) can be accepted for their knowledge or communicational skill.

> In bulletin boards like The Well, people connect with strangers without much of the social baggage that divides and alienates. Without visual cues about gender, age, ethnicity, and social status, conversations open up in directions that otherwise might be avoided. Participants in these virtual communities often express themselves with little inhibition and dialogues flourish and develop quickly.
>
> (Poster 1995a: 90)

From this, some make the bolder claim that with online communication in 'cyberspace' or virtual reality, not only can we not be seen, but we are liberated to present our identities in new ways, or more profoundly, develop new identities – playful identities in which gender, race, species even, become fluid. Sherry Turkle has addressed the individual's sense of self in computer networked communication. She sees networks as potential 'identity workshops' in which identity is refracted through role-play and remote interaction with other users: 'The self is not only decentered but multiplied without limit. There is an unparalleled opportunity to play with one's identity and to "try out" new ones' (Turkle 1996: 356).

From this, early cybercultural studies sometimes made the bolder claim that in online communication in cyberspace, not only can we 'float free of biological and sociocultural determinants', but in some way our bodies are left behind in 'incorporeal interaction' (Dery 1994: 3). Thus not only can we present ourselves as a different gender, race or species, we could be disembodied (see **5.4.4**). While the fevered predictions of the early 1990s about the imminent uploading of human consciousness to cyberspace may have faded, current academic and popular debates on digital culture often still assume a fundamental separation between actual space and virtual space, and between the actual domestic, everyday lives of the users and players of virtual spaces and their presence (through avatars for example) within the virtual.

Does then the everyday engagement with Internet media escape established patterns of play and the negotiations and constructions of identity in 'old' media consumption? On what notions of historical, technological or cultural change are these incorporeal virtual identities based? Alluquere Roseanne Stone asks 'what is new about networking?' and gives two possible answers. The first is 'nothing', i.e. communicating via a computer network is little different from using the telephone (though this overlooks the possibility that early telephony might in itself have been a profound proto-cybercultural experience!). The second possible answer is 'everything': networks could be seen as more like public theatre than 'old' media, as new arenas for social experience and dramatic communication, 'for qualitative interaction, dialogue and conversation' (Stone 1995: 16). Stone asserts that the second answer is true and argues that this has profound implications for our sense of our selves as bodies in space, our sense of 'presence'. She argues that the relationship between the material nature of the body – the 'physical envelope' – and the identity with which it once seemed coterminous is 'embedded in much larger shifts in cultural beliefs and practices [including] repeated transgressions of the traditional concept of the body's physical envelope and of the locus of human agency' (Stone 1995: 16). For Stone, these larger shifts are symptomatic of nothing less than the end of the 'mechanical age', and the beginning of the 'virtual age' (Stone 1995: 17). Others concur. Mark Poster is one contemporary writer on new media who sees the advent of electronic media as analogous in historical importance to that of movable type. New media mark the end of the modern era and usher in postmodern subjectivity:

In the twentieth century electronic media are supporting an equally profound transformation of cultural identity. Telephone, radio, film, television, the computer and now their integration as 'multimedia' reconfigure words, sounds and images so as to cultivate new configurations of individuality. If modern society may be said to foster an individual who is rational, autonomous, centered, and stable . . . then perhaps a postmodern society is emerging which nurtures forms of identity different from, even opposite to those of modernity. And electronic communications technologies significantly enhance these postmodern possibilities.

(Poster 1995a: 80)

Cutting across cybercultural (and postmodernist) thought we can see quite diverse assumptions about relationships between the individual or subject, media technology, and historical and cultural change. The question we must now ask is: what role might media technologies play in effecting or facilitating changes in identity or subjectivity? As Poster indicates above, the development of print through movable type in the mid-fifteenth century is generally seen as the first mass medium and is often cited as a key factor in the development of modern rationality and subjectivity, and the undermining of the medieval religious world (see also McLuhan 1962, Birkerts 1994, and Provenzo 1986).

It could be argued that the epochal shift from the mechanical to the virtual is not quite so clear cut. Poster for example seems confused as to whether his 'postmodern possibilities' are the product of new media in particular, or electronic media (including television and radio) in general. The above quote suggests the latter, but elsewhere he specifically identifies digital media as the point of rupture. Against the 'alienation' of 'one-way' broadcast media, he posits the many-to-many system of the Internet:

> the question of the mass media is seen not simply as that of sender/receiver, producer/consumer, ruler/ruled. The shift to a decentralized network of communications makes senders receivers, producers consumers, rulers ruled, upsetting the logic of understanding of the first media age.
>
> (Poster 1995a: 87–88)

Stone, however, is clear on the distinction between old and new. It rests on the networked structure of new media use. Thus 'one-to-one' telephone conversations and 'one-to-many' model of broadcast media are superseded by 'many-to-many' communications facilitated by Internet media

4.4.3 Virtual ethnography

A comprehensive understanding of relationships between identity, technologies, and everyday life must draw on ethnographic approaches and description. The ethnography of new media cultures faces distinct challenges. There are questions of the *sites*, as well as the subjects, of ethnographies of new media cultures. Christine Hine outlines an established view of ethnography as 'the sustained presence of an ethnographer in the field setting, combined with intensive engagement with the everyday life of the inhabitants of the field site, which make for the special kind of knowledge we call ethnographic' (Hine 2000: 63–64). Traditional ethnography then is site-specific: Miller and Slater argue that even Internet ethnography can be sited in actual places, 'by investigating how Internet technologies are being understood and assimilated somewhere in particular . . .' (Miller and Slater 2000:1). How then to conduct an ethnography that describes both actual and virtual spaces?

Hine makes (after Clifford Geertz) a key distinction between two broad and contradictory approaches to 'traditional' ethnography:

> The ethnographer is able to use this sustained interaction to 'reduce the puzzlement' (Geertz, 1993: 16) which other people's ways of life can evoke. At the same time, ethnography can be a device for inducing that same puzzlement by 'displacing the dulling sense of familiarity with which the mysteriousness of our own ability to relate perceptively to one another is concealed from us' (Geertz, 1993: 14).
>
> (Hine 2000: 64)

This latter strategy, of inducing puzzlement (perhaps denaturalising, 'making strange') is particularly suggestive for the study of the researcher's own culture (or subcultures or groups thereof). Hine is clear that her intentions, in studying the Internet, are thus oriented; such an approach allows for the description and articulation of the familiar and the strange, the established and the novel. The following case study exemplifies this.

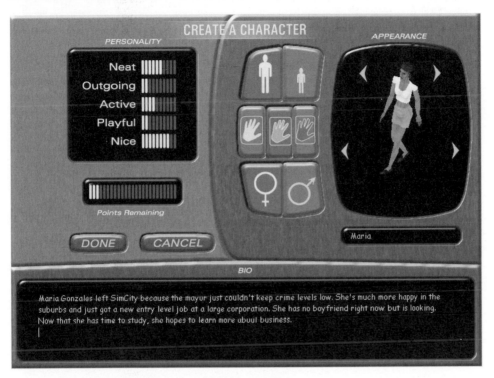

4.12 Identity play? *The Sims*.

There is now a substantial body of 'virtual ethnographic' research, the most interesting of which traces the interpenetration of virtual and actual worlds (see for example Hine 2000, Slater 1998, Taylor 2006, Dixon and Weber 2007). The attention of this research to the textures of actual/virtual cultures and events is rich and productive, but it can be noted that its primary concern is often with the conversations and relationships between human participants and the broader contexts of language and culture that position them. Explicit attention is rarely given to the nature or specific effects of the technologies that facilitate or afford these cultures and identity games in the first place. This accounts for new media studies' focus on networked communication, on the relationships between humans across the various Internet media. It also explains the reluctance to study direct relationships between the human and the technological in digital environments, for example that between player-avatars and the non-human agents (bots) in online games. There are important exceptions to this general rule. For example, Turkle's assessment of the possibilities of identity play online is based very much in her earlier work on the relationship between computer users, their identities, their computers and the programs (including games) they were using. It is not only information and images that this technology allows us to experiment with and manipulate, she argues, but also the user's personality, identity and sexuality (Turkle 1984: 15). Here then identity play is

CASE STUDY 4.6: Cyberferret and play with virtual gender

Caroline Bassett's ethnographic study 'Virtually Gendered: life in an online world' (1997) undermines assumptions that virtual worlds (and our identities within them) fully escape the actual world, that visitors to them leave behind their sociocultural contexts. She notes the diverse and ostensibly emancipatory presentations of self in the playful virtual environment of Xerox's PARC research centre online 'world': LambdaMOO. As with other MUDs, LambdaMOO has a text-based interface, and citizens present themselves through three basic attributes: name, gender and appearance, all represented to other users as textual description. They can also 'build' themselves a textual home, its design reflecting their new identity. For example exploring ambiguity and androgyny:

Neuterworld.

A bland, white room. Clean air is sucked into your nostrils and unclean exhalation is sucked out of the room through the huge roof mounted extractor fan. A sense of peace pervades the whole room. Bara is here.

Bara.

A tall, dark individual of slight build. This person is curious in that it is impossible for you to tell whether it is male or female!

It is sleeping.

(Bassett 1997: 541)

Whilst sympathetic to the possibilities of MUDs and related online communication forms, Bassett questions uncritical notions of new free-floating identities in cyberspace, observing that whilst some participants do experiment with very different characteristics, or multiple 'identities', this is by no means practised by all. Thus while some take advantage of the transgressive genders allowed by the MUD:

E looks content, and eir eyes beam at you with a kind of amusement . . . the black suede mini hugs Peri's hips and barely covers eir crotch, black suede glistening in the light or lack there of. Carrying bodysuit, nipple clamps . . .

E carries a [hash] note on Eir gender in Real Life . . .

(Bassett 1997: 545)

Most adhere to stereotyped constructions of masculinity or femininity:

Beige Guest

One luscious babe, with a flowing mane of brilliant red hair, with crystal emerald eyes, and the most enchanting smile on earth.

(Bassett 1997: 546)

Bassett notes that it is probable that such hyperfeminine presentation is almost certainly that of a male participant. Even shifting identity to an inanimate object or animal does not automatically mean an escape from the gendered structures of Real Life:

Cyberferret is a ferret . . . with several cybernetic implants. One leg is bionic, and his entire skeletal system is made of titanium. He is looking for something to KILL!

(Bassett 1997: 549)

Cyberferret aside, most online identities within LambdaMOO are, regardless of their play with gender, overwhelmingly presented as being white, attractive and young. This counters any straightforward assumption that identity construction is free from real life constraints and distinctions. Bassett draws on Judith Butler's concept of identity formation as 'performative', that is to say that identity (and in gender in particular) is not so much constructed as constantly materialised through acts in language.

Despite this, Bassett argues for two progressive readings of 'the small world' of Lambda. The first is that it highlights gender as constructed and 'unnatural', and second she implies that Real Life discourses are not entirely dominant in cyberspace, that Lambda does provide 'spaces for disruption, for the possibility of gender-play, and for the emergence of new forms of multiple subjectivity' (Bassett 1997: 550). Identities and subject positions persist across the actual and the virtual, but not without the possibility of transformation and play.

effected through the feedback between individual and machine, not between individuals through networks. This raises a couple of important points. The cybercultural paradigm of free-floating identity play in virtual worlds is not necessarily predicated on remote communication between humans: the technological imaginary of networked virtual reality is rooted in the interactive engagement with the space of the computer game. It follows then that, at the very least, new media studies' conceptualisation of identity and subjectivity should encompass the direct relationship between human and machine as well as the relationships between humans facilitated by machines.

For example, the characteristics of online 'identity' have shifted somewhat with the advent of graphically sophisticated persistent virtual worlds of *Second Life* and games such as *World of Warcraft*. Rather than the player's descriptive skills, the avatar is developed through the software conventions and defaults of the world itself and time, application, aptitude and technical resources are required to produce a more customised avatar. To engage fully in these worlds and realise their ludic and creative potential also requires substantial investments of time, effort and ability (and money). In *World of Warcraft* this means the forging and maintenance of teams of players to undertake quests, levelling up through the acquisition (within the diegesis of the game) of financial, armorial and supernatural resources. Similarly in *Second Life*, to build a house, and to learn how to make (and then distribute or sell) virtual objects, requires many hours learning the software, developing skills, networking and expertise.

Whatever identity play might be evident in these everyday virtual practices, it is only one of a broader range of playful (and work-like) activities and processes, shaped by the affordances of the software and the social (and game) rules established by both the corporations that run these worlds (for *World of Warcraft* and *Second Life*: Blizzard and Linden Labs respectively) and the protocols and norms established, negotiated and fought for by the players themselves (in this sense these graphic virtual worlds are similar to social networking sites). Tanya Krzywinska suggests that

> Identity play is only one aspect [of *World of Warcraft*], however, and for many it tends to tail off after a while as it is harder to maintain the more you play. Transformational elements do not simply operate in terms of identity play; becoming more skilled at playing the game, making for a greater sense of agency and acting as an *apparent* foil to the forces of determination, is also a form of pleasure-generating transformation.
>
> (Krzywinska 2007: 117).

What is needed is a model of enquiry that factors in both the intangible nature of subjectivity and the materiality of the technologies and techniques with which subjectivity is interwoven.

CASE STUDY 4.7: Gender and technicity in *Quake*

4.13 Monstrous feminine bodies, armour, and the technicities of skinning and drawing. Left: *Quake* skin by kind permission of Milla, Right: Machogirl. Videogame character designed by 10 year old girl, London 1995

Relationships between identity and everyday technologies are *material* as well as imaginary. An awareness of computers may offer ways of thinking about the self, but users, programmers and players are changing, working with, their subjectivity in learning to manipulate the hardware and software. Taste and preference, self-presentation and performance in popular technoculture are inseparable from the embodied nature of technical expertise and dexterity.

Videogame culture is a clear example of this. One may think of oneself as a gameplayer, as others might think of themselves as film buffs, or as music fans, but a player identity can only be fully inhabited through marked levels of technical competence. The videogame is an unforgiving medium: while it is possible to sit through a demanding art film for example, attempting to decode its images and intentions, if a player does not understand the game's interface or hasn't the experience or dexterity to handle its controls or solve its puzzles, then they are stuck, not players at all.

There are other barriers to a gameplaying identity, particularly in collective, online games. Helen W. Kennedy has studied the gendered culture of the online FPS *Quake*, both the games themselves and the Internet forums, fan websites, communities and amateur production of game elements that surround the games. Her interviews with female players reveal a range of strategies deployed to gain entry to this predominantly (and sometimes aggressively) masculine culture (Kennedy 2007, see also Dovey and Kennedy 2006). As well as developing expertise in playing the game itself, these include setting up websites, forming women-only 'clans' for multiplayer competition, and designing 'skins', graphics that can be loaded into the game to transform the appearance of the player's avatar. Kennedy points out that while these women are individually and collectively negotiating and constructing the possibilities for femininity in the hypercharged and ultraviolent killing floors of *Quake*, these identities are inseparable from the material technocultural phenomena of both the intense embodied pleasures of gameplay and the acquisition and exploitation of technical knowledge in the design of skins and websites.

> You have to be able to use the mouse for more than just point and click you have to sort of be able to use it around space which is a bit different and it's easy to end up looking at the ceiling or getting stuck in corners and becoming frag bait. Oh, yeah, and your left and right hands are doing totally different things, you've got to really know where all the keys are . . . at first I couldn't get it all sorted out, changing weapons, jumping, moving around and shooting it was all a bit much and my mouse hand would be doing one thing and I'd have to look at the keyboard to try and find the right keys . . . then after a while it all sort of clicks and you're just staring at the screen and your hands are going like crazy and you just sort of do it all on automatic and you feel like it's you in there, sneaking round corners and fragging that poor little eyeball on legs to bits . . . (Interview with author, Xena, *Quake Interviews*, December 2001).
>
> (Kennedy 2007: 123)

The virtual world of *Quake* is populated by figurations of cyborgs (not least those created by these female gameplayers themselves), but, Kennedy argues, gameplay, gameplayers and game culture are literally cyborgian, a circuit of 'machines, code and bodies' (Kennedy 2007: 127). Identity then is 'technicity', which here encapsulates 'taste, technological competence and the use of technology as a means through which to form and express individual and group identities' (Kennedy 2007: 137). Expertise, knowledge, dexterity, training, aptitude, preference, and creative practices are all techniques in the technological sense, and are all the stuff of everyday work and play. They are shaped by, and shape, bodies, minds and machines.

4.4.4 The subject of technology

To make sense of the varying claims of these theories of changing identities in relation to media technologies, it is important to be clear what is meant by identity – or rather at least to be clear that it is not clear what is meant by identity. Within Cultural and Media Studies 'identity' as a concept is generally interchangeable with 'subjectivity' (Hall 1997; Butler 2000). Sometimes the terms have different connotations. Whereas, for example, an individual designing a MySpace page or writing their daily blog post may choose aspects of their interests and personal life to present as their identity, their *subjectivity* may be seen as less accessible to conscious manipulation, as more fundamental to that individual's place in the world and its hierarchies. Subjectivity, then, may be established through broader historical and cultural contexts, and positions individuals within the power structures of gender, class, and race.

Though central to modern notions of individuality and liberty, it should be noted that the word 'subject' also carries connotations of subjection, of being an individual constituted within or by power structures, 'a subject of the Crown' for example. So, on the one hand this is a concept which constitutes an internal, private sense of self in individuals, but on the other it refers to the positioning of the individual within society. Michel Foucault's work is particularly influential here. He argues that these two concepts of the subject are not contradictory but inseparable: the very rationality celebrated by the Enlightenment is not a universal principle, but a discourse which positions some individuals as rational but others as criminal or insane (Foucault 1989).

Descartes' famous dictum 'Cogito ergo sum' (I think therefore I am) is emblematic of the Enlightenment subject's ideal existence in the higher realms of thought and reason. As we will see, this philosophical separation of mind and body, or Cartesian dualism, has proved immensely popular in thinking through the status of thought and communication in cyberspace

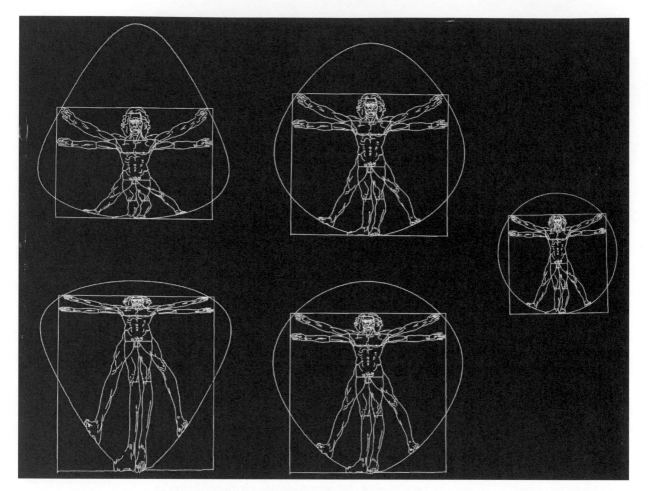

4.14 Charles Csuri, 'Leonardo Two' (1966). Renaissance man, distorted by computer algorithms.

The subject is a historical category of existence, emerging in the Renaissance, the beginning of the modern world. It can be seen as marking the end of the medieval worldview of a static, God-ordained universe of fixed hierarchies in which individuals and social classes, along with angels, animals and minerals, all had their immutable place:

> The Enlightenment subject was based on a conception of the human person as a fully centred, unified individual, endowed with the capacities of reason, consciousness and action, whose 'centre' consisted of an inner core [identity] which first emerged when the subject was born, and unfolded with it, while remaining essentially the same – continuous or 'identical' with itself – throughout the individual's existence.
>
> (Hall *et al*. 1992: 275)

With the Reformation, the emerging social and economic forces of mercantile capitalism increased the mobility of individual traders, and with the beginnings of urbanisation established social relationships were shaken, requiring new relationships between individuals and society. The category of an autonomous individual helped to make sense of this new, non-natural order. Ideas of the freedom of the rational individual informed both the French Revolution and the development of liberalism in economics and politics.

If the subject, then, is the figure of Man (Hall *et al.* (1992) point out that the Enlightenment subject was generally assumed to be male) in the modern world, and if subjectivity is changing in some fundamental way, the argument runs that we must be seeing the emergence of a postmodern subject. Hall describes how this putative new subject is conceptualised as 'having no fixed, essential or permanent identity. Identity becomes a "movable feast": formed and transformed continuously in relation to the ways we are represented or addressed in the cultural systems which surround us.' This is not always the liberating, pluralising of identity celebrated in postmodernist identity politics however. It could be catastrophic hyperreality: 'as systems of meaning and cultural representation multiply, we are confronted by a bewildering, fleeting multiplicity of possible identities, any one of which we could identify with – at least temporarily' (Hall *et al.* 1992: 277).

These diverse histories and hierarchies of subjective change are important to bear in mind as they underlie any idea of what subjective change might be today. All of the key positions covered here reject any idea of historical or cultural change as smooth and evolutionary. All are based on an understanding of distinct periods in history. Foucault, for instance, in charting the history (or 'archaeology') of knowledge, sees a profound break in our ideas of self in the Enlightenment, which established the rational and ostensibly universal principles on which the modern Western world is based. Other arguments seem to imply a modernist subject (i.e. late nineteenth century to mid-twentieth) rather than this modern one (i.e. Enlightenment or post-Renaissance), seeing the coming of industrial society and mass urbanisation as an environment that necessitates subjective change. Some discourses see different qualitative levels of change, some more significant than others. Marxists, for example, might see the modern subject as emerging with capitalism at the end of the feudal era. Subsequent changes, corresponding to changes of the mode of production (e.g. the shift from mercantile to monopoly capitalism), while perhaps significant, would not then be seen as fundamental. Feminists, while charting similar shifts in the modern world, may see the far older power structures of patriarchy as being the most significant.

There are contradictions here: on the one hand online communications create or realise a fluid, decentred subject, while on the other, by stripping away 'superficial' corporeal markers of identity we approach something like a 'truthful' essential self constituted in ideal communication with other disembodied but authentic identities. N. Katherine Hayles notes connections between recent cybercultural notions of identity and the long-established Enlightenment subject. Both, she argues, are based on the notion that

> embodiment is not essential to human being . . . Indeed one could argue that the erasure of embodiment is a feature common to both the liberal human subject and the cybernetic posthuman. Identified with the rational mind, the liberal subject possessed a body but was not usually represented as being a body. Only because the body is not identified with the self is it possible to claim for the liberal subject its notorious universality, a claim that depends on erasing markers of bodily difference, including sex, race, and ethnicity.
>
> (Hayles 1999: 5 quoted in Kitzmann 1999)

For Judith Butler it seems that the construction of identity is effected through subjects organising together according to affinities in a process of *identification*. Here then identity is the social appearance of the subject (Butler 2000). Identity is sometimes used more specifically in the analysis of media consumption (Tomlinson 1990), and a different inflection of the term identification is central to Film Studies' theories of the relationships between film spectators and film images (Metz 1985).

Subjects and media technologies

There are precedents for linking changes in the subject to changes in media technologies. The development of print through movable type in the mid-fifteenth century is generally seen as the first mass medium. It is often cited as a key factor in the waning of the medieval religious world, and hence the development of modern rationality and subjectivity (McLuhan 1962; Birkerts 1994; Provenzo 1986). The role of the mass media and specific media technologies in the second half of the twentieth century is articulated differently across the diverse debates in cultural theory, yet there is a general assumption that contemporary culture in the developed world is characterised by an increasing prevalence of mediated forms and images, with concomitant effects on life, experience, political activity and so forth (see e.g. Jameson 1991, Harvey 1989).

As we have seen, even in mainstream Cultural and Media Studies media technologies are often assumed to be instrumental in a shifting sense of identity in numerous ways, including the following: the provision of media images and narratives for identity construction (Kellner 1995); consumption as an active practice of identity bricolage (Hebdige 1979; Willis 1990), constructed through the images and consumer goods individuals 'choose' (Tomlinson 1990); all processes given new impetus by the interactive and reproductive power of digital software (Chandler 1998), or by a shift from the 'broadcast' model of mass media to the non-hierarchical networks epitomised by the Internet (Poster 1995b). Where Cultural and Media Studies and related disciplines turn their attention to new media, they explore how identity can be 'constructed' in cyberspace or virtual worlds and how individuals engage in virtual communities (Hine 2000; Bassett 1997; Slater 1998; Green and Adam 2001).

On a less epochal timeframe and register, film theory since the late 1960s has established a quasi-cyborgian model of media subjectivity in which the film spectator is one component in the 'cinematic apparatus', both physically and psychically positioned by the film, its mode of projection, and the cinema auditorium. The position of spectator within the cinema auditorium (in the dark, looking at the large screen in front whilst the images are projected overhead from behind) produces an array of ideological effects, not least that of identification with the camera:

> that which has looked, before the spectator, at what the spectator is now looking at . . . The spectator is therefore interpellated by the filmic text, that is the film constructs the subject, the subject is an effect of the film text.
>
> (Hayward 1996: 8)

4.4.5 Cyborgs, cyberfeminism and the posthuman

Cyborgs

> A cyborg is a rather slippery thing.
>
> (Kember 1998: 109)

Donna Haraway's influential essay 'A Manifesto for Cyborgs: Science, Technology, and Socialist Feminism in the 1980s' is a thorough postmodernist interrogation of binary oppositions, identifying:

self/other, mind/body, culture/nature, male/female, civilized/primitive, reality/appearance, whole/part, agent/resource, maker/made, active/passive, right/wrong, truth/illusion . . . [as dualisms] systemic to the domination of women, people of color, nature, workers, animals.

(Haraway 1990: 218)

These categories are not only excluded from, and dominated by, the universalising myth of the Western subject; importantly, they are positioned as 'others' to define this subject, 'to mirror the self'. Monsters such as those in classical myth demonstrate the ambiguities of self-definition through the other: the centaur, half human, half animal represents 'boundary pollution'. The cyborg then is a contemporary monster, but from the standpoint of a post-modernist politics of difference, one to be celebrated.

The 'challenge to western either/or epistemology' is conducted through an 'ironic political myth' of the cyborg. This creature is 'a cybernetic organism, a hybrid of machine and organism' (Haraway 1990: 191). It is deliberately ambiguous, encompassing fictional cyborgs such as *Robocop*; the increasing material intimacy between human bodies and machines (in medicine, warfare, or in miniaturised consumer electronics); a conception of networks as complex systems in which categories of biology and machines blur, and a postmodernist, 'post-gender' subject position. This latter is facilitated precisely by the cyborg's ambiguity. It is not reducible to either the natural or the cultural, and therefore is neither entirely male nor female. Haraway cites *Blade Runner*'s heroine, the replicant Rachel, as an image of the fundamental confusion the cyborg generates around distinctions between the technical and the natural, and questions of origins, of mind and body (Haraway 1990: 219). The cyborg comes into being through 'replication' rather than organic reproduction, so it lends itself to the 'utopian tradition of imagining a world without gender' (Haraway 1990: 192). This then is an attempt to think beyond difference, beyond the dualisms that structure the modern subject, an attempt in which science and technology, and particularly information technology, are central.

Haraway is careful to insist that her cyborg is at once an ironic fiction and a way of thinking about actually existing phenomena. As N. Katherine Hayles puts it:

> [Haraway's] cyborgs are simultaneously entities and metaphors, living beings and narrative constructions. The conjunction of technology and discourse is crucial. Were the cyborg only a product of discourse, it could perhaps be relegated to science fiction, of interest to SF aficionados but not of vital concern to the culture. Were it only a technological practice, it could be confined to such technical fields as bionics, medical prostheses, and virtual reality. Manifesting itself as both technological object and discursive formation, it partakes of the power of the imagination as well as the actuality of technology.

(Hayles 1999: 114–115)

This articulation of the actual and the metaphorical is very important and is often blurred in research based on Haraway's essay. In addition to the fictional cyborgs of science fiction cinema and literature, Hayles distinguishes between 'actual cyborgs' (for example people fitted with pacemakers) and 'metaphoric cyborgs' (Hayles 1999: 115). The 'adolescent game player in the local video game arcade' exemplifies the 'metaphoric' cyborg for Hayles, and we will return to this everyday technocultural entity later in this section.

It is useful to point out here that Hayles's use of the term 'metaphoric' in this context might be misleading. In strict cybernetic terms the gameplayer is not metaphorically but *actually* part of a feedback loop with the videogame. See **4.5.5** and **5.4.4** for the cybernetic nature of videogame play

The cyborg has generated substantial comment (Gray *et al.* 1995; Gray 2002; Zylinska 2002; Balsamo 1996), though it should be noted that media technologies are rarely discussed in cyborgian terms. There are notable exceptions (often in relation to videogames, e.g. Friedman 1995, 1999; Ito 1998; Lahti 2003; Dovey and Kennedy 2006; Giddings and Kennedy 2006)

Posthumanism

All this said, while the use of the term 'cyborg' here makes links with salient concepts, debates and disciplines, and suggests new couplings or hybridities of the human and the technological in contemporary everday life, it may ultimately prove misleading. It implies, and is often taken to mean, a discrete, bounded entity (a cybernetic *organism*); a monster no doubt, but one generally more or less human in origin and form. Think of the cyborg's fictional figurations: Robocop and the Terminator for example. Part man and part machine no doubt, but reassuringly humanoid in form and, as the films unfold, increasingly 'human' in emotional and moral terms. Similarly, however bewildered or decentred postmodernist subjects feel themselves to be, they – and their crisis – are still fundamentally *human*.

> It is comforting . . . and a source of profound relief to think that man is only a recent invention, a figure not yet two centuries old, a new wrinkle in our knowledge, and that he will disappear again as soon as that knowledge has discovered a new form.
>
> (Foucault 1970: xxiii)

In this often-quoted sentence Foucault suggests a more profound sense of change in the subject, one that has been picked up in recent theoretical developments that resonate with new media and technocultural theory, developments that are sometimes loosely bracketed together as posthumanism. Posthumanism can however be divided into three (overlapping) approaches. First the term refers to a critique of the notion of humanism and the human subject within critical theory (Badmington 2000); second it refers to a range of debates around science and technology that are researching into, or predicting, changes in the human body and its relationship with technology and technoscience in the present and the near future. There are distinct echoes of early uncritical cyberculture in some manifestations of this aspect of posthumanism or 'transhumanism' (see for example the 'extropian' movement http://extropy.org/ with its New Age worldview, unqualified optimism about technological progress, and corporate ambitions). Third, 'posthumanism' is used within critical cyberculture (particularly cyberfeminism) and some STS-influenced debates to draw on both of the first two and to address critically the relationships between technology and the human. Not surprisingly this discussion has been termed 'critical posthumanism' (Didur 2003). Critical posthumanism is often concerned with the cultures and implications of biotechnology, reproductive technologies and genetics (Halberstam and Livingston 1996; Thacker 2005; Davis-Floyd and Dumit 1998) and has been greatly influenced by the work of Donna Haraway.

Critical posthumanism is, then, an articulation of a number of interlinked concepts:

- the cyborgian notion of the posthuman as marked by material, corporeal change (whether through prosthetics or genetic manipulation);

- the challenge cybernetics makes to the established sense of the human body's boundaries – for example, 'the idea of the feedback loop implies that the boundaries of the autonomous subject are up for grabs, since feedback loops can flow not only within the subject, but also between the subject and the environment' (Hayles 1999: 2);

- the cyberfeminist critique of the Enlightenment subject, as founded on a Western epistemology of binary divisions (not least that of male–female), and the (more or less) ironic proposition that fictional cyborgs and actual technologies offer alternative ways of thinking about identity;

- post-structuralist critiques of post-Enlightenment humanism. Poster argues that 'We are moving beyond the "humanist" phase of history into a new level of combination of human and machines, an extremely suggestive assemblage in which the figures of the cyborg and cyberspace open vast unexplored territories' (Poster 1995b).

Cyberfeminism

> Perhaps, ironically, we can learn from our fusions with animals and machines how not to be Man, the embodiment of Western logos.
>
> (Haraway 1990: 215)

'Cyberfeminism' is not a movement as such; the term covers a diverse, even contradictory range of feminist theories on technological change and gender. These theories – and, again, Haraway's cyborg in particular – have been influential on many studies of new media. For cyberfeminists the recognition and critique of the gendered nature of the Enlightenment human subject is central. 'Posthumanism' here then is a political gesture towards rethinking the relationships not only between the human and the technological, but between men and women and the technological.

Though in quite different ways, the works of Donna Haraway and Sadie Plant have addressed the sexual politics of new technologies and subjectivities through an enquiry into what it means to be human, each seeing technological change as potentially liberating. Both draw on science fictional ideas of the embodied cyborg, though Plant's model of a blurring of boundaries between the biological and the machinic is predominantly one of networks rather than bodies. She sees the history of the computer's development as one of ever-expanding complexity, to the point at which this complexity is indistinguishable from the complex systems of both nature and culture:

> Parallel distributed processing defies all attempts to pin it down, and can only ever be con-tingently defined. It also turns the computer into a complex thinking machine which converges with the operations of the human brain . . . Neural nets are distributed systems which function as analogues of the brain and can learn, think, 'evolve' and 'live'. And the parallels proliferate. The complexity the computer becomes also emerges in economies, weather systems, cities and cultures, all of which begin to function as complex systems with their own parallel processes, connectivities and immense tangles of mutual interlink-ings.
>
> (Plant 2000: 329)

Plant isn't speaking metaphorically here, she is asserting that machines not only appear to take on the characteristics of biological systems, including the human brain, but that to all intents and purposes no meaningful distinction between the natural and the machinic can now be made. For Plant the Internet, or matrix, is inherently feminine and manifests

> lines of communication between women, long repressed, . . . returning in a technological form . . . The immediacy of women's communion with each other, the flashes of intuitive exchange, and the non-hierarchical system which women have established in the net-working practices of grass roots feminist organisations: all these become the instant access of telecommunication, the decentred circuits and dispersed networks of informa-tion.
>
> (Plant 1993: 13–14)

Plant's project is, like that of Haraway, to question and 'think beyond' the structuring binaries of Western thought, and again in particular the masculine subject as agent of history. Both draw on post-structuralist theories. Plant develops the ideas of French theorist Luce Irigaray who argued that, apparently paradoxically, machines and women are bracketed together in binary opposition to men. For though not 'natural' as such, machines are, like women, things existing to benefit man, 'mere things on which men worked', or objects of exchange (Plant 1993: 13). In opposition to men, they too have been seen as having no agency or self-awareness. Following this logic, then, Plant asserts that there is only one *homo sapiens* ('Man') and that 'Woman is a virtual reality'. The implication here is that women have always been positioned as some kind of biological-machinic hybrid, and that it is only with the emergence of information technology that this association ceases to be repressive. Instead it marks a revolution that doesn't so much undermine the male modern subject as sweep him away, in 'a fluid attack, an onslaught on human agency and the solidity of identity . . . It is the process by which the world becomes female, and so posthuman' (Plant 1993: 17).

Sarah Kember is critical of Sadie Plant's analysis of the relationships between the human and the machine in the age of networked communication, arguing that collapsing any distinction between life and information – a concept she terms 'connectionism' – runs the risk of conflating the complex systems of nature with social systems such as economies. While connectionism 'offers a rhetoric of resistance to control and authority which is based on the destruction of boundaries', Kember sees it as fundamentally anti-political in that the assertion of such systems as 'selforganizing, self-arousing' (Plant 1995: 58) denies any social or historical context. For Kember, Haraway, by contrast, seeks to 'trouble and revise the restricted rationality of conventional Western forms of knowledge' without recourse to connectionism (Kember 1998: 107; see also Squires 1996).

> While cars are not commonly thought of as media, driving is one of the most familiar and mundane experiences of contemporary technoculture, and we might remember McLuhan's assertion that the wheel is a medium, an extension of the body, or to be more precise, the foot

CASE STUDY 4.8: Everyday cyborgs – driver cars

4.15 Virtual car drivers and the Nintendo Wii.

As befits something so monstrous, the cyborg is heteromorphic. For Donna Haraway it is chimerical, an ironic yet Utopian being made from actual and symbolic parts. However for this study of everyday technoculture we can be less ambiguous. Contemporary life in the developed world is a near constant set of overlapping and nested relationships between the human mind and body and non-human processes and entities. A number of STS-influenced sociologists have discussed the everyday technoculture of cars and their drivers in cyborgian terms. Tim Dant usefully adopts the term *assemblage* from ANT to denote these impermanent but significant couplings of the human and the nonhuman (Dant 2004, also Haraway 2004, Latour 1999). These 'car/drivers' (Lupton 1999), or 'driver-cars' (Dant 2004), then, are assemblages of human and machinic components within a technologised environment of roads and street furniture, more than the sum of their parts:

The driver-car is neither a thing or a person; it is an assembled social being that takes on properties of both and cannot exist without both . . . The car does not simply afford the driver mobility or have independent agency as an actant; it enables a range of humanly embodied actions available only to the driver-car.

(Dant 2004: 74)

For Deborah Lupton 'when one is driving, one becomes a cyborg, a combination of human and machine' (Lupton 1999: 59). The contemporary technocultural phenomenon of road rage is bound up with this cyborg ontology:

When other car/drivers invade our space, appear to put us in danger, when they touch our hybrid bodies with their own or yell at us, our sense of being in a private space within a public sphere is violated.

(Lupton 1999: 70)

Angry drivers, Lupton suggests, force the breakdown of the automotive actor-network, threatening 'the complex social order of the road and its heterogeneous network of human, non-human and hybrid actors' (Lupton 1999: 70). This is an example of ANT applied to everyday here-and-now technoculture. It describes a network of the human and the nonhuman as characteristic of the most familiar and mundane activities:

Many of our engagements with machines challenge notions of the accepted dichotomy between human and non-human, between self and other. Drawing a distinction between the 'animate' and the 'inanimate' and 'human' and 'non-human', therefore, suggests dichotomies which perhaps should be viewed as continual or hierarchical categories. Actors may better be conceptualized as the products of networks of heterogeneous factors interrelating with one another.

(Lupton 1999: 58–59)

Though ostensibly similar to Lupton's car/driver, Dant's driver-car is terminologically, and ultimately conceptually, distinct. He is clear the driver-car is not a cyborg: he makes a distinction between the *cyborg* as a human augmented by 'feedback systems incorporated into the body that can be used to replace or enhance human body parts' and *assemblages*, the temporary constitution of human and nonhuman actors (Dant 2004: 62). The assemblage 'comes apart when the driver leaves the vehicle and . . . can be endlessly re-formed, or re-assembled given the availability of the component cars and drivers' (Dant 2004: 62). In denying any cyborgian characteristics to the driver-car assemblage, Dant reinscribes a solidly humanist position, arguing that 'human subjectivity is in no sense constituted by getting into a car; it is a temporary assemblage within which the human remains complete in his or her self' (Dant 2004: 62).

Conversely, Lupton's vision of the car/driver as one actor-network circulating eccentrically within and across many others indicates that there is little humanist reassurance in stepping out of the driver-car:

the network of social relations, norms and expectations around car use, such as road rules, and material and spatial aspects such as the physical nature of roads, the presence of traffic lights and of other cars, represent everpresent structuring features of car use. Cyborg subjectivities, therefore, are not simply about how we, as bodies/selves, interact with our machines, but about how we interact with other cyborgs as part of a cyborg 'body politic'.

(Lupton 1999: 59)

4.4.6 Issues and conclusions

The notion that there are important shifts in the nature of identity or subjectivity attendant on the advent of digital media is evident across the diverse conceptual frameworks of new media studies. There is little agreement over the precise nature of these shifts, their historical and technological location, and their epochal import, but each – in different ways – makes claims for the importance of these shifts in understanding everyday life in a digital technoculture. We have seen then:

- profound claims for transformation of the underpinnings of everyday life, its politics and possibilities: sense of self, gender, body and identity in a new media world;

- demands to see the self in everyday life not as an autonomous subject but as, to varying degrees and with diverse conclusions, embroiled in networks, in intimate relationships with machines and media;

- that the science fictional figures of the posthuman and the cyborg have a descriptive and nonmetaphorical purchase on mundane, everyday technocultural relationships.

4.5 Gameplay

This section aims to do three main things: to look at the videogame as an extremely successful new medium in its own right, of central significance to the everyday consumption of new media; to serve as an extended case study applying the key concerns of this part of the book to the consumption of one new medium; and to explore the significance of play as central to, yet in significant ways apart from, everyday life.

Videogames are the first popular computer-based medium. Pre-dating the home computer, games devices such as the 'tennis' game Pong were first plugged into television sets in 1972. They brought with them fears and fascination – a sense that everyday life was meeting the future: new ways of relating to machines, new images and worlds, frightening narratives of symbolic violence and addiction. This section they will be studied as:

- consumer media technology, shaped by and shaping everyday activities and dynamics;

- new media devices and texts, offering interactive pleasures and possibilities;

- games, inviting the analysis of play as a particular mode of use or consumption that troubles established concepts of everyday space and time, reality, identity and ideology;

- computer media, whose consumption and meanings in everyday life are inseparable from their status as digital technologies, and which suggest that popular computer media and communication technologies more generally might be thought of as playful;

- suggestive of new ways of thinking about the intimate relationships between the human and the technological in new media culture – as everyday lived and embodied cyberculture.

4.5.1 New media's other

OK, you're haunted. You're seeing Cyber-Demon Lords in your dreams. You can't get to that Soul Sphere in the Military Base, and it's driving you nuts. You're a hopeless Doom addict. A Doomie. Yeah, it hurts. And yet . . . who would have thought going to Hell could be so much fun?.

(Barba 1994: v)

These are the opening sentences from *Doom Battlebook*, a manual and **cheats** guide for the popular computer and video game released in 1993. *Doom* is a first-person shoot-em up (or FPS), a game in which the player's point of view is apparently through the eyes of the character he or she controls in the game. The premiss of the game is simple: the player must guide the character through maze-like corridors of a science fiction environment, shooting any creature he meets. Weapons and power-ups (ammunition, first-aid kits, armour) are collected along the way to prolong the slaughter, and the whole experience is one of horror, panic, and the temporary satisfaction of annihilating a room full of enemies, satisfaction soon forgotten as the next level is explored. *Doom* is a grimy post-industrial universe of bubbling toxic waste and slimy metal walls. Perhaps now regarded by gameplayers as quaint in its simplicity, despite (by today's standards) low-resolution graphics and pixellated monsters, the game still generates controversy. As it is now over fifteen years old, the game highlights the longevity of the videogame as a popular new media form, and *Doom*'s conventions (navigable 3-D space, first person perspective, weaponry and health pickups, the possibility of networked play, etc.) are still widely used in contemporary videogames such as the *Halo* and *Quake* series.

Doom is an early example of an often-vilified new medium, which, since its introduction, has been the focus of fears of cultural and social change, particularly around childhood and youth. Seen as encouraging anti-social play in violent and morally dubious computer environments and narratives, videogames become everything that threatens an idealised children's culture. Against 'spontaneous play' on beaches and in woods, a 'play world of the natural child [that is] open and friendly', is set the play world of 'the "electronic child" . . . hemmed in by conflict and fear' (Stutz 1995). Although videogames are now taken more seriously, reviewed alongside television programmes and films in the press for example, they can still at times elicit very similar reactions. More recently the *Grand Theft Auto* series has proved controversial, and *Manhunt 2* was banned in the UK, achieving an 18 certificate only after court action by the game's producers Rockstar.

Many of these anxieties and moral outrages follow the well-established patterns of the 'media scares' – video-nasties, comics, pinball and penny-dreadfuls have all in their time epitomised the new and dangerous (Barker 1984). Videogames add to this panic the threat of the computer's increasing influence in everyday life. These anxieties are evident in academic and theoretical discourses as well. Videogames are generally presented as a problem to be solved, threatening a future of hyper-gendered identities or a technoconsumerist 'Nintendo generation'. Cultural theorists are not immune from such dread. Julian Stallabrass articulates a nightmare of a cybernetic capitalism and the implosion of the public and private:

> There is a shadowy ambition behind the concept of the virtual world – to have everyone safely confined in their homes, hooked up to sensory feedback devices in an enclosing, interactive environment which will be a far more powerful tool of social control than television.
>
> (Stallabrass 1993: 104)

This paranoia about compelling, immersive and cybernetic relationships between computer games and their players, coupled with the games' status as commercial media, was widely felt:

> Nintendo games . . . privatise rather repulsive fantasies of conflict and image; they delimit the imagination and offer only servile participation. The hypnotic alienation it perpetuates hardly suggests that technology has any progressive features.
>
> (Druckrey 1991: 18)

Or Donna Haraway, in her 'Cyborg Manifesto':

> The new technologies seem deeply involved in the forms of 'privatization' . . . in which militarization, right-wing family ideologies and policies, and intensified definitions of corporate (and state) property as private synergistically interact. The new communications technologies are fundamental to the eradication of 'public life' for everyone. This facilitates the mushrooming of a permanent high-tech military establishment at the cultural and economic expense of most people, but especially of women. Technologies like video games and highly miniaturized televisions seem crucial to production of modern forms of 'private life'. The culture of video games is heavily orientated to individual competition and extra-terrestrial warfare. High-tech, gendered imaginations are produced here, imaginations that can contemplate destruction of the planet and a sci-fi escape from its consequences. More than our imaginations is militarized; and the other realities of electronic and nuclear warfare are inescapable.
>
> (Haraway 1990: 210–211).

In **4.2.2** above we saw how the videogame, for some, exemplifies a post-Fordist colonisation and commodification of everyday time and space, while simultaneously manifesting its 'simulatory hyperreal' cultural correlative (Kline *et al*. 2003: 75)

The constitution of fields of study in new media (CMC, cybercultural studies, media educationalism, etc.) has, until recently, tended to marginalise or exclude popular, commercial and commodified versions of digital media and information technologies. Within education they are a dangerously seductive distraction from learning, or at best offer themselves as Trojan Horses or sweeteners for the real business of computer use. Within cybercultural discourses they haunt the fringes of MUDs and hypertext as gendered, commodified toys, as other to the online heterotopias of identity play. It is evident that discourses celebrating new media may do so in denial of certain key contexts for the development of new media as popular cultural forms.

For example, in an essay on the game *Myst*, David Miles identified interesting precedents for the game's interactive narrative structure and atmosphere. The list is impressive: the gothic novel, *Parsifal*, Verne, modernist literature (Gide, Robbe-Grillet, Borges), Homer, early cinema. The essay is a perceptive and imaginative attempt to take the computer game seriously, and to think of what its future might be. However, in doing so it elided the very 'low' cultural pleasures that have popularised and developed the form. For Miles *Myst* was not a 'videogame' but an 'interactive multimedia novel on CD-ROM' (Miles 1999: 307). Non-violent, sedate and intellectually challenging, *Myst*, though published in the same year as *Doom*, seems to belong to a different world. While the computer or videogame may well, as Miles hoped, offer art and literature new forms and aesthetics, to forget that *Myst* is still a computer game, and as such the hybrid offspring of less prestigious cultural forms (pinball machines, science fiction, fantasy and horror literature, toys, television), is to miss the central significance of the videogame to new media.

In both popular and academic discourses, videogames are often explicitly posited as emblematic of the troubled status of our understanding of the real world in media culture. The principal example is the 1991 Gulf War. The thorough control of news media by the coalition states, and the spectacle of 'smart' weapons and video footage from missiles at their point of impact epitomised a popular notion of 'simulation' as a conflation of digital and video imaging technology and a sense of a remote, mediated experience (by both domestic audiences and Western military). This 'simulation' was explicitly figured in terms of videogames, as

In recent years the academic study of video and computer games has flourished with international conferences, new journals and scholarly publications. See for example the journals *Game Studies* (http://www.gamestudies.org) and *Games and Culture*, and the Digital Games Research Association (http://www.digra.org). Key books include Dovey and Kennedy 2006, Juul 2005 and Taylor 2006

General Norman Schwartzkopf's phrase 'the Nintendo war' resonated across the news media and academic discourses (Sheff 1993: 285). The notion of the videogame war has persisted in the reporting of the second Gulf War (see Consalvo 2003).

Doom is often implicated in this blurring of the real and the mediated in violent events. Frequently cited in media scares around youth culture, particularly in the United States, the game has been blamed (along with other commercial youth-oriented media, particularly popular music) in the shooting of school students by classmates in Littleton, Colorado in 1999. Widely quoted in press and television reports on the killings, the military psychologist Lt.-Col. David Grossman argues that, just as *Doom* is used by the US Marines as a training simulator, so it 'trained' these disturbed adolescents to kill. Moreover, the videogame's immersive mode of consumption encouraged a disastrous breaking down of the distinction between fantasies and reality. In a *New York Times* article reprinted in the *Guardian*, Paul Keegan discussed Grossman's views, concluding:

> And that's what makes shooters [first person shoot-em ups] unlike any other form of media violence we've seen before. You're not just watching a movie, you're in the movie. You're not just empathising with Arnold Schwarzenegger as he blasts the bad guy to smithereens, you're actually pulling the trigger.
>
> (Keegan 2000: 3)

This, then, is an extreme form of realism – the interactive manipulation of pixellated icons of hyperbolic violence mapped directly, unmediated, on to real-world behaviour. Such claims do not stand up to serious scrutiny, but they do highlight, through their resonances with certain discourses of VR and cyberspace, the underlying sense in the technological imaginary of interactive media of an idealist (whether Utopian or Dystopian) notion of the end of media. The shoot-em up genre can be seen then as the 'repressed' of the cybercultural enthusiasm for interactivity – losing oneself in the medium can be creative and liberating, but is haunted by the possibility that this immersion can be hypnotic, seductive, 'mindless' as well as bodiless.

In this section we will challenge this marginalisation and argue that the study of videogames offers us analytical and critical purchase on the forms and consumption of new media technologies in general.

4.5.2 Videogames as new technology

Rather than being a marginal form of new media, videogames (as media texts and as new modes of play and consumption) are indivisible from the dissemination and popularisation, and even the development, of personal computing, its software and interfaces, its practices and meanings. The relationship between the emergence of home/personal computers and videogames is tangled and complex; in what follows we suggest some key strands.

Instrumental play

Games software was central to the practices of early home computing, not only as entertainment but also as demonstrative of the power and possibilities of the new machines. As we have seen, home computers were distinctly 'open' devices. Games would be bought, copied, or written by users as much to see what the computer could do, exploring graphics, sound and interactivity, as for the pleasures of gameplay itself. In a broader sense, home computer use has continued to be characterised by a kind of exploratory play with computer or software systems, whether or not game software itself was being used. Indeed, play in this

See Norris (1992). For a fascinating account of an attempt to challenge this scare around youth culture in the US, see Jenkins (2001) on his testimony to the Senate Commerce Committee

Levy (1994) identifies a 'hacker ethic', a kind of politics of computer programming as serious play. Many of the elements of this unwritten hacker manifesto – free exchange of information, mistrust of authority, celebration of meritocracy – are evident in subsequent cultures of Internet development and the open source movement. Even the origin of the term 'hacker' is ludic. Deriving from MIT jargon for prank, a hack is 'a project undertaken or a product built not solely to fulfil some constructive goal, but with some wild pleasure taken in mere involvement . . . to qualify as a hack, the feat must be imbued with innovation, style, and technical virtuosity' (Levy 1994: 23)

general sense is a significant strategy for learning the computer's system. The governmental, educational and commercial discourses of the promotion of computer use since the 1980s have, sometimes anxiously, emphasised this 'instrumental play' – promising the purchasers of home computers that the information age can be fun. The experience of interacting with and controlling a computer, primarily through play, would link user and machine in the spare bedroom with the historic forces of the information revolution (**4.3.1**).

It could be argued that the relationship between computer games and personal computing is even more significant. The origins of personal computing lie in the philosophy and innovations of the first 'hackers', students at MIT in the late 1950s. These students challenged official uses of the institution's mainframe computers (statistical analyses, scientific simulations, and so on); instead they would develop non-instrumental ways of exploring the computers' potential. This exploration ranged from using the mainframe to play single-track classical music to programming the lights on the front of the machine to allow a game of computer ping-pong. Such play was not always wilfully trivial however – they also experimented with the possibilities of artificial intelligence in chess programs.

On one level these hackers were, like the home computer hobbyists to follow, 'just seeing what the machine would do'. However, in experimenting with real-time computer interaction and animation, through the design of games, they established a new mode of computer use which ultimately resulted in PC graphical user interfaces (see also **3.6**). Some recognised the implications of computer games early on. As MIT researcher Stewart Brand observed, after watching *Space War!* in 1972, ten years after its creation: 'Ready or not, computers are coming to the people. That's good news, maybe the best since psychedelics' (quoted in Ceruzzi 1999: 64).

Hacking as consumption

Not only have computer and video games played a significant role in turning computer technology into domestic computer media, they have, through their generation of new modes of interaction with screen-based information and communication, leaked out into many other everyday technologies and media – from the PC *Minesweeper* games and 'desktop' puzzles to the games-derived interfaces and 'help' screens on photocopiers, digital photo booths, and mobile phone text-messaging. Tamagotchi, DVD games, board games with DVDs, videogames on mobile phones, on digital cable channels, sites devoted to Flash-based games, games within other applications such as social network sites (applications that are in themselves playful in nature), and so on.

From this observation, a number of questions can be posed:

1   If computer and video games have made computer technology accessible and popular, have they, in so doing, effectively commodified computer technology, turning the radical hacker ethic into consumerist entertainment?

2   What are the implications of the study of media technology as games and its consumption or use as play?

3   Could the recognition of videogames as central to the information revolution require us to look again at the long-established discursive oppositions between work/education and play, instrumental use and consumption, games and everyday life?

CASE STUDY 4.9: *Doom* as media, technology and new cultural economy

To draw together commercial entertainment, key hacker tenets (free access to code, the hands-on programming imperative), new consumption practices and new Internet-based production and marketing models, we will again enter the fun hell that is *Doom*.

As mentioned above, the US Marine Corps adapted this game as training simulator software. However they also then marketed their customised version as a game. While this circularity may seem a useful example of the thesis that the boundaries between war, power, media and entertainment are now thoroughly blurred, it also allows us to make more specific observations. The job of converting the game into training software (and back again) was facilitated by the innovative way in which *Doom* was distributed. First, the initial levels of the game were given away, made available for download from the Internet (Manovich 1998). Second, in hacker tradition, the publishers made the code and file formats for the game's design freely available, allowing players (as had always been the case with early, simpler, computer games) to modify levels, add new enemies or construct new levels themselves.

Comparing *Doom* to *Myst* (both published in 1993), Lev Manovich argues that there is a fundamental difference between them that is not to do with violent content or cultural pedigree, but rather cultural economy. Whereas *Myst* invited its players to 'behold and admire' its images and narratives, *Doom* asked its players to take them apart and modify them. In this sense *Doom*, then, is a good example of computer media designed for creative and enabling engagement by its users. As Manovich puts it, the game 'transcended the usual relationships between producers and consumers' (Manovich 1998).

Online gaming has developed from *Doom*'s office-based, multi-player networks to *Quake* tournaments on LANs or the Internet, and the technical and aesthetic legacy of its 3-D interface and game engine is evident in the current popularity of MMOGs and other networked virtual worlds such as *Second Life*.

Programming as play

To address question 1 above, the focus must be shifted from the technologies themselves, to the practices of their use. Hacking as play has been seen as inseparable from the demands (in terms of expertise and time) of programming. For the producers and users of early home computers it was assumed that computer use meant programming. To run the most elementary game or application required a grasp of programming languages such as BASIC, and a grasp of coding was seen as central to the realisation of the potential of computers. Leslie Haddon has differentiated between 'computer games' and 'videogames' (arcade machines, or early dedicated consoles) on just such grounds. The keen player/programmer could intervene into the code of the home computer game, using 'pokes' or cheats to explore the game environment or change parameters (Haddon 1992: 89).

By the late 1980s however, as the micro gave way to IBM-compatible or Apple Macintosh personal computers with DOS (later Windows) and the Apple GUI, programming ceased to be needed in everyday computer use, and, partly as a consequence, the distinction between computer and video games became less clear. Today, the PC is regarded by videogame manufacturers as one platform alongside the various competing dedicated videogame consoles. The most popular games are adapted across these platforms.

Another example of an earlier (in this case much earlier) computer game with far-reaching implications for the development of popular, personal computing and the Internet, is *Adventure* (1967). An interactive story, set in a Tolkeinesque fantasy world, with forking paths followed according to the player's choice, luck, or ability to solve puzzles. As well as remaining popular in its own right for decades, it has been influential on a number of more recent game genres, and is an early example of interactive narrative

Not only did this shareware marketing strategy continue and extend the long established gaming culture of cheats and patches, it was also the inspiration for Netscape's early conquest of Internet browsing through free availability of its software (Herz 1997: 90)

However, not all computer-mediated play and games fall within the videogame mode. Traditional games such as chess, bridge, quizzes have also been adapted. Recent advances in the secure handling of money online has led to the increasingly popular phenomenon of online poker games

CASE STUDY 4.10: *Pokémon*: videogames as new (mass) media

4.16 Pikachu, I choose you!

To explore the issues arising from popular new media's implication within commercial entertainment culture we will return to the multi-platform worlds of *Pokémon* as a case study.

Beginning life in 1996 as a game for the Nintendo Gameboy hand-held videogame console, *Pokémon* went on to achieve dramatic success as a card collecting and trading game, and grew to a merchandising franchise worth $5 billion a year. The 'Pocket Monsters' feature in a television series, animated feature films, videogames on all Nintendo consoles, and all the other licensed products of children's media culture. It is estimated that, at the phenomenon's height, half of all Japanese seven- to twelve-year-olds were regular players. Even before it had been released in the UK, *Pokémon: the First Movie* had overtaken *Lion King* as the most successful animated film (*Guardian*, 20 April 2000). After pornography, *Pokémon* was the most searched for subject on the web in 1999 (*Guardian Editor*, 21 April 2000).

Pokémon is an example of the transmedial 'entertainment supersystem' or convergent 'media mix' discussed above in **4.3.3**. Marsha Kinder developed her notion of the 'entertainment supersystem' through studying Teenage Mutant Ninja Turtles, a children's media craze of the late 1980s. Like the Turtles, *Pokémon* is based around ritualised conflict (and, like the Turtles a decade earlier, has had its products banned from schools for apparently provoking real fights). However, *Pokémon* has exceeded even the Turtles in its saturation of children's media and everyday lives:

> The real reason for the game's astounding success probably has more to do with the breathtakingly clever way in which Nintendo and its franchisees have created a self-referential world in which every product – every trading card, computer game, movie, cartoon and hamburger box – serves as propaganda for all the others.
>
> (Burkeman 2000: 2)

The idea that we are seeing the emergence of a global commercial popular culture is a familiar one. This global culture is, however, commonly viewed as evidence of US cultural dominance, with talk of Disnification or McDonaldisation as the analogue in the cultural sphere to globalisation in the economic sphere. *Pokémon* and *Teenage Mutant Ninja Turtles*, however (along with other supersystems such as *Power Rangers*), are evidence of a meeting and hybridisation of Eastern and Western popular cultural forms. Even before *Pokémon*, the videogame was perhaps the most thoroughly transnational form of popular culture, both as an industry (with Sony, Sega and Nintendo as the key players) but also at the level of content – the characters and narratives of many videogames are evidence of relays of influence between America and Japan.

Nintendo, in its pre-videogame incarnation as playing card manufacturer, introduced the first Disney licensing into Japan soon after the Second World War, and a tremendous boom in (the already established) Japanese animation industry followed. As Disney took European folktales, stripped them of their original religious motivations, and animated them with the anxieties and morals of a Western bourgeoisie, so Japanese *anime* (animated films) and *manga* (comics) took Disney images, with their graphic resonances with traditional Japanese art, and charged them with very different philosophies.

MacKenzie Wark asserts that videogames are 'primers in junk consumerism' (Wark 1994). If we accept this analysis, then the *Pokémon* card game could also be seen as an education in market economics. There are over 150 characters in each iteration of the gameworld, each with their own card, and the manufacturers ensure competition and trade between players (and sales) by restricting the supply of certain cards. This exploitation of the established children's culture of collecting has been widely criticised: 'the result is a particularly pure form of kiddie capitalism, in which acquisition is no longer just a means to further play, but the very essence of play itself' (Burkeman 2000: 2).

However, this trading aspect also makes it a sociable game, with its own improvised playground-level practices and the emergence of local cultural economies such as collectors' fairs and game tournaments. To determine whether *Pokémon* can in any way be seen to exceed 'kiddie capitalism' – whether its status as one of the most effective of the 'ideal commodities' of videogames means it reduces childhood and play to a nightmare of commodification and manipulation – we would need to study in more detail the ways in which the games are played and articulated in children's everyday lives. In her studies of similar media mix cultures in Japan (discussed in **4.3.3** above) Mizuko Ito puts the issue thus:

> The rise of global communication and media networks is tied to an imagination that is more commercially driven, fantasy-based, widely shared, and central to our everyday lives *at the same time* as it is now becoming more amenable to local refashioning and mobilization in highly differentiated ways.
>
> (Ito, undated)

A vivid example of this refashioning of commercial media by everyday imagination is provided by Julian Sefton-Green's study of the consumption of the *Pokémon* game-universe by his 6-year-old son, Sam (Sefton-Green 2004). The study offers significant insights into computer games as distinct media forms and their play as distinct cultural practices. For example, Sam's Gameboy sessions alternated with intense periods of study, poring over *Pokémon* magazines, rehearsing plots and remembering cues. He learned all the maps within the Poké-world and the locations of secret keys and potions. Obsessive discussion about how to get his *Pokémon* characters to grow levels (evolve) and to have enough strength and/or hit points to defeat the enemy he knew he was going to face . . .

> Towards the end of the game he did get very frustrated with his ability to defeat the Elite 4 (the penultimate challenge) and eventually he sought help. About 75 hours into the game, on a visit to the home of family friends who had older children (and Gameboys), Sam asked for their assistance. The older boys gave him some advice and also allowed him to hook his Gameboy to one of their machines to swap characters; taking pity on him, they gave him a well-developed Golduck (level 60). At that point, Sam essentially saw the game as a personal individual challenge and because he was not part of a larger community of players he seemed indifferent to the social dimension provided by this aspect of the game. Crucially, from his perspective, when he was given the Golduck, he also learned a 'cheat': 'You go to Viridian City and talk to this person who tells you how to train Pokémon. Then you go to Cinnabar Island and swim along the right hand edge. When you find a Missingo it changes to what's top of your list [of objects carried with you] to more than a hundred; and if it's rare candy [which enables Pokémon to evolve] you can grow your Pokémon.'
>
> (Sefton-Green 2004: 147)

This cheat 'transformed his attitude to the game' and he completed it and other versions much more quickly. The 'cheat' then is a complex actor, at once a software technology, a videogame media convention, a gameplay tactic, and a social resource.

Not only are games and their playing distinct from television and television viewing, but moreover, they require on some level an understanding of their distinct nature as interactive computer media 'texts' or technologies. Sefton-Green describes the experience of the *Pokémon* game as one of tension between the game's imaginative world (its diegesis) and its formal constitution as a logical (software) system. For example a hyperpotion powerup might be saved for a favourite character, Butterfree, rather than given to the more strategically powerful Vaporeon:

> For Sam, part of the challenge of the game was learning to see it as a discrete rule-bound process in and of itself and not as a natural phenomenon that could be addressed following the logic of the TV series.
>
> (Sefton-Green 2004: 151)

In his play, Sam does not differentiate between old and new media. He made up songs about his favourite Pokémon, played with Pokémon toys in the bath and enacted Pokémon-style battles with friends. Though books and magazines are as much a part of Sam's engagement with the Poké-world as videogames are, Sefton-Green suggests that we may be seeing different kinds of engagement with 'old' media in these videogame play cultures: Sam is an intense autodidact, educating himself in the minutiae of a simulated world, but devours this printed material not only to immerse himself in an imaginative fantasy world, but as information or tools for play.

This Poké-world reveals a vision of a transformed everyday life/media culture, newly populated with alien species, shot through with 'colourless energy' and hyperpotions, and governed by the conflicting systems of children's media drama and software logic. Sam lives in an ecology that is both virtual and actual; an ecology simultaneously playful and very serious.

4.5.3 Play, media and everyday life

Play is a key term in the development of popular computer media and in theories of identity and subjectivity in digital culture. As we have seen it underpins cybercultural shifting subjectivities, notably online 'identity play', and is a foundational concept in important areas of new media research and history: exploratory, ludic computer programming and robotics are seen as educationally progressive (Papert 1980, 1994); play and games are central to the development of personal computing via the ethics and aesthetics of the early hackers (Levy 1994); and the necessary experimentation of early home computer use (Haddon 1988a). While it is clear that these playful, creative activities are to be understood as distinct from, or opposite to, the instrumental uses of computer media (word processing, spreadsheets, work-related emails etc.), the concept of play itself is rarely defined or reflected on. Moreover implicit assumptions about play can be put to ideological use; anxieties about videogames are often bound up in contradictory assumptions about the value, and types of, play. The most popular mode of non-instrumental engagement with computer media, videogame play, provokes, as we have seen, profound anxieties and wild assumptions of militarised imaginations, servile participation and hypnotic alienation.

Play has not been exposed to sustained study in Media Studies either, though there are notable and useful exceptions and these will be briefly surveyed below. In Cultural and Media Studies too then the value of play in a mediated everyday life is often ambiguous – perhaps creative and resistant, but also worryingly conformist or rule-bound. The exemplars of media form and consumption from which Media Studies has developed some of its key concepts tend to be news media and drama, not entertainment or ludic media such as comedy or game shows. The popularity of videogames as a media form offers the opportunity to foreground play in a number of ways: as a mode of cultural practice in general; as a mode of media consumption; as a way into analysing the forms and conventions of ludic media and media games; and as a way of thinking about the 'consumption' of computer media as non-instrumental 'uses' of technology. One of the first projects of the field of Game Studies has been to locate and synthesise disparate theories of play and games from across the humanities and social sciences (Salen and Zimmerman 2003; Dovey and Kennedy 2006; Perron 2003).

This section will not attempt a comprehensive survey of theories of play but will suggest some implications of taking play seriously as a cultural phenomenon of central significance to new media studies as well as to the study of videogame culture. It will concentrate on notions of games and play as:

- fundamental to culture, yet undertheorised;

- an ambiguous yet central aspect of – both part of and separate from – the space and time of everyday life;

- a distinct yet ambiguous form of entertainment and communication media, and their consumption (not least with the advent of new media); and

- a concept with the potential to confuse a series of distinctions underpinning Cultural and Media Studies and new media studies, including consumption/production, real/fantasy, rules/freedom, ideology/critique, meaning/nonsense, as well as generating or repurposing a few new ones – for example, simulation/representation.

Theories of time, space and games

The literature of play operates at the margins and in the interstices of the humanities and social sciences. In his book *Homo Ludens* (1986 [1938]), the cultural historian Johan Huizinga suggested that play is not an ephemeral, inconsequential activity, but an essential, central, factor in civilisation. Religious rituals, sport and drama, to name but three near-universal cultural realms, are all characterised by types of play – for Huizinga play and games can be very serious activities. The human then is not characterised primarily by rational thought and self-awareness (*homo sapiens*) or creativity and the use of technology (*homo faber*) but by play (*homo ludens*).

Though central to culture, play is always, according to Huizinga, separate from ordinary or real life, it is 'a stepping out of "real" life into a temporary sphere of activity with a disposition all of its own' (Huizinga 1986: 8). Separated from the materially necessary activities of work and the satisfaction of bodily needs, it occurs in *interludes* in daily life. Play is not ephemeral however; through its often regular repetitions and rituals (football matches on Sunday, crossword puzzles in coffee breaks) it is integral to everyday life. Play is distinct from other areas of everyday life both temporally and spatially, 'It is "played out" within certain limits of time and place',

> the arena, the card-table, the magic circle, the temple, the stage, the screen, the tennis court, the court of justice, etc. are all in form and function play-grounds, i.e. forbidden spots, isolated, hedged around, hallowed, within which special rules obtain. All are temporary worlds within the ordinary world, dedicated to the performance of an act apart.
>
> (Huizinga 1986: 10)

CASE STUDY 4.11: Playing the Internet

Sonia Livingstone recounts a story from her research, an account illustrative of the fundamentally enmeshed relationships between technology, media, imaginative play, 'real' and 'virtual' space:

Two eight year old boys play their favourite multimedia adventure game on the family PC. When they discover an Internet site where the same game could be played interactively with unknown others, this occasions great excitement in the household. The boys choose their fantasy personae, and try diverse strategies to play the game, both co-operative and competitive, simultaneously 'talking' online (i.e. writing) to the other participants. But when restricted in their access to the Internet, for reasons of cost, the game spins off into 'real life'. Now the boys, together with their younger sisters, choose a character, dress up in battle dress, and play 'the game' all over the house, going downstairs to Hell, The Volcanoes and The Labyrinth, and upstairs to The Town, 'improving' the game in the process. This new game is called, confusingly for adult observers, 'playing the Internet'.

(Livingstone 1998: 436)

This brief account is tantalisingly illustrative of the fundamentally enmeshed relationships between technology, media, imaginative play, 'real' and 'virtual' space. Yet the 'Internet game' is offered as an interesting aside to the article's primary research concerns, and its implications are left unexplored. It is a reflection of the problem discussed in **4.3.4** above that new technologies may be visible and available for analysis at moment of 'impact' (or breakdown) but not once 'adopted' and naturalised. But it is also perhaps a problem of describing, assessing and theorising *play* as a mode of being in mediated everyday life.

These children have not left the real world for cyberspace, they have at once invented new games with new media, and demonstrated a powerful sense of continuity with play and games pre-dating digital culture, playing with and performing in space that is both actual and imaginary. Technology, media, performance, consumption, family and gender relationships are all intertwined in the ambiguous time and space of play.

Rules of the game: *ludus* and *paidia*

Roger Caillois developed Huizinga's ideas and his categorisation of types of play and games has been particularly influential on Game Studies' consideration of play theory. He categorised what he saw as the fundamental elements of play: *agon* – competitive play, as found in many sports and games from football to chess; *alea* – games largely based on the workings of chance; *mimicry* – role play or make-believe; and *ilinx* – or 'vertigo', dizziness and disorder, evident in children rolling down hills or screaming (Caillois 1962: 25). These categories are not mutually exclusive and are often evident as pairs within particular games. For example, though *agon* and *alea* are opposites, one relying on skill and dedication, the other on luck, they are both present in many card games.

Cutting across these categories is an axis that measures the underlying qualities of particular games or types of play. One pole on this axis is *ludus*, and the other *paidia*. Ludus denotes modes of play characterised by adherence to strict rules: 'calculation, contrivance, subordination to rules'. Paidia is the opposite: 'true' creative play – 'active, tumultuous, exuberant, spontaneous' (Caillois 1962: 53). Thus chess can be placed near the ludus end of this axis, whereas the imaginative and improvised make-believe of young children would sit at the opposite pole of paidia. It is the political or moral values given to positions on this ludus–paidia axis, rather than the categories of agon, alea, mimicry and ilinx, which often underlie popular and academic anxieties about videogame play. Videogames are generally, in this sense, ludic: rule-bound and apparently not offering much space for spontaneity or innovation. As the influential critic of videogames, Eugene Provenzo put it,

[c]ompared with the worlds of imagination provided by play with dolls and blocks, [video] games . . . ultimately represent impoverished cultural and sensory environments for the child.

(Provenzo 1991: 97)

Significantly however Caillois himself does not privilege paidia over ludus. For him, ludus is fundamentally linked with the development of civilisation. Rules, he asserts, transform play 'into an instrument of fecund and decisive culture' (Caillois 1962: 27). On a more everyday level, the ludic is also evident in more respectable games and activities such as chess, crossword puzzles, even detective stories. Many videogames share this intellectual play – the solving of puzzles for no apparent reason than the pleasure of doing so. Moreover, even ludic games need room for improvisation:

the game consists of the need to find or continue at once a response which is free within the limits set by the rules. This latitude of the player, this margin accorded to his action is essential to the game and partly explains the pleasure which it excites.

(Caillois 1962: 8)

Sherry Turkle identifies a relationship between the paidia of fantasy, and the rule-bound ludic in videogames. Science fiction and fantasy fiction are extremely influential on the development of video and computer games, not only at the level of symbolic content (spaceships and monsters), but through the operations of an analogous tension between the fantastical or imaginative, and the logical and rule-governed.

A planet can have any atmosphere, but its inhabitants must be adapted to it . . . You can postulate anything, but once the rules of the system have been defined they must be adhered to scrupulously.

(Turkle 1984: 77)

Similarly, the logic of the videogame world is that events may well be surprising, but they shouldn't be arbitrary. Ultimately, then, she argues that computer games are rule-governed rather than open-ended (Turkle 1984: 78; see also Provenzo 1991: 88ff).

What do games mean?

The place of games and play in culture is ambiguous. For Caillois, while games are fundamental to civilisation, 'play and ordinary life are constantly and universally antagonistic to each other' (Caillois 1962: 63). For Marshall McLuhan games are at once communication media, a popular art form, and a collective modelling of society:

Games, like institutions, are extensions of social man and of the body politic, as technologies are extensions of the animal organism . . . As extensions of the popular response to the workaday stress, games become faithful models of a culture. They incorporate both the action and the reaction of whole populations in a single dynamic image.

(McLuhan 1967: 235)

They are not simple representations of a culture though. McLuhan's games share with those of Caillois an ambiguous relationship with the social world, they exist within it but distinct from it:

> Games are a sort of artificial paradise like Disneyland, or some Utopian vision by which we interpret and complete the meaning of our daily lives. In games we devise means of non-specialized participation in the larger drama of our time.
>
> (McLuhan 1967: 238)

Games then are separate from the world in time and space, played within boundaries and bound by rules. However in important ways they are part of the world: they may figure or model their larger social context, and of course they are part of the world in that people play games everyday – they are no less real for being distinct from other cultural activities. Moreover this notion of the game dynamically modelling real world relationships or forces resonates with simulation as a computer media form. Simulation finds particular expression in particular genres of videogame (from *SimCity* and *SimAnt* to the current popularity of *The Sims*) but is, in highly significant ways, integral to all videogames.

In fact, for Caillois, the separation of play from other areas of everyday life is essential. The danger in games comes not from restrictive rules, but rather from their 'corruption' if their autonomy from the real world is undermined: for example, the horoscope's aleatory blurring of reality and chance, or the vertiginous corruptions of drug and alcohol consumption. It is precisely the sharp delineation between fantasy and reality that protects the player from alienation from the real world (Caillois 1962: 49).

See **1.2.6** Simulated

Games mean nothing: ludology to simulation

> Video games are a window onto a new kind of intimacy with machines that is characteristic of the nascent computer culture. The special relationship that players form with video games has elements that are common to interactions with other kinds of computers. The holding power of video games, their almost hypnotic fascination, is computer holding power.
>
> (Turkle 1984: 60)

If, on the one hand, videogames spring from mass media, and on the other, media consumption in general can be seen as playful, can the videogame be analysed as a specific new medium, and do its ludic practices have any distinct critical purchase? In shifting the emphasis to games as a specific set of cultural forms, rather than play as a general mode of consumption, we can see that videogames do mark a significant new medium: mass media as games. That is to say, though boardgames may draw on entertainment themes and images, they are not as thoroughly imbricated in, or formally similar to, the images and action of moving image media: film, animation and television. There is in the content of videogames a semiotic complexity at the level of content not evident in chess or golf or *Cluedo*.

However, despite evident continuities and connections between videogames and other popular media, we might ask whether established methods of media theory are fully adequate to the study of videogames. Where distinctions are made between videogames and earlier electronic media, they tend to be drawn along questions of the mode of consumption or spectatorship of these interactive, 'immersive' forms. The videogame as computer-based medium, and its interactive consumption, requires specific critical attention.

> A jaundiced figure floats across the screen. He is constantly searching for things to eat. We are looking at a neo-Marxist parable of late capitalism. He is the pure consumer. With his obsessively gaping maw, he clearly wants only one thing: to feel whole, at peace with

himself. He perhaps surmises that if he eats enough – in other words, buys enough indus-trially produced goods – he will attain this state of perfect selfhood, perfect roundness. But it can never happen. He is doomed forever to metaphysical emptiness. It is a tragic fable in primary colours.

(Poole 2000: 189)

As Steven Poole demonstrates in his tongue-in-cheek (though telling) interpretation of the symbolic content of *Pac-Man*, videogames may not be 'representational' in the same way as other popular visual media. Visually *Gran Turismo* represents a car race (or more accurately it remediates television's representations of motor racing), but playing the game is little like watching a race on television. The pleasures of controlling and responding to the screen rep-resentations follow the logic of the game itself, a logic of variables within a system. Videogames are, in the strict sense of the word established in **1.2.6**, simulations.

  While the pleasures of many videogames cannot be entirely separated from the material dynamics and processes they simulate – and part of the pleasure of a videogame like *Doom* is the sense of more directly engaging with or intervening in (even 'controlling') popular media images and action – they cannot be analysed only in terms of methodologies of film or tele-vision textual analysis. Neither *Monopoly* nor *SimCity* are accurate models of the complex systems of property markets or urban development. Each is a game, with its own structure and economy set up to defer and grant pleasure, to facilitate the solitary passing of time, or social interaction. Whatever the narrative potential for the videogame, its conventions and modes of play are inseparable from its status as computer media. Playing a videogame requires an understanding of, even a decoding of, its structure or system. This system (of levels, of architectural organisation, of points, timing of events, of non-player characters' AI, etc.) is itself, of course, a highly complex semiotic system, which could feasibly be thought of as radically independent from the particular set of images or scenarios textured-mapped over it. For example, the *Doom* 'engine', as we have seen, has been used as the basis for a number of quite different interactive environments.

  Underneath the flashy graphics, cinematic cut-scenes, real-time physics, mythological back-stories and everything else, a videogame at bottom is still a highly artificial, purposely designed semiotic engine.

(Poole 2000: 214)

Media play

Earlier in this Part it was suggested that the notion of popular media 'consumption' might not be fully adequate to an understanding of videogame play. Recent work in Media Studies has suggested that *play* might be a productive term for thinking about media 'consumption' more generally. Roger Silverstone for instance regards the mass media and play as inseparable:

  We are all players now in games, some or many of which the media make. They distract but they also provide a focus. They blur boundaries but still somehow preserve them. For, arguably we know, even as children, when we are playing and when we are not. The thresholds between the mundane and the heightened spaces of the everyday are still there to be crossed, and they are crossed each time we switch on the radio or television, or log on to the World Wide Web. Playing is both escape and engagement. It occupies protected spaces and times on the screen, surrounding it and, at some further remove. While we can enter media spaces in other ways and for other purposes, for work or for information, for example, while they exist to persuade as well as to educate, the media are a principal site in and through which, in the securities and stimulation that they offer the viewers of the world, we play: subjunctively, freely, for pleasure.

(Silverstone 1999a: 66)

The fort/da game refers to Freud's observations of his eighteen-month-old grandson throwing a wooden reel on a string out of his cot, and pulling it back in, making sounds Freud took to be 'fort' (gone) and 'da' (there). Freud interpreted this as the infant playing out his anxieties over his mother's absence and return

For John Fiske, the pleasure of engagement with the texts and images of the media is the 'active' consumer's articulation of the relationship of the real world and media representations and is both creative and playful. However playing with the boundary between the real and the representation in media consumption can also be an anxious activity. Fiske cites arguments that children's control of television sets (changing channels, switching the set on and off) is a kind of electronic fort/da game. Children will also playfully explore the distinction between the symbolic and the real in the content of programmes – satirising representations they do not approve of (Fiske 1987: 231).

Both of these elements of play – the anxious and the performative – are also evident in, indeed central to, videogame play. They raise the question of the political dynamic of play in general and videogame play in particular: what is the relationship between the activity, performance and pleasure of the player, the specific rules of the game and broader social rules and ideologies? For John B. Thomson, the everyday politics of individual identities in the dominant symbolic systems (ideologies or discourses) can be discussed in ludic terms, 'Like a game of chess, the dominant system will define which moves are open to individuals and which are not' (Thompson 1995: 210). Whilst for Fiske, playing with the rules is an emancipatory activity:

> The pleasures of play derive directly from the players' ability to exert control over rules, roles, and representations – those agencies that in the social are the agencies of subjection, but in play can be agents of liberation and empowerment. Play, for the subordinate, is an active, creative, resistive response to the conditions of their subordination: it maintains their sense of subcultural difference in the face of the incorporating forces of the dominant ideology.

(Fiske 1987: 236)

In a response to political and press condemnation of videogame arcades (or video parlours) in Australia in the 1980s, Fiske and Jon Watts expand on this politics of play. They argue that there is a contradiction

> centred in the technical nature of the games themselves, in that they offer disapproved of versions of activities that are normally highly valorised by society at large: they position the player in interaction with a machine (the reference for this is clearly the production line) and they position him in front of an electronic screen like that of the television set. Clearly, the similarities to two such central social activities as manufacturing and television-watching cannot be responsible for the parlours' antisocial image, but they provide us with a starting point for our investigation, which must concern itself with inversions of the normal, not with reproductions of it.

(Fiske and Watts 1985)

It is interesting to note that in the two decades since this essay was published the electronic screen has become the technological locus of work as well as leisure. The salient point here is that playful activities that 'look like' non-playful activities (whether these activities are the virtual violent activities on screen or the activities of the player in front of the machine) are not necessarily analogues for those non-playful activities. Like a medieval festival they might turn the world upside down.

However, if play as cultural practice so thoroughly suffuses contemporary media consumption and identity construction, there is a danger of losing any sense of it as a critical or analytical term in understanding new media. It should also be noted that these examples of attention to play in Media Studies, welcome as they are, are speculative, sketches for a potential field of enquiry. They do not draw on, and do not conduct, ethnographic research into media play. Game Studies is beginning to undertake both theoretical and empirical research into play however. The work of the anthropologist Victor Turner on play, for example, has been used to examine the communication in, and talk around, the multiplayer game *Counterstrike* (Wright, *et al.* 2002, see also Dovey and Kennedy 2006: 34–35). More often though, play is introduced as part of efforts to define games, whether for the purposes of defining the key concepts of Game Studies (Walther 2003), of the analysis of games as a distinct cultural form (Juul 2003) or to inform the game design process (Salen and Zimmerman 2003).

4.5.4 Playing with a computer

We have suggested that the development of personal computing is bound up in playful practices and identified some characteristics of videogames as new media, distinct from other screen-based popular media. What does it mean though, to play with a computer?

> Play is sometimes invoked or factored in to support studies of which it is not the main object of research. Studies of fan fiction use a notion of play to articulate the creativity of such practices around the scaffolding of the source text (Jenkins 1992; Hills 2002). Matt Hills uses the psychologist D. W. Winnicott's theories of play as a 'third space' between the subject and object (for instance the child and his or her toy) in his work in this field

4.17 Game code: *Evil Alien*. Reproduced from COMPUTER SPACE GAMES by permission of Usborne Publishing Ltd, © 1982

Interactivity as gameplay

While action games are perceived as crude and one-dimensional, it must be remembered that game events unfold, through play, in real time. Key aspects of established narrative visual media (cinema and television drama), such as timing, plot, character development and depth, the controlled revelation of narrative information to the viewer, etc. are all extremely limited by interactivity. The player is not only immersed in but is also 'responsible' for the onscreen events. If the game ends it is because of the player's failure, not the deeply established reassurance of narrative closure. It could be added that, contrary to the prevalent critical view of games such as *Doom* or *Grand Theft Auto* as an uncomplicated desire for control and mastery, gameplay is characterised as much by anxiety, even fear, as by triumphant machismo. Players lose constantly, replay and are 'killed' again.

There is a contradiction, or at least a tension, here between the player's awareness of the conventions and thorough artificiality of this experience, and the real, often visceral fear this experience can provoke. We know this from horror films – we are quite conscious, from the music and other signs, that something is about to jump out, but this knowledge only seems to heighten the experience rather than defuse it. The videogame compensates with other features, depending on the genre: *Tomb Raider* (a mixture of reflexes, lateral thinking and spatial awareness), *Silent Hill* (atmosphere), or *Tetris* (reflexes and panic).

Learning

Whilst all media consumption requires knowledge of particular codes, and is always an active process, 'decoding' or learning is foregrounded in the interactive playing of videogames. The process of learning the codes and conventions, the ways of understanding and playing the game must take place with each genre of game. Each genre has its own mode of interaction – and each game within the genre invents its own variations, different combinations of buttons to press or peripherals to add. Mastering the controls of each game is essential, and a fundamental pleasure in its own right. Videogames are, as Provenzo says, 'literally teaching machines that instruct the player . . . in the rules . . . as it is being played' (Provenzo 1991: 34).

It is not just the controls and rules that the player must learn. Each videogame is a semiotic universe – every element from backgrounds to characters, walls, trees, etc. is coded and its place within the meaning of the world and its playing decided. Nothing is incidental or random. Again we return to the peculiarly non-immersive quality of videogame play – to some degree, the more sophisticated the representation of an immersive world, the more aware the player must be of its artifice. The graphic and conceptual simplicity of *Tetris* may leave the player, hours later, with a feeling of having been in a trance, but to play *Tomb Raider*, for example, is to learn the semiotics of virtual world construction. The environments are like stage sets: painted backdrops, with some elements that appear to function as we would expect their referents in the real world to (doors that open, stairs that can be climbed, etc.). Some elements do not – windows and doors can serve only a decorative function. Move Lara Croft up close to a foliage-covered wall of architectural ornament and it is revealed as pixellated graphics mapped onto the regular polygonal units that structure these artificial realms.

Identification

> it is often assumed in popular descriptions of game-playing that a facile process of iden-
> tification occurs . . . given that one appears to play many games in the first person and
> that one is 'rewarded' by maintaining the 'life' of this character, it is all too easy to assume
> an identification between player and role, but characters in computer games are rarely
> complicated personae.
>
> (Sefton-Green, quoted in Green *et al*. 1998: 27)

This active engagement with the very structure of the videogame in its playing suggests that
established critical frameworks for understanding the relationship of the media spectator to
media text are not enough. Theories of cinema spectatorship, founded on the assumption
that viewers identify with the film's main protagonist, may initially appear useful to studying
gameplay, given the videogame player's interactive control of the game's characters.
However, as the shift from second to third person in this instruction book indicates, this is not
a straightforward connection:

> Infiltrate without being seen by your enemies. You're Solid Snake and you've got to single-
> handedly infiltrate the nuclear weapons disposal facility, which is being occupied by a
> group of terrorists. If the enemy spots Snake, they will call in reinforcements and go after
> him. You can't win a firefight against superior numbers, so try to avoid unnecessary bat-
> tles whenever you can.
>
> (Konami's *Metal Gear Solid* instruction book, 1999)

The consumption of this new medium can only be understood if the videogame is theorised
as software as well as media text – as computer-based media. As Poole argues, the player
of *Pac-Man* is 'having a conversation with the system on its own terms' (Poole 2000: 197).

In this Part of the book we have already touched on the complexities of videogame play
and identity and the cybernetic relationship between players and game technologies. The following two case studies explore these issues further and in relation to the symbolic and
abstract systems of the videogame as computer media object.

CASE STUDY 4.12: Identifying with the computer in simulation games

Ted Friedman has explored this question of the videogame player's identification with the texts, images and worlds of this new medium. He focuses on the successful genre of simulation games, games in which complex social, historical, geographical, or fantastical inter-actions are modelled by the computer (for example, *Populous*, *SimCity*, *Theme Park*, *SimAnt*, *Civilisation*, etc.). Sometimes known as 'God games', the player is usually 'omniscient', the interface is a bird's-eye view or isometric map-like representation of the game's world over which the player can scroll. The player is not, however, omnipotent. The object is not to control the simulation fully, but instead to intervene within the unfolding complex developments (geo-politics, city development or fantastical evolutionary processes, etc.), to shape these dynamic forces according to each game's algorithms. The game may be extremely open-ended – the *SimCity* player chooses the kind of urban environment they wish to encourage, and there is often no obvious end, solution or victory. The player, therefore, does not 'identify' with any individual protagonist, as they might if watching a film. Instead, Friedman argues, in the game *Civilisation II*, the player has to juggle numerous different roles at the same time, 'king, general, mayor, city planner, settler, warrior, and priest to name but a few' (Friedman 1995). We cannot here talk, as film theory might, about occupying subject positions in our iden-tification with this game. For Friedman, rather, the player must identify 'with the computer itself . . . the pleasures of a simulation game come from inhabiting an unfamiliar, alien mental state: from learning to think like a computer' (Friedman 1999).

As we have seen, the interactive playing of a game does not allow the player free rein:

> computers 'teach structures of thought', 'reorganize perception'. Simulation games in particular aestheticize our cybernetic con-nection to technology. They turn it into a source of enjoyment and an object for contemplation . . . Through the language of play, they teach you what it feels like to be a cyborg.
>
> (Friedman 1999)

Here, then, we see videogames not as ephemeral digital toys but as offering unique opportunities for engaging with and making sense of the complex and intimate relationships – networks even – between people and computer media and technology.

Ted Friedman (1999) 'Civilisation and its Discontents: simulation, subjectivity, and space', in Greg Smith (ed.) *On a Silver Platter: CD-ROMs and the promises of a new technology*, New York: New York University Press, pp. 132–150. Available online: http://www.duke.edu/~tlove/civ.htm (accessed 6/11/00)

CASE STUDY 4.13: Identifying with codes and demons

The complex shifting of focus and identification necessary to play videogames is clearly indicated in an Australian study of the implications of children's videogame culture for education. Two twelve year old boys were asked to play a favourite Nintendo game (*Super Ghouls and Ghosts*). One of the friends played the game and the other observed and offered commentary. Their dialogue is revealing of the complexities of their engagement with the game:

Louis: What is the game play about? What are you actually doing here?

Jack: Well, you're . . . what you do is you go around shooting zombies, with weapons like daggers, arrows. . .

Louis: Like medieval-time weapons?

Jack: Yes.

Louis*:* Yeah, OK – What is your favourite level that you have encountered?

Jack: My favourite level has to be the first level . . .

Louis: The first level . . . Easy?

Jack: Yes, it's fairly easy.

Louis: Now, do you like playing the game normally, or do you like having it with the codes inputted?

Jack: I like playing it with . . . both.

Louis: Oh, OK . . . What kind of codes would you put in for the action replay, which we have at this moment, Da Dah!!!!

Jack: I would, I would put . . . 'continuous jumping', which means you can just jump, and jump, and just keep jumping . . .

Louis: . . . and jump, and jump, and jump, and jump . . . What else? Infinite energy, is that a code?

Jack: I'd make it immune, I'd make myself immune to my enemies. That means no enemies could rip me.

Louis: Oh, that's alright. I like how that goes.

(Green *et al.* 1998: 27)

A little later:

Jack: Like, how about . . . I wish I was Knight Arthur. Could you please explain who Knight Arthur is?

Louis: He is the character you play in this story. I wish I could be Knight Arthur with my little pro-action replay plugged in . . . and I would turn on, I'd turn on the action again. I'd put in, let's see, 70027602 in the code importer, and you would get, you'd be immune to enemy attacks if . . . I can walk around it going through flames and lava and big demons like hydras and things.

(Green *et al.* 1998: 28)

The researchers are particularly concerned with questions of the kinds of 'literacy' demonstrated here – as the children switch between text and images on screen and on printed pages. They point out that these children have a clear sense that they are playing a game, that they see themselves separately from the game's characters. 'Identification', then, is with the game as program, the boys are engaging with its semiotic structure, simultaneously articulating the iconography (medieval weapons, etc.), its conventions (levels, bosses), and knowledge external to the game (codes and cheats). Playing such games involves the simultaneous mapping of the game as software, as simulated space, and as symbolic environment, within their social circuits and resources.

It is worth noting the sheer complexity of this gameplay – within the same breath the boys are talking in terms of symbolic content (monsters and knights), virtual space, identification with characters/avatars, yet they are also engaging with the game as software, simultaneously ludic and algorithmic, offering tactical variations within a system (cheats): a manipulation of the gameworld at the level of program as well as symbolic content.

Videogame play is bound up in the materiality and imaginary of cyberculture. William Gibson's sketch of intense arcade players is an ur-moment in the genesis of cyberpunk and his insight and the implications of it for understanding cyberculture more generally are discussed in detail in Part 5 of this book

4.5.5 Cybernetic play

Ted Friedman has seen the cybernetic loops between game and player as only a particularly intense example of those of computer use more generally:

> What makes interaction with computers so powerfully absorbing – for better or worse – is the way computers can transform the exchange between reader and text into a feedback loop. Every response you make provokes a reaction from the computer, which leads to a new response, and so on, as the loop from the screen to your eyes to your fingers on the keyboard to the computer to the screen becomes a single cybernetic circuit.
>
> (Friedman 1995).

In similar terms, James Newman points out that

> Importantly, the . . . relationship between player and system/gameworld is not one of clear subject and object. Rather, the interface is a continuous interactive feedback loop, where the player must be seen as both implied and implicated in the construction and composition of the experience.
>
> (Newman 2002: 410).

This notion of digital game playing as cybernetic takes us beyond notions of the 'interactivity' of popular new media and has far-reaching consequences. In these terms interactivity can be seen as players choosing pathways or objects via interfaces and menus, perhaps not so far removed from other forms of media consumption. To describe digital gameplay as cybernetic though is to suggest a much more intense and intimate relationship between the human and the machine, and a relationship in which neither partner is dominant, or, as Newman intimates, clear distinctions between them become unsustainable. Player and software are a circuit. It is not surprising then that the monstrous figure of the cyborg stalks through discussions of the nature of videogame play (see also Lahti 2003 and Giddings and Kennedy 2006).

As we have seen, for Ted Friedman the player is taught how to think 'like a cyborg', and for Katherine N. Hayles the adolescent videogame player is a 'metaphoric' cyborg. In her work on female *Quake* players Helen W. Kennedy is clearly using this terminology literally (**4.4.3** above). For her, gameplay is cybernetic, 'networks and flows of energy which are entirely interdependent', in gameplay 'there is no player separate to the interface and game world, there is a fusion of the two into a cyborgian subjectivity – composed of wires, machines, code and flesh' (Kennedy 2007: 126). The fact that this videogame-and-player loop is temporary or intermittently constructed (i.e. it exists as such only in particular moments of gameplay) should not detract from either its reality or its technocultural significance. In these terms then the event of videogame play can be thought of as *literally* cyborgian, not only a human subject in a technologised environment, but rather as the human as one element in an event assembled from and generated by both human and nonhuman entities.

This not only challenges a fundamental tenet of Media Studies – that media messages or communication are always only socially (not physically or technologically) determined, it also suggests that gameplaying in particular (but also technocultural relationships more generally) must be conceived of in ways which fundamentally challenge existing ways of theorising the relationships between humans and (media) machines (and the physical world).

4.6 Conclusion: everyday cyberculture

By exploring the everyday use of, and play with, popular new media, it quickly becomes clear that these new technologies do not mark the end of everyday life and relationships; the 'real world' is not left behind for the blinking lights, geometries and disembodiment of a fictional cyberspace. Instead we see a much more complex – and interesting – picture. The communication vectors of the Internet, the dynamic spaces of videogames, the 'technological imaginary' of all of these are interwoven, fitting into the architecture of the home, movement through the urban environment, established patterns of gender, family and social life, and dramatised by both the instrumental fantasies of hardware and software producers and the action filled narratives of popular culture. Slotting into, or levering open, everyday realities, flickering between technology and media, cyberspace and everyday space are enmeshed and interpenetrating, 'continuous with and embedded in other social spaces' (Miller and Slater 2000: 4).

This section has drawn on theoretical and empirical approaches to the study of everyday life and society from the humanities and social sciences, and Cultural and Media Studies in particular. Yet throughout it became clear that key humanist tenets of these intellectual frameworks are limited and do not fully address the specific questions raised by digital media technologies nor do they adequately describe the texture and circuits of everday digital culture. In particular the following issues were raised:

- How 'newness' and change might be identified, described and theorised in the context of the ostensibly mundane and persistent spatiotemporal and technosocial relationships that constitute the domestic environment;

- How an understanding of the specific nature of digital media as soft and hard technologies can inform the study of popular digital culture, both in terms of commercial media objects and in terms of lived experience;

- How an attention to play as a ubiquitous, yet elusive, mode of cultural engagement is similarly central to everyday cyberculture;

- How digital media effect new intimacies between minds, bodies and machines;

- How alternative theoretical resources are required to conceptualise relationships of agency and effect between heterogeneous actors without always assuming the primacy of human agency.

This last issue demands further enquiry. It asserts that culture has always been technoculture, and thus has marked ontological implications for the study of the historical and social nature of technology. Part 4 has explored some aspects of the networks and relationships that constitute contemporary cyberculture at the level of everyday experience. The monstrous figure of the cyborg has been repeatedly invoked, as it stalks through discussions of corporeality and identity. In Part 5 we will more fully interrogate the history and philosophy of technoculture in general and cyberculture in particular.

Bibliography

Aarseth, Espen *Cybertext: perspectives on ergodic literature*, Baltimore, Md.: Johns Hopkins University Press, 1997.

Aarseth, Espen 'Computer game studies: year one', *Game Studies* 1.1 (July) http://www.gamestudies.org (accessed July 2001).

Abbott, Chris 'Making connections: young people and the internet', in *Digital Diversions: youth culture in the age of multimedia*, ed. Julian Sefton-Green, London: UCL Press, 1998, pp. 84–105.

Adorno, Theodor *The Culture Industry: selected essays on mass culture*, London: Routledge, 1991.

Akrich, Madeleine 'The de-scription of technological objects', in *Shaping Technology / Building Society: studies in sociotechnical change,* eds Wiebe Bijker and John Law, Cambridge Mass.: MIT Press, 1992, pp. 205–223.

Alloway, Nola and Gilbert, Pam 'Video game culture: playing with masculinity, violence and pleasure', in *Wired Up: young people and the electronic media*, ed. Sue Howard, London: UCL, 1998, pp. 95–114.

Aronowitz, Stanley, Martinsons, Barbara, Menser, Michael and Rich, Jennifer *Technoscience and Cyberculture*, London: Routledge, 1996.

Atkins, Barry *More than a Game: the computer game as fictional form*, Manchester: Manchester University Press, 2003.

Badmington, Neil ed. *Posthumanism,* Basingstoke: Palgrave Macmillan, 2000.

Balsamo, Anne *Technologies of the Gendered Body: reading cyborg women*, Durham N.C. and London: Duke University Press, 1996.

Balsamo, Anne, 'Introduction', *Cultural Studies* 12 (1998): 285–299.

Banks, John 'Controlling gameplay', *M/C journal: a journal of media culture* [online], 1(5) (1998). Available from http://journal.media-culture.org.au/9812/game.php (accessed 20/9/05).

Barba, Rick *Doom Battlebook*, Rocklin, Calif.: Prima Publishing, 1994.

Barker, Martin *Video Nasties*, London: Pluto Press, 1984.

Bassett, Caroline 'Virtually gendered: life in an online world', in *The Subcultures Reader*, eds Ken Gelder and Sarah Thornton, London: Routledge, 1997, pp. 537–550.

Baudrillard, Jean *Simulations*, New York: Semiotext(e), 1983.

Baudrillard, Jean *The Revenge of the Crystal*, London: Pluto Press, 1990.

Bazalgette, Cary and Buckingham, David *In Front of the Children: screen entertainment and young audiences*, London: BFI, 1995.

Bell, David *An Introduction to Cybercultures*, London: Routledge, 2001.

Bell, David and Kennedy, Barbara eds *The Cybercultures Reader*, London: Routledge, 2000.

Benedikt, M. ed. *Cyberspace: first steps*, Cambridge, Mass.: MIT Press, 1991.

Bernstein, Charles 'Play it again, Pac-Man', *Postmodern Culture* 2.1 (September 1991) http://www.iath.virginia.edu/pmc/text-only/issue.991/pop-cult.991 (accessed July 2002).

Bijker, Wiebe *Of Bicycles, Bakelites, and Bulbs: toward a theory of sociotechnical change*, London: MIT Press, 1997.

Bijker, Wiebe and Law, John eds *Shaping Technology/Building Society: society studies in sociotechnical change*, Cambridge Mass.: MIT Press, 1992.

Bingham, Nick, Valentine, Gill and Holloway, Sarah L. 'Where do you want to go tomorrow? Connecting children and the Internet', *Environment and Planning D – Society and Space* 17.6 December (1999): 655–672.

Birkerts, Sven *The Gutenberg Elegies: the fate of reading in an electronic age*, London: Faber and Faber, 1994.

Bloch, Linda-Renee and Lemish, Dafna 'Disposable love: the rise and fall of a virtual pet', *New Media and Society*, 1(3) (1999): 283–303.

Boddy, William 'Redefining the home screen: technological convergence as trauma and business plan' at the *Media in Transition* conference, MIT, 8 October 1999. http://media-in-transition.mit.edu/articles/boddy.html (accessed May 2001).

Bolter, Jay David and Grusin, Richard *Remediation: understanding new media*, Cambridge, Mass. and London: MIT Press, 1999.

Bromberg, Helen 'Are MUDs communities? Identity, belonging and consciousness in virtual worlds', in *Cultures of Internet: virtual spaces, real histories, living bodies*, ed. Rob Shields, London: Sage, 1996.

Buckingham, David *After the Death of Childhood: growing up in the age of electronic media*, Oxford: Polity Press, 2000.

Buick, Joanna and Jevtic, Zoran *Cyberspace for Beginners*, Cambridge: Icon Books, 1995.

Bukatman, Scott *Terminal Identity*, Durham, N.C.: Duke University Press, 1993.

Bull, Michael 'The world according to sound: investigating the world of Walkman users', *New Media and Society*, 3(2) (2001a): 179–197.

Bull, Michael 'Personal stereos and the aural reconfiguration of representational space', in *TechnoSpaces: inside the new media*, ed. Sally Munt, London: Continuum, 2001b

Burgin, Victor, Kaplan, Cora and James, Donald *Formations of Fantasy*, London: Methuen, 1986.

Burkeman, Oliver 'Pokemon power', *Guardian G2*, 20 April 2000, pp. 1–3.

Burkeman, Oliver 'The internet', *The Guardian*, 2 January 2008, online at http://www.guardian.co.uk/g2/story/0,,2234176,00.html (accessed Feb. 2008).

Burnett, Robert and Marshall, P. David *Web Theory: an introduction*, London: Routledge, 2003.

Butler, Judith 'Subjects of sex/gender/desire', in *The Cultural Studies Reader* (2nd edn) ed. Simon During, London:

Routledge, 2000, pp. 340–353.

Caillois, Roger *Man, Play and Games*, London: Thames and Hudson, 1962.

Cameron, Andy 'Dissimulations; illusions of interactivity', http://www.hrc.wmin.ac.uk/hrc/ theory/dissimulations/t.3.2 (accessed January 2002).

Carr, Diane 'Playing with Lara', in *Screenplay: cinema/videogames/interfaces*, eds Geoff King and Tanya Krzywinska, London: Wallflower Press, pp. 171–180.

Casas, Ferran 'Video games: between parents and children', in *Children, Technology and Culture: the impacts of technologies in children's everyday lives*, eds Ian Hutchby and Jo Moran Ellis, London: Routledge, 2001, pp. 42–57.

Cassell, Justine and Jenkins, Henry *From Barbie to Mortal Kombat: gender and computer games,* Cambridge, Mass.: MIT Press, 1999.

Ceruzzi, Paul 'Inventing personal computing', in *The Social Shaping of Technology: how the refrigerator got its hum*, eds Donald MacKenzie and Judy Wajcman, Milton Keynes: Open University Press, 1999, pp. 64–86.

Chandler, Daniel 'Video games and young players' (1994) http://www.aber.ac.uk/media/Documents/ short/vidgame.html (accessed May 2000).

Chandler, Daniel 'Personal home pages and the construction of identities on the web', http://www.aber.ac.uk/media/Documents/short/webident.html (1998) (accessed May 2000).

Chandler, Daniel and Roberts-Young, Dilwyn 'The construction of identity in the personal homepages of adolescents' (1998) http://www.aber.ac.uk/Documents/short/strasbourg.html (accessed May 2000).

Cockburn, Cynthia 'The circuit of technology: gender, identity and power', in *Consuming Technologies: media and information in domestic spaces*, eds Roger Silverstone and Eric Hirsch, London: Routledge, 1992.

Cockburn, Cynthia and Furst Dilic, Ruza *Bringing Technology Home: gender and technology in a changing Europe*, Milton Keynes: Open University Press, 1994.

Collins, Jim *Architectures of Excess: cultural life in the information age*, London: Routledge, 1995.

Consalvo, Mia 'It's no videogame: news commentary and the second Gulf War', in *Level Up: digital games research conference* [online], eds Marinka Copier and Joost Raessens, Utrecht: Faculty of Arts, Utrecht University, 2003. Available from http://oak.cats.ohiou.edu/~consalvo/consalvo_its_no_videogame.pdf (accessed April 2006).

Cooper, Hilary 'Fleecing kids', *Guardian*, 10 June 2000.

Copier, Marinka 'The other game researcher: participating in and watching the construction of boundaries in game studies', in *Level Up: digital games research conference*, eds Marinka Copier and Joost Raessens, Utrecht: Faculty of Arts, Utrecht University, 2003, pp. 404–419.

Cunningham, Helen 'Mortal Kombat and computer game girls', in *In Front of the Children: screen entertainment and young audiences*, eds Cary Bazalgette and David Buckingham, London: BFI, 1995.

Daliot-Bul, Michal 'Japan's mobile technoculture: the production of a cellular playscape and its cultural implications', *Media, Culture & Society*, 29(6) (2007): 954–971.

Dant, Tim 'The driver-car', *Theory, Culture & Society*, vol. 21(4/5) (2004): 61–79.

Darley, Andrew *Visual Digital Culture: surface play and spectacle in new media genres*, London: Routledge, 2000.

Davis-Floyd, Robbie and Dumit, Joseph eds *Cyborg Babies: from techno-sex to techno-tots*, London: Routledge, 1998.

De Certeau, Michel *The Practice of Everyday Life*, London: University of California Press, 1988.

De Certeau, Michel 'Walking in the city', in *The Cultural Studies Reader*, ed. Simon During, London: Routledge, 1993, pp. 151–160.

Dery, Mark ed. *Flame Wars – the discourse of cyberculture*, London: Duke University Press, 1994.

Dewdney, Andrew and Boyd, Frank 'Computers, technology and cultural form', in Martin Lister, *The Photographic Image in Digital Culture*, London: Routledge, 1995.

Dibbell, Julian 'Covering cyberspace', Paper delivered at the *Media in Transition* conference at MIT, Cambridge, Mass. (1999) http://media-In-transition.mit.edu/articles/dibbell.html (accessed June 2000).

Didur, Jill, 'Re-embodying technoscientific fantasies: posthumanism, genetically modified foods and the colonization of life', *Cultural Critique* 53 (2003).

Dixon, Shanly and Weber, Sandra eds *Growing Up Online: young people and digital technologies*, New York, Palgrave Macmillan, 2007.

Dovey, Jon ed. *Fractal Dreams: new media in social context*, London: Lawrence & Wishart, 1996.

Dovey, Jon and Kennedy, Helen W. *Game Cultures: computer games as new media*, Milton Keynes: Open University Press, 2006.

Downey, Gary Lee, Dumit, Joseph and Williams, Sarah 'Cyborg anthropology', in *The Cyborg Handbook*, eds Chris Hables Gray with Steven Mentor and Heidi J. Figuera-Sarriera, London: Routledge, 1995, pp. 341–346.

Druckrey, Timothy 'Deadly representations, or apocalypse now', *Ten-8* 2(2) (1991): 16–27.

du Gay, Paul, Hall, Stuart, Janes, Linda, Mackay, Hugh and Negus, Keith *Doing Cultural Studies: the story of the Sony Walkman*, London: Sage, 1997.

Dyson, Esther *Release 2.0: A design for living in the digital age*, London: Viking, 1997.

Economic and Social Research Council *Virtual Society? The social science of electronic technologies Profile 2000*, Swindon: Economic and Social Research Council, 2000.

Edge, Future Publishing, 'XBox from concept to console', September 2000, pp. 70–77.

Edge, Future Publishing, 'XBox comes out of the box', February 2001, pp. 7–13.

Ellis, John *Visible Fictions: cinema, television, video*, London: Routledge & Kegan Paul, 1982.

Facer, K., Furlong, J., Furlong, R. and Sutherland, R. 'Constructing the child computer user: from public policy to private practices', *British Journal of Sociology of Education* 22.1 (2001a): 91–108.

Facer, K., Furlong, J, Furlong, R. and Sutherland, R. 'Home is where the hardware is: young people, the domestic environment and "access" to new technologies', in *Children, Technology and Culture*, eds Ian Hutchby and Jo Moran-Ellis, London: Falmer Press, 2001b, pp. 13–27.

Facer, Keri, Sutherland, Rosamund, Furlong, Ruth and Furlong, John, 'What's the point of using computers? The development of young people's computer expertise in the home', *New Media and Society*, 2(2) (2001): 199–219.

Featherstone, Mike *Consumer Culture and Postmodernism*, London: Sage, 1990.

Featherstone, Mike and Burrows, Roger *Cyberspace, Cyberbodies, Cyberpunk: cultures of technological embodiment*, London: Sage, 1995.

Feenberg, Andrew and Bakardjieva, Maria, 'Virtual community: no "killer implication"', *New Media and* Society, 6(1) (2004): 37–43.

Fidler, Roger *Mediamorphosis: understanding new media*, London: Sage, 1997.

Finnemann, Niels Ole 'Modernity modernised', in *Computer Media and Communication: a reader,* ed. Paul A. Mayer, Oxford: Oxford University Press, 1999.

Fiske, John *Television Culture*, London: Methuen, 1987.

Fiske, John 'Cultural studies and the culture of everyday life', in *Cultural Studies*, eds L. Grossberg, Cary Nelson and Paula Treichler, London: Chapman and Hall, 1992.

Fiske, John and Watts, Jon 'Video games: inverted pleasures', *Australian Journal of Cultural Studies* [online], 3 (1) (1985). Available from http://wwwmcc.murdoch.edu.au/ReadingRoom/serial/AJCS/3.1/Fiske.html (accessed 7/2/06).

Fleming, Dan *Powerplay: toys as popular culture*, Manchester: Manchester University Press, 1996.

Flew, Terry *New Media: an introduction* (2nd edn), Oxford: Oxford University Press, 2005.

Flynn, Bernadette, 'Geography of the digital hearth', *Information, Communication and Society*, 6(4) (2003): 551–576.

Foucault, Michel *The Order of Things*, London: Tavistock, 1970.

Foucault, Michel *Madness and Civilisation: a history of insanity in the age of reason*, London: Routledge, 1989.

Frasca, Gonzalo 'Simulation versus narrative: introduction to ludology', in *The Video Game Theory Reader*, eds Mark J. P. Wolf and Bernard Perron, London: Routledge, 2003, pp, 221–236.

Friedman, Ted 'Making sense of software', in *Cybersociety: computer-mediated communication and community*, ed. Steven G. Jones, Thousand Oaks, Calif.: Sage, 1995.

Friedman, Ted 'Civilisation and its discontents: simulation, subjectivity and space' (1999) http://www.gsu.edu/~jouejf/civ.htm (accessed July 2002). Also published in *On a Silver Platter: CD-ROMs and the promises of a new technology*, ed. Greg Smith, New York: New York University Press, 1999, pp. 132–150.

Fuller, Mary and Jenkins, Henry 'Nintendo and New World travel writing: a dialogue', in *Cybersociety: computer-mediated communication and community*, ed. Steven G. Jones, London: Sage, 1995, pp. 57–72.

Furlong, Ruth 'There's no place like home', in *The Photographic Image in Digital Culture*, ed. Martin Lister, London: Routledge, 1995, pp. 170–187.

Gelder, Ken and Thornton, Sarah *The Subcultures Reader*, London: Routledge, 1997.

Giddings, Seth, 'Playing with nonhumans: digital games as technocultural form', in *Selected Papers from Changing Views: Worlds in Play*, eds Suzanne Castells and Jen Jensen, Vancouver: Simon Fraser University, 2005.

Giddings, Seth 'I'm the one who makes the Lego Racers go: studying virtual and actual play', in *Growing Up Online: young people and digital technologies*, eds Shanly Dixon and Sandra Weber, New York: Palgrave/Macmillan, 2007.

Giddings, Seth and Kennedy, Helen W. 'Digital games as new media', in *Understanding Digital Games*, eds Jason Rutter and Jo Bryce, London: Sage, 2006, pp. 149–167.

Giddings, Seth and Kennedy, Helen 'Little Jesuses and fuck-off robots: on aesthetics, cybernetics and not being very good at *Lego Star Wars*', in *The Pleasures of Computer Gaming: Essays on Cultural History, Theory and Aesthetics*, eds Melanie Swalwell and Jason Wilson, Jefferson N.C.: McFarland, 2006.

Gray, Ann *Video Playtime: the gendering of a leisure technology*, London: Routledge, 1992.

Gray, Chris Hables ed. with Mentor, Steven and Figuera-Sarriera, Heidi J. *The Cyborg Handbook*, London: Routledge, 1995.

Gray, Chris Hables *Citizen Cyborg: politics in the posthuman age*, London: Routledge, 2002.

Gray, Peggy and Hartmann, Paul 'Contextualizing home computing – resources and practices', in *Consuming Technologies – media and information in domestic spaces*, eds Roger Silverstone and Eric Hirsch, London: Routledge, 1992, pp. 146–160.

Green, Bill, Reid, Jo-Anne and Bigum, Chris 'Teaching the Nintendo generation? Children, computer culture and popular technologies', in *Wired up: young people and the electronic media*, ed. Sue Howard, London: UCL Press, 1998, pp. 19–42.

Green, Eileen and Adam, Alison *Virtual Gender: technology, consumption and identity*, London: Routledge, 2001.

Haddon, Leslie 'Electronic and computer games – the history of an interactive medium', *Screen* 29.2 Spring (1988a): 52–73.

Haddon, Leslie 'The home computer: the making of a consumer electronic', *Science as Culture* no. 2 (1988b): 7–51.

Haddon, Leslie 'The cultural production and consumption of IT', in *Understanding Technology in Education*, eds Hughie Mackay, Michael Young and John Beynon, London: Falmer Press, 1991, pp, 157–175,

Haddon, Leslie 'Explaining ICT consumption: the case of the home computer', in *Consuming Technologies – media and information in domestic spaces*, eds Roger Silverstone and Eric Hirsch, London: Routledge, 1992, pp. 82–96.

Haddon, Leslie 'Interactive games', in *Future Visions: new technologies of the screen*, eds Philip Haywood and Tana Wollen, London: BFI, 1993, pp. 123-147.

Hakken, David *Cyborgs@Cyberspace: an ethnographer looks to the future*, London: Routledge, 1999.

Halberstam, Judith and Livingston, Ira eds *Posthuman Bodies*, Bloomington: Indiana University Press, 1996.

Hall, Stuart 'Encoding, decoding', in *The Cultural Studies Reader* (2nd edn), ed. Simon During, London: Routledge, 2000 [1973], 507–517.

Hall, Stuart 'Minimal selves', *ICA Documents 6: Identity*, London: ICA, 1987, pp. 44–46.

Hall, Stuart ed. *Representation: cultural representations and signifying practices*, London: Sage, 1997.

Hall, Stuart, Held, David and McGrew, Tony *Modernity and its Futures*, Cambridge: Polity Press, 1992.

Haraway, Donna 'A manifesto for cyborgs: science, technology, and socialist feminism in the 1980s', In *Feminism / Postmodernism*, ed. Linda J. Nicholson, London: Routledge, 1990.

Haraway, Donna *The Haraway Reader*, London: Routledge, 2004.

Harries, Dan ed. *The New Media Book*, London: BFI, 2002.

Harvey, David *The Condition of Postmodernity: an enquiry into the origins of cultural change*, Oxford: Blackwell, 1989.

Hayles, N. Katherine, 'Virtual bodies and flickering signifiers', *October*, 66 (1993). Available from: http://www.english.ucla.edu/faculty/hayles/Flick.html (accessed 3/3/05).

Hayles, N. Katherine, 'Narratives of artificial life', in *Futurenatural: nature, science, culture*, eds George Mackay *et al.*, London: Routledge, 1996, pp. 146–164.

Hayles, N. Katherine *How We Became Posthuman: virtual bodies in cybernetics, literature and informatics*, London: University of Chicago Press, 1999.

Hayward, Susan *Cinema Studies: the key concepts*, London: Routledge, 1996.

Hebdige, Dick *Subculture: the meaning of style*, London: Methuen, 1979.

Heim, Michael 'The erotic ontology of cyberspace' [online], chapter from *The Metaphysics of Virtual Reality*, New York: Oxford University Press, 1993, pp. 82–108. Available from: http://www.cc.Rochester.edu/college/FS/Publications/ (accessed 5/3/00)

Heise, Ursula K. 'Unnatural ecologies: the metaphor of the environment in media theory', *Configurations*, 10(1) (2002): 149–168.

Herz, J. C. *Joystick Nation: how video games gobbled our money, won our hearts and rewired our minds*, London: Abacus, 1997.

Highmore, Ben *Everyday Life and Cultural Theory*, London: Routledge, 2001.

Hills, Matt *Fan Cultures*, London: Routledge, 2002.

Hine, Christine *Virtual Ethnography*, London: Sage, 2000.

Howard, Sue *Wired-Up: young people and the electronic media*, London: UCL, 1998.

Huffaker, David A. and Calvert, Sandra L. 'Gender, identity and language use in teenage blogs', *Journal of Computer-Mediated Communication*, 10(2) (2005) http://jcmc.indiana.edu/vol10/issue2/huffaker.html (accessed Jan. 2008).

Huhtamo, Erkki 'From kaleidoscomaniac to cybernerd: notes toward an archaeology of media', in *Electronic Culture: technology and visual representation*, ed. Timothy Druckrey, New York: Aperture, 1996.

Huizinga, Johan *Homo Ludens: a study of the play element in culture*, Boston: Beacon Press, 1986.

Hutchby, Ian and Moran-Ellis, Jo *Children, Technology and Culture*, London: Falmer, 2001.

Ito, Mizuko 'Inhabiting multiple worlds: making sense of SimCity 2000 ™ in the fifth dimension', in *Cyborg Babies: from techno-sex to techno-tots*, eds Robbie Davis-Floyd and Joseph Dumit, London: Routledge, 1998, pp. 301-316.

Ito, Mizuko 'Mobilizing the imagination in everyday play: the case of Japanese media mixes', draft of chapter to appear in the *International Handbook of Children, Media, and Culture*, ed. Sonia Livingstone and Kirsten Drotner, undated. http://www.itofisher.com/mito/ito.imagination.pdf (accessed Jan. 2008).

Jameson, Fredric *Postmodernism, or the Cultural Logic of Late Capitalism*, London: Verso, 1991.

Jenkins, Henry *Textual Poachers: television fans and participatory culture*, London: Routledge, 1992.

Jenkins, Henry 'X logic: respositioning Nintendo in children's lives', *Quarterly Review of Film and Video* 14 (August 1993): 55–70.

Jenkins, Henry, '"Complete freedom of movement": video games as gendered play spaces' [online], in *From Barbie to Mortal Kombat: gender and computer games*, eds Henry Jenkins and Justine Cassell, Cambridge, Mass.: MIT Press, 1998. Available from: http://web.mit.edu/21fms/www/faculty/henry3/publications.html (accessed 21/9/05).

Jenkins, Henry 'Professor Jenkins goes to Washington' (11 June 2001) http://web.mit.edu/21fms/www/faculty/henry3/profjenkins.html.

Jenkins, Henry *Convergence Culture: where old and new media collide*, New York: New York University Press, 2006.

Jensen, Klaus Bruhn 'One person, one computer: the social construction of the personal computer', in *Computer Media and Communication: a reader*, ed. Paul A. Mayer, Oxford: Oxford University Press, 1999, pp. 188–206.

Jha, Alok, 'Live longer, live better: futurologists pick top challenges of next 50 years', *The Guardian*, Saturday 16 February 2008, http://www.guardian.co.uk/science/2008/feb/16/genetics.energy (accessed Feb. 2008).

Jones, Steven G. ed. *Cybersociety: computer-mediated communication and community*, London: Sage, 1995.

Jones, Steven G. ed. *Virtual Culture: identity and communication in cybersociety,* London: Sage, 1997.

Jones, Steven G. ed. *Cybersociety 2.0: revisiting computer-mediated communication and community,* London: Sage, 1998.

Jones, Steven G. ed. *Doing Internet Research: critical issues and methods for examining the net,* London: Sage, 1999.

Juul, Jesper 'The game, the player, the world: looking for a heart of gameness', in *Level Up: digital games research conference*, eds Marinka Copier and Joost Raessens, Utrecht: Faculty of Arts, Utrecht University, 2003.

Juul, Jesper *Half-Real: video games between real rules and fictional worlds*, Cambridge, Mass.: MIT Press, 2005.

Keegan, Paul 'In the line of fire', *Guardian G2,* 1 June 2000, pp. 2–3.

Kellner, Douglas *Media Culture: identity and politics between the modern and the postmodern*, London: Routledge, 1995.

Kelly, Kevin *Out of Control: the new biology of machines*, London: Fourth Estate, 1995.

Kember, Sarah *Virtual Anxiety: photography, new technologies and subjectivity*, Manchester: Manchester University Press, 1998.

Kember, Sarah *Cyberfeminism and Artificial Life*, London: Routledge, 2003.

Kennedy, Helen W. 'Lara Croft: feminist icon or cyberbimbo? on the limits of textual analysis', *Game Studies* 2(2) (2002) http://www.gamestudies.org/0202/ (accessed 10/10/04).

Kennedy, Helen W. 'Female *Quake* players and the politics of identity', in *Videogame, Player, Text*, eds Barry Atkins and Tanya Krzywinska, Manchester: Manchester University Press, 2007, pp. 120–138.

Kinder, Marsha *Playing with Power in Movies, Television and Video Games: from Muppet Babies to Teenage Mutant Ninja Turtles*, Berkeley: University of California Press, 1991.

Kitzmann, Andreas 'Watching the web watch me: explorations of the domestic web cam' (1999), http://web.mit.edu/comm-forum/papers/kitzmann.html.

Kline, Stephen, Dyer-Witheford, Nick and de Peuter, Greig, *Digital Play: the interaction of technology, culture and marketing*, Montreal: McGill-Queen's University Press, 2003.

Kroker, Arthur *The Possessed Individual – technology and postmodernity*, London: Macmillan, 1992.

Krzywinska, Tanya, 'Being a determined agent in (the) *World of Warcraft*: text/play/identity', in *Videogame, Player, Text*, eds Barry Atkins and Tanya Krzywinska, Manchester: Manchester University Press, 2007, pp. 101–119.

Lahti, Martti 'As we become machines: corporealized pleasures in video games', in *The Video Game Theory Reader*, eds Mark J.P. Wolf and Bernard Perron, London: Routledge, 2003, pp 157–170.

Lally, Elaine *At Home with Computers*, Oxford: Berg, 2002.

Landow, George P. *Hypertext – the convergence of contemporary critical theory and technology*, Baltimore, Md.: Johns Hopkins University Press, 1992.

Landow, George P. *Hyper/Text/Theory*, Baltimore, Md.: Johns Hopkins University Press, 1994.

Latour, Bruno, 'Technology is society made durable', in *A Sociology of Monsters*, ed. John Law, London: Routledge, 1991, pp 103–131.

Latour, Bruno 'Where are the missing masses? the sociology of a few mundane artefacts', in *Shaping Technology / Building Society: studies in sociotechnical change,* eds Wiebe Bijker and John Law, Cambridge Mass.: MIT Press, 1992, pp. 225–258.

Latour, Bruno *We Have Never Been Modern*, London: Harvester Wheatsheaf, 1993.

Latour, Bruno *Pandora's Hope: essays on the reality of science studies*, London: Harvard University Press, 1999.

Laurel, Brenda *Computers as Theatre*, Reading, Mass.: Addison-Wesley, 1993.

Law, John ed. *A Sociology of Monsters*, London: Routledge, 1991.

Law, John 'Notes on the theory of the actor network: ordering, strategy and heterogeneity', Lancaster: Centre for Science Studies, Lancaster University (1992) http://www.comp.lancs. ac.uk/sociology/papers/Law-Notes-on-ANT.pdf (accessed July 2008).

Lea, Marin *The Social Contexts of Computer Mediated Communication*, London: Harvester-Wheatsheaf, 1992.

Levy, Steven *Hackers – heroes of the computer revolution*, Harmondsworth: Penguin, 1994.

Lievrouw, Leah and Livingstone, Sonia *The Handbook of New Media*, London: Sage, 2002.

Lister, Martin ed. *The Photographic Image in Digital Culture*, London: Routledge, 1995.

Livingstone, Sonia 'The meaning of domestic technologies', in *Consuming Technologies – media and information in domestic spaces*, eds R. Silverstone and E. Hirsch, London: Routledge, 1992, pp. 113–130.

Livingstone, Sonia 'Mediated childhoods: a comparative approach to young people's media environments in Europe', *European Journal of Communication* 13.4 (1998): 435–456.

Lohr, Paul and Meyer, Manfred eds *Children, TV and the New Media: a research reader*, Luton: University of Luton Press, 1999.

Lunenfeld, Peter *The Digital Dialectic: new essays on new media*, Cambridge, Mass.: MIT, 1999.

Lupton, Deborah 'Monsters in metal cocoons: "road rage" and cyborg bodies', *Body and Society*, 5(1) (1999): 57–72.

Mackay, Hugh *Consumption and Everyday Life: culture, media and identities*, London: Open University Press/Sage, 1997.

MacKenzie, Donald and Wajcman, Judy *The Social Shaping of Technology: how the refrigerator got its hum* (1st edn), Buckingham: Open University Press, 1985.

MacKenzie, Donald and Wajcman, Judy *The Social Shaping of Technology* (2nd edn), Buckingham: Open University Press, 1999.

Manovich, Lev 'Navigable space' (1998) http://www.manovich.net (accessed January 2001).

Manovich, Lev *The Language of New Media*, Cambridge Mass.: MIT Press, 2001.

Marks Greenfield, Patricia *Mind and Media – the effects of television, computers and video games*, London: Fontana, 1984.

Mason, Paul 'Kenya in crisis', BBC News Online, 8 Jan 2007, http://news.bbc.co.uk/1/hi/technology/6241603.stm.

Mayer, Paul A. *Computer Media and Communication: a reader*, Oxford: Oxford University Press, 1999.

McAffrey, Larry *Storming the Reality Studio – a casebook of cyberpunk and postmodern fiction,* Durham, N.C.: Duke University Press, 1991.

McLuhan, Marshall *The Gutenberg Galaxy: the making of typographic man*, London: Routledge, 1962.

McLuhan, Marshall *Understanding Media: the extensions of man*, London: Routledge, 1967.

McNamee, Sara 'Youth, gender and video games: power and control in the home', in *Cool Places: geographies of youth cultures,* eds Tracey Skelton and Gill Valentine, London: Routledge, 1998.

McRobbie, Angela 'Postmodernism and popular culture', in *Postmodernism*, ed. Lisa Appignansesi, London: ICA, 1986.

Metz, Christian *Psychoanalysis and Cinema: the imaginary signifier*, London: Macmillan, 1985.

Miles, David 'The CD-ROM novel *Myst* and McLuhan's Fourth Law of Media: *Myst* and its "retrievals"', in *Computer Media and Communication: a reader*, ed. Paul Mayer, Oxford: Oxford University Press, 1999, pp. 307–319.

Miles, Ian, Cawson, Alan and Haddon, Leslie 'The shape of things to consume', in *Consuming Technologies – media and information in domestic spaces,* R. Silverstone and E. Hirsch, London: Routledge, 1992, pp. 67–81.

Miller, Daniel and Slater, Don *The Internet: an ethnographic approach*, Oxford: Berg, 2000.

Miller, Toby *Popular Culture and Everyday Life*, London: Sage, 1998.

Moores, Shaun 'Satellite TV as cultural sign: consumption, embedding and articulation', *Media, Culture and Society* 15 (1993a): 621–639.

Moores, Shaun *Interpreting Audiences: the ethnography of media consumption*, London: Sage, 1993b.

Morley, David, *Family Television: cultural power and domestic leisure*, London: Comedia, 1986.

Morley, David 'Where the global meets the local: notes from the sitting room', *Screen* 32.1 (1991): 1–15.

Morley, David and Robins, Kevin *Spaces of Identity – global media, electronic landscapes and cultural boundaries*, London: Routledge, 1995.

Morris, Sue 'First-person shooters: a game apparatus', in *ScreenPlay: cinema/videogames/interfaces*, eds Geoff King and Tanya Krzywinska, London: Wallflower, 2002, pp. 81–97.

Morse, Margaret *Virtualities: television, media art, and cyberculture*, Bloomington: Indiana University Press, 1998.

Murray, Janet *Hamlet on the Holodeck: the future of narrative in cyberspace*, New York: The Free Press, 1997.

Negroponte, Nicholas *Being Digital*, London: Hodder & Stoughton, 1995.

Negroponte, Nicholas 'Beyond digital', *Wired*, 6.12 (December 1998), http://www.wired.com/wired/archive/6.12/negroponte.html (accessed June 2001).

Newman, James 'In search of the videogame player: the lives of Mario', *New Media and Society*, 4(3) (2002): 405–422.

Nixon, Helen 'Fun and games are serious business', in *Digital Diversions: youth culture in the age of multimedia*, ed. Julian Sefton-Green, London: UCL Press, 1998.

Norman, Donald A. *The Design of Everyday Things*, New York: Basic Books, 2002.

Norris, Christopher *Uncritical Theory: postmodernism, intellectuals and the Gulf War*, London: Lawrence and Wishart, 1992.

Nunes, Mark, 'What space is cyberspace? the Internet and virtuality', in *Virtual Politics: identity and community in cyberspace*, ed. David Holmes, London: Sage, 1997, pp. 163–178.

Oftel Residential Survey, online at http://www.statistics.gov.uk/STATBASE/ssdataset.asp?vlnk=7202.

O'Riordan, Kate, 'Playing with Lara in virtual space', in *Technospaces: inside the new media*, ed. Sally R. Munt, London: Continuum, 2001, pp. 124–138.

Papert, Seymour *Mindstorms: computers, children and powerful ideas*, London: Harvester Press, 1980.

Papert, Seymour *The Children's Machine: rethinking school in the age of the computer*, London: Harvester-Wheatsheaf, 1994.

Penley, Constance and Ross, Andrew eds *Technoculture*, Minneapolis: University of Minnesota Press, 1991.

Perron, Bernard 'From gamers to player and gameplayers', in *The Video Game Theory Reader*, eds Mark J.P. Wolf and Bernard Perron, London: Routledge, 2003, pp. 195–220.

Plant, Sadie 'Beyond the screens: film, cyberpunk and cyberfeminism', *Variant* 14, Summer (1993): 12–17.

Plant, Sadie 'The future looms: weaving women and cybernetics', in *Cyberspace Cyberbodies Cyberpunk: cultures of technological embodiment*, eds Mike Featherstone and Roger Burrows, London: Sage, 1995.

Plant, Sadie 'On the matrix: cyberfeminist simulations', in *The Cybercultures Reader*, eds David Bell and Barbara M. Kennedy, London: Routledge, 2000, pp. 325–336.

Poole, Steven *Trigger Happy: the secret life of video games*, London: Fourth Estate, 2000.

Popper, Frank *Art of the Electronic Age*, London: Thames & Hudson, 1993.

Poster, Mark *The Mode of Information: poststructuralism and social context*, Cambridge: Polity Press, 1990.

Poster, Mark 'Postmodern virtualities', in *Cyberspace Cyberbodies Cyberpunk: cultures of technological embodiment*, eds Mike Featherstone and Roger Burrows, London: Sage, 1995a.

Poster, Mark 'Community, new media, post-humanism', Undercurrent 2 (Winter 1995b) http:// darkwing.uoregon.edu/~ucurrent/2-Poster.html (accessed July 2000).

Provenzo, Eugene F. Jr. *Beyond the Gutenberg Galaxy: microcomputers and the emergence of post-typographic culture*, New York: Teachers College Press, 1986.

Provenzo, Eugene F. Jr. *Video Kids – making sense of Nintendo*, Cambridge, Mass.: Harvard University Press, 1991.

Pryor, Sally 'Thinking of oneself as a computer', *Leonardo* 24.5 (1991): 585–590.

Raessens, Joost and Goldstein, Jeffrey *Handbook of Computer Game Studies*, Cambridge, Mass.: MIT Press, 2005.

Rheingold, Howard *Virtual Reality*, London: Mandarin, 1991.

Rheingold, Howard *The Virtual Community – finding connection in a computerised world*, London: Secker & Warburg, 1994.

Robins, Kevin, 'Cyberspace and the worlds we live in', in *Fractal Dreams: new media in social context*, ed. Jon Dovey, London: Lawrence & Wishart, 1996, pp. 1–30.

Robins, Kevin and Webster, Frank 'Cybernetic capitalism: information, technology, everyday life', http://www.rochester.edu/College/FS/Publications/RobinsCybernetic.html (accessed July 2000). The print version appears in *The Political Economy of Information*, eds Vincent Mosco and Janet Wasko, Madison: The University of Wisconsin Press, 1988, pp. 45–75.

Robins, Kevin and Webster, Frank *Times of the Technoculture: from the information society to the virtual life*, London: Routledge, 1999.

Roden, David, 'Cyborgian subjects and the auto-destruction of metaphor', in *Crash Cultures*, eds Jane Arthurs and Iain Grant, Bristol: Intellect, 2003, pp. 91–102.

Ross, Andrew 'Hacking away at the counterculture', in *Technoculture*, eds Constance Penley and Andrew Ross, Minneapolis: University of Minnesota Press, 1991.

Rutter, Jason and Bryce, Jo *Understanding Digital Games*, London: Sage, 2006.

Salen, Katie and Zimmerman, Eric *The Rules of Play: game design fundamentals*, Cambridge Mass.: MIT Press, 2003.

Sanger, Jack, Wilson, Jane, Davies, Bryn and Whittaker, Roger *Young Children, Videos and Computer Games: issues for teachers and parents*, London: Falmer Press, 1997.

Sefton-Green, Julian *Digital Diversions: youth culture in the age of multimedia*, London: UCL Press, 1998.

Sefton-Green, Julian *Young People, Creativity and New Technologies: the challenge of digital art*, London: Routledge, 1999.

Sefton-Green, Julian 'Initiation rites: a small boy in a Poke-world', in *Pikachu's Global Adventure: the rise and fall of Pokemon*, ed. J. Tobin, Durham, N.C.: Duke University Press, 2004, pp. 141–164.

Sefton-Green, Julian and Parker, David *Edit-Play: how children use edutainment software to tell stories*, BFI Education Research Report, London: BFI, 2000.

Sheff, David *Game Over – Nintendo's battle to dominate an industry*, London: Hodder & Stoughton, 1993.

Shields, Rob ed. *Cultures of Internet: virtual spaces, real histories, living bodies*, London: Sage, 1996.

Silverstone, Roger, *Television and Everyday Life*, London: Routledge 1994.

Silverstone, Roger *Why Study the Media?*, London: Sage, 1999a.

Silverstone, Roger 'What's new about new media?, *New Media and Society* 1.1 (1999b): 10–82.

Silverstone, Roger and Hirsch, Eric 'Listening to a long conversation: an ethnographic approach to the study of information and communication technologies in the home', *Cultural Studies* 5.2 (1991): 204–227.

Silverstone, Roger and Hirsch, Eric *Consuming Technologies – media and information in domestic spaces,* London: Routledge, 1992.

Skirrow, Gillian 'Hellivision: an analysis of video games', in *High Theory/Low Culture – analysing popular television and film*, ed. Colin MacCabe, Manchester: Manchester University Press, 1986, pp. 115–142.

Slator, Don 'Trading sexpics on IRC. embodiment and authenticity on the internet', *Body and Society* 4.4 (1998): 91–117.

Spigel, Lynn, 'Media homes: then and now', *International Journal of Cultural Studies* 4(4) (2001): 385–411.

Springer, Claudia, 'The pleasure of the interface', *Screen*, 32(3) (1991): 303–323.

Springer, Claudia *Electronic Eros: bodies and desire in the postindustrial age*, London: Athlone, 1996.

Squires, Judith, 'Fabulous feminist futures and the lure of cyberspace', in *Fractal Dreams: new media in social context*, ed. Jon Dovey, London: Lawrence & Wishart, 1996, pp. 194–216.

Stallabrass, Julian 'Just gaming: allegory and economy in computer games', *New Left Review* March/April (1993): 83–106.

Sterling, Bruce *Mirrorshades – the cyberpunk anthology*, London: HarperCollins, 1994.

Stern, Susannah R. 'Adolescent girls' expression on web home pages: spirited, sombre and selfconscious sites', *Convergence: the journal of research into new media technologies* 5.4 Winter (1999): 22–41.

Sterne, Jonathan 'Thinking the Internet: cultural studies versus the millennium', in *Doing Internet Research: critical issues and methods for examining the Net*, ed. Steven G. Jones, London: Sage, 1999, pp. 257–287.

Stone, Allucquere Rosanne *The War of Technology and Desire at the Close of the Mechanical Age*, Cambridge, Mass.: MIT Press, 1995.

Strathern, Marilyn 'Foreword: the mirror of technology', in *Consuming Technologies – media and information in domestic spaces*, eds Roger Silverstone and Eric Hirsch, London: Routledge, 1992, pp. vii–xiii.

Stutz, Elizabeth 'What electronic games cannot give', *Guardian*, 13 March 1995.

Sudnow, David *Pilgrim in the Microworld: eye, mind and the essence of video skill*, London: Heinemann, 1983.

Sutton-Smith, Brian, *Toys as Culture*, New York: Gardner Press, 1986.

Sutton-Smith, Brian, *The Ambiguity of Play*, Cambridge, Mass.: Harvard University Press, 1998.

Taylor, T. L. *Play Between Worlds: exploring online game culture*, Cambridge, Mass.: MIT Press, 2006.

Terry, Jennifer *Processed Lives: gender & technology in everyday life*, London: Routledge, 1997.

Thacker, Eugene *The Global Genome: biotechnology, politics and culture*, Cambridge, Mass.: MIT Press, 2005.

Thompson, John B. *The Media and Modernity: a social theory of the media*, Cambridge: Polity Press, 1995.

Thrift, Nigel 'Electric animals: new models of everyday life?', *Cultural Studies* 18(2.3), May/March (2004): 461–482.

Thurlow, Crispin, Lengel, Laura and Tomic, Alice *Computer Mediated Communication*, London: Sage, 2004.

Tobin, Joseph 'An American Otaku (or, a boy's virtual life on the net)', in *Digital Diversions: youth culture in the age of multimedia*, ed. J. Sefton-Green, London: UCL Press, 1998, pp. 106–127.

Tomlinson, Alan ed. *Consumption, Identity and Style: marketing, meanings and the packaging of pleasure*, London: Routledge, 1990.

Trend, David ed. *Reading Digital Culture*, Oxford: Blackwell, 2001.

Turkle, Sherry *The Second Self-Computers & the Human Spirit*, London: Granada, 1984.

Turkle, Sherry *Life on the Screen: identity in the age of the internet*, London: Weidenfeld & Nicolson, 1995.

Turkle, Sherry 'Constructions and reconstructions of the self in virtual reality', in *Electronic Culture: technology and representation*, ed. Timothy Druckrey, New York: Aperture, 1996, pp. 354–365.

Turkle, Sherry, 'Cyborg babies and cy-dough-plasm: ideas about self and life in the culture of simulation', in *Cyborg Babies: from techno-sex to techno-tots*, eds Robbie Davis-Floyd and Joseph Dumit, London: Routledge, 1998, pp. 317–329.

Turkle, Sherry, 'What are we thinking about when we are thinking about computers?', in *The Science Studies Reader*, ed. Mario Biagioli, London: Routledge, 1999, pp. 543–552.

Turner, Victor *From Ritual to Theatre: the human seriousness of play*, New York: PAJ Publications, 1982.

Walkerdine, Valerie. 'Video replay: families, film and fantasy', in *Formations of Fantasy*, eds Victor Burgin, Cora Kaplan and Donald James, London: Methuen, 1986.

Walther, Bo Kampmann 'Playing and gaming: reflections and classifications' [online] *Game Studies* 3(1) (2003), http://www.gamestudies.org/0301/ (accessed 19/10/05).

Wardrip-Fruin, Noah and Harrigan, Pat eds *First Person Media: new media as story, performance, and game*, Cambridge, Mass.: MIT Press, 2003.

Wark, McKenzie 'The video game as emergent media form', *Media Information Australia*, 71 (1994). Available at http://www.mcs.mq.edu.au/Staff/mwark/warchive/Mia/mia-video-games.html (accessed 28/8/00).

Weinbren, Grahame, 'Mastery (Sonic c'est moi)', in *New Screen Media: cinema / art / narrative*, eds Martin Reiser and Andrea Zapp, London: BFI, 2002, pp. 179–191.

Wheelock, Jane 'Personal computers, gender and an institutional model of the household', in *Consuming Technologies – media and information in domestic spaces*, eds Roger Silverstone and Eric Hirsch, London: Routledge, 1992, pp. 97–111.

Wiener, Norbert *Cybernetics: or the control and communication in the animal and the machine*, Cambridge, Mass.: MIT Press, 1961.

Williams, Raymond *Television: technology and cultural form* (2nd edn), London: Routledge, 1990a [1975].

Williams, Raymond *Problems in Materialism and Culture*, London: Verso, 1990b.

Willis, Paul *Common Culture: symbolic work at play in the everyday cultures of the young*, Milton Keynes: Open University Press, 1990.

Winner, Langdon, 'Do artifacts have politics?', in *The Social Shaping of Technology* (2nd edn), eds Donald MacKenzie and Judy Wajcman, Milton Keynes: Open University Press, 1999, pp. 28–40.

Winnicott, D. W. *Playing and Reality*, Harmondsworth: Penguin, 1974.

Winston, Brian *Media Technology and Society: a history from the telegraph to the internet*, London: Routledge, 1998.

Wise, J. Macgregor, 'Intelligent agency', *Cultural Studies* 12(3) (1998): 410–428.

Wolf, Mark J. P. and Perron, Bernard eds *The Video Game Theory Reader*, London: Routledge, 2003.

Wolfe, Tom 'suppose he is what he sounds like, the most important thinker since newton, darwin, freud, einstein, and pavlov what if he is right?', *The New York Herald Tribune* 1965, online at http://digitallantern.net/mcluhan/course/spring96/wolfe.html (accessed Jan 2008).

Woolgar, Steve, 'Why not a sociology of machines? The case of sociology and artificial intelligence', *Sociology,* 19(4) (1985): 557–572.

Woolgar, Steve, 'Configuring the user: the case of usability trials', in *A Sociology of Monsters: essays on power and technology and domination*, ed. John Law, London: Routledge, 1991, pp. 58–99.

Woolley, Benjamin *Virtual Worlds – a journey in hype and hyperreality*, Oxford: Blackwell, 1992.

Wright, Talmadge, Boria, Eric and Breidenbach, Paul 'Creative Player Actions in FPS Online Video Games: Playing Counter-Strike', *Game Studies* 2(2) (2002). http://www.gamestudies.org/0202/ (accessed 7/9/04).

Yates, Simeon J. and Littleton, Karen 'Understanding computer game cultures: a situated approach', in *Virtual Gender: technology, consumption and identity*, eds Eileen Green and Alison Adam, London: Routledge, 2001, pp. 103–123.

YouGov 2006 *The Mobile Youth Report* online at http://www.yougov.com/archives/pdf/CPW060101004_2.pdf.

Zylinska, Joanna ed. *The Cyborg Experiments: the extensions of the body in the media age*, London: Continuum, 2002.

5 Cyberculture: Technology, Nature and Culture

Introduction

New media form part of cyberculture, but they are not all there is to it. 'Cyberculture', a frequently used term, suggests something about the sort of culture we are dealing with: it is a culture in which machines play a particularly important role. Nobody who has heard the term is unaware of the other constituents of that culture: other than communications networks, programming, and software there are also the issues of artificial intelligence, virtual reality, **artificial life**, and the human–computer interface. The works of fiction that gave a cultural context to the computers, such as William Gibson's *Neuromancer* (1986), Richard Kadrey's *Metrophage* (1989), Pat Cadigan's *Synners* (1991), and Bruce Sterling's *Schismatrix* (1985), or the films that provided its characteristic images, from Ridley Scott's *Bladerunner* (1982, 1992) to the Wachowski brothers' *The Matrix* (1999), routinely not only play out plots concerning computers and computer media but also explore the construction and politics of artificial life (*Bladerunner*), the complexity and technological resources of organic bodies (*Neuromancer*, *Matrix*), and even, with Cadigan's (1991) famous online stroke, the indissociability of biological and technological systems: hence the 'syn-' part of her title.

As such fictions make often shockingly clear, cyberculture thus marks a threshold at which concepts, theories and practices stemming from cultural and media studies confront concepts, theories and practices stemming from the sciences – notably from **biotechnology**, robotics and AI research, genetics and genomics. Driving through this heady mix of concepts and traditions is, of course, the extraordinary pace of contemporary technological change. Our newspapers now routinely announce some new marriage of biology and technology in the form of intelligent prosthetics, implant technologies, cloning, and so on, while we are suffering new physical (repetitive strain injury) and psychological disorders (in-tray anxiety, information sickness) as a consequence of the ubiquity of computation.

Cyberculture, then, consists in a mass of new technological things, a wide range of imaginative fictions that have, as it were, seeped through the screens so that they may seem like realistic descriptions of our bewildering everyday lives. Moreover, it brings the theories and practices of the sciences into direct contact with those of cultural and media studies. Accordingly, it has given rise to questions concerning which of these traditions is better suited to characterise the emergent culture: popular science books vie with works in media studies, philosophy, cultural theory, and so on, over how precisely to characterise the seemingly unprecedented mix of culture and technology that is cyberculture. All involved in this contest seem beset with a certain theoretical anxiety, so that the flow of ideas, fictions, concepts and technologies has become seemingly inexhaustible.

Such anxieties, and the sudden confluence of culture and technology that fuel them, are not, however, new. The fictions, sciences and philosophies, alongside the sweeping changes

For more on the fictions surrounding cyberculture, see McCaffery (1992)

We have seen (**1.6.3–1.6.5**) one reason why this is so by revisiting the McLuhan–Williams problematic concerning electronic technology (particularly television) and its impact on culture, and the ensuing marginalisation of questions of media and technological determination, of media and technology as environments for human action, and so on

1.6.3 Williams and the social shaping of technology
1.6.4 The many virtues of Saint McLuhan
1.6.5 The extent of the 'extensions of man'

in everyday life during the Industrial Revolution, were beset by a similar range of problems, and suffered a similar sense of cultural disorientation. So too, the rise of clockwork mechanisms, and the aggressively materialistic theories that accompanied them, upset the sense of humanity's place in the natural and divine order, changing medicine and psychology into branches of mechanics. Indeed, as far back as the first century AD cultures were awash with hypotheses and experiments concerning bringing machines to life.

In many other parts of the book we have sought to understand new media as subject to control and direction by human institutions, skill, creativity and intention in broadly the same terms as we have always assumed traditional media to be. But, in turning to the phenomenon of cyberculture, and the histories that feed it, we will be meeting other traditions of thought, some of surprising longevity, and their contemporary manifestations which do not always sit comfortably alongside this humanist emphasis. This being the case, no full account of the culture of new media can be given without exploring the flow of ideas from the other fields that inform cyberculture.

The proximity and traffic between the discourses about new media and cyberculture are reason enough to pay them full attention in this book, but there is another reason which may be more important. This is that many of the questions that the emergence of new media have given rise to are actually versions of larger and more fundamental questions about the relationship of culture to technology and technology to nature. These are not questions that media studies, in general, concerns itself with.

However, a number of studies and bodies of thought that attempt to address the nature of everyday life and experience in advanced technological societies under the name of 'cyberculture' or 'cybercultural studies' do have some things to say about culture, technology and nature. Indeed, these three categories and the shifting relations between them can be said to lie at the very heart of cyberculture. We may be used to dividing 'nature' from 'culture', and we routinely base our academic investigations on attending to one or the other realm, but the advent of technology troubles this simple distribution of academic labour, and compels us to ask the question of how to approach 'the question of technology' at all.

It is to these ideas, histories and theories that we now turn. While the ideas at the centre of cyberculture can all too easily seem to be either enjoyable or trite and naive, near-delirious imaginings of science fiction authors and screenwriters, it has also been recognised that 'cyberpunk' science fiction offers an address to many current developments in science, technology and culture that the divided academic world often fails to catch. As one media theorist has put it, 'cyberpunk can . . . be read as a new form of social theory that maps the consequences of a rapidly developing information and media society in the era of techno-capitalism' (Kellner 1995: 8). Thus, cyberpunk fiction is accorded the status of a sociology of new media cultures. Conversely, Kellner goes on to recommend that we read actual sociologies of media-saturated society, such as those by the notorious theorist Jean Baudrillard, as actually being a form of 'dystopic science fiction'. Kellner's view stands like a warning: we are about to enter a sphere in which distinctions between science fiction, sociology and philosophy can become hard to maintain.

We will not, however, merely be spinning bizarre riddles or presenting cyberculture as the realm of delirium some critics (including one of this book's authors!) have energetically insisted it is. Our attempt here is to take the reader behind the scenes of cyberculture by tracing the conceptual roots and histories of some theories and ideas concerning nature, culture and technology, automata and living machines, the actual and the virtual, and so on. It will then explore some core developments in the contemporary studies of science, technology and culture that place developments in new media in a very different light to that which we, by and large, shed upon it in other parts of the book.

5.1 Cyberculture and cybernetics

> Gibson's fictions show, with exaggerated clarity, the iceberg of social change sliding across the surface of the late twentieth century, but its proportions are vast and dark.
>
> (Bruce Sterling, 'Preface' to Gibson [1988])

As Bruce Sterling reminds us, for cyberculture, computers as media and technologies of communication are just the tip of these arch-cyberpunks' iceberg of social change. It is cybernetics, the scientific source of the 'cyber' prefix, that points to the less visible, 'vast and dark proportions' of this iceberg. For cybernetics is interested in both 'animals and machines', in technology and biology. The biology that has, for centuries, been culturally inter-twined with its technologies is now spliced with them, and has even itself become a source of technologies, as cybernetic digitality has spread like a cancer from telephones to genomes, faxes to foods. Cyberculture therefore combines cybernetics' interest in technology and biology, in physical and living things, with, as Kellner has it, an interest in mapping the consequences of this conjunction of technology, nature and culture.

Accordingly, section **5.2** will address technology as physical, **5.3** will focus on technology and biology, and **5.4** will offer a critical account of theories of cyberculture, paying particular attention to which theoretical perspectives provide a map that encompasses technology, nature and culture, the three points on our compass. The first section, meanwhile, explores some of the problems attendant upon finding a framework in which to address these three points, and will ask some orienting questions to help us navigate across these terrains.

5.1.1 Technology as real and material: media studies' blindspot?

However we think about it, technology is something real. Real in the obvious, material sense: we can touch it, it does things, it performs certain actions, it makes yet other actions possible, we rearrange our work and leisure around it, and so on. New technologies do produce highly tangible changes in the way everyday life is conducted (**4.1.1–4.1.3**): they affect the way in which labour power is deployed, how money is invested and circulates, how business is done (**3.18**, **3.19**), how and where identities are formed (**4.3.1–4.3.3**) and so on. In such ways, technology, both in its forms and its capacities, profoundly affects human culture.

However, as we have seen (**1.6**), most media theorists are highly sceptical of such a claim. The very question 'how does technology affect us?' is traditionally criticised within media studies as being based upon a naive idea; the idea that technology itself determines anything is dismissed as faulty thinking, and then receives little attention. This has led both to a general blindness concerning the history and philosophy of technology in general, and a relative absence of studies that seek to understand technology's role within cultural and media studies.

At times of significant change in media technologies such as we are now witnessing, this very 'taboo' leads, in turn, to sudden outbursts of techno-enthusiasm and the making of vastly overinflated claims. Concentrating on what happens only at the very moment of new media technology's 'newness' means that questions of technology slip into the background once they are no longer new. When this happens, cultural and media studies can revert to its

For the moment, a realist view is one that includes the cultural consequences of non-human things on the basis of the physical being that machines and humans share. The concept of 'realism' is further discussed in section **2.7** in the context of filmic realism

This 'rolling back' of techno-hype is normally achieved by stressing issues of how social power, investment, use and reception of technologies limits and directs their application, not by seeking to understand the material nature of technology in history default state in which technology is a marginal issue and it again slips off the agenda. It then becomes too easy to regard technology as something that in itself requires no further attention. The recurring moment of inflated claims has been criticised and passed. The 'silly season' is over again. In short, not asking questions, seriously and consistently, about technology produces a cycle of boom and bust in cultural and media studies.

The current advent of a 'new' set of media technologies therefore brings with it an unsettled problematic – that of how physically real technologies are understood within cultural and media studies – and affords an opportunity to develop a means of viewing technology and its cultural effects within a realist framework.

5.1.2 Studying technology

A consequence of sidelining questions of technology within media studies, except to roll back undisciplined euphoria and ideological overstatement by techno-enthusiasts, means that the field of media studies has largely failed to develop a means of addressing technology as a real and material phenomenon.

The current emergence of new media technologies highlights this lack. The major focus on technology within cultural and media studies is in the manner that discourses surround and construct its cultural meaning (this is dealt with in **1.5**). While such studies tell us a great deal about what technology means to particular cultural groups, they tell us much less about technology itself, and do not therefore provide an adequate means of studying it in itself. Indeed, such studies are often underpinned by the conviction that 'in itself' technology is nothing; it is just a collection of dumb stuff without purpose or meaning until a culture provides them. In this part of the book we recognise that technology is not only culturally constructed as a unit of meaning, it is also physically constructed and physically constructive of a vast array of cultural phenomena. Therefore, to be a realist about technology entails asking what technology really is.

5.1.3 What is technology?

So, the fundamental aim of this section is to answer a deceptively simple and frequently dismissed question: what is technology? Of course, we all take it for granted that we have a serviceable knowledge of what technology is, since we are surrounded by it. Technology itself is therefore no stranger to us, as we are more or less familiar with individual technological things. Consider, however, the topic of this book. The occasion for writing it at all is the relatively sudden appearance of what are generally referred to as new media technologies. Section **1.3** has critically discussed the sense of newness regarding 'new media', and **1.5** analyses the discursive construction of 'new media', but we now need to build on these discussions and address the sense in which the technologies themselves are 'new'; that is, what precursors they have in the history of technology.

In the attempt to provide an answer to this question it is important to consider how we may go about it. For example, we may answer straightforwardly, 'technology is another word for machinery'. But such an answer tells us nothing other than that the two terms are substitutable; any sentence containing the word 'technology' can substitute 'machinery' for it without loss of meaning. But this tells us nothing more about technology, but only how the word functions in the English language. Such an approach answers a semantic question, a question about the meaning and use of a word. If we want to know something about technology that is not simply semantic, then, we need to use other approaches than ones that involve us getting lost in a dictionary! We can immediately see, then, that answering this question involves attention to the means we employ to answer it (and that the substitution of terms does not get us very far). We can, for example, ask those around us to contribute elements to a definition of technology. Such contributions are likely to include:

1   constructed for some specific purpose;

2   mechanical, thermal, electrical or digital;

3   artificial rather than natural;

4   automates human labour;

5   a natural human capacity;

. . . and so on. Such contributions to a definition may be more or less complex, but when we bring them together as we have above we find that some elements of these possible answers contradict each other. For example, is technology a natural thing (5), because it is in the nature of human beings to produce it (even primitive humans used sticks to dig with)? Or is it a wholly artificial thing (3), since it must be constructed by humans, and is not to be found in nature? Such an approach does not solve the problem of knowing what technology is, but it can help sharpen up how we ask the question.

5.1.4 How to proceed?

If then, in asking 'what is technology?' we also have to ask how we should ask this question (in other words, how can we go about getting a meaningful answer), the following sections will advance slowly, making each stage of the process as clear as possible. We should also be clear that in moving from stage to stage, from observation to observation, we will inevitably be making an argument.

We will try to be clear about the stages in the argument we make or how we arrive at any specific point. It is important to see that the answers we arrive at need not be regarded as final and absolute, since they are bound to be the consequences of the argument we adopt. We recognise that other arguments will arrive at different answers. However, whatever the answers given, the important thing is that this section maps out the coordinates within which an answer to the question 'what is technology?' needs to be given.

We are bound to meet a number of problems in what follows. Our aim will not be to solve such problems straightaway, but rather to grasp them, to feel our way around them, as though they were three-dimensional things. In this way, we hope to make something that appears to be so abstract and slippery (the meaning of technology) quite concrete. But, it will take a little time! We start this journey by considering a big idea about what technology is not – nature.

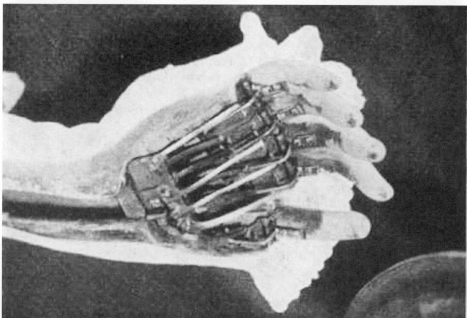

5.1 (top) Terminator hand from *T2* (1992). Courtesy of The Ronald Grant Archive. (below) Jaquet-Droz, Androïde hand (1769).

5.1.5 Technology and nature: the cyborg

We are now familiar with the idea of the living machine: the cyborg. The sight of Arnold Schwarzenegger stripping away his skin to reveal the machinery beneath its surface is becoming as familiar to us as the revelation of skin beneath clothing. We may be less famil-iar with the fact that the cyborg has a history stretching back to the first century AD. What this history tells us is that technology has always been intimately involved with a fascination for the possibility of creating life. A very old idea, in which Terminator-style cyborgs, together with current projects in the biological sciences and in the field known as artificial life or Alife, are the latest manifestations. On the face of it, nothing could be further apart than technological and biological things. Technology is by definition artificial, and biology, by definition, investigates the natural. What then is it about technology that relates it to the creation of living things?

As cyborgs, clones, and prosthetics call into question the settled edge between the biological and the technological in the contemporary world, so too in the seventeenth century the entire natural universe, and all the things in it, were thought of in accordance with the technology that was then predominant: clockwork. The question of whether humans are little more than natural machines was initially posed, in an explicit form, in the seventeenth and eighteenth centuries (**5.3.2**). The same question now echoes in the problems explored through figures such as the 'replicants' in the film *Bladerunner*. Others have argued that, in much the same way that human beings (nature) evolved from apes, technology too has evolved (**5.3.5**, **5.4.3**).

It seems then, that while drawing a line between technology and nature may seem like a good place to start if we wish to define technology, under examination even this line turns out to be questionable. There is a long history of doubting the distinction. It is less an answer to our question than a source of problems. From the question of what technology is, then, we derive further questions about the relationships between technology and nature, between physical machines, artifice, and physical things in general.

5.1.6 Technology and culture

If defining technology by opposing it to nature is not as straightforward as it may at first seem, how far do we get by opposing technology to another big idea or category of things: culture? In looking at the question this way we are immediately returned to the problem that we mentioned above: the tendency for cultural and media studies to dismiss the role that technology plays in shaping culture. (The question of whether technology is an agent which causes social and cultural change (technological determinism) formed the crux of the debate between McLuhan and Williams (**1.6**).) We are going to view this debate as unsettled. We now find, much to the scorn of some media theorists, that a magazine such as *Wired* (which adopted McLuhan as its patron saint), insists that the new technologies are literally changing the world. Such a view is not only touted by the 'digerati' who contribute to *Wired*, but is also argued by academic cyberneticians such as Kevin Warwick.

Warwick's scenario of a future dominated by machine life (Warwick 1998: 21ff.) forms the basis of the nightmare presented in films such as *Matrix*. Similarly, cyberpunk fictions such as William Gibson's *Neuromancer* (1986) present technologically driven futures whose outlines are just visible in the contemporary world. The possibility of the technological determination of culture appears to be far from exhausted in some quarters.

Let us then consider that while it may seem self-evidently true that humans put machines together, does it automatically follow that humans and their cultures remain in control of them? The view that human beings (or human cultures and societies) are in control of their machines works well as long as we consider simple machines or tools, but it works less well when we consider complex machines or systems of machinery. On an industrial assembly line, the human operator may have remained in limited control of a region of that machinery laying under their hands (riveting, panel-beating, etc.), but what was the relation between the entire system of machinery and the humans working on it?

Kevin Warwick, Professor of Cybernetics at the University of Reading, UK, has not only argued that, within the next half century, machines will be at least as intelligent as humans, he has also, as he puts it, 'upgraded' his body with cybernetic implants. The first, in 1998, consisted of a one-way communications chip surgically inserted into his arm. This enabled him to 'communicate' with the computers in his home and workplace, causing doors to spring open, his computer to boot itself up and greet him, the lights and television to come on, and so forth. The second, in 2001, is a two-way chip, not only sending, but also receiving signals. This is also one of a pair, the other being inserted into his wife's arm, enabling signals to be sent directly from nervous system to nervous system. The experiment is designed to show whether or not sensations such as pain are physically communicable

Marx distinguishes the instrument or tool, 'which the worker animates', from large-scale machinery, in which 'it is the machine that possesses skill and strength in place of the worker . . . The worker's activity . . . is determined and regulated on all sides by the movement of the machinery' (1993: 693). See **5.2.1**.

Now, at the beginning of the twenty-first century, we also need to consider the extent to which digital technologies swiftly become invisible components that facilitate many of our actions and transactions in everyday life – a situation that makes new technologies less like discrete machines that we use and more like a technological environment, in which questions of control may pass from the hands of their users to the systems themselves (as in automated defensive missile-deployment systems or the automated stock market).

While we can, and need to, criticise and resist the deployment of technologies in the service of interests which are damaging to societies and to people (e.g. maximising profit by replacing human labour that an economic system deems too 'expensive' with cheaper machine labour or the escalation of deadly states of conflict), this does nothing to undermine the fact that technologies have profound effects on both the form and the functions of human cultures. Indeed, once technology becomes environmental (the phrase is McLuhan's – see **1.6**), as has been increasingly apparent since the Industrial Revolution in the nineteenth century, it makes increasingly less sense to distinguish technology from culture as cultures become increasingly technologised. Thus, while we might have become used to defining technology against culture, we can see that this is also problematic. Culture has become inextricably bound up with complex technological systems and environments. The very term 'cyberculture' stands for something like this: not a culture that is separate from technology but one in which these spheres fuse.

To sum up: as with the distinction between technology and nature, we again find ourselves faced with a problem when we consider the relations between technology and culture. In trying to define technology against nature and against culture, we end up with a series of problems. In order to begin examining these problems it will be helpful to reconsider the relations between all three terms that we are dealing with: nature, technology and culture.

5.1.7 Nature and culture

The now commonplace division of things into the realms of 'nature' and 'culture' has been a fundamental intellectual habit since the nineteenth-century German philosopher, Wilhelm Dilthey, carved up knowledge into the natural or physical sciences (*Naturwissenschaften*) and the cultural or human sciences (*Geisteswissenschaften*). Following this division, we are likely to agree with another seminal thinker of the nineteenth century, Karl Marx, when he states that, 'nature builds no machines' (1993: 692). It is still largely the case that, if we were asked if technology belongs to the realm of nature, we would almost certainly answer 'no'. We are, in fact, apt to experience difficulty with the very question. The question seems not to make sense. Can we therefore conclude that if technology is definitely not nature, it is solely a cultural phenomenon?

5.1.8 A problem with binary definitions

The question: 'does technology belong to the realm of nature or to that of culture?' is a troubling one because it suggests that the nature–culture divide, which has become 'second nature' in the humanities, is assumed to be a binary relation. A binary relation is an opposition of two terms where the difference between the terms is thought to tell us something about each of them. So, what it is to be 'feminine' gains some meaning by not being 'masculine', and what it is to be 'strong' gains meaning if we know what being 'weak' means. However, there is more to binary oppositions than that. Such oppositions also exhaust the field of possibilities that we can think of. Thus, 1 and 0 exhaust the elements (although not the combinations) of any binary system, just as 'guilty' and 'innocent' exhaust the system of legal verdicts under English law. However, our examination so far must lead us to consider whether a simple opposition of 'nature' to 'culture' can exhaust the field of possibilities regarding how one relates to the other. Just as black and white, while an opposition, does not exhaust the field of all possible colours that, in fact, lie between them and out of which each is constituted. Failure to pay attention to this simple point has resulted, in recent years, in a fundamental confusion with regard to what a binary relation is, so that we feel we have already explained something when we say 'it's a binary opposition'.

Many theorists in the human sciences, including media studies, have sought to retain such a binary relation between 'nature' and 'culture'. For example, in his *The Elementary Structures of Kinship* ([1949] 1969) the structural anthropologist Claude Lévi-Strauss declares that rather than 'confidently repudiating' the distinction between nature and culture, as many sociologists and anthropologists have done, he wishes to offer a 'more valid interpretation' of it and thus to save it ([1949] 1969: 9).

Through his new interpretation, Lévi-Strauss reinforced the binary opposition between nature and culture. His argument is exemplified by his treatment of the way that the practice of incest is prohibited in all human societies. He observes that the prohibition of incest has both 'the universality of . . . instinct, and the coercive character of law and institution . . . Inevitably extending beyond the historical and geographical limits of culture, [it is] coextensive with the biological species' ([1949] 1969: 10). In this way, the question then arises, is incest prohibition natural or cultural, inborn or invented, given or constructed?

If the prohibition is universal, it is tempting to regard this as evidence that it is a natural phenomenon, an attribute we humans are born with. Yet, at the same time, is not a prohibition, by definition, something cultural; a law or institution the observation of which is enforced? If an aversion to incest were natural, there would be no need of coercion or enforcement in its prohibition. As incest is actively prohibited must it therefore be cultural and not, after all, natural? One answer to this conundrum is that 'incest prohibition' demonstrates that the sphere of culture has its own universal laws, much as the sphere of nature does (as in the universal laws of physics, for example). So, here again we meet the idea that nature and culture are not governed by the same laws. While this may lie at the root of our present problem, it also offers scope and validity to the human or cultural sciences as independent of the physical sciences. Human societies are not, the argument goes, governed by the same forces that shape the natural world and are therefore a quite separate field of enquiry and explanation.

We have seen how the binary nature–culture distinction helps to make sense of a phenomenon such as a prohibition, and why, if this is established as a universal law (like the law of gravity in earth-bound physics), it provides the study of culture and society with solid ground, with its own puzzles, problematics and processes to explain. However, if we substitute the object that interests us, 'technology', for 'incest prohibition' in Lévi-Strauss's account, then the question becomes cloudy again.

Unlike a prohibition, a technology cannot be reduced to an outcome of a society's coercive and enforcing arrangements for behaviour, or the universal laws of the cultural anthropologist. While a society might control and legislate about the uses of technologies, these also necessarily function in accordance with certain physical laws (there needs, for example, to be contact or communication between parts of a machine if it is to function). Thus, even if we accept (with Marx) that it is only in human cultures that we find the construction and invention of machines, does this mean that technology is nothing more than a fact of culture? Is it solely an extension of the capacities of culture, or is it solely an

The irony of this is that the very reduction that humanism wishes to achieve – that the sum total of actions in the world are achieved solely by the speaking animal – was always conceived as a critical gesture; in Williams, for example, it was intended to demonstrate the falsity of the idea that machines act without human intervention, so that when we are tempted to describe machines as active, as determinant – mere descriptions, these – we look instead for the human behind them, and the will to profit that guides their manipulations of objects. In Marx, the struggle against the 'self-acting mules' with which industrialisation threatened to render human makers redundant, is intended to bring about the conscious realisation on the part of labouring humanity that we alone are capable of making, since 'nature builds no machines' (Marx 1993: 706) exploitation of given physical phenomena (as steam-power exploits the combustibility of minerals, or nuclear power the fissionability of atoms)? A little thought will show that technology is both. It is physical (like nature) and invented (like culture). Technology 'belongs' exclusively to neither sphere. For this reason, we begin to see why it would be useful to accept that nature and culture, where technology is concerned, do not exhaust the field of things.

5.1.9 We have never been binary: Latour and 'actor-network theory'

Bruno Latour, an anthropologist of science, has sought to address precisely this problem. In his 1993 book, *We Have Never Been Modern*, he offers a diagnosis of modernity as a condition in which the humanities have become so embroiled in questions of the social, linguistic and discursive construction of meanings that we have forgotten how to ask questions about what things are.

At the root of this situation there lies a prejudice. The prejudice is that of humanism, which Latour argues is reductive 'because [it] seek[s] to attribute action to a small number of powers' – human powers – 'leaving the rest of the world with nothing but simple mute forces' (1993: 138). All that exists, meanwhile, exists only in 'the linguistic play of speaking subjects' at the expense of the material and technological world (1993: 61). In other words, we humans talk about talk, while things maintain their onward march beneath the level of our scrutiny.

We routinely discuss signs apart from what they are signs of, representations apart from what they represent, meanings apart from matter, and ideologies that mask realities, so that the world we inhabit now seems to be composed exclusively of linguistic, textual or interpretative acts. At the same time, a glance at a newspaper reveals how complex interrelations between this human world and non-human things (the environment, the life-span of the sun, the actions of viruses and, crucially, the actions of technology) have become. Is the HIV virus a textual construct? It involves certain constructions of meaning, certainly ('God's plague visited upon sexual deviants'; 'originating from human–animal intercourse in Africa', and so on); but is there not also a thing there, the virus itself? Latour's point is not that we should dismiss the discourses and address ourselves only to things; he is not suggesting that the virus's meaning is a pointless distraction from its biochemical properties and that we should therefore run from our libraries to laboratories. Rather, his point is that texts, meanings and intentions cover only a limited proportion of the surfaces of things. A full account of a thing must therefore situate it in the network of other things, texts, discourses and institutions of which it is part. Studying the HIV virus therefore entails attention being paid to the literature, science, journalism, politics, hospital organisation, medical research, funding arrangements, the sociology of scientific breakthroughs, the aetiology of infection, the genetic structure of the virus, and so on. Instead of thinking about things in isolation from meanings, or of meanings in isolation from things, reality is composed of networks in which human things (meanings, texts, discourses, institutions, signs) interact constantly with non-human things (viruses, biochemistry, immune systems). Crucially, for Latour, what knits all these things together are the various technologies that facilitate these interactions: the technologies of medical research and intervention, communication and transportation systems, genomic technologies, and so on. Since networks are not stimulated into action exclusively by human actions, but also by non-human things, including the technological forms available to us, Latour sets out the concept of non-human agency against the humanist understanding of agency we find in contemporary social theory.

5.1.10 Media as technology

Having seen how and why a distinction is drawn between nature and culture, as the basis of the natural and cultural sciences, it may be that rather than ask what 'realm' technology belongs to we should ask what field(s) of study technology as such falls under. The question 'what is technology?' can then be answered in a number of different ways, depending on what field one is answering it from.

When looked at as a physical object, technology is the concern of the natural and applied sciences, since no technology can work unless it successfully exploits a set of physical laws. Thus a steam engine works by creating pressure from the combustion of a mineral fuel in a boiler, which drives a system of wheels and gears by way of a condenser and a system of valves. Each of these processes exploits combustible materials, the differentials between heat and cold sources, and so on, without which the engine would not work. But technologies do also have a high degree of cultural 'presence'; they are invested with meaning (see **1.1** and **1.5**). This is what is foregrounded when technologies are looked at as cultural phenomena and is one reason why they are not thought of as only physical machines. A prime example of this is the sense the cultural or human sciences give to the term 'media'.

A medium is seldom treated as something 'in itself'. Even if the apparatus or the material nature of a technology is paid attention, as part of an analysis of what a medium is (Williams [1977] does so in 'From Medium to Social Practice'; in film theory, the 'apparatus' also supplies such attention (see **2.7**)), cultural and media studies mainly looks at a medium as an instantiation of certain economic, communicational, political, commercial, or artistic interests. On the other hand, the physical sciences, even of the applied variety, do not address such technologies as 'media' but only ever as an arrangement of electrical circuits, functions, transmitters, pattern and noise. It is as if what is foregrounded in the physical or natural sciences becomes background in the cultural or human sciences, and vice versa, thus maintaining a blind spot between nature and culture.

Many cultural and media theorists seek strenuously to police the divide between nature and culture. This is done by wholly removing technology from the sphere of nature and subsuming it under the category of culture. The substantial argument, for example, behind Raymond Williams's idea of what he calls 'cultural science' (1974: 119ff.) is that, since cause and effect explanations cannot be transferred from the effect of cues hitting billiard balls to matters of social change, or from science to history, the idea of 'technological effect' must be dropped altogether in favour of an account of social change that concentrates on the intentions and purposes of the groups who use technologies in the act of changing things.

This is humanism. The argument is that, instead of asking questions of cause and effect, that belong wholly to the physical sciences, the business of cultural science is to ask questions of agency. Agency replaces cause as an explanatory principle since the concept of agency involves not only the causing of an action but the desires, purposes and intentions behind it. Agency, on such a view, is exclusively therefore the property of socially interacting humans, restricting cultural science to the study of human actions, and ruling out of court the actions of anything else. Williams's cultural science, as Latour says of the modern humanities, is cut off from the physical world. Strictly speaking, there can be no cultural study of technology, only of its human uses. Conversely, the media as technology cannot be said to have any direct 'effects' on culture at all, since it is made up of the actions, purposes, desires and intentions of human agents.

This is why cultural and media studies in general feels confident about rejecting the notion that watching, say, a graphically violent movie, video or TV broadcast can be said to have an

This is one way to characterise a strong version of social construction: the world as we know it is the world that we know only insofar as we talk about it, and are aware of how we talk about it. Accordingly, from our present perspective, social constructionism is a form of humanism. Ian Hacking, in *The Social Construction of What?* (Cambridge, Mass.: Harvard University Press, 1999), pp. 1–34, carefully and clearly unpicks the varieties and uses of social construction. He argues that theorists seldom if ever put forward a positive account of constructionism, but only provide constructionist accounts of things – for example, gender – when their contingent and historical character, and the ideological motives they serve, have been forgotten

In this way, although we are in pursuit of a more realist view of technology, we need again to consider what the study of culture (or 'cultural studies') takes as so important; the way that discourses (in this context whole sets of historical disciplines) frame, select, and make sense of reality in different ways (see **1.5**)

1.1 New media: do we know what they are?
1.5 Who was dissatisfied with old media?
2.7 Digital cinema
1.6 New media: determining or determined?

effect on the watcher, such that s/he then goes out and guns down the neighbourhood or murders a child. In this argument, however, the reluctance to transfer the language of 'cause and effect' from merely physical phenomena to human actions betrays, on both sides, a fundamental and necessary blindness to the role of technology. Implicit in the idea of causation is not just that event *x* causes event *y*, but rather that between them there is a sequence of physical events, a causal chain. However, the idea that human beings, who are after all equally physical as mental animals, are subject to no physical effects from phenomena they experience by way of the interaction between their senses and technologies, is as ludicrous and unsustainable as the idea that they are 'caused' to murder, maim and torture by viewing 'video-nasties'. Moreover, since Williams's arguments are held by traditional media and cultural studies to have won the day over McLuhan's technological determinism, they continue to frame the media and cultural studies approach to technology today. If we want, therefore, to ask questions of the technological elements of cyberculture, we need to remain critically aware of the humanism Williams bequeathed to media studies' approach to them (see **1.6**).

Here we see two approaches to the question of 'what is technology' enter into an apparently unresolvable conflict: on the one hand, the apparent 'scientism' of the regular statistics and surveys that demonstrate that, for example, 'videogame violence causes real violence'; on the other, the humanism of 'there are no causes in culture, only agents and their purposes'. These certainly provide two answers to the question 'what is technology?' – on the one hand, it is a set of machines that cause certain predictable effects; on the other, it is a means by which socially embodied purposes are achieved – but they bring us no closer to a satisfactory answer. What they do tell us, however, is that neither the insistence on pure, physical causality, of the sort modelled on the collisions of billiard balls, nor the equal and opposite insistence on no causality, only human agency, provides the frameworks necessary to answer it. We shall therefore explore other theoretical frameworks in what follows. To begin this process we shall revisit the issues at the heart of the Williams–McLuhan problematic: causality and technological determinism. If Williams's arguments bequeathed media studies a problematic humanism, has something been overlooked in the account of technological and cultural change McLuhan offered that might help us to answer the question, 'what is technology?'

5.2 Revisiting determinism: physicalism, humanism and technology

Introduction

In **1.6.4**, we noted that by tracing the influence of central theses in McLuhan's work we arrive at the idea of a physicalist understanding of new media and cultural studies. It is the physical aspects – especially as regards the new technologies and the physical relations of humans to them – that 'mainstream' cultural and media studies has proved to be unable to address. Yet this is an aspect of cyberculture that science fiction has been able to address. In his introduction to a seminal collection of cyberpunk fiction, author and manifestoist Bruce Sterling notes the following:

> Traditionally there has been a yawning gulf between the sciences and the humanities: a gulf between literary culture, the formal world of art and politics, and the culture of science, the world of engineering and industry. But the gap is crumbling in an unexpected fashion. Technical culture has gotten out of hand. The advances of the sciences are so deeply radical, so disturbing, upsetting and revolutionary, that they can no longer be contained. They are surging into culture at large; they are invasive; they are everywhere.
>
> (Sterling, in Gibson 1988: xii)

This is our starting point for the considerations of technology that follow. Its purpose is to re-establish the physical continuity between bodies, technologies and images – between nature, technology and culture – that is necessary to examining the effects of the new technologies. Nor can such an account avoid attending to the role of the sciences in cyberculture, as Sterling alerts us. In this light, it is clear that the physicalist basis of McLuhan's theses, if not the specific theses themselves, offers the prospect of a framework within which cyberculture, in the inclusive sense Sterling gives it, may be examined. Moreover, from the example of Sterling we can see that such a basis is not merely a product of theorising about electronic technologies in the 1960s but is actually a core element of contemporary cyberculture. The contemporary centrality of such theorising is further demonstrated, in the popular realm, by the magazine *Wired* canonising McLuhan as its 'patron saint', and in the increasing amount of 'new media' research being done around McLuhan (Levinson 1997; De Kerckhove 1997; Genosko 1998).

If McLuhan retains a powerful presence in cyberculture, Williams's ideas on technology have, as we have argued (see **1.6.3**), effectively defined the theoretical stance of mainstream cultural and media studies and the humanities in general. The core of the problem remains that of technological determinism, which continues to haunt the humanities' treatment of the question of technology. Thus cultural historians of technology (Smith and Marx 1996), anthropologists (Dobres 2000), as well as culturalists (MacKenzie and Wajcman [1985] 1999), continue to devote books to arguing that physical devices do not have determining effects on culture. This alone demonstrates that technological determinism remains an important issue.

One reason why this is so is that the new media are not simply new media but also new technologies. For that reason the question of the place of technology in culture has again become central. Cyberculture, as Sterling testifies, has reintroduced into culture at large an array of concerns that have become alien to cultural and media studies, but which are important elements of attending to technology in general, and to the inalienably technological component of that culture. Amongst such concerns are the histories and philosophies of science, as well as those sciences that rely on technology to investigate the physical world.

In the next section, therefore, we suggest ways in which a physicalist basis for cyberculture can provide important links between the histories of science, technology and culture, and thus address the question of technological determinism – whether technology causes, or human agents intend, the social changes that accompany technological change – from the point of view of cyberculture.

5.2.1 Physicalism and technological determinism

We have argued (**1.6.3**, **1.6.4**) that the encounter between the cultural approaches to technology exemplified by Williams and McLuhan in the 1960s constitutes an enduring core of intellectual resources for contemporary addresses to cyberculture. In this section, therefore, we will revisit this problematic one final time in order to examine what is at stake in the concept of technological determinism. However, we should not be under the impression that the two approaches are only to be found in Williams and McLuhan. On the contrary, as we have seen, they continue to underwrite much contemporary debate around the issue of technological determinism (see Dobres 2000; MacKenzie and Wajcman [1985] 1999; Smith and Marx 1996). The virtue of addressing the problematic as it arises in Williams and McLuhan is that Williams in particular is concerned to argue the case against determinism through from first principles, while McLuhan offers a clearly deterministic counterposition. Finally, this latter is one that has been resumed in recent years in order precisely to address issues arising from

1.6.4 The many virtues of Saint McLuhan
1.6.3 Williams and the social shaping of technology

cyberculture and digital media that mainstream cultural and media studies is ill-equipped to confront.

We have seen in **5.1.10** that the basis of the humanities' challenge to technological determinism is humanism. We saw that this challenge consists in the critique of the concept of cause applying to the cultural realm, and its replacement with the concept of 'agency'. Causes obtain only in the physical world, not in the cultural. If, however, there is merit to a physicalist approach to technology in culture outlined in **1.6**, then it is that it places culture within rather than outside the realm of physical causation. The consequences of this move are far reaching indeed, insofar as, just as Sterling insists, mapping cyberculture entails making ourselves passingly familiar not just with cultural accounts but with scientific and philosophical ones as well. Moreover, it will help us to see that 'cyberculture' is not a wholly new cultural phenomenon in its catholic inclusiveness, but rather just the latest in a long line of historical technocultures.

Yet the histories of philosophy and the sciences tell us there is not only one kind of cause. Aristotle distinguished four causes; the early moderns attempted to replace these four with just one; the contemporary sciences recognise at least two kinds of causation. Thus, when we say 'technology causes social change' we might be using one of any number of concepts of cause. Our first task will therefore be to map out some of the salient historical and contemporary concepts of cause, and then to ascertain which sense of causality Williams ascribes to what he takes to be McLuhan's determinism. Following this, we will attempt to characterise what senses of causality are involved in a range of theories of technology.

Nor is 'determinism' a simple, monolithic concept. Again, there are varieties of determinism. Mathematical determinism is not the same as historical determinism, for example. Even within the relatively restricted range of technological determinism, at least three versions of this theory have been distinguished (Bimber, in Smith and Marx 1996), while chaos theory is based not on randomness but on physical systems that are deterministic yet unpredictable (see **5.4**).

Finally, we will ask what varieties of agency are there, and can they be restricted to humans alone? Under what concept of agency can machines be accounted agents?

Each of these concepts is like a set of co-ordinates on the map of cyberculture that this section is concerned to draw. Knowing what these co-ordinates are will help us orient our way through that fraught terrain, but it will also help us to distinguish the routes other theorists take through it. Finally, it will enable us to locate the core questions of any technoculture, from the hydraulic age to the mechanical, and from the industrial age to the cybernetic.

5.2.2 Causalities

In this section we will meet three different types of cause. The concept of cause is important in examining technological determinism, insofar as the latter thesis attempts to explain *what causes cultural change* by way of technological change. However, what kind of cause is this? Does technology cause cultural change in the same way as the impact of one billiard ball on a second causes the latter to move? Do we search for the cause of cultural change in the same way that investigators seek the cause of an accident? Or is the cause of technological change itself deeply embedded in the natural blueprint of humanity, as Bergson, for example, argues?

Already it is clear that the question of causality is complex. The concepts of causality we will be looking at are:

- teleological
- mechanical
- non-linear

Each of these stems from a period in the history of the natural sciences. The point of examining them here is that it opens up two questions, which we will answer below:

1   What kind of causality does Williams impute to McLuhan's technological determinism?

2   What alternative concepts of causality are there?

Ultimately, what is at stake is whether technology can be examined on a physicalist basis, or whether, by dint of its cultural presence, we must, as traditional media studies does, give up this basis. Accordingly, we will carefully note in the following accounts the difficulties in transposing them from the realm of nature, where scientists and philosophers have deployed them, to that of culture.

Teleological causality

After Aristotle identified teleology as a form of causality in the fifth century BC, it became the dominant mode for explaining the natural world until the sixteenth and seventeenth centuries. Even in the contemporary natural sciences, particularly in biology, teleology continues to cause controversy amongst scientists. In the context of new media, however, we come across teleology whenever a history is concocted to explain that the modern computer, for example, is really the perfected form of an older technology. The story is then told of how the abacus is, in fact, the computer in germ, and that it took several thousand years for the abacus to unfold its potential and become the computer (see **1.4.1** for a critical discussion of teleological modes of explaining new media).

1.4.1 Teleological accounts of new media

Using the above example, we can see that teleology argues that the computer exists in some form in the abacus and that the abacus was destined or determined to become the computer over time. While this sounds improbable when applied to inanimate things like the abacus and the computer, it sounds much more plausible when applied to living things. Consider, for example, the acorn. As it grows, the acorn becomes an oak tree, and cannot become anything else. Thus we can see that the telos – the 'end' or 'goal' – of the acorn is the oak tree. If we accept this, we are arguing that the oak is the cause of the acorn, which is the argument that Aristotle put forward, calling such a cause a final cause (the oak is what the acorn finally becomes), and explanations of final causes, teleological explanations.

Consider the differences between these two examples: first, applied to the acorn and the oak, the teleology in question is internal to the acorn. However, applied to the abacus and the computer, the teleology is external to the abacus. In other words, there is nothing in an abacus *per se* that determines it to become a computer, as an acorn is determined to become an oak. Applied to the acorn, then, we are dealing with a kind of cause; applied to the abacus, merely with an explanation. That is why teleological arguments feature more regularly in contemporary biology than they do in the history of technology. This does not mean that there cannot be a teleology of technology; it may simply be that the processes by which technologies develop are insufficiently understood.

Mechanical causality

Teleological explanations of natural phenomena fell into disrepute in the sixteenth and seventeenth centuries – the dawn of the modern period. This period witnessed such a great increase in clockwork technologies that it sought to explain the world as a clockwork phenomenon:

> It is my goal to show that the celestial machine is not some kind of divine being, but rather like a clock . . . In this machine nearly all the various movements are caused by a single, very simple magnetic force, just as in a clock all movements are caused by a single weight.

> (Kepler 1605, cited in Mayr 1986: 61)

This conception of the world made philosophers sceptical of such 'occult causes' as teleology, requiring instead that there be evidence of causation. The basis of mechanical causation is that in order for anything to be called a cause there must be contact between it and the thing it causes to move. For example, winding a watch causes the hands to move, since the action of winding coils a spring, the subsequent unwinding of which turns cogs that in turn move the hands on the watch's face. But the watch cannot be said to cause a reorganisation of the social observance of time ('clocking on', timetabling, and so on), since there is no contact between the mechanical parts of the watch and the institutions that adopt it as an organising principle.

However, many philosophers, well into the eighteenth century, sought to explain the workings of human beings in terms of clockwork mechanisms as well, thus eradicating the distance between the material world of physics and the human world. Amongst the consequences of this view was that life itself began to be seen as something that could be created in technological form. We will explore the mechanical age's attitudes to 'artificial life' in section **5.3**.

5.3 Biological technologies:
the history of automata

Non-linear causality

Mechanical causality works in what is called a linear fashion. This means two things:

- all actions are reversible: watches are wound from an inert state to which they return as they unwind, at which point they are ready to be rewound;

- there is always a chain of causes, leading from event X to event Y to event Z, and so on.

However, certain physical phenomena are not reversible: living things, for example, unlike watches, cannot be revivified once they die; life is a one-way street, as it were. If humans are to all intents and purposes walking, talking clockworks, then how is it we cannot be rewound? Living things proved such a problem to the mechanical world-view that philosophers despaired of finding 'a Newton of the blade of grass'.

Related to this point, if life is a one-way street, then how does it start? What causes life? If we are dealing with an individual creature, then we can say 'its parents', but if we are dealing with life in general then there is no obvious explanation. In the eighteenth century, philosophers thus sought the 'vital force' that caused life in the same way that all physical events on the earth could be explained by the actions of the gravitational force. Towards the end of that century, the philosopher Immanuel Kant concluded that we cannot avoid viewing living things as if they were 'natural purposes' (Kant [1790] 1986, §5), thus reintroducing teleology at the end of mechanism's long reign.

Second, how can we explain phenomena that appear to be effected not by causal chains but by cyclical behaviours? For example, what causes an amoeba to exist? Amoebas reproduce by dividing themselves into two new amoebas. Thus one amoeba is the cause of two more, each of which in turn is the cause of two further amoebas. The process has no beginning or end, but continues indefinitely. This is not so much a chain as a cycle, in which the effect (two amoebas) of reproduction is also its cause (two more amoebas).

Cybernetics and non-linearity

For cybernetics, non-linearity comes in two sorts: negative and positive feedback. Since cybernetics is concerned, like the thermodynamics on which it is based, with minimising loss (of energy, for thermodynamics; of information, for cybernetics), negative feedback is viewed as the source of maintaining order against the corrosive forces that threaten to destabilise it. These forces are always present since, just as energy always tends to dissipate according to thermodynamics, so too for cybernetics information always tends to become noise, or order, disorder. Some noise, disorder or energy loss is therefore inevitable, but order is maintained by negative feedback. Such feedback always 'tends to oppose what the system is already doing, and is thus negative' (Wiener [1948] 1962: 97). What the system is already doing, however, is losing information or increasing disorder, since this is in the nature of systems. This process can however become self-amplifying, multiplying geometrically the quantity of noise or disorder in the system, and leading to the system grinding to a halt or going out of control. This latter process is called positive feedback. (See **5.4**.)

5.4 Theories of cyberculture

The problem, then, with mechanical causation is that it did not explain all events in the physical world, and left biology almost entirely out of account. At best, therefore, mechanical causality accounts only for a region of physical events.

Both the origin of life and the amoeba's reproductive cycle are examples therefore not of linear but of non-linear causality. Somehow, life emerges, and amoebas keep dividing. These one-way processes are irreversible (life cannot be restarted; amoebas cannot divide less). While late nineteenth-century scientists conceded life was a non-linear phenomenon, the study of such phenomena has only really emerged in the last quarter of the twentieth century. The contemporary sciences that study non-linear phenomena concern themselves with what is called emergence: how order arises out of chaos (Prigogine and Stengers 1985), how organised life emerges from a chemical soup (Kauffman 1995); how mountains form (Gould 1987), and so on. Non-linear accounts have also been given of overtly social phenomena, such as how crowds develop, economic behaviour (Eve *et al.* 1997), and so on. In all cases, something coherent and organised arises not from a single cause but from any number of factors that converge to form a 'looping' or feedback structure, giving rise to what is called a 'self-organising' phenomenon.

We can see, then, that from the apparent limitation of mechanical explanation to a small region of physical phenomena, and the apparent limitation of teleology to living things alone, non-linear causality seems to work across the supposed boundary between the natural and cultural worlds. This is not, of course, an uncontroversial point, since many people would be reluctant to see what seemed to them to be utterly chance occurrences (finding oneself part of a crowd; going on a shopping spree) turn out to be functions of underlying organisations. But it is no more difficult to accept than that our beliefs and opinions, our desires and identities, are the fruits neither of nature nor choice, but of the effects of the economic, political and ideological structures of our culture.

Chaos, complexity and non-linearity

Cybernetics, concerned as it is with communication and control, tended to be concerned to eliminate positive feedback as system-disruption, noise, and the eventual collapse of the system, and to construct devices that maintained an equilibrium between positive feedback (change) and negative feedback (control). Beyond a certain threshold of positive feedback, this equilibrium was fatally disrupted, leading only to systems failure and breakdown. The recent study of chaotic phenomena, however, is interested not in phenomena in equilibrium but in those that are far from equilibrium. The study of non-linear phenomena in chemistry, for example, led Ilya Prigogine to discover processes that took place apparently spontaneously in far from equilibrium conditions. Prigogine called such phenomena dissipative structures: 'dissipative' because they take place not when a system is in an equilibrium state but once positive feedback has dissipated that system; and 'structures' since these same dissipative processes give rise to spontaneous order. A frequently used example of such a process is the so-called 'chemical clock':

> Suppose we have two kinds of molecules, 'red' and 'blue'. Because of the chaotic motion of the molecules, we would expect that at a given moment we would have more red molecules, say, in the left part of a vessel. Then a bit later more blue molecules would appear, and so on. The vessel would appear to us as 'violet', with occasional irregular flashes of red or blue. However, this is not what happens with a chemical clock; here the system is all blue, then it abruptly changes its colour to red, then again to blue. Because all these changes occur at regular time intervals, we have a coherent process.
>
> (Prigogine and Stengers 1985: 147–148)

The example of the chemical clock thus demonstrates that there are such spontaneously arising pockets of order; that once systems go into chaotic positive feedback they do not merely collapse but rather give rise to new and different orders. Prigogine and Stengers therefore call this process 'self-organisation'. They go on to locate such processes in biology, such as in the growth and reproduction of unicellular organisms (amoebas).

Conclusion: Williams and McLuhan on causality

What concept of causality does Williams therefore impute to McLuhan's technological determinism? Although he does discuss the need for 'a very different model of cause and effect' (1974: 125) – which will turn out to be the replacement of the concept of causality with that of agency – Williams does not make explicit what model of causality he is ascribing to McLuhan's technological determinism. We can, however, infer what kind of 'model' he is using if we examine what he sees as the consequences of such a determinism:

> If the medium – whether print or television – is the cause, all other causes, all that men ordinarily see as history, are at once reduced to effects. Similarly, what are elsewhere seen as effects, and as such subject to social, cultural, psychological and moral questioning, are excluded as irrelevant by comparison with the direct physiological and therefore 'psychic' effects of the media as such.
>
> (Williams 1974: 127)

If X is a cause, then it cannot be at the same time an effect: we can thus see that Williams is using a linear conception of causality, ruling out teleology and non-linearity (of the sort, for example, found in cybernetics). From our discussion of concepts of causality, this leaves mechanical causality. Is this the conception of cause Williams is working with? Two points he makes support this view:

1   He calls the effects McLuhan describes 'physiological'.

2   He qualifies these physiological effects as 'direct'.

It is really (2) that makes it clear that the causality Williams has in mind is indeed mechanical, since 'direct physiological' effects means that these effects are produced by a physically proximate cause. Non-linear causality is indirect: causal, but unpredictable. If we add this to the idea that a cause cannot simultaneously be an effect, then we get the image of the causal chain that is the preferred explanatory mode of modern science between the sixteenth and eighteenth centuries. The argument has nothing to say, therefore, about other forms of causality, and *deals only with one view of determinism*.

Moreover, by tying 'physiology' to the version of causality he criticises as inadequate for understanding social practices, Williams effectively rules out the physical in any form having any influence whatever upon culture. Yet this is surely not true: one clear reason for the emergence of factories during the late eighteenth and early nineteenth centuries must be that the large machines they housed required their parts to be physically proximate to one another – an engine will not drive a conveyor belt unless they are connected by cogs. The physical form of a technology therefore constrains and determines how it can be used.

Through this analysis, therefore, we have opened up a route for studying technology in a physicalist manner that is not vulnerable to the sophisticated criticisms Williams levelled at McLuhan. We have not yet asked, however, what model of causality McLuhan is dealing with. While McLuhan is notoriously oblique (although not without reason), we can find repeated references to technologies creating new environments, to technologies as extensions, having physical effects on their users, and so on. However, in the first essay of *Understanding Media*, McLuhan writes:

[A]s David Hume showed in the eighteenth century, there is no principle of causality in mere sequence. That one thing follows from another accounts for nothing . . . So the greatest of all reversals occurred with electricity, that ended sequence by making things instant. With instant speed the causes of things began to emerge to awareness again . . . Instead of asking which came first, the chicken or the egg, it suddenly seemed that a chicken was an egg's idea for getting more eggs.

(McLuhan 1967: 20)

In other words, McLuhan disavows 'sequence', and is not therefore dealing with the causal chain beloved of mechanism. Further, the instantaneity of, for example, electronic communications, brings causality to the fore again, since it makes us ask, if two events happen instantaneously, can we say that one causes the other? Just as the idea of the sequence of causes and effects recedes from attention, therefore, the idea of causes being effects of effects, and of effects being causes of causes, arises. Thus McLuhan's conception of the causality employed in electronic technologies is non-linear. Given electronic technologies, then, our environment becomes non-linear. Similarly, however, given mechanical technologies, our environment becomes mechanical. In other words, the technology in question

Nor is this cross-border traffic between the sciences and the humanities one-way. Friedrich Engels, for example, noted that Marx considered that Darwin's work on evolution provided the naturalistic basis for 'dialectical history' (Engels 1964: 7). Engels went on to extend this principle, and to write *Dialectics of Nature*, providing a dialectical account of the natural world causes events in accordance with its physical principles: there are mechanical causes at work in cultures that are predominantly structured by mechanical machines, and electronic causes at work in those primarily structured by electronic machines.

While McLuhan does not spell this out, the crux of the point is this: that it is the physical principles of a given technology that cause it to be used in certain ways. These uses then amplify the impact of the technology on the culture, so that mechanical technologies will produce mechanised cultures, electronic technologies, cultures based on instantaneity, and so on. Moreover, since the use of particular technologies extends our bodies and senses, human beings tend necessarily to be unaware of the impact the technologies are having: they become our nature. Importantly, then, the conception of causality at work here is not direct, but it is physical. To clarify:

1   the physical method of working of a technology determines its possible uses, so that

2   that determination of possible uses becomes amplified through its use, so that

3   the governing technology of an age will shape the society that uses it accordingly.

5.4 Theories of
cyberculture

This is a cybernetic understanding of the relations between humans and machines, which we will explore further in **5.4**.

To summarise: the version of causality Williams accuses McLuhan of working with is not the same version of causality that McLuhan is actually working with. Williams holds that determinism implies a mechanical causality, whereas McLuhan is actually working with a non-linear causality based on cybernetics (**5.4**).

5.2.3 Agencies

When Williams argues that McLuhan is a technological determinist, he bases this accusation on a certain type of cause, one that he identifies as stemming from the realm of 'physical facts' (1974: 129), that is, from the field of study proper to the natural sciences. Williams's own answer to the question of what causes cultural change does not therefore dispense with the concept of causality, but invokes an alternative concept – agency.

5.2.2 Causalities

As we have seen in **5.2.2**, however, there is no settled view regarding one kind of causality operative within the physical realm. Similarly, there is more than one account of agency. This section will discuss two basic kinds of agency: (1) humanist and (2) non-human.

The humanist concept of agency

At the root of the determinism problem is the question of what it is to ascribe agency to something. Williams, coming from a Marxist–humanist background, considers agency to be the ultimately reducible preserve of human beings as cultural actors. Contemporary cultural theory agrees almost entirely with this, viewing all other conceptions of agency as mystifications and distortions of our actual relations to things and to societal or cultural forms. If, accordingly, we were to accept the view that agency may indeed be ascribed to non-human phenomena, then we would be obscuring the reality of the situation, where in fact things are never innocently what they are, but serve some social purpose, follow an agenda of one or other interest group, or what have you. Let us call this the 'crime boss' theory of culture, in which we must be ever alert for the distortions of real cultural forms by mere ideological trappings, lest we find ourselves unwittingly serving a purpose contrary to our interests. In the loosest terms, this is what lies behind Marx's description of the factory system as inaugurating the dominance of dead over living labour, or machines over labouring humanity: such an arrangement serves the production process of capital, and has no other purpose than to line the pockets of the increasingly wealthy at the expense of the mass of labouring humanity.

At the root of this lies the view that it is indeed possible to reacquire one's total agency, to remove the shackles that bond us to the false gods of work, money, pain and misery, and to assume the mantle of free agents with which nature has endowed us but industrial culture steals. Such a view may justly be called humanism, since it jealously restricts agency to human beings as a matter of principle, despite any and all evidence to the contrary.

Non-human agency

What grounds, however, could there be to extend the concept of agency to non-human things? Before answering this, it is worth noting the following concerning humanism:

1   that since at least the eighteenth century human agency or 'free will' has been behind an attempt to isolate mere natural causality (that storms arise, that volcanoes erupt, that the earth circles the sun, that all earthbound phenomena are governed by the laws of gravity, and so on) and to add to it a form of causality specific to our freedom, to the fact that our choices and actions matter;

2   that this project survives in any attempt to isolate concepts of agency, and in consequence to argue against the view that machines themselves do anything of note to humans, without humans having already done something fundamental to machines;

3   that it takes no account of the extent to which human agency, even thus isolated, could be said to be independent of factors entirely beyond (restricted) human control.

It is by virtue of this last characteristic that Marx set such store by human consciousness, by the tricks that it plays on us, by things that appear to us and what we therefore think: not all our acts demonstrate agency, and those that do it takes hard work – becoming conscious of our real situation – to realise. We must labour to become conscious of our lost or alienated agency in order that we may resume it in resolute acts of will.

Thus the determinist ascription of agency to technology (it is technology that acts, and we who are acted upon) is perceived by the Marxist not as an evocation of real processes but as their distortion through reproducing the ideology of technology that causes events to occur, cultures to form and so on, over which we humans have little or no say. In truth, says the Marxist, this is simply a renunciation of our own agency, made palatable by the suggestion of inevitability. If, however, it were to turn out, as determinism suggests, that technology simply does drive history, then the suggestion that human consciousness and action are not the stage in which history is played out suffers irreparable damage, and Marx's 'historical materialism' becomes humanist idealism.

The three points listed on p. 307, however, serve to demonstrate the culturalist separatism that humanism has established between the worlds of culture and nature. The former is made up of institutions, beliefs, intentions and purposes, and the latter of blind causes. The sociologist of science Bruno Latour, however, has recently argued that to analyse the contemporary world, it is necessary to break down culturalist separatism and to establish in its stead a theory of how it is that technological and natural artefacts become agents. Thus Latour draws together the natural and the human sciences, and generalises the concept of agency to attach to 'non-humans'. Latour's '**actor-network theory**' disputes the notion that anything has agency on its own. Rather, agency is acquired by a thing being a component of

Marx and materialism

Marx is concerned to defend his brand of 'historical materialism' from what he calls 'crude' materialism. Crude materialism 'regards as the natural properties of things what [historical materialism regards as] social relations of production amongst people' (Marx 1993: 687). The proponents of such 'crude materialism' include Dr Price and his 'notion of capital as a self-reproducing being' (ibid.: 842), and Andrew Ure's definition of the factory as conveying the idea of 'a vast automaton, composed of numerous mechanical and intellectual organs' (ibid.: 690). Marx himself, on the other hand, is not such a 'crude materialist' when he writes of 'living machinery' (ibid.: 693) or that 'capital employs machinery' to promote its 'metabolism' (ibid.: 701), since he is only describing how such machinery 'confronts the individual', and how 'machinery appears . . . as alien, external' to living labour. This is because the latter lacks an understanding of 'the science that compels the inanimate limbs of the machinery . . . to act purposefully' (ibid.: 693–695). In other words, Marx compels humanity to recognise these illusions as illusions (machines are not really alive) and to become conscious of the power we possess as a human being to dominate the machines, and equally to understand our power to imagine they dominate us. Thus, according to Marx, living machines, self-acting mules, automata comprising intellectual and mechanical organs, occur only in the minds of labouring humanity, and can therefore be controlled merely by how we think about them (of course, Marx says that such changes have as a consequence an action that seizes control of human destiny).

a larger system (a network). Such systems dominate, he argues, the contemporary landscape: wherever we look, we see social action taking place not as a result of individually or collectively willed human actions but rather due to the relations between humans and the increasing quantity of non-human things that populate the cultural landscape. The consequence, however, of accepting Latour's account of how non-humans acquire agency is to abolish any sense in which the cultural field in general remains an exclusively human concern. Can we really therefore accept an account of agency that grants it to things?

To update this question, it lay behind philosopher Hubert Dreyfus's mistakenly arrogant challenge to a computer that it could never beat him at chess, since it necessarily lacked intelligence. Upon losing, Dreyfus then redefined what counted as intelligence to what could not be algorithmically coded, or turned into a program. *L'affaire Dreyfus*, as it has subsequently become known, demonstrated that humanists will do anything to safeguard their specialness, even when there is nothing special left, other than to invent games without rules to frustrate Deep Blue. However, does the computer in question possess agency of any sort, or are its actions entirely dependent on its makers? Black-and-white answers to this question are insufficient to answer it, since at the very least the actions of machine (Deep Blue), human (Kasparov, Dreyfus) and game are importantly interdependent: none acts without the others. And this is precisely Latour's point: it is as false to argue that a machine on its own has agency as it is to suggest that only humans do; rather it is the network as a whole that acts, effects and determines. Thus, he writes of large-scale social (legal, educational, medical), commercial (corporations, markets), political (governments) or military institutions that they are 'actors [or "agents"] of great size . . . macro-actors . . . made up of a series of local interactions' (Latour 1993: 120–121). Humans are not therefore agents that create the networks, rather we are only involved in 'local interactions' that make up these macro-actors: IBM, the Red Army, and so on.

The cost and benefit of this extension of agency from humans to things is to give up on the humanist view that there are machines on one side, humans on the other, and that the machines are taking over! This is precisely the anxiety that lies behind the presentation of intelligent and independent machines in popular culture, from *Terminator* to *Tetsuo*; but it also, perhaps surprisingly, underwrites serious-minded speculations such as Kevin Warwick (1998) offers, concerning a future governed entirely by machines. But this humanism is also the source of almost all the critical approaches cultural and media studies has at its disposal to address cultural phenomena: Marxist humanism, as we have seen, rests on precisely this bedrock (see Feenberg [1991] and Mitcham [1994] for accounts of the critical and the humanist approaches to technology, respectively). The stakes involved in the issue of agency are therefore considerable.

Note, however, that Latour leaves the question of whether agency exists at all, intact. In other words, he renegotiates the source of social action from humans alone to humans and non-humans, but allows thereby that purposeful social action does take place. That is, Latour stops short of outright determinism. We will now consider the varieties of determinism, before drawing **5.2** to a close.

5.2 Revisiting determinism: physicalism, humanism and technology

5.2.4 Determinisms

Some theorists cast serious doubt on even the validity of the concept of agency, suggesting that it is ludicrous to imagine that 'there exists at all, in the whole of reality, the sort of agency that can begin or purposively redirect causal chains, not merely serve as one more link inside them' (Ferré 1995: 129). Such a view is an example of a very straightforward determinism that suggests that every event has a cause, and that ultimately the very idea of voluntary action or choice is therefore illusory: there is no agency, that is, only causality.

This is the starkest form of determinism, but not the only form. As Williams understands it, technological determinism answers a question as to the causes of social change. He then interprets this to mean either that human agency causes social change, or, since technology is simply another physical thing, social change is just another instance of physically caused changes. We have, moreover, seen that Williams is operating with only one view of causality here, that of linear or mechanical causality. We have suggested already that this is not what McLuhan is getting at, but the point that remains to be considered is whether, without retreating wholly to a point where the only causes of social effects are mechanical, technology can be seen as determining. This is why we examined other concepts of causality. In this section, therefore, we will examine the kinds of determinism left out of the account by Williams's critique of McLuhan. These are:

- soft determinism;

- from soft to hard determinism.

We will see that soft determinisms tend to emphasise the formative role played in technologically determinist societies by non-technological factors, and do not therefore rule out the role of agency in principle. But we will also see that such accounts pave the way for a kind of historicised hard determinism modelled on non-linear causation.

Soft determinism
In *Does Technology Drive History?* (Smith and Marx 1996), a collection of essays taken from a 1994 symposium between historians, sociologists and theorists held on the topic of technological determinism, the editors arrange versions of determinism, following the philosopher

William James, according to 'hard' and 'soft' poles. 'At the hard end of the spectrum', they write, 'agency (the power to effect change) is imputed to technology itself' (ibid.: xii), whereas 'soft determinists begin by reminding us that the history of technology is a history of human actions' (ibid.: xiii). Neither version, however, disputes the deterministic outcome of technology, since in both cases what may begin as an aid to human life ends up dictating what form it must take (consider how the car has changed the form and function of the city). What they dispute is the kind of agency or the kind of causality involved in technological determinism. Hard determinists, that is, insist that the cause of technological deterministic effects is itself technological. Soft determinists insist conversely that while determinism is the outcome, the agency that produces that outcome is not itself technological but consists additionally in a variety of factors: economic, political and social.

There are many soft-deterministic accounts of the role of technology in culture. The social theorist Jürgen Habermas (1970), for example, argues that what he calls 'capitalist **techno-science**' becomes deterministic due to the fact that its goals are strictly compatible with capitalism's, insofar as both triumph the validity of 'instrumentalist' – whatever gets the job done – behaviour over all other claimants to validity. Thus social justice, judgements and beliefs, since they do not simply aim to get something done, lose cultural authority due to the successes of capitalist technoscience. We can see what Habermas means by the instrumental form of reasoning embodied in technoscience if we consider why it is that social services such as schools are required to deliver 'results' for their pupils, and have their own value assessed by these results; or why 'efficiency gains' must be made in hospitals, etc. The purpose of schools is not to educate but to gain high grades for their pupils; the purpose of hospitals is not to cure the sick but to become efficient treatment centres for clients who want a job done.

Therefore **technoscience** is deterministic not in its origins (it required the collaboration of capitalism to become the dominant form of social organisation) but in its effects, since once established, it defines its own goals – to get the job done – and expands its influence into all forms of social activity. While the situation, as far as Habermas is concerned, is therefore deterministic (everything is defined in terms of technoscientific instrumentalism), it is not irrevocable, since behind this deterministic situation lies the capitalist will. Habermas therefore takes a classically humanist path, rejecting the idea that technology (or science) is determining on its own, and arguing instead for the human capacity for self-determination through instituting rational deliberation regarding the proper ends of society.

Similarly, the philosopher Jean-François Lyotard (1984), who accepts Habermas's view that technoscience has become determinant, argues that he offers a solution that no longer holds for the information economy. What the information economy consists in, argues Lyotard, is precisely the subjection of language – the medium in which Habermas's 'rational deliberation' is to take place – to technoscientific imperatives. In other words, once capitalism has got into our sentences, there is no longer any point in communicating unless we are going to get something done thereby. Moreover, these imperatives have been irrevocably settled into the social structure due to computerisation, since computers are precisely information processing devices. Since the computer has become a dominant technology for commercial and communicational purposes, this in turn alters the goals of communication from rational exchange to gaining information. Both Lyotard and Habermas therefore offer deterministic accounts of the social role and function of technology, given the social deployment of those technologies. In other words, their determinisms suggest that 'there's no going back', although Habermas argues that, if we cut through the ideology that promotes instrumentalism – getting the job done – as an imperative, the technoscientific tide can be turned, whereas Lyotard insists that it cannot.

Note the echo of this selfaugmentation in the concept of self-organisation

From soft to hard determinism

1.6.4 The many virtues of
Saint McLuhan

Soft determinists are therefore concerned to highlight technological determinism as an effect of social forces, rather than as their cause. But the key issue they raise, regardless of identifying the causes of a deterministic situation, is that technological determinism now need not imply that it was always so. Such accounts therefore make room for those who argue that while societies have not always been technologically determined, they become so at specific historical junctures.

Precisely such a process was ascribed to technological change by Jacques Ellul in his book *The Technological Society*, published in France in 1954. Ellul calls this process the 'self-augmentation of technique'. He writes:

> At the present time, technique has arrived at such a point in its evolution that it is being transformed and is progressing almost without decisive intervention from man . . . [T]his is a self-generating process; technique engenders technique.

> (Ellul [1954] 1964: 85, 87)

This is a version of determinism in which, given the interaction of technique by technique (for Ellul, 'la technique' includes not only hard technologies such as machines, but soft technologies like statistical census methods, bureaucracies, political, medical, carceral and educational institutions and so on), technology simply 'reacts upon' technology, exponentially increasing its forms beyond the control of designers, policymakers and so on. As he puts it, 'when a new technical form appears, it makes possible and conditions a number of others' ([1954] 1964: 87). As an example of such a process, consider what the replacement of valves with microchips has made possible and conditions: instead of room-filling immobile computing devices we have laptops and mobile Internet access devices, which makes possible (albeit not actual) a universally accessible global communications network, which in turns makes possible the extension of monitoring and surveillance techniques, the replacement of physical travel to work with remote access points, deregulating the culture of the office, global finance crashing, new cultural and political potentials for action, new non-terrestrial forms of corporate expansionism, and so on.

On this reading, technology not only becomes its own governor, but begins to establish the physical framework for technological and cultural activity in general, making possible and necessitating not only further new technological forms but also new cultural ones. When, that is, a new technological form is introduced (the steam engine, the factory, the telegraph, the computer), the extent to which it spreads throughout a culture will determine in turn the extent to which subsequent technologies must conform with its principles of operation: there could be no place for a steam computer in a digital environment, for example; digital environments require digital augmentation. Similarly, manufacturing economies in information-rich environments tend to die out, whereas computer manufacture generally takes place in information-poor economies (see Castells [1996] 2000; Plant 1997).

Technical self-augmentation then, acts not merely to increase the quantity of technics but reacts on itself, creating a positive feedback that carries everything else along with it, causing therefore qualitative change. Ellul's account thus suggests that technological determinism is not an historical constant, but that it arises at a certain stage of technological development, where technology saturates the environment. At such a point, humans cease to create technologies as an extension of their own capacities and start instead to respond to the imperatives of the technologies they have created. Technology now 'engenders', as Ellul puts it, itself.

Such an account of 'local' determinism also figures largely in the mathematics of chaos and complexity theory. In these accounts, determinism is not a global condition, but pertains only within the confines of a given region of phenomena. Lyotard, who coined the term 'local determinism' (1984: xxiv), borrows its formulation from the catastrophe mathematician René Thom, who writes: 'The more or less determined character of a process is determined by the local state of the process' (Thom 1975: 126; cited by Lyotard 1984: 56)

Box: Chaos, complexity and non-linearity, p. 334
5.3.5 Life and intelligence in the digital age

This form of artificial intelligence is not the only technology that has been described as self-organising. Marx, for example, scolds Dr Price for his 'crude materialism' when the latter suggests that capital becomes a 'self-reproducing being' (Marx 1993: 842), yet he simultaneously describes the factory as a 'self-moving automaton, a moving power that moves itself' (ibid.: 692); Ellul's self-augmentation thesis, and Bergson's idea that technology 'reacts upon' itself, basically describe the same phenomenon

There is not a huge distance here between the prompting of human intervention by technological demand and machines becoming self-aware, a constant of science fiction from the intelligent computer Hal, in *2001: A Space Odyssey*, to Skynet, the self-aware computer intelligence in *Terminator 2*. However, in the former example the computer is engineered to be intelligent; in the latter it becomes so of its own accord as a result of surpassing a critical mass: it self-organises, to use Prigogine and Stengers's term.

Finally, therefore, we must ask in what sense this is a hard determinism. First, in the sense that Smith and Marx give to the term, technology, on Ellul's account, does become the cause of technological determinism, although this was not always the case. In other words, to demonstrate the technological determinist position we no longer need to construct a history in which all technologies have caused all social changes, but only identify those historical junctures at which technology, as it were, becomes self-organising.

Second, Ellul's is a hard determinism in the sense that it uses a model of causality that obtains in the physical as well as in the social world: that of self-organisation, or nonlinear causality. In the **Box** on p. 334, we saw how non-linear processes are involved in cybernetics and in chaos and complexity theories, and noted that these non-linear processes have been described as 'self-organising'. Self-organising processes in the natural world arise not from a single cause, but from the emergence of order in a chaotic environment. One school of thought in artificial intelligence research, for example, looks not to programme intelligence into a computer, but to prompt it to learn, in the same manner as does a human infant. By connecting several processors together, and having them fire information at each other in a more or less random manner, the idea is that intelligence will 'emerge' or 'self-organise' (see **5.3.5**).

Consider the following account of the emergence of robotic intelligence:

[We] may without much difficulty imagine a future generation of killer robots dedicated to understanding their historical origins. We may even imagine specialized 'robot historians' committed to tracing the various technological lineages that gave rise to their species. And we could further imagine that such a robot historian would write a different kind of history than would its human counterpart. While a human historian might try to understand the way people assembled clockworks, motors and other physical contraptions, a robot historian would likely place a stronger emphasis on the way these machines effected human evolution . . . The robot historian of course would hardly be bothered by the fact that it was a human who put the first motor together: for the role of humans would be seen as little more than that of industrious insects pollinating an independent species of machine-flowers that simply did not possess its own reproductive organs during a segment of its evolution.

(De Landa 1991: 2–3)

Here we can see how actions that are themselves effects (machines assembled by humans) can become in turn the causes of further effects (the evolutionary direction of biological and technological 'species'). We need not, however, resort to robo-history in order to find similar processes. This is precisely the order of effects found in any complex biological system (plants, animals, humans) in which effects become causes in turn. If we consider the growth of any organism, for example, it is clear that in no sense is this the consequence of a single cause. Again, it is worth noting that such processes are found equally in the natural world (storms, chemical clocks, the formation of mountains) as in the cultural (riots, market behaviours, settlement patterns). Thus self-organisation and technological self-augmentation provide a physicalist account of 'hard' technological determinism that yet remains sensitive to historical contingencies. At the same time, rather than restricting agency to humans, this account notes that the formation of purposes is itself a self-organising process, and that there is no reason therefore not to ascribe agency to non-humans.

5.3 Biological technologies: the history of automata

In the game of life and evolution, there are three players at the table: human beings, nature and machines. I am firmly on the side of nature, but nature, I suspect, is on the side of the machines.

(Dyson 1998: 3)

Introduction

Having looked at the physicality of technology in **5.2**, this section will focus on the relations between biology and technology. While the popular figure of the cyborg suggests that the cybernetic age is the first time in history that biology and technology could (potentially) be combined, and while a lot of criticism in fact supports precisely this view, as we shall see there is a long history to the idea of living machines. As cyberneticist Norbert Wiener writes:

At every stage of technique, the ability of the artificer to produce a working simulacrum of a living organism has always intrigued. This desire to produce and to study automata has always been expressed in terms of the living technique of the age.

(Wiener [1948] 1962: 40)

Following Wiener's lead, this section will primarily be concerned to outline the history of automata – of 'self-moving things' (**5.3.3**) – in order to display the relations between technology and biology at each stage of technological development. It will also, however, be posing questions concerning the biological and the technological in general.

Since the seventeenth century, mechanical monsters, demonic machines and living instruments have populated not only fictions, fairground spectacles of often dubious authenticity, magic lantern shows and cinema, but also engineering projects, physiological researches, and computing projects. From Julian de La Mettrie's *Man-Machine*, to Frankenstein's monster, to 'cellular automata' and De Landa's Terminator-type 'robot historian', living technology preoccupies the furthest reaches of each epoch's technological capacities and imaginary. In keeping with the lesson of the previous section (**5.2**), that we must pay attention to the physical underpinnings of culture if we are to understand the interaction between humans, machines and material nature, then it becomes necessary that we focus on a given technological culture's means for realising artificial life. Therefore, the rest of this section will chart the forms of autonomous or 'animate' machines – automata – whose spectres haunted, or whose matter constructed, life in Europe throughout various epochs of technological development.

Cyberculture may not, therefore, be the first time in history that a living machine stands on the horizon of a culture's technological capacities, but it perhaps encompasses a larger range of technological interventions in biology than previous ages. As we shall see, amongst the consequences of the influence of cybernetics has been a conception of life as information (DNA and genomics – **5.3.5**), and a conception of biology as technology, or of 'biotechnology'. At the same time, both in fiction and reality, there has been a renewed push to create living technologies, whether in the form of the cyborg, or of the field of scientific research known as 'artificial life' or 'Alife'.

5.3.1 Automata: the basics

Throughout the history of automata certain concepts recur, forming a core of what sorts of things automata are. Particularly crucial here are two sets of differences: between tools and machines, on the one hand, and between *simulacra* and *automata* on the other.

Tools and machines

The former differentiation places the technological object along a scale of dependency relative to its user, with the hand-tool almost entirely dependent and the industrial machine almost entirely independent. The hand-tool needs to be moved by an external source, whereas the machine moves itself. In this sense, only machines can be automata. But there are also machines that use tools, or that automate functions hitherto requiring an external, human user. For example, the robots used in car manufacture use tools formerly wielded by humans, such as riveters, paint guns, and so on. A technology's dependency need not therefore always be on human users; nor is a human always the user of a technology – Marx, for example, argued that with industrialisation machines position humans as the dependent ones, reversing the situation between user and used, with humans possessing a low degree of independence in relation to the machines. Potentially, then, humans can become tools of machines, as Aristotle pointed out:

> Now instruments are of various sorts; some are living, others lifeless; in the rudder, the pilot of the ship [the kybernetes] has a lifeless, in the look-out man, a living instrument; for in the arts [techne] the servant is a kind of instrument. Thus too, a possession is an instrument for maintaining life. And so . . . the slave is a living possession, and property a number of such instruments; and the servant is himself an instrument for instruments.
>
> (Aristotle, *Politics* book 1, 1253b; in Everson 1996: 15)

Simulacra and automata

Thus, some twenty-five centuries ago, we find Aristotle taking the idea of 'living instruments' seriously. He continues:

> For if every instrument could accomplish its own work, obeying or anticipating the will of others, like the statues of Daedalus, or the tripods of Hephaestus, which, says the poet, 'of their own accord entered the assembly of the gods'; if, in like manner, the shuttle would weave and the plectrum touch the lyre, chief workmen would not want servants, nor masters slaves.
>
> (Aristotle, *Politics* book 1, 1253b; in Everson 1996: 15)

Homer's account of 'tripods', from which Aristotle quotes, contains further mentions of Hephaestus's mechanical wonders. A lame smith, Hephaestus, has undertaken to extend his thus limited capacities by mechanical means, extending himself, as it were, through these 'twenty tripods . . . fitted with golden wheels . . . so he could have them moving of their own accord'. He also sees to some of his more immediate needs with mechanical maids:

> They are made of gold, looking like living girls; they have intelligent minds, and have learnt their handiwork from the immortal gods. So they busied themselves in support of their master.
>
> (Homer, *Iliad* 18, in Hammond 1987: 304–305)

5.3.5 Life and intelligence in the digital age

In section **1.2.6** of this book, the term 'simulation' is distinguished from 'imitation'. 'Simulacrum' as used here should not be understood as being related to the above sense of 'simulation'; strictly speaking, in terms of automata, the simulacrum is the imitation, whereas the automaton proper 'simulates' in the sense of section 2. We shall therefore only use 'simulacrum' and its cognate 'simulation' in this section to refer explicitly to the history of automata, since the distinction features throughout the literature (see Glossary)

1.2.6 Simulated

While digital simulacra of living systems (Alife is less concerned with biological individuals than with the systems they compose) become increasingly accurate, Alife's strong claim to instantiate or realise life poses questions to the very foundations of biology: to what extent is biology in principle limited to the study of 'life as we know it'?

Here we have two sets of classical distinctions in the history of automata. In Aristotle, we have the distinction between living and lifeless instruments; in Homer, that between the tripods that *move of their own accord* and the maids who look like 'living girls'. In many ways, these distinctions are interconnected: what *moves of its own accord*, the 'self-moving thing', is a precise translation of the word *automaton*. Living things are therefore 'natural automata' or 'natural machines', as the philosopher, mathematician and calculator-maker G.W. Leibniz was still calling them in the early eighteenth century (*Monadology* ([1714] 1989) §64), and as early computer theorists called them in the middle of the twentieth (von Neumann [1958] 1999). Thus, although he elsewhere differentiates 'natural' from 'unnatural' things in that the former, unlike the latter, 'contain within themselves' their own 'source of movement and rest' – that is, *move of their own accord* (*Physics* bk. II.1, 192b), automata are differentiated by Aristotle not according to whether they are biological or technological, but simply according to whether they have the power of autonomous motion. Thus, a slave may be biological, but the power of autonomous motion he possesses as a natural being may be inactive in him *because he is a slave*, an 'instrument' or extension of the master. Similarly, as his consideration of Hephaestus' devices shows, Aristotle sees nothing inherently impossible in the idea of self-moving technological things. Of the latter, there are therefore two types – the automaton or self-moving thing pure and simple (the tripod), and the automaton that *looks like something living* (the maid).

This same distinction was made in 1964 by the historian of science and technology Derek J. de Solla Price in the following terms: *simulacra* are 'devices that simulate' other things (spiders, humans, ducks) and *automata* are 'devices that move by themselves' (1964: 9). Arguably the only new distinction in the history of automata is that introduced by artificial life (Alife) researchers between *simulation* on the one hand and *instantiation* or *realisation* on the other. The distinction is neatly summed up in this comment by one of the major figures in Alife research, Christopher G. Langton:

> We would like to build models of life that are so lifelike that they would cease to be models of life and become examples of life themselves.
>
> (Langton citing Pattee, in Boden 1996: 379)

History of automata

AD1	Pneumatic and hydraulic automata, pneumatic theatre
9th–11th cent.	Water-clocks
14th cent.	Early mechanical clocks
17th cent.	Mechanism and the clockwork universe: natural and artificial automata, calculators, 'machine man'
18th cent.	Clockwork automata; mechanical pictures; chess-playing, writing, and speaking automata; physiological automata
19th cent.	Life as electricity, manufactures as automata; fairground automata, intelligent engines
20th cent.	Intelligent machines, cellular automata, cyborgs, robotics

Early automata

The history of automata is generally dated as having begun with the construction of hydraulic and pneumatic automata, worked by the pressure of water and air in pumps and pipes. Such automata were constructed in Ancient Greece, Byzantium, Old Iran and Islam, where they adorned temples, courts and monuments. The best known of these ancient automata are two works by Hero of Alexandria in the first century AD. The first was his fountain or *pneumatikon*. A device now so commonplace as to escape our attention, the fountain worked by building air pressure in a container part-filled with water. When the pressure was released, it drove the water up and out of a vertical pipe, forming the crown of a fountain (Ferré 1995: 47). To consider the shock and entertainment this gave rise to, consider that in nature water never moves *upwards*. The second of Hero's automata was the mechanical theatre, as narrated in his book on automata, in which pneumatic and hydraulic forces propelled figures into movement, performing small scenes. Hero's automaton theatre was reconstructed, following its author's instructions, in the fifteenth century, and contained a mechanism sufficiently complex to narrate five scenes of the actions of the Gods Nautilus and Athene on Greek shipping. The construction of such technologised spectacles creates grounds for reconsidering the history of moving or *kinematic* pictures as stretching back to the first century AD, as Deleuze (1989) notes. Hero's automaton theatre, that is, connects automata not only to the history of puppet shows but also and more directly to the technologies of mechanical paintings of the eighteenth and nineteenth centuries, the first examples of moving images.

5.2 Hero of Alexandria's Automata: the mobile theatre, first century AD.

5.3 The first moving images: an eighteenth-century mechanical picture: front and rear views (Chapuis and Droz 1958: 142–143). Conservatoires des Arts et Metiers

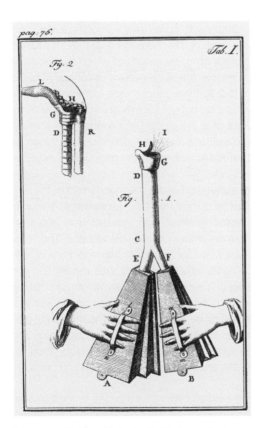

5.4 Lungs and bellows. Understanding the human body as composed of machines was an important aspect of mechanistic thought in the seventeenth and eighteenth centuries. (Hankins and Silverman 1995: 194). Courtesy of the University of Washington Libraries

Pneumatic, non-simulacral automata went on to become objects of intense scientific and popular scrutiny, extending as far as the great Arabic water-clocks of the ninth century. The next major work on automata after Hero's, however, was Al-Jazari's *Treatise on Automata*, dating from the twelfth century. During that same century, it is said that Thomas Aquinas, shocked at the spectacle of a moving, speaking head made of baked clay by Albertus Magnus, smashed it, thinking it a great evil (White 1964: 124–125). But it was not until the rise of the mechanical clock in the fourteenth century that automata suddenly increased in the complexity of their operations. Enormous clocks were built, such as Giovanni di'Dondi's great 16-year project completed in 1364. This measured not only the passage of time, but also the movements of the sun and the planets (White 1964: 126). Already the suspicion was dawning that clockwork was more than a means to describe or model natural phenomena, but instead, the very mechanism of nature itself.

5.3.2 Clockwork: technology and nature, combined

Mechanism

Clockwork is the technology proper to the period of mechanism and the mechanical philosophy from the seventeenth century to the mid-eighteenth. This was the period in which philosophers and scientists devised the ambition of explaining all nature in terms of clockwork. The same period of history saw Newton's mechanism become the truly dominant worldview, which was to remain dominant, albeit with some major modifications, until Einstein's Relativity Theory in the early twentieth century. Mechanism constituted a triumph over the mere theorising, on the basis of Aristotle's texts, by means of which the medieval period had attempted to explain natural phenomena. Medieval natural philosophy utilised Aristotle's concept of 'final causes' or *teleology* (**5.2.2**). Final causes were extremely useful in explaining the 'what' of things (why a thing is what it is), but not for examining the detail of the how it became what it is; that is, it was exactly not what the moderns understood as science. In place of recognisably modern scientific explanations it offered definitions of things as *potentials* inhering in the essences of things that are actualised in the growth and development of that thing.

To dispose of the concept of final causes in explaining nature, the mechanists of the seventeenth and eighteenth centuries insisted that *all things must be explained in terms of motion and the interrelations of parts*, thus replacing 'final' with 'efficient' (or 'effecting') causes. As to the cause of motion, however, there was considerable debate. The most extreme of mechanists left no room in the natural world for any other than mechanical, efficient causes. This was a giant clockwork universe, and God's role was merely to have created it, after which it ran its own course. Although mechanism typically resulted in making the concept of a divine being redundant, it is worth noting that even Newton considered that the forces by which motion was caused in the first place were ultimately the domain of theology rather than natural science. However, in a godless universe of mechanical motion and parts, all things within it must be explained in similar terms. For the mechanists, then, as Thomas L. Hankins puts it, 'there was no basic difference between one's watch and one's pet dog' (Hankins 1985: 114).

It was in consequence only a matter of time before philosophers began to explain even the most complex of physiological functions in mechanical terms, and, thereafter, to attempt the construction of artificial life forms based on clockwork principles. While at first these were strictly physiological demonstration models (cf. Hankins and Silverman 1995) showing the heart as a pump, the lungs as bellows, each linked by pipes and valves, the resultant 'automata' acquired great fame and value beyond their scientific and medical relevance to philosophers.

Man-machines: de la Mettrie and Descartes

During the reign of the mechanical philosophy, since the alternative to animals and man being clockwork creatures was that they were infused with divine sparks of life, the construction of automata became a profession of the secular triumph of the natural sciences. Accordingly, many physiologists and philosophers regarded living mechanical automata as an inevitable consequence of their philosophies: if science has shown that nature is mechanical, and has enabled us to make mechanical things, then science can construct artificial automata after the pattern of nature's own. Thus, the military field-surgeon, physiologist and philosopher Julian Offray de La Mettrie's 1747 manifesto-like treatise *Machine Man* considered and rejected all those views that did not accept that animate nature and machine-life were one and the same substance. He wrote:

> Let us conclude boldly that man is a machine and that there is in the whole universe only one diversely modified substance . . . Here is my system, or rather the truth, unless I am very much mistaken. It is short and simple. Now if anyone wants to argue, let them!
>
> (la Mettrie [1747] 1996: 39)

It was in precisely this vein that the French *philosophes* of the eighteenth century were to trumpet scientific materialism over the mystifications of theology, leading, for example, Denis Diderot to advance the hypothesis that between rock and spider, spider and man, there were no essential differences in kind, but only in the degree of their organisation and complexity. Life, accordingly, was to be explained by an increase in the complexity of the organisation of matter, and intelligence by a still higher increase (Diderot 1985: 149ff.).

Disputes such as this were nothing new, however. Debates between physicalists and theists regarding the natural or divine causes of life were a constant feature of the philosophical and scientific landscape of the seventeenth century. What was new was that physicalist theories were being demonstrated by the construction of automata that replicated or simulated the functions of the various organs in the human body. Thus, as the philosopher René Descartes wrote in his 1662 *Treatise on Man*:

> I suppose the body to be just a statue or a machine made of earth . . . We see clocks, artificial fountains, mills, and other similar machines which, even though they are only made by men, have the power to move of their own accord in various ways.
>
> (Descartes [1662] 1998: 99)

Note that here Descartes specifically speaks of machines that 'move of their own accord', thus taking up the implication in Aristotle that there is nothing in principle impossible in the idea of self-moving, and thus effectively biological, technologies (**5.4.1**). Descartes now extends this supposition to understanding all the bodily machine's functions: the nerves are like the pipes in the mechanical parts of fountains; the muscles, engines and the tendons are springs; the blood, or 'animal spirit', to water and the heart to its source, a pump; respiration is like the movement of a clock or mill; perception, the passage of a visual impulse to the brain, is the impact of moving parts on one another, and so on (Descartes [1662] 1998: 106). Taking up the challenge of Descartes' hypotheses, Athanasius Kircher began construction of a mechanical speaking head for the entertainment of Queen Christina of Sweden (in whose service

5.2.2 Causalities

Consider also in this light the newer voice-magic displayed by Stephen Hawking's artificial speaking machine

Descartes died), but never completed it. Announcing it in his *Phonurgia nova* ('New Voice-Magic') of 1673, he affirmed that the head would move its 'eyes, lips and tongue, and, by means of the sounds which it emitted, [would] appear to be alive' (Bedini 1964: 38). Such machines involved solving the problem of how to reproduce the functions of several different organs mechanically: the larynx, tongue, lips and palate, and the lungs, so their successful construction was neither physiologically nor technologically as trivial as the prospect of such machines might now seem. That said, of course, the technology we ritually implant in our bodies to replace failing organs, such as the heart, follows the same precepts as its eighteenth-century precursors, as do the clumsier yet functionally identical dialysis machines that stand in for the failed functions of human kidneys. The absolute lack of change in our thinking about such technologies has only recently been highlighted by the attempt to grow replacement organs in, as it were, organic factories, such as pigs' bodies. With a little genetic engineering, pig hearts can be made compatible with human bodies, thus enabling the transfer of organic rather than mechanical hearts. The apparent newness of these 'xenotransplantation' biotechnologies demonstrates instead a 300-year-old historical continuity, rooted in the attempt to construct mechanical organs which has held sway over medical and physiological thinking since Descartes and La Mettrie first promoted the idea of the human body as a machine. Even by the late eighteenth century, however, speaking heads with moving parts were finally built by, among others, the architect of the famous chess-playing automaton, Baron von Kempelen (Bedini 1964: 38; Hankins and Silverman 1995: 186ff.).

Before this time, however, a French surgeon and anatomist named Claude-Nicolas le Cat constructed an automaton 'in which one can see the execution of the principal functions of the animal economy, circulation, respiration, secretions' (Hankins and Silverman 1995: 183). This was constructed in order to settle a scientific question of the effects of the common therapeutic practice of 'bleeding' a patient in order to relieve the patient of her symptoms. If the automaton were to settle the question (as both Le Cat and François Quesnay, his adversary, agreed it would), then it must have been held to be not simply a visually accurate model of the human digestive and circulatory system but rather a physiologically accurate one. Thus even from the proposal for such a model, we can see the extent to which Descartes' physicalist and mechanistic physiological principles were by this time not being treated as wild hypotheses but as the basis of a scientific physiology. The seventeenth and eighteenth centuries thus witnessed a plethora of similar models of respiration, blood circulation and the like.

Vaucanson's duck

Sustaining the same goal of realising biological physiological systems in mechanical devices, Jacques de Vaucanson attempted in the 1730s to construct 'a moving anatomy' to reproduce all the major organic functions. This attempt reached an initial completion in the 'artificial duck of gilt brass' of 1738, 'which drinks, eats, quacks, flounders in water, digests and excretes like a live duck' (Vaucanson, cited in Bedini 1964: 37). In this mechanical bird, according to Diderot's *Dictionary of the Sciences* of 1777,

> the food is digested as in real animals . . .; the matter digested in the stomach is led off by pipes to the anus, where there is a sphincter allowing it to pass out. The inventor does not set this up as a perfect digestive system capable of manufacturing blood . . . to support the animal . . . [but] only to imitate the mechanics of the digestive process in three things, firstly, the swallowing of the food, secondly the maceration, cooking or dissolving of it, and thirdly the action causing it to leave the body in a markedly changed form.
>
> (Diderot, cited in Chapuis and Droz 1958: 241)

The duck made its author instantly famous and wealthy, and brought about his election to the French Académie, where he was in charge of patenting new inventions in industry. Amongst these was Jacquard's automatic pattern-weaving loom, which was to play its role in Ada Lovelace's first attempts at understanding and creating what is now called programming. By 1805, however, Goethe reported having seen the duck, now 'completely paralysed' and incapable of digestion, like a dying animal condemned never finally to die, at the home of the new owner (cited in Chapuis and Droz 1958: 234).

 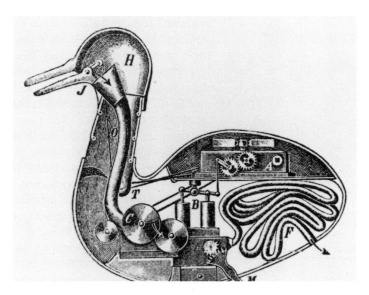

5.5 Vaucanson's mechanical duck (1738). Courtesy of The British Library

Between the development of physiological automata and the early nineteenth century, when Goethe's comments on the gilt brass duck were written, automata gradually fell from scientific and philosophical grace, due to shifts amongst the community of scholars away from the Newtonian philosophy that gave mechanism its principal grounding. If mechanism gave a false view of biological phenomena, then the important questions about life could no longer be solved by mechanical means. It was during the late eighteenth and early nineteenth centuries that researches in galvanism (named after the Italian discoverer of 'animal electricity' or galvanism, Luigi Galvani) and electricity began to displace mechanical devices as the principal technologies of life, as we can see if we consider the role played by electricity as the 'life force' that 'galvanises' Frankenstein's monster into life. During this same period, however, mechanical automata began to acquire a significance far removed from the rarefied environments of scholarly dispute. While Vaucanson's brass duck convinced the editors of the 1777 edition of the *Encyclopédie* of the physiological validity of mechanism, the duck won more fame from public exhibition than from the scientific community. Thus Vaucanson became rich by it, and von Kempelen financed his serious-minded attempts to automate voice production with deliberately scientifically fraudulent devices for public entertainment, such as his famous chess-player of 1769.

The Jaquet-Droz Androïdes
The popularity of such devices returned attention from the scientific to the spectacular uses of automata. As early as 1610, mechanical automata were being produced that simulated

spiders, birds, caterpillars and so on. Even before this, however, mechanical automata were produced as ornaments of the true automaton, the clock. These were automata that, rather than automating organic functions, simulated living things in clockwork. Thus, in 1773, thirty years after Vaucanson sold his automata and moved on, Pierre and Henri-Louis Jaquet-Droz produced what the *Encyclopédie* distinguished from physiological automata by calling them 'androids' – human-like things. Amongst the Jaquet-Droz androids or simulacra, are a writer (Chapuis and Droz 1958: 293–294; 396), an artist (ibid.: 299–300) and a musician (ibid.: 280–282). Of these life-size simulacra or androids, the writer writes messages of up to forty characters in length, the artist draws four sketches (a dog, a cupid, the head of Louis XIV and profiles of Louis XVI and Marie Antoinette [Bedini 1964: 39]), and the musician plays five tunes, composed by Henri-Louis Jaquet-Droz, on an organ (Chapuis and Droz 1958: 283).

Further such simulated artists, along with magicians and acrobats, were commissioned and constructed (by the firm of Jaquet-Droz and the automaton maker Henri Maillardet) for specific purposes of public and popular exhibition, and commanded high prices (Jaquet-Droz's second musician of 1782 was sold to the London office of Jaquet-Droz's own firm for 420 pounds sterling [Chapuis and Droz 1958: 284]). While at that time simulacra towards the end of the eighteenth century were principally regarded as entertainments, these entertainments themselves contained both the source of and the fuel for further debate and often reflected on the automaton's status as a mechanical artefact. If automata appeared to be and to act as living things, then to what extent are they not what they appear? Of particular note here is one of the messages that Jaquet-Droz's writing android composed, seizing provocatively on a passage from Descartes' *Meditations*. In it, the author, looking down from his window onto people crossing the square, notes that all he is then observing is hats and coats, which as well as dressing men could equally well 'conceal automata' ([1641] 1986: 21). What differentiates those automata from me is simply that 'I am a thing which thinks'. Since I am thinking, I must exist. Jaquet-Droz's automaton writer writes: 'I am not thinking . . . do I not therefore exist?'

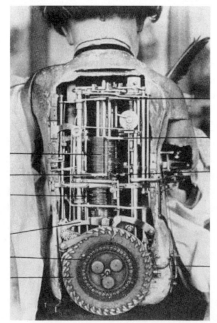

a   b

c

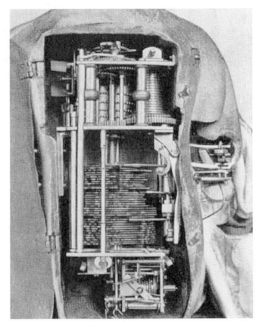

d

e

f

5.6a–f: Writer, draughtsman and musician (Chapuis and Droz 1958: 293–294; 299–300; 280–282)

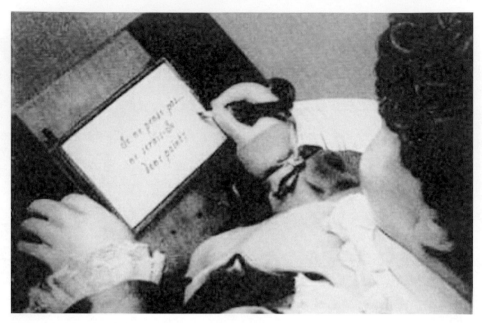

5.7 The writer's board reads 'I am not thinking . . . do I not therefore exist?' Chapuis and Droz 1958: 396

Popular mechanics: the ends of automata

Thus, if physiological automata were used for the scientific scrutiny of the mechanisms of living bodies, simulacral automata, or androids, result in queries being levelled regarding the nature of intelligence or the workings of the mind. While this shift from automata to androids occurs in the context of a shift away from mechanism and towards a more dynamic and vital-ist world-view in the sciences of the period, it also sees mechanical simulacra acquiring an unprecedented popularity in fairgrounds and popular theatres.

Even as late as the mid-nineteenth century, automata were constantly exciting audiences, although the nature of these audiences had begun to change: in place of the courts and aris-tocrats who initially delighted in these marvels, or the laboratories and scientists attempting to create life, automata became the preserve of fairgrounds and mass spectacles, touring not through the courts and palaces of Europe, but through its fairs and theatres. As early as 1805, we note the poet Wordsworth reeling disgustedly from the 'parliament of monsters' to be observed at fairs.

> All moveables of wonder, from all parts
> Are here – Albinos, painted Indians, Dwarfs,
> The Horse of knowledge, and the learned Pig,
> The stone-eater, the man that swallows fire,
> Giants, Ventriloquists, the Invisible Girl,
> The Bust that speaks and moves its goggling eyes,
> The Wax-work, Clock-work, all the marvellous craft
> Of modern Merlins, Wild Beasts, Puppet shows,
> All out-o'the-way, far-fetched, perverted things,
> All freaks of nature, all Promethean thoughts
> Of man, his dullness, madness, and their feats

All jumbled up together, to compose
A Parliament of Monsters.
                    (Wordsworth, *Prelude* [1805] 1949)

Wordsworth's repugnance notwithstanding, interest in mechanical automata had not waned by the mid-nineteenth century, when Charles Babbage used to visit John Merlin's London Mechanical Museum to watch the mechanical silver lady who danced there (Shaffer, in Spufford and Uglow 1996). Between the heyday of mechanism and Babbage's time, however, clockwork or mechanical automata had fallen from scientific grace to become fairground attractions on a par with stone-eaters, fireswallowers, invisible girls, and puppet shows. The 'parliament of monsters' thus found at fairground spectacles degenerates further still, so that the marvels that had once replaced cathedral building as a statement of a culture's glory, pride and ability, became by the late nineteenth century, as Norbert Wiener notes, little more than adornments 'pirouetting stiffly on top of music boxes' ([1948] 1962: 40), and by the twentieth, as wind-up toys such as Atomic Robot Man.

Even such toys as pirouetting dancers and wind-up robots betray their lineage in the extraordinary mechanical creatures of the eighteenth century, and provide an ironic image of our perspective on that era's apparent naivety: imagine thinking that humans and other animals were mere mechanical creatures!

Following a period in which the popularity of such mechanical simulacra has reduced them to the status of playthings and ornaments, in the contemporary world the distinction between *simulating* intelligence and automating biological systems in technological form has resurfaced (**5.3.5**).

5.3.5 Life and intelligence in the digital age

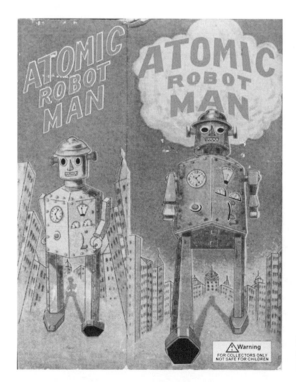

5.8 Atomic Robot Man: a 1990s reproduction of a 1950s mechanical toy. Courtesy of Schilling Inc.

5.3.3 Self-augmenting engines: steampower against nature

Continuities and breaks in the history of automata

Recounting the devolution of mechanical automata from being royally commissioned miracles in the eighteenth century to becoming fairground spectacles by the nineteenth and decorations or toys by the mid-twentieth, it is easy to imagine that there is a great historical rupture between their demise as serious objects of study and the rise of the cybernetic automata of John von Neumann and Norbert Wiener in the mid-twentieth century. For example, as Silvio Bedini put it:

> A study of the history of automata clearly reveals that several of the basic inventions produced for these attempts to imitate life by mechanical means led to significant developments culminating in modern automation and cybernetics.
>
> (Bedini 1964: 41)

> The terms 'normal' and 'crisis' are here taken from Kuhn (1962). They will be discussed further at **5.4.3**.

5.4.3 Cybernetics and culture

5.2.4 Determinisms

In other words, from the 1352 Strasbourg clock and the complex automata of the eighteenth century, 'to electronic and cybernetic brains, the road of evolution runs straight and steady' (Price 1964: 23). But such easy assumptions, especially in an age which automatically accepts the idea of historical discontinuities or ruptures, should not be made without examination.

We shall adopt two principles in offering this history of automata. First, that this history is discontinuous, marked by 'normal' and 'crisis technologies'; and second, carrying over from our discussion of Ellul's conception of the history of technology (**5.2.4**), we will note the broadening cultural impact of technology as it enters phases of 'self-augmentation'. Notably, we will see this in the discussion below of the steam technologies driving the Industrial Revolution.

Continuing to tack close to the line of life, however, we shall see that during the age of steam power and industrialisation, the conception and construction of automata change unrecognisably. If a Vaucanson or a von Kempelen were to be transported from the eighteenth to the nineteenth century they would not recognise the later century's machines as automata at all, for these latter no longer look like us.

Androides and intelligence

As has already been noted, d'Alembert's and Diderot's famous *Encyclopédie* (1751–1765) contains entries on both '*automates*' and '*androïdes*'. Some seventy years later, David Brewster repeated the same classifications in the 1830 *Edinburgh Encylopaedia*, 'automata' and 'androides' (Poe 1966: 381; Chapuis and Droz 1958: 284). The same distinction is effectively made by Price during the second half of the twentieth century, although this time between 'simulacra (i.e., devices that simulate) and automata (i.e., devices that move by themselves)' (Price 1964: 9). The self-moving and the man-like, however, do not exhaust the field of the automaton. As can be seen from the fictions and automata of the late eighteenth century and the early nineteenth, attention had shifted somewhat from the earlier century's concern with *physiology* to the nineteenth century's fascination with *intelligence*. So, while Price suggests that 'the very existence' of automata 'offered tangible proof . . . that the natural universe of physics and biology was susceptible to mechanistic explanation' (1964: 9–10), the distinctions between automata on the one hand and androides and simulacra on the other seems to leave the question of intelligence outside the realm of what could be explained mechanically. What these distinctions therefore overlook in the history of technology is such experimental devices as calculators, many of which were invented and produced by Pascal and Leibniz in the seventeenth century, and Johannes Müller in the eighteenth. In this, Price adheres to a version of mechanistic explanation offered by René Descartes ([1641] 1986), who argued that the only thing not reducible to mechanism was the human mind. It is precisely this contention, however, that the history and development of technologies even prior to the mid-seventeenth century when Descartes was writing, undoes. Thus from Pascal to Charles Babbage's Difference and Analytical Engines of the mid-nineteenth century there extends a line of development in the technological embodiment of intelligence. Not only does this line of development tie the clockwork age to the computer age – thus perhaps providing a missing link between those periods – it also prepares the way for one of the chief themes of the 'philosophy of manufactures' during the industrial age: the question of intelligence as governance. Moreover, Babbage's proto-computers seem less of a historical surprise, less an act of lone genius than the development of potentials inherent in already existing mechanical devices. We will return to the technological embodiment of intelligence as a component of steam technologies.

Why there are no steam simulacra

However, a version of the same distinction offered by Diderot, the *Edinburgh Encyclopaedia*, and finally by Price (1964), between those automata that do and those that do not resemble human form, was offered closer to our own time by Jean Baudrillard. In 1976, he distinguished automata from robots, on the grounds that where the former looks like a human the latter need not, so long as it *works* like one ([1976] 1993: 53–55). Baudrillard offers this as proof of a shift in the ideals of simulation, of artifice. In the age of automata, immediately prior to the French Revolution, machines resembled human form; by the Industrial Revolution, Baudrillard argues, machines no longer resemble their makers' bodies but rather their functions. With functionalism, he writes, 'the machine has the upper hand' ([1976] 1993: 53) since the very idea of the machine is functional perfection. Such functionalism in the construction of automata is not new, however, but stretches back to the nineteenth century. In 1847, the physicist Herman von Helmholtz wrote:

> nowadays we no longer attempt to construct beings able to perform a thousand human actions, but rather machines able to execute a single action which will replace that of thousands of humans.
>
> (cited in Bedini 1964: 41)

In this passage we can already see the passage to the 'self-acting mules', the great mechanical triumph of dead over living labour, that Marx witnessed in the practical, developmental logic of industrialism. The replacement of thousands of units of living, human labour with dead, machine labour, brings an end to the technologies of automation being applied to the charming ornamental devices adorning the clocks and snuff-boxes of the eighteenth century, and gave rise to the productivist rule of the physics of steam and connecting-rods over questions of will, intelligence and physiology.

'Man' remains the focus of eighteenth-century science; by the nineteenth century, however, that role has been rescinded, and granted instead to the machine. It is precisely this shift from simulacra to functional automata that differentiates the age of clockwork from that of steam. That is why, although we can trace, as it were, precursor-forms of the cyborg of contemporary fictions back to the mechanistic experiments and contrivances of the eighteenth century, with the rise of steam machines there are no longer any steam simulacra, but only steam *automata*.

5.9 A steam cyborg? *Steampunk* issue 1, Cliffhanger/DC Comics 1999

Indeed, the development of technology during the nineteenth century completely disregarded the humanist conceit of the mechanical simulacrum or android, following a trajectory which takes technology further away from the anthropomorphism of the android and from simulacra of any sort, the nearer it comes to becoming a true automaton.

Reversing nature

The abandonment of the android notwithstanding, in whatever terms the distinction is made, it is intended to divide those automata or machines that resemble human beings from those that do not, *but are automata nevertheless*. To understand why this is so, consider the inscription on **Figure 5.10**: Athanasius Kircher designed this 'clock driven by a sunflower seed' (Hankins and Silverman 1995: 14) in 1633. But it is less the details of this (fraudulent) invention that matter than what it tells us concerning the proximity of technology to nature during that period when the mechanical philosophy dominated. Technology such as that deployed in the construction of automata being the *artificial* realisation of *nature's own mechanism* made it possible not only to conceive of naturally harmonious devices; it also, as already noted by a surgeon such as La Mettrie, led to an understanding of living bodies in terms of mechanism. After the mid-eighteenth century, however, there emerged a new understanding of life, one that emphasised a distance between life and clockwork, where the mechanists saw only an increasing proximity. Thus, at the turn of the nineteenth century, the name 'biology' was given to the field of study that had opened up, dividing living from non-living bodies.

With the introduction of a distinct science called biology, and the consequent division of living from non-living things, life was no longer conceived as produced through mechanism alone. There had to be something else, a vital force or a major difference between organic and inorganic matter. The scientific grounds for the construction of mechanical simulacra of living, even human bodies had disappeared, leaving no further motive for their production than entertainment. Thus, instead of constructing machine life in human form, nineteenth-century physiologists began to measure living bodies as heat engines, and engines that functioned poorly when compared with other machines. Key to this shift was a new evaluation of respiration, the 'paramount function . . . providing the energy that powers the living being . . ., liberat[ing] heat and energy in a form useful to the organism' (Coleman 1977: 119). Marx makes this understanding of the organism clear: the machine, he writes, 'consumes coal, oil etc. . . . just as the worker consumes food' (1993: 693). If the intake of calories (literally, units of heat) provides machinery and organism with energy, then the use of this energy could be comparatively measured as units of work. Understood in accordance with this function, the organism becomes 'an energy-conversion device, a machine' (Coleman 1977: 123), one whose efficiency could be measured against others.

As a mode of analysis, many biologists argued, this was fine; but it told us nothing about life itself, how it arises, how it differs from lifeless things. Such analyses provide mere evidence of the energy-efficiency of biological heat engines. As biology was therefore turning away from technology for purposes of understanding life, engineers and industrialists simultaneously began to see the relative inefficiency of biological as opposed to technological heat engines. If, in working, functions currently allotted to humans could be given to machines, then a net increase in functional efficiency could be gained. The steam age no longer modelled machines on man, but measured humans against machines.

However, we should not conclude that the mechanists' aim of producing artificial yet living things becomes a quaint relic of an age ignorant of biology, just as the alchemists had been ignorant of chemistry. On the contrary, freed from the constraints of the simulation of life as it is, all life was redefined in accordance with the functioning of machines that, in Baudrillard's words, now 'had the upper hand' ([1976]1993: 54). Life was now imagined as it could be by 'philosophers of manufacture', engineers, politicians, and industrialists, spawning enormous social engineering projects. The steam-driven, mechanical pandemonium unleashed by large-scale industrial engines renounced the uncanny or distasteful status of man's double to achieve real dominion over human life and social organisation, producing, in Thomas Carlyle's words, 'a mighty change in our whole manner of existence' (in Harvie *et al.*, 1970: 24). Where under mechanism art and nature were conjoint, as Kircher's print of the sunflower clock makes so abundantly clear, steam power predominantly offered a means to reverse nature.

'Biology' as the 'science of life' emerged simultaneously in works by Gottfried Rheinhold Treviranus and by Jean Baptiste de Lamarck published in 1802. Prior to 1750, Foucault asserts, 'life did not exist' (1970: 127–128). That is, there could be no biology because there was no understanding of living things separate from the understanding of non-living things

New automata: engines and factories

Consider, for example, the first practically applied steam engine, assembled by Thomas Newcomen in the eighteenth century. It was used to reverse the flow of water into mines, a task that had hitherto been performed by slaves. Similarly, the steam engine enabled boats to navigate upstream in freshwater, rather than struggling against it with oars (Wiener [1958] 1987: 140). Effectively an autonomous power source, the steam engine made possible enormous gains against nature, improving hugely on inefficient human functioning. Moreover, it was in this sense that the 'philosophers of manufacture' in the early nineteenth century – Andrew Ure, Charles Babbage and Dr Price, for example – were led to speak of factories as automata, as 'moving powers that moved themselves'. In the factory, the automaton no longer resembles living bodies as did mechanical simulacra, but, as Baudrillard notes, *duplicates* their functions in order, as Helmholtz confirms, to *replace* them. Not only did the great steam engines that powered the range of machines incorporated into a factory supply them with motive force, cause the movements of these machines, they also exerted their iron will over the hitherto independent will of machines' human users; indeed, 'the worker's activity . . . is determined and regulated on all sides by the movement of the machinery, and not the opposite' (Marx 1993: 693). As engines reversed nature, factories became autonomous entities. By giving up being simulacra of humans, automata become relatively automous, acquiring social and physical agency, their movements, as Marx noted, 'determining' the worker, 'and not the opposite' (1993: 693).

5.10 Sunflower clock: 'art and nature conjoined'. Courtesy of the University of Washington Libraries

Automata and social engineering

The reasons for this acquisition of power over human labour stem ultimately from a division in the kinds of machines that Charles Babbage noted in his 1832 *On the Economy of Machinery and Manufactures*, between '(1) machines employed to produce power; (2) machines whose purpose is simply to transmit power and to perform the work' (1832: 10–11). While other forces – social, political, economic, and so on – undoubtedly drove the factory into realisation, it was simply a physical necessity that machines of the first type be physically connected to machines of the second type: *mechanised labour, in other words, necessitated centralisation*. As Norbert Wiener notes concerning the technological form of early factories, 'the only available means of transmission of power were mechanical. The first among these was the line of shafting, supplemented by the belt and the pulley' ([1958] 1987: 142). Indeed, he further notes that factories had barely changed even by the time of his own childhood at the turn of the twentieth century.

It is this technological necessity that made the rise of the factory as a relatively isolated, closed system of machinery necessary in turn, and that therefore gave rise to factories physically isolated in new, industrial spaces. In other words, a steam engine, no matter how powerful, can only drive those other machines to which its power is physically transmitted. It is this, in turn, that meant that human workers had to be situated in relation to the machine, rather than the other way around as was the prevailing situation in the hand- or foot-powered machines of earlier, mutually remote, cottage industries. Hence there arose the issue of the role of the human will and the human agent in these 'manufactories'. Rather than being the agents employing machinery to their own purposes, living workers were 'pushed to the side of the production process' (Marx 1993: 705), and merely 'watched attentively and assiduously over a system of productive mechanisms' (Ure 1835: 18). In consequence, rather than users external to the machine, they became the machine's 'intellectual organs', subject eventually to the 'will' of the engine that drove their actions. Thus Ure:

> In its most rigorous sense, the term [factory] conveys the idea of a vast automaton, composed of numerous mechanical and intellectual organs operating in concert and without interruption, towards one and the same aim, all these organs being subordinated to a motive force which moves itself.
>
> (Ure 1835: 18–19)

The steam automaton no longer looks like us at all, it no longer excites uncanny fears of our doubles; rather, it uses humans as subsidiary power sources devoted to an aim dictated to them by the mechanical arrangement of the automaton's parts. Humans for the first time become components of systems of machinery. It is worth noting, at this point, that the subordinate position of living with respect to non-living automata echoes Aristotle's definition of a slave as not a self-moving thing by virtue of being a tool of the master (**1.6.4**). This definition makes the 'master' interchangeably human *or* technological, the only condition being that the master *is that which moves itself*, and the slave that which is moved accordingly. With industrial machines, then, mastery is usurped by technology.

Real and imaginary systems

While the worker is a part of the machine, a component-circuit designed by an alien will, the owner is not; rather, the factory is a realisation of his designs. It thus becomes possible to dismiss the idea of the technological system as a 'fancy' or a merely 'imaginary machine', as Adam Smith argued. Thus, although Marx's and Ure's great, steam automata subjugated the worker's body to the machines, even as its 'intellectual organs' or 'conscious linkages', the intellectual labour of the design and implementation of such automated systems of machinery still lay very firmly in the human domain. In accordance with this humanist view, Adam Smith further distinguishes *actual* machines from *imaginary* systems of machinery in the following terms:

> a machine is a little system created to perform as well as to connect together in reality those different movements and effects which the artist has occasion for. A system is an imaginary machine invented to connect together in fancy those different movements and effects which are already in reality performed.
>
> (Smith [1795] 1980: 66; emphasis added)

But whose 'fancy' is this? Not, of course, that of the worker, but of what Simon Shaffer calls the 'enlightened mechanics' (Clark *et al.* 1999: 145) that governed Diderot's and Smith's philosophy of manufactures. Just as the Enlightenment prized the exercise of reason above all else, such enlightened mechanics likewise prized *intellectual* over *manual* production, 'imagining' evermore mechanised forms of labour, as enlightened social order required. Thus Adam Ferguson, on the Enlightenment's ideal worker:

> Many mechanical arts require no [intellectual] capacity. They succeed best under a total suppression of sentiment and reason, and ignorance is the mother of industry as well as of superstition. Reflection and fancy are subject to err, but a habit of moving the hand or the foot is independent of either. Manufactures, accordingly, prosper most where the mind is least consulted, and where the workshop may, without any great effort of the imagination, be considered as an engine, the parts of which are men.
>
> (Ferguson [1767] 1966: 182–183)

Enlightened mechanists such as Ferguson, Smith and Diderot, then, were social engineers who commanded the division of labour between manual workers and machines as a single, rationally governed system. The question remains, however, whether such systems of machinery as *turn humans into simulacra of machines* in the mechanical repetition of their labour, remain *imaginary* creatures of fancy, as Smith and Ferguson argue, or whether the factory constitutes, as Ure, Babbage and Marx argue, a *real automaton that contains conscious linkages*, insofar as the whole factory is a self-moving machine. Following the idea of functional automata, we are no longer dealing with the mechanical simulation of human form or intelligence, but rather with their incorporation into a real, rather than an imaginary, system of machinery.

1.6.4 The many virtues of Saint McLuhan

Real technologies of governance

There are, however, other, more specifically technological developments that solve the problem, posed by Adam Smith, of the merely imaginary or the actually technological status of the 'system'. Both have to do with the role of the 'conscious linkages' in systems of machinery. In the late eighteenth century, as the 'enlightened mechanists' were writing, the problem of the *control* of machines was always solved by a human supervisory presence. Intelligence was needed to keep a watch over the machines, since they could not be self-correcting. Machines could overheat, run out of coal, or simply fall apart if there were no human supervisor to ensure their correct functioning. Indeed, this regularly happened to early steam engines. Consider, however, this account of an 'automatic furnace' constructed in the seventeenth century:

It is reasonably safe to state that cybernetics was already in a stage of potential realisation in the creations of the seventeenth century. Probably the first major step in this direction was taken with the design of thermostatic controls for chemical furnaces . . .,credited to Cornelius Drebbel (1573–1633) of Holland. A sketch in a manuscript dated 1666 shows an automatic furnace . . .; this used a thermostat filled with alcohol joined to a U-tube containing mercury. With the increase of heat, the alcohol expanded, forcing the mercury upward to raise a rod and by means of levers to close a damper. When the heat fell too low, the action was reversed by the contraction of the alcohol . . . This is unquestionably the first known example of a feedback mechanism which led to the self-control of mechanical devices.

(Bedini 1964: 41)

The technological problem of self-control was equally a problem for the industrial application of steam technology. The engineer James Watt introduced what he called a 'governor' into his engines to enable control of their speed. Norbert Wiener writes:

[Watt's] governor keeps the engine from running wild when its load is removed. If it starts to run wild, the balls of the governor fly upward from centrifugal action, and in their upward flight they move a lever which partly cuts off the admission of steam. Thus the tendency to speed up produces a partly compensatory tendency to slow down.

(Wiener [1954] 1989: 152)

Such devices, evincing what cybernetics calls 'negative feedback' (Wiener [1948] 1962: 97), certainly enable the production of self-controlling machines, but they do not seem to supply a direct answer to the question of the imaginary rather than the technological status of systems of machinery. What they do indicate is that functions hitherto thought to be the sole province of living intelligence, such as monitoring and control, can be automated and thus ceded to machines. Wiener even suggests that machines able to respond correctively to their own functioning, or to environmental changes, effectively possess sense-organs. However, the systemic automation of the intelligence needed to run a series of interrelated machines cannot be achieved with the same technologies as Drebbel's thermostat or Watt's governor.

It is Babbage in particular whose writings and inventions point up a solution to our problem: human agency remains the 'prime mover' of 'automatic' systems of machinery *only insofar as intelligence remains itself non-mechanical*. In this light, inventions that embodied intelligence in technological artefacts, such as Pascal's, Leibniz's and Müller's calculators, supply the missing link between the history of automata to cybernetics. And it was left to Ada Lovelace, 'the Queen of Engines', and the daughter of the poet Byron, to rejoin the history of automated intelligence to the factory system and early industrialisation in textiles. At this point, then, we must revert from the non-simulacral automata that characterise the rise of industrial machines to the last wholly simulational project regarding automata to date. That is, the automation of intelligence.

5.3.4 The construction of inanimate reason

The history of artificial intelligence begins with mechanical calculators. But calculators can simulate only one function of human intelligence, while human intelligence is capable of a high number of functions. Artificial intelligence comes one step closer to realisation, therefore, with the idea of the programmable; that is, a multifunctional machine. Here the efforts of Ada

Lovelace to establish the language and capacities of programming from her own mathematical researches, her mentor Babbage's Difference and Analytical Engines, and Jacquard's pattern-generating automatic looms, form a crucial historical juncture between *calculating* and *programming* in the history of artificial intelligence.

The first attempts to automate intelligence, as opposed to physiological functions, take the form of *calculating* devices. Although devices such as the abacus or 'Napier's Bones' – sticks of different lengths with correspondingly different numerical values – considerably pre-date the mechanical calculators of the seventeenth and eighteenth centuries, it is only by this date that questions arise concerning the possibility of automating intelligence. Intelligence had been overtly acknowledged as the distinguishing feature of human beings since Aristotle, so the prospect of automated intelligence or 'inanimate reason' was a high-stakes venture.

The Pascaline and Leibniz's mechanical reasoner

The earliest mechanical calculators, however, were intended merely as labour-saving devices. The philosopher and mathematician Blaise Pascal began to design calculators, known as Pascalines, in 1642. Rather than automating intelligence, Pascal's intent was to free the mind from the burden of laborious calculation, specifically that of his government official father. The Pascalines were simple devices to facilitate error-free addition. While some have called them 'the first true digital computer' (Price 1964: 20), given their limited range of functions, this may be true only insofar as these were devices for computing digits, for they were primarily manually operated like the abacus. The Pascaline did, however, contain one feature that distinguished it from earlier 'arithmetical instruments' and made it into what can justly be described as a 'calculating machine', as one Dionysius Lardner wrote in an essay on 'Babbage's Calculating Engine' printed in the *Edinburgh Review* in 1843. Once again, we note the classical distinction between an 'instrument' or tool and a 'machine', based on the

5.11 The 'Pascaline' (1642), a semi-automatic calculator by Blaise Pascal. © Science Museum/Science and Society Picture Library

quantity of actions the latter can perform independently of its user. Thus, what distinguished Pascal's machine from a mere tool was that it contained a mechanical means to solve the problem of 'carrying' a number from, say, the column of single units to the column of tens. According to Lardner's account, Pascal's machine

> consisted of a series of wheels, carrying cylindrical barrels, on which were engraved the ten arithmetical characters . . . The wheel which expressed each order of units was so connected with the wheel which expressed the superior order [i.e., 10s rather than 1s], that when the former passed from 9 to 0, the latter was necessarily advanced one figure; and thus the process of carrying was executed by mechanism.
>
> (Lardner [1843], in Hyman 1989: 106)

While Pascal's machine automated addition, in 1673 the philosopher, scientist and mathematician G.W. Leibniz showed a prototype of his mechanical calculator, the *calculus rationator*, to the Royal Society of London. As well as addition and subtraction, this calculator could multiply and divide automatically, by way of Leibniz's 'stepped reckoner', containing cogs of different lengths which mechanically realised those functions (MacDonald Ross 1984: 12–13). Noting that Leibniz himself never published a detailed account of his calculator's mechanism (although one of his calculators remains extant in the Hanover State Library), Lardner concludes that, unlike the Pascaline, 'it does not appear that this contrivance . . . was ever applied to any useful purpose' ([1843], in Hyman 1989: 108). However, Leibniz's calculator was not, like Pascal's, a utilitarian device constructed to save time and reduce error; its real significance was that it demonstrated that reasoning could be mechanised. The calculator itself, therefore, was a by-product of this larger project, a project which led Norbert Wiener, among others, to herald Leibniz as 'the patron saint of cybernetics' ([1948]1962: 12).

 Leibniz had noted that there was a similarity between all kinds of reasoning – moral, legal, commercial, scientific and philosophical – and calculation: like the latter, all reasoning followed rules. Unlike arithmetic, however, the terms in which broader forms of reasoning were conducted were unsuitably vague and general. In other words, while 1 + 1 could easily be automated, problems that involved concepts could not. This is because concepts were not simple like numbers, but had content. What Leibniz therefore sought to do was to break down this content into its basic elements and thus to discover the formal logic by which reasoning worked – the 'language of thought' as artificial intelligence researchers now call it – and to define the major concepts employed in terms of numerical or alphabetic values. When, for example, contemporary logicians say 'X is P' (bananas are yellow; men are mortal, etc.), they are using precisely the kind of 'universal characteristic' comprising 'all the characters that express our thoughts' that was Leibniz's lifetime project. Once such a universal characteristic was completed it would form the 'grammar and the dictionary' of 'a new language which could be written or spoken' (Leibniz [1677] 1951: 16). Once all our thoughts were given numerical expression, and given the rules of calculation in general (i.e., reasoning), it would, Leibniz reasoned, be possible to mechanise reasoning in its entirety, and thus to produce a reasoning machine. Thus, amongst Leibniz's experiments in constructing such languages is his invention of binary notation, in which all numbers are expressed as combinations of zeros and ones, such as all digital computers operate on. Although Leibniz drew up a plan for a calculator that used this binary arithmetic, he never produced such a machine. It is not simply the machines he produced, however, but the convergence between the idea of a formal, universal language and the construction of reasoning machines that is represented by Leibniz's calculator. As far as Leibniz was concerned, the mechanical calculator thus becomes the mechanical reasoner, the forerunner of artificial intelligence. As Wiener has it,

> It is therefore not in the least surprising that the same intellectual impulse which has led to the development of mathematical logic has at the same time led to the ideal or actual mechanization of processes of thought.

> (Wiener [1948] 1962: 12)

Thus, while Leibniz states that the universal characteristic is a tool to 'increase the power of the human mind' ([1677] 1951: 16), increasing the clarity, certainty, and communicability of our ideas, glimpsing the prospect of a larger calculator to mechanise all reasoning, he thought of engraving it with the legend 'Superior to man', and that in comparison with this, previous calculators 'are in fact mere games' (Leibniz [1678] 1989: 236). Leibniz is not a constructor of calculators for their own sake, therefore, but rather a forerunner of programming, computer construction and, as the logical conclusion of these latter, artificial intelligence.

Ada and Babbage: programmable engines

Leibniz, however, never constructed his mechanical reasoner. All that remains of it is his tentative draft (MacDonald Ross 1984: 30). To some extent, this was also the fate of Charles Babbage's Difference and Analytical Engines. Although he, with the help of engineer Joseph Clement, constructed a demonstration model of about one-seventh of the size of the completed Difference Engine in 1832, none was satisfactorily completed during his lifetime. However, the problem which Babbage faced was not the theoretical one of whether such mechanical reasoners were possible, but rather the state of the mechanical arts of the mid-nineteenth century. Babbage could not find engineers capable of cutting the brass components of his engines with sufficient accuracy, all but disabling the project's realisation. Of course, other factors – financial, lack of obvious applications, and political resistance – contributed to the lack of a working Analytical Engine, as has been suggested (see Woolley 1999: 273ff.); however, as Ada Lovelace's far-reaching analyses of that Engine show, what it causes us to imagine is precisely the interconnections between these new technologies and extant ones. Had they been fully realised, however, these machines, and especially the Analytical Engine, had the potential to turn the period of the Industrial Revolution into the first computer age, as William Gibson and Bruce Sterling's novel *The Difference Engine* (1990) hypothesises.

While the two engines have been celebrated as the precursors of modern computing, their significance might, as with that of Leibniz's calculator, lie elsewhere. First, it is important to distinguish between the functional repertoire of the two machines. The Difference Engine, the first such calculating engine on which Babbage worked from the 1820s on, was so called because it worked on the method of iterating finite differences. In other words, it calculated according to a formula that, as it were, was hardwired – or more accurately, perhaps, 'hard-cogged' (Spufford, in Spufford and Uglow 1996: 169) – into its mechanical structure. If the differences between terms could be specified as a formula, then it could be added or subtracted to produce numbers bearing the same relation to each other as to all the other numbers it could derive. The derivation of each number, or of each number thus similarly related, involved repeating or 'iterating' the 'programme' as a whole. The embodiment of such calculative possibilities in mechanical form was already a considerable advance on previous calculators – of which Babbage might well have said, as did Leibniz of the calculators preceding his own, that they were 'in fact mere games' (Leibniz [1678] 1989: 236). Although

5.12 Charles Babbage's Difference Engine No. 1 built by Joseph Clement in 1832. Difference Engine No. 2 was only assembled in 1991 by the London Science Museum. © Science and Society Picture Library

it was manually operated by means of a handcrank, the engine's subsequent operation was entirely automatic, yielding its results without further human intervention. If it could be driven by a steam engine, then even this minimal intervention could easily have been removed.

Despite the gravity of its achievements, however, the Difference Engine had a profoundly practical intent: it was designed to calculate and print the mathematical tables on which human 'computers' had to rely for such tasks as calculating navigation, annuities, and so on, without the frequent errors of calculation or transcription that occurred in the production of tables. Babbage himself not only wrote such a table, but amassed a collection of some 300 volumes of them, through which he regularly trawled for such errors as he wished to eliminate through the 'unerring certainty of mechanism' (cited in Swade 1991: 2). However, as he notes in a letter announcing the project of the Difference Engine to the President of the Royal

Society, Sir Humphry Davy, a M. Prony of France had established a means for producing such tables through the method of the division of labour (Hyman 1989: 47; see also Daston 1994: 182–202). Prony's method was to have mathematicians draw up a simplified formula, which was then applied by a mass of non-specialist workers – known at the time as 'computers' – to calculate the results of the arithmetical operations the formula specified. Upon witnessing Prony's 'arithmetical factories' in operation, Babbage remarked, in a tellingly prescient vision of the steam automata that Marx and others would argue factories became, 'I wish to God these calculations had been accomplished by steam' (cited in Woolley 1999: 151).

However, while the Difference Engine could realise the long-held dream of automated calculation by 'hardcogged' machines, as with Leibniz's mechanical reasoner, Babbage's Engines were not to be mere calculators but incidental by-products of larger-scale projects. That project was the automation not simply of calculation but of analysis. Thus the Analytical Engine, the Difference Engine's successor, was a machine that not only calculated, but also 'decided' what formula to use in order to do those calculations. It was in effect a programmable computer, whose programs could include instructions for the utilisation of subsequent programs without human intervention. Because this was such a difficult idea to grasp, even for those versed in mathematics and mechanics, Babbage encouraged Luigi Menabrea, an Italian military engineer whom he had encountered while presenting his Engine work in Italy, to publish his 'Sketch of the Analytical Engine' in 1842. A year later, Ada Lovelace translated them into English and published them with notes that far outweighed the slim essay they accompanied.

Although controversy arises surrounding both the extent to which the Analytical Engine can be compared to a computer (Hyman 1989: 242–243), and the real contribution made by Ada Lovelace to the development of programming (Woolley 1999: 276ff.; Plant 1997; Hyman 1989: 243), it is Ada's analysis of the machine's functioning and possibilities that make most apparent what advances in inanimate reason Babbage's second engine had made. She writes of the Anlaytical Engine as

> the material expression of any indefinite function of any degree of generality and complexity . . . ready to receive at any moment, by means of cards constituting a portion of its mechanism (and applied on the principle of those used in the Jacquardloom), the impress of whatever *special* function we may desire to develop or tabulate.
>
> (Lovelace 1843, in Hyman 1989: 267)

In other words, the Analytical Engine has no particular set function, as the Difference Engine does (the latter is, essentially, an 'Adding machine', according to Ada Lovelace), but can be programmed to perform any computable function. In this, it resembles the 'universal machine' described by Alan Turing in 1936, and thus forms the true (if inactual) forerunner of contemporary computing. The means by which it is 'programmed' are those Jacquard 'devised for regulating . . . the most complicated patterns in the fabrication of brocaded stuffs' (1843, in Hyman 1989: 272): punched cards. 'We may say', Ada wrote accordingly, 'that the Analytical Engine *weaves algebraical patterns* just as the Jacquard-loom weaves flowers and leaves' (1843, in Hyman 1989: 273).

In one sense, the relation of the Analytical to the Difference Engine is the same as that between Leibniz's calculator and the project of which it formed a part. Ada even echoes Leibniz's language: the Analytical Engine, she writes, does not occupy common ground with mere 'calculating machines'. It holds a position wholly its own . . . In enabling mechanism to combine together general symbols . . ., a uniting link is established between the operations of matter [i.e., the Engine itself] and the abstract mental processes of the most abstract branch of mathematical science. A new, a vast, and a powerful language is developed for the future use of analysis . . .

(Lovelace 1843, in Hyman 1989: 273)

As regards what can be called its functional indeterminacy – the fact that it is equally well-suited to carrying out several operations – the Analytical Engine thus most closely approximates the modern computer, as we have already remarked. Indeed, as also noted, Alan Turing's first computers were just such 'universal machines' (Turing 1936; Hodges 1992, 1997), capable of enacting many processes and 'hardcogged' for none. Programmability, the distinction between a 'storehouse' and a 'mill', the terms Ada gave to those functions now called *memory* and *processor* (1843, in Hyman 1989: 278–281), where everything seems set up in advance so that *all* the Analytical Engine is is the precursor of the modern computer, just as all Leibniz's machine was, was an expensive labour-saving calculator. Lovelace, however, saw it as something infinitely more: the Analytical Engine was as improbable and yet as realisable as the idea of a 'thinking or of a reasoning machine' (1843, in Hyman 1989: 273). Following Leibniz and Lovelace, however, we must note that, as it were, the circuit of history that Babbage began but never completed, is not closed by the construction of a working Difference Engine in 1991 (Swade 1991, 2000). The Analytical Engine has never yet been built – although a partial model was under construction at the time of Babbage's death in 1871. Neither does the functional similarity of Babbage's designs and those of Turing, for example, who oversaw the construction of the earliest computers (Colossus in 1942 and ENIAC in 1946; Hodges 1997: 24–31), and who cited the Analytical Engine as precisely such a 'universal machine', imply that Babbage's second Engine has been superseded by subsequent developments. Viewing the 1991 Difference Engine as the *completion* of its 1832 counterpart, and the Turing machine or the modern computer as the *completion* of Babbage's designs of the mid- to late nineteenth century, locks these machines, along with those of Pascal and Leibniz, into the prehistory of current technologies, which therefore become those same designs, perfected.

Gibson and Sterling's fictional account of a mid-nineteenth-century computer age is sometimes read as precisely this kind of operation: take a machine that remained unrealised in its time, have it realised then, and see the age of information powered by steam! The past becomes nothing other than the prehistory of present, cybernetic perfection, a 'virtual history' that in reality remained inactual (Spufford and Uglow 1996: 266ff.). However, this is a virtual history constructed not to account for present perfections but for future imperfections: it is the prehistory of the world inhabited not by us, but by the cyberpunk futures these and other authors began to invent in the 1980s (Gibson 1986; Sterling 1986). What Spufford and others overlook in offering such an account is the otherwise bizarre conclusion to their virtual history. It ends not with computing, but with corporate bodies in the present age becoming self-aware. London, 1991:

a *thing* grows, an autocatalytic tree, in almost-life, feeding through the roots of thought on the rich decay of its own shed images, and ramifying, through myriad lightningbranches, up, up, towards the hidden light of vision,

Dying to be born,

The light is strong,

The light is clear;
The Eye at last must see itself
Myself . . .
I see:
I see,
I see
I
!

(Gibson and Sterling 1990: 383)

Spufford views the Difference Engine in precisely this way. Taking it as a 'collaboration between [the] times' when it was designed and built, he writes that it thus forms part of the history of computing only 'retrospectively' (Spufford and Uglow 1996: 267–268), and only therefore insofar as it was, as of 1991, completed

Of course, this is fiction; but it points up an important objection to the kind of virtual history that, for example, Spufford and Uglow (1996), Warwick (1998) and De Landa (1991) engage in. That is, first, that in doing retrospective histories the object from which the perspective is articulated is a contingent object: there is no absolute end-point of technological development reached in contemporary computing, nor any end point of technological evolution reached in futural robotic histories. In a sense, this is to make the same point as Leibniz does about the true value of his calculator, and as Lovelace does about that of Babbage's Analytical Engine: both refuse a reductive explanation of their machines' functional capacities, and argue instead for other virtualities those machines possess. In both cases, as in Gibson and Sterling's novel, those virtualities have to do with *artificial intelligence*, as though this were a virtual property of *all* technology.

CASE STUDY 5.1: Chess and 'inanimate reason'

Baron von Kempelen's celebrated Chess-Playing Automaton was contrived in 1769 as an entertainment for the Royal Court of his native Hungary. A mechanistic physiologist, von Kempelen also constructed a speaking automaton, featuring mechanically reproduced lungs, voice-box, mouth, tongue and lips, to better understand the functions of its organic counterpart and to re-engineer these in mechanical form. Less renowned than the chess-player (to which its subsequent owner, Johann Maelzel, the inventor of the metronome, ironically added a voice-box), the speaking automaton was a genuinely mechanical device, reproducing speech without hidden human intervention (Hankins and Silverman 1995: 178–220).

However, it was the mystery surrounding the precise mode of *human* intervention in the chess-player's operations that excited the greatest curiosity when von Kempelen, and later Maelzel, took it on extended tours of the cities of Europe and the United States. 'It is quite certain', wrote Poe, 'that the operations of the Automaton are regulated by *mind*', but the most pressing problem was 'to fathom the mystery of its evolutions'; that is, 'the manner in which human agency is brought to bear' ('[1836] 1966: 382–383). While others had sought principally to expose the secret hiding place of the child or dwarf who inhabited the chest upon which the chess-player was mounted, Poe demonstrates 'mathematical[ly] . . ., *a priori*' that the Automaton could be no 'pure machine' from the fact that no mechanism could either predict its antagonist's moves, or allow an indeterminate time to elapse between the moves of its antagonist. In other words, unlike a mathematical calculation or the performance of a rhythmic piece of music, there is neither a determinate sequence of events (each move will depend upon the machine's antagonist) nor a set period of time (the antagonist's moves will each take a different length of time to consider and execute). It could not, in other words, be 'programmed' in advance to carry out specific moves at specific points. Baron von Kempelen himself admitted as much in his own account of the chess-player as 'a very ordinary piece of mechanism – a *bagatelle* whose effects appeared so marvellous from the boldness of the conception, and the fortunate choice of the methods adopted for promoting the illusion' (ibid.: 382). Poe's own assessment of the inventor's intelligence is given dubious recognition in a short story entitled 'Von Kempelen and his Discovery', in which the eponymous hero is presented as an alchemist fulfilling the dream of turning base metal into gold (ibid.: 72–77). Like the alchemist then, according to Poe, von Kempelen possessed a genius for the false, which made him a false genius.

If the fate of the first chess-playing mechanism was to expose the necessity of human intervention in a game that has often been seen as synonymous with intelligence, this is not the same fate shared by its machine successors. The first of these, constructed in the 1920s by the then president of the Spanish Academy of Science, Torrès y Quevedo, was an electrical 'adaptation of the mechanical inventions which moved the earlier automata' (Chapuis and Droz 1958: 387). It worked by responding to changing electrical contacts between the chess pieces and the board and, as Chapuis and Droz note, 'there is nothing more exciting than to watch this struggle between the machine and the man, who inexorably will be defeated', referencing Chapuis's silent film, *Le Joueur d'échecs* ['The Chess-Player'] of 1930, in which one such contest is recorded (Chapuis and Droz 1958: 387). Moreover, by virtue of the contacts by which the machine receives information from its antagonist's actions, the machine has acquired what Chapuis and Droz call, following Norbert Wiener, 'artificial senses' (1958: 389).

5.13 Torrès y Quevedo's 1920s chess-playing machine.

Curiously, the same comparison as Poe made in 1836 between *artificial intelligence* and *alchemy* was made 130 years later in an essay that was to be the undoing of the reign of human over machine intelligence. Philosopher Hubert Dreyfus wrote 'Alchemy and artificial intelligence' as an attack on the entire artificial intelligence research programme, specifically insofar as such researchers were attempting to develop chess-playing computers. As he recounts in *What Computers Can't Do* (1979), Dreyfus challenged any machine to beat him at chess, and lost. A mere quarter of a century later, in 1996, an individual who can only now be described as having been the world's greatest *human* chess-player, Gary Kasparov, accepted a challenge from IBM's supercomputer, 'Deep Blue' – and was defeated. There is therefore an entire history of chess-playing automata. Every challenge has been a spectacle, as though we were testing fate to maintain us as the only intelligent species on the earth. But coextensive with these spectacles there have been real developments in artificial senses and intelligence. Although an appropriate description of von Kempelen's automaton, and despite postdating Quevedo's machine, it now seems that Walter Benjamin was wrong when he noted, in the first of his 'Theses on the Philosophy of History' (written in 1940), that the materialism represented by the automaton could only win philosophically by virtue of the wizened theologian hidden in the mechanism (1973: 255): after *L'Affaire Dreyfus* and Kasparov, materialism is the only game in town.

Just as automata provide a history of artificial life, calculators provide a history of artificial intelligence. While both research programmes derive essentially from work done in the last quarter century or so, their respective histories stretch further back, as the foregoing sections show. The next section will therefore consider the current state of these 'sciences of the artificial' (Simon [1969] 1996) and draw out the questions artificial life and intelligence pose regarding the relations between nature and culture that technology brings into play.

5.3.5 Life and intelligence in the digital age

5.3 Biological technologies: the history of automata
5.3.4 The construction of inanimate reason

As noted in the introduction to **5.3**, the digital age demonstrates a vast range of crossovers between the biological and the technological. Apart from the 'sciences of the artificial' (Simon [1969] 1996) – artificial intelligence (AI) and artificial life (Alife) – there is also the rise of 'molecular cybernetics' (Monod 1971) or genetics, and the various biotechnologies, in which organic matter becomes a technology in its own right. We will briefly survey AI and Alife, therefore, before moving on to discuss genetics and biotechnology.

AI

Can machines think? Scientists say 'yes', humanists 'no'. AI researchers confidently predict that genuinely intelligent machines will be created – it's just a matter of time. So if we rephrase the question from 'can machines think?' to 'can they think now?', we must surely – scientist and humanist alike – answer 'no'. However, remember what happened to Hubert Dreyfus when he argued thus: a computer beat him at chess. Consider what this computer does. It calculates the possible moves against the consequences of those moves every time its opponents make a move of their own. The machine then calculates the most logical move to make in order to win the game, and prompts its human helper to execute that move. Is the machine thereby thinking? 'Not really', we are likely to answer, 'it's just calculating, treating chess as a series of maths problems'. Yet isn't this precisely what a human chess-player does when s/he reflects on the game, weighing up the possible moves and selecting the one most likely to achieve a win? Even if we concede this, however, we are likely to assert, 'there's nothing like thinking going on in the computer, only electrical charges exchanging input and output signals'. But isn't this exactly as the brain works?

There are two main approaches to AI:

1   Classical AI or 'good-old-fashioned-AI' (GOFAI), which is concerned to imitate human intelligence in machines.

2   Connectionist AI or 'neural networks', concerned to bring about machine intelligence, regardless of whether or not it resembles human intelligence.

Classical AI

Classical AI seeks to translate what it calls 'the language of thought' into a computer program. In principle, any consistent reasoning can be turned into a program using the intermediary of logic. What logical analysis enables AI researchers to do is to construct Leibniz's 'universal characteristic' (**5.3.4**) as program code, thus enabling thought to be realised in machines. In consequence, much classical AI has concentrated on the development of 'expert systems' to replace or augment existing human experts. Such systems are produced by gathering as much information as possible from human experts in a given field (medical diagnosis, for example), and then boiling down the information into logical form.

EXPERT SYSTEMS

The chess-playing computer, Deep Blue, that defeated Gary Kasparov in 1996, is one culmination of this kind of GOFAI research. The other culminating technology is the expert system, a 'software superspecialist consultant' (Dennett 1998: 15). Such AIs have already been produced, and with startling results, as Dennett reports:

> SRI in California announced in the mid-eighties that PROSPECTOR, an SRI-developed expert system in geology, had correctly predicted the existence of a large, important mineral deposit that had been entirely unanticipated by the human geologists who had fed it its data. MYCIN, perhaps the most famous of these expert systems, diagnoses infections of the blood . . . And many other expert systems are on the way.
>
> (Dennett 1998: 16)

Expert systems are computer programs formed from the sum total of available knowledge in a given field. The most extreme case is Douglas Lenat's CYC project, an attempt to build a 'walking encyclopaedia' containing *all* knowledge, a project whose expected completion Lenat measures not in person-hours but in person-*centuries*, since all the various bits and pieces of 'knowledge' must be individually encoded into CYC's program, the most enormous database ever imagined.

SIMULACRA OF INTELLIGENCE

In terms of the distinctions we made in **5.3.1**, classical AI seeks to produce a simulacrum of human intelligence, or of 'the language of thought'. For critics such as Hubert Dreyfus (1979), however, the idea that this amounts to thinking is simply false. He insists that any really intelligent machine (which he thinks is impossible in principle) must demonstrate more than just the *logical* elements of human thinking. A truly intelligent machine would have to be capable of actual conversation, with all the vagaries, hints, jokes, blind alleys and false starts that are features of human conversations. This would be evidence of intelligence idling, rather than working towards some particular intelligent function (calculating the number of atoms in a table, for example, or predicting sites of mineral deposits). Dreyfus's implicit criticism of classical AI, therefore, is that true intelligence is more than logical functions: it must be capable of 'non profit-making' behaviour. In other words, a truly intelligent machine would have to be capable of real stupidity.

However, Dreyfus and classical AI alike share the view that AI must be about replicating human intelligence in machines, by copying it into programs that are then downloaded into the computer. This is the approach rejected by Connectionist AI.

Connectionist AI

Neural networks or connectionist AI, however, follow the other line of simulation that runs through the mechanistic physiologies of the eighteenth century: the simulation not of functions (such as intelligence) but of organs (hearts, lungs, voice-boxes; **5.3.3**). Instead of modelling high-level cognitive functions like intelligence, connectionist AI asks: how do biological *brains* work? Dennett puts the issue starkly:

> If . . . [classical] AI programs appear to be attempts to model the mind, Connectionist AI programs appear to be attempts to model the brain.
>
> (Dennett 1998: 225)

5.3.1 Automata: the basics

5.3.3 Self-augmenting engines: steampower against nature

Neural nets therefore attempt to model the brain's physical apparatus. Brains consist of neurones (brain-cells) firing electrochemical signals to each other in what appears to be a rather scatter-gun manner. No neurone taken on its own is *intelligent*, however, although neurone activity is obviously essential to the realisation of intelligence in brains. Intelligence might not, connectionists reasoned, be intelligent *all the way down* to brain architecture, but might *emerge* at a higher level of complexity from the interactions of these 'stupid' bits and pieces called neurones. A better way, therefore, to create intelligent machines might be to simulate brain architecture using computers. Thus, instead of trying to program intelligence into a single computer working through a CPU, connectionists build what are called *neural nets*, in which several computers are linked together, each playing the role of a 'neurone', sending signals to many others at once.

In the jargon, classical AI is 'top-down', in that it imposes a program on the machine; connectionist AI is 'bottom-up', in that it wants the machine to 'grow' intelligence.

Like classical AI, neural net or connectionist AI has had its successes: although classical AI could easily turn chess-playing into a program, it could not do anything with face-recognition. Humans recognise faces in microseconds, but if you pause to consider how many actions a computer would have to perform in order to distinguish one face from amongst many – how many comparisons, examinations, analyses of nose-length, eye-colour and so on – and what mammoth database it would have to possess to facilitate these comparisons, facial recognition becomes, from the programmer's point of view, an awesomely vast task. This is because brains do not run through a series of instructions, one after the other, in order to execute 'face-recognising'. Memory (Reagan's face) and perception ('Reagan's face!') work simultaneously. Exploiting this idea, connectionist AI researchers have been able to build face-recognising neural networks. Instead of having the information programmed in, the neural net must *learn* to recognise a face. Neural nets, given only a basic operating code (much as humans are born with – the hardwired ability to suckle, make noise, breathe and excrete), are 'trained' to pick up relevant traits and to discard irrelevant ones, until the face is literally imprinted on its memory. This 'evolutionary' approach to learning in order eventually to realise intelligence differs strongly therefore from the 'program-in, intelligence-out' approach of classical AI. Connectionists hope that, given neural nets that are sufficiently parallel (that possess a quantity of 'neural' connections comparable to biological brains), intelligence may eventually *emerge*.

Since connectionism regards intelligence as an *emergent property*, it is based on an understanding of the brain as a complex, dynamical system. In such a system, highly complex things can and do emerge from very simple things, like a chemical clock from a mixture of two chemicals, or like intelligence from the interaction of stupid neurones. Neural networks are therefore not just simulations of biological brains, but actual, technological brains.

Alife

Alife's computer-based history can be traced back to Alan Turing and John von Neumann, the designers of Colossus and ENIAC, respectively. Turing was convinced that the development of organic forms (morphogenesis) must be computationally modellable and therefore really computational, writing a paper to that effect in 1952. Beginning in the 1940s, von Neumann designed what he called 'cellular automata', composed of 'cells' of information capable of self-replicating – much like living or 'natural automata' (Boden 1996: 5–6). Although John Horton Conway developed his *Game of Life* in the late 1960s, AI dominated the sciences of the artificial from the 1950s on, until Alife regained some prominence in the 1980s due to the work of Thomas Ray and Chris Langton, both of whom implemented Alife

Poundstone (1985) gives instructions for how to program this game into an IBM PC. Similarly, Dawkins (1991) provides his own Alife evolutionary simulation in *Blind Watchmaker: the Program of the Book*. Dawkins developed his influential theory of 'the selfish gene' (Dawkins 1976) on the basis of observations of a computer model of evolutionary behaviour (see Dennett 1998: 233n). Later in that work, Dawkins went on to propound an influential but contested evolutionary model of cultural phenomena such as ideas, musics, behaviours and social codes (1976: 206) programs and began to theorise about the field. Ray proposed in 1989 that the 'virtual organisms' grown in his Tierra program ought to be 'set free' to roam and replicate wherever they might find a niche on the net (Robertson *et al.* 1996: 146). Outside the computer, however, Alife has had a long career, based on whatever technology happens to be 'the living technique of the age' (Wiener [1948] 1962: 40). Such approaches, which assume their current form in robotics (Warwick 1998; Dennett 1998: 153–170), are therefore known as 'hard Alife', while computationally based work is called 'soft Alife'. A third area, exemplified by the developments in reproductive technologies and 'genetic engineering', is sometimes known as 'wet Alife'. Apart from simulating biological brains in technology, one field of wet Alife known as 'neuromorphic engineering' is concerned to build 'brainlike systems . . . using real neurones' (Boden 1990: 2). In this context, biology simply becomes another technology.

Alife and biology

There are two reasons why Alife in general and Dawkins's simulations in particular are viewed as relevant methods for studying genetic behaviour, one stemming from biology itself and the other from computer science. First, the biological reason. Ever since Crick and Watson decrypted the structure and behaviour of DNA in 1966, evolutionary biologists have generally accepted that there is a strong parallel between information processing and the activity of DNA. DNA is a code that is translated and carried by 'messenger RNA' to form new strands of DNA, much as information is the product of messages translated into codes, transmitted, and retranslated into messages.

Crick and Watson laid out the chemical structure and behaviour of the genetic code in 1966. Within a few years, biologists were already avowing the informational basis of life. Some, such as Jacques Monod, went so far as to rename genetics as 'microscopic cybernetics' (1971). Clearly, such a cybernetics must differ significantly from the version of it made famous for media studies through Shannon and Weaver. Such cybernetics aims above all at the reduction of noise to zero, and therefore at maximal information content. If all noise were eliminated from the reproductive process, for example, then there could be no evolutionary change, and the appearance of any and all offspring could be predicted on the basis of the genetic information taken from its parents. If, on the other hand, there were nothing but noise, there would remain no basic structure that all members of a given species exemplified. Thus reproductive or molecular cybernetics must consist of a simultaneous maintenance of perfectly reproducible information (giving humans, for example, the correct number of limbs) *and* a certain amount of noise (accounting for change and the appearance of individuals).

Using a science fiction of a Martian exobiologist attempting to distinguish living things from machines on earth, Monod runs through many characteristics shared by all things, organic and technological. He shows how, to the Martian biologist, every apparently distinguishing characteristic fails. If we say, for example, that technological things will show their manufactured character in the fact that their structure is exactly identical in all instances, the same is manifestly true of crystals, bees and humans, all of which show exactly the same amount of structural invariance and complexity as do technological things. One part, therefore, of molecular cybernetics is devoted to the maintenance of order, repeating the structure of the species in all individuals. Monod's 'structural invariance' is therefore like cybernetic restraint, scrupulously maintaining order by the same processes of feedback inhibition and activation as a thermostatic device. Moreover, organisms, like crystals, are composed of 'self-replicating machines' such as von Neumann defined (**5.3.5**), whereas artefacts – human-made technologies, Monod says – are not so clearly so. This yields a degree of 'freedom' for the morphogenetically autonomous object – freedom, that is, from external

Deleuze and Guattari's theory of biology–technology relations is profoundly influenced by Monod's cybernetics, which they cite repeatedly throughout *Anti-Oedipus* ([1974] 1984]

5.3.5 Life and intelligence in the digital age

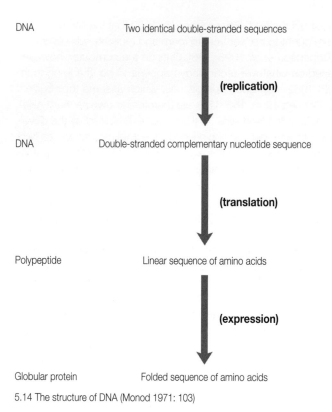

DNA   Two identical double-stranded sequences

(replication)

DNA   Double-stranded complementary nucleotide sequence

(translation)

Polypeptide   Linear sequence of amino acids

(expression)

Globular protein   Folded sequence of amino acids

5.14 The structure of DNA (Monod 1971: 103)

causation: each organism applies its own restraints to itself as it develops. Finally, organic cybernetics achieve such autonomy through 'teleonomy', by which Monod understands 'being imbued with project' *by nature* – 'such as', he adds, 'the making of artefacts' (1971: 20), thus repeating Marx's formulation of *homo faber*. Neither of these latter are of themselves, however, absent from artefacts. Alife is composed entirely of self-replicating machines, while the problem of identifying the source of the project with which a thing is imbued is made manifest by the example of the camera. Is the project of capturing images inherent in the camera itself or in the eye? Since the functions of both are in the end identical, although the hardware is different in each case, there can be no quick solution to the problem. Monod's answer to this is not to decide once and for all which objects projects do or do not reside in, but rather to suggest that the differences between technological and biological things lie in a quantitative threshold, which he calls a thing's 'teleonomic level' which is set by the quantity of information that must be transferred in order to realise that object (1971: 24–25). Clearly, this is higher in a complex biological individual than in any technological thing (although this is not necessarily so – consider the complexity of information transfer in a fully functional neural net).

Monod's account of microscopic cybernetics therefore offers provisional means for identifying organisms as distinct from machines. But the rationale for his assertion that the organism is composed of many molecular cybernetic systems stems from the fact that he derives the two major functions – teleonomy and invariance – from actual constituents of biological systems:

The distinction between teleonomy and invariance is more than a mere logical abstraction. It is warranted on grounds of chemistry. Of the two basic classes of biological macromolecules, one, that of proteins, is responsible for almost all teleonomic structures and performances; while genetic invariance is linked exclusively to the other class, that of nucleic acids.

(Monod 1971: 27)

Once again, then, the distinction between the 'natural' construction of humanity and its construction of artefacts turns out, as we saw in our analysis of Marx's extensionalism, to be a mere quantitative threshold. Just as at a certain point technological extensions of human functions begin to alter those functions in turn, so too, at a certain point, the quantity of information transfer involved in the production of things is all Monod can assure us separates technological from biological systems. Nothing could make this issue clearer than the Human Genome Project.

The Human Genome Project is an attempt to map the entire gene sequence for a 'typical' human. It has been competitively pursued over the last decade by two groups: The Wellcome Institute, a UK-based charitable institution that wants full and immediate disclosure, via the net, of all their findings, and Celera Genomics, a US-based biotechnology company, which has been patenting in a piecemeal fashion those segments of the genome it has decoded. This battle between publicly funded academe and privately funded profit-making corporate culture has something of an epically cyberpunk quality about it. We are witnessing the genesis (almost literally) of genetic capitalism, the patenting of life. It is entirely imaginable that, for example, if Celera-patented genomic byproducts were purchased for, say, infertility treatments, ownership of the resultant offspring could be legally contested. All that is needed now is a cultural sub-group of genome-hackers, disaffected biotechnology consultants, and a novel, perhaps entitled *Genomancer*, to spark – or perhaps catalyse – an entire new literary sub-genre. Moreover, given implants such as Kevin Warwick has been experimenting with since 1998, we can imagine patented genome-strings downloaded into implants to get past security systems, only to leak into the implantee's body.

From the current perspective, however, what is fascinating about the genome is the fact that it has been impossible to produce until such time as computing had reached what, after Monod, we might call a sufficiently high teleonomic level. The genome must, moreover, be housed in a computer memory, since human memory is insufficient for the job. This makes the genome a properly hybrid creature: it is a blueprint of human life that can only be realised as a blueprint in a technological medium. Here 'man' has been extended so far he has seeped into the machines. It is the role of these machines to set about reorganising the blueprint for manufacturing humanity, to eliminate imperfections and enhance existing capacities. Genomic propaganda regularly promises cures for cancer, longevity enhancement, an end to birth defects, and so on, although these remain for the moment of a science fictional order. There are already a variety of genetic anomalies available on the market: Dupont's Oncomouse™, a patented cancer experiment that is no longer a creature of nature but of commerce. GM foods, of course, are a well-known political horror story, prompting fearsome predictions of the rise of Franken-pharms to replace agriculture with pharmiculture. Each of these developments is contested, however, in official and unofficial manner, resulting in truly bizarre demographic combinations: bioethics committees composed of priests, politicians, scientists and lawyers deciding on the paths permissible for the re-engineering of the species, and modified grassroots political protest groups campaigning against such 'double helix hubris' (Harpignies 1994). In each case of biotechnology, be it the genome or Flavr Savr, the

See Haraway (1997) for an analysis of Oncomouse, and Myerson (2000) for a discussion of Haraway's work regarding actually existing hybrids. For a general, critical overview of 'Frankenphaming', see Harpignies (1994)

5.3.2 Clockwork: technology and nature, combined
5.3.3 Self-augmenting engines: steampower against nature

world's first commercially available GM vegetable (or is it a fruit?), however, the important thing to note is the extension of technology into nature. No longer content to sit idly by while culture and nature struggle over their two cultures, technology, and especially corporate biotechnology, has entered the fray, cyberneticising everything.

Perhaps when a new version of Monod's *Chance and Necessity* is written (it was reissued in 2000), the visitor trying to distinguish technology from biology will be itself technological, not just of another species, therefore, but another phylum.

Alife and computation

Computer science did not have to wait long for intimations of artificial life. John von Neumann, who designed the computer ENIAC (along with Turing's Colossus, the first actual computer in history), was, like Vaucanson and von Kempelen (**5.3.2**), Diderot and Babbage (**5.3.3**), interested in constructing artificial automata that not only replicated various aspects of natural automata but, crucially, that reproduced. He thus asked:

> What kind of logical organisation is sufficient for an automaton to reproduce itself? Von Neumann had the familiar natural phenomenon of self-reproduction in mind when he posed [this question], but he was not trying to simulate the self-reproduction of a natural system at the level of genetics and biochemistry. He wished to abstract from the natural self-reproduction problem its logical form.
>
> (A.W. Burks on von Neumann, cited by Langton in Boden 1996: 47)

In other words, if Dawkins is concerned to *imitate* the actions of various evolutionary strategies, von Neumann was concerned to *construct automata* – which were called *cellular automata* – that had an appropriate reproductive strategy for their environment. This same distinction is core to artificial life. Chris Langton, author of what is widely regarded as the field's 'manifesto' (Langton, in Boden 1996: 39–94) writes that artificial life

> attempts to (1) synthesise the process of evolution (2) in computers, and (3) will be interested in *whatever emerges from the process, even if the results have no analogues in the natural world*.
>
> (Langton, in Boden 1996: 40; emphasis added)

If biology understands life *as it is* by taking living things apart (analysis), Alife wishes to understand life *as it could be* by putting it together (synthesis), in whatever way it happens. Alife is therefore referred to by Thomas Ray, for example, as 'synthetic biology' (in Boden 1996: 111–145). Both Langton and Ray, therefore, espouse what is called 'strong Alife', rather than its 'weak' variety, the concern of which is, as is Dawkins', merely to *simulate* 'life as it is'.

From 'self-moving things' to 'self-organisation'

The history of automata, from hydraulic or pneumatic, clockwork, galvanic or calorific, constantly runs close to the line of life that animates or drives these attempts to construct artificial life forms. Alife crosses this line, turning biological things into technologies (wet Alife) and technological things into biological ones (strong Alife). The very phrase 'synthetic biology' shows that the line dividing simulacra from automata, and technology from nature, has been crossed. Science is no longer exclusively concerned merely to understand the natural world; it actively desires to construct an artificial one. It is technology that has made it possible to cross this line; specifically, as point (2) of Langton's definition of Alife states, computing technology.

At the very beginnings of the digital computer in the 1940s and 1950s, Alan Turing began to work on computers and biology, and John von Neumann began to work on cellular automata. Cellular automata are pieces of code that are not only self-moving (automata), but self-replicating. Margaret Boden describes the cellular automaton as

> a computational 'space' made up of many cells. Each cell changes according to the same set of rules, taking into account the states of neighbouring cells. The system moves in time-steps [i.e., according to fixed periods], all the cells normally changing . . . together . . . After each global change, the rules are applied again . . .
>
> (Boden, in Boden 1996: 6)

Then the whole process begins again, ad infinitum. With the cellular automaton, von Neumann therefore succeeded in giving computational form to biological reproduction. Not only did the automaton change with each cycle of global changes, every time the cycle was repeated different changes resulted. Thus, from a simple set of initial instructions, cellular automata produced complex and unpredictable forms. What changed the forms the CA thus produced was the state of all the cells undergoing transformation, not an overall program with instructions that the CA change in some predetermined manner. Such phenomena are known as *self-organising*, insofar as it is the phenomena themselves, and not an overarching program, that organise themselves into a non-preprogrammed form.

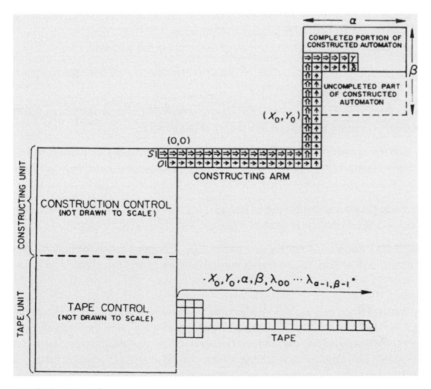

5.15 CA from Virtual Organisms.

5.3.6 Conclusion

Technology does not, as it were, veer away from the physical towards serving a purely human culture. On the contrary, by emphasising the difference between tools and machines, used and user, servant and master, we have seen that there is no historical constancy in the human user being the master, and the non-human technology, the servant. A machine, in other words, uses tools just as humans do; and, just as humans can be tools for human masters, so too they can be tools for non-human machines. This is not to say that there are never (or have never been) periods when control of machines did devolve to human users, merely that such periods tend to come under threat during times of large-scale technological expansion, or what Ellul (1964) calls technological self-augmentation.

Rather than veering from the physical to culture, technology veers towards the physics of living things, towards life. Always at the limit of a culture's technological imaginary, machines approximate life throughout history, whether in a form that *looks like us* (simulacra) or one that does not (automata). While the cyborg is the most widespread contemporary cultural mani-festation of this tendency, it is not the only one, as we have seen. Rather, the devolution of automata from simulacra has meant that cyborgs, almost always given human form, pose the wrong questions about the prospects of 'artificial life'. By forsaking the prospect of the living simulacrum (like the figure of the 'double' that runs throughout a certain species of uncanny literature), the science of Alife is attempting to grow life-forms from the ground up, that do not resemble previously existing creatures but resemble their mechanisms. This has been made possible by the increasing proximity, during the age of information, of genetics and compu-tation, the online marriage of which has given us the genome.

By placing the automaton centre-stage in histories of technology, we can see the con-stancy of this tendency towards life. However, it is not a continuous or cumulative tendency. Technological change forces new technologies to start again.

What we can learn therefore from the history of automata is the following:

- that the cyborgs of contemporary culture are importantly *not new*, but have precursors at every stage of technological development;

- that therefore *life* and *technology* have converged and diverged throughout history, form-ing an important constant throughout the history of technology;

- that every time the question '*what is technology?*' is answered, history is rewritten to suit, and the answers assume the status of a set of unbreakable assumptions ('normal' tech-nology);

- that these assumptions – and that view of history – are disrupted and problematised with every change in the technological base of a given culture ('crisis' technology);

- finally, that during periods of normalised technology, the oppositions of human and machine, nature and artifice, nature and culture, the physical and the human, go unex-amined.

To emphasise: these phenomena are historically cyclical, recurring at every technological age, as Wiener says. For the present, *digital machines represent for us a crisis technology, inso-far as all the old stabilities regarding the relations between nature, culture and technology are once again disrupted*. This creates uncertainties for the cultural analysis of physical things, of course, but at the same time it provides us with opportunities to re-examine what has been taken for granted since the cultural approach to technology became normalised, and to reopen the questions that led it to become so. The histories of previous periods of crisis tech-nologies provide us with glimpses into the form those problems have taken, and therefore provide guides as to how we might contemporarily pose those, and perhaps new, problems. Since history, however, is not theoretically innocent, but laden with often unacknowledged assumptions, it is also necessary to look at the theories those histories are made to subserve. In consequence, this is the task to which the following section now turns.

5.4 Theories of cyberculture

Introduction

The science of cybernetics lies at the artificial heart of cyberculture. It is concerned with con-trol and communication in animal *and* machine – in biology *and* technology. Although popularly associated only with digital technologies, cyberculture actually encompasses the relations between nature and technology, as we have seen. Since we have now looked at technology and biology, we will begin by taking a closer look at cybernetics. We will then move on to look at a number of theories of cyberculture itself; that is, the attempts to map it across the three domains that have structured Part 5: technology, nature and culture.

5 Cyberculture: technology, nature and culture

5.4.1 Cybernetics and human–machine relations

A short history of classical cybernetics

Cybernetics grew up, towards the end of the Second World War, around the work of a group of mathematicians, engineers and physicists investigating problems of communications sys-tems and anti-aircraft targeting systems. The latter problems were the special preserve of Norbert Wiener, who wrote concerning them to Vannevar Bush, a computing pioneer, in 1940. Wiener was a mathematician and physicist working on problems of prediction, and therefore control: in order to target a moving object, that object's trajectory and speed need to be calculated quickly. Never attack the enemy where he is, but where he will be. Vannevar Bush and John von Neumann, another cyberneticist, were pioneers in computing machines, working on replacing mechanical calculating procedures (**5.3.5**) with electronic ones. Von Neumann, together with economic theorist Oscar Morgenstern, also developed an influential model of economic behaviour known as 'games theory', spreading cybernetics into the social world. Finally, in common with all cybernetics, Claude Shannon, working at the Bell Telephone Labs, was interested in the theoretical design and practical installation of maximally efficient communications systems. Shannon and Weaver's model of communications has since achieved infamy in media studies as less a theory of communication than of *propaganda* (Fiske 1990: 6–7), in that it is concerned only with the *successful* and *one-way* communica-tion of information. Less pejoratively, however, this account of cybernetic theories of communications highlights the relation between communication and control. To understand this it is necessary not to think of all communication as verbal or symbolic. Communication takes place, argues cybernetics, when a signal produces a response, such as when a tongue of flame singes the flesh on your arm, and you withdraw it. This is not a message to be under-stood, but one inducing an action or reaction. It is this dimension which has drawn most fire from media studies commentators as it seems to reduce the idea of communication to one of mere 'response' or 'reaction'.

5.3.5 Life and intelligence in the digital age

However, in order to see the contribution that cybernetics makes to an understanding of human–machine relationships, we must take note of three main principles in its accounts of the processes of control and communication. These are:

1   Feedback, positive and negative.

2   Restriction produces action, not choice.

3   Information varies inversely as noise.

FEEDBACK

Feedback occurs in two ways: first, negatively. Negative feedback is what keeps a system operational within fixed parameters. For example, when a thermostat cuts power to a heat source it is doing so to prevent overheating. When it sends a signal to the heat source to bring it back online, it does so to prevent cold. As a consequence, a given temperature is maintained within a certain range of fluctuations: we could say that it is fundamentally conservative in that respect. Negative feedback is so-called because it 'negates' the tendency to continue heating, or to discontinue heating altogether.

Second, positive feedback is the type we are familiar with from live electronic music. The signal is too close to the source, reacting back on it to amplify the amount of noise (as opposed to information) produced by the system. If unchecked, positive feedback will continue to amplify until the speaker is destroyed. Similarly, if a steam engine without a governor were to keep building up pressure it would become an explosive rather than a motive force. Positive feedback leads to the eventual collapse of the system in which it is generated. But while the system survives it, positive feedback constantly changes the state of the system, and sometimes introduces surprising and unpredictable behaviours on the part of that system. In short, all change can be understood as the product of positive feedback.

RESTRICTION

When cyberneticists discuss control they are interested in preventing positive feedback and maximising negative feedback. The maximal state of negative feedback is total predictability in the system: it will never do anything remotely unexpected, and will continue indefinitely to serve its appointed purpose. For this reason, an action is never a consequence of an agent's choice but rather of the restriction of all possible actions bar one. This is interesting not only from the point of view of efficiently functioning machines but because it is based upon the realisation that the operation of a machine may lead to several possible outcomes; and the task of cybernetics is to see how only one of these, a preferred outcome, can be ensured. In this sense, cybernetics is 'realist' about producing an 'actual' outcome from a range of possible outcomes. This, as we will see, is important when discussing what is meant by the 'virtual' (see **5.4.2**).

5.4.2 Cybernetics and the virtual

For the moment, the important thing to grasp is this. We noted earlier that Wiener was interested in prediction systems, and with this sense of cybernetic restriction we get some sense of how it is that cybernetics sees things: any current state of affairs – what we might call the 'present actual' – is the consequence of eliminating alternative futures. If these alternatives need to be eliminated or negated it can only be because they in some sense exist in the present as potential outcomes, which would happen were they not checked. In other words, they exist as inherent tendencies. The important thing about such a view is that it incorporates the possible into the present, and produces the actual by splitting the present and discarding what remains. Control is not only conservative, then, it is also predictive, and *this sense of the future acting on the present* has become a core theme of cyberfictions.

INFORMATION AND NOISE

Classical cybernetics was principally concerned to eliminate noise from communications channels. One good way to understand what noise is, is to consider a telephone signal: when it is clear, and neither the apparatus nor environmental obstacles interfere (producing feedback in the first instance, and distorting or eliminating the phone signal in the second), the greatest amount of information is produced (both callers can hear each other perfectly). Simply put, the more interference in the signal, the less information is received. The clearest signal would therefore produce maximum information, and the least clear, the most noise. In any signal, however, there is always some noise, and the more information transmitted, therefore, the more the noise increases. For classical cybernetics, noise is a bad thing, and no information can result as noise increases.

POST-CLASSICAL CYBERNETICS

Cybernetics is not confined to the interests of geeks in Second World War military command, communication and control (otherwise known as C3; see De Landa 1991). Its proponents theorised about serial and parallel computing, and produced early valve computer systems. Symptomatic of the principal development, however, is cybernetics' concern with questions of learning. Gregory Bateson, in the late 1960s and 1970s, for example, was putting forward the notion that perfect replication of a message (i.e. perfect information retrieval) amounted to zero learning, echoing the adage that 'one repays one's teachers badly by imitation'. Learning always involves deviation, departure from a norm, and so on. While this may not sound startling, it opens important new questions.

First, it suggests that restriction, in the sense discussed above, not only destroys alternatives in order to arrive at perfect responses but also takes cues from information received and builds on them. Although cybernetics sees control as negative feedback, eliminating all but one response, learning involves positive feedback, producing new responses.

Second, taken alongside John von Neumann's theoretical account of the differences between parallel and serial computing, positive feedback devices became extremely interesting for artificial intelligence researchers (**5.3.4**). Rather than asking, in a cybernetically negative way, 'how can we ensure that the war machine – i.e., soldiers, tanks, planes, communications systems, strategies, and so on – obeys our commands to the letter?', they began to ask, in a cybernetically positive manner, 'how can we get machines to learn?' (**5.3.5**).

Third, the virtues of positive feedback began to be explored in other fields, notably chemistry and genetics. In chemistry, for example, questions began to be asked about spontaneously emerging 'order out of chaos', something many phenomena seemed to exhibit, but of which there was no available theoretical model. Hence there arose approaches such as non-linear, or 'far from equilibrium' dynamics (**5.2.2**). In genetics, perfect information transfer would mean no change from generation to generation, thus annihilating the genetic basis of evolution, which depends on change, and there could be no genetic means of accounting for mutation. Imperfect transcriptions therefore became a focus of research, explicitly premissed on positive feedback, and on change rather than control.

Fourth, rather than a principle of negation, therefore, selection became a positive principle. In answering the question 'why this outcome rather than another?', scientists' attention switched from a process of enforcing desired outcomes to seeking desirable ones. As Manuel de Landa puts it, every far-from-equilibrium phenomenon is formed as if it were in the wake of a kind of 'guiding head' or 'searching device' (de Landa 1993: 795) that eventually 'selects' a particular order. As opposed to the negative method of applying constraints to the system, this positive method cannot guarantee a particular outcome. Thus, storm-chasers learn to recognise the signs of impending storms, but there is no guarantee that a storm will occur, or that it will occur where it seems most likely. The storm has a life of its own.

PCs are serial computers, insofar as they have one central processing unit (CPU) through which all tasks must be processed, one after the other. A parallel computer involves several processors, and conducts several tasks at once. When von Neumann made this distinction, he considered computers to be inherently serial, but brains – 'natural automata'– to be inherently parallel. See von Neumann ([1958] 1999)

5.3.4 The construction of inanimate reason
5.3.5 Life and intelligence in the digital age

If this use of the phrase 'war machine' sounds metaphorical, evoking only the efficiently co-ordinated actions of bodies of soldiers, aircraft, tanks, etc. towards a single target, consider the US Gulf War pilots' complaints of 'information overload' from their cockpits. In the latter, the pilot no longer surveys a natural, but a simulated, vista, and receives more information from on-board computational devices than human neurophysiology proved capable of dealing with. The 'war machine' is no metaphor. See de Landa (1991)

5.2.2 Causalities

Storm-chasers feature not only as the heroes of Jan de Bont's film *Twister* (1998), but also in Bruce Sterling's novel *Heavy Weather* (1995). Sterling offers excellent illustrations of the above ideas throughout that work. Again, Sterling's *Distraction* (1999) provides a host of examples of such runaway processes. Set around the exploits of a political fixer in the US after its entire online economy has been wiped out by a Chinese electromagnetic pulse, the novel's hero expends all his energies trying to tap sources of disorder and to turn them into new forms of order, new political structures. These structures are not known in advance, but occur only within the specific process of which he makes himself part. As regards feedback in fiction, David Porush (1985) argued that cybernetic fictions (such as Thomas Pynchon's *Gravity's Rainbow* or *The Crying of Lot 49*) consist in a series of structures that contain their own momentum, and thus build like feedback rather than progressing like standard linear narratives (beginning, middle, end). More recently (in Broadhurst-Dixon and Cassidy 1997), Porush has made the same point in such a way as to involve the reader in the feedback: any text causes changes in the reader's brain, that in turn cause changes in the reader's normal cognitive behaviours. In this sense, it is always true to say 'that book changed my life'

Finally, since cybernetics never discriminated against a component of a system as to whether it was biological or technological, feedback ceased to be confined to the study of communications in general and instead began to find applications in chemistry, biology, economics, AI, Alife, sociology (Eve *et al.* 1997), politics and literary studies. It is arguably from the prevalence of runaway positive feedback that cyberculture, concerned as it is with rapid and unstoppable change, takes its cues.

The smallest circuit

Gilles Deleuze, a philosopher often associated with cyberculture (see for example Lévy 1998; Critical Art Ensemble 1995; Genosko 1998; Ansell-Pearson 1997), took the work of Bergson ([1911] 1920), who reduced cinema from an emergent art form to a producer of 'mechanical thinking', and sought to demolish its intellectual significance, as the philosophical basis of his own two-volume work on cinema (Deleuze 1986; 1989). In that work he put forward his thesis concerning the 'mental automaton' that is produced by the combination of cinematic spectacle and viewer. Deleuze takes this combination seriously, saying that this mental automaton consists of a body made of nerves, flesh and light. It is formed because the cinema is a device that creates a feedback circuit between organic bodies and sensory stimuli (sounds, images), that is so complete it forms a new system. It does this because the cinematic sign creates the shortest, most intense circuit between nerve signals and impulses. Once the circuit has formed, these impulses no longer come from the screen to the viewer, but form circuits with the brain that form in turn other circuits, mixing a multitude of cinematic signs with bodies. Crucial to this mental automaton is that it is a new system formed *in situ*, rather than a mere bringing together of separate organic and technological systems.

Deleuze's conception of the automaton demonstrates its allegiances to cybernetics in that it is not about bodies, but circuits. Moreover, rather than explaining its emergence as the effect of a cause, Deleuze presents the circuit as formed given simple contact between the brain and the cinema. The circuit, in other words, is self-organising (**5.2.4**). Further, the 'mental automaton' is physical, involving new circuits of neurones and light. From this, all the others devolve, in increasing degrees of complexity – sign and nerve, image and physical action. Being the shortest circuit, finally, it 'loops' more frequently than the others, thus forming a *subject* emerging from the circuit that experiences all the others. Deleuze thus develops a conception of a cybernetic subject that is neither reducibly technological nor biological, that self-organises, and that not only forms the basis for reconceiving debates about media effects and the causal force of images but also suggests that there is space neither for agency nor mechanical determinism (such as Deleuze finds, to an extent, in Bergson's critique of the cinema).

We can see then that Deleuze undertakes to develop Bergson's 'mechanical thinking': cinema is not the flat presentation of events unfolding mechanically in time, annulling our own sense of 'lived time', but rather a positive feedback circuit that forms a cybernetic subject specific to the physical environment that is the cinema: the 'mental automaton'.

Hybrids

Barring the mental automaton, all the cybernetic devices we have examined thus far – factory and worker, steam engine and governor, the telephone and the callers, pilot and aircraft, and any machine whatever – consist of combinations of parts that can be undone: the steersman (kybernetes) leaves his ship, workers leave factories, audiences leave cinemas, soldiers go on leave and detach themselves from the war machine, and so on. Although Plant (1997), for instance, insists that all cybernetic systems constitute cyborgs simply by virtue of utilising technological and biological components, the cyborg itself, as figured in cyberculture more generally, is not so detachable.

Here we return to the distinction between automata that look like humans (simulacra), and those that do not (**5.3.2**). Factories, war machines, cinema circuits, and so on, do not look like humans but are automata in the strict sense, in that, once 'plugged in', they are *self-moving things*. Almost invariably, however (although there are notable exceptions, such as the cybernetic systems that run *The Matrix*), contemporary cyborgs do look like humans. Arnold Schwarzenegger's *Terminator* cyborgs vaguely resemble humans, as does *Robocop*, Stelarc, *Steampunk*'s Cole Blacquesmith. *Star Trek: the Next Generation*'s Lieutenant Data not only looks human, but notoriously wants to become more so – something the *Star Trek* franchise has demonstrated an alarmingly soapy determination to achieve, even humanising their unstoppably inhuman cybernetic nemesis the Borg through the figure of *Voyager*'s Seven of Nine. Despite the questions of body boundaries posed by Allucquere Rosanne Stone (1995) concerning the precise limits of Stephen Hawking's body, the physicist remains manifestly human.

However, cyberpunk fiction focuses less on shiny metal cyborgs like the Terminator, or on the oily iron and muscle cyborgs known to Marx, than on the technology of the implant. Beginning with the contemporarily well-known artificial heart, *Neuromancer*'s world contains artificially grown organs of all sorts, machine implants like eyes that record and playback the light stimuli they receive, undernail razors, flip-top nano-filament containing thumbs, and so on. Technology ceases to be big, but becomes instead invasive, sticky. Like the contact lens, it sinks quickly beneath the horizon of our attention as soon as it descends below the skin.

We are, of course, mixing fictional and factual sources of cyborgs here. But key to this discussion is not whether a fictional cyborg has less reality than a factual one; rather, it concerns identifying the *prevalent type* of the cyborg in contemporary culture, whether manifest in images, narrative, surgeries or laboratories.

Thus, rather than the simple, separable cyborg (pilot and aircraft, ear and hearing aid, etc.), Kevin Warwick, Professor of Cybernetics at the UK's Reading University, has been conducting experiments with invasive cybernetic technologies, with the express purpose of 'upgrading' himself to become a cyborg. He has already tried implanting a transmitter chip beneath the surface of his skin, as well as, more recently, a receptor chip. The purpose of these experiments is to interface the body and technology directly, through the medium of the electricity that nervous impulses and computer signals share. He hopes to create direct, person-to-person (or cyborg-to-cyborg) communications links, as well as ultimately, thought-operated computation. Such experiments concern direct neural interfaces linking technology and biology indissociably, changing what counts as a biological and a technological system. That this technological trajectory was first announced in cyberpunk fiction matters little. What does matter is that such fiction, and such experiments, bear witness to the indissociability of biology and technology that is cybernetics' core insight.

While Warwick explicitly calls the creature he is becoming a cyborg, others maintain the use of the alternative term *hybrid*. Donna Haraway, famous for her 'Manifesto for Cyborgs' (Haraway 1991), is one such theorist. By emphasising the hybrid, Haraway effectively re-biologises the militarily-tainted discourses of cybernetics. A hybrid is a biologically grafted organism (a new variety of rose, or a new breed of show dog), a mix of species. Of course, we are already familiar with the way that biotechnology has technologised the biological, making hybrids a bio-technological product. The Flavr-Savr tomato (Haraway 1997: 56), for example, the first GM foodstuff available on the US market, is raw (or should that be 'cooked'?) biotech, rather than 'nature's own' (Myerson 2000: 24).

Deleuze is often thought important *vis-à-vis* cyberculture for two reasons. One is the concept of the 'desiring machine' he and analyst Félix Guattari invented in their *Anti-Oedipus* ([1974] 1984); the other is Deleuze's own repeated engagements with the concept of the virtual, beginning with his 1966 book on Bergson (Deleuze 1988), and running through *Difference and Repetition* ([1968] 1994). We will address the latter concept in **5.4.2**

5.4.2 Cybernetics and the virtual
5.2.4 Determinisms
5.3.2 Clockwork: technology and nature combined

It is not an objection to the 'self-moving' status of automata that they need a power source. As Marx says, the machine 'consumes coal, oil etc. . . . just as the worker consumes food' (1993: 693)

Other hybridisers such as Bruno Latour (1993), whose work is a direct attempt to generate an anthropology of non-human things – that is, to frame the non-human social agents such as machines, viruses, mudslides, and so on, within a culture that does not reduce them to tools of humanity – insist that the hybrid is not necessarily an individual organism, but something much larger. His view is that human and non-human things form hybrid entities by virtue of the networks they share (**5.2.3**). Nothing is any longer purely human, not because of physical changes to the human being itself but because of changes to the environment in which humans live. We live in a bio-technological world where we are indissociably networked with other things, so that for every social action we engage in, there are agents that are human as well as agents that are not (machines, weather systems, viruses, institutions, and so on). Latour thus proposes a shift away from attention to a world which is somehow purely human to a world which is resolutely and increasingly hybrid.

5.2.3 Agencies

What both the scientist and the cultural theorist, Warwick and Haraway, share with the world of cyberpunk fiction is an acknowledgement that the grafts between biological and technological parts and systems are becoming far more intimate. Cyborg components belong to a scale beneath that of the organism thus cyborganised: no longer is man spliced to machine by way of a steering wheel, a rudder, or a conveyor belt; instead, the machines have got you 'under their skin'. On this view, shared by novelists, scientists and cultural scientists, humanity faces the reconstruction of the species for the first time in its existence.

5.3 Biological technologies: the history of automata

All the elements present in cyberculture's prehistory, then, which we encountered in **5.3**, remain present within its contemporary manifestation: automata that look like us (simulacra) and automata that don't; artificial life and natural technologies; debates on what lives and what causes, what determines and what acts. The distinction between the hand-held tool (the 'extension of man') and the environmental, 'self-augmenting' machine (**5.3.1**) reappears in contemporary cyberculture as that between micro and macro technologies: cyborgs as technologically enhanced biological units, and cyborgs as biologically powered technological units.

5.3.1 Automata: the basics

The machinic phylum

The above issues stem entirely from considering the interlacing of biology and technology that is at the centre of cybernetics. However, cybernetics is not the only theoretical approach premissed on such a synthesis. For example, Deleuze and Guattari's concept of the machinic phylum places their thinking about machines on a firmly biological footing.

It is often assumed that their use of the term 'phylum' must be metaphorical; however, it is absolutely to be understood in the context of supplying a microbiology, a morphology, and an ecology of machines. Each of these three fields signals a scale in machine connections, beginning with the smallest (the permanently coupling desiring machines), up to the largest (the mechanosphere), with the phylum intermediate between them. By placing the machinic phylum on such a biological footing, however, machines become fundamental to the possibility of biology.

They take their concept of desiring machines from three sources: from Marx, they take the idea of material production; from Freud, the idea of desire; from Monod, the idea of microscopic cybernetics. Desiring machines are not to be understood as occupants of individual psyches but as the molecular assemblers of things, just as for Monod proteins and nucleic acids build bodies. Similarly, they are not metaphors, but real, producing not fantasies, as Freud would have us believe, but reality. 'The unconscious is not a theatre', they write, 'but a factory' (Deleuze and Guattari [1974] 1984: 311). Instead of identifying the machines with the already individuated psyche, so that 'we' human individuals simply become machines or machine-like, they identify them with the microscopic, pre-individual processes that form all chemical and biological bodies. These are the machine processes underlying all things. Thus the psychoanalytic focus on the subject is overturned in favour of the pre-personal material production of the realities of body and world. At the same time, Marx's grounding of material reality in the actions and productions of social human beings gives way to a microscopic material reality that is truly machinic: nature not only builds machines, it is machines. Monod, finally, is taken literally, but without his illegitimate attempts to maintain the superiority of complex bodies over molecular processes.

Just as they undercut the level of the individual, so they leap from these molecular assemblers to their next category in the biology of machines – the phylum. Where we hear and read a great deal about cyborgs as 'new species', they remain, on such views, members of the same phylum (a higher order of classification than species). In other words, with the concept of the machinic phylum, they are indicating that the real issue does not lie in the alterations wrought upon a single species – man – but on the phylum, a higher order of classification that is principally concerned with formal similarities and differences rather than with individuation. Species are defined as individuals by heredity: only members of the same species produce offspring. Phyla are not defined by heredity, but by shared form or characteristics. The machinic phylum therefore comprises all those things that share machinic form. We do not ask, under the rubric of the machinic phylum, what a machine is, but rather *what are the variations in its forms*. Cybernetics constitutes, in this sense, a characteristic morphology of self-regulating, self-producing assemblages, regardless of their material components, and is thus an attempt at a machinic phylum. Just as Wiener saw the remit of cybernetics extending from animal to machine, so too Deleuze and Guattari see 'a single machinic phylum . . . as much artificial as natural' (1988: 407). The phylum forms the basis on which all singular things are effected, cut from its flow, as it were. Because they are concerned only with one species (life) and with one phylum (the machinic), Deleuze and Guattari effectively ignore individual things in favour of constant variations of components. All organisms, in this sense, are cybernetic from the outset, and in consequence, cyborgs and artificial life forms do not constitute new species but merely constantly changing states of matter and organisation. And the machine is the very paradigm of this constant disassembly and reassembly: machines are not species *of* life, they *are* life in its purest state.

If everything belongs to the machinic phylum this seems to leave little room for the mechanosphere. However, Deleuze and Guattari use the latter concept to reject the idea of a purely biological evolution: 'There is no biosphere . . ., but everywhere the same Mechanosphere' (1988: 69). What this means is that everything that is organised matter – organic or otherwise – is a machine, differently realised. How a particular machine is put together, and what from, is always a question of technology and can never be reduced to biology. Their view of the relation between technology and biology, then, is one that usurps the role of biology as the science of life, and argues that the true science of life is technological in nature.

These are complex ideas, and perhaps the best way to sum up Deleuze and Guattari's work on the question of biology and machine relations is the following: life is nothing but machines.

In all this, Deleuze and Guattari are profoundly influenced by two 1950s works by Gilbert Simondon: *The Mode of Existence of Technical Objects* and *The Individual and its Physico-Biological Genesis*. Simultaneously biological and technological, Simondon's work in both contexts concentrates on the processes of concretisation that lead to the production of a biological or technological thing. In both cases, the thing becomes actual by restrictions placed on the matter from which they are formed by feedback processes that inhere in matter that is becoming organised. Thus a biological entity emerges because the materials it is made of are restricted in their pairings (i.e., molecule X cannot bind with molecule Z, but only with A), and turn these restrictions into a repeated pattern. A technological object comes into existence in exactly the same way. Core to both is the fact that they do not represent the total actualisation of all the potential inherent in the systems they constitute: the parts of a machine (for example, an internal combustion engine) or the functions of organic bodies (a beating heart, for example) can be reassembled to form a bomb, or be replaced by a mechanical device. More technically expressed, machines are functionally underdetermined. The sense in which these undeveloped potentials nevertheless exist in a virtual state will be core to our next section.

5.4.2 Cybernetics and the virtual

Perhaps no term has flourished more under cyberculture than the word *virtual*. Virtual reality machines, no matter how primitive they are, have become a central feature in the cybernetic landscape, since Jaron Lanier began using the term to denote the VR technology with which we are currently familiar: headset, data-gloves and treadmill. As a consequence, we tend simply to identify the 'virtual' with these, and indeed with practically any computer-based technologies, whether entertainment platforms or military training assemblages. It becomes hard to see just how the two terms 'virtual' and 'reality' add up to more than just 'simulation', and even harder to see that the two terms form an apparent oxymoron. It is the gap between VR machines and the concept of the virtual that this section is intended to open up for discussion.

> For more on Lanier, and the prehistory of the term VR, see Rheingold (1991), and Heim (1993: chs 8–9). Heim further discusses some of the issues regarding the virtual and the real which we address below

In a strong sense, it is the *ontological* claim inherent in the concept of virtual reality that we wish to examine here. To explain: consider the everyday sense in which we say a task has *virtually* been completed, or that one thing is *virtually* the same as another. Such uses indicate that the task or the things in question are *almost* but *not really* complete, the same, and so on. If we attach this significance to the term virtual reality, then we see an immediate problem: almost real but not quite? In one sense, this seems a perfectly reasonable definition of virtual reality, something that *looks* and *behaves* like the real thing, but which isn't. On the other hand, if we take the 'reality' in virtual reality, this suggests something more than the everyday sense of the 'virtual' as *almost real but not*. It suggests that the virtual is a kind of reality, as distinct, perhaps, from 'real reality', which is the clumsy phrase Pat Cadigan has the characters in her novel *Synners* (1991) use in order to make a clumsy distinction between the world online and off. Now, how can something which is *almost real but not really real* be at the same time something that is a *kind of reality*? The everyday sense of the virtual is cast into doubt by the addition of 'reality'.

While this problem may seem to be of merely academic (in the pejorative sense) interest, in fact many things hinge on settling the issue regarding the reality of the virtual. First, and most obviously, what exactly are we doing when we enter a virtual reality environment and interact with objects within it? We assess the reality of an object in the real world in accordance with the evidence of our senses of sight and touch: if a desert traveller sees an oasis but upon reaching it notices that it has vanished, then the oasis is not real but a mirage. As in real reality, therefore, if we can touch a virtual object, albeit with the aid of a dataglove, is it not real? If it is not real, are we *not* interacting with anything at all, but merely *deluded* about what our senses are telling us, as though taking a dream for reality? In this sense, VR technologies would amount to *insanity engines*, propagating illusions that we mistake for the real. Clearly, then, virtual realities are more than mere illusions.

Moreover, forgetting for the moment the status of the environment we enter, what of the status of the real-world technologies we use to enter it, or the programs that are these virtual environments? Clearly, the illusions with which we interact are produced by complex and very real interactions between hardware (data-gloves, treadmill and headset), software (the actual program we are running) and our senses (how we experience these interactions). Even the simulated everyday world that Neo and his compatriots in *The Matrix* inhabit is produced by very real connections between machines, programs and nervous systems, and cannot therefore be discounted as illusory. Without these machines, there would be no simulation. Therefore, simulations are importantly real by virtue of the technologies necessary to producing them, and the effect they have upon us.

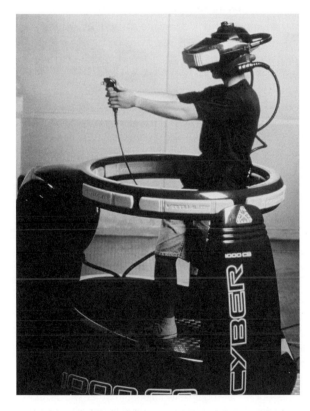

5.16 A Virtual Reality machine and user, as seen from real life.

Deleuze and the virtual

What we learn from virtual reality *machines* is that we can no longer use the term 'real' as though it were the *opposite* of the virtual, or the illusory. By adding the terms together, we get differentiations within reality; different kinds of reality, rather than a contrast with it. On what are these different types of reality based? First, consider the sense in which a task that is virtually completed is, in an everyday sense, *almost* completed. The reference to time is clear: the task's completion is just about *upon* us, but is not yet. In this sense, a reference to the virtual includes future states as a part of the real; the future has a kind of reality which is virtual, but not *actual*. This is the sense of the 'virtual' that Gilles Deleuze maintains: the virtual is real, but inactual. That is, it has real existence but not in the same way as the things that are *actually* around us.

Traditionally, however, the *actual* is the opposite of the potential. When, for example, we say that 'an acorn is a potential oak tree', we are saying that the acorn *will become* an oak tree, that the oak realises the potential of the acorn. Another way of putting this would be to say that the potential of the acorn ceases to exist as it becomes an oak; that is, that it no longer exists as potential. Thus Deleuze further distinguishes the virtual from the potential: a thing potentially exists if it *might* or *could* exist; it is a *real possibility*, as we say. If we conceive of the virtual as *potential* existence, we implicitly suggest that this potential is realised in the thing that it becomes, and therefore that the virtual exists only insofar as it eventually ceases to be virtual as it becomes actual. But this is to suggest that the virtual has no existence of its own, that there is no sense in which the virtual is real. It also suggests that there is a predictable relation between virtual and actual things, so that, for example, a car is the actualisation of a particular virtual thing which can therefore become nothing but that car. It is as if the virtual car is the actual car in an imperfect or incomplete state. This would mean that there are a bunch of virtual cars queuing in the sky, as it were, waiting to take the exit to the earth. Such an image of the virtual merely doubles the actual world, and has to wait to become real rather than being real itself.

However, if we want to insist that the virtual is not just inactual (i.e. *not* yet real, but real as it is), then clearly the reality of the virtual must lie elsewhere than in the *potential* existence of a certain thing. What is the virtual if it is not an inferior copy of the actual? Ultimately, such a virtual reality stems from cybernetics. We can see precursors, however, to this idea in Gilbert Simondon's account of the 'mode of existence of technical objects', as the title of his (1958) book has it.

Simondon and the virtual-real

Simondon argues that in analysing any complex machine it must be broken down into its constituent parts, many of which are functionally independent of the actual (i.e., the current) function or use of the whole machine (see Dumouchel 1992). To define a machine by its function is to abstract that function from the range of functions of which it is capable. In other words, nothing in the machine itself predetermines it to functioning in the way it actually does. The inactualised capacities are *real virtualities* of the machine. In this way, complex technical objects provide a material basis for differentiating between the actual and the virtual, where it is the actual that is an abstraction from the virtual rather than the virtual being the abstract or potential existence of the machine.

Perhaps the best illustration of this idea is the status of computers as 'universal machines', which is how Alan Turing defined the computer in 1936. They are so called precisely because they do not have just one, but rather multiple functions. In other words, since it is a universal machine, a computer's possible functions can never be exhausted by any particular application or program. Simondon's point, however, extends to regard all complex technologies as essentially universal machines. That is, if we define a machine by its use, we mistake the complex interplay of its subsystems (for example, explosive chemical mixtures, electrical sparking, and cooling systems in a car's internal combustion engine) for a single system determined to certain functions, whereas each of these subsystems can of course form part of other machines (bombs, light bulbs and refrigerators). The history of any given machine is formed by the passage – or evolution – from the technical potentials to the concretisation of the various potentialities or virtualities the machine exploits. According to Simondon, therefore, in any given piece of technology there are complex relations between actual and virtual machines, all of which are, however, real.

If we consider simple machines in similar terms, by contrast, such as tools, we note that they have become, in Simondon's words, 'hypertelic'; that is, their purpose has become overdetermined to a single function. This means that they can no longer be used for anything other than a severely restricted range of tasks (consider how few functions a hammer has as compared to a computer). All the virtualities the tool exploits – the resistance and density of certain alloys, the conjunctions of wood and metal, the combination of hammer and claw, and so on – have been concretised, resulting in so rigid and inflexible a relation between the sub-systems it exploits that these can no longer be dissociated (if just one part is damaged the whole is irremediably dysfunctional). A complex machine, then, is distinguished from a simple machine by the range of virtualities that it instantiates. This means in turn that the use of a technical object always seizes on an abstraction of the concrete machine from its virtualities, virtualities which, however, define and materially constitute the machine as such.

While this may seem improbably abstract, Simondon is essentially viewing complex machines from the standpoint of how cybernetic devices work. The point has often been made that cybernetics does not work through choice or purpose – that is, through positively selecting a purpose or object – but rather through restraint: we get a false picture of cyber-netics if we consider it steering towards a single goal. In other words, a system does not produce what it does by virtue of opting for a single outcome, but by preventing or 'restrain-ing' other possible outcomes (this is another way of saying that cybernetic systems work by minimising noise – see Bateson 1972: 399–400). It is as though a cybernetic device deselects virtualities in order to arrive at a realised function (e.g., amplifying a signal by acting on the noise). If this is the case, then a system is an actualised region of the virtual-real.

In both Simondon and cybernetics, then, the virtual is considered as a real space that remains both real and inactual. The actual is something that as it were is cut from this space by virtue of the actions of deselection performed upon it. Both Simondon and cybernetics, then, take the virtual to be real, but there are many who do not, and who in consequence dis-pute the ascription of 'reality' to the virtual.

Critiques of the virtual

One way to critique the virtual is to argue that it is not a real space at all, and certainly not one that we can inhabit. The idea of a 'virtual community' has, for instance, come in for consid-erable hammering. Critics argue that, instead of being a real community, a virtual community is a way of escaping the real-world decay of community. The virtual community therefore exists only insofar as it mystifies the community whose absence requires its replacement. Such critics consider 'virtual' to mean little more than 'illusory', 'mythical' or 'ideal': these terms all apply to the virtual, they argue, which is something that, because it seems real, is taken so to be, but which really is not. Virtual communitarians are therefore avoiding the real world, not interacting in a segment of it.

Of course, there is something going on when messages are exchanged across great dis-tances, and responses from anonymous correspondents are elicited. That something, however, is akin to claiming that a telephone line constitutes an alternative reality, or that, for that matter, a book constitutes a world. In reality, books and telephones only do this *in the imagination*, since there are no real, offline differences produced in the real world. Thus crit-ics do not go so far as to deny the existence of the virtual, but merely to say that such existence as it has it shares with phenomena like delusions, hallucinations, dreams or illusions that become public, much like Gibson's definition of cyberspace as a 'consensual hallucina-tion' (1986: 12).

However, to argue that, whatever the appearance of community, for example, in the vir-tual world, there are no actual communities formed is a bit like arguing that changes in the social order of, for example, Mars, are not real because they do not affect what happens on earth. By extension, it is akin to arguing that changes in the social order of Burma are not real because they do not have any effect on the social order in Canada. What such critics are guilty of is mistaking the virtual-real as only real insofar as it forms a part of 'real reality' here and now. If the effects of the virtual remain virtual, then by definition they are not real. The virtual, however, cannot be regarded as a mere dreamscape, or an hallucination in itself; rather, by virtue of its *consensual* character (in Gibson's oft-quoted phrase), it must of necessity be real (something unreal cannot be shared). Instead of arguing that the virtual is *not* real, therefore, the topic for debate must be the limitations of the virtual, and the possible solutions to these limitations.

The theoretical grounds for arguing in this critical manner ultimately stem from the idea that the 'virtual' is just a *name*, that it therefore is nothing in itself but merely an unreal add-on that tells us something about its users' relation to what is really real. Such a theory is called *nominalist*, in that it insists that what is denoted by the term is reducible to an attitude towards reality, and has no physical or real embodiment. We shall see how such nominalist accounts fare when we consider the relations between cyberculture and the body (**5.4.4**).

5.4.4 Cyberculture and the body

What is virtual technology?

Let us return to the computer, and Alan Turing's definition of the computer as a 'universal machine'. What this means is that any programmable function can be implemented on a universal machine. It is the medium in which Leibniz's universal calculus is finally installed (**5.3.5**). Woolley suggests therefore that the computer itself is a 'virtual machine':

5.3.5 Life and intelligence in the digital age

> [the computer] is an abstract entity or process that has found physical expression. It is a simulation, only not necessarily a simulation of anything actual.
>
> (Woolley 1992: 68–69)

This is not to say that in some sense the computer does not exist, but rather that, like Simondon's complex machines, it exists primarily in a virtual state. Only component functions of the computer or the complex machine are ever actualised, rather than the whole machine. Of course, this does not mean that the computer as such is not actual, but only that it is never actual as the totality of functions of which it is capable. In this sense, the computer itself serves as a paradigm case of a virtual technology, but at the cost of alerting us to the fact that, as Simondon suggests, all complex machines – technologies that contain technological parts – are also themselves virtual machines in the same sense: technological parts can be separated and recombined endlessly, without exhausting their virtual functions in any given combination of them. Nevertheless, the actual machine does not contain these virtual functions as actual components of itself; the virtual components of a machine are real insofar as they are virtual, since the actual machine does have a specific function. Simondon's point is that in reality this is not all there is to it. The virtual, as Deleuze puts it, is like structure; it cannot be considered actual in itself but must be considered a real part of the machine, since if it were not the machine would have no structure.

Unlike nominalism, then, this view cannot reduce structure to a helpful name for an abstract account of a thing. For a nominalist, a machine does not have a structure like humans have skeletons, but has a structure insofar as it can be analysed in structural terms. The Deleuze–Simondon–cyberneticist view is therefore called realist insofar as it takes the virtual to be real in itself, and not to depend on what is actual for its reality. Everything virtual is real, in Deleuze's crystal-clear formulation of virtual realism: 'the virtual is not opposed to the real, but to the actual' ([1968] 1994: 208).

5.4.3 Cybernetics and culture

Crisis technology

In **5.1**, we discussed the view that cyberculture represents in some sense a revolutionary moment in the history of technology, and that cybernetic machines are therefore 'crisis technologies'. These terms, as stated in **5.3.3**, stem from historian and philosopher of science Thomas Kuhn's famous account of *The Structure of Scientific Revolutions* (1962). Kuhn's theory slices the history of scientific inquiry into two distinct periods: normal science, during which work goes on as usual, and crisis science, during which more questions than answers accumulate, and the basic theories and assumptions held by science – what Kuhn calls a scientific paradigm – come in for interrogation. Following a period of crisis science there occurs a scientific revolution or 'paradigm shift'. Crucially, Kuhn claims that the questions asked by scientists under the old paradigm can no longer be asked in the new one: the objects investigated under the old paradigm are simply no longer members of the new paradigm. Scientific paradigms are therefore **incommensurable** – literally, they lack all common standard of measure. A contemporary chemist, for example, has not acquired a better means to measure the ether; for the contemporary chemist, the ether does not exist, although it did until the early twentieth century.

The example of the ether makes clear the extent to which the objects of scientific scrutiny have a contested reality: such objects are deemed by Kuhnian accounts of science to have no independent reality, but rather to be theory-dependent. It is useless, say Kuhnians, to debate the extra-theoretical reality of theory-dependent entities (such as ether, or the thousands of species of subatomic particles physicists hypothesise about), since it is their usefulness to a dominant theory that establishes their status as real (useful). It is for this reason that Kuhnian accounts of science are antirealist (we would contemporarily say **constructionist**) concerning the objects of that science.

Although the question of technology differs from that of scientific objects insofar as technologies are uncontroversially real, there are important parallels with Kuhn's antirealist story of science. It is only at points of crisis in the development of new technologies that they become subject to investigation as such. During periods of normal technology the machines are deselected as objects of theoretical scrutiny, prompting accounts of them that emphasise their social constructedness in accordance with broader contexts of their political and social usefulness to a particular project. This is precisely the account of technology that Williams, for example, offers. Such accounts of technology are importantly anti-realist in that they argue machines are themselves socially or politically dependent, since their reality is a matter of *how they are implemented or deployed*, rather than a question pertaining to technology itself. It is only during periods of rapid technological change, or 'crisis technology', that machines seem to rise up and confront us as 'an alien power, as the power of the machine itself' (Marx 1993: 693). Anti-realists would argue that to be realist about machines in such a manner amounts to abstracting them from all social context, or to being duped into thinking that the purposes given to the machines by their developers and deployers are somehow purposes that inhere in the machines themselves. Realists, meanwhile, would argue that the question of the determination of a given machine to a specific purpose (manufacture, militarism, etc.) is secondary to the capacities of the machine itself, as Simondon, for example, argues (**5.4.2**).

Whichever line of argument we take it is important to realise that the argument arises only in the context of crisis technology and almost never in that of normal technology. In other words, it is only because of technological change that such arguments are made.

5.1 Cyberculture and cybernetics

5.3.3 Self-augmenting engines: steampower against nature

5.4.2 Cybernetics and the virtual

Figurative technology

The arguments that we are exploring in this section, that technologies have determinations beyond, or independently of, their social uses, can be called realist arguments. To grasp what is involved here it is important to understand the thinking behind 'anti-realist' or 'constructionist' viewpoints, in the sense these terms acquire from Kuhn's account of the history of science.

We can do this by considering the work of Claudia Springer. In her analysis of the concept and popular figure of the cyborg (1996), Springer argues that the most culturally representative cyborg in existence is Arnold Schwarzenegger. This is not just because he played the Terminator in the films of the same name, but also because his own, living, muscular body suggests the figure of the cyborg: it is a machined body, armoured against breakdown, whether by metal or muscle. The question is *how* has this body come to stand for the cyborg? Surprisingly, perhaps, Springer argues that the cyborg-status of Schwarzenegger's body is conferred upon it by commercial cinema's maintenance of conventional gender roles. The cinematic cyborg carries the cultural ideal of the masculine gender to its logical conclusion as a body armoured against intrusion and weakness, hard and unstoppable. Cyborgs are not really machines, therefore, but culturally forceful figures that reinstate a model of masculinity that can be traced back to the masculine ideal of the armoured, military body (see Theweleit 1986).

Springer's concern is not therefore to account for the cyborg as a technological possibility or actuality, but to locate it within the broader social and gendered relations that give rise to it. It is important to realise that constructionist and technologically anti-realist accounts such as Springer's are not confined to analysing *fictional* cyborgs. On the contrary, they emphasise the social constructedness of 'real' cyborgs. Springer also subjects scientific research into artificial intelligence (**5.3.5**) to the same analysis as she brings to bear upon filmic representations. Debates, for example, about the nature of human consciousness have a long history of separating 'mind' from 'body', which have in turn informed constructions of gender by associating the female with the body and the male with the mind, and have elevated cognitive above sexual activity. In this way the task for the anti-realist or constructionist cultural analyst is to see how the historical gendering of the mind and body is being manifested and continues in cyberculture – in the claim that interactive media are more active (male and intellectually alert) rather than passive (female and bodily), or in AI research, in which (certainly in its classical variant – **5.3.5**) scientists seek intelligence in software (mind, male) rather than wetware (body, female). As a consequence, such constructionist analysis is in danger of making it seem irrelevant whether AI is actually real, or whether it is a project, a dream, a fantasy or a fiction. For the cultural constructionist they all share and promote the same sexist ideology at work in society at large.

Ideological technology

Our third example of constructionist accounts of technology is accounts which seek to show that ideas about the progressive power, the inevitability or autonomy of technology, are driven and shaped by capitalism. Such ideas about technology are seen to be an expression of an economic and political system pursuing its own interests in extracting profit out of human labour. Such accounts argue that we are presented with a false picture of the inevitability of things, which prevents us from overthrowing the tyranny of machines over human beings, and that, therefore, the determinist view, or picture of how things stand, is ideological. There is a long tradition of such accounts of the effects of technology on society which stems from the economic and social theories of Marx.

5.3.5 Life and intelligence in the digital age

For further constructionist, antirealist accounts of technology, see Terranova (1996b), Ross (1991), Balsamo (1996), and, to a large extent, any work based on Haraway's famous account of the 'cyborg myth' (1991)

Such accounts share with the 'figurative' kind the agenda of political criticism of technology: for both, technology has no independent reality outside of the social relations that form it. To political analysts of technology, history demonstrates that the horror and social pandemonium produced by the onslaught of new machinery are symptoms of the social agendas of those that deploy it. Thus, if we look at the rise of the factory during the Enlightenment period (**5.3.4**), we can see that technology serves both as a means and as an ideal for organising the production of goods. The distinction drawn between mechanical and intellectual labour not only separates humanity from machines but also separates control from productive activity. Workers become cogs in a machine whose design reflects the social and economic agenda of factory owners. To the owners, this is merely the establishment of an appropriate social order, reflecting the priority of mind over muscle. On the other hand, for the workers, the machine is a new and inhuman governor of their lives and their labour. However, accounts of technology as ideology will argue that both views, those of the capitalist and those of the labourer, are false. This is because the owners are wrong when they claim that technology embodies rationality and social order, and the worker has a false relation to the same machinery insofar as the new order s/he experiences is not an irrevocable force of governance but a potential means to reorganise human work and productive activity.

So the primary aim of such accounts is to insist that technology can only be understood within the context of the organisation of human productive activity. Further, they will argue that accounts that fail to do this are ideological, not real. However, from the kind of 'realist' standpoint that we have been outlining in the previous sections, the purpose of such criticism of technology as ideology is not able to establish the true nature of technology itself; rather, it is concerned to reveal technology's uses and revolutionary potentials, and the forms of organisation it makes possible.

Such a view of technology stems ultimately from Marx's analyses of machinery as 'dead labour', and informs much cultural analysis of technology.

For such accounts, the distortions of human life introduced by technology can only be understood against the historical constant of human productive activity itself. It is thus only by 'revolutionising the mode of production' (Marx and Engels 1973: 104) that the interests of all human beings as workers will be put before those of the owners of technology and seekers of profit, allowing technology to be used for wider human ends.

THE FRANKFURT SCHOOL AND TECHNOLOGICAL RATIONALITY

The social theorists and philosophers of the Frankfurt School – chiefly, Adorno and Horkheimer (1996), along with Marcuse (1968) and their successor Habermas (1970) – extend the humanistic basis of the Marxist account of technology with their critique of what they call 'technological rationality' or 'instrumental reason'. They see such technological rationality or 'instrumental reason' exemplified in the military and in economic production. Importantly, they also see it in the 'culture industry', where the arts, humanities and critical thought ceased to be questioning or subversive of the established social order, and became instead so many commodities produced for a mass market.

They argue that instrumental reasoning has no other purpose than achieving goals, and that this leads to a radical impoverishment of the possibilities of thought, culture and social life. Everything becomes a machine, not merely metaphorically but in its fundamental modes of operation.

They see the roots of this situation in the eighteenth-century Enlightenment (Adorno and Horkheimer 1996), where the glorification of pure reason removed social constraints such as religion or objective morality from its use and at the same time therefore, with nothing else to

---

5.3.4 The construction of inanimate reason

Two members of the Frankfurt School, Marcuse (1968) and Habermas (1970), reject the idea that science and technology are necessarily symptoms or products of instrumental reason. Thus Marcuse calls for alternative sciences and technologies, while Habermas calls for a rethinking of how they are deployed, and the means by which their deployment is rationally constrained. Putting forward a view of rationality concerned with communication rather than with means–ends (instrumental) reasoning, therefore, Habermas advocates the creation of discursive institutions to humanise the applications of science and technology, leading, he proposes, towards a more generous conception of rationality than Horkheimer and Adorno allow for

Feenberg (1991) provides a recent version of this account of technology. It is worth noting that Habermas's own successor, Niklas Luhmann (1995), rejects the critical approach common to Habermas and the earlier Frankfurt School, and instead conceives of 'social systems' in a broadly cybernetic model

aim for, ends up establishing reason as a means to achieve a subject's purposes, whatever they may be. In terms of reason alone, they argue, a situation is reached where there is no longer any difference between making a film, wooing a lover, or engineering the Final Solution.

In short, all are plans transformed into actions, and their rationality is measured merely in the appropriateness of the means to ends. Under the tyranny of instrumental reason, Adorno and Horkheimer (1996) argue, all culture becomes mechanical, and technological and scientific advance is merely symptomatic of this instrumentalisation.

All these accounts conceive of technology as a symptom of broader social issues. Adorno and Horkheimer see technology as, above all else, an expression of an increasingly instrumental culture in which goals have become separated from wider human and moral values. They urge that this situation can only be thwarted by a radical project of self-criticism on the part of that culture as a whole (a prospect of which Adorno was massively sceptical), while Habermas considers the uses of technology as potentially reflecting a broader and non-instrumental usage of human reasoning (1970). At the basis of each of these accounts of technology, therefore, there lies a conception of a properly human life laid waste by a technology under the sway of 'inhuman' capitalism or mechanised thought. Therefore accounts that focus on opposing humans and machines tend to be antirealist about technology in order to emphasise the priority of their human users. The question we must ask, therefore, is whether these accounts constitute theories of technology at all, or whether instead they are theories of human nature (as in Marx) or human culture (as in Springer, in Adorno and Horkheimer, in Marcuse and in Habermas).

5.4.4 Cyberculture and the body

Disembodiment

It has been a commonplace anti-realist criticism of cyberculture in general and cyberpunk fiction in particular that it promotes a new form of disembodied, purely mental existence. By asking the vexing question 'What do cyborgs eat?', for example, Margaret Morse (1994) highlights the tendency to repudiate the body that can be found throughout cybercultural phenomena, from the magazine *Mondo 2000* to William Gibson's *Neuromancer*. Other critics have been less cautious in their formulations, leading some to insist on the dangerous 'disembodied ditziness' (Sobchack 1993: 583) inherent in cyberpunk; or to follow Springer (1996: 306) in disparaging its 'willed obliteration of bodies'; or merely to entertain 'the possibility of a mind independent of the biology of bodies' (Bukatman 1993: 208) ambivalently proffered by cyberspace.

But what would such a thing as 'a mind released from the mortal limitations of the flesh' (Bukatman 1993: 208) be? Not only is a disembodied mental existence, Bukatman's version of cyberspace as a 'celebration of spirit', a facile misunderstanding of cybernetics, it is also inconceivable unless we acknowledge, with Descartes and popular Christian mythology, that mind, spirit or what have you *could* have independent, that is, non-biological existence. Bukatman seeks to get around this cartesianism by stating that in cyberspace, although 'consciousness becomes separated from the body . . ., it becomes a body itself' (1993: 210); but this does little more than reiterate Descartes' argument that mind, though immaterial, is nonetheless a *thing* (*res cogitans*), albeit in less clear terms.

Meanwhile, Gibson's fiction, the repeated target of critics of cyberpunk's supposed advocacy of 'the bodiless exultation of cyberspace' (Gibson 1986: 12), takes considerable care to position such views of the possibilities of cyberspace within the perspective of Case, the 'console cowboy', who, as a result of an assault on his nervous system by a nervetoxin given him as a punishment, is now reduced to living as an exile from cyberspace, in the 'prison of his own flesh'. In other words, such positions are given as a character's mourning for a loss that was itself *physically* induced by way of the nerve-toxin. Possibilities for alternative or enhanced embodiment are presented throughout the novel as poor substitutes, despite their technological sophistication, for the sheer complexity, the 'infinite intricacy' of the body's bio-chemical structure (Gibson 1986: 285).

Bukatman's gestures towards the possible impact of complex technologies on the modes of survival of organic bodies, along with the criticisms of cyberpunk's 'disembodied ditziness', seem to fall between two chairs: the reflex criticism of received mind–body dualism, and maintaining an *ambivalence* as regards these possibilities. Gibson's own fictions may often seem to share this sophisticated blend of cultural criticism, the heady potentials of comput-ing technology, and embodied, animal ambivalence; however, Case's realisation of the body's importance is based not on its animal confrontation with a technological world but instead on the degrees of complexity afforded by technological with regard to biological platforms. When, for example, Dixie, an artificial intelligence or uploaded personality ('ROM construct'), asks Case to do him a favour and 'erase this goddam thing' (1986: 130), it is because of the poor fit between the construct's memories and his actuality. His entire body has been removed, like his friend's frostbitten thumb, and the newly immobile program *feels* its absence, albeit artificially. This points to limitations in the technological platform that are not inherent in it, indicating instead a relative paucity of information as compared with the bio-logical body. Conceiving of the issue of the relation between body and technology in this manner does not create essentialist divisions between the two, but rather places both on the properly cybernetic footing of informational complexity.

These instances create a context in which it makes sense to interrogate the place of the body in cyberculture. To be sure, there has been a great deal of such interrogation (**5.3**): questions regarding the nature of cyborg bodies, the role of physical activity in VR, and the sexuality of online avatars, have excited a great deal of comment in the last few years. However, perhaps by virtue of the critical component of cultural analysis, such accounts have in the main remained within the ambit of humanism, even if their principal agenda is to advocate 'posthumanism'. While this latter term is more often employed by the more evangelical wings of cyberculture (such as the Extropians, *Mondo 2000*, or Timothy Leary), it has also been subject to more critical scrutiny in, for example, N. Katherine Hayles's *How We Became Posthuman* (1999). As the pronoun in Hayles's title indicates, the concern of posthumanism, whether critical or evangelical, still orbits around the centre of human being, making such an approach extremely vulnerable to Marxist or Frankfurt School criticism. However, if we examine the manner in which Gibson's fiction relates biology and technology, we see that it does not centre around the question 'what is it to be human?', but rather, 'what is the relative complexity of information as encoded by biological and technological objects?' As discussed above (**5.4.2**), there has been a sig-nificant intertwining of biology and information technology since the late 1940s, which has taken the contemporary forms of genomics, on the one hand, and biotechnology, on the other. Apart from the fact that such questions are implicit in that text of Gibson's most often criticised for its anti-body, pro-technology, culturally and historically masculinist dualism, but have not received the same critical attention, there are two further reasons to pursue such an approach:

1   It avoids the pitfalls of treating new technologies, and the changes that ramify from them, in terms of the critical models these technologies contest.

5.3 Biological technologies: the history of automata

5.4.2 Cybernetics and the virtual

2   It attempts to integrate cyberculture as a purely cultural phenomenon with scientific and technological attempts to eradicate the boundary between biology and technology.

Finally, if (1) is a *theoretical issue*, (2) invests this theory with a practical significance: that is, whatever the theoretical adequacy of the models used by cultural and media studies, commercial biotechnology has already condemned humanism to history, and is challenging discursive with physical **constructionism**.

Cybernetic bodies 1: gaming, interactivity and feedback

Gibson has often been reported as remarking that the idea of cyberspace came by noticing the way that videogamers were involved with their machines. Given that this is the situation from which Gibson began to populate cyberspace with novel bio-technological entities, it makes sense to begin our examination of cybernetic bodies by revisiting that games arcade in Vancouver:

> I could see in the physical intensity of their postures how *rapt* the kids inside were. It was like one of those closed systems out of a Pynchon novel: a feedback loop with photons coming off the screens into the kids' eyes, neurones moving through their bodies, and electrons moving through the video game.
>
> (Gibson, in McCaffery 1992: 272)

Again, just as with the biological and the technological objects discussed immediately above, we do not see here two complete and sealed-off entities: the player on the one hand and the game on the other. Rather, there is an interchange of information and energy, forming a new circuit. Although this is merely a description of an impression, it poses a question concerning the much-hyped property of interactivity (**1.2.2**) in computer gaming: what if the relation between user, program and technology were closer to the cybernetic circuit Gibson describes than to the voluntarist narrative underpinning the options, choices and decisions on the part of the user such games are said to demand?

1.2.2 Interactivity

In a cybernetic circuit there is no point of origin for any action that circuit performs. In other words, it would make little sense to talk of one component of a circuit initiating that circuit. By definition, a circuit consists in a constancy of action and reaction. In gaming, for example, not only is there the photon–neurone–electron circuit Gibson evokes, there are also macroscopically physical components of that circuit, such as the motions of finger, mouse or stick. Motions of a finger, prompted as much by changes in the display as by any 'free will' on the part of the player, also provoke series of neuroelectrical pulses resulting in hand–arm–shoulder–neck movement, even in wholebody motion, for which the individual whose body it is, is far from responsible. Through the tactile and visual interface with the machine, the entire body is determined to move by *being part of the circuit of the game*, being, as it were, *in the loop*. If games in general, as McLuhan suggests, are 'machine[s] that can get into action only if the players consent to become puppets for a time' (1967: 253), this is true above all of computer gaming, where users become, in Gibson's terms, 'meat puppets' by virtue of their dependency on the physical aspects of the circuit.

See **5.4.1** for Deleuze's emphasis on the cybernetic idea of the shortest circuit

5.4.1 Cybernetics and human–machine relations

Noting that cybernetic control works by eliminating possible actions rather than prompting particular ones (**5.4.1**), we begin to gain a picture of what is physically going on in gaming: the circuit serves to reduce the possibilities of motion and action and to amplify the remaining actions through a delicate balance of feedback mechanisms: just enough positive feedback to produce local changes, and enough negative feedback to ensure global stability on the part of the game circuits. Cybernetically, then, interactivity is a false description of a process of the programmed elimination of possible actions, not of creating possibilities of actions.

The most important aspect of this account of gaming is that it shifts attention from the interactions between two discrete entities towards the cybernetic processes that, as it were, edit parts from each to create an indissociable circuit of informational-energetic exchange. Gaming, we could say, is here not an action, nor even an *inter-action*, but literally a *passion* – a 'being-acted-upon'. Consider the extent to which cultural and media studies argues for a conception of the viewer, user or spectator as active. Even interactivity (as we noted in **5.4.3**) contains a measure of activity that makes it a more desirable state than passivity. This is because, when one is passive, one is acted upon. This sense of 'passivity' draws on the root of the word – *pathe* – which it shares with 'pathology', 'sym-pathy', 'patient', and so on. In ancient Greek philosophy, if a person was 'pathic' they were precisely being acted upon. However, there is another sense of 'passion', involving an absorbing pleasure that blinds the 'patient' to everything else. It is in *both* senses that the term can be used here; as a passion in which the gamer surrenders to being acted upon by the game, its apparatus, its signs, its action-prompts and so on. The term thus preserves the 'inter' of 'interactivity', and yet instead of ascribing the hard duty of action to the gamer, ascribes to her a passion for letting the game take her over. It is surely this that Gibson saw in the Vancouver arcade.

Of course, even if we accept this reformulation of what happens in gaming as a cyber-netic circuit, we also have to recognise that such circuits are temporary, coming into operation, if recurrently, for only a matter of minutes or hours, apparently far removed from the cyborgs we are said to become as we grow more intimate with our machines. However, we have such machine-passions in all our technological interactions; as McLuhan noted, for example, 'one of the benefits of motivation research has been the revelation of man's sex rela-tion to the motorcar' (1967: 56). It is the passional conduct of gaming that explains the 'rapt' physical intensity of the players Gibson saw in the Vancouver arcade; but it also suggests something much broader concerning human–machine relations, on the one hand, and the dependent circuits formed by parts of each, on the other. That is, it suggests that cybernetic bodies are not whole organic bodies that have technological parts added to them, but bodies which have abstracted from them into passional circuits with parts of other bodies.

In many ways, arguments about interactivity replay those concerned with whether tech-nology or human, social purposes form the principal historical actors: whichever way we argue these cases, we conclude that one, and only one, component of human–machine rela-tions contributes action to history, while the other plays a merely supporting role, and is acted upon by the active one. Such concerns are explicit in Marx, for example, when he writes that with industrial machinery, man 'steps to the side of the production process, instead of being its chief actor' (1993: 705), and in the very idea of machinery as 'self-activating objectified labour' (1993: 695). Indeed, the entire history of technology amounts to a series of attempts to produce precisely this kind of self-acting machine (**5.3**). Thus, in its broadest terms, the ideal of interactivity is an attempt to resolve the confrontation of machine and human into a more collaborative view of history. In the same terms, the cybernetic view of gaming is also non-confrontational; but it is less collaborative than it is constructivist – that is, it is concerned with the formation of new circuits. In terms that Deleuze and Guattari borrow from Monod, cybernetics is **molecular** rather than **molar**: it concerns the small circuits of photons, neu-rones and electrons rather than relations between a ready-made and whole subject, on the one hand, and its incomplete, otherwise inert technological objects on the other.

5.4.3 Cybernetics and culture

5.3 Biological technologies: the history of automata

Cybernetic bodies 2: prosthetics and constructivism

Accounts of actual cyborgs often begin by focusing on the prosthetic devices we regularly incorporate into our bodies, or that are formed by incorporating our bodies into larger technological devices. Effectively a version of the theory that technology constitutes a physiological or sensory extension of our bodies (**1.6.4**, **5.4.2**), such an account will tend to highlight how it is that humans have already become cyborgs through the use of pacemakers, contact lenses, hearing aids and prosthetic limbs, on the one hand, and of cars, factories and cities on the other. The general point being made in such accounts is that humans are no longer separable from the technologies that biologically and environmentally saturate our lives. In contrast with the 'molecular' account of gaming above, we can call this a 'molar' account of the cyborg, since it concentrates on whole machines that become part of us (pacemakers etc.), or that we form part of (cars etc.). In other words, it maintains that cyborg bodies are formed by the incorporation of whole bodies into whole machines, and vice versa. Indeed, this is characteristic of the extension theory of technology in general: there must be something to be extended, and something to do the extending.

However, if we take the example of gameplaying used above, in what sense can the cybernetic body thus formed be accounted for within the extensionalist or prosthetic theory of the cyborg? Instead of looking at what physiological or sensory functions of the organic body are extended by the prosthetic of the machine, we focused on the loop of constant information and energy exchange formed between parts of the machine and parts of the user's body. An example will be useful to make the issues clear. Just as the gaming example was drawn from fiction, so this example will be drawn from the arts.

The artist Stelarc stages performances in which various mechanical and digitally controlled devices are attached to his body. On the surface, then, this looks like a classic, prosthetic case of extensionalism. One such device is called the Stimbod. The Stimbod is a 'touch screen muscle stimulation system' (Stelarc 2000: 568), a computer map of the performer's body, attached to it by electrodes and stimulators. By touching points on this map of the body, the performer's body is in turn stimulated to move (hence 'Stimbod') by an electrical current sent through the electrodes attached to that body. This turns the performer's body into an 'involuntary body'. In one sense, it is clear that the performer's body has its sensory field and muscular activation extended by the Stimbod, since by virtue of the machine it is subject to stimuli it would otherwise not receive. On the other hand, the Stimbod connects muscles, sensors, pixels and finger into an electrical-informational circuit that does not so much change the existing body as construct a new one. Further components, moreover, can be added: in 1995 Stelarc put the Stimbod on the web and attached the sensors and stimulators to the involuntary body, allowing remote access to that body's musculature. Similarly, by recording the motions thus produced, a muscular memory is effectively produced *in the computer* which can be deployed independently of the touch-screen interface. Stelarc calls this new body a 'collaborative physiology' (2000: 569), making it clear that, rather than simply extending an existing organic body with a technological one, a *new physiological entity* is thus constructed from this network of organic and technological parts, combined into a circuit of information and energy exchange.

As with the gaming circuit, the Stimbod-Involuntary Body circuit remains impermanent; it is something from which the performer's body, like the gamer's, can be detached whole and unchanged. The technological components in this sense remain prosthetic. It is also important to note, however, the sense Stelarc's performances give to the idea of the *construction* of cybernetic bodies from physical parts of heterogeneous origin. Here the construction is not only molar, composed of whole entities, but also molecular, composing the body of the performance.

1.6.4 The many virtues of Saint McLuhan
5.4.2 Cybernetics and the virtual

See **5.4.2** for the role of cybernetics in biological theory in general, and biotechnology in particular

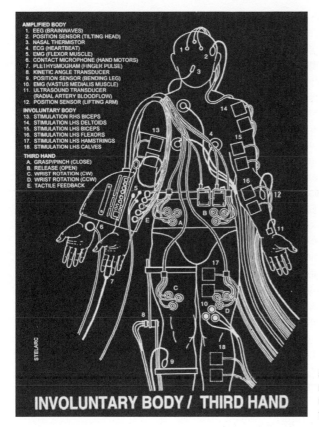

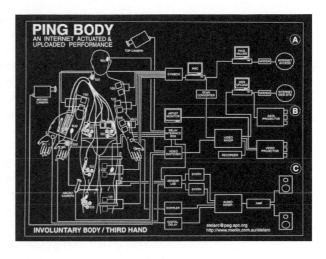

5.17 Stelarc's STIMBOD – a touch-screen interface for the remote manipulation of the body. Information from the touch-screen is sent to receptors attached to the body's muscles, and a signal from these stimulates the muscle to contract, forcing the body to move.

By dint of the separability of bodies, such phenomena as gaming and the Stimbod do not seem to back up claims made to the effect that the cyborg marks the 'end of humanity' in some sense. Stelarc himself, echoing claims made by cyberneticists such as Kevin Warwick, notes that technology potentially transforms the relationship between the evolution of the species and the physical alteration of its members. Technology, he writes, 'provides each person with the potential to progress individually'. Because one can technologically transform one's body, and since the limits of such transformations are marked only by technological thresholds and questions of surgical practice, the technological transformation of the human body will mean that 'it is no longer of advantage to either remain "human" or evolve as a species' (2000: 563).

To some extent, such an approach to the cybernetic body underscores an agenda it shares with biotechnology. Just as for Stelarc the problems of the human body stem from its inefficiency with regard to the technological environment it has fashioned, so, as its name implies, for biotechnology, the difference between biological and technological objects has all but disappeared: biological components carry out specific tasks, and are therefore subject to replacement by technological parts (such as pacemakers) that perform those same functions, or can themselves be deployed in contexts other than those in which they naturally function. In this context, we may consider the stem cell. Stem cells are undifferentiated according to particular functions, but differentiate into the various tissues and muscles only later in the development of the organic body. Biotechnologists therefore reason that undeveloped stem cells may be used to 'regrow' damaged areas of the body, irrespective of what areas these are. Although this has recently been attempted as a cure for Parkinson's disease, and met with disastrous results (patients reported a marked improvement in their condition throughout the first year following treatment, but subsequently developed new disorders as the stem cells continued to grow, leaving the biotechnologists and surgeons with no clue as to what to do to halt this runaway process), what is important from the present perspective is the sense that biological entities have become, under biotechnology, components for the technological reconstruction of bodies.

Cloning presents a similar attitude to the technology of the body: cells whose nuclei have been removed can be turned into engines for the production of new creatures by means of refilling the empty cell with new nucleic material. The biotechnological procedure known as transgenics, for example, often fills thus enucleated cells with hybrid genetic matter, so that we can 'grow' pigs with human DNA, making inter-species organ transplants possible by diminishing the risk of the host body's rejection of foreign organic matter.

We can see then that all biotechnological phenomena emphasise the proximity between biological and technological function, just as the uses of technology in altering or complementing human biology can potentially be indefinitely extended. In both cases, we note a use of constructivism that, unlike its discursive or ideological variant, is profoundly physical. Both non-organic technology and biotechnology provide means for constructing or reconstructing bodies that go beyond the limits of the prosthetic devices that provide us with examples of actual cyborgs. This helps to clear up the reason we may feel that while *technically* a woman with a pacemaker *may* be defined as a cyborg, this is a kind of loose extension of the term, and is not really what we mean by it. A wholly constructed creature composed of biological and technological components, on the other hand, is exactly what we mean by the cyborg.

5.4.5 Implications for the humanities

As we conclude this section, it is worth revisiting two issues arising from the examples selected:

1   the relation between individual and social biotechnological constructivism;

2   the question of cyberculture's often criticised quest for disembodiment.

The relation between individual and social biotechnological construction

Once we have absorbed the various ways in which cyborgs can be constructed, we begin to notice that even now there are issues affecting the likely paths such constructivism will follow. We noted above that Stelarc suggests that technology provides the individual with the potential to progress apart from the species' evolutionary processes. Stelarc thus raises a fundamental problem concerning the relation between constructivism and freedom. We can best approach this issue by way of the example of cosmetic surgery.

Most cosmetic surgeries fall into two types: first, reconstructive surgery, following a burn or some other accident, and second, elective surgery, which concerns the removal of undesired features, or the creation of desirable ones. The first is palliative, undoing damage done to a body; the second is aesthetic, remodelling the face and gross body parts in accordance with an ideal. The last of these is perhaps the second millennium's version of pre-photographic portraiture, in which the artist commissioned would abide by the wishes of his patron-sitter to 'iron out' or 'improve' aspects of the sitter's appearance for purposes of producing a better portrait. That cosmetic surgery does approach the condition of art is often noted, and a London reconstructive surgeon recently employed a portraitist to capture his work in various stages of completion, providing his patients or subjects with a non-clinical visual account of their progress.

Like portraiture in painting, elective surgery has also tended to correspond to certain ideals of 'beauty': how long will it be before we see a rise in the fortunes of Rubensesque elective surgical techniques? To highlight this fact, the French performance artist Orlan subjects her face to frequent surgical alterations that *do not* correspond to these ideals; instead, she implants horns, ridges, and other grotesque features into her face. Similarly, the surgeon who provided artist Mark Pauline, of the Survival Research Laboratories, with a prosthetic thumb to replace the one he lost during a performance, later became disenchanted with medicine for its lack of creativity, despite its plastic potential, and joined the artist's group.

Such examples of the proximity of art and surgery remind us of the body's plasticity, its malleability, and thus pose a question to elective surgery: why treat it as a means to impose an ideal upon one's face and body rather than using it to treat the body as a site of experiment, as both Orlan and Stelarc do? Of course, posing such a question, as Orlan explicitly does, has the effect of highlighting the gendered social pressures that result in the maintainance of the ideal female form by surgical means. As she puts it in the text of one of her performances, 'I Do Not Want to Look Like . . .':

> many damaged faces have been reconstructed and many people have had organ transplants; and how many more noses have been remade or shortened, not so much for physical problems as for psychological ones? Are we still convinced that we should bend to the determinations of nature? This lottery of arbitrarily distributed genes . . .
>
> (Orlan 1995: 10)

As does Stelarc, Orlan proposes her work as a plastic challenge to nature's provision; unlike Stelarc, her work also engages the social pressures on women's bodies, and so does not place as much weight on the category 'individual' as does the former. Nonetheless, Stelarc's work does confront and name a major social issue concerning the age of constructivism both he and Orlan usher in. 'In this age of information overload', he writes,

> what is significant is no longer freedom of ideas, but freedom of form . . . The question is not whether society will allow people freedom of expression, but whether the human species will allow individuals to construct alternate genetic coding.
>
> (Stelarc 2000: 561)

Stelarc effectively recasts the issue of human freedom in biotechnological terms. Biotechnology itself, however, has other ideas. The recent competition between the public sector, in the form of the Wellcome Institute, and the private sector, in the form of Celera Genomics, Inc., to decode the human genome has predictably resulted in victory for the latter. While the significance of this event itself is great as regards the future of state health-care provision and drug or treatment prices, it is of importance here insofar as it demonstrates that the pressure against the biotechnological individual freedom Stelarc champions is likely to come from the corporate environments that can afford to sponsor the research. If biotechnology in general is producing a more constructivist ethos as regards the human body, then one of the major components of this constructivism will be financial. Perhaps species-difference will replace class as the front line of constructivist social struggle.

Cyberculture's quest for disembodiment

Finally, we are now in a position to return to the issue raised at the beginning of **5.4.4** concerning cyberculture's quest for disembodiment. While there may be a *sense* of disembodiment attaching to the use of computers for accessing cyberspace, the gaming example that Gibson provides, and our exploration of it, shows that far from disembodiment it is a question of the constitution of other, cybernetic circuits. Indeed, cyberculture in general is a highly physicalist environment in which the lines dividing biology from technology are erased by biotechnology, art and surgery. If cyberculture has a bias, then, it is not towards disembodiment but towards physicality. As Bruce Sterling (in Gibson 1988: xii) says concerning cyberpunk fiction, the traditional 'yawning gulf between . . . literary culture, the formal world of art and politics, and the culture of science, the world of engineering and industry' is crumbling, and in its place looms the cybernetic culture that combines them.

The challenges posed by cyberculture, then, consist not only in providing theories that can articulate the products or texts of that culture, but in providing theories that can reintegrate the long-severed intellectual and practical relations between the worlds of science, engineering, technology and the humanities. It is for that reason that this final part of the book has taken a broad view of cyberculture, as Sterling asserts cyberpunk does, and has included the history and philosophy of science and technology, alongside theoretical questions arising from both the humanities and the scientific contexts concerning the cybernetic objects that are not only a part of popular culture but actually populate our world.

5.4.6 A plea for realism: on causes in culture

'What is technology?' Some proposals and conclusions

In asking the question '*what is technology*?', we have pursued a single string of arguments throughout this section (because these arguments are pursued throughout the section, the section numbers following each proposition below (**P1-4**) are intended only to provide the reader with initial statements of each):

1   that culture is not a domain separable from nature, since nature underlies the very possibility of any culture at all (**5.1.7–5.1.8**);

2   that technology can no more be separated from nature (it depends on physical laws) than from culture (it *possibilises* cultural expression and expression-possibilising technologies are referred to as *media*) (**5.1.6**);

3   that media do not exhaust the field of cultural technologies (**5.1.9**); and

4   that in consequence, approaches to technology deriving from the culturalism that tends to define post-Williams cultural and media studies are importantly flawed (**5.1.10**).

These arguments have been augmented by pursuing technological histories other than those expressly belonging to media histories. Hence our detailed examination of **artificial life** (**5.3**) has not only concentrated on its contemporary, digital expression, but equally on the hydraulic, clockwork, and thermal approaches by means of which the same problem has been approached throughout history. What conclusions can we draw from all this?

An initial conclusion we hope the reader will have drawn is that things are more complex than their names suggest. When we call something a 'medium', a 'machine', a 'subject', an 'agent' or a 'cause', what we are thus naming may not resemble the ideas we may previously have formed about it. As an example, consider the differences between the chess-playing automata discussed in **Case study 5.1**, and the passional, gaming 'cyborgs' we analysed in **5.4.4**: while the former are clearly separable machines, the latter consist in circuits of organic and non-organic elements – eyes, brains, fingers, nerves and screens, pixels, electrons and circuitries – forming a 'whole' that is neither recognisable as a whole nor in any of its parts. How different everything looks if we track its parts, rather than assume it to be the whole it resembles: the passional circuit is not the chance encounter of two ready-made individuals, but a rearrangement of parts from each into a new, and largely invisible, whole. It is such rearrangements, as we have seen in **5.4.2**, that the French philosopher of science and techology Gilbert Simondon says are 'overdetermined' when, under the influence of habitual usage, we reduce the *reality* of the technology used to the function that it possesses through that use, as though its parts were inflexibly tied to that use and incapable of any other functions. Consider for example the novel uses to which a holidaying surgeon on a transatlantic flight put a plastic water bottle, some straws and a miniature of whisky when a fellow passenger suffered a loss of breathing: straw and bottle became and artificial respirator, the wound necessary to insert it sterilised by the whisky. Therefore, to put this conclusion (**C1**) in simple form, we should

C1. *never assume that the names we give things correspond to the things so named.*

What this section proposes, then, is that technology consists in a rearrangement of existing parts, some from nature, some from culture, some from existing technologies. What unites these parts, as the example of the 'passional circuits' we encountered in our analysis of gaming (**5.4.4**), is a flow of energy diverting the course of causes and effects into new arrangements.

In addition to Simondon's theory of complex technologies and the discussion of 'passional circuits', consider Jutta Schickore's recent (2007) study of the history of microscopy as an example of what we are examining. The book is entitled *The Microscope and the Eye*, and its title is informative: a history of the microscope on its own might chart its invention, its development, early experiments with it, its eventual uses, and its effects in terms of the progress of scientific knowledge. The microscope would remain, in such a history, an isolated technological artefact, complete in itself, with no relation to its immediate biological environment other than what is revealed concerning it through the microscope's lens. Yet the microscope is inconceivable without the eye through which its findings can be realised; Schickore's book therefore concentrates equally on the eye, on the 'nerves and the retina' (2007: 1) that both made it work, and that the microscope in turn reveals to other eyes. The microscope exploits the properties of glass, brass, nerves, retinas and brains, the sciences of chemistry and biology, and the practises of lens-grinding and industrial manufacture. It is inseparable from the development of science, and from the institutions and practices it unites. The simple recombination of all these elements is precisely what a technology effects.

Take a third example: the Visible Human Project (see also Cartwright in Biagioli, ed., 1999). A human body is cut into nanometer-thin slices, scanned into a computer, and then recombined into a complete, 3-D movable and searchable image of the entire human body. A cutting technology, an imaging technology, and an animating technology are all involved in this artefact's production, of course; but so too are the body thus cut, the penal and judicial systems that made it available, the medical institutions into which this reassembled body has entered its second life. The VHP recombines sciences, legal systems, and biological entities into a multi-parented entity that itself, in turn, re-enters the world as a medical-scientific technology. The key thing is that we do not get at its reality for so long as we consider it through the lenses of resemblance, but only when we consider its complexities, its embededness, its causes and its effects. The technology is not just what produces the VHP, it is also what it effects.

These examples should serve to make concrete the further conclusions this section will draw. But the reader should bear in mind that this is the conclusion to the entirety of this section of the book, and that its roots lie way back at the book's beginnings. We draw our conclusions, therefore, from *all* the examples therefore considered throughout Part 5.

If we now return, then, to the start of our investigations, we come back to the question of the relations between culture, technology and nature with which it began. Critical readers may well have asked themselves, '*why* is it necessary to re-examine these relations?' There are two reasons why we should, the first relatively complex, and the second relatively simple.

To take the complex reason first, we should remind ourselves of what we noted at **5.1.2** (see also the glossary entry on **Realism**) concerning the study of technology in general: 'to be a realist about technology entails asking what technology really is'. This is the realism for which this concluding section pleads: we should attend not simply to the *social constructedness* of technological phenomena, but to the extended effects they create, the causes they exploit and the rearrangement of parts and processes they effect. We have seen that the social constructivism arguments do not achieve this, since they wish to exempt discussion of causality from the analysis of technology. It is therefore necessary, we argue, at least to supplement this with a realist perspective on technology. In presenting these arguments, we draw our terms from their use not in the discussion of cinema genres or the arts, but from their use in the philosophy of science. A realist, in such a context, considers scientific theories to be theories of nature itself, of physical reality, whereas an anti-realist argues we must give up on access to reality since the complexity of our theoretical and experimental apparatus means that we only gain access to what we construct (for a discussion of these terms, see Hacking 1983, and his pointed rejection of anti-realism in Hacking 1999). Insofar as we are here offering arguments against social constructivism, offering realism as the alternative is easily comprehensible. We therefore set out here the argument that this kind of philosophical approach to the problem is not only a helpful, but also a necessary addition to the analysis of technology in culture.

The simpler – or, at least, the more direct – answer to the question *why* we need to re-examine the relations between nature, culture and technology is the following:

C2. *because any address to technology that omits any of these elements can produce at best a partial, and at worst a false account of technology.*

Consider again, for example, Schickore's addition of the eye and the nerve to the history of the microscope: such 'contextual' additions are often simply social – the experimental environment of science conveniently meshes with a political, economic or military agenda, for instance; or the broader history of vision as it involves the arts is considered. Seldom, however, do biological components of technological entities enter into consideration. If we do not take the retina–nerve–brain complex into account when analysing what the microscope is, however, not only are its actual workings only partially presented, but the important bio-technological connection, which embeds the technology not only in culture, but also in nature, is lost. To put the same point more starkly, an approach to technology that asks not *what technology is* but, for example, *how have technologies been imagined or used* can provide at best a portrait of technologies as *imagined* or *used*; or at worst, *not a portrait of technologies at all.*

We might therefore draw the conclusion that technology is *simply not* what cultures imagine it to be. Such a conclusion, however, would be premature, since it would already have decided what technology *is not*, and therefore relies on an implicit assumption about *what it is.* Technology is irreducibly embedded not only in nature, but also in cultural or social systems (consider the role of the penal and judicial systems in the production of the VHP, for instance). From these considerations, we can however conclude the following: that such a portrait of technology is *partial* when this is all it examines, and is *false* when it claims this is *all* technology is. This is the reason we have argued, both in sections **5** and **1.6**, that the 'cultural science' theory of technology, which accounts for it *solely* as a social formation made up of diverse social purposes, is *false* if it is taken as the claim that *such purposes are all that technology is*.

Once again we see why the question 'what is technology' is so important: when this is the question orienting inquiry, the inquirer will be alert to the likely partiality of all stock responses (see the list of such responses in **5.1.3**). This is because, implicit in the question is what we should call a *realist assumption*. To ask 'what is *x*?' – that is, is to ask not just what *x* might appear to be to such-and-such a socially or historically specific group, but rather, what *x* is – is to ask what *x* REALLY is or, in other words, to launch an inquiry into the nature of reality. Again, therefore, from the consideration of technical objects, social and cultural locations and uses, and the biological and mineral actuators of these objects, we arrive at the requirement for a philosophical consideration of the question, as no *partial* answer to it is adequate to its nature.

However, such questions are risky. Asking 'what something *is*' is likely to earn the inquirer the label of 'essentialist', a label that serves in effect to excommunicate that inquirer from the field to which she intended to make her contribution. However, just as we should *never assume that the names we give things correspond to the things themselves* (**C1**), neither should it be assumed that 'essentialism' is what its users and abusers assume it to be. Strictly speaking, an essentialist is one who argues that a thing is what it is because it possesses an unchanging and separable essence. Thus, a human being is a human being because regardless of its accidents (sex, height, weight, colour, etc.), the entity in question satisfies the essence of being human – which, according to Aristotle, for example, is to be a rational, social, talking, featherless biped. Similarly, if the question is 'what is technology?', answering this in such terms as 'the *essence* of technology is . . .', is only one way of answering that question. Therefore,

C3. *not all realism is essentialist.*

What, then, does a realism about technology involve? If answers to this question can be partial, then evidently realism involves not reducing the whole answer to any one of technology's parts (machine, user, context, history, connection with natural causes and artificial effects). This is why we have argued not only that no reducibly culturalist answer to the question 'what is technology?' can be adequate, but also that

C4. *any adequate answer to the question 'what is technology?' must address it both from the cultural and the physical dimensions.*

Simply put, this is a 'realist' approach for two reasons: first, because it does not claim that technology is either *only* cultural or *only* physical; and second, because *technology is really* both cultural and physical. By extension, therefore:

C5. *reality comprises cultural, physical and technological phenomena.*

The next stage in our inquiry is therefore *how* these phenomena combine in reality.

What is reality, *really*?

This is the position at which Bruno Latour (1993, 1999) has influentially arrived. Although, as we shall note below, Latour has been appropriated in some quarters as a constructivist, Latour describes what he does as 'realist'. Thus, as we saw in **1.6.6**, Latour argues that a 'more realistic realism' (1999: 15) has the virtue of being *maximally inclusive* of the elements – cultural, technological and physical – that make up reality. Accordingly, Latour argues that reality is not comprised of single elements (be they physical or social), but rather of many and diverse kinds of elements, and the networks they form. One important consequence of this account is that discursive, representational and semiotic entities are as real as atoms, forces and chemical elements. Reality becomes a 'flat field', so that rather than comprising a physical or material level about which culture creates a second, representational and discursive level, discourses and representations are simply found 'alongside' chemicals, minerals and atoms. The following passage expresses this flat reality well:

> We are aiming at a *politics of things*, not at a bygone dispute about whether or not words refer to the world. Of course they do! You might as well ask me if I believe in Mom and apple pie or, for that matter, if I believe in reality!
>
> (1999: 22)

'Of course I'm a realist', says Latour; but of what kind? Latour's realism includes things in the world, the world itself, and words that refer to the world. This is why Haraway (1989: 7) is simply wrong to conclude that Latour 'radically rejects all forms of epistemological realism and analyzes scientific practise as thoroughly social and constructionist'. Haraway is wrong not because she calls Latour a constructionist, but because she does so at the expense of, rather than because of realism. Just as 'of course' he's a realist, so too he is 'of course' not going to conclude that constructions are not real: Latour's realism includes both epistemological realism ('of course words refer to the world!') and the constructed ('we are aiming at a politics of things'). Moreover, it would be equally wrong to assume, as many do and as Haraway implies in the above cited comment, that the only form of construction is social. The whole point of a 'politics of things' lies precisely in the fact that things construct networks that involve physical elements as much as representational or referential ones. Consider in this regard the gaming cyborg analysed in **5.4.4**; or the VHP discussed above: of course they represent, and of course they refer, just as of course they are things. Latour's realism then concludes that not all construction is social, just as not all politics are human:

> [R]ealism became even more abundant when nonhumans began to have a history, too, and were allowed the multiplicity of interpretations, the flexibility, the complexity that had been reserved, until then, for humans.
>
> (1999: 16)

Insofar as Latour's realism does not eliminate one set of concerns in favour of another, it is evidently a helpful way for realists to analyse the complex combinations of technology and culture that shapes our reality. However, some problems remain. By inserting the inclusivist conjunction 'both . . . and . . .' between social *and* physical things, such a realism seems to imply that some things are physical, and some not. Reality, on such a view, is made of both of the physical (metal things, fleshy things, mineral things) and the non-physical (representing things, referring things). Yet while words refer, they are also physical (written or spoken; patterns of ink on paper, pixels on a screen, or air through lungs, larynx and ear, and electrical patterns in brains); while images represent, they are also physical (pixels on a screen, light on plastic, or paint on canvas or paper). Clearly then, representing things are as physical as non-representing things. If Latour is suggesting otherwise, his account of reality is a dualist one. If he is not suggesting that representing or referring things are non-physical, then how can a distinction be made between the cultural and the physical?

How might Latour's realism be rescued from the dualist threat of the separability thesis? We could argue that although all cultural things are physical, *not all physical things are cultural*. Only some things, in other words, refer or represent, not all. This is precisely, however, what Latour's 'politics of things' rules out. Things have their own politics because they *act* even if they don't represent. Consider again the microscope and the eye. Neither component simply or reducibly represents, but both act, and act in particular ways. Were this not the case, then the microscope–eye connection simply would not work. Because it is the *actions* of things that constitute their politics, we are reminded that politics cannot be reduced to representations or images or references.

If then the realist must refuse a distinction between culture on the one hand, and nature and technology on the other, then does the view that all culture is necessarily physical eliminate what the human and social sciences have long regarded as their own domain, namely, a 'social reality'? *Only* if this is regarded as a separable domain, quite apart from that, for example, studied by physics, chemistry or biology. The separability thesis is best exemplified by Williams's withdrawal of culture from nature and technology on the grounds that 'there are no causes in culture' (**5.1.10**). We can now more clearly see the force of conclusion **C2** above, that we must reject as partial or false any account of technology than rests on such prior exclusions. Coupled with this claim, Latour's realism shows that there are actions in nature and technology just as much as there are in culture. Drawing a lesson for cultural and media studies from this politics of things, we can say that the political or cultural extends far further than the limits representation or reference might draw around them. Thus, there are indeed things *out there*, and they act on and through us long before we have a chance to 'construct' them. Latour's realism consists precisely in this politics of things, and it has a greater range than the cultural politics of representation.

For proponents of culturalism, however, if we reject the separation of nature and technology from culture, the worry is that adopting such a realism would entail that social reality as such would disappear, only to be replaced by some form of 'cultural physics'.

Precisely this worry has, for example, greeted attempts to study social phenomena in biological terms. For example, the field known as 'sociobiology', taking its name from biologist E. O. Wilson's controversial *Sociobiology: The New Synthesis* (1975), argues that there is no distinction between animal and human behaviour, since both are governed by evolutionary imperatives (Dennett 1995 argues for the virtues of a modified sociobiology). For this reason, human cultures can and should be explained in biological terms. On a more specifically cultural level, so-called 'cognitive film theorists' propose that audience response to film screenings ought to be studied in terms of theories derived from philosophical approaches derived from the cognitive neurosciences (see Grodal 1997, Smith 1995).

Such approaches are examples of the view that it is only the natural sciences (evolutionary biology, cognitive psychology) that supply us with valid theories, and for this reason, is known as *scientism*. Clearly, Latour's 'more realistic realism' neither argues for a cultural domain separate from the natural world, nor for a scientism to replace social explanations of phenomena. Rather, his solution to the separability problem is supplied in that the theory's aim of *including* natural, technological and cultural phenomena is achieved by presenting these phenomena not as entities from separate domains, but as elements of the networks they form. In other words,

C6. *there are no entities that are exclusively cultural or physical.*

Which is why we have argued (see Propositions 1 and 2, above) that culture is not a domain separable from nature. Granted that realism entails we cannot divide culture from physics, doesn't this entail a strong physicalist thesis that, namely, all of reality, cultural as well as technological, is ultimately grounded in nature?

Latour is very unwilling to accept this. He maintains, against this physicalism, that it is *networks* that construct reality. His realism suggests an *ontology* – a theory of what exists – comprised not of things, but of 'hybrids' or networks, composed of 'gods, people, stars, electrons, nuclear plants and markets' (1999: 16).

An ontology for realist theories of technology in culture

Before we answer the question posed at the end of the last paragraph, we should return to our guiding question – 'what is technology?' Are we now, after all these detours, able to answer it? Bearing our realist propositions in mind and paying particular attention to the discussions forming section **5.2**, we notice that the core theme of that section – causality – is missing from the list of possible answers to the question 'what is technology?' supplied in **5.1.3**. Causality, withdrawn from the cultural address to technology since Williams, lies at the core of a realist theory of technology and will finally provide an answer to the question of what it is.

Why argue that 'causes' are central to a realist definition of technology? There are two main reasons, one based on attending to precisely what technology is, the other providing the basis for an alternative to the 'thing'-based ontology that creates the dualist problem we saw in Latour's realism.

Common to most of the definitions of what technology is offered in **5.1.3** is the assumption that technology is, indeed, a thing or set of things:

1   whether it is something constructed for some purpose;

2   whether it is mechanical, thermal or digital;

3   whether artificial or natural;

4   whether it has the effect of alienating human labour; or

5   is a natural human capacity.

Of these definitions, only (4) does not consider technology as a *thing*. Rather, it is considered from the perspective of its *effects*: whatever technology 'is', it has such-and-such a set of effects. It was Marx who offered this account of technology, and he did so, because like Latour, Marx thought it importantly false to consider technology as simply a 'thing'. Unlike Latour, Marx argues this is inappropriate on the basis of a view of technology as *nothing at all* before it is set to work *in accordance with a particular set of purposes*. Here, of course, Williams would enthusiastically agree with Marx's assessment of the question; but Williams would further propose that in fact, this is precisely what technology is, and in so doing would supplant this with definition (1), returning technology to the status of a thing. What then is it that Marx spotted and Williams did not?

In defining technology from the perspective of its effects, Marx ultimately substitutes its 'thing' status for that of a *force* or an *action*. That is, he replaces the question 'what is technology?' with the question 'what does technology do?'. This is certainly a realist theory of technology insofar as whatever a technology is or might be, common to all technologies is that they have effects. Even the self-destructive 'anti-technologies' that figure, for instance, in Jean Tinguely's 1960 sculpture *Homage to New York* cause events to occur – the self-destruction of the technology itself.

Marx's is *not* a realist theory, however, insofar as it ascribes these effects to 'purposes' rather than causes in general. As we saw in **5.2.2**, the theory of causality that defines it in terms of purposes is called 'teleology', and teleology is only one kind of cause. Therefore, there are more and other causes besides purpose. This being the case, the realist is compelled to reject as 'partial' the account of technology as purpose, but importantly, is not similarly compelled to throw the causal baby out with the teleological bathwater. *Nor is the realist compelled*, as is the mechanist, *to deny that there do exist purposive causes*, only, to repeat, that these are not the *only* causes there are.

What, then, does it mean to define technologies as having effects? First, it means: technology *does things*. It assembles repeatable actions. Second, however, it means that to have effects at all, technology must mesh with some physically exploitable causes: the steam engine, for instance, exploits the physical properties of combustible materials in a boiler and then puts the resulting pressures to work. All these effects obey the laws of heat and energy known as thermodynamics. *There are no technologies that do not exploit physical causes*. We are now in a position to offer the first step towards a realist definition of technology:

D1. *technology exploits causes to produce repeatable effects, and is thus more a set of powers than it is a thing.*

Technology, in other words, is the manipulation of causes. Technology is by definition an engine of change. If it does not manipulate causes, it is not a technology, since it simply cannot *work*. The first thing that we note concerning this definition is that insofar as it meshes with the physical world, this definition establishes the *necessity of the physical dimension with regard to any consideration of technology*, and that included amongst this physical dimension are the *effects* the particular exploitation of causes produces. The second thing to note is that it provides a means to approach the ontology necessary to a realist account of technology, one that gets us past the 'thing' problem we encountered via Latour's realism, but that does not thereby sacrifice technology's physicality. Causes, that is, are forces, processes and actions that are physical without being things; they are *powers* always routed through things. Thus causes establish physical routes through things that do not resemble those things.

To make this idea clearer, consider the example discussed in **5.4.4** of the 'passional circuits' established in gaming: this circuit of causes works not by combining two whole things – the human player and the machine played – but rather by looping photons, neurones and electrons, light, eyes, fingers and electronics into a new entity. What defines this entity is not the entities it is made from, but the circuit that constructs it. The resulting circuit is physical and cultural, but resembles no hitherto existing entity in either domain. At a larger scale, consider the technology that enabled and determined the form that industrialisation took in Britain during the nineteenth-century: steam technologies require constant part-to-part contact, including the labour force required to fuel, maintain and serve this larger, inherently social technology. The resulting entirely new social and cultural forms that thus emerged can be charted through the circuits of coal, steel, and, as Lyotard has shown, a complete reworking of the human senses: 'look at the English proletariat, at what capital, that is to say their labour, has done to their body . . ., the strange bodily arrangement of the skilled worker with his job and his machine' (1993: 111).

This established, we must now return to the question of Latour's reluctance to answer the question as to the nature of the networks he wants to use as the basis of his proposed ontology. The problem his network ontology encounters concerns precisely the nature of these networks: if the answer to the question were 'networks are physical', then they could be explained wholly in terms of their physical components, rendering the cultural components obsolete. This is why we often gain the impression from reading Latour's analysis of networks that they are primarily descriptive. However, our analysis of the role of causality in defining technology, while making the physical primary, results not in explanations of cultural phenomena simply in terms of preexisting theories from physics or from biology, because it does not acknowledge

(a) that there are discrete physical, biological, or cultural kinds or domains of things; nor that

(b) things have ontological priority over causes; but rather that

(c) causes are powers that produce new things.

The lessons we learn from being realists about technology are first that technology is as technology does. Second, that because technology exploits physically available causes, to consider things technologically and realistically means to follow these causes through their various transformations, both natural and artificial. Although any separable 'social' or 'cultural reality' is a casualty of this approach, the richness of the resulting hybrids is as breathtaking as it is ubiquitous, as such new phenomena as the Visible Human Project, Oncomouse or stem-cell engineering attest. Each of these are new phenomena created by the rediscovery of causes through new ways to manipulate them: the VHP splices parts of the criminal justice system, a human body, and new imaging technologies; Oncomouse is genetic manipulation coupled with commerce and intellectual property law; stem-cells recontextualise the machines that make bodies in the first place, in order to generate new body parts. These are as much cultural as they are physical phenomena, and they are remaking us as we learn increasingly to remake things.

Although we began this book by examining the ubiquity of newness (cf. **1.4.4**), in the end, precisely this attests to the permanent actions of technology on culture. In order to examine these things, causality must be returned to the study of culture. Because the readers and the authors of this book alike are living through a period of what we have called 'crisis technology' (**5.4.3**), we are fortunate to be able to see some of these changes before these technologies become 'normal' in turn. The visibility of technology affords us the opportunity of reviewing our approach to technology in culture, and of seeking, instead of sweeping it under a discursive carpet, to encompass the wider realities in which they enmesh our cultures. Such a realism *simply takes as much as it can concerning a given phenomenon into account* when seeking to explain it. After decades of seeking to exclude causes from culture, realists see, all too clearly, that they operate at its very core.

Bibliography

Adorno, Theodor and Horkheimer, Max *Dialectic of Enlightenment*, trans. John Cumming, London: Verso, 1996.

Ansell-Pearson, Keith *Viroid Life*, London: Routledge, 1997.

Aristotle *The Politics and The Constitution of Athens*, ed. Stephen Everson, Cambridge: Cambridge University Press, 1996.

Aristotle *The Physics*, ed. Robin Waterfield, Oxford: Oxford University Press, 1996.

Babbage, Charles *On the Economy of Machinery and Manufactures*, London: Charles Knight, 1832.

Balsamo, Anne *Technologies of the Gendered Body: reading cyborg women*, Durham N.C.: Duke University Press, 1996.

Barnes, Jonathan ed. 'Eudemian ethics', in *The Complete Works of Aristotle*, vol. 2, Princeton: Princeton University Press, 1984.

Basalla, George *The Evolution of Technology*, Cambridge: Cambridge University Press, 1989.

Bateson, Gregory *Steps to an Ecology of Mind*, New York: Ballantine, 1972.

Baudrillard, Jean *Symbolic Exchange and Death*, London: Sage, [1976] 1993.

Baudrillard, Jean *The System of Objects*, London: Verso, 1996.

Baudrillard, Jean *Simulacra and Simulation*, Ann Arbor: University of Michigan Press, 1997.

Bedini, Silvio 'The role of automata in the history of technology', *Technology and Culture* 5.1 (1964): 24–42.

Bell, David and Kennedy, Barbara M. *The Cybercultures Reader*, London: Routledge, 2000.

Benjamin, Walter *Illuminations*, London: Fontana, 1973.

Bergson, Henri *Creative Evolution*, London: Macmillan, [1911] 1920.

Bergson, Henri *The Two Sources of Morality and Religion* London: Macmillan, [1932] 1935.

Bertens, Hans *The Idea of the Postmodern: a history*, London: Routledge, 1995.

Biagioli, Mario ed. *The Science Studies Reader*, New York: Routledge, 1999.

Blackmore, Susan *The Meme Machine*, Oxford: Oxford University Press, 1999.

Boden, Margaret *The Philosophy of Artificial Intelligence*, Oxford: Oxford University Press, 1990.

Boden, Margaret *The Philosophy of Artificial Life*, Oxford: Oxford University Press, 1996.

Braudel, Fernand *Capitalism and Material Life 1400–1800*, New York: Harper and Row, 1973.

Broadhurst-Dixon, Joan and Cassidy, Eric, eds *Virtual Futures: cyberotics, technology and posthuman pragmatism*, London: Routledge, 1997.

Bukatman, Scott *Terminal Identity*, Durham, N.C.: Duke University Press, 1993.

Butler, Samuel *Erewhon*, New York: Signet, 1960.

Cadigan, Pat *Synners*, London: Grafton, 1991.

Carter, Natalie Interview with Kevin Warwick, Videotape, 2001.

Castells, M. *The Rise of the Network Society*, London: Blackwell, [1996] 2000.

Chapuis, Alfred and Droz, Edmond *Automata: a historical and technological Study*, Neuchâtel: Editions du Griffon, 1958.

Clark, William, Golinski, Jan and Schaffer, Simon *The Sciences in Enlightened Europe*, Chicago: University of Chicago Press, 1999.

Coleman, William *Biology in the Nineteenth Century. Problems of form, function and transformation*, Cambridge: Cambridge University Press, 1977.

Critical Art Ensemble *Electronic Civil Disobedience and Other Unpopular Essays*, New York: Semiotext(e), 1995.

D'Alembert, Jean and Diderot, Denis *Encyclopédie, ou Dictionnaire raisonné des arts, des sciences et des métiers*, Paris: Briasson, David, Le Breton et Durand, 1777.

Darwin, Charles *Origin of Species*, Harmondsworth: Penguin, 1993.

Daston, Lorraine 'Enlightenment calculations', *Critical Inquiry* 21.1 (1994): 182–202.

Dawkins, Richard *The Selfish Gene*, London: Granada, 1976.

Dawkins, Richard *Blind Watchmaker: the Program of the Book*, PO Box 59, Leamington Spa, 1991.

De Kerckhove, Derrick *The Skin of Culture*, Toronto: Somerville House, 1997.

De Landa, Manuel *War in the Age of Intelligent Machines*, New York: Zone, 1991.

De Landa, Manuel 'Virtual environments and the emergence of synthetic reason', in *Flame Wars*, Special edition of *South Atlantic Quarterly* 92.4, ed. Mark Dery, Durham, N.C.: Duke University Press, 1993, pp. 793–815.

De Landa, Manuel *A Thousand Years of Non-linear History*, New York: Zone, 1997.

Deleuze, Gilles *Cinema 1: the movement image*, trans. Hugh Tomlinson and Barbara Haberjam, London: Athlone, 1986.

Deleuze, Gilles *Bergsonism*, trans. Hugh Tomlinson, New York: Zone, 1988.

Deleuze, Gilles *Cinema 2: the time-image*, London: Athlone, 1989.

Deleuze, Gilles *Difference and Repetition* London: Athlone, [1968] 1994.

Deleuze, Gilles and Guattari, Félix *Anti-Oedipus*, London: Athlone, [1974] 1984.

Deleuze, Gilles and Guattari, Félix *A Thousand Plateaus*, London: Athlone, 1988.

Dennett, Daniel *Darwin's Dangerous Idea*, Harmondsworth: Penguin, 1995.

Dennett, Daniel *Brainchildren: essays on designing minds*, Cambridge, Mass.: MIT Press, 1998.

Dery, Mark ed. *Flame Wars*, Special edition of the *South Atlantic Quarterly* 92.4, Durham, N.C.: Duke University Press, 1993.

Descartes, René *Meditations* ed. John Cottingham, Cambridge: Cambridge University Press, [1641], 1986.

Descartes, René, 'Treatise on man', in *The World and Other Writings* ed. Stephen Gaukroger. Cambridge: Cambridge University Press, [1662], 1998.

Diderot, Denis *Rameau's Nephew and D'Alembert's Dream*, Harmondsworth: Penguin, 1985.

Dobres, Marcia-Anne *Technology and Social Agency*, Oxford: Blackwell, 2000.

Dreyfus, Hubert *What Computers Can't Do*, New York: Harper and Row, 1979.

Dumouchel, Paul 'Gilbert Simondon's plea for a philosophy of technology', *Inquiry* 35 (1992): 407–421.

Dyson, George *Darwin Among the Machines: the evolution of global intelligence*, Harmondsworth: Penguin, 1998.

Ellul, Jacques *The Technological Society*, New York: Vintage, [1954], 1964.

Engels, Friedrich *Dialectics of Nature*, trans. Clemens Dutt, London: Lawrence and Wishart, 1964.

Eve, Raymond E., Horsfall, Sara and Lee, Mary E. eds *Chaos, Complexity and Sociology: myths, models and theories*, London: Sage, 1997.

Feenberg, Andrew *Critical Theory of Technology*, London: Routledge, 1991.

Ferguson, Adam *An Essay on the History of Civil Society*, ed. Duncan Forbes, Edinburgh: Edinburgh University Press, [1767] 1966.

Ferré, Frederic *Philosophy of Technology*, Athens, Ga.: University of Georgia Press, 1995.

Fiske, John *Introduction to Communication Studies* (3rd edn), London: Routledge, 1990.

Foucault, Michel *The Order of Things*, London: Tavistock, 1970.

Foucault, Michel *Discipline and Punish*, trans. Anthony Sheridan, Harmondsworth: Penguin, 1979.

Foucault, Michel *Birth of the Clinic*, London: Routledge, 1986.

Foucault, Michel *Technologies of the Self*, ed. Luther H. Martin, Huck Gutman and Patrick H. Hutton, London: Tavistock, 1988.

Galison, Peter 'The ontology of the enemy: Norbert Wiener and the cybernetic vision', *Critical Inquiry* 5.1 (1994): 228–266.

Genosko, Gary *McLuhan and Baudrillard*, London: Routledge, 1998.

Gibson, William *Neuromancer*, London: Grafton, 1986.

Gibson, William *Burning Chrome*, London: Grafton, 1988.

Gibson, William 'An interview with William Gibson', in *Storming the Reality Studio: a casebook of cyberpunk and postmodern fiction*, ed. Larry McCaffery, Durham, N.C.: Duke University Press, 1991, pp. 263–385.

Gibson, William and Silverman, Robert *Instruments of the Imagination*, Cambridge, Mass.: Harvard University Press, 1995.

Gibson, William and Sterling, Bruce *The Difference Engine*, London: Gollancz, 1990.

Gillespie, Charles Coulston *Genesis and Geology*, Cambridge Mass.: Harvard University Press, 1992.

Gleick, James *Chaos*, London: Cardinal, 1987.

Gould, Stephen Jay *Time's Arrow, Time's Cycle*, Harmondsworth: Penguin, 1987.

Grodal, Torben *Moving Pictures. A New Theory of Film Genres, Feelings and Cognition*, Oxford: Oxford University Press, 1997.

Habermas, Jürgen *Towards a Rational Society*, London: Heinemann, 1970.

Hacking, Ian *Representing and Intervening*, Cambridge: Cambridge University Press, 1983.

Hacking, Ian *The Social Construction of What?* Cambridge, Mass.: Harvard University Press, 1999.

Hankins, Thomas L. *Science and the Enlightenment*, Cambridge, Cambridge University Press, 1985.

Hankins, Thomas L. and Silverman, Robert J. *Instruments and the Imagination*, Princeton, N.J.: Princeton University Press, 1995.

Haraway, Donna *Primate Visions: gender, race and nature in the world of modern science*, London: Verso, 1989.

Haraway, Donna *Simians, Cyborgs and Women: the reinvention of nature*, London: Free Association, 1991.

Haraway, Donna *Modest Witness @ Second Millennium: FemaleMan meets OncoMouse*, London: Routledge, 1997.

Harpignies, J.P. *Double Helix Hubris: against designer genes*, New York: Cool Grove Press, 1994.

Harvie, Christopher, Martin, Graham and Scharf, Aaron eds *Industrialization and Culture 1830–1914*, London: Macmillan, 1970.

Haugeland, John *Mind Design: philosophy, psychology and artificial intelligence*, Cambridge, Mass.: MIT, 1981.

Hayles, N. Katherine 'Narratives of artificial life', in *Futurenatural. Nature, Science, Culture*, ed. George Robertson *et al*. London: Routledge, 1996, pp. 146–164.

Hayles, N. Katherine *How We Became Posthuman: virtual bodies in cybernetics, literature, and informatics*, Chicago: University of Chicago Press, 1999.

Heim, Michael *The Metaphysics of Virtual Reality*, Oxford: Oxford University Press, 1993.

Hodges, Andrew *Turing: the Enigma*, London: Vintage, 1992.

Hodges, Andrew *Turing. A natural philosopher*, London: Phoenix, 1997.

Hoffman, E.T.A. 'Automata', in *The Best Tales of Hoffmann*, ed. E. F. Bleiler, New York: Dover, 1966.

Homer *The Iliad*, ed. Martin Hammond, Harmondsworth: Penguin, 1987.

Hughes, Thomas P. 'Technological momentum', in *Does Technology Drive History?* eds Merritt Roe Smith and Leo Marx, Cambridge, Mass.: MIT Press, 1996, pp. 101–113.

Hyman, Anthony *Science and Reform: selected works of Charles Babbage*, Cambridge: Cambridge University Press, 1989.

Kadrey, Richard *Metrophage*, London: Gollancz, 1989.

Kant, Immanuel *Critique of Judgement*, trans. Werner S. Pluhar, Indianapolis: Hackett, [1790] 1986.

Kauffman, Stuart *At Home in the Universe*, Harmondsworth: Penguin, 1995.

Kay, Lily E. *Who Wrote the Book of Life?*, Stanford, Calif.: Stanford University Press, 2000.

Kellner, Douglas *Baudrillard: a critical reader*, Oxford: Blackwell, 1994.

Kellner, Douglas *Media Cultures*, London: Routledge, 1995.

Kelly, Kevin *Out of Control*, New York: Addison-Wesley, 1994.

Kleist, Heinrich von 'On the marionette theatre' in *Essays on Dolls*, ed. Idris Parry, Harmondsworth: Penguin, [1810] 1994.

Kuhn, Thomas *The Structure of Scientific Revolutions*, Chicago: University of Chicago Press, 1962.

La Mettrie, Julian de *Machine Man and Other Writings* ed. Ann Thompson, Cambridge: Cambridge University Press, [1747] 1996.

Langton, Christopher G. 'Artificial life', in *The Philosophy of Artificial Life*, ed. Margaret Boden, Oxford: Oxford University Press, 1996, pp. 39–94.

Lardner, Dionysius 'Babbage's Calculating Engine', *Edinburgh Review* CXX ed. Anthony Hyman, Cambridge: Cambridge University Press, [1843] 1989, pp. 51–109.

Latour, Bruno *We Have Never Been Modern*, trans. Catherine Porter, Hemel Hempstead: Harvester-Wheatsheaf, 1993.

Latour, Bruno 'Stengers's shibboleth', Introduction to Isabelle Stengers' *Power and Invention: situating science*, Minneapolis: University of Minnesota Press, 1997, pp. vii–xx.

Latour, Bruno 'One more turn after the social turn', in *The Science Studies Reader*, ed. Mario Biagioli, New York: Routledge, 1999, pp. 276–289.

Leibniz, G. W. 'Towards a universal characteristic' in *Leibniz. Selections*, ed. Philip P. Wiener, New York: Scribner's, [1677] 1951.

Leibniz, G. W. 'Letter to Countess Elizabeth' in *Leibniz: Philosophical Essays*, eds Robin Ariew and Daniel Garber, Indianapolis: Hackett, [1678] 1989.

Leibniz, G. W. *Monadology*, eds Robin Ariew and Daniel Garber, Indianapolis: Hackett, [1714] 1989.

Lenoir, Timothy 'Was the last turn the right turn? The semiotic turn and A.J. Greimas', in *The Science Studies Reader*, ed. Mario Biagioli, New York: Routledge, 1999, pp. 290–301.

Levinson, Paul *Digital McLuhan*, London: Routledge, 1997.

Lévi-Strauss, Claude *The Elementary Structures of Kinship* Boston: Beacon Press, [1949] 1969.

Lévy, Pierre *Becoming Virtual: reality and the digital age*, New York: Plenum, 1998.

Levy, Steven *Artificial Life*, London: Jonathan Cape, 1992.

Lovelace, Ada 'Sketch of the Analytical Engine invented by Charles Babbage, Esq. by L.F. Menabrea of Turin, with notes upon the memoir by the translator', Scientific Memoirs (1843), in *Science and Reform: selected works of Charles Babbage*, ed. Anthony Hyman, Cambridge: Cambridge University Press, 1989, pp. 243–311.

Luhmann, Niklas *Social Systems*, trans. William Whobrey, Stanford, Calif.: Stanford University Press, 1995.

Lyotard, Jean-François *The Postmodern Condition: a report on knowledge*, trans. Geoff Bennington and Brian Massumi, Manchester: Manchester University Press, 1984.

Lyotard, Jean-François *Libidinal Economy*, trans. I. H. Grant, London: Continuum, 1993.

MacDonald Ross, George *Leibniz*, Oxford: Oxford University Press, 1984.

MacKenzie, Donald A. and Wajcman, Judy *Social Shaping of Technology*, London: Open University Press, [1985] 1999.

Mandelbrot, Benoit *The Fractal Geometry of Nature*, New York: Freeman, 1977.

Marcuse, Herbert *One Dimensional Man*, London: Sphere, 1968.

Marx, Karl *Capital*, Volume 1, London: Lawrence and Wishart, 1974.

Marx, Karl *Grundrisse*, trans. and ed. Martin Nicolaus, Harmondsworth: Penguin, 1993.

Marx, Karl and Engels, Friedrich *The Communist Manifesto*, Harmondsworth: Penguin, 1973.

Mauss, Marcel *General Theory of Magic*, London: Routledge and Kegan Paul, 1974.

Mayr, Otto *Authority, Liberty and Automatic Machinery in Early Modern Europe*, Baltimore, Md.: Johns Hopkins University Press, 1986.

McCaffery, Larry ed. *Storming the Reality Studio: a casebook of cyberpunk and postmodern fiction*, Durham, N.C.: Duke University Press, 1992.

McLuhan, Marshall *The Gutenberg Galaxy*, London: Routledge and Kegan Paul, 1962.

McLuhan, Marshall *Understanding Media: the Extensions of Man*, London: Sphere, 1967.

McLuhan, Marshall *Counterblast*, London: Rapp and Whiting, 1969.

Mitcham, Carl *Thinking Through Technology*, Chicago: University of Chicago Press, 1994.

Monod, Jacques *Chance and Necessity*, London: Fontana, 1971.

Morse, Margaret 'What do cyborgs eat? Oral logic in an information society', *Discourse* 16.3 (1994): 87–121.

Myerson, George *Donna Haraway and GM Foods*, London: Icon, 2000.

O'Brien, Stephen 'Blade Runner: if only you could see what I have seen with your eyes!', *SFX* 71 (December 2000): 7–9.

Orlan '"I do not want to look like . . .": Orlan on becoming-Orlan', tr. Carolyn Ducker, *Women's Art* 64 (1995): 5–10.

Plant, Sadie *Zeros and Ones: digital women and the new technoculture*, London: Fourth Estate, 1997.

Poe, Edgar Allan 'Maelzel's chess-player' in *The Complete Tales and Poems of Edgar Allan Poe*, ed. Mladinska Knijga, New York: Vintage, [1836] 1966.

Porush, David *Soft Machine: Cybernetic Fictions*, New York: Methuen, 1985.

Poundstone, William *The Recursive Universe: cosmic complexity and the limits of scientific knowledge*, New York: William Morrow, 1985.

Price, Derek J. de Solla 'Automata and the origins of mechanism and mechanistic philosophy', *Technology and Culture* 5.1 (1964): 9–23.

Prigogine, Ilya and Stengers, Isabelle *Order out of Chaos*, London: Flamingo, 1985.

Ray, Thomas S. 'An approach to the synthesis of life', in *The Philosophy of Artificial Life*, ed. Margaret Boden, Oxford: Oxford University Press, 1996, pp. 111–145.

Rheingold, Howard *Virtual Reality*, London: Secker and Warburg, 1991.

Robertson, George, Mash, Melinda, Tickner, Lisa, Bird, Jon, Curtis, Barry and Putnam, Tim, eds *Futurenatural. Nature, science, culture*, London: Routledge, 1996.

Ross, Andrew *Strange Weather: culture, science and technology in the age of Limits*, London: Verso, 1991.

Schaffer, Simon 'Babbage's intelligence: calculating engines and the factory system', *Critical Inquiry* 5.1 (1994): 203–227.

Schaffer, Simon 'Babbage's dancer and the impressarios of mechanism', in *Cultural Babbage: time, technology and invention*, eds Francis Spufford and Jenny Uglow, London: Faber, 1996, pp. 53–80.

Schaffer, Simon 'Enlightened automata', in *The Sciences in Enlightened Europe*, eds William Clark, Jan Golinski and Simon Schaffer, Chicago: University of Chicago Press, 1999, pp. 126–165.

Schickore, Jutta *The Microscope and the Eye. A History of Reflections 1740–1870*, Chicago and London: University of Chicago Press, 2007.

Simon, Herbert *The Sciences of the Artificial*, Cambridge, Mass.: MIT, [1969] 1996.

Simondon, Gilbert 'Technical individualisation', in *Interact or Die*, eds Joke Brouwer and Arjen Mulder, Rotterdam V2 Publishing/Nai Publishers, 2007, pp. 206–215.

Simondon, Gilbert *Le Mode d'existence des objets techniques*, Paris: Aubier, 1958.

Smith, Adam *Essays on Philosophical Subjects*, Oxford: Clarendon Press, [1795] 1980.

Smith, Anthony *Goodbye Gutenberg: the newspaper revolution of the 1980s*, Oxford: Oxford University Press, 1981.

Smith, Merritt Roe and Marx, Leo eds *Does Technology Drive History*, Cambridge, Mass.: MIT, 1996.

Smith, Murray *Engaging Characters. Fiction, Emotion and the Cinema*, Oxford: Clarendon Press. 1995.

Sobchack, Vivian 'New age mutant ninja hackers: reading Mondo 2000', in , Special edition of the *South Atlantic Quarterly*, 92.4, ed. Mark Dery, Durham, N.C.: Duke University Press, 1993, pp. 569–584.

Springer, Claudia *Electronic Eros: bodies and desire in the postindustrial age*, London: Athlone, 1996.

Spufford, Francis and Uglow, Jenny eds *Cultural Babbage: time, technology and invention*, London: Faber, 1996.

Stelarc 'From psycho-body to cyber-systems: images as post-human entities', in *The Cybercultures Reader*, eds David Bell and Barbara M. Kennedy, London: Routledge, 2000.

Stengers, Isabelle *Power and Invention: situating science*, Minneapolis: University of Minnesota Press, 1997.

Sterling, Bruce *Schismatrix*, Harmondsworth: Penguin, 1985.

Sterling, Bruce ed. *Mirrorshades*, New York: Ace, 1986.

Sterling, Bruce *Heavy Weather*, London: Phoenix, 1995.

Sterling, Bruce *Distraction*, New York: Ace, 1999.

Stone, Allucquere Rosanne *The War of Desire and Technology at the Close of the Mechanical Age*, Cambridge, Mass.: MIT Press, 1995.

Swade, Doron *Charles Babbage and his Calculating Engines*, London: Science Museum, 1991.

Swade, Doron *The Cogwheel Brain*, New York: Little, Brown, 2000.

Tapscott, D. and Williams, A. *Wikinomics: How Mass Collaboration Changes Everything*, London: Penguin Books, 2006.

Terranova, Tiziana 'Digital Darwin: nature, evolution and control in the rhetoric of electronic communication', *Techoscience: New Formations 29*, eds Judy Berland and Sarah Kember (1996a): 69–83.

Terranova, Tiziana 'Posthuman unbounded: artificial evolution and high-tech subcultures', in *Futurenatural. Nature, science, culture*, eds George Robertson *et al*. London: Routledge, 1996b, pp. 165–180.

Theweleit, Klaus *Male Fantasies*, vol. 2, Minneapolis: Minnesota University Press, 1986.

Thom, René *Structural Stability and Morphogenesis*, New York: W.A. Benjamin, 1975.

Turing, Alan 'On computable numbers', *Proceedings of the London Mathematical Society*, series 2.42 (1936): 230–265.

Turing, Alan 'Computing machinery and intelligence', *Mind* 51 (1950): 433–460, in *The Philosophy of Artificial Intelligence*, ed. Margaret Boden, Oxford: Oxford University Press, 1990

Turing, Alan 'The chemical basis of morphogenesis', *Philosophical Transactions of the Royal Society of London* B 237 (1952): 37–72.

Ure, Andrew *The Philosophy of Manufactures*, London, 1835.

von Neumann, John *The Computer and the Brain*, New Haven and London: Yale University Press, [1958] 1999.

Ward, Mark *Virtual Organisms: the startling world of artificial life*, London: Macmillan, 2000.

Warwick, Kevin *In the Mind of the Machine*, London: Arrow, 1998.

White, Lynn *Medieval Technology and Social Change*, Oxford: Oxford University Press, 1964.

Wiener, Norbert *Cybernetics: control and communication in animal and machine*, Cambridge, Mass.: MIT Press, [1948] 1962.

Wiener, Norbert *The Human Use of Human Beings*, London: Free Association, [1958] 1987.

Wiener, Norbert *The Human Use of Human Beings*, London: Free Association, [1954] 1989.

Williams, Raymond *Television, Technology and Cultural Form*, London: Fontana, 1974.

Williams, Raymond *Marxism and Literature*, Oxford: Oxford University Press, 1977.

Wilson, Edward O. *Sociobiology: The New Synthesis*, Cambridge Mass.: Harvard University Press, 1975.

Woolley, Benjamin *Virtual Worlds: a Journey in hype and hyperreality*, Oxford: Blackwell, 1992.

Woolley, Benjamin *The Bride of Science: romance, reason and Byron's daughter*, London: Macmillan, 1999.

Wordsworth, William 'Prelude', in *The Poetical Works of William Wordsworth*, vol. V, eds E. de Selincourt and Helen Derbyshire, Oxford: Oxford University Press, 1949.

Ziman, John M. ed. *Technological Innovation as an Evolutionary Process*, Cambridge: Cambridge University Press, 2000.

Glossary

Actor-network theory
Actor-network theory derives from the work of Bruno Latour (see especially Latour [1993] for an excellent account of it). It has been highly influential in the field of 'science studies', but has also, through Donna Haraway (1989, 1991, 1998), become an important component of cybercultural studies. Actor-network theory offers a means to treat not merely of cultural things, but also of physical things. Thus it presents an alternative to (a) transforming technology into a discursive entity in order to discuss it in terms of cultural and media studies; and (b) treating cultural phenomena as irrelevant from the point of view of engineering and the sciences. It gives, therefore, ideally equal treatment to human and non-human agents in the analysis of highly technologised sociocultural phenomena. In Carl Mitcham's (1994) terms, it bridges the gulf that exists between 'humanities philosophy of technology' and 'engineering philosophy of technology'. The goal of the theory is to provide a symmetrical account of the relations between human and non-human actors, although changes in these relations become difficult to model in accordance with this demand for symmetry, since they are often precisely not symmetrical.

Affordance
The term 'affordance' derives from design theory. It refers to the possible ways in which artefacts and materials can be used, the actions or processes they facilitate. Affordances are determined primarily by the physical properties, shape and scale of artefacts, rather than their cultural significance or meanings.

Algorithm
A series of instructions – a recipe or formula – used by a computer, or a program, to carry out a specific task or solve a problem. The term is generally used in the context of software to describe the program logic for a specific function. The two important factors in determining how to design an algorithm are the accuracy of the result and the efficiency of the processing.

Analogue
A form of representation, such as a chemical photograph, a film, or a vinyl disc, in which a material surface carries continuous variations of tone, light, or some other signal. Analogue representation is based upon an unsegmented code while a digital medium is based upon a segmented one in which information is divided into discrete elements. The hands of a traditional (analogue) clock which continuously sweep its face, in contrast to a digital clock which announces each second in isolation, is a common example.

Artificial intelligence (AI)
One of the two main 'sciences of the artificial' (Simon 1996) artificial intelligence is an ongoing research programme aiming to produce intelligent programmes (soft AI), or artificially intelligent things (robotics, hard AI). The two main branches of the first are Good Old Fashioned AI (GOFAI; see Haugeland 1981), and connectionism.

Artificial life (Alife)
Otherwise called 'synthetic biology', artificial life does not seek to understand life as it is but to create life as it could be. This can be in any one of three forms: hard Alife, or robotics; soft Alife or online 'creatures'; and wet Alife or engineering life from the ground up. The most extreme form of soft Alife argues that virtual 'creatures' are already alive, albeit in a silicon, rather than a carbon, environment. See Langton in Boden (1996), Ward (2000), Terranova and Hayles in Bird *et al.* (1996).

ASCII (American Standard Code for Information Interchange)
ASCII is a standard developed by the American National Standards Institute (ANSI) to define how computers write and read characters. The ASCII set of 128 characters includes letters, numbers, punctuation, and control codes (such as a character that marks the end of a line). Each letter or other character is represented by a number: an uppercase A, for example, is the number 65, and a lowercase z is the number 122.

Authorship
The idea that the meaning and quality of a text or other product is explained by name, identity and inherent abilities of the individual person who made it rather than seeing a text as the outcome of wider cultural forces or its meanings arising in the act of its being read.

Avatar
Originally the incarnation of a God in Hinduism. A visual representation of a participant in a shared digital environment (e.g. in online chat). It can look like a person, an object, or an animal. An interface for the self.

Bandwidth
Capacity to carry information. It can apply to telephone or network wiring as well as system buses, radio frequency signals, and monitors. Bandwidth is most accurately measured in cycles per second, or hertz (Hz), also as bits or bytes per second. So, for example, we might describe certain kinds of transmission capabilities as a narrow bandwidth carrying small amounts of data slowly, and others as wide bandwidth, carrying large amounts of data fast.

Biotechnology
Biotechnology, at once a scientific, a corporate and an artistic concern, consists in various approaches to re-engineering organisms for new purposes. Cloning, crop re-engineering, xenotransplantation, genomics and transgenics derive their principal impetus from the informational nature of genetic transfer, whose greatest artefact thus far is the human genome. It features heavily in cyberpunk fiction, as well as in the work of performance artists such as Orlan and Stelarc.

Browser
Viewing software that interprets HTML. A variety of extensions allow the display of other formats for audio, video and animation.

Bulletin board system
A computer that many users can connect to through phone lines and associated telecommunications networks. Usually has email and message conferences, as well as files and chat. A BBS may or may not have connections to other computers. A common communication 'space' for people with similar interests or goals.

Canon, canonical
A cultural product or collection of products (books, works of art, theories, buildings), which has come to be a defining product in the orthodox history of a discipline or practice.

Cartesian grid
A schema or conception of space defined by the co-ordinates of height, width, and depth, a cubic, gridded, measurable space: the classical, mathematical representation of three-dimensional space.

CGI
Computer-generated imagery. The term is commonly used to describe computer animation and special effects in film and television production.

Chaos
Chaos theory stems from mathematical researches into unpredictable phenomena arising in otherwise determinist systems. A determinist system is one in which, given a knowledge of the initial state of the system, its future may be accurately predicted or modelled. The famous 'butterfly effect', which occurs when tiny changes in a system (a butterfly in Florida flaps its wings) give rise to large-scale effects (there is a storm in China), is therefore both deterministic (it arises from given causes) and unpredictable (these causes cannot be modelled). Chaos theories are important here because they enable us to model technological determinism without forsaking the complexity of social and technological relations, on the one hand, and, on the other, emergent determinisms, such as Ellul (1964) and de Landa (1991) argue for.

Cheats
In computer and video games, to 'cheat' is to use a code or password to either gain access to another section or level of the game, or to change certain of the game's parameters. For example, a cheat may give the player more 'lives'. Originally included in games by programmers to facilitate testing of games before publication, they quickly became part of game culture as shared knowledge between players, and also support the production of published guides and magazine supplements. More recently 'patches' have added to the possibilities of manipulating the computer game. Available from the Internet for example, patches change a game's parameters more significantly, adding new levels or different characters.

Commodities, commodification
A commodity is a product or service that is bought or sold. In the Marxist sense used within this book, the commodity form underpins the capitalist market and, to a greater or lesser extent, modern society. For Marx, commodities were not simple objects, but, once they were exchanged in markets they took on values and a 'life of their own'. Commodification is, on one level, the process described above, but it is often applied to questions of the commercialisation of culture – for example, it might be argued that with the arrival of advertising, online shopping, etc. the World Wide Web has been 'commodified'.

Community
Our sense of belonging to social groups which often extend beyond the boundaries of specific place to include taste, consumption, shared interests and shared discursive codes. Used here to describe groups of Internet users sharing a common interest connected via networked digital media.

Computer-mediated communication (CMC)
Simply the activity of communicating with other individuals or groups using digitised information transmitted through telephone and other telecommunications links such as cable, and satellite. This covers everything from email, to participation in shared communication forums such as newsgroups or bulletin boards, chat rooms and avatar-based communication spaces online. A major site of study in the development of new media studies.

Connectionism
Connectionism is one of the major branches of AI research. As opposed to 'Good Old Fashioned AI', which is effectively concerned to model intelligent functions in software, it understands intelligence as a function of the structural complexity of brains, and seeks to reproduce that complexity in artificial forms. In connectionist computation, instead of pushing all tasks through a single central processing unit (CPU), it 'connects' several, on the understanding that each CPU represents not a whole brain, but rather a brain cell or neurone (see the papers by Clark and Cussins in Boden [1990]). Like many of the sciences of the artificial, cyberculture has provided an occasion for it to migrate from the sciences into culture at large (see Plant 1997).

Constructionism
An important theoretical approach to social and cultural phenomena, constructionism consists in the rejection of the idea of firm foundations for concepts such as 'identity', 'gender', and so on, in favour of trying to understand them as emerging from social and cultural interaction, usually (but not always), of a linguistic or discursive character. It is therefore highly opposed to any and all forms of physicalism or essentialism, which it regards as making unwarrantable claims to authority on the grounds of a presumed 'prelinguistic' or 'prediscursive' access to an unconstructed real. Not to be confused with *constructivism*.

Constructivism
This concept, derived from the philosophical work of Gilles Deleuze and Félix Guattari (1988) and Isabelle Stengers (1997), arises on the back of the inroads into physical re-engineering that have been made by the sciences of the artificial – AI and Alife – and by biotechnology. These sciences show us that things themselves are constructed, and can therefore be reconstructed. Unlike constructionism, however, it emphasises that the construction in question is physical, not merely discursive or social.

Convergence
Term used to describe the ways in which previously discrete media forms and processes are drawn together and combined though digital technologies. This occurs both at the levels of production and distribution. At the level of production, for example, newspapers, music, and television once had very different physical production bases but could all now be substantively produced using the same networked multimedia computer. Second, at the level of distribution previously discrete networks are absorbed into the single process of online networks – news, music, entertainment can all be accessed through the Internet. Third, convergence also refers to the ways in which media ownership is increasingly concentrated through mergers of corporations that would previously have operated in different sectors (e.g. Time-Warner and AOL).

Cyberculture
We use this term in two related, but distinct, ways in this book. In the first it is taken to refer to the complex of 'culture + technology' derived from the history of cybernetics. This is because cybernetics is concerned with information systems not only in machines but also, as Norbert Wiener ([1948] 1962) has it, in animals and in social structures.

Accordingly, the term does not only refer to a culture with digital machines, but applies equally to industrial and mechanical cultures.

Second, cyberculture is used to refer to the theoretical study of cyberculture as already defined; that is, it denotes a particular approach to the study of the 'culture + technology' complex. This loose sense of cyberculture as a discursive category groups together a wide range of (on many levels contradictory) approaches, from theoretical analyses of the implications of digital culture to the popular discourses of science and technology journalism.

What unites these approaches is the assertion that technology, particularly computer technology, and culture are profoundly interrelated in the contemporary world.

Cybernetics

Cybernetics, according to Norbert Wiener ([1948] 1962), who coined the term, is the science of 'control and communication in the animal and the machine'. Already, then, heralding the rise of the concept of the 'cybernetic organism', or cyborg, cybernetics views the states of any system – biological, informational, economic, political – in terms of the regulation of information. This occurs in two ways. Most systems are governed by negative feedback, whereby systems reinforce their stability by reference to an optimal state of the system that negates other states (i.e. resists change). For example, a thermostat responds to both heat and cold in order to ensure an optimal temperature. On the other hand, processes governed by positive feedback are said to be in a runaway state, where minute changes become self-amplifying and change the overall state of the system. An example of this latter would be any process of historical change. Although cybernetics fell into disrepute in media studies due to the rejection of Shannon and Weaver's essentially one-way theory of communication, cyberculture has predictably seen a rise in its fortunes. See Plant (1997).

Cyberpunk

A genre of science fiction that has had a marked influence on the theoretical study of digital technologies and networks. William Gibson's novel *Neuromancer* is particularly influential, as is the film *Bladerunner*; both are characterised by gritty, noir-influenced narratives and a fascination with new, intimate relationships between the human body or mind and technologies. Gibson's cyberspace is a key example, as is the figure of the cyborg. A similar genre is evident in Japanese popular culture. Examples familiar to Western audiences include the animated film *Akira*, and the comic *Bubblegum Crisis*. The influence of cyberpunk themes is evident in a wide range of popular fantasy texts, from *Pokémon* to *Robot Wars*. The term has also been taken to refer to an actual youth subculture in the 1980s – of post-punk streetwise hackers. Other cyberpunk writers include Pat Cadigan, Bruce Sterling and Neal Stephenson.

Cyberspace

A term coined by science-fiction writer William Gibson to describe his fictional computer-generated virtual reality in which the information wealth of a future corporate society is represented as an abstract space. Pre-dating the Internet as a popular phenomenon, Gibson's cyberspace has been widely interpreted as prophetic (though he says he got the idea from watching children playing videogames). The word is also used in very general terms to cover any sense of digitally generated 'space', from the World Wide Web to virtual reality.

Cyborg

Cybernetic organism. Refers to a wide range of actual and fictional hybrids of the human and the machine, from the use of medical implants such as pacemakers to the technologically enhanced individuals of science fiction. The figure of the cyborg has become one of the defining moments of recent cinematic culture, as well as a central figure in theorising 'post-human' relationships with technologies. Arnold Schwarzenegger stripping living flesh from his titanium-alloy frame is as familiar an image in cyberculture as the gamer in the arcade that set Gibson's fictions off towards cyberspace. The concept originates from work done by Manfred Clynes in 1960, who was seeking a solution to the problems posed by the sheer volume of information an astronaut must process, along with the environmental difficulties of space flight. A machine-mediated human, Clynes reasoned, would be better placed than an unaided human, to cope with these problems. As the examples show, key to the cyborg is the conjunction of biological and technological elements. Notions of the implications of these hybrid entities are similarly various: they may offer new ideas for thinking about the individual in the technologised postmodern world (e.g. Haraway 1990), or offer solutions to a perceived redundancy of the unenhanced human body in the near future (e.g. the work and ideas of the artist Stelarc).

Desktop

Another term for the PC or Apple Mac Graphical User Interface. These GUIs use the desktop and stationery as a metaphor – hence files are stored in folders, unwanted files are placed in a wastebin, and so on.

Diegesis

All of the narrative elements in a film that appear to emanate from the fictional world of the film itself – the words the actors speak, the music whose source we can see in a scene. A non-diegetic element, for example, would be a voice-over.

Digital

New media are also often referred to as digital media by virtue of the fact that media which previously existed in discrete analogue forms (e.g. the newspaper, the film, the radio transmission) now converge into the unifying form of digital data. They can now all be either converted to or generated as a series of numbers which are handled by computers in a binary system. Media processes are brought into the symbolic realm of mathematics rather than those of physics or chemistry. Once coded numerically, the input data in a digital media production can immediately be subject to the mathematical processes of addition, subtraction, multiplication and division through algorithms contained within software.

Discourse, discursive

Discourses are elaborated systems of language (conversations, theories, arguments, descriptions) which are built up or evolved as part of particular social behaviours (e.g. expressing emotion, writing legal contracts, practising medicine). The suggestion is therefore that ideas do not circulate in a vacuum but are bound up with forms of social practice and institutional power. Discourses, like the words and concepts they employ, can then be said to construct their objects because they lead us to think about them and know them in particular ways. 'Discursive', as used in this book, refers to the way members of a culture invest meaning in and think, talk, and write about new image and communication technologies.

Dispersal

Used in this book to characterise some aspects of new media which, by contrast with traditional mass media, exist in a more diffuse and fragmented way within the culture at large. Networked-based communications are more dispersed than centralised means of distribution. New media production resources are more widely dispersed than centralised mass media production resources.

Dotcoms

Businesses attempting to use the Internet as their primary marketplace. The term comes from the widespread use of URLs as company brands, for example Boo.com (when spoken aloud: 'boo dot com'). Dotcoms generated a great deal of excitement and speculation in the late 1990s, excitement that soon proved misplaced.

Dystopian

Usually used in discussions about new media that see developments in technology as primarily malign. The opposite of utopian.

Email

A system of servers and software that allows messages to be sent to a particular individual in accord with agreed standards.

Embodiment

Referring to the assertion that human knowledge and experience is inseparable from the biological and socially constituted human body, this term is generally used to counter assumptions or claims, in the study of new technologies, that the body is becoming less important – for example, that we 'leave our bodies behind' when we enter Virtual Reality.

Enlightenment

An intellectual and historical period in Europe dating from the early eighteenth century. Enlightenment thought challenged the intellectual dominance of the Church and a religious worldview in the name of reason and science. The Enlightenment attitude to technology – that it was inherently progressive and a force for reason and moral good – has been challenged recently in postmodernist thought. Postmodernism is sometimes seen, then, as amongst other things, the end of the 'Enlightenment project'.

Ethnography
The empirical study of ways of life of particular groups or cultures through participant observation. In the study of new media this may involve established media audiences methodologies (interviews, observations of media use, etc.) or the development of new methodologies to study online communities.

Flaming
The practice of sending abusive messages to one with whom one disagrees. An aggressive use of email, bulletin boards or chat rooms.

Frankfurt School
A group of scholars and critics associated with the Institute for Social Research founded in Frankfurt in 1923, before dispersing during the Nazi period and returning to Frankfurt in 1953. Leading authors include Theodor Adorno, Herbert Marcuse, Max Horkheimer, Walter Benjamin and Jurgen Habermas. These writers all engage in a critical theory using the Marxist idea of 'critical theory'; that is to change as well as to describe the world. Of particular historical significance insofar as they were the first scholars to write about the culture industry seeing it as part of a system which produced passive consumers rather than active citizens.

Genre
Used in media studies to describe particular groups or categories of text that are recognisable to producers and to audiences (typically, for example, 'the western', 'the soap opera', 'the romance'). The identity of the genre resides in shared textual characteristics, common signs that the reader would expect to be able to identify within similar kinds of texts. Characterised in the contemporary period as much by the breakdown of specific genre boundaries in the circulation of 'hybrid' texts produced in the search for innovative media products – for example, reality TV documentary programmes of emergency service activities that combine highly fictionalised action techniques with factual actuality footage.

Hackers
Popularly understood to mean destructive and anti-social computer experts (usually youthful) breaking into computer networks and designing computer viruses, and the subject of media scares in the 1980s. However, the term originates in the computer research facilities of US universities in the late 1950s. These hackers, though often given to pranks, were not so much anti-social as instrumental in the development of personal computing and, with their 'ethic' of open-source coding and anti-authoritarianism, influential on later discourses of computer media, especially around the Internet.

Home computer
Or microcomputer. Pre-dating the personal computer and its move from office to home in the mid- to late 1980s, home computers were first produced at the end of the 1970s. Whereas PCs are either IBM or Apple Mac compatible, home computers were based on a wide range of platforms. In the UK, Clive Sinclair's ZX80 and ZX81 were among the first popular models.

HTML (HyperText Markup Language)
HTML is a collection of formatting commands that create hypertext documents or web pages. A web browser interprets the HTML commands embedded in the page and uses them to format the page's text and graphic elements. HTML commands cover many types of text formatting (bold and italic text, lists, headline fonts in various sizes, and so on), and also have the ability to include graphics and other non-text elements.

Humanism
Everything is by man and for man: this is perhaps the most straightforward characterisation of humanism. In more detail, humanism is the theoretical (and political) prioritisation of the subject over the physical and/or social forces that act upon it. This is a problem for cyberculture, since it is concerned with precisely the technologies with which subjects interact, or which, many argue, act on humans in culture. Some theorists, such as Bruno Latour (1993), therefore argue that it is necessary to grant the status of agency to non-human entities, such as machines, animals, institutions, diseases, and so on (see *actor-network theory*).

Hyperreality, hyperrealism
As used by postmodernist thinkers Umberto Eco and Jean Baudrillard, hyperreality as a concept is a response to the problematic theoretical status of the 'real world' in contemporary media culture. For Eco it refers to an emerg-

ing culture of 'fakes' in the US in particular (waxwork museums, theme parks, animatronics), whereas for Baudrillard it is synonymous with simulacra – hyperreality is not a distortion of reality, rather it has superseded reality. Hyperrealism is also a term for a dominant aesthetic in animation in which realist cinematic codes (of narrative and visual imagery) are adopted, but exaggerated, in animation.

These two terms, though distinct, come together in critical studies of the products of the Walt Disney Corporation. Eco and Baudrillard both use Disneyland as a case study of hyperreality, and it is Disney's animated films which are the prime exemplars of hyperrealism.

Hypertext

A kind of writing facilitated by computer technology in which documents and parts of documents are linked together to allow the reader to follow his or her own 'path' through a body of information or a narrative. Developed by Ted Nelson in the 1960s (though often regarded as originating in the ideas of Vannevar Bush, Roosevelt's science adviser, at the end of the Second World War), the hypertext model forms the basis of the organisation of the World Wide Web.

ICT (Information and communications technologies)

Used to denote that range of technology associated with the distribution of information in both *analogue* and *digital* formats.

Idealism

See *Materialism*.

Immersion

While normally referring to being under the surface of, or 'in' a body of liquid, in the present context it refers to the experience of being inside the world of a constructed image. The image is not before the viewer on a surface from whose distance they can measure their own position in physical space. Rather, it appears to surround them. By extension the term is used to describe the experience of the user of certain new media technologies (particularly VR, but also videogames) in which the subject loses any sense of themselves as separate from the medium or its simulated world.

Incommensurability

The concept of incommensurability stems from Thomas Kuhn's famous work, *The Structure of Scientific Revolutions* (1962). In it, Kuhn argues that during periods of large-scale change in scientific theories, the new theory does not explain the same phenomena as the old theory did. The two theories – or paradigms – are therefore said to be incommensurable in that they do not measure the same phenomena, nor can they be subsumed under a common measurement (this is what the word 'incommensurable' literally means). Implicit in this is the further idea that the entities to which theories refer do not really exist, but are only functional terms within a given theory (that is, they are said to be theory dependent). Thus Kuhn's argument is often used in support of constructionist positions.

Information revolution

See *Knowledge economy*.

Instrumental, instrumentalism

As used in this book, the instrumental refers to the use of media technologies for practical, educational or productive ends, rather than for pleasure or entertainment. In general terms, instrumentalism concerns the 'editing out' of social, political and economic phenomena that have no clear output. Under technoscience, for example, such outputs are measured by efficiency gains alone. Recently, educational policies in a number of countries have emphasised the instrumental uses of learning for the knowledge economy at the expense of more abstract notions of knowledge as an end in itself.

Interactive

Technically the ability for the user to intervene in computing processes and see the effects of the intervention in real time. Also used in communications theory to describe human communication based on dialogue and exchange.

Interface

Usually used to denote the symbolic software that enables humans to use computers, and to access the many layers of underlying code that causes a software to function (e.g. the desktop).

Internet
The collection of networks that link computers and servers together.

IRC
Internet Relay Chat – chat room technologies that allow many users to type text into a common 'conversation' in more or less real time.

Keynesianism
A theory associated with the work of the twentieth-century British economist John Maynard Keynes. Keynes argued amongst much else that in times of economic slump it was the duty of Government to carry on spending and maintain demand for goods so as to avoid further economic decline.

Knowledge economy
The widely expressed thesis that, at the end of the twentieth century, the industrialised world is undergoing some kind of economic restructuring. The depth and significance of this 'revolution' is argued over, depending on the theoretical or political position of the commentators, but there is a widespread sense that information, knowledge, intellectual property, etc. are increasingly important factors in late capitalist political economy. ICTs are usually seen as instrumental in these changes, precisely because of the significance of information processing and communication.

Long Tail, The
A theory of the way conventional media economics have changed due to the Internet and network culture. Traditionally, companies and producers of all types strove to capture mass markets; bigger markets were better markets. The theory of the 'long tail' argues that the economic basis of production is changing in ways that unlock market diversity as networked communications allow producers to connect with a multiplicity of smaller niche markets. As search technologies place the most obscure product at the fingertips of specialist consumers, lower volume products attain a margin of profitability to challenge that of the mass market (see Anderson 2006).

Materialism
Two concepts of materialism are relevant in this book: 1 the doctrine that we are dealing always with physical things, whether we are looking at machines, meanings, or effects. Further, materialism is the doctrine that all is matter, such that automata could be constructed from metal, or that machines need no 'soul', 'mind' or 'personality' in order to be intelligent; 2 derived from Marxist thought, a materialist approach within cultural and media studies is one that foregrounds the economic and social contexts and determinants of cultural and media forms. These forms then are understood as historically situated and the product of conflicting power relationships. They may well function ideologically, distorting our understanding of the real, material relations that govern our work, leisure and lives. This sense of materialism sets itself against idealism – an approach which assumes an inherent logic or teleology to particular cultural phenomena. To an idealist, technocultural change (for example, developments in cinematic realism) is the gradual, but inevitable, realisation of a true essence, independent of historical or social contingencies (for example, the assumption that CGI will one day exactly replicate the look of conventional cinematography).

McLuhanite
Associated with the claims and ideas of Marshall McLuhan – in particular the idea that media systems have transformative effects on human subjectivity and society.

Microcomputer
See *Home computer*.

Modernism
Modernism takes shape definitively as a series of artistic (e.g. impressionism, cubism, futurism) and philosophical (i.e. Marxism) movements that were themselves responses to the problems and crises of social life brought about by the mass industrialisation and urbanisation of nineteenth-century Western countries. In this book the term is more often used to refer to the kinds of centralised methods of state and economic organisation and their associated mass media systems developed in the first half of the twentieth century.

Modernity

The condition of being modern – derived originally from the upheavals in Western thought that date from the eighteenth-century Enlightenment, i.e. a sense that to be 'modern' is to be against traditional hierarchies of state, monarch and religion and to be for the novel, the innovative and the progressive.

Molar, molecular

This pair of contrasting (not opposing) terms was borrowed, by Deleuze and Guattari (1984, 1988), from Jaques Monod's use of them in his (1971) account of 'molecular cybernetics'. First, molar phenomena (subjects, bodies, objects) are composed of molecular ones. If we concentrate our theories of things on molar phenomena, as for example humanism must, being essentially based on human actions, we therefore start from a position of several autonomous things, each disconnected from the other. If we start, however, from the molecular level, we do not merely start with smaller items, we start with connective phenomena, from which larger-scale entities may arise. While the contrast may appear to be between large and small entities, it really lies between isolated entities and connectivity. The example of gaming is used to discuss this contrast in **5.4.4**.

Monetarism

A theory associated with the work of the twentieth-century US economist Milton Friedman who erroneously argued that control of the supply of money would in itself control inflation.

MOO

See *MUD*.

MP3 (Motion Picture Export Group Layer 3)

A popular format for encoding sound, widely used for the digitisation of music.

MUD

Multi-User Dungeon (sometimes also 'domain' or 'dimension'). Dating from the early 1980s, an online role-playing environment originally derived from Dungeons and Dragons type games. Normally textbased, Multi-User Dungeons allow numerous people to play and interact in the same game scenario at the same time. Also MOO, Multi-User Object-Oriented spaces in which users built an environment in 'object-oriented' language which allowed pre-coded navigation through text-constructed 'spaces'. Increasingly replaced by shared spaces in which users speak to each other and interact through 'avatars' in, for example, online gaming.

Neo-liberalism

Used to describe the economic theory that argues for a return to completely free and open markets as the best way of ordering society. Originating in the US in the late 1970s as a response to crises in the post-war economic consensus, neo-liberalism aggressively seeks to turn as many goods and services as possible into commodities and to find as many markets as possible for trading those commodities. Characterised by a critique of state regulation of both the economy and social questions, neo-liberalism attacks the postwar consensus on welfare, as well as media regulation, for example. Neo-liberal attitudes were evident in the promotion and celebration of the 'new economy' of the dotcom phenomenon of the late 1990s.

Networked

Denotes a collection of computers connected to each other. May be as few as two PCs.

Newsgroups

Name given to the topic-specific information and opinion exchange sites on the Internet that are collectively known as 'Usenet News'. The newsgroup has the quality of an unending text conversation in which the messages respond to and comment on previous messages. Some newsgroups have an editorial control policy run by a discussion 'moderator'; others are simply open to anyone to say anything.

Nominalism

Nominalism is opposed to the philosophical sense of realism. Kuhn's incommensurability thesis, for example, could be said to be nominalist insofar as it makes the entities referred to by theories into mere names (hence nominalism) of things, rather than names of real entities. Similarly, then, all constructionist accounts of things are philosophically nominalist, diverting attention from what really exists to the ways they are named or constructed through discourse.

Online
To be logged on to a server.

Paradigm
The term 'paradigm', like incommensurability, stems in its contemporary usage from Thomas Kuhn (1962). In its loosest sense, it refers to the set of beliefs and opinions about particular knowledges that are regarded as 'established'. In this sense, the paradigm operates as a kind of 'horizon of askable questions' at a certain cultural–historical juncture. More specifically, it refers to the explicitly formulated governing ideas of the time; eighteenth-century physics, for example, had mechanism as its paradigm. In this instance, the paradigm identifies the genuine problems that arise within it. A paradigm shift occurs when the problems begin to outnumber the solutions, thus turning critical attention on the paradigm itself. Kuhn calls this situation one of 'crisis'. A new paradigm will then arise that solves these new problems at the expense of the old paradigm. MacKenzie and Wacjman (1999) make use of Kuhn's language in this context.

PC (personal computer)
Originating in the early 1980s on the one hand as computer enthusiasts such as Steve Jobs and Steve Wozniak moved out of the home computer culture and founded the Apple Corporation and on the other as companies such as IBM moved from the institutionalised mainframe market towards producing smaller individualised computers.

Physicalism
Physicalism, in the present context, can be taken to be a theory of technology that prioritises its physical aspects, and the conjunction of these aspects with the physical aspects of humans. Physicalist theories therefore emphasise the technological artefacts themselves, along with the body, the senses, and the physical environment in which they are located. Accordingly, it is philosophically realist, rather than nominalist. Such a view, we argue in **1.6.4**, is held by McLuhan, and by many of those who exploit his work in the context of cyberculture. The interaction between humans and machines is therefore a physical moment as well as whatever symbolic dimensions it may have.

Post-structuralism
'Structuralism' is the name given to a dominant strand of French literary and cultural investigation from the 1950s through to the 1970s. In media studies it is associated with semiotics as a method for reading texts as sign systems. In general it is a method that sees all phenomena as determined and made meaningful through the operation of underlying structures and systems which have their own grammar. Post-structuralists have tended towards the rejection of such 'totalising' theoretical approaches, through, for example, deconstruction, feminism and postmodernism. In particular in this book the term is used to denote the idea that the human subject is not a fixed identity but is in a permanent process of becoming through language and text. The post-structuralist method challenges the idea that there is a permanent fixed or stable subject.

Postmodernism
The term 'postmodernism' is used in a tremendously wide range of discourses to account for an equally wide range of phenomena. It can mean a particular change in the aesthetics of certain cultural forms from the late 1970s and early 1980s (postmodern architecture for example), or postmodern culture as symptomatic of fundamental economic or cultural change. This change might be the end of the Enlightenment project for example, or the product of a restructuring of global capitalism in the latter half of the twentieth century. Many accounts of postmodernist culture are predicated on a notion of the significance (or dominance) of a commodified media culture. In all of these concepts, moreover, there is a sense of a blurring of boundaries between previously distinct or opposite phenomena: between high culture and popular culture, the local and the global, the public and the private.

Prosumerism
The term 'prosumer' is originally from the video industries referring to technologies aimed between the consumer domestic market and the professional production market. By extension used here to refer to technologies of media production that are economically within the range of the domestic consumer but technically capable of producing work for large-scale distribution.

Public sphere
The model of disinterested open public conversation based in rational critical debate identified by Jurgen Habermas as evolving in eighteenth-century Europe (1989). More recently interpreted as the communicative space which is open and accessible to the maximum numbers of a society and which therefore provides the foundation for democratic governance and culture.

Realism

Realism is used here with two distinct but overlapping meanings. The first, derived from literary theory, film and media studies, refers to the idea that representations either conform to realism as a generic form (believability, 'realistic' scenes and characters), or that they are coherent references to a reality beyond the representation itself, thus transcending or denying their status as representations by appearing as a 'window on the world'. Second, realism is also the philosophical view opposed to constructionism. Whereas, for example, a constructionist viewpoint would take the phenomena under consideration to be products of the discourses used in their consideration, to be theory-dependent, the contrary realist view would be that things exist whether or not they are objects within a discourse or theory. The realist is therefore committed to the view that things are not reducible to ways of speaking or representing them.

Referentiality

The manner in which representations refer to things in the real world. How a representation depicts or denotes an object or event existing in the physical world.

Remediation

A central idea for thinking about 'new' media since the concept of remediation suggests that all new media, in their novel period, always 'remediate'; that is, incorporate or adapt previously existing media. Thus early cinema was based on existing theatrical conventions, computer games remediate cinema, the World Wide Web remediates the magazine, etc. Originally from Marshall McLuhan (1964: 23–24), but more recently usefully applied by Bolter and Grusin (1999).

Science and Technology Studies

A broad interdisciplinary field concerned with the relationships between science, technology and society. Researchers include sociologists and anthropologists, historians and philosophers. Its emphasis on the operations and agency of technology and other material phenomena marks its difference from the articulations of technology and the social usually offered by the humanities and social sciences.

Server

A computer that provides the information, files, web pages, and other services to the client that logs on to it.

Simulacrum, simulation

There are two main uses of these terms in this book. The first derives from the history of technology. In the history of technology, automata are divided into two classes: automata and simulacra. Simulacra are self-moving things that look like something they imitate (Vaucanson's duck, for example, or anthropomorphic robots like Star Wars' C-3PO – see **5.3.2**), and self-moving things that do not resemble anything in particular (factories, cellular automata, fountains, clocks, and so on). This use of simulacrum gives it a realist slant: it names one kind of automaton, or self-moving thing, but the simulacrum is itself as real as the thing it imitates.

The second and more common use of the term here derives from the work of French postmodern theorist Jean Baudrillard (1983) who argued that the sign and what it refers to had collapsed into one another in such a way that it had become impossible to distinguish between the real and the sign. According to Baudrillard, simulacra are signs that can no longer be exchanged with 'real' elements, but only with other signs within the system. For Baudrillard reality under the conditions of postmodernism has become *hyperreality*, disappearing into a network of simulation. This has been conceptualised as a shift from the practice of 'imitation' (or 'mimesis', the attempt at an accurate imitation or representation of some real thing that lies outside of the image or picture) to that of 'simulation' (where a 'reality' is experienced that does not correspond to any actually existing thing). A simulation can be experienced as if it were real, even when no corresponding thing exists outside of the simulation itself.

Spam

The email equivalent of junk mail. Usually offering commercial services and opportunities.

Spectacle, the spectacular

As well as its commonly understood reference to visually striking (though perhaps superficial) cultural forms and texts (blockbuster films, firework displays), the 'spectacular' has a specific intellectual pedigree in cultural theory. The French theorist Guy Debord developed the Marxist concept of the commodity to explain the persistence of post-war capitalism. If commodities are products alienated from their producers through the operations of markets and money, the spectacle is the commodification of (consumer) society as a whole – a profound alienation: 'capital accumulated until it becomes an image'. Advertising, cinema, publicity and the media are just aspects of the general form of the spectacle.

Structuralism

Structuralism is a mode of thinking and a method of analysis practised in twentieth-century social sciences and humanities. Methodologically, it analyses large-scale systems by examining the relations and functions of the smallest constituent elements of such systems, which range from human languages and cultural practices to folktales and literary texts.

Technoculture

Technoculture generally refers to cultural phenomena in which technologies or technological forces are a significant aspect. The essays in Penley and Ross's book *Technoculture* (1991) for instance cover medical and reproductive technologies and discourses, computer hacking and viruses, erotic manga, hip hop music and culture, art, and cyberpunk. The term 'techno-popular culture' has been used in ethnographic research on young people and computer media (see Facer, Sutherland and Furlong 2003). However it is also argued that any a priori distinction between technology and culture (i.e. as two largely separate phenomena that come together at certain junctures) should be questioned. Bruno Latour for instance asserts that society has always been an indissoluble network of technological and human entities .

A distinction can be made then between 'technoculture' and 'cyberculture'. Cyberculture (or 'digital culture') generally refers only to digital age technologies (though it is important to note that the science of cybernetics does not restrict itself to computer technologies), whereas technoculture might be used to refer to all cultural and social formations and phenomena if society is (and always has been) constituted by humans, machines and tools. Cyberculture therefore can refer specifically to the nexus of humans, culture and digital technology, and technoculture to broader and/or older formations of the cultural and the technological. In some STS discussions the term 'sociotechnical' is used (Bijker and Law 1992; Berg 1994) rather than technoculture. Both foreground the argument that social, cultural and technological phenomena and entities are inextricably linked and as such are largely commensurate.

Technological determinism

Technological determinism remains, as MacKenzie and Wajcman ([1985] 1999) argue, the 'dominant account' of technology in everyday or 'common sense' culture. In its bluntest form, it argues that technology drives history – that is, that social arrangements are determined by technological ones. However, there are other accounts of technological determinism, such as that offered by Ellul (1964). He argues that technology does not directly drive history, in a billiard-ball manner, but rather that given a certain degree of complex interrelatedness, technology becomes determinant at a certain stage in history. This is also the view of Thomas Hughes (see Smith and Marx 1996), who argues that it is not individual technologies or technology in general that are determinant, but rather technological systems in which there is a high degree of interrelatedness. See **5.2** for a variety of accounts of determinism.

Technological imaginary

The concept of a technological imaginary draws attention to the way that (frequently gendered) dissatisfactions with social reality and desires for a better society are projected onto technologies as capable of delivering a potential realm of completeness. It is used here, therefore, as a characteristic of many of those arguments for new media that see them as a solution to social and cultural ills.

Technology

Commonly used to describe socially or economically useful artefacts and associated processes – therefore as 'tools' or machines which extend the capabilities of the human body. Usually perceived as derived from applied scientific development. However, also used here in a wider sense to imply technology not only as object but also as a process that includes the socially constructed knowledges and discourses that enable the technology to function.

Technoscience

Technoscience refers to the conjunction of technological success with general social effectiveness: what works in technology becomes the model of how we ought to think about what works socially, economically, educationally, and so on. Because its efficiency becomes its own criterion of success, technoscience tends to become the dominant ideological position, as argued by Jurgen Habermas (1970). This view of technoscience is further amplified and explored by Jean-François Lyotard (1984), where it is given the status of one of the chief determinants of the 'postmodern condition' in matters of science, politics, philosophy, and so on.

Teleology

Arguments, theories or histories that explain the nature of something not by their original cause but by ideas about the purpose or 'end' that something appears to have. In this context an example would be that virtual reality is the 'end' to which cinema was striving as a stage in a long historical drive to achieve perfect illusions of reality.

Text, textual

In media studies a 'text' means more than a written text. It is used to refer to any artefact or product (a TV programme, a video game), even an activity or performance (a dance), which has structure, specific qualities, meaning and which can be analysed and 'read'. 'Textuality' – the properties of texts.

Ubiquitous computing

Term used to describe the diffusion of computing technologies throughout our environment through increasing miniaturisation and the development of 'smart' (i.e. predictive) computing applications. Therefore the idea that computers will soon be an embedded function of our physical environments.

Usenet

See *Newsgroups*.

Utopian

Usually used in discussions about new media that see developments in technology as primarily beneficial. The opposite of *dystopian*.

Virtual

The concept of the virtual is in widespread, but varying use. First, it is the name of a branch of technologies, most specifically of virtual reality. Here, the sense of virtual is almost synonymous with 'simulation', if we understand this as meaning something that is 'not really real'. Accordingly, virtual reality becomes a simulated reality, more or less a fantasy world we can step in and out of by virtue of the technologies that allow humans to access it. However, the idea of a 'not really real reality' seems confusing (see Heim [1993] for an analysis of this sense of the virtual), not least because we enter VR by way of real machines, and experience it through our bodies. In what sense then can we say that virtual reality is not real? Such accounts of the virtual leave this physical aspect out of the picture. In contrast to this sense of the virtual, a growing field of theory, much of it informed by Gilles Deleuze's (1994) philosophical analyses of the concept, argues that the virtual is that part of the real that is not actual. 'Actuality' here means both real and current; that is, if we identify the real only with what is current, then future and past states cannot be real. Yet whatever future events will actually befall us, the future itself remains a permanently real and inactual presence. We can therefore say that the future has a kind of reality that is not actual but virtual. This sense of the virtual is in turn given physical form by the processes of feedback that are key to cybernetics.

Visuality

The culturally and historically specific way in which vision is practised. The manner in which vision (and the various modes of attention that we commonly identify: seeing, looking, gazing, spectating and observing) is historically variable. It reminds us that 'vision is an active, interpretative process strongly governed by communities and institutions, rather than an innocent openness to natural stimuli' (Wood 1996: 68).

Windows

A Graphical User Interface combined with an operating system. It provides both the software to make the various parts of the hardware interact with each other and allows the input of commands and the output of results in forms accessible to non-specialists. The windows metaphor, of multilayered frames offering data access, has become the standardised interface for PCs. Originally developed by Apple Mac and later imitated by Microsoft.

Index

eBooks –

due for return on or before the

A library at your fingertips!

eBooks are electronic versions of printed books. You can store them on your PC/laptop or browse them online.

They have advantages for anyone needing rapid access to a wide variety of published, copyright information.

eBooks can help your research by enabling you to bookmark chapters, annotate text and use instant searches to find specific words or phrases. Several eBook files would fit on even a small laptop or PDA.

NEW: Save money by eSubscribing: cheap, online access to any eBook for as long as you need it.

Annual subscription packages

We now offer special low-cost bulk subscriptions to packages of eBooks in certain subject areas. These are available to libraries or to individuals.

For more information please contact webmaster.ebooks@tandf.co.uk

We re continually developing the eBook concept, so keep up to date by visiting the website.

www.eBookstore.tandf.co.uk